Constructions of Gender in Religious Traditions of Late Antiquity

Constructions of Gender in Religious Traditions of Late Antiquity

Edited by
Shayna Sheinfeld
Juni Hoppe
Kathy Ehrensperger

LEXINGTON BOOKS/FORTRESS ACADEMIC
Lanham • Boulder • New York • London

Published by Lexington Books/Fortress Academic
Lexington Books is an imprint of The Rowman & Littlefield Publishing Group, Inc.
4501 Forbes Boulevard, Suite 200, Lanham, Maryland 20706
www.rowman.com

86-90 Paul Street, London EC2A 4NE, United Kingdom

Copyright © 2024 by The Rowman & Littlefield Publishing Group, Inc.

"Because of Her We All Die: Eve in Early Jewish and Early Christian Reception" by Sara Parks is originally from *The Routledge Companion to Eve*, 1st Edition by Caroline Blyth and Emily Colgan, Copyright © 2023 by Routledge. Reproduced by permission of Taylor & Francis Group.

All rights reserved. No part of this book may be reproduced in any form or by any electronic or mechanical means, including information storage and retrieval systems, without written permission from the publisher, except by a reviewer who may quote passages in a review.

British Library Cataloguing in Publication Information Available

Library of Congress Cataloging-in-Publication Data Available

ISBN 9781978714557 (cloth : alk. paper) | ISBN 9781978714564 (epub)

∞™ The paper used in this publication meets the minimum requirements of American National Standard for Information Sciences—Permanence of Paper for Printed Library Materials, ANSI/NISO Z39.48-1992.

*To those who have had to remain unseen or hidden and
to those who are still marginalized because of your
gender, we see you and honor your identity.
To those who plant sparks of resilience and who open doors to
embrace all expressions of gender, we see you and thank you.*

Contents

Acknowledgments   ix

Introduction   xi
Shayna Sheinfeld, Juni Hoppe, and Kathy Ehrensperger

1   Why Should an *Androginos* Not Become an Enslaved Hebrew?: Tannaitic Reasoning about the *Androginos* within the Roman World   1
    Bernadette J. Brooten

2   Because of Her We All Die: Eve in Early Jewish and Early Christian Reception   23
    Sara Parks

3   The Feminine as an Intellectual Category in Gnosticism: Proposing a Methodological Framework   55
    Lavinia Cerioni

4   Explicit and Implicit Gender Laws—"Incest" in Qumranic and Tannaitic Literature: A Comparative Reading of Lev 18:13   73
    Federico Dal Bo

5   Torah, Gender, and Rabbinic Expertise   99
    Krista N. Dalton

6   Constructions of Gender in Origen of Alexandria   115
    Ilaria L.E. Ramelli

7   One of the Boys: Jerome's Fabulous Frontier Masculinity   161
    Matthew R. Anderson

8	Queen Helena of Adiabene through the Centuries *Sarit Kattan Gribetz*	195
9	"For Rachel I Will Return the Israelites": Maternal Grief and Loss in the Early Jewish Imagination *Sari Fein*	237
10	The Body as a Wonderland: Rabbinic Talk of the Human Body as a Sex/Gender Construction *Daniel Vorpahl*	257
11	Shush Shelamzion, Your Brother Shimon Is Speaking!: A Peculiar Pattern of Palestinian Passivation *Andrew W. Higginbotham*	281
12	Eve in Early Christian Armenian Tradition *David Zakarian*	301
13	The Stillborn Messiah and the Non-Viable Redeemer: Gender and Judeo-Christian Entanglement *Ruth Kara-Ivanov Kaniel*	323
14	Tying Knots of Fortitude to Withstand Your Beauty: Women as Temptresses and Tests of Fortitude in Sufi Literature *Matthew R. Hotham*	345
Index		365
About the Contributors		377

Acknowledgments

This edited volume came together after the 12th Nangeroni Meeting of the Enoch Seminar which was held virtually on July 19–22, 2021. This conference was organized by Shayna Sheinfeld, Kathy Ehrensperger, Juni Hoppe, and Joshua Scott and sponsored by the Enoch Seminar in collaboration with the Encyclopedia of Jewish-Christian Relations (EJCR) project of the Abraham Geiger Kolleg, Potsdam. While the conference was originally supposed to take place in June 2020 in Berlin, like so many events during the first years of the COVID-19 pandemic, we postponed and finally made the decision to hold the conference online the following summer, recognizing the increased challenges of doing scholarship during this time, especially for women, caregivers of children (a disproportionate number of whom are women), the immunocompromised, people with disabilities, and racialized populations.[1] As we did during the conference, we also want to acknowledge here in this volume not only the challenges of doing work during a global pandemic while having to manage childcare/homeschooling but also the extreme stress, uncertainty, and sadness that we have lived through. Many of us lost loved ones to COVID-19 and have loved ones (or ourselves) who suffer from its long-term complications. Many of us were cut off from our support networks (let alone our access to scholarship)[2] and/or were unable to support our own family and friends who were in need during this time. Conversely, learning to meet virtually and work remotely shone a spotlight on the stark, often gendered inequities that the "normal" expectations of academia exacerbate, from toxically gendered work environments to inequities of finance, mobility, and neurotypicality. In many ways, these challenges make the virtual meeting and the content of this volume all the more important—that this level of scholarship and collaboration produced during this time is truly a feat.

While the pandemic highlighted and exacerbated inequalities at all levels, not everything that came out of it was bad. Virtual events became more common, and hosting an online conference brought together scholars who may not have otherwise been able to participate in an international meeting for any number of reasons. While we still had to negotiate time zones (even between the chairs), we worked hard to make sure that there were punctual start and end times, as well as breaks, to allow for scholars from multiple time zones and with various other demands on their time to join us. With the care that we tried to bring to our decisions, we created a successful online conference, developed common space to share bibliographic and other recommendations, and with all who participated built an intentional community of scholars.

We are grateful for the participants who helped to create a truly inclusive feminist conference: one committed to collaboration, to supportive and intellectually engaging discussion, and to lifting one another up. Original participants included Matthew Anderson, Jennifer Barry, Albert Baumgarten, Gabriele Boccaccini, Catherine Bonesho, Catherine Bronson, Bernadette Brooten, Lavinia Cerioni, Federico Dal Bo, Krista N. Dalton, Carly Daniel-Hughes, Magdalena Díaz Araujo, Kathy Ehrensperger, Sari Fein, Erin Galgay, Andrew Higginbotham, Alexandra Hoffmann, Juni Hoppe, Matthew Hotham, Allison Kanner-Botan, Sarit Kattan Gribetz, Maia Kotrosits, Sara Parks, Sara Omar, Ilaria Ramelli, Joshua Scott, Shayna Sheinfeld, Angela Standhartinger, Jillian Stinchcomb, Michal Bar-Asher Siegal, Alison Vacca, Daniel Vorpahl, Lily Vuong, Meredith Warren, and David Zakarian. While not every participant was able to publish a paper in this volume, we acknowledge all of you in the productive exchange of ideas we shared for four days in July 2021, and we see your comments and feedback present in the ideas found in this volume. We would like to express a special thank you to Joshua Scott for all of his technical and organizational support and to Gabriele Boccaccini for his leadership in the Enoch Seminar.

NOTES

1. Data is still being analyzed on the results of pandemic on scholarship for minoritized populations. An early report by Deryugina, Shurchkov, and Stearns highlights the increase of the gender gap in academia (Tatyana *Deryugina, Olga Shurchkov, and Jenna Stearns,* "COVID-19 Disruptions Disproportionately Affect Female Academics," *AEA Papers and Proceedings* 111 [2021]: 164–68).

2. We are grateful for the groups and individuals who stepped up on social media during the pandemic to help disseminate hard-to-access scholarship to those who needed it.

Introduction

Shayna Sheinfeld, Juni Hoppe, and Kathy Ehrensperger

The idea for this conference and subsequent collection of scholarship emerged toward the end of the 10th Nangeroni meeting of the Enoch Seminar held in Rome (2018) on "Gender and Second Temple Judaism."[1] We realized at that time that the conversation was just getting started, and there was a rich and relevant body of material just out of reach beyond the arbitrary restriction of the Second Temple period. Ideas about honed terminology, the importance of jettisoning the notion of "neutrality" to historical scholarship that ignores gender (and other lenses), and the problems of disciplinary silos where scholars of early Islam, Ancient Judaism, Rabbinics, and Early Christianity are not necessarily in conversation even when there would be clear benefit are areas that we saw could be expanded upon. This second meeting on Gender created space for interdisciplinary and intersectional discussion and this resulting collection of contributions contains some of the scholarship influenced by this interaction.

Although this is not clearly evident in the conference title, the key focus was on aspects of gender in "monotheistic" traditions in the geographical realm of the Mediterranean and the Near East during a time period when the religious traditions now known as Judaism, Christianity, and Islam were not yet discernible as distinct, separate communities, but when boundaries were fuzzy and cultural and religious multilingualism were widespread rather than the exception. The focus on these particular traditions indicates that despite the attempt not to assume the existence of the traditions from a contemporary point of view, it proves hermeneutically difficult to step outside one's present location. Hence, noticeably absent in this collection is a specific focus on the wider "religious" context of these particular traditions, often labeled as "paganism," or constructed as the "other" over against which the "monolatrist/monotheistic" traditions are supposed to have demarcated themselves. It is evident that here boundaries are fuzzy, if they exist at all. These "other" traditions may be present here and there in one or the other of the contributions of this volume as, for example, in Lavinia Cerioni's chapter on the examination of the feminine as an intellectual category in Gnosticism and Bernadette Brooten's comparative look at *androgyni* in Jewish and Roman sources, but they are not in focus per se and in their own right. Of course, no conference and no collection of essays can be comprehensive, but the fact that only after the conference we became really aware of this gap indicates that this volume represents a specific monolatrist/monotheistic perspective indebted to the existence of the contemporary three monotheistic religious traditions.

TIME: THE QUESTION OF PERIODIZATION

Turning to the period from 300 BCE to 1000 CE in the regions of the Mediterranean and the Near East it becomes evident that it is difficult to provide clear rationales for any chronological demarcation. It certainly was a period during which political, social, cultural, linguistic, and religious traditions enriched, differentiated, and transformed each other in multiple rhizomatic interactions. It was the aim of both conferences to focus on gender as a decisive aspect in all these interactions, but we considered it impossible to cover such a vast time span and the diversity of aspects in the space of just one conference and conference volume. Hence, as noted, we decided to split the topic along an admittedly rather arbitrary chronological boundary, using traditional labels for the respective periods, Second Temple Judaism for the first, and Late Antiquity for the second period in view.

Evidently the chronological as well as the geographical boundary labels are meant to be indications rather than clear demarcations. Although it could be argued that the Second Temple period began with the building of the Second Temple under Persian Rule and ended with the fall of the Temple in Jerusalem in 70 CE it is often assumed that the more decisive final event was the suppression of the Bar Kokhba revolt in 135 CE, when any hope for a restoration of the Temple and a return to Jerusalem faded into a distant future for Jews. But even this is messy: while there was certainly disruption, there is also evidence of much continuity in Judaism from before the destruction of the Second Temple into what is often now called the rabbinic period.

The focus of the subsequent conference and conference volume presented here is on what has been traditionally referred to as Late Antiquity, but admittedly the periodization of Late Antiquity is even fuzzier than that of the Second Temple period. It can certainly not be marked by some key event in Jewish history and does not line up nicely with the end of the so-called Second Temple period. In recent years a multiplicity of publications have addressed the issue of the label as well as the periodization of Late Antiquity.[2] Some see the beginning of the period marked by Constantine and the end by the rise of Islam. A traditional view maintained that Late Antiquity arose out of the redefinition of the imperial Roman ideological model of the superiority of the "High Empire," an empire that saw its sovereignty contested in many ways after 230 CE and that with Constantine began to be reformulated from a Christian point of view.[3] This perspective views the period predominantly through the lens of the Christianization of the Roman Empire. There are variations to this perspective, when, for example, Peter Brown proposed to see the beginning of the period in the reign of Marcus Aurelius, and ending with Mohammed.[4] Political aspects play an important role in such periodization, and it is noteworthy that key male figures are exclusively named as chronological boundary markers, highlighting the patriarchal perspective inherent in our views of history. Whichever historical event or development is chosen as a demarcation, there remains a certain arbitrariness in such periodization. The focus on Christianization has been fundamentally challenged as it obscures if not obliterates the fact that this was part of a manifold process of religious transformations which involved what we distinguish today and call pagan, Christian, Jewish, Manichean, Zoroastrian, and Islamic traditions. These transformations involved and affected religious traditions in different and hardly equal ways.[5] It renders any periodization according to Christian parameters questionable, without denying the significance of the change of Christianity from minority to majority position. An interesting proposal has been presented by Garth Fowden. He extends the longue durée of Late Antiquity of Peter Brown in both directions, conceptualizing the period as the "First Millenium."[6] His aim is not only an expansion of the timeline but rather a re-focussing of our perception away from its fixation on Greek and Roman Antiquity, the Middle Ages and the Renaissance, to include Islam. This requires that geographically the scope is also widened from a focus on the Eastern Mediterranean (as Brown had done), to what he calls the "Eurasian Hinge," encompassing the Arabian Peninsula, the Syrian desert, the Iranian Plateau, and the eastern Mediterranean.[7] The key characteristic of the period, according to Fowden, is the interaction of three traditions of the book, Judaism, Christianity, and Islam. Fowden's periodization comes closest to the period the contributions of this volume cover, but they do not neatly fit into any of the precise periodizations mentioned above. They span from about 200 BCE (see Federico Dal Bo's contribution on incest in Qumran and early Rabbinic Literature) into what sometimes also is labeled as early Middle Ages (ca 900 CE), with influence beyond this period (see Ruth Kara-Ivanov Kaniel's contribution on The Stillborn Messiah and the Non-Viable Redeemer and Matthew R. Hotham's contribution on women as temptresses in Sufi traditions). While we, the editors, use the traditional labels, we are aware that we do so as scholars raised and located in the Western university system. This is not a problem per se, as there is no point of view from nowhere. Thus, the discussion presented here concerning the historical period in view is one from precisely this perspective. However, we wish to stress that clearly this is but one possible perception of the period and the space in view here. From the perspective of other traditions, the periodization would be different. But for the purpose of academic communication in the context of Western university systems, we will operate with the terms used here, remaining very aware that this is a construction from a particular perspective. It should be acknowledged that no clear criteria for a beginning and end of "Late Antiquity" can be identified and thus the chronological boundaries remain fuzzy. However, in this volume the period labeled Late Antiquity is seen as encompassing the time span from roughly the second or third to the ninth century CE with some chapters reaching beyond these dates in either direction, in some sense corresponding to Fowden's First Millennium.

In terms of characteristics of the time and space subsumed under the term Late Antiquity, the perception of decline, fall, and catastrophe which described and evaluated events in the Roman Empire from an elitist political view of imperial power have widely although not entirely been abandoned since Peter Brown's *The World of Late Antiquity* mentioned above.[8] However, not only the time span in question but also the label itself that is applied for this period (with its fuzzy boundaries), deserves a moment of pause. What is "late" in relation to what? And what is actually meant by "antiquity?" In Western Europe, a periodization emerged with Petrarca who described his own time in relation to what went before as a re-birth of an idealized classical antiquity, hence referred to these periods as Antiquity, and the Modern Age (Renaissance) set over against the so-called dark Middle Ages.[9] Evidently, the use of such and similar terminology has its roots in the European history of science where in the wake of the Humanist enthusiasm for ancient Greek and Roman traditions these were considered to be the roots of, and in many cases normative for (European) civilization. As with many terms now prevalent in scholarly discussions, the term "Late" Antiquity initially emerged in German scholarship.[10] Similar to the term Spätjudentum, applied to Jewish traditions after the Babylonian exile, the term "late" here indicates more than something that is later in terms of chronological time, but encompasses a value judgment in that what comes after is of lesser value, actually being a decline from an ideal, in the case of Jewish traditions, the ideal of a so-called prophetic religion,[11] in the case of Late Antiquity, a decline from what was considered to have been the pinnacle of the idealized Greek and Roman traditions. There is a problem with the term "Antiquity" as well in that Classical Antiquity was supposed to have ended with the rise of Alexander the Great and the so-called Hellenization of the eastern Mediterranean, a process which was already seen as one of decline compared with the Classical period. However, the period of Hellenism is certainly not seen as equal to the period of Classical Antiquity, hence what "antiquity" refers to in the term Late Antiquity seems rather unclear as well. As noted, these terms and periodization of history have temporal and local roots, and are now common in scholarly discourse, but should not be considered universal.[12] But when time is conceptualized as linear, periodizations help to somehow locate oneself in the now in relation to before and after. They are heuristic devices with specific functions in specific contexts. They are used here to facilitate academic communication, with the caveat that, in intercultural academic discourse, they may also hinder such communication, and thus should be critically assessed and used with caution. We consider it important to critically consider the limitations of the current academic framework rather than assuming its universal validity especially if we take seriously that we interact as colleagues from different locations and traditions.

SPACE: THE QUESTION OF LOCATION

Similarly imprecise and to some extent problematic is the issue of the geographical demarcation in view. Along with the challenge of a periodization focused on Christianization came a challenge to the accompanying focus on the realm of the Roman Empire, that is, the Mediterranean Basin.[13] Although the gravity of the Roman Empire cannot be ignored for the period, it did not provide the geographical or cultural boundaries of the world, despite claims that it spanned the entire *oikoumene*, and represented the peak of human civilization. The space in question spanned from the Atlantic to the Indus for sure, including the Sassanid Empire as a significant power, and from the Danube and Rhine valleys to North Africa, Egypt, and south of it. Trade routes expanded even further, hence the interactions between peoples through small-scale networks were as significant if not more significant than official networks secured by armies. Although diverse regions under imperial control often served suppliers of resources for their various overlords at times, they retained particular traditions, creatively interacting with majority or dominating ideologies and thus were essential players in the diversity of interactions and transformations during Late Antiquity. What could be seen as boundaries of empires guarded by armies from one perspective were permeable and porous pathways from the perspective of small networks of communities in everyday life.[14]

There can be no doubt of course that in such a vast space over such a long period of time societies and traditions undergo changes on a significant scale. The great narratives of rise (of Christianity) and fall (of the Roman Empire) may be too narrowly focused and too simplistic to grasp the diversity of processes, interactions, and events during this time, but in terms of religious history this should not distract from what Stroumsa has called "the theological and ritual dynamism" of the period.[15] He identifies a "passage from polytheistic systems to monotheistic and dualistic ones," and a "move from rituals centered upon sacrifices in temples to rituals established upon scriptures, in churches, synagogues, and mosques."[16] But these dynamics did not unfold only, possibly not even predominantly on the big stage, but were lived in diverse communities. As Michel de Certeau has emphasized, people in their everyday lives "make innumerable and infinitesimal transformations of and within the dominant cultural economy in order to adapt it to their own interests and their own rules."[17] These processes were not merely conflictual, as previously assumed for example, between paganism and Christianity, possibly not even predominantly so, but rather were processes of appropriation by people in their everyday life.[18] Far from being linear processes, interactions over time and space continued, transformed, and appropriated traditions, and interactions could be antagonistic as well as cooperative and cannot really be captured by a model of cause and effect, but rather by models which depict processes as rhizomatic in multiple ways and directions.[19]

It is being recognized widely, that in and through these processes of appropriation identities were transformed, but the categorization of collective identities as static impermeable groups is not a helpful tool to understand these interactions and processes, neither socially, politically nor in terms of religious traditions. There were communities, but they were porous in many aspects and remained intertwined in numerous ways. Important were the processes in which categories were developed to make sense and find a place in the world.[20] Although differentiation did emerge, it was more by integrating practices and positions known, thus re-configuring rituals and theological ideas in transformation processes. What is sometimes called a remainder of pagan practices is revealing the perspective of the "victorious" or imperialist agenda, but in the processes of transformation in everyday life such labels would have been meaningless. These processes were localized rather than universal, and as is evident in the chapters presented, reveal illuminating insights when analyzed as such.

Although the cultures and societies that flourished during this time in this vast space (*les vastes espaces*)[21] cannot be subsumed under any kind of unity as such, they shared ideas and held common views. Interestingly there was one shared idea in all its diversity among many of the religious traditions prevalent: revealed texts were seen as authoritative and providing guidance for life in human as well as human-divine interactions.[22] These texts with their narratives, poetry, hymns, and rules were part of community-forming processes. These communities were intertwined, living alongside each other, at times hostile, at times hospitable, and involved in discussions and debates. Although, as noted, monotheistic views gained momentum, it has been challenged that this was the hallmark of the period. Stroumsa argues that even this aspect should be seen in a process-oriented way in that the diversity of polytheistic perceptions was not replaced with some pure monotheism (which was by the way not the hallmark of Christianity alone[23] and not simply due to its eventual dominance) but was negotiated in multiple ways and adapted to everyday life. The communal interaction that continued and fostered the dynamics of change was enabled by the fact that in and with their cultural differences, the communities all took part in a shared religious language or *koine* whether expressed in Latin, Greek, Aramaic/Syriac, Armenian, or Arabic. In this *koine*, ideas, stories, and practices circulated among diverse communities, were interpreted, transformed, and adjusted to localized perceptions. The cultural differences and adaptations are thus not only evidence for differentiation between communities but also of shared traditions across all the multiple fuzzy boundaries. It seems that the common language and the notion of a revealed book are aspects that eventually emerged as characteristics and became the hallmark of different communities in their diversity. They left traces of their interactions with their respective "holy scriptures" in ever-increasing interpretive texts, which thus reflect these processes at a literary level.

The focus of this volume is on some examples of the implications of these processes in terms of gender studies.

GENDER: INTERSECTIONAL PERSPECTIVES

Today, as in antiquity, we all operate within the oppressive structures of patriarchy, which works in tandem with other systems of oppression.[24] Patriarchy is our reality, and it was the reality of the authors of ancient texts and the contexts in which ancient folks lived and breathed.[25] The diverse methodological approaches found in the following chapters attempt to move beyond the descriptive into the analytical, considering, as the title of this volume suggests, the "constructions" of gender in late antique religious traditions. This implies that although texts are the product of particular times and places, it is difficult, and in many of the texts discussed here, next to impossible to locate and date them precisely. The analyses presuppose socio-historical relevance without drawing precise conclusions concerning their function. They are thus analyzed as literary products which construct gendered discourses. We begin, then, with the premise that gender is not a fixed "given," but a fluid and cultural construct.[26] Characteristics attributed to the categories male and female meander along a slope of symbolic as well as material effect. Like today, there was no non-gendered discourse in the time period concerned. The categorization was seen as natural, beyond what in contemporary discourses might be labeled as social, sociological, or cultural. That is, how gender is portrayed and written about in the texts and ideas examined in this volume reflects cultural norms or is proscriptive of gendered ideals of the time periods and geographic locations in which they were produced. Likewise, as scholars each of us brings our own contemporary notions of gender to our readings, regardless of our goals or hermeneutical lens.[27] Inevitably, arguments that do not claim to address questions of gender in fact bring contemporaneous (and patriarchal) understandings of gendered ideas, language, roles, and norms into the argument. As noted, no one is without gendered notions.

One of our methodological goals in this volume is to highlight the constructed nature of gender in the texts and contexts from Late Antiquity, as viewed with contemporary intersectional lenses.[28] This is no easy task, and the authors of the contributions in this volume vary in how they approach this challenge. As gender is deeply ambiguous and variegated, complicated by time and context, each chapter is unique in its questions, methodology, and implications. For example, in her chapter on the first woman, Sara Parks explores the variety of interpretations of the character of Eve in ancient Jewish and early Christian reception history. From "everywoman" to lover to the entryway through which evil and death entered the world, Eve became a tool that many (male) authors used in order to represent their own agendas. In early Christian Armenian traditions, however, the uses of Eve as first woman are relatively neutral, avoiding the "blame game" employed by some Jewish and other Christian interpretations, as David Zakarian argues. Constructions of gender of the "other," too, can be used as a way to self-describe a particular "in" group. Krista Dalton explores how the rabbis construct the rabbinic self through interactions with a woman and a non-rabbinic Jewish man, while Matthew Hotham disrupts notions of Sufism as "gender-egalitarian" by examining how in two instances, women are framed as tests of spiritual fortitude for early Sufi men. Each of the contributions works to explore and expose construction of gender(s) within the fuzzy boundaries of various traditions, geographies, and time periods.

SUMMARY OF CONTRIBUTIONS

Similar to the 10th Nangeroni Meeting and the conference volume emerging from it, the goal of this volume is to highlight the relevance of gender-sensitive approaches in the period of Late Antiquity. Since during this period significant perceptions and ideals of the three monotheistic traditions emerged or were claimed or attributed normative status, further analyses through a gender-sensitive lens is a high desideratum. The authors of the essays presented here are committed to such a research agenda, to which this volume contributes a few snapshots, although only one contribution on Islam from the conference was submitted for inclusion in this volume, and we as

Introduction xix

the editors recognize this dearth. We look forward to continued discussions among a variety of scholars who study Islam, Christianity, and Judaism, as we had at the conference.

The contributions are presented in a roughly chronological order. Given that the dating of the texts discussed here is in many cases vague or controversial, or that some contributions cover a wide swath of time and text, chronology can only be an imprecise rule of thumb and is not meant to be taken literally.

In chapter 1, Bernadette J. Brooten deals with the question of "Why Should an *Androginos* Not Become an Enslaved Hebrew?" in her analysis of Tannaitic reasoning about people with both female and male genitals. Since *androgyni* and *hermaphroditi* could be sexually exoticized for entertainment in the Roman world, the Tannaim might have been concerned that Jewish enslavers could penetrate an *androginos*.

In chapter 2, "Because of Her We All Die: Eve in Early Jewish and Early Christian Reception," Sara Parks discusses Eve's early Jewish and Christian interpreters who were much more interested in employing Eve to promote their own views than in showing any loyalty to the text of Genesis.

In chapter 3, "The Feminine as an Intellectual Category in Gnosticism," Lavinia Cerioni proposes a feminine methodological framework that allows for a grouping together of Gnostic texts and accounts for similarities and differences in the texts of the Nag Hammadi library.

Federico Dal Bo's "Explicit and Implicit Gender Laws" in chapter 4 presents a typological analysis of discussion of incest in Qumranic and Tannaitic literature. He argues that both sets of literature generally agree on the prohibition of incest but offer different hermeneutical rationale for it.

In chapter 5, "Torah, Gender, and Rabbinic Expertise," Krista N. Dalton considers how the production of a gendered rabbinic self was inextricably bound up in the construction of Torah expertise and demonstrates how looking past the "naturalness" of the rabbi as Torah expert reveals a contingent relational process that produced both gender and expertise.

Ilaria L. E. Ramelli examines "Constructions of Gender in Origen of Alexandria" by investigating Origen's reflections on women's relation to God and Christ and the divine transcendence of gender categories, the destiny of gender differences in the other world, as well as on the role of women in the Church and their presence in the orders of the diaconate and presbyterate in chapter 6.

In chapter 7, "One of the Boys: Jerome's Fabulous Frontier Masculinity," Matthew R. Anderson builds on postcolonial approaches to Jerome by proposing that a useful way to examine his constant reinvention of his gendered persona is through an "aware-settler" or "settler-colonial" hermeneutic that highlights the intended permanence of settlement, its complex mutuality with Indigeneity, and the importance of narratives of heroic virtue to settler identity.

In chapter 8, Sarit Kattan Gribetz explores "Queen Helena of Adiabene through the Centuries" and the reasons that she remained an enduringly compelling figure in Rabbinic sources, early Christian writings, and Toledot Yeshu stories.

Sari Fein considers the role of Rachel as a mourning mother in the Late Antique Jewish midrash *Lamentations Rabbah* in "'For Rachel I Will Return the Israelites': Maternal Grief and Loss in the Early Jewish Imagination" in chapter 9.

In chapter 10, Daniel Vorpahl examines halakhic, metaphorical, and narrative manifestations of the human body in "The Body as a Wonderland: Rabbinic Talk of the Human Body as a Sex/Gender Construction," alongside selected examples from the Babylonian Talmud to convey the relevance of the body-gender relation within these fields of discourses of the Amoraic period.

In chapter 11, "Shush Shelamzion, Your Brother Shimon Is Speaking!: A Peculiar Pattern of Palestinian Passivation," Andrew W. Higginbotham examines the figure of Queen Salome Alexandra who is silenced by the later (male) writers who deign to remember her. Higginbotham highlights how the earlier sources are more likely to silence or erase Queen Salome, while later sources restore her agency.

David Zakarian argues in chapter 12, "Eve in Early Christian Armenian Tradition," that while in neighboring Christian traditions Eve's figure was deployed for the symbolic construction of "woman" as God's creation who is inferior to man, the Armenian church adopted a relatively neutral stance toward her.

In chapter 13, "The Stillborn Messiah and the Non-Viable Redeemer: Gender and Judeo-Christian Entanglement," Ruth Kara-Ivanov Kaniel explores the motif of a "non-viable Messiah" as a concept that reflects gendered collective identities and cultural personalities by discussing Jewish and Christian reactions to controversial issues surrounding a Messiah who possesses "feminine "attributes.

Matthew R. Hotham's contribution in chapter 14, "*Tying Knots of Fortitude to Withstand Your Beauty*: Women as Temptresses and Tests of Fortitude in Sufi Literature," explores how women are framed as sources of temptation and tests of spiritual fortitude for early Sufi men.

NOTES

1. Kathy Ehrensperger and Shayna Sheinfeld (eds.), *Gender and Second-Temple Judaism* (Lanham: Lexington Books/Fortress Academic, 2020).

2. Averil Cameron, "The 'Long' Late Antiquity: A Late Twentieth-Century Model," in *Classics in Progress. Essays on Ancient Greece and Rome*, ed. Timothy P.

Wiseman (Oxford: Oxford University Press, 2002), 165–91; Chris Wickham, *Framing the Early Middle Ages: Europe and the Mediterranean 400–800* (Oxford: Oxford University Press, 2006); Edward James, "The Rise and Function of the Concept 'Late Antiquity'," *Journal of Late Antiquity* 1 (2008): 20–30.

3. For a discussion see Hervé Inglebert, "Introduction: Late Antique Conceptions of Late Antiquity," in *Oxford Handbook of Late Antiquity*, ed. Scott F. Johnson (Oxford: Oxford University Press, 2012), 3–28.

4. Peter Brown, *The World of Late Antiquity from Marcus Aurelius to Muhammad* (London: Thames and Hudson, 1971).

5. Guy Stroumsa, *The Crucible of Religion in Late Antiquity* (Tübingen: Mohr Siebeck, 2021); Maijastina Kahlos, *Religious Dissent in Late Antiquity 350-450* (Oxford: Oxford University Press, 2019), 10.

6. Garth Fowden, *Before and After Muhammad: The First Millennium Refocused* (Princeton: Princeton University Press, 2013), 50.

7. Fowden, *Before and After Muhammad,* 100–04.

8. As with the question of periods, the question concerning the characteristics of the period has triggered a high volume of publications in recent years. Cf. also the discussion by Clifford Ando, "Decline, Fall, and Transformation," *Journal of Late Antiquity* 1 (2008): 31–60.

9. Stefan Rebenich, "Late Antiquity in Modern Eyes," in *A Companion to Late Antiquity*, ed. Philip Rousseau (Malden: Wiley-Blackwell, 2009), 77–92, here 77; Fowden, *Before and After,* 51.

10. For an excellent overview see Nora K. Schmid, Nora Schmidt, and Angelika Neuwirth, *Spätantike. Von einer Epoche zu einem Denkraum* (Wiesbaden: Harrassowitz Verlag, 2016) and Konrad Schmid, "The Rise and Fall of the Notion of 'Spätjudentum' in Christian Biblical Scholarship," in *Protestant Bible Scholarship: Antisemitism, Philosemitism and Anti-Judaism,* ed. Arjen F. Bakker, René Bloch, Yael Fisch, Paula Fredriksen, and Hindy Najman (Leiden: Brill, 2022), 63–78.

11. Schmid, "Rise and Fall."

12. Averil Cameron, *From the Later Roman Empire to Late Antiquity and Beyond* (London: Routledge, 2023), 145–48.

13. For a critical discussion of "Mediterraneanism" see William V. Harris, "The Mediterranean and Ancient History," in *Rethinking the Mediterranean*, ed. William V. Harris (Oxford: Oxford University Press, 2005), 1–42; Seth Schwartz, *Were the Jews a Mediterranean Society?* (Princeton: Princeton University Press, 2011), 21–25; also Fowden, *Before and After,* 93–126.

14. Kahlos, *Religious Dissent,* 87. On networks and network theory see Anna Collar, *Religious Networks in the Roman Empire: The Spread of New Ideas* (Cambridge: Cambridge University Press, 2014); Michal Bar-Asher Siegal and Yossi Yovel, "Network Analysis Reveals Insights about the Interconnections of Judaism and Christianity in the First Centuries CE," *Humanities and Social Sciences Communications, Nature* 10, no. 191 (2023): 1–9.

15. Stroumsa, *Crucible*, 2.

16. Stroumsa, *Crucible,* 2.

17. Michel De Certeau, *The Practice of Everyday Life* (Berkeley: University of California Press, 1984), xiii–xiv.

18. On appropriation as a concept for understanding transformations during the period in question see Jitse H. F. Dijkstra, "Appropriation: A New Approach to Religious Transformation in Late Antiquity," *Numen* 68 (2021): 1–38; also Marian Füssel, "Die Kunst der Schwachen: Zum Begriff der 'Aneignung' in der Geschichtswissenschaft," *Sozial. Geschichte. Zeitschrift für historische Analyse des 20.und 21. Jahrhunderts* NF 21 (2006): 7–28.

19. For one example of how Judaism and Christianity continued to interact, separate, and come back together, see Adele Reinhartz, "A Fork in the Road or a Multi-lane-highway?: New Perspectives on the 'Parting of the Ways' Between Judaism and Christianity," in *The Changing Face of Judaism, Christianity, and Other Greco-Roman Religions in Antiquity*, ed. Ian H. Henderson and Gerbern S. Oegema (Gütersloh: Gütersloher Verlagshaus, 2006), 280–95.

20. Kahlos, *Religious Dissent*, 86.

21. Stroumsa, *Crucible*, 1.

22. Inglebert, "Introduction," 17; Stroumsa, *Crucible*, 8.

23. Cf. Stephen Mitchell and Peter Van Nuffelen (eds.), *Monotheism between Pagans and Christians in Late Antiquity* (Leuven: Peeters, 2010).

24. Blossom Stefaniw, "Feminist Historiography and Uses of the Past," *Studies in Late Antiquity* 4, no. 3 (2020): 260–83, here 263.

25. Stefaniw, "Feminist Historiography," 265–66.

26. Judith Butler, *Gender Trouble: Feminism and the Subversion of Identity* (New York: Routledge, 2010), 8–10.

27. Including the so-called "objective" historical-critical lens. Sara Parks, Shayna Sheinfeld, and Meredith J. C. Warren, *Jewish and Christian Women in the Ancient Mediterranean* (Abingdon, Oxon: Routledge, 2022), 27–28. For a comprehensive analysis of the way contextual readings affect interpretive methods, especially from traditionally marginalized perspectives, see Fernando F. Segovia, *Decolonizing Biblical Studies: A View from the Margins* (United Kingdom: Orbis Books, 2000).

28. The introduction to our first conference volume highlights many methodological approaches and concerns that are applicable to the study of religions beyond the Second-Temple period. See Shayna Sheinfeld, "Gender and Second-Temple Judaism: Challenges and Possibilities," in *Gender and Second-Temple Judaism*, ed. Kathy Ehrensperger and Shayna Sheinfeld (Lanham: Lexington Books/Fortress Academic, 2020), 1–21.

BIBLIOGRAPHY

Ando, Clifford. "Decline, Fall, and Transformation." *Journal of Late Antiquity* 1 (2008): 31–60.

Bar-Asher Siegal, Michal and Yossi Yovel. "Network Analysis Reveals Insights about the Interconnections of Judaism and Christianity in the First Centuries CE." *Humanities and Social Sciences Communications* Nature 10, no. 191 (2023): 1–9.

Brown, Peter. *The World of Late Antiquity from Marcus Aurelius to Muhammad.* London: Thames and Hudson, 1971.

Butler, Judith. *Gender Trouble: Feminism and the Subversion of Identity.* New York: Routledge, 2010.

Cameron, Averil. "The 'Long' Late Antiquity: A Late Twentieth-Century Model." In *Classics in Progress. Essays on Ancient Greece and Rome*, edited by Timothy P. Wiseman, 165–91. Oxford: Oxford University Press, 2002.

Cameron, Averil. *From the Later Roman Empire to Late Antiquity and Beyond.* London: Routledge, 2023.

Collar, Anna. *Religious Networks in the Roman Empire. The Spread of New Ideas.* Cambridge: Cambridge University Press, 2014.

deCerteau, Michel, *The Practice of Everyday Life.* Berkeley: University of California Press, 1984.

Deryugina, Tatyana, Olga Shurchkov, and Jenna Stearns. "COVID-19 Disruptions Disproportionately Affect Female Academics," *AEA Papers and Proceedings* 111 (2021): 164–68.

Dijkstra, Jitse H. F. "Appropriation: A New Approach to Religious Transformation in Late Antiquity." *Numen* 68 (2021): 1–38.

Ehrensperger, Kathy and Shayna Sheinfeld (eds.). *Gender and Second-Temple Judaism.* Lanham: Lexington Books/Fortress Academic, 2020.

Fowden, Garth. *Before and After Muhammad. The First Millennium Refocused.* Princeton: Princeton University Press, 2013.

Füssel, Marian. "Die Kunst der Schwachen: Zum Begriff der 'Aneignung' in der Geschichtswissenschaft." *Sozial. Geschichte. Zeitschrift für historische Analyse des 20.und 21. Jahrhunderts* NF 21 (2006): 7–28.

Harris, William V. *Rethinking the Mediterranean.* Oxford: Oxford University Press, 2005.

Hervé, Inglebert. "Introduction: Late Antique Conceptions of Late Antiquity." In *Oxford Handbook of Late Antiquity,* edited by Johnson, Scott F., 3–28. Oxford: Oxford University Press, 2012.

James, Edward. "The Rise and Function of the Concept 'Late Antiquity'." *Journal of Late Antiquity* 1 (2008): 20–30.

Kahlos, Maijastina. *Religious Dissent in Late Antiquity 350-450.* Oxford: Oxford University Press, 2019.

Mitchell, Stephen, and Peter Van Nuffelen (eds.). *Monotheism between Pagans and Christians in Late Antiquity.* Leuven: Peeters, 2010.

Parks, Sara, Shayna Sheinfeld, and Meredith J. C. Warren. *Jewish and Christian Women in the Ancient Mediterranean.* Abingdon Oxon: Routledge, 2022.

Rebenich, Stefan. "Late Antiquity in Modern Eyes." In *A Companion to Late Antiquity*, edited by Philip Rousseau, 77–92. Malden: Wiley-Blackwell, 2009.

Reinhartz, Adele. "A Fork in the Road or a Multi-lane-highway? New Perspectives on the 'Parting of the Ways' Between Judaism and Christianity." In *The Changing Face of Judaism, Christianity, and Other Greco-Roman Religions in Antiquity*, edited by Ian H. Henderson and Gerbern S. Oegema, 280–95. Gütersloh: Gütersloher Verlagshaus, 2006.

Schmid, Konrad. "The Rise and Fall of the Notion of 'Spätjudentum' in Christian Biblical Scholarship." In *Protestant Bible Scholarship: Antisemitism, Philosemitism and Anti-Judaism,* edited by Arjen F. Bakker, René Bloch, Yael Fisch, Paula Fredriksen, Hindy Najman, 63–78. Leiden: Brill, 2022.

Schmid, Nora K., Nora Schmidt, and Angelika Neuwirth. *Spätantike. Von einer Epoche zu einem Denkraum.* Wiesbaden: Harrassowitz Verlag, 2016.

Schwartz, Seth, *Were the Jews a Mediterranean Society?* Princeton: Princeton University Press, 2011.

Segovia, Fernando F. *Decolonizing Biblical Studies: A View from the Margins.* United Kingdom: Orbis Books, 2000.

Sheinfeld, Shayna. "Gender and Second-Temple Judaism: Challenges and Possibilities." In *Gender and Second-Temple Judaism,* edited by Kathy Ehrensperger and Shayna Sheinfeld, 1–21. Lanham: Lexington Books/Fortress Academic, 2020.

Stefaniw, Blossom. "Feminist Historiography and Uses of the Past." *Studies in Late Antiquity* 4, no. 3 (2020): 260–83.

Stroumsa, Guy. *The Crucible of Religion in Late Antiquity.* Tübingen: Mohr Siebeck, 2021.

Wickham, Chris. *Framing the Early Middle Ages: Europe and the Mediterranean 400–800.* Oxford: Oxford University Press, 2006.

1

Why Should an *Androginos* Not Become an Enslaved Hebrew?

Tannaitic Reasoning about the Androginos *within the Roman World*

Bernadette J. Brooten

In this chapter, I will examine early rabbinic discourse on gender variation within its broader cultural context, which may help in understanding why ancient Jewish sages held some of the legal opinions that they did. I will particularly focus on why these rabbis held that a person with both male and female genitalia should not be sold or sell themselves into slavery (Tosefta, Tractate Bikkurim 2:6).

A number of early rabbinic texts concern individuals whose physical or perceived genitals and reproductive capacities resist classification into a gender binary.[1] These earliest rabbis (first century BCE to early third century CE), called "Tannaim," apparently see an *andrōginos* (from Greek *androgynos*) as a person with the capacity to penetrate and to be both vaginally and anally penetrated and a *tūmtūm* as one with a skin over the genitals that can be broken to reveal male or female genitals. In addition, they write of eunuchs, of men whose testicles are crushed or whose penis is severed, and of infertile women. They enumerate which commands, prohibitions, and obligations apply to an *androginos* and to a *tumtum*.[2] The Tannaim also raise legal questions about eunuchs, women who do not mature sexually, and so on, but ultimately treat them either as male or as female.[3] Rabbinic genders, then, if we can speak of such, number four: male/man, female/woman, *androginos,* and *tumtum*.[4]

Such pioneering scholars of the Talmud as Charlotte Elisheva Fonrobert, Sarra L. Lev, Gwynn Kessler, and Max K. Strassfeld have opened up a field that has proven to be central for understanding gender, and they have laid the groundwork for this chapter.[5]

I will focus my attention on the *androginos*, who poses significant problems for the sages in deciding which laws to apply, because rabbinic modes of applying some of the commandments are binitarian. The noun *androginos* is grammatically masculine, and the Tannaim nearly always apply the masculine pronoun to such a person, but that in no way solves their problem of deciding which gendered commandments apply to such a person.[6] Although called "he," an *androginos* is legally feminine in some ways. The rabbinic sages construe some commandments to apply only to men, some only to women, and some to both. I will locate rabbinic treatments of the *androginos* within ancient Mediterranean culture as a whole by surveying the range of meanings of the Greek *androgynos* and Latin *androgynus*,[7] along with several other comparable and related terms, by comparing the early sages' treatment of gender variation, and by asking why. Secondly, as a case study of the value of viewing the rabbinic representations of the *androginos* with others in the world around them, I will try to ascertain why one early rabbinic text disallows an *androginos* from entering into slavery.

TANNAITIC TEXTS ON THE *ANDROGINOS* IN COMPARISON WITH GREEK AND LATIN ONES

What May a Jewish *Androginos* Do and Not Do? Their Mother? What About an Animal Who is an *Androginos*?

The Tannaim debate whether an *androginos* may marry a man or a woman, the length of a mother's impurity after the birth of a baby *androginos*, whether an *androginos* may be alone with men or alone with women, whether an *androginos* may serve as a witness, whether an *androginos* may be sold as an enslaved Hebrew, and much more. Beyond this, they discuss whether an animal who is an *androginos* qualifies to be sacrificed as a firstborn male or whether it may instead be slaughtered.[8] The Tannaim sometimes base their opinions on a particular construal of scripture, but they often do not explain their reasoning. One text summarizes majority and occasionally minority legal views on commandments that apply or do not apply to an *androginos* in: (1) the ways in which an *androginos* is like a man, (2) the ways in which an *androginos* is like a woman, (3) the ways in which an *androginos* is like both, and (4) the ways in which an *androginos* is like neither (t. Bikk. 2:2–6; Mishnah, Tractate Bikkurim 4:1–5 [not in all manuscripts]).

The Tannaim hold that an *androginos* may marry a woman (in the active form of the verb, *nōsē*, used when a man marries a woman), but not be married as if a woman (*nissa*) (m. Yevamot 8:6; m. Bikk. 4:2 [not in all manuscripts]; t. Bikk. 2:3). Confirming that an *androginos* is like a male with respect to marriage, the Mishnah teaches that a priest (*kōhēn*) who is an *androginos* and marries an Israelite woman (i.e., not of the priestly class) confers upon her the right to eat the priestly offerings, just as if the priest were male (m. Yev. 8:6). An *androginos* may also eat the priestly offerings in their own right, albeit not the Holy Things (t. Yev. 10:2).

After giving birth, a mother is to sit for a period of impurity, which Leviticus calculates as a week for a baby boy and two weeks for a baby girl (Lev 12:2–5). In the context of discussing how Leviticus applies to miscarriages or beings born from human mothers in the shape of other species or infants otherwise not clearly a human boy or a human girl, the Tannaim address the obligations of the mother of an *androginos* or a *tumtum*. She, they say, sits out her days of impurity for a male and a female (m. Niddah 3:5).[9] Apparently, either they view the infant as both female and male, or they doubt the infant's gender. In either case, observing the purity regulations for both ensures fulfilling the biblical commandment.

According to the Tosefta, like men, an *androginos* is not allowed to be alone with women and, like women, not allowed to be alone with men (t. Bikk. 2:3–4). The rabbinic concept here is gender segregation, *yichud*.[10] On the assumption that sexual intercourse is liable to take place if a man and a woman are alone together in a room, the Tannaim ordain that a man may not be alone with (one or) two women, but that a woman may be alone with two men (m. Qiddushin 4:12), but not one. Rabbi Yehudah presents a minority opinion in prohibiting a woman from being alone with two men, although the majority of his fellow rabbis allow it (t. Qidd. 5:10). Apparently, the second man secluded with a woman may or may not guard his fellow from transgressing the rabbinic precept. The Tannaim are assuming that female and male desire and behavior differ from each other. When formulated for the *androginos* in t. Bikk. 2:4, there are no minority opinions, and "like women" assumes that women are uniformly prohibited from being alone with a man. Rabbinic sources represent aspirations for how Jewish law should be followed, rather than descriptions of what Jews are actually doing. In the vision of t. Bikk. 2:3–4, an *androginos* will not be close friends with either a man or a woman, because an *androginos* may not be secluded with either a man or a woman. According to m. Qidd. 4:14, a man "whose business [or: occupation] is with women, may not be alone with women," which would render it impossible for an *androginos* to work wool, grind grain, put up food, or cook together with one or two women. An *androginos*, who, like women, is not allowed to be alone with a man, would be unable to work in a workshop with a man, go into a hut together when tending sheep out in the fields, or stay at an inn together. The specter of illicit sex is more prominent for the *androginos* than for women or men. An unmarried man may sleep together with another unmarried Jewish man, because "Israel is not suspected" of sexual relations between males (t. Qidd. 5:10; cf. m. Qidd. 4:14 and b. Qidd. 82a), but an *androginos* may not. Apparently, either a Jewish man is suspected of the desire to have sexual relations with an *androginos*, or a Jewish *androginos* is suspected of the desire to have sex with a Jewish man, or both. Thus, the Tannaim sexualize an *androginos* to a greater extent than Jews with unambiguous genitalia.

Like women, an *androginos* may not serve as a witness (t. Bikk. 2:4; m. Bikk. 4:3 [not in all manuscripts]). The doubt implied by having female genitals apparently excludes an *androginos* from witnessing, a powerful function that could lead to a punishment or a court-ordered fine.

The Torah ordains that Israelites redeem their firstborn son from being sacrificed to God and that they sacrifice the male firstling among their animals.[11] The animals sacrificed shall possess no blemish (*mūm*).[12] After discussing all manner of blemishes that an animal might have, the rabbis of the Mishnah agree that an animal that is a *tumtum* or an *androginos* may not be sacrificed and may not be slaughtered elsewhere. R. Ishmael says, "There is no greater blemish than this," whereas the majority hold that, while such an animal does not count as a male firstling suitable for sacrifice, it may be used as a farm animal (m. Bekhorot 6:12). Perhaps R. Ishmael also viewed a human *tumtum* or *androginos* as having a blemish greater than all others.

Androgynoi/i in Greek and Latin Sources: Effeminate Men and Monsters: From Portents of Evil to Entertainment

In the world surrounding the early rabbis, *androgynos/us* can have multiple meanings, of which I will discuss those most relevant to the earliest rabbinic discussion. Some contribute to historical depth, while others help to understand what the Tannaim are not doing. Joseph Marchal, configuring some of the following sources in relation to others more explicitly erotic, expertly demonstrates a sometimes dazzling incoherence in Roman-period conceptualizations of ancient androgyny.[13]

Within Greek medicine, the Hippocratic Corpus, which dates from the Hellenistic period, but continues to be read in the time of the early rabbis, classifies men and women based on behavior, character, and physical appearance. Three types of male and three types of female offspring can result from the mixing of specific types of female and male seeds:

(1) men "brilliant in soul and strong in body";
(2) brave men, less brilliant than the first type; and
(3) men-women (Greek *androgynoi*, plural of *androgynos*); and
(1) women who are very female and fair;

(2) women bolder than the first type, but modest; and
(3) mannish women (*andreiai*) who are bolder than the other two types.

When speaking of physical appearance, this medical writer is not referring to variation in genitals, but rather to strength in men and beauty in women. Behavior and character are equally important: brilliance in soul, bravery, modesty, and boldness. On the side of both the men and the women, the list ranges from the ideal very male and very female to the *androgynoi* and the mannish women. Striking is the fluidity of this medical description.

In contrast, in the Tannaitic conceptualization of both an *androginos* and a *tumtum*, physical strength, beauty, concepts of brilliance or lack thereof in the soul, bravery or lack thereof, or modesty plays no role. Rather than representing an *androginos* or a *tumtum* on a behavioral, attitudinal, and aesthetic scale, the Tannaim assume that the reader knows that these terms apparently refer to a physical variation of the genitals, and that they are human souls like other human beings. The Tannaim create nuance and place an *androginos* and a *tumtum* on a spectrum, but one with man and woman, not a spectrum ranging from braver and stronger men to *androgynoi* or more modest and beautiful women to mannish women. Unlike the Hippocratic Corpus, the Tannaim concern themselves with an infant's genital appearance. Bravery, boldness, and modesty are not yet apparent, and the Tannaim show no evidence of considering such factors in any case.

In some Greek conceptualizations, an *androgynos* can also mean a person who begins life as female and later lives as male, which results in a change in behavior and dress.[14] Greek writer Diodoros of Sicily (first century. BCE) treats *androgynos* and *hermaphroditos* as synonyms, arguing, however, that such a person is not a *dimorphos* (two-formed one), that is, fully female and fully male. Diodoros writes of one Heraïs, born a girl and married to a man, whom he calls a *hermaphroditos* and of whom he reports that others assumed that she had been having male-male, that is anal, sex with her husband. Heraïs becomes ill and suffers pain until a tumor in her groin bursts, revealing male genitalia. A physician surgically completes the transformation, so that he becomes Diophantos. Diodoros further reports on a woman named Kallo who, not having an opening in her female orifice, was "forced to submit to unnatural sex," that is, presumably anal sex, until she developed a tumor, on which the physicians performed a technically quite remarkable surgical transformation to maleness, so that he became Kallon. Diodoros also reports on an Italian who had married an *androgynos*, similar to the two aforementioned persons, and of another such person at Athens. Diodoros stresses that he is presenting these cases not to entertain his readers, but rather to improve them, to make them realize that such a person is not a "monster" (*teras*). With horror, he reports of people who had burned them alive. He disputes the view of some people that hyenas are both female and male and alternate in behaving as females and as males. Instead, Diodoros asserts that no living creatures can be both female and male, that monsters (*terata*) are born, but that they do not live to adulthood.[15]

Unlike Diodoros, the early rabbis do assume that living creatures can be both female and male. In Diodoros's terms, they assume that a *dimorphos* can exist, terming such a person an *androginos*. In contrast, the early rabbinic *tumtum*, while conceptually related to the *androginos* and often mentioned along with the latter, is not an *androginos/hermaphroditos*. Further, the Tannaim do not speak of a *tumtum* or an *androginos* being anything like a monster (*tera*), and they do not discuss anyone killing such a person. Does this mean that none of their fellow Jews harbored fear or disgust at the sight of such a person, for example, at the public baths, when urinating in a field or elsewhere, or as a child running naked, or that persons with genital variation never experienced violence against them for their appearance? In a world shaped by binary thinking, perhaps such persons did encounter fear, disgust, and even violence. The Tannaim do not speak in these terms or encourage such behavior, although the binary legal structures that they created laid the foundations for it.

Somewhat along the lines of the Hippocratic Corpus, Philo of Alexandria (first century BCE to first century CE) defines an *androgynos* in behavioral terms, including erotic behaviors. Philo discusses Leviticus 18:22 and 20:13, which prohibit anal intercourse between males and place it under the death penalty. Philo assumes that his readers will understand the verses to refer to pederasty, a form of male-male relations well known in Philo's world and accepted by some. In the most vociferous of condemnations, Philo calls the boy participant an *androgynos*, who should be "suffered not to live for a day or even an hour."[16] On the assumption that the adult male would assume that he is not at fault, since he has not betrayed his manliness, Philo writes that the (adult) lover should know that he is subject to the same penalty. Why? Because he pursues a pleasure that is contrary to nature and because he teaches the boy unmanliness (*anandria*) and softness or effeminacy (*malakia*). The adult lover effeminates/emasculates the bloom of boys' prime.[17] Philo goes on to speak of the powerful public presence of non-Jewish *androgynoi* in marketplaces, religious processions, and religious rites, some of whom mutilate their genitals out of a desire to be completely transformed into women, for which they receive even greater honor, when they should actually be punished as criminals.[18] For Philo, these *andyogynoi*, like the penetrated boys, are agents; they themselves desire to have their genitals cut. In neither case does Philo consider power relations. Philo does not envision anyone else cutting them so that these *androgynoi* can entertain others.

Early rabbinic discourse differs from that of Philo. In discussing male-male intercourse (*mishkav zakur*), the Tannaim take Lev 18:22 and 20:13 to refer to one specific behavior, namely a male anally penetrating another male. In its earliest stage, Lev 18:22 and 20:13 likely penalizes only the insertive male, not the receptive one.[19] Some Tannaim take it this way (m. Sanhedrin 7:4; m. Keritot 1:1), although other rabbis, while also assuming an insertive party (*shōkēv*) and a receptive one (*nishkav*), place both under the penalty (Sifra, Qodashim 10:11).[20] The Tannaim show no interest at all in whether the insertive participant teaches the receptive one unmanliness or softness/effeminacy. In contrast to Philo's view, for them, the receptive party is not an *androginos* by virtue of being penetrated. Illustrating this difference is R. Eliezer, who deems the penetrator of an *androginos* subject to stoning, just like the penetrator of a male (m.Yev. 8:6).

Latin literature differs further and reflects societal change over time. Pliny the Elder (first century CE) treats *androgyni* and *hermaphroditi* (Greek loan words in Latin) as synonyms, observing, "Persons are also born of both sexes combined—what we call *hermaphroditi*, once called *androgyni* and classed as portents or monstrosities [*prodigia*], but now as entertainments [*delicia*]."[21] Pliny represents a broader historical transition that occurred roughly between the Roman Republic and the Empire, which began in 27 BCE, away from killing *androgyni*. Recall that Diodoros sought to end that practice in the late Republic. Pliny presents *hermaphroditi* as being both female and male, rather than as transitioning from one to the other, as Diodoros of Sicily has it. The previous classification of an *androgynus* as a *prodigium*, portent or monstrosity, however, echoes Diodoros of Sicily and suggests danger, risk, a being from which one might shrink back or violently assault.

The classification of an *androginus* in Pliny's time as a *delicium* suggests treating such an individual as a pet or as a darling. In elite Roman society, both masters and mistresses could keep enslaved children (not necessarily children whose genitals differed from those of the majority population) as darlings, *delicia*.[22] Owners apparently sometimes required enslaved children to appear nude at symposia and around the house.[23] Several Roman emperors are reported to have kept enslaved *delicia* children, which may have been known to Jews paying close attention to the emperors who determined Jewish fates. Emperor Augustus (27 BCE –14 CE) is said to have kept boys who were attractive in appearance or speech, especially Moors and Syrians, and to have disliked persons with disabilities.[24] A late antique source has Augustus consorting with twelve "catamites" (Latin: *catamiti*) and twelve girls.[25] Emperor Vitellius (69) also had his darlings.[26] Some suspected Emperor Titus (79–81) of unchastity because of the crowds of favorite boys and eunuchs around him; he is said to have once cherished his *delicati*, but then to have tired of them.[27] A "Caesar's boy" is said to have served Emperor Domitian (81–96).[28] Some

Romans were particularly drawn to disabled *delicia*, and a "monster (*terata*) market" existed in Rome and perhaps elsewhere, where buyers sought out three-eyed or ostrich-headed persons.[29]

Although Pliny does not designate persons who begin life as one sex or gender and then later live as another as *androgyni* or *hermaphroditi*, he does give several accounts of women who first understand themselves to be women and then later as men right after his discussion of *androgyni* and *hermaphroditi*.[30]

In line with Pliny's report that people in the past, but not the present, saw an *androginos* as a monster, a marvel, a wonder, the Tannaim, almost all of whom lived in the imperial period of Roman history, do not treat the *androginos* as a monster or comparable. I will shortly discuss whether they saw an *androginos* as at risk of being treated as entertainment.

Greek writer Phlegon of Tralles in Asia Minor (second century CE), a freedman of Emperor Hadrian (117–138), defines two distinct types of *androgynoi*, those born with both female and male genitalia, and successive *androgynoi*, those who begin their life identified as one sex and gender and then behave and understand themselves as another. Phlegon thereby follows in the line of Diodoros in designating such persons as *androgyni*. When a Lokrian woman married to Polykritos, a high-ranking Aitolian, gives birth to an infant with both male and female genitalia, the infant's relatives take it to the agora, where some in the assembly suggest that it portends a breach between the Aitolians and the Lokrians. Phlegon terms the infant a "monster" or "portent" (*teras*). In the end, the now-deceased Polykritos returns as a ghost to devour the infant. Otherwise, the assembly may have killed the infant, such as by burning it alive.[31] In addition, Phlegon discusses an *androgynos* born in Rome in 125 BCE, concerning whom the Senate has the priests read the Sibylline Oracles, which describe monsters/portents (*tera<te>*) and in which the Sibyl declares that a woman will bear an *androgynos* with all of the male and female parts. The Sibyl provides detailed instructions for rituals to propitiate the deities, but this time, no one speaks of killing the infant.[32]

Phlegon also presents six stories of persons who begin life one way and end it another, at least two of them mythical (Teresias and Kaineos/Kainis).[33] They apparently count as oddities, but not as monsters or portents who present a religious danger to society and may need to be killed. In one story, Phlegon speaks of an *androgynos* in Antioch, a young bride from whom male genitalia burst forth.[34] This individual may be an *androgynos* because the genitals appear first to be female and later male, or because the female genitals remain after the male ones burst forth. Other *androgynoi* include the betrothed Philotis in Mevania, Italy, who in 53 CE sees himself and is seen as a man when male genitals appear, and an *androgynos* in Epidauros first named Sympherousa (f.) and then Sympheron (m.).[35]

Whereas Phlegon subdivides the *androgynos* into (1) persons with both female and male genitals and (2) persons who begin life as one sex and gender and later live as another, the Tannaim place somewhat parallel the *androginos* and the *tumtum*. As seen above, a mother of either a *tumtum* or an *androginos* remains impure for the period of a baby boy and for the period of a baby girl (m. Nid. 3:5). Similarly, a man who vows that he will be a Nazir (person under a vow to do certain things) (see Numbers 6) if a son is born to him, but who instead has a daughter, a *tumtum*, or an *androginos* is not a Nazir, because none of these counts as a son (m. Nazirim 2:7).

In contrast, however, to Phlegon's narratives concerning the infant whom the assembly would have killed and concerning the Senators seeking guidance in the Sibylline Oracles about rituals to propitiate the deities, the early rabbis do not expect their community to purge itself of an infant *androginos* through killing, nor do they see such a person as a divine omen. For the ancient sages, an *androginos* is a human creature whose variation raises halakhic questions. The Mishnah states that if the potential Nazir says, "when I will have a son," but then has a daughter, a *tumtum*, or an *androginos*, that father is not a Nazir. If, however, he instead says "when I will have a child (*walad*)," then even the birth of a daughter, a *tumtum*, or an *androginos* obligates the man to follow through on his vow (m. Naz. 2:7). A *tumtum* and an *androginos* are simply children, not portents or omens. They do not enjoy the prized status of sons, but they are no less a father's children than his sons.

Julius Obsequens (ca. fourth century) reports on portents/omens (*prodigia*) that occurred in the much earlier Republican Period of Roman history. He recounts tales in which the inhabitants of a specific town or city, apparently to avert evil from the community, cast into the sea or into a river infant or older *androgyni*, sometimes on the orders of the diviners.[36] Only in the Etruscan city of Arretium does Obsequens report on two *androgyni* whose killing he does not describe. Many lightning strikes follow, then supplication ceremonies, and lustration songs by twenty-seven virgins, perhaps to ward off further harm.[37]

Beyond Diodoros of Sicily and Phlegon, Livy, Tacitus, Pliny the Younger, and Aulus Gellius also discuss cases of persons moving from female to male, of whom it is uncertain whether they are male or female, and of persons with two sets of genitalia.[38] Favorinus of Arelate (ca. 80–160; today's Arles), academic philosopher and sophist, could have been an *eunuchus* or could have had both female and male genitals. Second- and third-century writers variously describe him as beardless[39] and an academic eunuch,[40] or as a beardless *androthēlys* (man-female) with a high-pitched voice.[41] The Suda, a tenth-century Byzantine lexicon styles Favorinus an *androgynos*, also known as a *hermaphroditos*.[42]

Like Diodoros of Sicily, Christian theologian Clement of Alexandria (ca. 150–ca. 215) rejects the idea that hyenas are truly both female and male or that humans can be so: "nature can never be forced to change."[43] Similarly, Clement claims that *hermaphroditoi* and *androgynoi*, a third sex, do not even exist.[44]

While for the early rabbis the *androginos* is apparently in the middle between man and woman or rather both/and, the Roman jurists base their legal opinions on the extent to which a *hermaphroditus* tends toward maleness, which gives such a person more rights. Like rabbinic legal thought, Roman law is often based on a binary: "There are many points in our law in which the condition of females is inferior to that of males."[45] Roman Jurist Ulpian (second–third century, from Tyre in Syria) writes: "It is asked: With whom is a *hermaphroditus* comparable? I rather think each one should be ascribed to that sex which is prevalent in their make-up."[46] So, whereas the rabbinic *androginos* is fully female and fully male, the *hermaphroditus* may be more female or more male. In the Justinian Digest, Ulpian's statement on the *hermaphroditus* follows immediately upon that concerning the inferior condition of women under the law. Like the rabbis, Roman jurists base themselves on the physical characteristics of the person. In the concrete case of whether or not a *hermaphroditus* may witness a will, Roman jurist Paul (second–third century.) writes, "it depends on their sexual development."[47] Ulpian elsewhere allows a hermaphrodite to institute a *posthumous* heir, "if the male characteristics in him are predominant."[48] Unlike the early rabbis, Roman jurists are only concerned with the ways in which a hermaphrodite is like a man, since being a man allows him to do things that a woman may not do.

Mathew Kuefler argues that some in late antiquity removed the threat posed by the ambiguity of a *hermaphroditus* by classifying such a person as masculine, citing these legal principles by jurists Ulpian and Paulus as evidence, whom Augustine helps to understand when he notes that *androgyni* and *hermaphroditi* are masculine and not feminine forms.[49] Kuefler, however, misconstrues the Roman legal discussion of *hermaphroditi* by failing to recognize that a masculine noun form does not legally disambiguate a human person. If Kuefler were correct that, as a Roman legal person, a *hermaphroditus* is masculine, then the jurists would simply declare every *hermaphroditus*, rather than just the one in whom the male sex is prevalent, to be capable of bearing witness or doing anything else that only a male may do.

In sum, the Roman jurists allow for a physical gender fluidity that apparently differs from the early rabbinic concept of the *androginos*.

Four late antique medical handbooks transmit surgical instructions that may well go back to Soranos of Ephesos (first–second century). In one of these, Paulus of Aegina (seventh century) teaches medical practitioners how to perform a castration and surgical corrections of *hermaphroditoi*, of which Paulus says there are four types, three male and one female, and a clitoridectomy on an adult woman with an "overly large" clitoris.[50]

Compare R. Yehudah, who says, "[If] a *tumtum* is torn (*niqra*) and is found to be male, he does not perform *chalitzah* (ritual with one's brother's widow), because he is like a *saris* (eunuch)" (m. Yev. 8:7). The verb *niqra* can mean both to be torn (perhaps envisioned as like the woman in Diodoros of Sicily who develops a tumor that bursts) or surgically operated upon. This could be a cutting, although R. Yehudah does not state that clearly.

So, with this one possible exception of R. Yehudah on the *tumtum*, the Tannaim, to my knowledge, have no interest in surgical interventions on an *androginos*, the equivalent of a *hermaphroditos*, and, unlike Paulus of Aegina's probably adopted text, they do not distinguish among differing male and female physical forms of *androgynoi/hermaphroditoi*.

CASE STUDY: WHY DOES THE TOSEFTA DISALLOW THE SALE OF AN *ANDROGINOS* INTO SLAVERY?

One element of Tosefta Bikkurim's halakhic pronouncements can illustrate in greater detail the value of situating Tannaitic texts on the *androginos* within a larger social and cultural context. T. Bikk. 2:6 states that an *androginos* "is not sold as an enslaved Hebrew, unlike both men and women" (אין נמכר לעבד עברי לא כאנשים ולא כנשים).[51] This clause echoes verses from Exodus, Leviticus, and Deuteronomy that regulate how both Hebrew women and Hebrew men are to sell themselves or be sold into slavery and how they are to be subsequently treated. Exod 21:2–11 allows and regulates the sale into slavery of a Hebrew man and his wife, and of a Hebrew daughter. Similarly, Deut 15:12–18 regulates the sale into slavery of a Hebrew man or woman. According to Lev 25:39–43, rather than as enslaved laborers, Israelites are to treat destitute fellow Israelites who have sold themselves as hired laborers. In Leviticus, permanent, unregulated slavery is reserved for persons from surrounding nations and for non-Israelites living in Israel. Because the Tosefta concerns itself only with an Israelite *androginos*, however, the question of a non-Israelite enslaved person does not apply here. The Tosefta employs biblical terms, namely "is sold"/"sells oneself" (נמכר; *nimkar*) and "enslaved Hebrew" (עבד עברי; *eved ivri*). Exodus, Deuteronomy, and Leviticus speak of selling and of being sold, but only Lev 25:39 uses the form *nimkar*.[52] In Lev 25:39, the "brother"/"sibling," presumably male or female (as in Deut 15:12), sells themself to their kin, that is, to a fellow Israelite, upon becoming so impoverished that they see no other choice. The Mekilta of R. Ishmael, a Tannaitic halakhic midrash on Exodus, interprets Lev 25:39 as self-sale and Exod

21:2 as sale by a court because the man in question had stolen and could not repay.[53] Similarly, the Sifra, a Tannaitic halakhic midrash on Leviticus, takes Lev 25:39 to refer to self-sale and stresses that an Israelite is only allowed to sell themselves if they are poor, not simply to save money for an animal, tools, or a house.[54] The specific terms *nimkar* and *eved ivri* may point to the biblical verses for which an *androginos* may not sell themself (Lev 25:39: *nimkar*) or be sold into slavery by a court for theft (Exod 21:2, *eved ivri*; cf. Deut 15:12). Alternatively, the Tosefta may be construing Exod 21:2 and Deut 15:12 to refer to all forms of debt-slavery, not restricting the meaning of the verses to a court sale for theft. In that case, the biblical term *eved ivri* could point to an *androginos* selling themself (*nimkar*) into debt-slavery, as seen in Exodus and Deuteronomy, rather than into the less harsh treatment as a hired laborer idealistically prescribed by Leviticus.

Why do the Tannaim prohibit enslavement? The non-sale of the *androginos* is part of a larger discourse concerning who may be sold into slavery in which gender and age are central. The Tannaim construe the word "father" in Exod 21:7 to mean that only a father, but not a mother, may sell a daughter.[55] In addition, they take "daughter" to refer to a minor daughter, and they exclude a father from selling his minor son.[56] According to Exod 21:8, 9, the girl is meant to become the sexual partner of the master or of his son. In his commentary on the Tosefta, Saul Lieberman suggests that an *androginos* may not be sold to become an enslaved Hebrew girl (*ammah ivriyah*), because the *androginos* is not suited to be wife to a master or his son. If a father sold his minor child who was an *androginos*, he would be running the risk of selling someone who may not be sold, that is, a minor son.[57]

Lieberman further argues that both an *androginos* and a *tumtum* are not sold because it is not proper to give them a wife (which may happen to an enslaved Hebrew man [Exod 21:4–5]). Recall, however, that an *androginos*, according to t. Bikk. 2:3, may marry a woman but is not married as a woman. Exodus envisions this enslaved Hebrew man as able to beget children, and Lieberman views an *androginos* and a *tumtum* as unsuited to beget sons and daughters.[58]

According to Lieberman, in their discussion of the potential enslavement of an *androginos*, these early sages apparently harbor doubt as to whether a minor *androginos* might actually be a boy and as to whether an adult *androginos* has a functioning penis and is able to sire children.

The Tannaim explicitly construe the Bible to mean that an adult woman may not be sold by the court for having stolen and subsequently being unable to pay the restitution for the theft. Exod 22:3 states that a thief will be sold for *his* theft. The Mekilta of R. Ishmael interprets Exod 22:3 to mean that a woman, unlike a man, may not be sold into slavery for stealing.[59] The later Babylonian Talmud explains that "shall be sold for his theft" excludes for *her* theft.[60] In addition, the Mekilta states that "a woman does not sell herself" (Neziqin 3: ואין אישה מוכרת עצמה).[61]

In sum, uncertainty and fluidity best describe the Tannaitic conceptualization of the potentially enslaved *androginos*. Because one does not know whether a minor *androginos* is to be seen as male (in which case he may not be sold by his father) or as female (in which case she may), a father may not sell that child. If the adult *androginos* be seen as female, she may not be sold for theft or sell herself. If male, he may be sold for theft and may sell himself. Because of fear of selling someone who may not be sold, the *androginos* may not be sold at all. Because there is doubt as to whether an *androginos* is female or male, one errs on the side of caution.[62] The doubt model differs from viewing an *androginos* as fully male and fully female, which t. Bikk. 2:2–6 might otherwise lead us to follow.

This exegetical reasoning is certainly rabbinic and may well explain the prohibition of sale into slavery as a Hebrew, but does it exhaust the meaning? Might other considerations also play a role? I propose a new reading based on both rabbinic thought and on rabbinic awareness of their cultural environment. Could the Tosefta be prohibiting the sale of an *androginos* into slavery to avoid Hebrew enslavers from sexually exploiting a type of person at heightened risk of being used for entertainment and of anally penetrating them? Could the rabbis of the Tosefta have suspected some of their fellow Jews of considering, as Pliny reports, an *androginos* to be a wonder or monster (*prodigium*) or of using them for entertainment or as a darling pet (*delicium*)?

As sources discussed here show, in the surrounding Roman world, *androgyni* were vulnerable to violence and could be used for entertainment, which likely implies sexual exploitation. The early rabbinic prohibition against the seclusion of an *androginos* with either women or men demonstrates their heightened concern about such a person's sexual acts. The Tannaim know well the close connection between sexual contact and enslavement and captivity.[63] A father sells his minor daughter for the purpose of sex and possibly marriage (Exod 21:7–11). A freedwoman is assumed not to be a virgin (e.g., m. Yev. 6:5; m. Ketubot 1:2,4; t. Yev. 6:6).[64] Tosefta Horayot observes that men do not want to marry a freedwoman, owing to the wantonness of an enslaved woman (2:11; see also m. Avot. 2:7). Maybe these rabbis were particularly concerned that an Israelite enslaver might anally penetrate their enslaved *androginos*.

Like early Christian male writers, the Tannaim are quite aware of sexual contact between masters and the enslaved and do not think well of it. Neither early Christian writers nor the Tannaim, however, penalize Christian or Jewish masters respectively for such behavior.[65] According to Exod 21:7–11, sex between the girl sold into slavery and the master or his son (whether within marriage or concubinage or outside of both) is a central expectation of the sale. If an Israelite/Hebrew master were to vaginally penetrate an *androginos* sold to them, that enslaved Hebrew would be lowered to the level of a woman, which the Tannaim show that they do not want by writing that an *androginos* marries actively, but is not married passively. Penetrating an enslaved person vaginally is, however, not biblically prohibited. If, however, the master anally penetrates an *androginos*, that master is transgressing the biblical prohibition of male-male anal penetration (Lev 18:22; 20:13). See the later Babylonian Talmud passage on the (vaginal and) anal penetration of an *androginos* (b. Yev. 83b–84a), insightfully analyzed by Max Strassfeld.[66] Prohibiting an *androginos* from being enslaved in the first place prevents such sexual acts from occurring.

CONCLUSION

The Tannaim participate in discussions in the Roman world about whether persons with both female and male genitals exist, affirming that they do. They apply the term *androginos* to such persons, but not to individuals who are treated as (usually) female from birth and then later as male. Unlike some others, especially from an earlier period, the Tannaim do not view an *androginos* as a monster or a divine portent requiring expiation or removal through killing the person or as entertainment or a *delicium*. They may, however, see an *androginos* as disabled (as having a blemish, *mum*). They may also be hypersexualizing an *androginos* by not allowing such a person to be alone either with women or with men, or they may be recognizing that the culture hypersexualizes such a person. Unlike the ancient medical literature, which presents gender variation as on a scale of more masculine to more feminine, based either on behavior and appearance, or on the specific genital anatomy, the Tannaim do not generally view one *androginos* as more feminine and another as more masculine. The Tannaim do not recommend surgery to make the body of an *androginos* conform to a binary ideal appearance or to enable an *androginos* to live as a woman or as a man. They do, however, through halakhah, make each *androginos* in some ways like men, in some ways like women, in some ways like both, and some ways like neither, so that each *androginos* participates, as it were, in multiple spectra.

Traditional explanations for not allowing an *androginos* to become an enslaved Hebrew, such as that they cannot have children or are otherwise prohibited from sale (by being a minor son or an adult woman), are compatible with Tannaitic thinking, but may not exhaust the reasons for the prohibition.

Out of an awareness that sexual contact between owners and their enslaved laborers occurs not infrequently, the Tannaim may be concerned that male Jewish enslavers might subject an enslaved Jewish *androginos* to what they view as male-male intercourse. An open question is why the Tannaim do not restrict such a sale to a female enslaver, who could not penetrate an *androginos* with her own penis–or she would be an *androginos* herself.

I hope to have shown that the material and historical circumstances of enslavement in the Roman world in which the Tannaim lived, as well as their neighbors' past and contemporaneous responses to humans with ambiguous genitalia, affected how the Tannaim responded to the *androginos*, especially when enslavement overlapped with a non-binary human form. In turn, no account of gender in the Roman world as a whole is complete without this Jewish legal thinking.

How might this interpretation contribute to current theoretical discussions? Both doubt (do not sell an *androginos* lest you sell a person of, e.g., disallowed gender) and concrete knowledge of enslavement and of Roman cultural conceptions of *androgyni/hermaphroditi* likely shape this teaching. Gwynn Kessler demonstrates how the rabbis rewrite scripture to move beyond a gender binary.[67] By rejecting the enslavement of an *androginos* out of uncertainty about whether that person is male or female, these rabbis rewrite biblical laws on enslavement to go beyond their distinctions between females and males. Doubt also evokes fluidity about the *androginos*'s body and gender, in other words, the "instability of sexed embodiment," as Max Strassfeld puts it.[68] If a major concern is the sexual vulnerability of an enslaved *androginos* as *delicium*, then, in this respect, the prohibition on selling an *androginos* aligns well with Charlotte Fonrobert's view that "the presence of a penis has greater defining power than a vagina."[69] So, too, does Strassfeld's observation that early rabbis define the anus of an *androginos* as male.[70] The Tannaim resemble their neighbors in disapproving of some sexual contacts between male enslavers and enslaved girls and women, but of never placing such behavior under any penalty. If they were concerned about the sexual use of an enslaved *androginos* as a *delicium*, then anal penetration was likely foremost in their thinking. Penetrating an enslaved *androginos*'s vagina, in contrast, conformed to the normal pattern of enslavers. I very much hope that other scholars will further analyze this Toseftan prohibition on selling an *androginos*, and that they will either incorporate it into current concepts or will alter these accordingly.

NOTES

1. I have greatly benefited from conversations and communications with Rabbinics scholars Sarra L. Lev, Gwynn Kessler, Max Strassfeld, Lynn Kaye, and Reuven

Kimelman. Both Kessler and Lev are preparing book-length manuscripts that will include extensive discussion of the *androginos*.

2. As is customary, I use *androginos* and *tumtum*, that is, without the diacritical (i.e., long) marks, throughout the remainder of this chapter.

3. Sarra L. Lev, "They Treat Him As a Man and See Him As a Woman: The Tannaitic Understanding of the Congenital Eunuch," *Jewish Studies Quarterly* 17, no. 3 (2010): 213–43; and Lev, "How the ''Aylonit' Got Her Sex," *AJS Review* 31, no. 2 (2007): 297–316.

4. Gwynn Kessler, "Rabbinic Gender: Beyond Male and Female," in *A Companion to Late Ancient Jews and Judaism: Third Century BCE to Seventh Century CE*, ed. Naomi Koltun-Fromm and Gwynn Kessler (Hoboken: Wiley, 2020), 353–70; and "Perspectives on Rabbinic Constructions of Gendered Bodies," in *The Wiley Blackwell Companion to Religion and Materiality*, ed. Vasudha Narayanan (Hoboken: Wiley, 2020), 61–89.

5. Max K. Strassfeld, *Trans Talmud: Androgynes and Eunuchs in Rabbinic Literature* (Albany: SUNY Press, 2022); and "Translating the Human: The *Androginos* in Tosefta Bikkurim," *Transgender Studies Quarterly* 3 (2016): 587–604; Kessler, "Rabbinic Gender," and "Perspectives"; Charlotte Elisheva Fonrobert, "Gender Duality and Its Subversions in Roman Law," in *Gender and Judaism in Islam: Common Lives, Uncommon Heritage*, ed. Beth Wenger and Firoozah Kashani-Sabet (New York: New York University Press, 2014), 4–125; and "Regulating the Human Body: Rabbinic Legal Discourse and the Making of Jewish Gender," in *The Cambridge Companion to the Talmud and Rabbinic Literature*, ed. Charlotte Elisheva Fonrobert and Martin S. Jaffee (Cambridge: Cambridge University Press, 2007), 270–94. See also: Lev, "They Treat Him," and "How the ''Aylonit'."

6. An exception occurs at t. Bikk. 2:6; m. Bikk. 4:5 (found only in some manuscripts).

7. Latin speakers borrowed the term *androgynus* from Greek, latinizing its ending.

8. Only male firstborns are sacrificed.

9. M. Nid. 3:5.

10. On *yichud*, see Gail Labovitz, "Ḥeruta's Ruse: What We Mean When We Talk about Desire," in *The Passionate Torah: Sex and Judaism*, ed. Danya Ruttenberg (New York: New York University Press, 2009), 229–34. Labovitz analyzes Babylonian Talmud Qidd. 80b–81b at length.

11. Exod 12:29; 13:2, 12, 13, 15; Num 18:15–18; Deut 15:19–21.

12. Deut 15:21.

13. Joseph A. Marchal, *Appalling Bodies: Queer Figures Before and After Paul's Letters* (Oxford: Oxford University Press, 2020), 37–45. See also Luc Brisson, *Sexual Ambivalence: Androgyny and Hermaphroditism in Graeco-Roman Antiquity*, trans. Janet Lloyd (French original: 1997; Berkeley: University of California Press, 2002); Maud W. Gleason, *Making Men: Sophists and Self-Presentation in Ancient Rome* (Princeton: Princeton University Press, 1995).

14. Lutz Alexander Graumann, "Monstrous Births and Retrospective Diagnosis: The Case of Hermaphrodites in Antiquity," in *Disabilities in Roman Antiquity: A*

Capite ad Calcem, ed. Christian Laes, Chris Goodey, and M. Lynn Rose (Leiden: Brill, 2013), 181–209, has found mainly instances of female to male.

15. Diodoros of Sicily 32.10.2–12.3 (Heraïs/Diophantos, ca. 145 BCE; Kallo/Kallon, ca. 115 BCE; see Bernadette J. Brooten, *Love Between Women: Early Christian Responses to Female Homoeroticism* (Chicago: University of Chicago Press, 1996), 277–80; revised German ed., with new foreword: *Liebe zwischen Frauen: Weibliche Homoerotik in hellenistich-römischer Zeit und im frühen Christentum*, trans. Gerlinde Baumann (Berlin: Lit, 2020), 313–16.

16. *On the Special Laws* 3:38.

17. *On the Special Laws* 3:39–40.

18. *On the Special Laws* 3:40–42.

19. Saul M. Olyan, "'And with a Male You Shall Not Lie the Lying Down of a Woman': On the Meaning and Significance of Leviticus 18:22 and 20:13," *Journal of the History of Sexuality* 5 (1994): 186–87, 179–206.

20. Sifra, Qodashim 10.11 first cites rabbis who reason that Lev 18:22, which mentions only the insertive partner, prohibits only him from male-male intercourse and not the receptive partner, but that Deut 23:18 and 1 Kings 14:24 prohibit the receptive partner from doing so. These rabbis find in Lev 20:13 the penalty for both, since, unlike Lev 18:22, Lev 20:13 mentions both. R. Akiva derives a prohibition for both partners in Lev 18:22 itself, namely by re-vocalizing the single verb "to lie" as meaning both "you shall not lie" and "you shall not be laid." This reasoning is based on the rabbinic view that no word in the Torah is superfluous.

21. Pliny, *Natural History* 7.4.34.

22. Christian Laes, "Desperately Different? *Delicia* Children in the Roman Household," in *Early Christian Families in Context: An Interdisciplinary Dialogue*, ed. David L. Balch and Carolyn Osiek (Grand Rapids: Eerdmans, 2003), 298–324; on *delicium* (Latin) used even as a technical term in Greek, see, e.g., Plutarch, *Life of Antony* 59.

23. E.g., Cassius Dio, *Roman History* 48.44.3, of Empress Livia.

24. Suetonius, *Lives: Augustus* 83.

25. Aurelius Victor, *Epitome of the Caesars* 1.22.

26. Suetonius, *Vitellius* 12. Asiaticus, said here to be one of Vitellius's *delicia*, is now an adult.

27. Suetonius, *Titus* 7.

28. Statius, *Silvae* 3.4.

29. Plutarch, *Moralia* 520C: *On Being a Busybody* 10.

30. Pliny, *Natural History* 7.4.36.

31. Phlegon of Tralles (flourished early second century), *On Marvels* 2.

32. Phlegon of Tralles, *On Marvels* 10 (125 BCE).

33. Phlegon of Tralles, *On Marvels* 4–9.

34. Phlegon of Tralles, *On Marvels* 6.

35. Phlegon of Tralles, *On Marvels* 7–8.

36. In his *Book of Prodigies*, Julius Obsequens apparently draws upon Roman historian Livy (ca. 59 BCE–17 CE). Obsequens reports on the years 190–11 BCE, but the original book would have included a longer time span. *Androgyni: Book of*

Prodigies, 22 (142 BCE), 27a (133 BCE), 32 (122 BCE), 34 (119 BCE), 36 (117 BCE; a ten-year old *androgynus* was drowned in the sea, twenty-seven virgins then lustrated, i.e., purified, the city with singing, and peace followed), 47 (98 BCE), 48 (97 BCE), and 50 (95 BCE).

37. Julius Obsequens, *Book of Prodigies*, 53 (92 BCE).
38. Livy, *Ab urbe condita* 24.10.10 (female to male; 214 BCE); 27.11.4–6 (uncertain; 209 BCE); 27.37.6 (uncertain; 207 BCE); 31.12.6 (uncertain; 200 BCE); 39.22.5 ("half-male" [*semimas*]; 186 BCE). Tacitus, *Annals* 12.64 ("two-formed" [*biformes*] persons; 54 CE); Pliny, *Natural History* 7.36 (female to male; 171 BCE; other females to males; unknown date).
39. Lucian of Samosata (ca. 120–ca. 180–200), *Demonax*.
40. Lucian of Samosata, *Eunuchus* 7.
41. Philostratos (ca. 170–ca. 250), *Lives of Sophists* 489.
42. The Suda, Phi 4.
43. Clement of Alexandria (ca. 150–ca. 215), *Paidagogos* 2.10.84.1.
44. Clement of Alexandria, *Paidagogos* 2.10.
45. *Digest* 1.5.8 (Papinian [142–212], Syria or Africa).
46. Digest 1.5.10 (Ulpian); trans. Alan Watson, *The Digest of Justinian* (Philadelphia: University of Pennsylvania Press, 1995).
47. *Digest* 22.5.15 (Paulus); trans. Watson.
48. *Digest* 28.2.6 (Ulpian); trans. Watson.
49. Augustine, *City of God* 16.8; Mathew Kuefler, *The Manly Eunuch: Masculinity, Gender Ambiguity, and Christian Ideology in Late Antiquity* (Chicago: University of Chicago Press, 2001), 22–23.
50. Paulus of Aegina, *Epitomae Medicae* 6.68–70; on the clitoridectomy, see Brooten, *Liebe*, 193–94, 196, 201; *Love*, 164–65, 171.
51. See also m. Bikk. 4:5 (not in all manuscripts).
52. Exod 21:2: "when you acquire" (תִּקְנֶה), Exod 7: "if a man sells his daughter" (יִמְכֹּר), Deut 15:12 "if your sibling, a Hebrew man or a Hebrew woman is sold to you" (יִמָּכֵר).
53. Mekilta, Neziqin 1, on Exod 21:2.
54. Sifra, Behar 7:1.
55. Exod 21:7; m. Ketubot 3:8; m. Sotah 3:8. See also b. Sot. 23b, which states that a mother may not sell her daughter, because Exod 21:7 says, "When a man sells his daughter."
56. Mekilta, Neziqin 3, on Exod 21:7.
57. Saul Lieberman, *Tosefta Ki-Fshuta: A Comprehensive Commentary on the Tosefta, Order Zera'im, Part II* (Jerusalem: The Jewish Theological Seminary of America, 1992), on t. Bikk. 2:6, 844.
58. Lieberman, *Tosefta*, on t. Bikk. 2:2, 844.
59. Mekilta, Neziqin 3, on Exod 21:7.
60. Mekilta, Neziqin 3, on Exod 21:7.
61. Mekilta, Neziqin 3, on Exod 21:7. The later Babylonian Talmud, however, explains that "shall be sold for his theft" excludes for *her* theft. Maimonides, *Mishneh Torah, Avadim* 1:2.

62. Sarra Lev is preparing a book manuscript in which she discusses differing Tannaitic models for viewing an *androginos*.

63. Catherine Heszer, "Part Whore, Part Wife," in *Doing Gender—Doing Religion: Fallstudien zur Intersektionalität im frühen Judentum, Christentum und Islam*, ed. Ute E. Eisen, Christine Gerber, and Angela Standhartinger (Tübingen: Mohr Siebeck, 2013), 303–23.

64. In t. Yev. 6:6, R. Yehudah requires a freedwoman to wait three months before marrying (on the assumption that she might be pregnant from her time of enslavement), but R. Yose allows her to marry immediately.

See Yael Wilfand, "Did Roman Treatment of Freedwomen Influence Rabbinic Halakhah on the Status of Female Converts in Marriage?" *The Journal of Legal History* 40 (2019): 182–202.

65. See, e.g., the sources found in Catherine Hezser, *Jewish Slavery in Antiquity* (Oxford: Oxford University Press, 2005), 191–201; Bernadette J. Brooten, "Enslaved Women in Basil of Caesarea's Canonical Letters: An Intersectional Analysis," in *Doing Gender, Doing Religion: Fallstudien zur Intersektionalität im frühen Judentum, Christentum und Islam*, ed. Ute Eisen, Christine Gerber, and Angela Standhartinger (Tübingen: Mohr Siebeck, 2013), 325–55; Kyle Harper, *Slavery in the Late Roman World, AD 275–425* (Cambridge: Cambridge University Press, 2011), 281–325; Margaret Y. MacDonald, "Beyond Identification of the Topos of Household Management: Reading the Household Codes in Light of Recent Methodologies and Theoretical Perspectives in the Study of the New Testament," *New Testament Studies* 57 (2011): 65–90.

66. Strassfeld, *Trans Talmud*, 98–110, 184–85.

67. Kessler, "Rabbinic Gender."

68. Strassfeld, *Trans Talmud*, 185, summarizing discussions throughout his book.

69. Fonrobert, "Regulating," 281.

70. Strassfeld, *Trans Torah*, 100–03.

BIBLIOGRAPHY

Brisson, Luc. *Sexual Ambivalence: Androgyny and Hermaphroditism in Graeco-Roman Antiquity*. Translated by Janet Lloyd. French original: 1997; Berkeley: University of California Press, 2002.

Brooten, Bernadette J. "Enslaved Women in Basil of Caesarea's Canonical Letters: An Intersectional Analysis." In *Doing Gender, Doing Religion: Fallstudien zur Intersektionalität im frühen Judentum, Christentum und Islam*, edited by Ute Eisen, Christine Gerber, and Angela Standhartinger, 325–55. Tübingen: Mohr Siebeck, 2013.

Brooten, Bernadette J. *Love Between Women: Early Christian Responses to Female Homoeroticism*. Chicago: University of Chicago Press, 1996; Revised German edition, with new foreword: *Liebe zwischen Frauen: Weibliche Homoerotik in hellenistich-römischer Zeit und im frühen Christentum*. Translated by Gerlinde Baumann. Berlin: Lit, 2020.

The Digest of Justinian. Translated by Alan Watson. Philadelphia: University of Pennsylvania Press, 1995.

Fonrobert, Charlotte Elisheva. "Regulating the Human Body: Rabbinic Legal Discourse and the Making of Jewish Gender." In *The Cambridge Companion to the Talmud and Rabbinic Literature*, edited by Charlotte Elisheva Fonrobert and Martin S. Jaffe, 270–94. Cambridge: Cambridge University Press, 2007.

Fonrobert, Charlotte Elisheva. "Gender Duality and Its Subversions in Roman Law." In *Gender and Judaism in Islam: Common Lives, Uncommon Heritage*, edited by Beth Wenger and Firoozah Kashani-Sabet, 4–125. New York: New York University Press, 2014.

Gleason, Maud W. *Making Men: Sophists and Self-Presentation in Ancient Rome*. Princeton: Princeton University Press, 1995.

Graumann, Lutz Alexander. "Monstrous Births and Retrospective Diagnosis: The Case of Hermaphrodites in Antiquity." In *Disabilities in Roman Antiquity: A Capite ad Calcem*, edited by Christian Laes, Chris Goodey, and M. Lynn Rose, 181–209. Leiden: Brill, 2013.

Harper, Kyle. *Slavery in the Late Roman World, AD 275–425*. Cambridge: Cambridge University Press, 2011.

Hezser, Catherine. *Jewish Slavery in Antiquity*. Oxford: Oxford University Press, 2005.

Hezser, Catherine. "Part Whore, Part Wife." In *Doing Gender—Doing Religion: Fallstudien zur Intersektionalität im frühen Judentum, Christentum und Islam*, edited by Ute E. Eisen, Christine Gerber, and Angela Standhartinger, 303–23. Tübingen: Mohr Siebeck, 2013.

Kessler, Gwynn. "Perspectives on Rabbinic Constructions of Gendered Bodies." In *The Wiley Blackwell Companion to Religion and Materiality*, edited by Vasudha Narayanan, 61–89. Hoboken: Wiley, 2020.

Kessler, Gwynn. "Rabbinic Gender: Beyond Male and Female." In *A Companion to Late Ancient Jews and Judaism: Third Century BCE to Seventh Century CE*, edited by Naomi Koltun-Fromm and Gwynn Kessler, 353–70. Hoboken: Wiley, 2020.

Kuefler, Mathew. *The Manly Eunuch: Masculinity, Gender Ambiguity, and Christian Ideology in Late Antiquity*. Chicago: University of Chicago Press, 2001.

Labovitz, Gail. "Ḥeruta's Ruse: What We Mean When We Talk about Desire." In *The Passionate Torah: Sex and Judaism*, edited by Danya Ruttenberg, 229–24. New York: New York University Press, 2009.

Laes, Christian. "Desperately Different? *Delicia* Children in the Roman Household." In *Early Christian Families in Context: An Interdisciplinary Dialogue*, edited by David L. Balch and Carolyn Osiek, 298–324. Grand Rapids: Eerdmans, 2003.

Lev, Sarra L. "How the ''Aylonit' Got Her Sex." *AJS Review* 31, no. 2 (2007): 297–316.

Lev, Sarra L. "They Treat Him as a Man and See Him as a Woman: The Tannaitic Understanding of the Congenital Eunuch." *Jewish Studies Quarterly* 17, no. 3 (2010): 213–43.

Lieberman, Saul. *Tosefta Ki-Fshuta: A Comprehensive Commentary on the Tosefta, Order Zera'im*, Part II. Jerusalem: The Jewish Theological Seminary of America, 1992.

MacDonald, Margaret Y. "Beyond Identification of the Topos of Household Management: Reading the Household Codes in Light of Recent Methodologies and Theoretical Perspectives in the Study of the New Testament." *New Testament Studies* 57 (2011): 65–90.

Marchal, Joseph A. *Appalling Bodies: Queer Figures Before and After Paul's Letters*. Oxford: Oxford University Press, 2020.

Olyan, Saul M. "'And with a Male You Shall Not Lie the Lying Down of a Woman': On the Meaning and Significance of Leviticus 18:22 and 20:13." *Journal of the History of Sexuality* 5 (1994): 179–206.

Strassfeld, Max K. "Translating the Human: The Androginos in Tosefta Bikkurim." *Transgender Studies Quarterly* 3 (2016): 587–604.

Strassfeld, Max K. *Trans Talmud: Androgynes and Eunuchs in Rabbinic Literature*. Albany: SUNY Press, 2022.

Wilfand, Yael. "Did Roman Treatment of Freedwomen Influence Rabbinic Halakhah on the Status of Female Converts in Marriage?" *The Journal of Legal History* 40 (2019): 182–202.

2

Because of Her We All Die

Eve in Early Jewish and Early Christian Reception

Sara Parks

INTRODUCTION

Eve has had a long and wide-ranging history of interpretation since her literary debut in Genesis 2–4. This chapter[1] traces the ancient Jewish and Christian period of that reception. Eve appears so frequently throughout the late Hellenistic and Roman periods that this is more "greatest hits" than complete catalog, but what emerges is that, while some references to Eve in early Judaism and Christianity are passing allusions to or reiterations of the tradition in Genesis, most depart significantly from it. Jews and Christians in the Hellenistic and Roman periods introduced numerous innovations, such as extrapolating from Eve to all women, singling her out from Adam as the cause of human downfall, and sexualizing her as a femme fatale or hapless assault victim. Some of these sharp departures from the Genesis accounts remain with Eve today.[2]

Recent monographs, from Barbara Deutschmann's work on gender dynamics in the creation accounts,[3] to Holly Morse's[4] and Helen Schüngel-Straumann's[5] monographs on Eve's reception history, affirm that the directions Eve took in ancient literary imaginations veered away from Genesis to suit authors' own purposes.[6] "Countless interpreters [claim] Genesis 2–3 as a prooftext for viewing women as inherently more sinful than men,"[7] but such readings are "variations of androcentrism reflecting their own culture."[8] Eve functions as a well-worn tool in the backpack of (male)[9] authors who wanted to comment on a range of topics; they found Eve "good to think with."[10] Many times, she was used to comment upon—or try to shape—the role of women.

Sometimes, such employment of Eve is relatively benign. For example, the book of Tobit (200s–175 BCE) mentions Eve to promote endogamous marriage. The context is a prayer offered by young Tobias just before he and Sarah go to bed on their wedding night under extremely dangerous conditions: a groom-murdering demon had killed seven of Sarah's previous would-be grooms (Tobit 3:8). Tobias and Sarah perform a ritual to banish the demon, then Tobias prays:

> Blessed are you, O God of our ancestors . . . You made Adam, and for him you made his wife Eve as a helper and support. From the two of them the human race has sprung. You said, "It is not good that the man should be alone; let us make a helper for him like himself." I now am taking this kinswoman of mine, not because of lust, but with sincerity. Grant that she and I may find mercy and that we may grow old together. (Tobit 8:5–7)[11]

The image of Eve in this text echoes the partnership assigned in Genesis 2:18, which Tobias cites, and references the first couple as parents of the human race (Gen 3:20). The text then shifts quickly back to an overall aim of the book of Tobit—the promotion of endogamy. The author of Tobit uses Eve to "think with" about Jewish marriage practice: it uses her associations with partnership and fecundity in order to discourage marriage to non-Jews. Here, Eve is not maligned but celebrated in the context of a wedding between kin.

This positive view of Eve, though, is out of line with most of her ancient interpreters. Eve was apparently ripe for the plucking for patriarchal and misogynistic views. This chapter surveys two main trends in Eve's reception in the hands of ancient Jewish and Christian thinkers. The first is the way that understandings of Eve as having *agency* are related to authors presenting her as *dangerous*, as though a woman with freedom who gives instruction to men is risky or deadly. The second is the way that allegorical readings of Eve (and femininity) as *sensual* are related to readings of Eve (and not Adam) as *sexual*. During this period, Eve's interaction with the serpent is sexualized, and she is reinvented as a femme fatale. Common across these two trends is a tendency to extrapolate from Eve to all women, with producers of texts mapping whatever views they have of women in general onto Eve, or, conversely, treating Eve as an aetiological explanation for "why women are like this."

It's All Eve's Fault (and Not Adam's)

Perhaps one of the best-known early Jewish innovations on Eve is the shifting of blame for sin and death from the primal *couple* onto the primal *woman*. Parker[12] and Deutschmann[13] notice that interpreters typically ignore Adam's shared responsibility for the events that take place in Genesis 3. Ben Sira (second century BCE) can be credited with the dubious honor of having been the first to exonerate Adam by declaring Eve the perpetrator of all ills, but many followed suit. The book of *Jubilees* (also second century BCE) excuses Adam with a simple addition to the Genesis plot. *Jubilees* retells Genesis in the style that some have called "rewritten Scripture"[14] and others have likened to fan fiction.[15] In its version of Genesis 2–3, Eve eats the fruit, then becomes aware of her "shame" and uses fig leaves to cover herself *before* going to find Adam (*Jubilees* 3:21). By having Eve don the leaves in advance, *Jubilees* implies that her decision to pull Adam in was deceitful and malicious.[16] Some later rabbinic texts also suggest that Eve *tricks* Adam into eating (Genesis Rabbah 19:5; Numbers Rabbah 10:4; Pirkei de Rabbi Eliezer 13).

1 Enoch exonerates Adam simply by not mentioning him in connection with the wicked angel Gaderel who introduced death into the world; it simply says Gaderel "misled Eve" (1 Enoch 69:6–7, translation by Isaac *OTP* 1983). Likewise, 2 Enoch 30:17 has God explain that "while [Adam] was sleeping, I took from him a rib. And I created for him a wife, so that death might come to him by his wife" (translation by Andersen *OTP* 1983).

The *Sibylline Oracles*, Book 1 (first to third century CE) also absolves Adam: "The woman first became a betrayer to him. She gave, and persuaded him to sin in his ignorance" (*Sibylline Oracles* I:42–44; translation by Collins *OTP*). Tertullian (c. 155–220 CE) calls Eve "the devil's gateway" and "the first deserter of the divine law," adding that Eve was targeted because "the devil . . . was not valiant enough to attack" Adam (*The Apparel of Women* 1.2). Likewise, 1 Timothy 2:14 (late-first to early-second century CE) states that "Adam was not deceived, but the woman was deceived and became a transgressor." In *The City of God*, Augustine (354–430 CE) doubles down on Adam's innocence:

> when he said: "And Adam was not deceived, but the woman was deceived' he must have meant that Eve had accepted what the serpent said to her as though it were true, while Adam refused to be separated from his sole companion even in a partnership of sin." (*The City of God* 4.14.11)

Thus, while Augustine admits that Adam has *sinned*, he sharply differentiates between Eve's and Adam's precise wrongdoing;[17] Eve was to blame for being duped by the serpent's words, whereas since Adam was "not deceived," his sin was . . . loyalty and affection for his partner? In other words, Augustine appears to reckon Eve's sin was stupidity and weakness, while Adam's was something more akin to gallant marital fidelity! Not only does this paint Adam in a much more positive light than Eve, but it may be suggesting to male readers that listening to women could spell their downfall.

EVE AS AGENT

Note that all of these examples portray Eve as a *victim* in relation to the serpent; she may be given agency in the moments where she consciously tricks Adam, but she is depicted as hapless when being convinced to eat the fruit herself. There are countless additional examples of Eve as passive pawn. In *Dialogue with Trypho* 79 (150–160 CE), Justin Martyr (c. 100–165 CE) places the serpent in the driver's seat: "the serpent beguiled Eve." Clement of Alexandria (c. 150–215 CE) also identifies Eve as the first victim of the active "deceiver." For Clement, Eve acts not as the *cause* of death in humanity, but rather as its first *casualty*: "it is one and the same deceiver who in the beginning carried off Eve to death, and now does the like to the rest of mankind" (Clement of Alexandria, *Exhortation to the Greeks*, 92.18–19).

However, many other interpreters start instead from the assumption that Eve is an *agent* of her own downfall—and, therefore, of humanity's. John Chrysostom (c. 349–407 CE) takes great pains to emphasize Eve's responsibility. In Schroeder's words, Chrysostom's *Homilies on Genesis* 1–17:

> lays great emphasis upon the woman's initiative in the original transgression, berating Eve for her impetuous behaviour (παρασυρεῖσα, "being carried away"), for her great inattentiveness (πολλὴ απροσεξία), and above all for her pride, "puffed up as she was with the hope of being equal to God and evidently dreaming of greatness."[18]

It is fruitful to use as a lens of inquiry the issue of whether Eve is depicted as a victim (thereby giving agency to the serpent) or as an active agent (often clothed in trickery or waywardness). Doing so reveals that portrayals of Eve as a deceitful temptress tend to extrapolate her guilt to all women, over and against Adam's (and men's), and to condition men to be wary of all women as dangerous Eves liable to destroy them.

In fact, there is only a single example in antiquity (aside perhaps from Genesis itself) that accords Eve agency without reducing her to a trope of warning to men; the Greek *Life of Adam and Eve* (GLAE; 100 BCE–700 CE). The *Life of Adam and Eve* is really a whole group of texts. They seem to have been extremely popular, given both their proliferation[19] and their rich and varied manuscript tradition in multiple languages.[20] The texts exist in two distinct recensions—the Greek Apocalypse of Moses and the Latin *Vita Adae et Evae*, which have a large overlap with each other.[21]

The *Life of Adam and Eve* (hereafter, the *Life*) vastly expands on the glimpse of Adam and Eve in Genesis 4–5 (with flashbacks to Genesis 2–3). Much of the account, which covers the time from the expulsion to their deaths, is told from the perspective of Eve. As such, this cluster of works treats Eve as a more fully developed character than almost any other ancient literature, apart from some stunning Nag Hammadi texts saved for later in the chapter.[22] Although all the versions of the *Life* share much in common, they (as well as their manuscripts) each vary by adding unique episodes.[23] It is in these many creative additions that we are given a window onto an Eve who experiences a range of emotions and thought processes, and takes decisive actions. She is blamed more than Adam as an agent in the downfall; in both 14.2 and 21.5, Adam asks her "what have you brought about among us?"[24] but she is exonerated by the fact that the serpent was disguised as one of the angels who frequent the garden, and so she believed she was listening to a messenger of God.[25] Eve is also complex in other ways in the *Life*; for example, she is depicted with prophetic abilities in chapter 2, when her prescient dream about Cain and Abel's conflict comes true. She gives voice to various prayers and undertakes acts of repentance throughout, such as her petition at the gates of Paradise with Seth (chapter 13) and her repentance in chapter 32. She understands a range of theological concepts such as the "day of resurrection" (chapter 10), and she actively works to protect the rest of humanity from the consequences of her mistakes by instructing her children in right living (chapter 30).

The *Life* is most interested in an aetiology for the presence of death, sin, and suffering,[26] but *en route* to this aim, the character of Eve is treated sympathetically and given direct speech, a range of complex emotions, and intellectual curiosity. Granted, Eve's main activity in the narrative is repentance; nevertheless, the complexity her character is given and the narration from her own perspective are extremely rare. In this sense, the *Life* allows Eve an active part in her own story.

The *Life* therefore stands apart from all other ancient literature with the possible exception of Nag Hammadi, because Eve is afforded a remarkable level of agency without her being entirely pinned with the guilt of the whole world or held up as a warning to all men about all women.[27] Her agency is employed in other ancient texts toward less sympathetic readings. During this period, Eve's character becomes fused with sensuality and sexuality; as she is sexualized, the presence or absence of agency can mean the difference between her being identified as a helpless victim or as a *femme fatale*.

Eve's Dangerous Agency

When depicted with agency in less complex ways than the *Life* and Nag Hammadi, Eve often represents patriarchal anxieties about uncontrolled women. In some cases, she is depicted as a naïve and passive *victim* of the serpent, and the lesson is that women's danger to men is in their weakness or foolishness. In other texts, though, it is frequently Eve, rather than the serpent, who is identified as the source of danger. She is thus sometimes specifically employed as a means of depicting women who take an active role as being dangerous to men. The message is: whether foolish or wise, weak or strong, women cannot be trusted and must be controlled. Ben Sira is perhaps the most vitriolic example of this view.

Jewish teacher and scribe Yeshua Ben Sira wrote his sapiential teachings in Hebrew in Jerusalem (c. 180 BCE); his grandson's translation of the teachings into Greek with the addition of a preface made their way into the Septuagint as the book of Sirach.[28] Ben Sira's vociferous misogyny is notorious.[29] For my purposes, he is most notable for one key innovation: he kicked off the longstanding malignment of Eve and exoneration of Adam by producing "the first explicit statement blaming Eve for bringing sin and death into the world."[30] The book of Sirach does not mention Eve's name, but there are three verses where she is likely implied: Sirach 25:24, 40:1, and 42:13.

Sirach 40:1 is a generalized introduction to the discussion of human woes: "Hard work was created for everyone, and a heavy yoke is laid on the children of Adam, from the day they come forth from their mother's womb, until the day they return to the mother of all." It is the other two verses (and the longer passages in which they occur) that concern innovations in Eve's reception. Sirach 25:24 gave this chapter its title: "From a woman sin had its beginning, and *because of her we all die*." For Ben Sira, the origin of sin is not shared with the serpent, Adam, the prohibition itself, or the God who provided it. Only "a woman" was to blame, and he does not even deign to name her.

This one-line reference to Eve is embedded in the context of a lengthy segment (25:13–26) discussing what horrible trials await a man whose wife is wicked. The section is a complaint about how troublesome, evil, angry, and dangerous women can be, bringing despair and scandal to their husbands. Ben Sira "would rather live with a lion and a dragon than live with an evil woman" (v. 16); he says that "any iniquity is small compared to a woman's iniquity" (v. 19), and a "dejected mind, gloomy face, and wounded heart come from an evil wife" (v. 23). The claim that "because of [Eve] we all die" (v. 24) comes near the end of the passage, which concludes with the advice that men should separate from a wife who doesn't "go as [they] direct" (v. 26). Here, Eve is listed as one example among many of a woman being the downfall of a man, despite the fact that Genesis doesn't exclusively associate Eve with sin, as has been made clear by Deutschmann, Gafney, and Morse recently,[31] and Trible and Bird long before them.[32] Ben Sira's decision "to read Eve as a sinner" in Genesis is an interpretive slant deriving from "silence and ambiguity" at most.[33] Ben Sira is, as far as I know, the very first to have closed off the ambiguity in Genesis and focused all blame onto Eve.

Ben Sira's third reference to Eve (42:13) is in the wider context of several verses devoted to the many problems that arise from daughters: "from garments comes the moth, and from a woman comes woman's wickedness."

Once again, Eve is not named, but she is probably the "woman" from whom "woman's wickedness" derives, especially given the earlier reference in 25:24. In neither passage is Eve the main focus; rather, she joins a barrage of examples that illustrate men's problems caused by women; the first passage lists the particular evils brought by wives, and this one focuses on the special evils brought by daughters.[34] Thus, Ben Sira did not place Eve at the center of all earthly ills by careful exegesis of Genesis, but rather tossed her in to prop up his existing negative views of women in the service of his "wise" advice to husbands and fathers. Subsequent interpreters were happy to take over his depiction of Eve as the primordial wicked woman; as a measure of the success of Ben Sira's misogynistic innovation, by the time of the rabbis, the figure of Eve automatically conjured images of women as the downfall of men, just as quickly as would a Siren or a Pandora.[35]

Eve as Everywoman

Another innovative element of Ben Sira's treatment of Eve is this association of Eve with all women. He not only blames Eve for the *first* case of wickedness, but sees every subsequent woman as a fresh opportunity for a man's downfall. Later ancient texts similarly assume a dangerous Eve within each woman. As Dan Clanton points out, "if Eve is to blame for the disobedient act in the garden, then the usual assumption is that somehow her actions reflect badly on other women."[36] Likewise, Elizabeth Clark writes of "the amalgamation of all women to 'woman' and the identification of 'woman' with Eve" as the most obvious example of "the universalizing tendency of ideology" in all Patristic literature.[37] Eve thus becomes a disastrous prototype for every man's interaction with women. For instance, Augustine asks: "What difference does it make whether it is in a wife or in a mother, provided that we nonetheless *avoid Eve in any woman?*" (*Letter* 243, translated by Teske, emphasis added). Augustine's contemporary Jerome (340s–420 CE) positions Eve as everywoman even more strenuously. In his letter to Nepotian, he tells clergy,

> a woman's foot must never cross the threshold of your humble lodging . . . Do not remain under the same roof with [women]; do not trust your chastity in the past. You cannot be a man more saintly than David, or more wise than Solomon. Remember always that a woman drove the tiller of paradise from the garden that had been given him. (Jerome, *Letters* 52, 5, translated by Wright)

For someone who frequently brags about his skills in Hebrew scriptural interpretation, it is interesting that Jerome describes the garden as having been given to Adam alone, and Eve as "driving" him from it.[38] Jerome goes on to instruct clergy to avoid having women enter their abode if they fall ill, as though in the process of ministering to their illness, women will slip a bit of forbidden fruit into the poor ailing man's medicine. Jerome has taken Eve's sole blame for the expulsion as a given; he does not even name Eve specifically, but simply refers to her as "a woman"—as though all women are likely candidates for the ruin of men.

This mistrust of everywoman via Eve again holds true in Augustine's *Sermon* 159A, where he cautions men destined for martyrdom to be on the lookout for loved ones who distract them from that prize. He says that they play the role of "serpent's agent," luring men from their divine destinies:

> Beware of Eve; she isn't in this instance your better half, but the serpent's agent. You were foolish enough to listen to her voice the first time, and you haven't even profited from the experience; but now this very same wife, to stop her husband winning the prize of martyrdom, with feminine cunning quotes to her husband the apparent authority both of the law and of the gospel. "Listen," says she, "to the commandment" . . . "What God has joined together, let not man separate (Mk 10:9)." . . . just see whether your wife is not separating you from God. (*Sermon* 159A, *On Honoring or Disregarding Parents*, 7; translation by Muldowney)

Tertullian, too, minces no words when, addressing women in general, he makes an extended comparison between his audience and Eve as he counsels women to:

> go about in humble garb, and . . . affect meanness of appearance, walking about as Eve mourning and repentant, in order that by every garb of penitence she might the more fully expiate that which she derives from Eve, the ignominy, I mean, of the first sin, and the odium of human perdition. And do you not know that you are (each) an Eve? The sentence of God on this sex of yours lives in this age: the guilt must of necessity live too. *You* are the devil's gateway: *you* are the unsealer of that tree: *you* are the first deserter of the divine law: *you* are she who persuaded him whom the devil was not valiant enough to attack. *You* destroyed so easily God's image, man. On account of *your* desert—that is, death—even the Son of God had to die. (*The Apparel of Women* 1.1, emphasis original)[39]

This is probably the most explicit ancient framing of Eve as everywoman. It not only condemns each woman for the perceived weakness and errors of Eve, but also manages to blame women alone for the crucifixion of Christ *and* slip in that it is *man*, not woman, who reflects "God's image." John Chrysostom (c. 347–407 CE) follows suit when he cautions that women have a "ready inclination to sin" and "the evil enemy can find many ways to creep in secretly" to tempt men through women. This is because "the eye of the woman touches and disturbs our soul, and not only the eye of the unbridled woman but that of the decent one as well" (*On the Priesthood* VI.8).[40] And the very title of Eastern Syriac theologian Narsai's diatribe, "On the Reproof of Eve's Daughters and the Tricks and Devices they Perform,"[41] shows the slide from Eve to all women and their depiction as dangerous to men due to a "natural" inclination toward trickery.

Some rabbinic texts participate in this extrapolation from Eve to all women too. Genesis Rabbah explains common women's activities, from wearing head-coverings, to leading funeral processions, to menstruating, by linking them to women's relationship to Eve and the first sin:

> Why does a man go out bareheaded while a woman goes out with her head covered? She is like one who has done wrong and is ashamed . . . therefore she goes out with her head covered. Why do they walk in front of the corpse? Because they brought death into the world . . . And why was the precept of menstruation given to her? Because she shed the blood of Adam . . . And why was the precept of "dough" given to her? Because she corrupted Adam, who was the dough of the world. (Genesis Rabbah 17:8; translation by Freedman and Simon)[42]

It is important to remember that the move from Eve to all women *is not a necessary one*, and some ancient texts avoid it. For instance, Gregory of Naziansus (c. 329—390 CE) accords both agency and blame to Eve, yet he does not see everyone assigned female at birth as automatically tainted. In the following passage, he uses Eve as a contrast in order to praise an admirable woman—his mother:

> She indeed who was given to Adam as a helper for him, because it was not good for man to be alone, instead of a co-worker became an enemy, and instead of a collaborator an opponent, and beguiling the man by means of pleasure, estranged him through the tree of knowledge from the tree of life. But she who was given by God to my father became not only, as is less wonderful, his co-worker, but even his leader, drawing him on by her influence in deed and word to the highest things.[43]

Here, Gregory accords Eve agency as the sensual beguiler of Adam, but he does not make the move to argue against women's leadership in general. Instead, he praises his mother as being the right kind of leader and positive influencer of her husband.

A SENSUAL EVE

So far, the examples I have shared blame Eve for sin and death, whether she is viewed as having been duped by the serpent (Justin Martyr, Clement of Alexandria) or as wielding some agency (Ben Sira, Augustine). I have also demonstrated the tendency to lump all other women in with Eve as a potential source of danger to men. But there have been some hints of another interpretive innovation which links the precise nature of Eve's wickedness, cunning, and danger to her perceived sensuality. As already shown, Gregory of Naziansus accuses Eve specifically of "beguiling the man by means of pleasure."

The most important proponent of Eve as an allegory for sensuality is Philo of Alexandria. This first-century Jewish philosopher wrote in Greek and produced a wide body of treatises and allegorical commentaries. Dorothy Sly, Holly Morse, and others have shown that Philo's treatments of Genesis, such as *Questions and Answers on Genesis* and *On the Creation of the World*, support his general tendency to dichotomize between inferior body/senses (Eve) and superior mind/soul (Adam). When the serpent suggests eating the fruit, Philo says that Eve gave in "without looking into the suggestion, prompted by a mind devoid of steadfastness" (*On the Creation* 156; translation by Colson and Whitaker). Philo provides an allegorical reading of the scene, whereby the serpent represents pleasure, Eve represents the senses, and "they, in turn, entice the mind, Adam."[44] For Philo, senses are prone to being deceived; Eve thus represents human failing. Since sensory perception is by nature passive and fallible, the senses are the entry point for sinful pleasures. Morse writes that Eve "becomes a figure of carnality, stupidity, and weakness" in Philo's writings, where she functions:

> as a facilitator of feminine carnal transgression . . . Philo understood Eve, specifically as female, to be the vehicle of sin, and . . . closely aligned her both literally and allegorically with weakness and lack of self-control. Philo responds to gaps and ambiguities in the biblical text to express disdain for the woman and the weakness he perceives in her, as well as allegorically aligning her with the inferior bodily senses.[45]

As both Morse and Sly demonstrate, Philo's allegorical reworking of Genesis 3 is deeply androcentric, as it tacitly assumes a heteronormative male gaze that perceives Eve's loveliness as a trap. The mind (Adam) is attracted through the senses (Eve) and ends up conceiving a child (vanity of thought):

> The Mind in us—call it Adam—having met with outward Sense, called Eve . . . approaches her for their mutual intercourse. She for her part takes in and catches as in a net the external objects of sense . . . Thus conceiving and being made pregnant, she straightway becomes in labour and bears the worst evil of the soul, vanity of thought. (Philo, *On the Cherubim* 56; translation by Colson and Whitaker)

If the allegory were to apply equally to all humans, regardless of gender, where all were exhorted to "be like Adam" (rational) and "not be like Eve" (governed by the senses), that would be one thing. However, as Sly points out, Philo explicitly maps the allegorical Eve and Adam onto women and men, respectively.[46] Like Ben Sira, then, Philo supports a hierarchical view of gender relations, where disaster will ensue if a man heeds the guidance of a woman. Thus, the character of Eve serves again as a handy example of alerting an assumed male audience to the consequences of listening to women.

Philo's use of Eve as everywoman to map dangerousness onto all women is an interpretive choice that not all texts make. For instance, Paul, Philo's first-century contemporary, also uses Eve's story as a caution, but for people of any gender. Eve is named only once in the genuine Pauline corpus, in 2 Corinthians 11:3: "I am afraid that as the serpent deceived Eve by its cunning, your thoughts will be led astray from a sincere and pure devotion to Christ." Note that Paul's usage does not make Eve every*woman*; it makes her every*person*; the Corinthian recipients are all addressed here. Paul's cautionary employment of Eve does not extrapolate from Eve to all women on the basis of gender. Unlike Philo, Paul by no means assumes that women are at all more likely than men to be led astray or to lead others astray. Neither does Paul lay the blame for the expulsion on Eve alone, given Romans 5:12 where he says that "sin came into the world through one man" (rather than one woman, as in contemporaneous texts).

A SEXUAL EVE

For Philo, Eve symbolizes the senses. Eve's connection to embodied experience and sensuality is important for understanding the permanent linking of Eve to *sexuality* that occurred in early Judaism and early Christianity. The sensual Eve easily becomes a sexual Eve—an agentic, dangerous, and hypersexualized temptress. Representing everywoman, she is a source of danger to everyman, because the key source of her dangerousness—as viewed through a heteronormative, androcentric lens—lies in her carnality.

Sexuality with Agency = Eve as Femme Fatale

The age-old femme fatale trope (which had not yet been named in antiquity, but which very much existed in figures such as Circe, Medea, Sirens, and Nymphs) refers to a stock female character who is as sexually attractive to men as she is deadly.[47] She is often held up as a warning, someone with whom a man consorts at his own grave peril. Caroline Blyth describes her as "the terrifying woman whose malignant eroticism has the power to intoxicate her victims and drag them mercilessly towards destruction."[48] Several female characters in biblical traditions were not femmes fatales in the narratives themselves, but become so through later accretions. Eve, Delilah, Jezebel, Judith, and Mary Magdalene are often hypersexualized in ways completely unwarranted by the earliest texts that mention them.[49] Some of these characters are sexualized in order to perpetuate the trope of women's dangerous sexuality. Eve, sexualized by Ben Sira and various later interpreters, very much became a femme fatale.

Christian theologian Origen (c. 185–253 CE) is like Philo in that he allegorizes the characters of the Eden narrative as a dichotomy between male/mind/reason and female/soul/body, with the masculine being superior to the feminine. Origen's Eve, though, is a "harlot" in pursuit of "carnal vices" (*Homilies on Genesis* 1.15). According to Morse, "Origen's understanding of the female soul is more explicitly sexual than Philo's" and "there is a shift in the allegorical interpretation of Eve between Philo and Origen, as readings of her weakness . . . become bound to an increasingly sexualized view of the female and, symbolically, Eve."[50] Origen, drawing on a growing tradition of female temptress figures,[51] is in the company of many other ancient interpreters who moved from the sensual to the sexual depiction of Eve; by making her into a monstrous sexualized bogeywoman, she could be used to control both men's sexuality through the threat of their downfall and women's sexuality through shame. Jean Higgins reminds us, though, that

> Gen 3:6b says nothing whatever about any temptation of Adam by Eve. Nor does Gen 3:17 lend the legend any serious support. The myth of Eve the temptress in its various forms cannot be explained except in terms of each commentator's own presuppositions and cultural expectations.[52]

Reading Eve as a temptress is not encouraged in Genesis.

Sexuality without Agency = Eve as Victim of Rape

Eve's depiction as a temptress who endangers men is not the only way she is sexualized during this period. Other texts sexualize her story in a different direction—Eve becomes a victim of sexual violence. These differing sexualizations of Eve depend, in part, on how much *agency* is accorded her. When Eve is agentic, her sexualization is often in the form of seducer and femme fatale who causes the downfall of men. But when Eve is an agentless victim, the sexualization of her narrative is as a tale of sexual assault by the serpent.

In her work on the reception of serpent traditions in early Jewish and early Christian writings, Hannah Wortzman takes for granted the general sexualization of the relationship between Eve and the serpent during the Hellenistic and Roman eras,[53] and is particularly interested in construal of the relationship as a seduction or rape. Evil enters the world through this sexual relationship between Eve and the serpent (who begins in the Hellenistic period to be conflated with the devil or Satan). Texts that support this reading include 4 Maccabees, the Enochic literature, the book of *Jubilees*, and various Nag Hammadi codices.[54]

4 Maccabees (first to second century CE) was referred to by some ancients as "On the Supremacy of Reason" (Eusebius, *Hist. eccl.* 3.10.6; Jerome, *De viris illustribus* 13). It continues in the tradition of 2 Maccabees, reworking the martyrdoms in 2 Maccabees 6–7 as a Stoic philosophical treatise. Its single reference to Eve is brief, but unusual, occurring in the context of a speech by the famous Maccabaean martyr mother which she delivers to her seven sons. The mother says,

> I was a pure virgin and did not go outside my father's house; but I guarded the rib from which woman was made. No seducer corrupted me on a desert plain, nor did the destroyer, the deceitful serpent, defile the purity of my virginity. (4 Macc 18:7–8)

Wortzman reads this passage as depicting Eve as "a victim of rape by Satanic forces."[55] What the mother means by "guarding the rib" is unclear, but a typical second-century focus on chastity and celibacy is certainly implicated. The mother's claim that *she* did not have "the purity of her virginity" defiled by the serpent seems to imply that Eve, on the other hand, did. This reflects an innovation in this period, whereby the specific moment when evil entered the world was when the serpent "beguiled" Eve *sexually*. Wortzman highlights other texts that construe the origins of evil in terms of Eve's seduction or rape by the serpent, including *Jubilees* and Enochic texts.[56] There are also numerous examples from rabbinic literature (such as Genesis Rabbah 18:6; b. [= Babylonian Talmud] Sotah 9b; b. Shabbat 145b–146, 196a; b. Avodah Zarah 22b; b. Yevamot 103b) where "the motif of Eve copulating with the primeval serpent"[57] is framed more as a seduction where the serpent "injected his lust into her."[58] The tradition of Eve copulating with the serpent, not implied in the Genesis accounts, was widespread and richly varied by early Roman times.

In many of these texts that construe Eve as a victim of sexual assault, she nevertheless still shares or even fully shoulders the blame.[59] In such texts, Eve's flawed connection with sense over reason, her naïve ability to be duped, her helplessness, or her inherent tendency to sin are presented as reasons to explain how she brought the encounter with the serpent upon herself (and, by extension, upon us all).

It is rare to find a text where Eve is an unequivocally positive character. However, the major exception can be found among the Nag Hammadi Codices (NHC), where Eve is both rape victim and blameless hero. (Please note that this paragraph contains a description of the assaults.) The Nag Hammadi text known as *On the Origin of the World* (NHC 13.2) is a highly imaginative retelling of the expulsion, in which both Eve and the serpent save the day while the Genesis stories of the rib and the tree are exposed as manipulative lies. The story begins with Adam helpless on the ground, unable to stand because he has no soul. Wisdom pities him and sends her daughter Eve to show him how to arise. The rulers of the world become jealous of Eve and conspire to rape her punitively and make her pregnant to produce vassals for them. The rulers then put Adam into a coma and, when he wakes, they tell him that Eve has come from his rib; this is intended to sow seeds of masculine domination in his mind as a further means of punishing Eve. But Eve is wise to their plan, and before they arrive to gang rape her, her spirit leaves her body and hides for refuge in the tree of knowledge, melding with it. The rapes unfold while Eve's spirit is detached from her body, and when her spirit re-joins her body, she finds she is indeed pregnant. The rulers are not yet satisfied that they have fully put Eve in her place, so they approach the couple with a lie: they will die if they eat from the tree of knowledge. But a benevolent serpent comes to help them; the serpent tells the truth about the tree. They eat and achieve enlightenment, realizing that the rulers are evil; they then begin a life together, fully aware of their love for each other, and redeem their children from enslavement through a balance of their shared wisdom.[60]

In this and other Nag Hammadi texts, there is no victim blaming around the rape of Eve; on the contrary, the rape is depicted as something terrible and difficult to endure, yet Eve goes on to survive and save humanity from the clutches of her assailants.[61] Gnostic readings of Eve are just as allegorical as Philo's, but here the feminine symbol is not denigrated as the problem for which patriarchy is the solution; rather, patriarchal hierarchy itself is a problem introduced by the evil rulers, for which a "dynamic relationship between masculine and feminine energies" is the solution.[62] Celene Lillie points out that Nag Hammadi's stories of the rulers' rape of Eve (including *On the Origin of the World*, *The Secret Revelation of John*, and *Reality of the Rulers*) "articulate a condemnation of this sexual violence, moving the locus of defilement from the victim to the perpetrator."[63] Lillie adds that, while "much of the Christian Testament and other early church writings are concerned with issues of sexual morality, chastity, and purity," these Nag Hammadi stories where Eve survives her rape provide a very different message than other streams of reception at the time.[64]

EVE AS A THINKING TOOL FOR VIRGINITY/CELIBACY

As Lillie correctly observes, the range of views on asceticism, especially sexual asceticism or chastity, is one of the liveliest topics for Christianity in the second century and onward. In this period, celibate roles became formal offices for women,[65] the first Christian orders of what we would now call nuns and monks appear,[66] and the traditions that pseudonymously claim to be in the lineage of Paul diverge sharply into two camps: the pro-chastity camp that can be seen in the Acts of Paul and Thecla and the works of Jerome; and the anti-ascetic camp that can be seen in the pseudo-Pauline pastoral epistles.[67] It is in this context that another development in the trajectory of Eve's sexualized reception takes place: her position as a thinking tool around virginity and celibacy.

Jerome, for instance, claims that Eve remained a virgin until the fall, and marriage only came about as a result of sin; therefore, a virginal state is preferred for everyone in imitation of paradise (*Letters* 22). He adds that: "Death came through Eve: life has come through Mary. For this reason the gift of virginity has been poured most abundantly upon women" (*Letters* 22). Eve is also a tool in pro-celibacy discourse in the Apocryphal *Acts of Andrew and Matthias*; there, Andrew has convinced Maximilla to cease having sex with her husband, and lauds her by comparison to Eve, as though Maximilla's celibacy somehow rights Eve's wrongs: "You healed her deficiency by not experiencing the same passions . . . Where Eve disobeyed, you obeyed" (*Acts of Andrew and Matthias* 37.5). He exhorts, "Just as Adam died in Eve through his complicity with her, so also I now live in you through your observing the commandment of the Lord" (39.7; both translations by Elliott). In this and many other early Christian texts, Eve is trotted out in myriad ways by authors wishing to weigh in on the raging asceticism debates.

One of the second-century trends to which Jerome's letters and the *Acts of Andrew and Matthias* point is a tendency to laud Mary by deeming her a new and better Eve. As Ashbrook Harvey points out, the trope of Mary as a second Eve follows on from Paul's description of Christ as a second Adam in Romans 5:12.[68] The modern "tendency to categorize women into two polar opposites"[69] might be credited in part to early Christian authors such as Justin Martyr, Tertullian, and Augustine, who employ Eve as a negative foil to Mary. This paired typology appeared frequently in early Christian discourse on asceticism and was most often used to laud virginity and chastity.[70] According to Lily Vuong, Justin Martyr (c. 100–165 CE) was "the first church father to advance the Eve–Mary comparison."[71] In addition to its use in sermons and commentaries, Lynda Coon notes that the Mary–Eve dichotomy was also employed in hagiographies of women saints, depicting their "before" and "after" progression from metaphorical Eves to metaphorical Virgin Marys.[72] By medieval times, Vuong reports that the typological twinning of "Eve, the disobedient and sinful mother of Cain" with "Mary, the obedient and chaste mother of Christ" is ubiquitous in art and literature, with the motif of "Mary treading on the head of the serpent and reversing the sin of Eve" being one of the most popular.[73]

Irenaeus (c. 130–202 CE) makes a parallel between Eve and Mary focusing on their "virgin" motherhood. According to Irenaeus, Eve is a virgin because Adam and Eve had not reached puberty in Eden and so they did not have sex (*Against Heresies* 3.22.4).[74] Jensen summarizes Irenaeus's "overt parallel between Mary and Eve" in *Against Heresies* (c. 175 CE):

> Mary's regenerative ability comes . . . from her obedience. In this she contrasts with the disobedient Eve, also a virgin (prior to her fall). One virgin mother becomes the source of life (salvation) and reverses the consequences (death) of the other's error. One mother (bearing a single child) thus redeems the act of the other (the mother of all living).[75]

The *Protevangelium of James* (mid-second to early-third century CE) contrasts Eve with Mary as well, but by comparing Adam to Joseph. Vuong observes that a main aim of this text is to explain why and how Mary came to hold "the paradoxical role of Virgin Mother."[76] It is Joseph who introduces the trope of juxtaposing Mary with Eve here, by comparing his own unfortunate lot to Adam's, when Mary falls illicitly pregnant while in his care. Joseph assumes the worst; he "threw himself to the ground in sackcloth, and wailed":

> Who took the virgin away from me and defiled her? Could it be that the story of Adam is being repeated in my case? For just as Adam was in the hour of his praising when the serpent came and found Eve alone and deceived her and defiled her, so too has the same happened to me. (*Protevangelium of James* 13:1, translation from Vuong)

Note that Joseph assumes Adam was not present while Eve was with the serpent, which means that Eve alone was not only "deceived" but also "defiled." This intersects Eve's blame with her sexualization and implicitly contrasts this against Mary's divine pregnancy.

In addition to Irenaeus and the *Protevangelium*, many other texts that make negative Eve–Mary comparisons also do so with a focus on Mary's marvelous offspring. Augustine's *Sermon* 232, for example, says: "Because man's fall was occasioned by womankind, man's restoration was accomplished through womankind" (*Sermon* 232, *On the Resurrection of Christ According to St. Luke*, Section 2; translation by Muldowney).[77] This and other similar texts seem to suggest that both Mary and Eve had supernatural *sexual* encounters which resulted in opposite conceptions: Eve birthing death, and Mary birthing life. For instance, the two women's comparison has overtly sexual connotations in Justin Martyr's *Dialogue with Trypho*. The *Dialogue* imagines both women as virgins who have sexual encounters with otherworldly beings (Mary with the Holy Spirit, and Eve with the serpent). Both conceive, but "Eve, who was a virgin and undefiled, having conceived the word of the serpent, brought forth disobedience and death" (*Dialogue with Trypho* 100).[78] Mary, on the other hand:

> received faith and joy, when the angel Gabriel announced the good tidings to her that the Spirit of the Lord would come upon her, and the power of the Highest would overshadow her: wherefore also the Holy Thing begotten of her is the Son of God; and she replied, "Be it unto me according to thy word." (*Dialogue with Trypho* 100)

Notice that Martyr feels the need to stress Mary's encounter with the "power of the Highest" was a *willing* one. No such comment is made about Eve's encounter with the serpent. But Eve's progeny was "disobedience and death" by contrast with Mary's progeny, "the Son of God." Here, Mary as willing vessel of life seems to be contrasted with Eve as *unwilling* vessel of death.[79] Readers may not often consider Mary's having been "overshadowed" by the "power of the Most High" (Luke 1:35) in a sexual light, but such connotations are clear, not only in *Dialogue with Trypho* but in the Lukan passage he references.[80] Martyr implies that Eve's dealings with the serpent involved non-consensual sex in contrast with Mary's express consent; Eve's children from the violent encounter are disobedience and death.

Tertullian, too, sets up an Eve–Mary contrast, also focusing on their offspring, but he does so by fashioning Eve into a mother of the first *murderer* so he can juxtapose this with Mary as mother of the redeemer.[81] In *The Flesh of Christ* 17.5, he writes that Eve gave birth "to the devil [Cain], the murderer of his brother," whereas Mary gave birth to "[Jesus] who should sometime bring salvation to his brother." In the same text, he insists that both Eve and Mary were virgins going into their separate encounters (with the serpent and with God, respectively), but "into Eve had crept the word . . . of death" and "the devil's word was to her a seed." For Mary, on the other hand, "God brought down into the womb his own Word, the good brother, that he might erase the memory of the evil brother." The virginal status of both Eve and Mary is also noted in the fifth-century Armenian text *History of the Armenians* (attributed to the pseudonymous author Agathangelos), which identifies Eve as a gateway for death and Mary as a gateway for life: "For as through the first virgin, Eve, death entered the world, so through this virgin, life will enter the world" (Agathangełos, *History* 79). Other theologians at the time[82] draw negative Eve–Mary comparisons, not only for the conceptions but for their *birthing* experiences too; Jennifer Glancy notes how often church fathers opined that Mary did not experience pain when giving birth to Jesus, a sign of her exemption from Eve's curse of labor pains.[83]

All of these (and many other) Mary/Eve pairings tacitly transfer the title of "mother of all living" onto Mary instead of Eve. What Eve has given birth to (through illicit coupling with the serpent) is mortality, sin, death, and curse. The upshot for patristic writers who juxtapose Eve with Mary is that Mary's virginity and submission are the antidote.

Although many patristic texts use Eve to promote chastity and celibacy, 1 Timothy, in contrast, sees Eve become a tool of anti-celibacy polemics. 1 Timothy is attributed to Paul but was written long after his death, as evidenced by its second-century concerns including reversals of both Paul's apocalyptic preference for celibacy and his endorsement of women in positions of leadership.[84] The letter's single reference to Eve is in the context of a passage that aims to simultaneously counteract Paul's exhortation against marriage (1 Corinthians 7:7–9) and his acceptance of women leaders (Romans 16:1–15; 1 Cor 11:4–5):

> Let a woman learn in silence with full submission. I permit no woman to teach or to have authority over a man; she is to keep silent. For Adam was formed first, then Eve; and Adam was not deceived, but the woman was deceived and became a transgressor. Yet she will be saved through childbearing. (1 Timothy 2:8–15)

This passage interprets the Genesis account hierarchically, with Adam in a higher position because he "was formed first" and Eve lower than him because she "was deceived and became a transgressor." Conveniently, gendered hierarchy is one of the text's central goals, seeking to bring Christ followers more in line with Roman household arrangements, so it is not surprising that the author sees it modeled in Eden as readily as Jerome saw celibacy there. The text reverses Paul's obvious comfort with women in powerful roles by admonishing women to "keep silent" and have no "authority over a man"; moreover, it also seeks to undo Paul's recommendation of celibacy with its astonishing claim that women "will be saved through childbearing."[85] Overall, the letter is part of the general goal in the pastoral epistles to root out behaviors that went against Roman norms, perhaps in order to distance the community from the Jewish rebellions against Rome.[86] Verse 5:23 tells its imagined recipient to "no longer drink only water, but take a little wine." Verse 5:3 says to "honour widows who are really widows," pushing back against the second-century trend of teenaged women skipping straight to the apparently liberating role of "widow" without ever having been married. 1 Timothy 5:9 attempts to set an age limit of sixty and above for the role, whereas an exasperated Tertullian struggles to at least not have virgin/widows younger than twenty (*The Veiling of Virgins* 9:2–3).

In 1 Timothy 2:14–15, Eve's curse is used to urge women away from celibate teaching roles and back to their duties as subservient child bearers. Sarah Fein suggests that if all women were cursed with pain in childbirth due to Eve's transgression, perhaps the author of 1 Timothy "provides all women with the opportunity for redemption by means of that same act."[87] This is clearly a case of "thinking with Eve" to serve patriarchal aims—in this case, to control and curtail real-life women.

In each of the examples I have discussed throughout this section, male writers contrast Eve with the "normative" femininity of the day, which allows them to argue about women's bodies. If they seek to promote celibacy and chastity, Eve and Mary are both depicted as virgins. If the authors disapprove of chastity as a choice for women, then Eve is used to remind women to submit to their husbands, since sin entered the world through a husband listening to his wife. None of these interpretations are faithful to Eve's title in Genesis as "mother of all living." Nor are they inevitable, but rather are conscious, crafted choices. The rabbis, for instance, do not assume Eve's virginity in paradise at all. A midrash implies this when it attempts to explain where Adam was when Eve was with the serpent: "Where was the man when this conversation was going on? Abba Halpurn bar Qoriah said, 'He had earlier had sexual relations, and now he was sleeping it off'" (Genesis Rabbah 1:201; translation by Neusner). The rabbis were having none of the early Christian debate over celibacy and asceticism; for them, it was a given that paradise included enjoyable sex.[88]

CONCLUSIONS

During the Hellenistic and Roman periods, the character of Eve underwent a variety of dramatic transformations, some of which have fallen away while others have lasted to the present. It is plain that loyalty to the Genesis accounts was by no means a concern; rather, Eve was overlaid with whatever views of women, gender, and sexuality a male author wished to promulgate.[89] As is predictable in patriarchal texts, Eve's gender and sexuality were often the central focus, whether she was envisioned as a femme fatale or as a virgin in paradise foreshadowing the celibate eschaton. Adam was often exonerated of responsibility for sin and mortality entering the world, and Eve was given full blame, along with all women by virtue of association.

Some overarching themes in these texts are that Eve represents everywoman; that Eve's transgression, when viewed through an androcentric lens, is somehow connected with sex and the sexuality of women in general, and that women, when they make their own decisions or have any power, present a danger for men. Almost all the texts in this survey assume that Eve is not simply a literary or historical figure but rather a figure useful for conveying one ideology or another to contemporaneous women (or, more often, to men). Philo, for example, uses Eve to talk about the nature of women as carnal and sensual in his endorsement of "masculine" virtues such as reason and self-control; Ben Sira uses her to support his belief that wives and daughters present a constant threat to husbands and fathers; 1 Timothy extrapolates from his reading of Eve that women should not be teachers and must funnel their energies only toward childbirth; and Augustine warns against wives and mothers who steer potential believers away from following Christ.

Philo's understanding of women as sensual and 1 Timothy's concern about womanly modesty both play into another common theme of these texts, which is the sexualization of Eve's interaction with the serpent. Some writers contrast a sexualized Eve with Mary to uplift the idea of virginity or chastity; others attach sexual violence to Eve's experience, painting her as gullible, weak, or overly sensual. Not all understandings of Eve as a sexual being are necessarily negative. Some rabbinic literature, for example, is accepting of human and female sexuality, assuming sex for pleasure in Eden. Gnostic texts anticipating a reunion of male and female forces could imply that a gendered balance of wisdom and power marks a shift to an enlightened state. These, and our few neutral examples, such as Tobit, might seem inconsequential considering how Eve's treatment has overwhelmingly made her a femme fatale; nevertheless, they highlight an important and frequently overlooked aspect of Eve's characterization during this time period: that imagining Eve as dangerous, as sensual, as sexual, or as wicked is a *choice*, and a choice that not all texts have made.

NOTES

1. Gratitudes: This research was funded by the Leverhulme Trust, in conjunction with the Department of Theology and Religious Studies at the University of Nottingham. The final draft was read in detail by Matthew R. Anderson, Caroline Blyth, and Meredith J. C. Warren, who gave invaluable advice on structure and suggested numerous additional primary sources. Shayna Sheinfeld was (and is always) a constant supportive sounding board. This chapter is reprinted here with generous permission from Caroline Blyth and Emily Colgan, eds., *The Routledge Companion to Eve* (London: Routledge, 2023).

2. For an eye-opening feminist analysis of Eve's use in modern branding, see Katie B. Edwards, *Admen and Eve: The Bible in Contemporary Advertising* (Sheffield: Sheffield Phoenix, 2012). This chapter does not provide an analysis of the Genesis accounts themselves, as there is by now a long history of feminist and womanist

analyses of the creation stories. It is here assumed that the extent to which misogynistic readings are located more in readers' assumptions than in the actual narrative is well known—as in, e.g., Helen Schüngel-Straumann, *Eva. Die erste Frau der Bibel: Ursache allen Übels?* (Paderborn: Ferdinand Schöningh, 2014).

3. Barbara Deutschmann, *Creating Gender in the Garden: The Inconstant Partnership of Eve and Adam* (Edinburgh: T&T Clark, 2022).

4. Holly Morse, *Encountering Eve's Afterlives: A New Reception-Critical Approach to Genesis 2–4* (Oxford: Oxford University Press), 2020.

5. Schüngel-Straumann, *Eva*.

6. See also Elaine Pagels, *Adam, Eve, and the Serpent: Sex and Politics in Early Christianity* (New York: Vintage, 1989) and Dan Clanton, *Daring, Disreputable, and Devout: Interpreting the Hebrew Bible's Women in the Arts and Music* (New York: T&T Clark, 2009).

7. Morse, *Encountering Eve's Afterlives*, 10.

8. Deutschmann, *Creating Gender*, 7.

9. On the unlikelihood of female authorship for any of our texts with the exception, perhaps, of the diary portions in Perpetua and Felicitas, see Ross S. Kraemer, "When Is a Text about a Woman a Text about a Woman?: The Cases of Aseneth and Perpetua," in *A Feminist Companion to Patristic Literature*, ed. Amy-Jill Levine with Maria Mayo Robbins (London: T&T Clark, 2008), 137–55, here 156–57.

10. The phrase "good to think with" was coined by Claude Levi-Strauss, *Le Totémisme Aujourd'hui* (Paris: Presses Universitaires de France, 1962). Using it to refer to male authors' use of female characters as conversation tools for discussing male-centred issues has become a handy shorthand in our field; this latter usage originates with Peter Brown, *The Body and Society: Men, Women, and Sexual Renunciation in Early Christianity* (New York: Columbia University Press, 1988), 153.

11. All English translations of biblical and apocryphal texts are from the NRSV; translations of the Pseudepigrapha are from Charlesworth's *OTP*. Dating follows Jonathan Klawans and Lawrence M. Mills, eds, *The Jewish Annotated Apocrypha NRSV* (Oxford: Oxford University Press, 2020); Amy-Jill Levine and Marc Zvi Brettler, *The Jewish Annotated New Testament*, 2nd ed. (Oxford: Oxford University Press, 2011); and Daniel M. Gurtner, *Introducing the Pseudepigrapha of Second Temple Judaism: Message, Context, and Significance* (Grand Rapids: Baker Academic, 2020).

12. Julie Faith Parker, "Blaming Eve Alone: Translation, Omission, and Implications of עמה in Genesis 3:6b," *JBL* 132, no. 4 (2013): 729–47, here 729.

13. Deutschmann, *Creating Gender*.

14. See Molly Zahn's assessment of whether "genre" is the best term for the frequent use of rewriting as a mode of textual production: Molly M. Zahn, "Genre and Rewritten Scripture: A Reassessment," *JBL* 131, no. 2 (2012): 271–88. For a critical account of the term's use, see Johannes Tromp, "Literary and Exegetical Issues in the Story of Adam's Death and Burial (GLAE 31–42)," in *The Book of Genesis in Jewish and Oriental Christian Interpretation*, ed. J. Frishman and L. Van Rompay (Louvain: Peeters, 1997), 25–42.

15. On pseudepigrapha as fan fiction, see Meredith J. C. Warren, "My OTP: Harry Potter Fanfiction and the Old Testament Pseudepigrapha," *Scriptura:*

Nouvelle Serie 8, no. 1 (2006): 53–66, and more recently Tom de Bruin, "Nostalgia, Novelty, and the Subversion of Authority in Testaments of the Twelve Patriarchs," *Transformative Works and Cultures 31: Fan Fiction and Ancient Scribal Cultures* (2019).

16. Clanton, *Daring, Disreputable, and Devout*, 9.

17. See Magdalena Díaz Araujo, "The Sins of the First Woman: Eve Traditions in Second Temple Literature with Special Regard to the Life of Adam and Eve," 91–112 in *Early Jewish Writings*, ed. Eileen Schuller and Marie-Theres Wacker (Atlanta: SBL, 2017), 91, who notes that in places where the blame is shifted onto Eve rather than shared by the couple, Eve is often "indicted for dissimilar transgressions" than Adam.

18. C. Paul Schroeder, "The Mystery of Love: Paradigms of Marital Authority and Submission in the Writings of St John Chrysostom," *St Vladimir's Theological Quarterly* 44, no. 2 (2000): 143–68, here 152.

19. Angela Standhartinger, "Manuscript and Gender: Eve's Testament in GLAE/Apoc. Mos. 15–30 and LLAE 45–60," *JSP* 31, no. 3 (2022): 215–46.

20. Gary A. Anderson and Michael E. Stone, *A Synopsis of the Books of Adam and Eve*, 2nd revised ed. (Atlanta: Scholars, 1999).

21. Gurtner, *Introducing the Pseudepigrapha*, 319.

22. Namely, *On the Origin of the World*, *The Secret Revelation of John*, and *Reality of the Rulers*.

23. So Standhartinger, "Manuscript and Gender," building on Christine Thomas, *The Acts of Peter, Gospel Literature, and the Ancient Novel: Rewriting the Past* (New York: Oxford University Press, 2003), 85ff.

24. John R. Levison, "Adam and Eve in Romans 1:18-25 and the Life of Adam and Eve," in *The Pseudepigrapha and Christian Origins*, ed. Gerbern Oegema and James H. Charlesworth (London: T&T Clark, 2008), 87–101, here 95.

25. Magdalena Díaz Araujo, "The Satan's Disguise: The Exoneration of Eve in the Greek Life of Adam and Eve 17:1–2," *Judaïsme Ancien* 5 (2017): 159–82; John R. Levison, "The Exoneration of Eve in the Apocalypse of Moses 15–30," *JSJ* 20, no. 2 (1989): 135–50.

26. Johannes Tromp, "The Story of our Lives: The qz-Text of the Life of Adam and Eve, the Apostle Paul, and the Jewish-Christian Oral Tradition concerning Adam and Eve," *NTS* 50 (2004): 205–23, here 214.

27. As Standhartinger points out in "Manuscript and Gender," the complicated and manifold manuscript tradition makes it difficult to say that the *Life* literature is positive or negative toward Eve from a feminist standpoint.

28. Benjamin G. Wright, "Ecclesiasticus, or the Wisdom of Jesus, Son of Sirach," in *The New Oxford Annotated Bible: NRSV with the Apocrypha*. 5th ed., ed. Michael D. Coogan (Oxford: Oxford University Press, 2018), 1479–81.

29. Tal Ilan, *Integrating Women into Second Temple History* (Peabody: Hendrickson, 2001), 155–74.

30. Eileen M. Schuller, "Introduction to the Apocrypha," in *Women's Bible Commentary*. Twentieth anniversary ed., ed. Carol A. Newsom, Sharon. H. Ringe, and Jacqueline E. Lapsley (Louisville: Westminster John Knox, 2012), 365–66, here 366.

31. See Deutschmann, *Creating Gender*; Wilda C. Gafney, *Womanist Midrash: A Reintroduction to the Women of the Torah and the Throne* (Louisville: Westminster John Knox, 2017); and Morse, *Encountering Eve's Afterlives*.

32. Phyllis Trible, *God and the Rhetoric of Sexuality* (Philadelphia: Fortress, 1978) and Phyllis Bird, "Images of Women in the Old Testament," in *Religion and Sexism*, ed. Rosemary Radford Ruether (New York: Simon and Schuster, 1974), 41–88.

33. Morse, *Encountering Eve's Afterlives*, 11.

34. Contra most interpreters, John Levison suggests in "Is Eve to Blame: A Contextual Analysis of Sirach 25:24," *CBQ* 47, no. 4 (1985): 617–23 that, given these passages are an extended warning to all husbands and fathers about the dangers of wicked wives and daughters, the "woman" causing wickedness and death here may not be Eve, but simply any ill-chosen wife or poorly managed daughter. Teresa A. Ellis has suggested in "Is Eve the Woman in Sirach 25:24?" *CBQ* 73, no. 4 (2011): 723–42 that as the woman is not named, she might as easily be Pandora. Morse critiques arguments that the woman in Sirach is anyone other than Eve (*Encountering Eve's Afterlives*, 27–31).

35. Samuel Tobias Lachs, "The Pandora-Eve Motif in Rabbinic Literature," *HTR* 67 (1974): 341–45.

36. Clanton, *Daring, Disreputable, and Devout*, 12.

37. Elizabeth E. Clark, "Ideology, History, and the Construction of 'Woman' in Late Ancient Christianity," in *A Feminist Companion to Patristic Literature*, ed. Amy-Jill Levine with Maria Mayo Robbins (London: T&T Clark, 2008), 101–24, here 111.

38. Jerome's Vulgate translation of Genesis 3:16 is similarly divergent from the Hebrew: he renders "you will turn to your husband" as something more like "you will be *under the power of* your husband" (*sub viri potestate eris*). So John Flood, *Representations of Eve in Antiquity and the English Middle Ages* (London: Routledge, 2011), 7. Jerome was also one of the first to leave out the phrase "with her" in Genesis 3:6b "and she gave also to her husband (with her) and he ate," which was common by the time of the so-called church fathers (Parker, *Blaming Eve Alone*).

39. Translation from the Tertullian Project. Versification from Turcan's Latin text. www.tertullian.org.

40. Cited in Patricia M. Rumsey, *'Lest She Pollute the Sanctuary': The Influence of the Protevangelium Iacobi on Women's Status in Christianity* (Turnhout: Brepols, 2020), 75.

41. On this and other Syriac treatments of Eve, see Susan Ashbrook Harvey, "Encountering Eve in the Syriac Liturgy," in *Syriac Encounters*, ed. Maria Doerfler, Emanuel Fiano, and Kyle Smith (Leuven: Peeters, 2015), 11–49.

42. Cited in Wojciech Kosior, "A Tale of Two Sisters: The Image of Eve in Early Rabbinic Literature and Its Influence on the Portrayal of Lilith in the Alphabet of Ben Sira," *Nashim: A Journal of Jewish Women's Studies & Gender Issues* 32 (2018): 118.

43. Quoted in Nonna Verna Harrison, *Grace and Human Freedom According to St Gregory of Nyssa* (Lewiston: Edwin Mellen, 1992), 124.

44. Dorothy Sly, *Philo's Perception of Women* (Atlanta: Scholars, 2020), 95.

45. Morse, *Encountering Eve's Afterlives*, 35–36.
46. Sly, *Philo's Perception of Women*, 95.
47. Edwards, *Admen and Eve*; Roche Coleman, "Was Eve the first femme fatale?" *Verbum et Ecclesia* 42, no. 1 (2021): a2138.
48. Caroline Blyth, *Reimagining Delilah's Afterlives as Femme Fatale: The Lost Seduction* (London: Bloomsbury, 2017), 9.
49. For example, the body of first-century texts that refer to Mary Magdalene do not give her age, but we can guess by naming conventions, and by her seemingly independent financial means, she is probably rather advanced in years. Yet depictions of her are virtually always youthful and sexy. Likewise, the texts give no reason to associate her with sex work or with the "sinful" woman who washed Jesus' feet, and yet the tradition has done both these things from the sixth century on. Mary Magdalene was sexualized in the tradition for the purposes of highlighting her dramatic "repentance," however, not to depict her as a femme fatale. On the hypersexualization of female characters into the extremes of either virgin or sex worker, see my interview in Vaillancourt (2019).
50. Morse, *Encountering Eve's Afterlives*, 37.
51. For a discussion of female temptresses in Qumran and sapiential literature, where an evil seductress in 4Q184 is not overtly an Eve or a Lilith, but is certainly a femme fatale, see Melissa Aubin, "'She Is the Beginning of all the Ways of Perversity': Femininity and Metaphor in 4Q184," *Women In Judaism: A Multidisciplinary Journal* 2, no. 2 (2001): 1–23.
52. Jean M. Higgins, "The Myth of Eve: The Temptress," *JAAR* 44, no. 4 (1976): 639.
53. Hannah Wortzman, "The Rape of Eve and its Spiritual Connotations in Early Jewish and Gnostic Literature," *Studies in Spirituality* 27 (2017): 57.
54. Marinus de Jonge and Johannes Tromp, *The Life of Adam and Eve and Related Literature* (Sheffield: Sheffield Academic, 1997).
55. Wortzman, "The Rape of Eve," 57.
56. Wortzman, "The Rape of Eve," 57.
57. Kosior, "A Tale of Two Sisters," 119.
58. Leila Leah Bronner, *From Eve to Esther: Rabbinic Reconstructions of Biblical Women* (Louisville: Westminster John Knox, 1994), 26.
59. Plus ça change . . .
60. I modelled this synopsis of NHC 13.2 on Celene Lillie's beautiful rendering in *The Rape of Eve: The Transformation of Roman Ideology in Three Early Christian Retellings of Genesis* (Minneapolis: Fortress, 2017), 2–3.
61. Of course, feminist biblical scholars like Trible and Edwards have argued from the Hebrew text of Genesis that Eve was more hero than villain there too (Trible, *God and the Rhetoric of Sexuality*, esp. 72–143; Karen Edwards, "The Mother of all Femmes Fatales: Eve as Temptress in Genesis 3," in *The Femme Fatale: Images, Histories, Contexts*, ed. Helen Hanson and Catherine O'Rawe (London: Palgrave MacMillan, 2010). 35–45.
62. Pagels, *Adam, Eve, and the Serpent*, 74–75.
63. Lillie, *The Rape of Eve*, 5.

64. Lillie, *The Rape of Eve*, 5.

65. On the official formation of Widow and Virgin (and their conflation in some circles), see, *inter alia*, Ute Eisen, *Women Officeholders in Early Christianity: Epigraphical and Literary Studies* (Collegeville: Liturgical, 2000), 143–57); Elizabeth Castelli, "Virginity and Its Meaning for Women's Sexuality in Early Christianity," *JFSR* 2, no. 1 (1986): 61–88; Charlotte Methuen, "The 'Virgin Widow': A Problematic Social Role for the Early Church?" *HTR* 90, no. 3 (1997)): 285–89; Steven L. Davies, *The Revolt of the Widows: The Social World of the Apocryphal Acts* (Dublin: Bardic, 1980).

66. On asceticism, virginity, and celibacy in early Christianity, see Castelli, "Virginity and Its Meaning," 61–88 and "Sex and Sexual Renunciation II: Developments in Research Since 2000," in *The Early Christian World*, 2nd ed., ed. Philip F. Esler (London: Routledge, 2017), 372–84.

67. Sara Parks, Shayna Sheinfeld, and Meredith Warren, *Jewish and Christian Women in the Ancient Mediterranean* (London: Routledge, 2022), 290.

68. Ashbrook Harvey, "Encountering Eve in the Syriac Liturgy," 12.

69. Vladimir Tumanov, "Mary Versus Eve: Paternal Uncertainty and the Christian View of Women," *Neophilologus* 95 (2011): 507.

70. Morse, *Encountering Eve's Afterlives*, 48.

71. Lily Vuong, *Gender and Purity in the Protevangelium of James* (Tübingen: Mohr Siebeck, 2013), 14.

72. Lynda L. Coon, *Sacred Fictions: Holy Women and Hagiography in Late Antiquity* (Philadelphia: University of Pennsylvania Press, 1997), 71–94, 145.

73. Vuong, *Gender and Purity*, 2.

74. See also Gary Anderson, "Celibacy or Consummation in the Garden? Reflections on Early Jewish and Christian Interpretations of the Garden of Eden," *HTR* 82, no. 2 (1989): 121–48; and Robin M. Jensen, "Mater Ecclesia and Fons Aeterna: The Church and her Womb in Ancient Christian Tradition," 137–55 in *A Feminist Companion to Patristic Literature*, ed. Amy-Jill Levine with Maria Mayo Robbins (London: T&T Clark, 2008), 140.

75. Jensen, "Mater Ecclesia and Fons Aeterna," 140.

76. Vuong, *Gender and Purity*, 18.

77. While this is not particularly in the context of a discussion about sexuality and celibacy, these topics lurk just under the surface. It is womankind that occasioned man's fall, rendering a gendered dichotomy. Further, it is a virgin that has accomplished "man's" restoration. It is unclear whether Augustine sees Eve as a parallel evil virgin to contrast with Mary, or as anti-virgin (sexually involved with the serpent).

78. Translations of Justin Martyr, *Dialogue with Trypho Are from Roberts-Donaldson*, accessed at http://www.earlychristianwritings.com/text/justinmartyr-dialogu-etrypho.html.

79. Just as early Christian tradition held that Joseph was not Jesus' "biological" father, some of the texts that sexualize Eve and the serpent seem to assume Adam was not the "biological father" of humanity. This could be a conflation of Watcher traditions with Eve traditions. The Watchers of Enochic literature are inspired by the *benei ha-elohim* ("sons of God") in Genesis 6:3 who found human women beautiful

and mated with them to create "mighty men" (Gen 6:4). On their reception, see Angela Harkins, Kelley Bautch, and John Endres, eds., *The Watchers in Jewish and Christian Traditions* (Minneapolis: Fortress, 2014). On the conflation over time between fallen angel traditions and Eve traditions (e.g., Cain as the offspring of evil angels), see Vita Daphna Arbel, *Forming Femininity in Antiquity: Eve, Gender, and Ideologies in the Greek Life of Adam and Eve* (Oxford: Oxford University Press, 2012), esp. 17–37.

80. Michael Pope considers the Lukan passage "especially sexually fraught." Pope shows "that Luke's introduction of Mary and his depiction of Gabriel's entrance make Mary an object of sexual advance and also sexual violence in a manner common in the LXX" and that "Gabriel's greeting to Mary and Mary's self-nomination as a slave further reinforce this violence"; Michael Pope, "Gabriel's Entrance and Biblical Violence in Luke's Annunciation Narrative," *JBL* 137, no. 3 (2018): 701.

81. Morse, *Encountering Eve's Afterlives*, 167.

82. In early Christian Syriac traditions, for some reason it is through the women's *ears* that the serpent enters Eve and the Holy Spirit enters Mary. Robert Murray, "Mary, the Second Eve in Syriac Tradition," *Eastern Churches Review* 3 (1971): 372–84.

83. Jennifer Glancy, *Corporal Knowledge: Early Christian Bodies* (Oxford: Oxford University Press, 2010), 163–273.

84. Jouette Bassler, *1 Timothy, 2 Timothy, Titus* (Nashville: Abingdon, 1996).

85. For an exploration of this notion of salvation from childbearing as part of a prolific ancient discourse around deities protecting from death during childbirth, see Emily Gathergood, "The Midwifery of God," PhD Dissertation, University of Nottingham, 2022.

86. As an example of this tendency, the chapter begins with a show of obeisance to the government; it calls for "supplications, prayers, intercessions, and thanksgivings" to be made for "kings and all who are in high positions, so that we may lead a quiet and peaceable life" (1 Tim 2:1–2). I call this the "nothing to see here, folks" tendency of many turn-of-the-second-century Christian texts such as Luke/Acts and the pastorals, which are trying hard to curb any notions that Jesus-followers are anything other than a fine, peaceable, upstanding Roman-style association, with venerable ancient roots.

87. Sarah E. G. Fein, "From Pain to Redemption: 1 Timothy 2:15 in its Jewish Context," 85–100 in *Gender and Second-Temple Judaism*, ed. Kathy Ehrensperger and Shayna Sheinfeld (Lanham: Lexington / Fortress Academic, 2020), 91.

88. Similarly, as mentioned above, various texts in the Nag Hammadi corpus like *On the Origin of the World*, *The Secret Revelation of John*, and *Reality of the Rulers*, also treat Eve's sexuality positively. Across the Gnostic corpus, the reunification of masculine and feminine, of which Adam and Eve are indicative, is necessary for true knowledge. See Lavinia Cerioni, "Feminine and Bridal Imagery in the Book of Baruch of the Gnostic Teacher Justin," in *From Jesus to Christian Origin,* ed. A. Destro, M. Pesce, and F. Berno (Turnhout: Brepols, 2019), 515–34.

89. Morse, *Encountering Eve's Afterlives*, 1–2, reflects on the reception of Eve as

evil, and easily manipulated, while her creative power has frequently been tainted by her association with sex and death. In other words, there has existed a divergence between the way we popularly think of Eve and how we might think of her based on the [Genesis] evidence.

BIBLIOGRAPHY

Agathangelos. *The Lives of Saint Gregory: The Armenian, Greek, Arabic, and Syriac Versions of the History Attributed to Agathangelos.* Translated by R. W. Thomson. Ann Arbor: Caravan, 2010.

Andersen, Francis I. "2 (Slavonic Apocalypse of) Enoch: A New Translation and Introduction." In *Old Testament Pseudepigrapha Vol. 1*, edited by James H. Charlesworth, 91–222. Garden City: Doubleday, 1983.

Anderson, Gary A. "Celibacy or Consummation in the Garden? Reflections on Early Jewish and Christian Interpretations of the Garden of Eden." *Harvard Theological Review* 82 (1989): 121–48.

Anderson, Gary A. and Michael E. Stone. *A Synopsis of the Books of Adam and Eve.* 2nd revised ed. Atlanta: Scholars, 1999.

Arbel, Vita Daphna. *Forming Femininity in Antiquity: Eve, Gender, and Ideologies in the Greek Life of Adam and Eve.* Oxford: Oxford University Press, 2012.

Ashbrook Harvey, Susan. "Encountering Eve in the Syriac Liturgy." In *Syriac Encounters*, edited by Maria Doerfler, Emanuel Fiano, and Kyle Smith, 11–49. Leuven: Peeters, 2015.

Aubin, Melissa. "'She Is the Beginning of all the Ways of Perversity': Femininity and Metaphor in 4Q184." *Women In Judaism: A Multidisciplinary Journal* 2 (2001): 1–23.

Augustine. *Sermons on the Liturgical Seasons.* Translated by Sister Mary Sarah Muldowney, R. S. M. Fathers of the Church 38. Washington: Catholic University of America, 1959.

Augustine. *Essential Letters.* Translated by J. Teske. New York: Augustinian Heritage Institute, 2021.

Bassler, Jouette. *1 Timothy, 2 Timothy, Titus.* Nashville: Abingdon, 1996.

Bird, Phyllis. "Images of Women in the Old Testament." In *Religion and Sexism*, edited by Rosemary Radford Ruether, 41–88. New York: Simon and Schuster, 1974.

Blyth, Caroline. *Reimagining Delilah's Afterlives as Femme Fatale: The Lost Seduction.* London: Bloomsbury, 2017.

Blyth, Caroline and Emily Colgan (eds.). *The Routledge Companion to Eve.* London: Routledge, 2023.

Bronner, Leila Leah. *From Eve to Esther: Rabbinic Reconstructions of Biblical Women.* Louisville: Westminster John Knox, 1994.

Brown, Peter. *The Body and Society: Men, Women, and Sexual Renunciation in Early Christianity.* New York: Columbia University Press, 1988.

Castelli, Elizabeth. "Virginity and Its Meaning for Women's Sexuality in Early Christianity." *Journal of Feminist Studies in Religion* 2, no. 1 (1986): 61–88.

Castelli, Elizabeth. "Sex and Sexual Renunciation II: Developments in Research Since 2000." In *The Early Christian World*, 2nd ed., edited by Philip F. Esler, 372–84. London: Routledge, 2017.

Cerioni, Lavinia. "Feminine and Bridal Imagery in the Book of Baruch of the Gnostic Teacher Justin." In *From Jesus to Christian Origins*, edited by A. Destro, M. Pesce, and F. Berno, 515–34. Turnhout: Brepols, 2019.

Charlesworth, James H. (ed.). *Old Testament Pseudepigrapha*, 2 vols. New York: Doubleday, 1983–1985.

Clanton, Dan. *Daring, Disreputable, and Devout: Interpreting the Hebrew Bible's Women in the Arts and Music*. New York: T&T Clark, 2009.

Clark, Elizabeth E. "Ideology, History, and the Construction of 'Woman' in Late Ancient Christianity." In *A Feminist Companion to Patristic Literature*, edited by Amy-Jill Levine with Maria Mayo Robbins, 101–24. London: T&T Clark, 2008.

Coleman, Roche. "Was Eve the First Femme Fatale?" *Verbum et Ecclesia* 42, no. 1 (2021): a2138.

Collins, John J. "Sibylline Oracles: A New Translation and Introduction." In *Old Testament Pseudepigrapha. Volume 1: Apocalyptic Literature and Testaments*, edited by James H. Charlesworth, 317–472. Garden City: Doubleday, 1983.

Coon, Lynda L. *Sacred Fictions: Holy Women and Hagiography in Late Antiquity*. Philadelphia: University of Pennsylvania Press, 1997.

Davies, Steven L. *The Revolt of the Widows: The Social World of the Apocryphal Acts*. Dublin: Bardic, 1980.

De Bruin, Tom. "Nostalgia, Novelty, and the Subversion of Authority in *Testaments of the Twelve Patriarchs*." *Transformative Works and Cultures* 31: *Fan Fiction and Ancient Scribal Cultures* (2019). https://doi.org/10.3983/twc.2019.1553.

De Jonge, Marinus and Johannes Tromp. *The Life of Adam and Eve and Related Literature*. Sheffield: Sheffield Academic, 1997.

Deutschmann, Barbara. *Creating Gender in the Garden: The Inconstant Partnership of Eve and Adam*. Edinburgh: T&T Clark, 2022.

Díaz Araujo, Magdalena. "The Satan's Disguise: The Exoneration of Eve in the Greek Life of Adam and Eve 17:1–2." *Judaïsme Ancien* 5 (2017): 159–82.

Díaz Araujo, Magdalena. "The Sins of the First Woman: Eve Traditions in Second Temple Literature with Special Regard to the Life of Adam and Eve." In *Early Jewish Writings*, edited by Eileen Schuller and Marie-Theres Wacker, 91–112. Atlanta: SBL, 2017.

Edwards, Karen L. "The Mother of all Femmes Fatales: Eve as Temptress in Genesis 3." In *The Femme Fatale: Images, Histories, Contexts*, edited by Helen Hanson and Catherine O'Rawe, 35–45. London: Palgrave MacMillan, 2010.

Edwards, Katie B. *Admen and Eve: The Bible in Contemporary Advertising*. Sheffield: Sheffield Phoenix, 2012.

Eisen, Ute. *Women Officeholders in Early Christianity: Epigraphical and Literary Studies*. Collegeville: Liturgical, 2000.

Elliott, J. K. "The Acts of Andrew and Matthias; The Acts of Peter and Andrew; The Acts of Andre and Paul." In *The Apocryphal New Testament*, edited by J. K. Elliott. Oxford Biblical Studies Online. Oxford: Oxford University, Press, 2021.

Ellis, Teresa A. "Is Eve the Woman in Sirach 25:24?" *Catholic Biblical Quarterly* 73, no. 4 (2011): 723–42.

Fein, Sarah E. G. "From Pain to Redemption: 1 Timothy 2:15 in its Jewish Context." In *Gender and Second-Temple Judaism*, edited by Kathy Ehrensperger and Shayna Sheinfeld, 85–100. Lanham: Lexington / Fortress Academic, 2020.

Flood, John. *Representations of Eve in Antiquity and the English Middle Ages*. London: Routledge, 2011.

Freedman, Harry and Maurice Simon, eds. *The Soncino Midrash Rabbah*. Chicago: Davka, 1995.

Gafney, Wilda C. *Womanist Midrash: A Reintroduction to the Women of the Torah and the Throne*. Louisville: Westminster John Knox, 2017.

Gathergood, Emily. *The Midwifery of God*. Ph.D. Dissertation. University of Nottingham. 2022.

Glancy, Jennifer. *Corporal Knowledge: Early Christian Bodies*. Oxford: Oxford University Press, 2010.

Gurtner, Daniel M. *Introducing the Pseudepigrapha of Second Temple Judaism: Message, Context, and Significance*. Grand Rapids: Baker Academic, 2020.

Harkins, Angela, Kelley Bautch, and John Endres (eds.). *The Watchers in Jewish and Christian Traditions*. Minneapolis: Fortress, 2014.

Harrison, Nonna Verna. *Grace and Human Freedom According to St Gregory of Nyssa*. Lewiston: Edwin Mellen. 1992.

Higgins, Jean M. "The Myth of Eve: The Temptress," *Journal of the American Academy of Religion* 44, no. 4 (1976): 639–47.

Ilan, Tal. *Integrating Women into Second Temple History*. Peabody: Hendrickson, 1999.

Isaac, Ephraim. "1 (Ethiopic Apocalypse of) Enoch: A New Translation and Introduction." In *Old Testament Pseudepigrapha. Volume 1: Apocalyptic Literature and Testaments*, edited by James H. Charlesworth, 5–90. Garden City: Doubleday, 1983.

Jensen, Robin M. "*Mater Ecclesia and Fons Aeterna*: The Church and her Womb in Ancient Christian Tradition." In *A Feminist Companion to Patristic Literature*, edited by Amy-Jill Levine with Maria Mayo Robbins, 137–55. London: T&T Clark, 2008.

Jerome. *Select Letters of St Jerome*. Translated by F. A. Wright. Loeb Classical Library 262. Cambridge, MA: Harvard University Press, 1933.

Klawans, Jonathan and Lawrence M. Mills (eds.). *The Jewish Annotated Apocrypha NRSV*. Oxford: Oxford University Press, 2020.

Kosior, Wojciech. "A Tale of Two Sisters: The Image of Eve in Early Rabbinic Literature and Its Influence on the Portrayal of Lilith in the Alphabet of Ben Sira." *Nashim: A Journal of Jewish Women's Studies & Gender Issues* 32 (2018): 112–30.

Kraemer, Ross S. "When Is a Text about a Woman a Text about a Woman?: The Cases of Aseneth and Perpetua." In *A Feminist Companion to Patristic Literature*, edited by Amy-Jill Levine with Maria Mayo Robbins, 137–55. London: T&T Clark, 2008.

Lachs, Samuel Tobias. "The Pandora-Eve Motif in Rabbinic Literature." *Harvard Theological Review* 67 (1974): 341–45.

Levine, Amy-Jill and Marc Zvi Brettler. *The Jewish Annotated New Testament*, 2nd ed. Oxford: Oxford University Press, 2011.
Levison, John R. "Is Eve to Blame: A Contextual Analysis of Sirach 25:24" *Catholic Biblical Quarterly* 47, no. 4 (1985): 617–23.
Levison, John R. "The Exoneration of Eve in the Apocalypse of Moses 15–30." *Journal for the Study of Judaism* 20, no. 2 (1989): 135–50.
Levison, John R. "Adam and Eve in Romans 1:18-25 and the Life of Adam and Eve." In *The Pseudepigrapha and Christian Origins*, edited by Gerbern Oegema and James H. Charlesworth, 87–101. London: T&T Clark, 2008.
Levi-Strauss, Claude. *Le Totémisme Aujourd'hui*. Paris, Presses Universitaires de France, 1962.
Lillie, Celene. *The Rape of Eve: The Transformation of Roman Ideology in Three Early Christian Retellings of Genesis*. Minneapolis: Fortress, 2017.
Methuen, Charlotte. "The 'Virgin Widow': A Problematic Social Role for the Early Church?" *Harvard Theological Review* 90, no. 3 (1997): 285–89.
Morse, Holly. *Encountering Eve's Afterlives: A New Reception-Critical Approach to Genesis 2-4*. Oxford: Oxford University Press, 2020.
Murray, Robert. "Mary, the Second Eve in Syriac Tradition." *Eastern Churches Review* 3 (1971): 372–84.
Neusner, Jacob. *Genesis Rabbah: Parashiyyot 1-33 on Genesis 1:1 to 8:14: The Judaic Commentary to the Book of Genesis: A New American Translation*, Vol. 1. Atlanta: Scholars Press, 1985.
Pagels, Elaine. *Adam, Eve, and the Serpent: Sex and Politics in Early Christianity*. New York: Vintage, 1989.
Parker, Julie Faith. "Blaming Eve Alone: Translation, Omission, and Implications of עמה in Genesis 3:6b." *Journal of Biblical Literature* 132, no. 4 (2013): 729–47.
Parks, Sara, Shayna Sheinfeld, and Meredith Warren. *Jewish and Christian Women in the Ancient Mediterranean*. London: Routledge, 2022.
Pope, Michael. "Gabriel's Entrance and Biblical Violence in Luke's Annunciation Narrative." *Journal of Biblical Literature* 137, no. 3 (2018): 701–10.
Rumsey, Patricia M. *'Lest She Pollute the Sanctuary': The Influence of the Protevangelium Iacobi on Women's Status in Christianity*. Turnhout: Brepols, 2020.
Schroeder, C. Paul. "The Mystery of Love: Paradigms of Marital Authority and Submission in the Writings of St John Chrysostom." *St Vladimir's Theological Quarterly* 44, no. 2 (2000): 143–68.
Schuller, Eileen M. "Introduction to the Apocrypha." In *Women's Bible Commentary. Twentieth Anniversary Edition*, edited by Carol A. Newsom, Sharon. H. Ringe, and Jacqueline E. Lapsley, 365–66. Louisville: Westminster John Knox, 2012.
Schüngel-Straumann, Helen. *Eva. Die erste Frau der Bibel: Ursache allen Übels?* Paderborn: Ferdinand Schöningh, 2014.
Sly, Dorothy. *Philo's Perception of Women*. Atlanta: Scholars, 2020.
Standhartinger, Angela. "Manuscript and Gender: Eve's Testament in GLAE/Apoc. Mos. 15–30 and LLAE 45–60." *Journal for the Study of the Pseudepigrapha* 31, no. 3 (2022): 215–46.

Thomas, Christine. *The Acts of Peter, Gospel Literature, and the Ancient Novel: Rewriting the Past*. New York: Oxford University Press, 2003.

Trible, Phyllis. *God and the Rhetoric of Sexuality*. Philadelphia: Fortress, 1978.

Tromp, Johannes. "Literary and Exegetical Issues in the Story of Adam's Death and Burial (GLAE 31–42)." In *The Book of Genesis in Jewish and Oriental Christian Interpretation*, edited by J. Frishman and L. Van Rompay, 25–42. Louvain: Peeters, 1997.

Tromp, Johannes. "The Story of our Lives: The qz-Text of the Life of Adam and Eve, the Apostle Paul, and the Jewish-Christian Oral Tradition concerning Adam and Eve." *New Testament Studies* 50 (2004): 205–23.

Tumanov, Vladimir. "Mary Versus Eve: Paternal Uncertainty and the Christian View of Women." *Neophilologus* 95 (2011): 507–21.

Vaillancourt, Philippe. "La Vierge et Marie Madeleine, une hypersexualisation aux antipodes." *Présence: Information Religieuse* (2019). http://presence-info.ca/article/academique/la-vierge-et-marie-madeleine-une-hypersexualisation-aux-antipodes.

Vuong, Lily. *Gender and Purity in the Protevangelium of James*. Tübingen: Mohr Siebeck, 2013.

Warren, Meredith J. C. "My OTP: Harry Potter Fanfiction and the Old Testament Pseudepigrapha." *Scriptura: Nouvelle Serie* 8, no. 1 (2006): 53–66.

Wortzman, Hannah. "The Rape of Eve and its Spiritual Connotations in Early Jewish and Gnostic Literature." *Studies in Spirituality* 27 (2017): 57–89.

Wright, Benjamin G. "Ecclesiasticus, or the Wisdom of Jesus, Son of Sirach." In *The New Oxford Annotated Bible: NRSV with the Apocrypha*. 5th ed., edited by Michael D. Coogan, 1479–81. Oxford: Oxford University Press, 2018.

Zahn, Molly M. "Genre and Rewritten Scripture: A Reassessment." *Journal of Biblical Literature* 131, no. 2 (2012): 271–88.

3

The Feminine as an Intellectual Category in Gnosticism

Proposing a Methodological Framework[1]

Lavinia Cerioni

INTRODUCTION

Ever since the words "women's studies" or "feminist studies" have made their long due appearance in early and late antique Christian studies,[2] investigating the role of the feminine in the history of Christianity has become a growingly pressing endeavor. In this chapter, I aim to illustrate the importance of investigating the feminine as an intellectual category—that is, as a means of conveying theological ideas—by also presenting a case study on the theological use of the feminine in Gnosticism.[3] Within Gnostic studies, the topic of gender (and women in particular) has drawn particular attention since the dawn of this field. Gnostic mythologies, so rich in female characters and feminine imagery, were fertile ground for the first studies on gender in early and late antique Christian studies.[4] This chapter builds on previous research and expands their scope to propose the use of the feminine as a theological interpretative framework for understanding the complex phenomenon of Gnosticism and its collocation within the first centuries of Christianity.

By using this approach to the feminine, I have a threefold aim. First, I would like to offer some methodological reflections on how approaching the feminine as an intellectual category fits within early Christian gender studies as a field. Second, as a result of my research on feminine imagery in Gnostic texts, I propose a working definition of Gnosticism. This definition challenges the dominant deconstructive perspective which dismisses the category of Gnosticism[5] and expands on the work of the few scholars—most recently Einar Thomassen—who are still attempting to make sense of Gnosticism, at the very least as *a working category*.[6] I argue that the different understandings of the feminine as an intellectual category among Gnostic movements represents a crucial theological framework to define the very essence of Gnosticism. Third, I present some of the most relevant Gnostic texts, thus showing the extent to which the feminine shapes the theological reflections of the second and fourth centuries. Through these texts, I show how feminine imagery played a crucial role in the negotiation of a Gnostic theological identity from the beginning and that there was not, nor has there ever been, a moment in which the feminine aspects of Gnostic theology have not been crucial in the identitarian intra-Gnostic and Christian debates.[7]

METHODOLOGICAL APPROACHES TO THE FEMININE IN THE HISTORY OF CHRISTIANITY

The terminology "gender studies" was born in the context of the Social Sciences and denotes a major interest in the social, cultural, and political status of women and, more recently, minorities.[8] In the past sixty years, scholars have been negotiating possible methodologies and approaches, thus creating variegated academic publications in need of constant methodological definition, as none of these different approaches to gender studies has a straightforward application in our field. For the larger part of the past sixty years, gender studies have been erroneously considered equivalent to feminist studies. In one of her last works, the renown feminist scholar Elisabeth Schüssler Fiorenza offered the following definition: "The f-word, 'feminist,' serves here as an umbrella term for gender, womanist, liberationist, postcolonial, Asian, African or Indigenous, Latina, queer, interreligious, and transnational studies and many other kyriarchy-critical perspectives and approaches."[9] In such a heterogeneous environment, it is crucial to define this chapter's research aim and approach. Promoting and participating in this ongoing debate, I concentrate on the feminine only, taking up the suggestion made by Elizabeth Clark in 2001 which has been so far neglected. Clark identified two general methodologies in the study of women in the history of Christianity: "women's history" and "gender studies." The first method has a defined historical outlook and traces the lives of real women throughout history. The second method has a close connection with feminist studies, that is, those studies which lay anti-kyriarchical claims and have the explicit intent to subvert the dominant masculine and patriarchal cultural paradigms. In the conclusion of her article, Clark reflects however on the very nature of the history of Christianity, a discipline which has texts as its primary sources, and defines Christian historians as "practitioners of a species of intellectual history."[10] In Clark's opinion, this poses an additional problem.

The current moment, more attentive to linguistic and social theory, is considerably less celebratory in its conclusions: we cannot with certainty claim to hear the voices of "real" women in early Christian texts, so appropriated have they been by male authors. Yet the direction in which I think interesting work is to be done examines how women and gender are constructed in these texts.[11]

This is indeed a challenge for the present study, that is, to investigate mainly "women-as-a-code." I intend to take here a historical approach which does not lay immediate political or anti-kyriarchical claims but wants to show how and to what extent the feminine as an intellectual category—that is, as a means of representing theological ideas—shaped the intra-theological debates of Gnostic theologians from the second to fourth centuries. Rather than focusing on the "real" women in Gnosticism, my aim is to investigate *in what way the feminine gender is used by Gnostic authors to portray God and the divine*. The present research has therefore a very narrow scope when compared with the immense variety of gender studies, as it aims at illustrating the use of one gender (the feminine) as a theological lens to interpret ancient Christian Gnostic texts. The feminine is here considered an intellectual category used by Gnostic theologians to convey their doctrines and intervene in the theological debates of their times. Even though numerous studies have been conducted on the role, functions, and theological significance of Gnostic female mythological characters, my approach contributes to expand our views on Gnosticism by acknowledging the existence of a theological negotiation which was entirely based on the use of gendered language as gateway for theological messages.[12] My analysis moves past the dominant masculine/spiritual and feminine/material Platonic and Philonic paradigms inherited by most Christian theologians of the first centuries to affirm that Gnostic theologians transcended it in response to the pressing need to make sense of a Christian God who exceeded some of the traditional intellectual and philosophical categories of the Hellenistic period.[13] Therefore, my approach to the feminine follows for the large part that interpretive line of "women-as-a-code," but it concentrates on the theological and philosophical implications of the feminine code, showing how this intellectual category shapes different theological doctrines. However, to make my case about the feminine, I believe it is first necessary to illustrate the definition of Gnosticism which emerged from the texts, as it is controversial in itself.

A DEFINITION OF GNOSTICISM

Since the first centuries of Christianity,[14] Christian and non-Christian writers who wanted to discern the definition, origin, identity, geography, and chronology of Gnosticism faced numerous problems due to the multifaceted nature of these movements. As pagan philosophers identified Gnostics as Christians[15] and Christian heresiologists saw them as Christian heterodox movements,[16] modern scholars of Gnosticism up to the beginning of the twentieth century have accepted the heresiological perspective. Indeed, few Gnostic primary sources were available up to the nineteenth century[17] and, thus, scholars took the heresiological accounts mostly for granted.[18] Even so, there were numerous uncertainties regarding the origin and identity of Gnosticism. With the discovery of the Nag Hammadi library in 1945, many believed that Gnostic studies were finally at a turning point.[19] But the library is a miscellaneous collection of works, some of which were not Gnostic, and it generated more confusion than clarity. It goes without saying that identifying a body of texts is crucial to define Gnosticism. As a matter of fact, Gnosticism presents the problem of the chicken and the egg: how can a definition be agreed if we do not agree on the body of texts to take into account?[20] In fact, a conference was held in Messina in 1966 with the sole purpose of defining Gnosticism. Notwithstanding the apparent consensus at the time, numerous scholars questioned the Messina conference's definition as the intrinsic structural equivocality of Gnosticism still impedes scholars to agree on the nature of Gnostic sources. The challenge is rooted in the scholarship to such an extent that most scholars have recently decided to dismiss the category of Gnosticism altogether,[21] following the arguments made by Michael Williams and Karen King.[22] They claimed respectively that, on the one hand, the Gnostic material is so variegated that it is impossible to trace a common essence; on the other hand, that Gnosticism has been fashioned as a strawman against which the so-called orthodox Christians erected the boundaries of their faith and, thus, does not provide a trustworthy account of these movements. Furthermore, they both contested that the widespread use of the words "gnosis" and "gnostic," which had and still has a wider application than the historical religious phenomenon, rendered the term fundamentally ambiguous.[23] As the definition of Gnosticism cannot be given for granted, I will illustrate briefly what I intend with it. Based on my research, I conclude the following:[24]

(a) Gnosticism is an equivocal Christian religious phenomenon which starts around the second century CE.[25]
(b) Gnostic movements are dualist systems, in which the inferior deity is the result of an intra-divine crisis caused by a female divine entity, often called Sophia.[26]
(c) The entire cosmos is dominated by a double movement of devolution/ reintegration. Part of humankind (usually identified with the Gnostics) retains a special position among created beings, sometimes expressed in

the terms of consubstantiality with the divine. The reintegration begins with the descent of a savior, often identified with Christ.
(d) The Gnostic cosmos—including all its inhabitants, whether deities or creatures—is organized in hierarchical levels, where the inferior level bears a *typological resemblance* toward the upper level.[27]
(e) The Gnostics aim at reuniting with God. This reunion is achieved thanks to the shared *feminine* identity between knower (the Gnostic) and known (the divine entity).
(f) Gnosticism is a syncretistic form of Christianity, borrowing from other religions and philosophies, especially Jewish apocalypticism and Middle-Platonic philosophies.[28]

Scholarship has also largely debated the existence of identifiable historical Gnostic sects. Besides Valentinianism,[29] evidence in this regard is not very solid. Information on the social structure of Gnostic movements relies almost exclusively on heresiological accounts, while there is little or no evidence in the original Gnostic sources.[30] For this reason, I deem more prudent to investigate the literary production of Gnosticism and identify common *mythologoumena* and *theologoumena*—namely, the foundational myths and the core theological doctrines—which do not necessarily correspond to identifiable historical Gnostic sects. In this regard, my investigation of feminine imagery confirms the validity of the scholarly distinction between two Gnostic paradigms: the so-called Classic Gnostic Mythologies (Ophitism, Barbeloitism, Sethianism)[31] and Valentinianism. Although the classification of the four major Gnostic movements can be traced back to heresiological taxonomies,[32] the following investigation on the use of feminine imagery suggests that each paradigm shapes the feminine according to their specific theological needs, thus legitimizing the use of this artificial classification.[33] However, such a classification should not be intended rigidly. In many instances, Gnostics texts display a combination of elements from different Gnostic paradigms that were used freely by theologians according to the specific need of each community.[34]

THE FEMININE AS A THEOLOGICAL FRAMEWORK

Gnosticism is one of the cases in Christian literature where feminine imagery becomes a defining factor for identifying theological variants. Indeed, the vast majority of Gnostic theologies are based on a devolution myth which stars Sophia (the last female aeon) as the main character.[35] Generally speaking, Gnostic femininity is theologically featured as representing God's paradoxical aspects, namely those divine features (e.g., generation, power, incarnation, passion) which were considered ill-suited to describe divinity according to the second and third centuries' philosophical and theological paradigms. Gnostic mythologies are often based on syzygies (male/female couples) in which, on the one hand, the male element is considered superior to the female element but, on the other hand, the true nature of God is represented by the unity of these two entities.[36] In this regard, I would like to stress that this fe/male vision of God grants greater importance to God's androgyny than mainstream Christianity. Representing God by means of syzygial couples has a fundamental countercultural stand as it overthrows gender-normative categories which were often proposed by mainstream Christianity.[37] Contrary to what one might assume, God's androgyny does not diminish the intellectual stand of binary gender categories: masculine and feminine become complementary categories which are even more necessary to picture a comprehensive image of God. Thus, the association of the feminine with instability and generation is most likely the reason why Gnostic mythologies envisioned a female entity causing the intra-divine rupture which originated the inferior world. Nonetheless, Gnostic female characters are far more complex than a superficial reading of these mythologies concedes. I summarize the feminine aspects of God in the following four characteristics: procreative ability, active force of the Father, subjection to passions, and spiritual guide. These four features are consistent throughout Gnosticism, albeit to different degrees of importance, and become the negotiating ground for the different Gnostic theologies. As feminine imagery is one of the determining factors that characterizes Gnosticism, my working hypothesis is that the manner in which a Gnostic author employs feminine imagery can be used to group different Gnostic works together, thus becoming an additional element to prove the existence of traceable coherent Gnostic *theologoumena* and *mythologoumena*. These are not scholarly categories fabricated by contemporary scholars, but genuine differences between Gnostic movements. In other words, we can make sense of Gnosticism also by identifying the degree and the kind of importance which is granted to the feminine by theologians.

Although Sophia's importance in Gnostic mythologies makes her the paradigm for feminine imagery, she is not the only female character. There are numerous others, like Barbelo, Incorruptibility, Holy Spirit, Church, Eve, Norea, and so on. However, these characters possess the above-mentioned theological feminine traits which make them all Sophia-like characters. In this respect, the *typological resemblance* is instrumental to understanding the similarities of Sophia-like figures: just like the cosmos is organized in degrading levels of perfections, each female character resembles the superior one to an imperfect degree.[38] Thanks to typological resemblance, all female characters assume specific theological meanings.

Classic Gnosticism[39]

In Ophitism, Barbeloitism, and Sethianism, the feminine plays a major generative, revealing, anthropological, and soteriological role.[40] In these mythologies, the generation of the divine world is entrusted to female aeons, who enact the Father's will. In the text of *Ap. John*, the female character named Barbelo is not only she who generates the entire divine world, but also one of the Trinitarian persons:

> I [am the Father], I am the Mother, and I am the Son.[41] [. . .] [The First Power], the glory of Barbelo, the perfect glory in the aeons, the glory of the revelation, she glorified the Virginal Spirit [. . .] This is the First Thought, his Image; she became the Womb of Everything for it is she who is prior to all of them, the Mother-Father, the First Man, the Holy Spirit, the thrice-male, thrice-powerful, the thrice-named androgynous one, and the eternal aeon among the invisible ones, and the first to come forth.[42]

In this quotation, although Barbelo embodies the generative power of God's power, she needs the male validation. Such a feature is so typical of the Gnostic representation of the divine to the point of making her the second person of this Gnostic Trinity. However, there are other cases in Gnostic texts where the appellative "Mother" does have such a positive connotation. In the case of Sophia, she is called mother of both Yaldabaoth, the false God, and of the spiritual church of the Gnostics.[43] Sophia's defection, caused by her desire to generate like the Father without the participation of her syzygial companion, is indeed the origin of the material world, which her deformed child Yaldabaoth created in a moment of monotheistic arrogance.[44] It is after this event that Sophia repents, and the totality of divine aeons sends down a savior to restore her into the divine world and in syzygial condition.[45] Nonetheless, Sophia is the reason for the existence of divine elements in humanity:

> And he (Yaldabaoth) said "If any other thing exists before me, let it become visible to me." And immediately Sophia stretched forth her finger and introduced light into matter; and she pursued it down to the region of chaos.[46]

Hence, the feminine is identified as the true origin of the Gnostic church for Sophia is their mother and their spiritual guide. This approach is further confirmed by the text of *Hyp. Arch.*, where the higher female aeon even serves as model for the creation of the first human being:

"Incorruptibility looked down into the regions (etc.)": so that, by the Father's will, she might bring the Pleroma into union with the Light. The archons laid a plan and said, "Come, let us create a man that will be soil from the earth." They modeled their creature as one wholly of the earth. [. . .] Now the archons [. . .] had taken [some soil] from the earth and modeled their

[man], after the body and after the [image] of God that had appeared [to them] in the waters. They said, "[Come, let] us hold of it by means of the form that we have modeled, [so that] it may see its male counterpart [*lacuna*], and we may size it with the form we have modeled" not understanding the power of God because of their powerlessness.[47]

In this account, Adam is created in the image of Incorruptibility to lure the female divinity into the lower world and trap her into materiality. This Gnostic rendering of the Genesis story implies that the entire creation is fashioned as feminine, at least to a certain extent. In addition, the feminine resides not in the material element of creation, which is here attributed almost exclusively to Adam, but in the divinity of human beings. In a similar account of the episode known as the "theophany above the waters" in *Orig. World*, Sophia assumes even a protological soteriological function:

> Since that day, all the authorities have honored the blood of the virgin. And the earth was purified on account of the blood of the virgin. But most of all, the water was purified through the likeness of Pistis Sophia, who had appeared to the prime parent in the waters. Justly, then, it has been said: "through the water." The holy water, since it vivifies the all, purifies it.[48]

This passage has strong baptismal imagery. The blood of the virgin, as the blood of Christ, purifies protologically the baptismal waters which are on the earth. Hence, Sophia becomes a soteriological agent who originally vivifies humankind. In other Ophite and Sethian works, similar salvific roles are usually attributed to other Sophia-like female figures, such as the spiritual Eve and Norea. These characters are directly involved in the process of revealing/knowing which leads humanity to God and act throughout history to reveal the existence of the true God and battle the power of Yaldabaoth:[49]

> And he (Adam) saw the woman beside him. And in that moment the luminous Epinoia appeared, and she lifted the veil which lay over his mind. And he became sober from the drunkenness of darkness. And he recognised his counter-image, and he said, "This is indeed bone of my bone and flesh of my flesh."[50]

This passage highlights the importance of Eve, here called the Epinoia of Light.[51] Her incarnation—that is, the incarnation of a spiritual divine being—makes Adam acknowledge his consubstantiality with the divine. This spiritual Eve is a soteriological agent insofar as she functions as the protological instructor of humankind who leads the way by revealing the fundamental knowledge of divine consubstantiality. It appears, therefore, that Gnostic works postulates two soteriological events, assigned respectively to Epinoia and to the savior. The difference between the two is that while the savior is *an eschatological soteriological agent*, Epinoia is the *protological soteriological agent*.

These few examples show that the feminine defines closely Ophite, Sethian and Barbeloite *mythologoumena* and *theologoumena* by serving as a literary code through which they engaged in complex theological issues, such as Trinitarian theology, theological anthropology, and soteriology.

Valentinianism

In Valentinianism, the feminine plays an important generative, revealing, Christological, and ecclesiastical role. Just like in Classic Gnosticism, female characters are involved in the generation of the Pleroma.[52] However, Valentinianism seems to focus more on God's transcendence than Classic Gnosticism, thus stressing the opposition and subordination of the female to the male element. In Valentinian texts, the role of the syzygy is highlighted,[53] but the syzygial work is credited to the male element, thus overshadowing the female contribution.[54] In this regard, the description of the Holy Spirit proposed in the *Gos. Phil.* is very interesting, as it is no longer associated to a Trinitarian female element, but to Sophia's double nature:

> The "Father" and the "Son" are single names, the "Holy Spirit" is a double name. [. . .] The Holy Spirit is in the revealed: it is below. It is in the concealed: it is above.[55] Echamot is one thing and Echmot another. Echamot is Sophia simply, but Echmot is the Sophia of death which is the one which knows death, which is called "the little Sophia."[56]

From a theological perspective, Valentinian Gnostics are re-shaping the above-mentioned Trinity conceived as Father-Mother-Son proper to Classic Gnosticism and associating the female Trinitarian person to an inferior, ambiguous, and disruptive character. In doing so, Valentinian Gnostics are indeed minimizing the contribution of the female aeon into the cosmological creation. However, this Valentinian shift in the interpretation of Sophia's role results in her assuming an unprecedented importance for Christology. In the texts of Theodotus's fragments, not only is she the helper and mystical bride of Christ,[57] who is also her saver, but she becomes the embodiment of Christ's sacrificial act:

> "Father," he says, "I deposit into thy hands my spirit." Sophia, he says, put forth a receptacle of flesh for the Logos, the spiritual seed; clad in it, the savior descended. Hence, at the Passion, he deposited Sophia with the Father, in order that he might receive her from the Father and not be held back here by those who have the power to unclad him. Thus, by the word already spoken of, he deposits the whole spiritual seed, the elect ones.[58]

Sophia is here identified with Christ's σαρκίον, the divine material and visible part of the Logos. In other words, Sophia is a type of the body and

Passion of Christ. The entire myth of Sophia's passion and disruption of the Pleroma is but a mythological rendering of Christ's own suffering. Sophia and Christ are the last syzygy to enter the Pleroma, thus showing the way to the elected Gnostics. For this reason, the Valentinian feminine imagery translates mainly into bridal and nuptial imagery, which finds its most evident expression in the mystical bridal chamber:

> If the woman had not separated from the man, she would not die with the man. His separation became the beginning of death. Because of this Christ came to repair the separation which was from the beginning and again united the two, and gave life to those who died as a result of the separation and united them. But the woman is united to her husband in the bridal chamber. Indeed, those who have been united in the bridal chamber will no longer be separated. Thus, Eve separated from Adam because it was not in the bridal chamber that she united with him.[59]

The status of perfection to which humankind aspires is gained by means of the reunion of the masculine and feminine in a unity, which is considered as the spousal union that takes place in the "bridal chamber" and typologically reproduces the composition of the Pleroma. In this theological paradigm, all human beings are considered as brides awaiting the arrival of the celestial bridegrooms, the angels.[60] Overall, I dare to say that the feminine is crucial in the theological articulation of the Valentinian system, as it is used to shape the core aspects of the Christian message.

CONCLUSION

In this chapter I provided two new perspectives. From a methodological point of view, I discussed the importance of considering the feminine as an intellectual category, that is, as a means to express theological ideas. By appreciating the theological value of this category, it is possible to cast new light on old problems, such as that of the definition of Gnosticism. In this regard, I showed that feminine imagery is a constitutive element of Gnosticism to such an extent that the "code" expressed by the feminine gender category becomes a key identity feature for Gnostic theologies. By using the feminine as an intellectual category, Gnostic authors expressed, underlined, and communicated their beliefs and theologies. The presented textual analysis showed that the use of feminine imagery was a genuine rhetorical tool of the early and late antique Christian theologians and not a modern superimposition on the texts.[61] Therefore, I argued that feminine imagery serves as a theological marker of Gnosticism as it is a common element to almost all Gnostic texts.

I explored how Gnostic feminine imagery is an essential part of their representation of the divine in both Classic Gnosticism and Valentinianism. Gnostic feminine imagery conveys some of the most original doctrines of these movements, which resorted to it in their attempt to cope with those aspects of the Godhead that they considered ambiguous and paradoxical. On the one hand, Classic Gnosticism largely uses feminine imagery in Trinitarian theology, by envisioning a female Trinitarian person who is involved in the creation of the divine world and of spiritual humanity. On the other hand, Valentinianism offers a more masculine interpretation of the Trinity, but it renders the core Christian belief in the redemptive function of Christ's Passion in utterly feminine terminology by identifying Sophia with Christ's suffering body. These few examples prove the importance of using the feminine as a theological framework in the study of early and late antique Christianity.

NOTES

1. This chapter is an overview of the working hypotheses developed in my monograph and it reflects further on the methodological aspects implied in the study of gender as an intellectual category, see Lavinia Cerioni, *Revealing Women. Feminine Imagery in Gnostic Christian Texts* (Turnhout: Brepols, 2021).

2. For two excellent surveys on the history of studies, see Elisabeth A. Clark, "Ideology, History, and the Construction of 'Woman' in Late Ancient Christianity," *Journal of Early Christian Studies* 2, no. 2 (1994): 155–84; and Elisabeth Schüssler Fiorenza (ed.), *Feminist Biblical Studies in the Twentieth Century* (Atlanta: Society of Biblical Literature, 2014).

3. On the problems surrounding the use of this category, see below.

4. See Simone Pétrement, *Le Dieu séparé: les origines du gnosticisme* (Paris: Cerf, 1984); Jorunn J. Buckley, *Female Fault and Fulfilment in Gnosticism* (Chapel Hill: University of North Carolina Press, 1986); Elaine H. Pagels, *Adam, Eve and the Serpent* (New York: Random House, 1988); Karen L. King (ed.), *Images of the Feminine in Gnosticism* (Philadelphia: Fortress Press, 2000).

5. Michael A. Williams, *Rethinking 'Gnosticism': An Argument for Dismantling a Dubious Category* (Princeton: Princeton University Press, 1996); Karen L. King, *What Is Gnosticism?* (Cambridge: Belknap Press of Harvard University Press, 2003).

6. Einar Thomassen, *The Coherence of "Gnosticism"* (Berlin: de Gruyter, 2020).

7. This is also the case of the very few Gnostic works (e.g., *Tri. Trac.* and *Gos. Truth*), where the absence of the feminine speaks louder than their eventual presence, see John D. Turner, *Sethian Gnosticism and the Platonic Tradition* (Louvain: Peeters, 2001), 754–60.

8. See Nancy A. Naples, *Companion to Women's and Gender Studies* (Hoboken: Wiley Blackwell, 2020), 6. This volume is an example of the various perspectives which have enriched gender studies in the past twenty years, as it explores "gender studies" in the full spectrum of its applications (e.g., Science, Culture, Society,

Economics, etc.). Moving away from an understanding of gender studies as a binary (masculine/feminine) constructed paradigm, Naples identifies the common denominator of gender studies in the close connection between postcolonial, postmodern, poststructural, and queer approaches, generating new intellectual formations in intersectionality and transnational feminist theories.

9. Elisabeth Schüssler Fiorenza, "Between movement and academy: Feminist Biblical studies in the twentieth century," in *Feminist Biblical Studies in the Twentieth Century*, ed. Elisabeth Schüssler Fiorenza (Atlanta: Society of Biblical Literature, 2014a), 1–17, here 1.

10. Elisabeth A. Clark, "Women, Gender, and the Study of Christian History," *Church History* 70, no. 3 (2001): 395–426, here 397. Even if there are some successful examples of ways to investigate the early and late antique Christianity by using other types of sources (for instance, the excellent work of Nicola Denzey Lewis, *The Bone Gatherers. The Lost Worlds of Early Christian Women* (Boston: Beacon Press, 2007) on the archeological and artistic evidence on women's patronage in Rome in the first centuries of Christianity), it is undeniably true that the vast majority of the sources at our disposal are literary works.

11. Elisabeth A. Clark, "The Lady Vanishes: Dilemmas of a Feminist Historian after the 'Linguistic Turn'," *Church History* 67, no. 1 (1998): 1–31, here 31.

12. Few studies on Gnosticism have explored this possibility, albeit tangentially, see Michael A. Williams, "Wisdom, Our Innocent Sister': Reflections on a Mytheme," in *Women and Knowledge in Early Christianity*, ed. Ulla Tervahauta (Leiden: Brill, 2017), 253–90; Tilde Bak Halvgaard, "Life, Knowledge and Language in Classic Gnostic Literature: Reconsidering the Role of the Female Spiritual Principle and Epinoia," in *Women and Knowledge in Early Christianity*, ed. Ulla Tervahauta (Leiden: Brill, 2017), 237–52.

13. On the complex relation between feminine, Platonism, and Gnosticism, see Emanuela Bianchi, "Receptacle/Chōra: Figuring the Errant Feminine in Plato's Timaeus," *Hypatia* 21, no. 4 (2006): 124–46; John D. Turner, "The Virgin That Became Male: Feminine Principles in Platonic and Gnostic Texts," in *Women and Knowledge in Early Christianity*, ed. Ulla Tervahauta (Leiden: Brill, 2017), 291–324; Turner, *Sethian Gnosticism and the Platonic Tradition*.

14. For some scholars even before then, see Edwin M. Yamauchi, "The Issue of Pre-Christian Gnosticism Reviewed in the Light of the Nag Hammadi Texts," in *The Nag Hammadi Library after Fifty Years: Proceedings of the 1995 Society of Biblical Literature Commemoration*, ed. Turner John D. and Anne McGuire A. (Leiden: Brill, 2001), 73–88.

15. See Plotinus' opinion in Porphiry, *Enneas* 9, 2.

16. This is indeed the case of all major Christian heresiologists, like Justin, Irenaeus, Hippolytus, Tertullian, and Epiphanius.

17. *Gos. Mary*, *Ap. John* and *Wis. Jes. Chr.* were already known thanks to the Berlin Codex.

18. This is indeed the case of the first major Gnostic scholars like Adolf Harnack, *History of Dogma*. Translated from the 3rd German edited by Neil Buchanan. 7 vols (Boston: Little, Brown, 1896–1905).

19. For the importance of using both Nag Hammadi and heresiological sources in the study of Gnosticism, see Thomassen, *Coherence*.

20. In this chapter, the texts presented have been acknowledged as Gnostic by the general consensus of the scholarly community, albeit a certain degree of manipulations during the centuries must be taken into account.

21. See the Westar Institute meeting report (https://www.westarinstitute.org/projects/christianity-seminar/fall-2014-meeting-report/) in Thomassen, *Coherence*, 2.

22. Williams, *Rethinking 'Gnosticism'*; King, *Gnosticism*.

23. See Andrew P. Smith, *A Dictionary of Gnosticism* (Wheaton: Quest Books, 2009).

24. This definition takes the moves from the Messina's definition of 1966 in Bianchi, "Receptacle/Chōra," 124–46, XXVI–XXVII:

> The Gnosticism of the second century sects involves a coherent series of characteristics that can be summarized in the idea of a divine spark in man, deriving from the divine realm, fallen into this world of fate, birth and death, and needing to be awakened by the divine counterpart of the self in order to be finally re-integrated. Compared with other conceptions of a "devolution" of the divine, this idea is based ontologically on the conception of a downward movement of the divine whose periphery (often called Sophia [Wisdom] or Ennoia [Thought]) had to submit to the fate of entering into a crisis and producing—even if only indirectly—this world, upon which it cannot turn its back, since it is necessary for it to recover the pneuma—a dualistic conception on a monistic background, expressed in a double movement of devolution and reintegration. The type of gnosis involved in Gnosticism is conditioned by the ontological, theological, and anthropological foundations indicated above. Not every gnosis is Gnosticism, but only that which involves in this perspective the idea of the divine consubstantiality of the spark that is in need of being awakened and reintegrated. This gnosis of Gnosticism involves the divine identity of the knower (the Gnostic), the known (the divine substance of one's transcendent self), and the means by which one knows (gnosis as an implicit divine faculty is to be awakened and actualized. This gnosis is a revelation tradition of a different type from the Biblical and Islamic revelation tradition).

25. In making this claim, I am denying the existence of what has been often labeled as proto-Gnosticim in the Pauline letters and Acts and also the so-called pre-Christian Gnosticism, see respectively Pheme Perkins, "Gnostic Motifs in the New Testament," in *The Gnostic World*, ed. Gary W. Trompf, Gunner B. Mikkelsen, and Jay Johnston (New York: Routledge, 2019), 90–99; and Carl B. Smith, "Ancient Pre-Christian 'Gnosticisms': The State of the Questions," in *The Gnostic World*, ed. Gary W. Trompf, and Gunner B. Mikkelsen and Jay Johnston (New York: Routledge, 2019), 63–78.

26. The few texts which do not present Sophia as the main characters—namely *Tri. Trac.* and *Gos. Truth*—do so consciously as they employ masculine imagery to mark a shift in the theological paradigms devised to represent God.

27. I mean typological in the Greek sense, as in τύπος (lit. impression, mold; fig. symbol) of the superior level. The term is borrowed from ancient Christian exegetes, who used it to indicate a specific exegetical device. However, I am here employing it in its cosmological and historical sense to indicate the similarities between levels

of reality in which the inferior cosmological level replicates the superior one. While I acknowledge that exegetical typology was theorized and employed by Gnostic and non-Gnostic writers alike, I claim that cosmological and historical typology is a proper feature of Christian Gnostic systems. Within Gnosticism, typology assumes more than a simple exegetical value, becoming the fundamental principle according to which the entire cosmos is ordained and the different levels of reality are organized. In other words, the Gnostic cosmos is divided into ontological levels, which maintain a certain similarity between themselves. For a detailed analysis of the Gnostic typological cosmology, see Cerioni, *Revealing Women*. The identification of these characteristics to the Gnostic system is a personal contribution, but it is largely based on the works of , François Sagnard, *La gnose valentinienne et le témoignage de saint Irénée* (Paris: Librairie Philosophique J. Vrin, 1947); Antonio Orbe, *La teologia dei secoli I e II. Il confronto della grande chiesa con lo gnosticismo* (Roma: Piemme, 1995); Manlio Simonetti, *Testi gnostici in lingua greca e Latina* (Milano: Lorenzo Valla, 1999); Christoph Markschies, *Gnosis: An Introduction* (London: T&T Clark, 2003); Gaetano Lettieri, "La mente immagine: Paolo, gli gnostici, Origene ed Agostino." in *Per una storia del concetto di mente*, ed. Eugenio Canone (Olschki: Firenze, 2005), 63–122.

28. Against King's objection to the use of syncretism when referring to Gnosticism—see (King, *Gnosticism*, 222–24). I tend to agree with the investigation regarding the importance of Platonism and Judaism for Gnostic movements, see (Turner, "Virgin") and Annette Y. Reed, *Fallen Angels and the History of Judaism and Christianity: The Reception of Enochic Literature* (Cambridge: Cambridge University Press, 2005).

29. There are numerous studies which prove extensively the existence of this Gnostic school, see particularly Christoph Markschies, "Valentinian Gnosticism: Toward the Anatomy of a School," in *The Nag Hammadi Library after Fifty Years: Proceedings of the 1995 Society of Biblical Literature Commemoration*, ed. John D. Turner, and Anne McGuire (Leiden: Brill, 1997), 401–38; and Einar Thomassen, *The Spiritual Seed: The Church of the "Valentinians"* (Leiden: Brill, 2006).

30. For the role of women in Gnostic communities, see Pagels, *Adam, Eve and the Serpent* and King, *Images*. More recently, scholars have claimed the monastic origin of the Nag Hammadi codices, see Hugo Lundhaug and Lance Jennot, *The Monastic Origins of the Nag Hammadi Codices* (Tübingen: Mohr Siebeck, 2015).

31. Here, I use the terminology "Classic Gnostic Mythology" for the sake of clarity. Nonetheless, I have some reservations about the use of the adjective "Classical," which delegitimizes other forms of Gnosticism and suggests not only the idea of a chronological precedence but also the theological primacy of these movements over the others—all assumptions that need to be proved further.

32. In particular, Clemens of Alexandria, *Strom* 7, 17(108), 1–2.

33. It is important to underline that the different ways of shaping the feminine imagery emerges from the texts and not the other way around. Moreover, the use of this category is common in Gnostic scholarship.

34. This has been extensively proved by Rasimus, who has identified the core doctrines of each movement of Classic Gnosticism. The most evident example is

Ap. John who is a combination of Ophite, Barbeloite and Sethian elements; Tuomas Rasimus, *Paradise Reconsidered in Gnostic Mythmaking* (Leiden: Brill, 2009).

35. In Gnostic mythologies, Sophia is the name attributed to the last production of the Pleroma, the fullness of the divine realm. She is a female aeon, who is considered part of the divine pantheon even if she is not united in syzygy with a male partner. The story begins when, being aware of her loneliness, Sophia becomes restless and begins searching for a suitable companion. During her quest, she oversteps the limits of her pleromatic conditions and leaps out of the Pleroma into the lower world. In falling outside of the Pleroma because of her uncontrolled desire, she gives birth to an abortion—often called Yaldabaoth or Demiurge—who does not resemble his mother and is ignorant of the world above. Being however extremely powerful, Yaldabaoth becomes the overlord (chief archon) of the inferior world, also generating several archons to help him in governing his realm. In doing so, he typologically and unwillingly reproduces the structure of the world above. Seeing the evils that she has brought into the world, Sophia regrets her decisions and appeals to the good grace of the Father. At this point, the Pleroma takes pity on her and sends down its perfect fruit, Christ, to rescue her. Christ is not only her savior but also her rightful companion, with whom she will ascend again to the Pleroma.

36. Such a way of envisioning genders can be traced back to Plato's philosophy, see Bianchi, "Receptacle/Chōra," 124–46.

37. See Mariano Troiano, *Eva, la serpiente y la Bestia instructora*, in *Mulier, quid ploras? Acts of the VII[a] Journadas de Estudios Patrísticos* (Buenos Aires: Biblioteca Augustiniana, forthcoming), who has kindly agreed to share with me his forthcoming publication.

38. The function of typological resemblance is expressed explicitly in Gnostic work, see *Ap. John* II, 14, 14–15, 13; *Hyp. Arch* II, 87, 8–11; *Orig. World* II, 102, 1–7; *Gos. Phil* 75, 3–9; *Ad. haer* I, 5, 3.

39. For the differences between the three Gnostic movements, see (Cerioni, *Women*, 45–98).

40. For a classification of the Gnostic works, see (Rasimus, *Paradise*, 62).

41. *Ap. John* II, 2, 13–15.

42. *Ap. John* II, 4, 36–5, 11.

43. See, for instance, *Ap. John* II,9,25–10,5; *Hyp. Arch* II, 94, 5–18.

44. *Ap. John* II, 10, 7–19; *Orig. World* II, 99, 29–101, 9; *Hyp. Arch.* II, 86, 27–87, 11.

45. *Ap. John* II, 14, 1–13; *Orig. World* II, 125, 14–31.

46. *Hyp. Arch* II, 94, 27–33.

47. *Hyp. Arch.* II, 87, 11–88, 1.

48. *Orig. World* II, 108, 25–109, 1.

49. *Ap. John* II, 20, 9–28; *Ap. John* II, 23, 4–10; *Hyp. Arch.* II, 89, 4–10; *Hyp. Arch.* II, 91, 34–92, 2.

50. *Ap. John* II, 23, 4–10.

51. Eve has many names in Gnostic mythologies, such as Epinoia of light, spiritual Eve, luminous woman, but it is always easily identifiable thanks to explicit reference to the biblical text of Genesis.

52. *Val. Exp.* XI, 22, 18–28; Irenaeus, *Ad. haer.* I, 1, 1.
53. It is particularly explicit in *Val. Exp.* XI, 36, 28–34 and XI, 39, 13.
54. This is indeed the case of Sophia and Christ in the one-Sophia Valentinian systems of *Val. Exp.*; *Exc. Theod.* (frag. 1–42) and Valentinus' system in *Adv. haer.* I, 11, 1.
55. *Gos. Phil.* II, 59, 11–19.
56. *Gos. Phil.* II, 60, 10–15.
57. *Val. Exp.* XI, 35, 30–37.
58. *Exc. Theod.* 1, 1–2.
59. *Gos. Phil.* II, 70, 10–2.
60. *Exc. Theod.* 21, 1–3.
61. Some scholars—e.g., (King, *Gnosticism*) and April D. De Conick, *Holy Misogyny: Why the Sex and Gender Conflicts in the Early Church Still Matter* (London: Continuum, 2011)—have claimed that this attention to the feminine is a characteristic proper only to movements which were rejected by the Catholic Church of the first centuries. By contrast, it seems to me that a theological presence of the feminine as an intellectual category—even if often not a positive one—is proper to many mainstream Christian theologians, such as Ambrose, Clement, Origen, Gregory of Nyssa. I believe this is a very fruitful research area which is yet to be explored.

BIBLIOGRAPHY

Bak Halvgaard, Tilde. "Life, Knowledge and Language in Classic Gnostic Literature: Reconsidering the Role of the Female Spiritual Principle and Epinoia." In *Women and Knowledge in Early Christianity*, edited by Ulla Tervahauta, 237–52. Leiden: Brill, 2017.

Bianchi, Emanuela. "Receptacle/Chōra: Figuring the Errant Feminine in Plato's Timaeus." *Hypatia* 21, no. 4 (2006): 124–46.

Buckley, Jorunn J. *Female Fault and Fulfilment in Gnosticism*. Chapel Hill: University of North Carolina Press, 1986.

Cerioni, Lavinia. "Tempo tipologico. La nozione di tempo nel Valentinismo." In "*XLVI Incontro di Studiosi dell'Antichità Cristiana*," 495–502. Rome: Nerbini, 2020.

Cerioni, Lavinia. *Revealing Women. Feminine Imagery in Gnostic Christian Texts*. Turnhout: Brepols, 2021.

Clark, Elisabeth A. "Ideology, History, and the Construction of 'Woman' in Late Ancient Christianity." *Journal of Early Christian Studies* 2, no. 2 (1994): 155–84.

Clark, Elisabeth A. "The Lady Vanishes: Dilemmas of a Feminist Historian after the 'Linguistic Turn'." *Church History* 67, no. 1 (1998): 1–31.

Clark, Elisabeth A. "Women, Gender, and the Study of Christian History." *Church History* 70, no. 3 (2001): 395–426.

De Conick, April D. *Holy Misogyny: Why the Sex and Gender Conflicts in the Early Church Still Matter*. London: Continuum, 2011.

Denzey Lewis, Nicola. *The Bone Gatherers. The Lost Worlds of Early Christian Women*. Boston: Beacon Press, 2007.

Harnack, Adolf. *History of Dogma*. Translated from the 3rd German edited by Neil Buchanan. 7 vols. Boston: Little, Brown, 1896–1905.

King, Karen L. (ed.). *Images of the Feminine in Gnosticism*. Philadelphia: Fortress Press, 2000.

King, Karen L. *What Is Gnosticism?* Cambridge, MA: Belknap Press of Harvard University Press, 2003.

Lettieri, Gaetano. "La mente immagine: Paolo, gli gnostici, Origene ed Agostino." In *Per una storia del concetto di mente*, edited by Eugenio Canone, 63–122. Olschki: Firenze, 2005.

Lundhaug, Hugo and Lance Jennot. *The Monastic Origins of the Nag Hammadi Codices*. Tübingen: Mohr Siebeck, 2015.

Markschies, Christoph. "Valentinian Gnosticism: Toward the Anatomy of a School." In *The Nag Hammadi Library after Fifty Years: Proceedings of the 1995 Society of Biblical Literature Commemoration*, edited by John D. Turner, and Anne McGuire, 401–38. Leiden: Brill, 1997.

Markschies, Christoph. *Gnosis: An Introduction*. London: T&T Clark, 2003.

Naples, Nancy A. *Companion to Women's and Gender Studies*. Hoboken: Wiley Blackwell, 2020.

Orbe, Antonio. *La teologia dei secoli I e II. Il confronto della grande chiesa con lo gnosticismo*, Roma: Piemme, 1995.

Pagels, Elaine H. *Adam, Eve and the Serpent*. New York: Random House, 1988.

Perkins, Pheme. "Gnostic motifs in the New Testament." In *The Gnostic World*, edited by Gary W. Trompf, Gunner B. Mikkelsen, and Jay Johnston, 90–99. New York: Routledge, 2019.

Pétrement, Simone. *Le Dieu séparé: les origines du gnosticisme*. Paris: Cerf, 1984.

Rasimus, Tuomas. *Paradise Reconsidered in Gnostic Mythmaking*. Leiden: Brill, 2009.

Reed, Annette Y. *Fallen Angels and the History of Judaism and Christianity: The Reception of Enochic Literature*. Cambridge: Cambridge University Press, 2005.

Sagnard, François. *La gnose valentinienne et le témoignage de saint Irénée*. Paris: Librairie Philosophique J. Vrin, 1947.

Schüssler Fiorenza, Elisabeth. "Between movement and academy: Feminist Biblical studies in the twentieth century." In *Feminist Biblical Studies in the Twentieth Century*, edited by Elisabeth Schüssler Fiorenza, 1–17. Atlanta: Society of Biblical Literature, 2014.

Schüssler Fiorenza, Elisabeth (ed.). *Feminist Biblical Studies in the Twentieth Century*. Atlanta: Society of Biblical Literature, 2014.

Simonetti, Manlio. *Testi gnostici in lingua greca e latina*. Milano: Lorenzo Valla, 1999.

Smith, Andrew P. *A Dictionary of Gnosticism*. Wheaton: Quest Books, 2009.

Smith, Carl B. "Ancient Pre-Christian 'Gnosticisms': The State of the Questions." In *The Gnostic World*, edited by Gary W. Trompf, and Gunner B. Mikkelsen and Jay Johnston, 63–78. New York: Routledge, 2019.

Tervahauta, Ulla. *Women and Knowledge in Early Christianity*. Leiden: Brill, 2017.
Thomassen, Einar. *The Spiritual Seed: The Church of the "Valentinians."* Leiden: Brill, 2006.
Thomassen, Einar. *The Coherence of "Gnosticism."* Berlin: de Gruyter, 2020.
Troiano, Mariano. *Eva, la serpiente y la Bestia instructora, in Mulier, quid ploras? Acts of the VII^a Journadas de Estudios Patrísticos*. Buenos Aires: Biblioteca Augustiniana, 2023 (forthcoming).
Trompf, Gary W. and Gunner B. Mikkelsen and Jay Johnston (eds.). *The Gnostic World*. New York: Routledge, 2019.
Turner, John D. *Sethian Gnosticism and the Platonic Tradition*. Louvain: Peeters, 2001.
Turner, John D. "The Virgin That Became Male: Feminine Principles in Platonic and Gnostic Texts." In *Women and Knowledge in Early Christianity*, edited by Ulla Tervahauta, 291–324. Leiden: Brill, 2017.
Turner John D., and Anne McGuire (eds.). *The Nag Hammadi Library after Fifty Years: Proceedings of the 1995 Society of Biblical Literature Commemoration*. Leiden: Brill, 2001.
Williams, Michael A. *Rethinking 'Gnosticism': An Argument for Dismantling a Dubious Category*. Princeton: Princeton University Press, 1996.
Williams, Michael A. "'Wisdom, Our Innocent Sister': Reflections on a Mytheme." In *Women and Knowledge in Early Christianity*, edited by Ulla Tervahauta, 253–90. Leiden: Brill, 2017.
Yamauchi, Edwin M. "The Issue of Pre-Christian Gnosticism Reviewed in the Light of the Nag Hammadi Texts." In *The Nag Hammadi Library after Fifty Years: Proceedings of the 1995 Society of Biblical Literature Commemoration*, edited by Turner John D. and Anne McGuire A., 73–88. Leiden: Brill, 2001.

4

Explicit and Implicit Gender Laws—"Incest" in Qumranic and Tannaitic Literature

A Comparative Reading of Lev 18:13

Federico Dal Bo

In this chapter, I address the notion of "incest" in Qumranic and Tannaitic literature as two virtually contemporary textual and historical realities. Nevertheless, these two dimensions only marginally overlap and had a quite different historical evolution.

On the one hand, Qumranic literature was strongly and idiosyncratically associated with the community of Qumran—that was constructed in late Hellenistic period, mostly included Essenes or an off-shot of the Essene movements and was destroyed at the end of the disastrous first Jewish-Roman war at the end of the first century of the common era. On the other hand, Tannaitic literature was associated with the intellectual class of the Pharisees—although these two categories overlap chronologically but are not entirely identical with each other—and was eventually included in the larger development of Rabbinic literature, becoming one of the main components of Jewish Law and Talmudic literature.

This obvious difference in the historical development of Qumranic and Tannaitic literatures calls for caution when examining how they treated specific legal issues with respect to contemporaneous actual or idealized Jewish societies. Therefore, the present examination should not be considered specifically historical but rather typological, since it is difficult to determine what the cultural, social, theological interactions between these two Jewish realities actually were.

In this chapter, I will argue that the Qumranites were pursuing a form of *religious radicalism* that implied making a series of linguistic and expressive choices that generally tended to shape sexuality as a social weapon for hegemonizing and controlling society. In addition, I will also argue that both Qumranic and Tannaitic literatures generally agree on the prohibition of incest in any form but also offer a quite different hermeneutical rationale for it. Interestingly, scripture conjugates verbs concerning the prohibition of incest exclusively in masculine gendered terms and extends it only implicitly onto women, as it is well known from linguistic studies. A linguistic counterpart to this neuter-to-male continuity may be found in gendered languages, where a word's neuter root also corresponds to the masculine form, however the feminine gender is generated by adding to the root.[1]

The prevalence of masculine gendered forms and inflections over the feminine ones—quite common in most Semitic languages—relies on the notion of "prior gender" that is not intrinsically discriminatory but rather reflects a linguistically imperfect way of determining biological gender, social gender, and class. For instance, the sociolinguistic scholar Deborah Tannen has appropriated the controversial notion of "genderlect"—the generic claim that gender is a relevant variable in human communication—and used it to explore the miscommunication between genders as a reflection of deeper differences in conversational styles, directedness, and indirectness in communication, allowing her to analyze communicative asymmetries in the interconnections between important variables, such as hierarchy and equality, closeness and distance.[2]

This linguistic imperfection plays a pivotal role in forming what Foucault calls *discourse*—as a historically contingent social system producing knowledge, meaning, and power. Therefore, the use of "prior gender" is not indifferent but has rather obvious consequences on taxonomy, epistemology, and gender hierarchy that eventually result in tolerating, suggesting, or even producing legal and social inequalities.[3]

The use of "prior gender" is typically accepted as a matter of fact. Notably, only the Qumranites explicitly assert that incest norms shall also pertain to women. Why is it so? Shall we suppose that any other Jewish community except the Qumranites were neglectful toward such a fundamental notion—incest?

A BIBLICAL PERSPECTIVE

It is well known that incest—here generally intended as a sexual relationship of any kind between close relatives—is severely regulated in the legislation from the book of Leviticus (Lev 18 and Lev 20). Yet, it cannot be overlooked that incest in terms of marriage is somehow tolerated in some passages from the book of Genesis due to its narrative function in designating the structure of kinship.[4]

In linguistic terms, incest is usually designated by the Hebrew term ערוה ("nakedness") and is associated with a specific prohibition: one should not "uncover" the "nakedness" of a forbidden sexual partner. Scholarship in Anthropology, Religious Studies, and Jewish Studies have already well proven that biblical incest norms functioned in defining and regulating both endogamy and progeny.[5] Their main purpose was limiting permitted partners and assuring a proper lineage. Notably, the biblical texts exclusively focus on the responsibilities of male householders who also tend to view women in this process as linguistically, ritually, and legally assimilated to "vessels" or "depositories" for men's children.[6]

More specifically, the Hebrew Bible also distinguishes between three different lists of forbidden sexual partners, according to the intensity of the degree of kinship: blood relatives (Lev 18:6–11), blood relatives' kin (Lev 18:12–16), and, finally, two people who are close kin to each other (Lev 18:17–18). Despite their alleged "moral character," the first function of the biblical norms on incest and sexual transgressions is social. These norms mostly pertain to—and therefore are fundamentally instrumental to—the definition of kinship. It is plausible to assume that biblical norms on incest implicitly provide a taxonomy of kinship from both a social and a juridical point of view. Thus, these norms provide a social and gender hierarchy, as they offer protection to core family members—according to a patriarchal and heteronormative point of view. Notably, the Hebrew Bible overtly forbids sexual relationships with those "blood relatives," as mentioned in the Code of Purity (Lev 21:2–3): mother, father, son, daughter, brother, and sister.

In her literary analysis of the book of Leviticus. *Recovering the Daughter's Nakedness*, Madeline McClenney-Sadler has also made manifest that biblical norms on incest play a decisive role in determining the structure of kinship, its social organization, and its gender hierarchy. These are described with a nomenclature that exhibits a rigid internal logic and consistency. The main purpose of incest legislation is not to reject its intrinsic "immorality." As evident from scripture itself, most of the stories from the patriarchal cycle include incestuous connections, which sometimes contradict modern "common sense." These narratives had a specific function: providing a precise taxonomy of kinship in ancient Near Eastern cultures. In short, because narratives in scripture seem to justify what is asserted legally, it is sometimes difficult to understand apparent ethical ambiguities in it.

As mentioned above, the biblical norms on incest usually open with an admonition that is spelled out in a stereotyped, technical language, that typically is morphologically masculine—probably as an imitation of the morphologically masculine but legally neutral Akkadian law collections—and is employed as a "prior gender" throughout the entire chapter:

> "None of you shall approach any that is the rest of his kin, to uncover their nakedness. I am the Lord" (אִישׁ אִישׁ אֶל־כָּל־שְׁאֵר בְּשָׂרוֹ לֹא תִקְרְבוּ לְגַלּוֹת עֶרְוָה אֲנִי יְהוָה). (Lev 18:6)

The present verse rules that close relatives are forbidden sexual partners. On the one hand, scripture prohibits sexual relationships with whoever "is near of kin to him." This prohibition is founded on the Hebrew idiomatic expression that literally designates "the rest of his flesh" and designates "blood relatives" as men either as masculine individuals or "custodians" of female individuals. Therefore, the taxonomy of incest is spelled according to the masculine "prior gender" but also includes the hierarchically subordinated women: mother, father, son, daughter, brother, and sister.

On the other hand, scripture also extends this prohibition to non-blood relatives, founded on the Hebrew idiomatic term ערוה ("nakedness"). The first prohibition, the one pertaining to close relatives, is directly connected to a divine command. In its strictest sense, it has no juridical rationale and is founded on the fear of God: "I am the Lord." The second prohibition—denoted by the expression אֶל־כָּל־שְׁאֵר בְּשָׂרוֹ (literally, "toward the rest of his flesh")—pertains to non-blood relatives, provides the very juridical rationale that was lacking in the first prohibition, and delineates the protected rights of a first person in relation to a second person that is the former's forbidden relative.

Though lacking a logical order, biblical norms on incest can be arranged not according to the intensity of the law but rather according to the intensity of the degree of kinship between forbidden partners. It is in this specific sense that the biblical norms on incest also provide a detailed taxonomy of kinship, from both a social and a juridical point of view. Therefore, it is evident that these norms, as well as the ones on blood manipulation, are founded on a social and gender hierarchy, offering protection of rights to the core family members.

However, the expressive rigidity—norms that are formally addressed only to males—determines several issues with the legal application of law. These norms actually provide neither the legal and juridical dynamics by which incest is consummated nor the reason why these forbidden forms of behavior happen to be stigmatized. It remains unclear whether women are considered active actors in an incest case and under which legal circumstances forbidden sexual relationships can be defined as incest. Consequently, most of these sexual transgressions are juxtaposed with the heterosexual matrimonial institution—whose heteronormative principle then functions as a proof case.

There especially is one relevant omission among the sexual transgressions mentioned in the book of Leviticus: the one between father and daughter—both as his legitimate or illegitimate daughter. This specific case is mentioned neither in the Hebrew Bible nor in the Mishnah. Yet, the case of incest between father and daughter is implicitly prohibited twice: once on account of one's loyalty to the Lord (Lev 18:6) and once on account of one's wife (Lev 18:17). The former argument presupposes that a daughter belongs to the "blood relatives," while the latter presupposes that interests and rights of one's wife are to be protected from competing also against her own daughter. This omission cannot be mistaken for leniency; rather, it presupposes the economics of ancient Israelite society.

Nevertheless, these juridical prescriptions often collide with the narrative passages from the Hebrew Bible that apparently describe the forefathers and foremothers of ancient Israel indulging in some of these acts, as the famous examples of Noah, Lot, Jacob, and Reuben easily demonstrate. Whereas later Rabbinic literature will try to harmonize this tension, the Hebrew Bible appears to leave it untouched.[7] This constituted a major issue for the Qumranites who also were avid readers of those texts that will later be included in the canonical scripture.

A QUMRANIC PERSPECTIVE

In the Pseudepigrapha and other early Jewish texts, the biblical prohibition of incest is mostly accepted as a basic principle of decent behavior.[8] These texts do not innovate beyond the biblical rulings on incest but rather manipulate the trope of incest in figurative terms and use it as a rhetorical allegation against the Gentiles and their secular powers, regardless of its realistic reliability (*Sib. Or.* 5:387–396 and 7:42–45).

The Qumranites paid special attention to the Levitical laws on incest but also considered the *Book of Jubilees* as an equally authoritative text as the—eventually canonized—texts of the Hebrew Bible.[9] More specifically, they applied the laws of incest equally to both males and females. They especially made this extension explicit and included the case of incest between the daughter of a brother and the brother of her father as equally culpable (CD 5:9–11). In addition to this, they also extended the prohibition of having intercourse with nieces, as already maintained in the *Book of Jubilees* due to specific narrative choices.[10] Consequently, they made the illicit nature of incest between a man and the daughter of his brother or sister explicit (CD 5 7b–11a, 6: 14–7:4). The Qumranites also extended the prohibition of intercourse with a family member to the prohibition of marrying her or him (11QTempl 66:11).

These supplementary rulings probably sought to provide uniformity from a redactional and rhetorical point of view and to neutralize the differences between biblical legal norms collected in the books of Deuteronomy and Leviticus (Deut 27, Lev 18, and Lev 20). The Qumranites explicitly condemned any illicit sexual act and strongly stigmatized it with derogative phraseology.[11] They extended biblical regulations on incest from male to female subjects by *explicating* their content. Their intention was to overtly state that incest is prohibited in any case—both involving male or female partners, in heterosexual and homosexual relationships. Nevertheless, this was not obvious according to a literal understanding of Levitical laws.

As it is well known, two very large fragments from what would later be identified as the *Damascus Document* had been published long before the initial discovery of the Dead Sea Scrolls in 1947. Solomon Schechter published them in his study under the title: *Fragments of a Zadokite work*.[12] This publication drew considerable attention for its importance. For the present chapter, it will be sufficient to focus exclusively on a small portion that reads as follows:

וגם מטמאים הם את המקדש אשר אין הם מבדיל כתורה ושוכבים עם הרואה את דם זובה
ומשה אמר אל אחות אמך לא תקרב שאר *vacat* לוקחים איש את בת אחיהם ואת בת אחותו
אמך היא ומשפט העריות לזכרים הוא כתוב וכהם הנשים ואם הגלה בת האח את ערות אחי אביה
vacat.והיא שאר[13]

> They also contaminate the sanctuary as they separate not according to the Law and lie with her who sees the blood of her issue. They take unto them a wife the daughter of their brother and the daughter of their sister. *vacat* But Moses said, "you shalt not approach the sister of your mother; she is your mother's near kin." And the law of incest for males is written, and like them are the females. And if a daughter of the brother uncovers the nakedness of the brother of her father, he is a near kin. *vacat*[14]

Schechter's careful and literal rendering of the passage especially emphasized the congruity between this still unknown sect and the Pharisaic vocabulary while designating sexual forbidden partners with עריות (literally "the naked ones") and the act of menstruating with the euphemistic technical expression הרואה דם ("whoever sees blood").

A more recent edition of the Hebrew text and an English translation was published under the title *The New Damascus Document* in 2006 by Ben Zion Wacholder. I quote his remarkable translation, but I also take the liberty to highlight some issues with the conventional bracketed *sic*:

וגם מטמאים הם את המקדש אשר אין הם מבדיל כתורה ושוכבים עם הרואה את דם
ומשה אמר אל אחות אמך לא תקרב *vacat* זובה ולוקחים איש את בת אחיהום ואת בת אחותו

שאר אמך היא ומשפט העריות לזכרים הוא כתוב וכהם הנשים ואם הגלה בת האח את ערות אחי
אביה והיא שאר *vacat*

They also defile the Temple, not separating (between clean and unclean) according to the Torah. And they lie with a menstruating woman [sic!] and marry the daughter of one's brother or sister. *vacat* However, Moses said, "You shall not come near the sister of your mother; she is a relation of your mother" (Lev 18:13) [sic!]. And the rules of incest are in male language, but they apply to women as well. Hence, if the brother's daughter uncovers the nakedness of her father's brother, she is a (forbidden) relation *vacat*.[15]

The most notable difference between Schechter's and Wacholder's versions—aside from a few linguistic choices—is the different treatment of an obscure quotation from scripture that the author of the *Damascus Document* attributed to Moses, as he openly says: "and Moses said" (ומשה אמר). While Schechter refrained from identifying the source, Wacholder is adamant in assuming that it is a quotation from the book of Leviticus—namely Lev 18:13. Given the hermeneutical importance of this verse, it is germane to pay more attention to this small, yet conclusive detail.

A MYSTERIOUS QUOTATION FROM SCRIPTURE

The question that first arises is whether this really is a quotation from the book of Leviticus, as Wacholder maintains. For clarity's sake, I report both versions emphasizing the notable differences in wording in italics (see Table 4.1):

The differences in wording are obvious and yet have somehow been neglected in recent editions of the *Damascus Document* that do not comment on it.[16] Some of them are probably only phraseological and can be justified as a matter of word economy or minor differences in wording: the elision of the term עֶרְוַת ("nakedness") in the quotation in the *Damascus Document* and the lack of the preposition כִּי, "because," are not negligible but can still be justified in terms of idiosyncratic phenomena in textual transmission. In other terms, they are notable differences that might only

Table 4.1 Lev 18:13 in Qumran and the Bible

Pseudo-Lev 18:13 in CD 5:8–9	Lev 18:13
אל אחות אמך אל אחות אמך לא תקרב שאר אמך היא You shall not *come near* the sister of your mother; she is a relation of your mother	עֶרְוַת אֲחוֹת אִמְּךָ לֹא תְגַלֵּה כִּי שְׁאֵר אִמְּךָ הִוא You shall not *uncover* the *nakedness* of the sister of your mother *because* she is a relation of your mother

reflect a specific difficulty in textual transmission but not necessarily more than this.

On the contrary, there is a striking difference in the choice of the main verb: while the *Damascus Document* reads לא תקרב ("you shall not come near") (Pseudo-Lev 18:13), Scripture reads לֹא תְגַלֵּה ("you shall not uncover") (Lev 18:13). How can this difference be explained?

Schechter suggested in his footnotes that the "nearest parallel" to this otherwise enigmatic quotation from scripture was, as anticipated, the very verse from the book of Leviticus. In quite similar terms, Israel Levy too suggested that the text was "corrupted," probably due to a false memory transmission. Nevertheless, he is cautiously inconclusive on the matter: "a supposer même que le verset était cité de mémoire, il est étonnant tout de même que, le prenant pour thème de discussion, on l'altère de la sorte."[17] Wacholder himself surprisingly suggests—if not imposes us to believe—that the quotation in the *Damascus Document* should be assimilated to the ordinary reading from the book of Leviticus.

In truth, this is a most important change in phraseology. Unfortunately, the recent edition of *The Biblical Qumran Scroll*—that provides a philologically reliable transcription of each identifiable fragment from scripture in consecutive biblical order together with the textual variants that are contained in the entire library of Qumran—does not include this verse from the book of Leviticus.[18] Since we have no "reconstructed" text, we can only speculate about the status of this passage in the Qumran library.

At first, there is one possible but admittedly implausible explanation: the text had been corrupted by some transmission error or the Qumran scribe might have been influenced from another similar verse. A possible candidate that is reasonably close in wording and content may be the following verse: "do not come near a woman during her period of uncleanness to uncover her nakedness" (וְאֶל־אִשָּׁה בְּנִדַּת טֻמְאָתָהּ לֹא תִקְרַב לְגַלּוֹת עֶרְוָתָהּ) (Lev 18:19).

Yet, one must resist this easy philological explanation, as if there were some sort of overall "dittography" during the editing of this passage from the *Damascus Document*. On the contrary, it is precisely a question of evaluating how deep the difference between the Pseudo-Leviticus quoted in the *Damascus Document* and the Masoretic text of the biblical book of Leviticus is.

The author of the *Damascus Document* is clearly using technical terminology. This is evident from his use of a legal terminology—a nuance that is unfortunately lost in Wacholder's still remarkable translation. Wacholder's rendering of the technical expression הרואה את דם (literally "whoever sees the blood") with a "menstruating woman" is contextually correct but prevents us from appreciating the subtle point that the Qumranites are raising. This translation overlooks an important phraseological and expressive feature in this text.

The Hebrew expression הרואה את דם ("whoever sees the blood")—a legal expression that is already extant in early Rabbinic literature, such as Mekhilta, Mishnah, Sifra, and Tosefta—is non-gendered and functionally neutral as it applies both to men and women. Accordingly, this phraseology allows for establishing a sort of legal and cultural symmetry between two legal entities: a man "who sees" his blood emission from his genitals, as a possible consequence of hematospermia, and a woman "who sees" her own blood, namely her menstrual blood, while this condition is more usually denoted with the expression נידה ("menstruating woman").

Yet, a more important point is the different connotation of the two negative verbs לא תקרב ("you shall not come near") (Pseudo-Lev 18:13) and לֹא תְגַלֵּה ("you shall not uncover") (Lev 18:13) as they occur in the *Damascus Document* and in Leviticus, respectively. As is well known, the negative verb לֹא תְגַלֵּה ("you shall not uncover") is usually used to indicate the prohibition of "uncovering" someone's body. Thus, it pertains exquisitely to the notion of having sexual intercourse as such, and therefore taking somebody's clothes off for the obvious reason of having coitus.

On the other hand, the negative verb לא תקרב ("you shall not come near") is less direct and designates a series of acts that may come to complete sexual intercourse but still include a series of middle-steps that might involve a series of erotic acts of different kinds: "approaching" the partner's body, engaging in non-penetrative sex, petting, and so on. The wider rationale involved by this verb suggests that any sexual and erotic act shall also be considered prohibited when someone's partner is menstruating, regardless of the nature of the sexual act—either a penetrative or a non-penetrative one. In this sense, then, the verb serves as a reinforcer of a sexual prohibition not to have any kind of sexual contact when the partner is menstruating.

Although there are no specific parallels to the reconstructed text from Leviticus that was used by the Qumranites, there are nonetheless several parallel passages that confirm how this distinction—between the two negative verbs לא תקרב ("you shall not come near") (Pseudo-Lev 18:13) and לֹא תְגַלֵּה ("you shall not uncover") (Lev 18:13)—was not only relevant but also largely accepted. In other words, there are some passages from Qumranic literature that can serve as true parallels to the text from this verse from Leviticus, as discussed recently by Baesick Choi. Notable differences, as usual, are highlighted in italics (see Table 4.2):[19]

These philological data are particularly relevant. On this basis, it is quite philologically implausible that the longer expression לֹא תִקְרַב לְגַלּוֹת ("you shall not come near to uncover") (Lev 18:19) may have persuaded the Qumranite scribe—either by omission, dittography, or a simple scribe's error—that the original Masoretic verse לֹא תְגַלֵּה ("you shall not uncover") (Lev 18:13) shall also be "altered" into the form לא תקרב ("you shall not come near") that

Table 4.2 "Uncovering Someone's Nakedness" in Qumran and the Bible

4Q251 17:3	Leviticus 18:13
את בת אחיו בת אחותו אל יגלה His brother's daughter or the daughter of his sister . . . let no man uncover . . .	עֶרְוַת אֲחוֹת אִמְּךָ לֹא תְגַלֵּה כִּי שְׁאֵר אִמְּךָ הִוא You shall not *uncover* the *nakedness* of the sister of your mother *because* she is a relation of your mother

is transmitted in the Qumranite version of Leviticus, as it is quoted in the *Damascus Document* (Pseudo-Lev 18:13). In other words, it is not impossible, albeit quite unlikely, that the difference between the two negative verbs לֹא תקרב ("you shall not come near") (Pseudo-Lev 18:13) and לֹא תְגַלֵּה ("you shall not uncover") (Lev 18:13) may have been caused by some issue associated with any form of textual transmission under the influence of the longer expression לֹא תִקְרַב לְגַלּוֹת ("you shall not come near to uncover") (Lev 18:19). On the contrary, I maintain that this deep change in wording rather manifests a profound ideological difference between the *literatures* that emerged from two chronologically subsequent Jewish realities—such as the community of Qumran that had elapsed before the Rabbis would eventually emerged as a cohesive group only several hundred years later.[20]

IDEOLOGY OF CHANGE IN QUMRAN: SHAPING SEXUALITY AS A SOCIAL WEAPON

The context of the passage from the *Damascus Document* clearly encapsulates the issue of having any kind of sexual relationships in general into the one in particular: having intercourse with a menstruating woman. This is stated from the beginning when the enemies of the Qumranites are harshly stigmatized: "lie with her who sees the blood of her issue" (ושוכבים עם הרואה את דם) (CD 5:7). What does it mean?

In my opinion, this is no occasional remark. On the contrary, as anticipated, I also maintain that the Qumranites were pursuing a form of *religious radicalism* that implied shaping sexuality as a social weapon for hegemonizing and controlling society—exerting a form of "bio-politics" in the precise sense of intersecting politics and human biology. In this respect, the verbal change from לֹא תְגַלֵּה ("you shall not uncover") (Lev 18:13) to לֹא תקרב ("you shall not come near") (Pseudo-Lev 18:13) is exactly instrumental to elevating any form of sexual transgression—say, having intercourse with a menstruating woman—to the highest taboo of the incest. In doing so, the Qumranites intended to strongly control sexual behavior and project their disciplined vision of sexuality unto the entire community—males and females alike, men and women alike.

This persuasive explanation for the verbal change from לֹא תְגַלֵּה ("you shall not uncover") (Lev 18:13) to לא תקרב ("you shall not come near") (Pseudo-Lev 18:13) also implies that the circumstance of this change is not philologically but rather ideologically motivated. In other terms, the author of the *Damascus Document* has deliberately *manipulated* the scriptural text for his own ideological benefit. Which one?

Using the verb לא תקרב ("you shall not come near") (Pseudo-Lev 18:13) rather than לֹא תְגַלֵּה ("you shall not uncover") (Lev 18:13) has a specific effect: merging two different categories of sexual transgression into one—having intercourse with a menstruating woman with committing incest. One should be careful in appreciating this juridically complex act of merging of two legal transgressions. The purpose of this rationale is not "downgrading" the issue of incest to having intercourse with a menstruating woman, as if spoiling someone's lineage were as inadvertent or negligible as having sex with a menstruating partner. On the contrary, the purpose exactly is the opposite: "elevating" a relatively mild sexual transgression—like having intercourse with a menstruating woman—to a serious social matter as incest. In doing so, the Qumranites also intended to reinforce their ideological juxtaposition by arguing that this strict discipline is equally applicable to both males and females. It is so due to a simple "analogy": וכהם ("and like them"). This clearly is a case of "integrative interpretation" that the Qumranines applied to produce (more) specific laws from pentateuchal verses and yet kept them at a biblical level of import.[21]

This suggests that the conflation of different categories of sexual transgressions—typically stigmatized by two different imperatives: לא תקרב "you shall not come near" (Pseudo-Lev 18:13) in place of לֹא תְגַלֵּה ("you shall not uncover") (Lev 18:13) but also occasionally conflated into a more complex phraseology לֹא תִקְרַב לְגַלּוֹת ("you shall not come near to uncover") (Lev 18:19)—points to *radicalize* the dimension of transgression. This conflation also implies that someone's *hermeneutical ability* to negotiate with these issues is inevitably eroded. The text does not only suggest that having intercourse with a menstruating woman is treated as seriously as an issue of incest but also extends the same rigor and discipline to the entire *society*—men and women alike, males and females alike, by means of a simple "likeness."

While analyzing the Hebrew of the Dead Sea Scrolls, Baasten has emphasized that a specific section from this passage—"the law of incest, written for males and like them [for] females"—plays a distinctive role: the first noun phrase is in extraposition, while the prepositional phrase is contrastive.[22] This exegesis suggests that the biblical text did not sound clear and precise enough to the Qumranites. In his examination of the attitudes toward sexuality in

Qumran, William Loader has also emphasized that the author was following a "converse logic." Accordingly, he argued that what was *written* for males was *likewise* applicable to women—and therefore had to be applied also to men and their nieces. It is plausible to assume that this kind of approach was explicitly directed against Tannaitic legislation that prohibited marriage between women and nephews but allowed marriage of uncles and their nieces, as normally maintained in several Rabbinic expositions.[23]

This custom—uncles marrying nieces—indirectly emerges also from a passage of the Mishnah that discusses Levirate marriage when the dead husband was married to more than one woman. The legal question emerging from the application of the Levirate marriage in the legitimate case of polygamy obviously is—which one of the wives shall be entitled to become pregnant from her dead husband's brother? The Mishnah comments on this legal case and distinguishes between different categories of women:

כֵּיצַד פּוֹטְרוֹת צָרוֹתֵיהֶן. הָיְתָה בִּתּוֹ אוֹ אַחַת מִכָּל הָעֲרָיוֹת הָאֵלּוּ נְשׂוּאָה לְאָחִיו, וְלוֹ אִשָּׁה אַחֶרֶת, וָמֵת, כְּשֵׁם שֶׁבִּתּוֹ פְּטוּרָה, כָּךְ צָרָתָהּ פְּטוּרָה.

> How do [these women] exempt their rival wives [from Levirate marriage]? His daughter or any one of those with whom relations are forbidden was married to his brother and [he] had another wife, and [he] died, just as his daughter is exempt [from Levirate marriage], so too her rival wife is exempt. (mYeb 1:2)

Polygamy constitutes a special case in the application of the Levirate marriage. There might be litigation between two—or more—wives surviving the same dead husband. Accordingly, the Mishnah accepts not only, as is obvious, polygamy but also, and especially, the marriage between an uncle and his niece as a legitimate marriage connection. Interestingly, a supplementary rationale to this otherwise problematic institution is also introduced in a supplementary source from the Babylonian Talmud: a *baraita*—an either actual or fictional early Hebrew tradition that was not included in the Mishnah at the time of its redaction. This *baraita* explicitly qualifies the marriage between an uncle and his niece in terms of non-sexual affection:

תָּנוּ רַבָּנָן הָאוֹהֵב אֶת אִשְׁתּוֹ כְּגוּפוֹ וְהַמְכַבְּדָהּ יוֹתֵר מִגּוּפוֹ וְהַמַּדְרִיךְ בָּנָיו וּבְנוֹתָיו בְּדֶרֶךְ יְשָׁרָה וְהַמַּשִּׂיאָן סָמוּךְ לְפִירְקָן עָלָיו הַכָּתוּב אוֹמֵר וְיָדַעְתָּ כִּי שָׁלוֹם אָהֳלֶךָ הָאוֹהֵב אֶת שְׁכֵנָיו וְהַמְקָרֵב אֶת קְרוֹבָיו וְהַנּוֹשֵׂא אֶת בַּת אֲחוֹתוֹ וְהַמַּלְוֶה סֶלַע לְעָנִי בִּשְׁעַת דָּחְקוֹ עָלָיו הַכָּתוּב אוֹמֵר אָז תִּקְרָא וַה' יַעֲנֶה תְּשַׁוַּע וְיֹאמַר הִנֵּנִי

> The Sages taught: whoever loves his wife like himself[24] and who honors her more than himself, and who instructs his sons and daughters in an upright path, and who marries them, about him the verse states: "and you shall know that your tent is in peace" (Job 5:24). Whoever loves his neighbors, and who draws his relatives close, and who marries the daughter of his sister and who lends a *sela'*

[coin] to a pauper at his time of need, about him the verse states: "then shall you call, and the Lord will answer; you shall cry, and He will say: Here I am" (Is 58:9) (bYeb 62b–63a).

The non-sexual understanding of a marriage between an uncle and his niece especially emerges from the use of the verb אהב ("to love") that is typically applied to the Lord (Deut 6:5), love for himself (Lev 19:18), love for someone's neighbor (Lev 19:18) and love for the stranger (Lev 19:34). This all suggests that, regardless of its actual social reality, the marriage between an uncle and his niece was not considered sexual, strictly speaking, but was rather encouraged for the sake of social and cultural cohesion.[25]

On the other hand, the Qumranites presumably shared their rejection of this kind of marriage also with the Sadducees—from whom we have no explicit writings but whose position on the matter can be conjectured on hermeneutical basis. As the late Aharon Shemesh convincingly suggested, the Qumranite rule to extend the law of incest also to women was also to be read against the pretension of adding new regulations on the matter. On the contrary, the *extension* of these regulations also to women tended to resolve the need for complementing Jewish law without formally relying on Oral law.[26] In this respect, their rejection of a marriage between an uncle and his niece was not only motivated by their strong apocalyptic expectations but also by a polemical attitude against the Pharisees—a sentiment that paired them with the Sadducees.[27] Besides, the Qumranites strongly emphasized the importance of keeping ritual purity. Accordingly, they developed a complex procedure of כרת ("banishment, excision") depending on the gravity of the transgression: a temporary banishment for minor and inadvertent transgressors and a permanent banishment for major transgressors. The temporary banishment pertained to those individuals who inadvertently failed to follow God's commandments. It lasted two years and probably also involved reduction of food rations. Notably, it was called הבדלה ("separation") from the "holy" community of Qumran, just as secular days are nowadays "separated" from Shabbat (1QS 9:2).

Thus, the Qumranites practiced differentiation in the application of banishment, prescribing either a temporary or a permanent one from the community. They differentiated between intentional and unintentional transgressions, just as the Rabbis did, but, unlike them, they also rejected the idea of atoning for inadvertent transgressions by bringing a sacrifice to the Temple in Jerusalem.

On the contrary, they considered this very institution defiling and unclean. Consequently, the institution of כרת ("banishment") was segmented into a temporary and a permanent banishment. Temporary banishment clearly served as a legal substitution for the biblical sin- and guilt-offering, prescribed for inadvertent transgressions. In this respect, the punishment by כרת ("banishment") was clearly different from any form of death penalty. On the other hand, temporary banishment was modeled on the biblical notion of exile:

> The idea that the temporary exclusion of an unwitting offender from the Community is a substitute for ritual expiation through sacrifice is based on the paradigm of Israel's exile; and according to the sectarian conception of history, that was the punishment for unintentional offenses.[28]

On the other hand, permanent banishment was usually decreed for capital offences—such as pronouncing the name of God, slandering the Sons of Light, complaining against the institutions of the community, and committing fornication with one's wife, that is, having intercourse with her not according to the sectarian laws of the Qumranites—but was still not assimilable to any form of death penalty.

The juxtaposition of legislation on incest and legislation on intercourse with women in their menstrual period is characteristic of Rabbinic literature but is also particularly frequent in the literature of Second Temple Judaism. As already anticipated, such juxtaposition also manifests a radical orientation, especially among the Qumranites: intercourse with a woman in her menstrual period is regulated as strictly as in cases of incest. This is evident from *The Temple Scroll* that stigmatizes these practices with unquestionable imperatives: "a man shall not take . . ." that is, "a man shall not marry . . ."[29] There are several reasons for using this terminology: providing uniformity from a redactional point of view and using a rhetorical point of view that neutralizes the differences between specific texts (especially Deut 27, Lev 18 and Lev 20) by using the formula "a man shall not take . . ."; introducing a legal stringency in the cases of incest, emphasizing the intentions of the books of Deuteronomy and Leviticus; finally, discussing the rules on incest on account of *The Temple Scroll*'s discussion of the rules on rape and its social ramifications such as the marriage to the rapist.[30] Also, the passage from the use of the term אשה ("woman") to the use of the term אשתו ("his wife") happens on an orthographic level and therefore reflects the textual history of the Masoretic Text.

A TANNAITIC PERSPECTIVE

Early Rabbinic literature is somewhat tolerant with respect to specific biblical institutions—such as polygamy—and treats the issue of having intercourse with a menstruating woman more moderately, as far as it is stigmatized but not as severely as a case of incest. Most of the core legislation to be found in the book of Leviticus, for instance, is devoted to limiting and punishing incest.

Early Rabbinic literature presents sexuality positively as included in the created order, while the restrictions for accessing it in space and time usually conform to biblical rulings without exhibiting the radicalism manifested in Qumranic literature. Like other early Jewish literatures, Tannaitic literature too agrees with most biblical injunctions on human sexuality. As already anticipated, this interest is especially manifested with elaborating in legal terms on specific cases and commenting on those aspects of biblical legislation—such as the case of an incest between father and daughter, the conflation of same-sex relations among males and pederasty, and the treatment of same-sex relations among females—that are considered either lenient, lacking details, or implicit, and otherwise dependent on interpretation.[31]

Nevertheless, Tannaitic literature usually exhibits some conceptual imprecision. The most notable one probably is the conflation between "person" and "act," so that incest as for intercourse during menstruation face the same kind of punishment.[32] This imprecise perception also supports—when it does not encourage it—a peculiar vision of sexuality and gender. Since the Rabbis assume that incest and deliberate intercourse during menstruation must be punished in the same way with כרת ("banishment"), then deliberate intercourse during menstruation is implicitly equivalent, in gravity and social stigmatization, to incest.

On the contrary, inadvertent intercourse is not to be punished similarly (mKer 2:6). The act of equating intercourse during menstruation with incest obviously sustains a repressive vision of sexuality. Tannaitic literature does not object, in principle, to this extension but does not consider it necessary to make it explicit. The extension of this prohibition from male to female partners in Tannaitic literature is only *implicit* and fundamentally depends on specific hermeneutical decisions, as it also emerges from later Amoraitic and Talmudic literature.

Notably, these prohibitions are expressed exclusively in the masculine, as already anticipated, and are never addressed directly to women. The original intention was probably rhetorical and consisted in *imitating* the phraseology of Mesopotamian legislation but was eventually interpreted ideologically and transformed into a specific assessment of gendered roles in Jewish society. Accordingly, Levitical law neither prohibits nor permits incest between the males of the family but rather condemns the seduction of a female member of the family. The lexical redundancy is usually disambiguated with the imperative: "you shall not approach his wife" (אֶל־אִשְׁתּוֹ לֹא תִקְרָב) (Lev 18:14). Accordingly, the nakedness of a female relative is not attributed to her, but rather to her husband. Consequently, intercourse with an aunt, a father's sister, for instance, would harm the rights of her husband, but not her own personal rights. The Mishnah systematically affirms this Tannaitic exegesis but eliminates any redundancy. Accordingly, biblical prohibitions are consequently abbreviated in the mishnaic narrative, as a commonly accepted exegetical move.

Yet, the mishnaic exegesis itself is also open to ideological additions. For example, while scripture reads that "the nakedness of your father, the nakedness of your mother, shall you not uncover; she is your mother; you shall not uncover her nakedness" (עֶרְוַת אָבִיךָ וְעֶרְוַת אִמְּךָ לֹא תְגַלֵּה אִמְּךָ הִוא לֹא תְגַלֶּה עֶרְוָתָהּ) (Lev 18:7), the Mishnah simply shortens it: "when one has intercourse with his mother" (הַבָּא עַל הָאֵם) (mKer 1:1). Similarly, when scripture reads that "you shall not uncover the nakedness of your father's brother, you shall not approach his wife" (עֶרְוַת אֲחִי־אָבִיךָ לֹא תְגַלֵּה אֶל־אִשְׁתּוֹ לֹא תִקְרָב דֹּדָתְךָ הִוא) (Lev 18:14), the Mishnah also abridges this verse and simply reads: "with the wife of his father's brother" (וְעַל אֵשֶׁת אֲחִי אָבִיו) (mKer 1:1). The implication is that whoever uncovers the nakedness of "your father" or "your father's brother" also uncovers the nakedness of a mother or wife and, conversely, uncovers a husband's nakedness.

We may thus note that a relevant omission among the sexual transgressions in the book of Leviticus is the incest between a father and his—either legitimate or illegitimate—daughter that is mentioned neither in the Torah nor in the Mishnah. Such an omission cannot be mistaken for leniency. It rather pertains to the presupposed economics of ancient Jewish society that regulates a woman's childhood, sexuality, and marriage under implicit economical categories. A woman is generally considered under the jurisdiction of a male either within her present or future family, her father, her brother or her (future) husband. In later Tannaitic exegesis this omission is amended through the assumption that the prohibition relating to a man's daughter is self-evident and may be deduced from the explicit prohibition of intercourse with a woman and her daughter: "you shall not uncover the nakedness of a woman and her daughter" (עֶרְוַת אִשָּׁה וּבִתָּהּ, לֹא תְגַלֵּה) (Lev 18:17).

It should also be noted that the Mishnah also rules against incest with the death penalty, as it emerges from the parallel legislations from Tractates *Makkot* and *Sanhedrin*. There also is an additional issue that cannot be explored in detail in the present paper: the incongruence between punishing incest with "banishment" (mKer 1:1) and punishing incest with the "death sentence" (mSanh 9:1). It cannot be overlooked that this incongruence mostly depends on the issue of determining the exact nature of four different forms of punishment: כרת (literally "banishment"), מתת הדין ("death sentence promulgated by a court"), מיתת בידי אדם ("death by the hands of man"), and מתת בידי השמים ("death by the hands of heaven"). The lexical and semantic differences among these four forms of punishment are disputed. The institution of כרת is sometimes assimilated to a form of "banishment" or considered as a euphemistic form for "excising" someone from the community to the extent that the Karaites assimilated it to מתת בידי אדם ("death by the hands of man")

(*Eshkol ha-Kofer*, no. 267; cf. also Jos. *Ant.* 3:12). On the other hand, death penalty is occasionally distinguished from כרת itself (bMak 28a).

The Mishnah severely rules against incest and reproduces *verbatim* the text of scripture, including it in the list of capital offences: "and these are those who are burned: whoever engaged in intercourse with a woman and her daughter . . ." (וְאֵלּוּ הֵן הַנִּשְׂרָפִין, הַבָּא עַל אִשָּׁה וּבִתָּהּ) (mSanh 9:1). It is notable that some Tannaim, as it is ruled in the Talmud from the Land of Israel, argued that the prohibitions of incest were transgressed through marriage and not simply by sexual contact:

הָאוֹנֵס וְהַמְפַתֶּה עַל הַנְּשׂוּאָה חַיָּב. אָמַר רִבִּי יוֹחָנָן. דֶּרֶךְ נִישּׂוּאִין שָׁנוּ. נָשָׂא אִשָּׁה וְאַחַר כָּךְ אָנַס אֶת אִמָּהּ חַיָּב. נָשָׂא אִשָּׁה וְאַחַר כָּךְ פִּיתָּה אֶת בִּתָּהּ חַיָּב

> Whoever rapes or seduces a married woman is guilty. Rabbi Yohanan said, one stated this for marriage. If he married a woman and then raped her mother, he is guilty. If he married a woman and then seduced her daughter, he is guilty. (yYeb 2:4 3d)

On the contrary, the Babylonian Talmud vehemently rejected this stringent ruling and objected that the wording of scripture mentions no marriage, and therefore considers any marital or extra-marital transgression of the rules on incest as a severe transgression:

הבא על אשה שנשא בתה לא קתני אלא הבא על אשה ובתה מכלל דתרוייהו לאיסורא ומאן נינהו חמותו ואם חמותו

> It is not taught [about the case of] whoever engaged in intercourse with a woman whose daughter he has married but rather [it is taught about the case of] "whoever engaged in intercourse with a woman and her daughter" (mKer 1:1) concluding [that] both of them are forbidden. Who are they? his mother-in-law and the mother of his mother-in-law. (bSanh 75a)

Nevertheless, despite the Rabbis' obvious concern with the implicit matter of incest between a father and his daughter, "the silence with regard to father-daughter incest is inexcusable, since all other kinds of sexual offences in the family are spelled out, albeit in a pure patrilinear manner."[33]

STRUGGLE FOR HEGEMONY AND APOCALYPTICISM?

After this brief examination of biblical, Qumranic, and Tannaitic literature, we could ask why there are so many differences among them despite the unsurprisingly consensus on the prohibition of incest.

As I have noted above, the prohibition of incest did not simply emerge as a sexual issue among permitted or prohibited intercourses but was rather strongly associated with the question of marriage as a social reality, and therefore was also projected onto—strictly speaking—non-sexual issues like inter-marriage, polygamy, and polyandry. In this respect, the prohibition of incest was not simply treated as a special kind of intercourse between specific kin members but was rather instrumental to supplementing the institution of marriage that was strictly normed according to patriarchal and heteronormative presuppositions. Besides, the same correction that the Qumranites suggested on the law of incest should probably be read as a polemic against? the Rabbinic and Tannaitic representation of marriage and was especially reflected as an emendation of the biblical text or a tendentiously rephrasing of a crucial scriptural passage.

This plausible intervention on the biblical text shall not to be mistaken for either an inadvertent scribal error or a fraudulent falsification of the Pentateuch but should rather be correctly appreciated for an "apocalyptical adaptation" of revelation to the coming end of times. This impending end of time also included a deep revision of the status of the Hebrew language. William M. Schniedewind has convincingly suggested that Qumranic Hebrew shall be regarded as a sort of "antilanguage"—whose fabrication requires a series of changes in orthography, prosody, and semantics.[34]

Yet, I have attempted to suggest here that the correction introduced by the Qumranites also reflects a specific understanding of the legal authority appointed to interpret scripture. I maintain that Qumranic and Tannaitic literature generally agree on the prohibition of incest, as this fundamentally depends on the acceptance of scripture as a veritable source. Scripture prohibits incest as clearly stated in the book of Leviticus, but typically spells its regulations in the masculine form, producing a series of hermeneutical issues.

Qumranic and Tannaitic literature generally agree on the prohibition of incest from a "doctrinal" point of view but disagree on the "hermeneutical" means of extending biblical regulations to a larger number of cases. While elaborating on the aforementioned Foucault's notion of "discourse"—in the strict sense of "the law of what it can be said"—I argue that Qumranic and Tannaitic literature referred to different "discourses" on sexuality, and therefore to a different notion of the relationship between power and knowledge. More specifically, Qumranic literature intended to make these regulations as *explicit* as possible in order to contrast the cultural hegemonic power of rising Rabbinic Judaism—for a simple reason: in front of an *explicit* law, there is room neither for hermeneutical negotiation nor for an intellectual class disciplining it. In this respect, as Vered Noam has convincingly argued, Qumranic law generally exhibits a "the unrefined, simple character" that strongly contrasts with the exegetical creativity and sophistication of almost contemporary Tannaitic literature.[35]

Accordingly, changes in biblical wording were not only hermeneutically justified but also ideologically required by the Qumranites who intended to isolate themselves from contemporaneous Jewry in a sectarian manner. Nevertheless, it is undisputed that the Qumranites considered scripture in general and prophetic books as the means of interpreting reality. Therefore, the interpreter was allowed to manipulate scripture with a large set of hermeneutical rules that included the use of forced or abnormal constructions, the introduction of a textual variance, letter permutation, letter substitution, and the use of acrostics.[36] These techniques were instrumental to providing a פשר or a "sectarian interpretation" of scripture. In doing so, the Qumranites intended not only to clarify a series of otherwise undetermined biblical norms but also to "unlock" their hidden, mysterious, and esoteric secrets by which to access a "deeper" revelation at a specific time, in a manner that, by principle, is no different from Paul's radical hermeneutics. In this sense, the hermeneutical dimension of פשר ("sectarian interpretation") was inherently connected to a specific time schedule designated by the term פתר ("periodization").[37] It is this deeper stratum of biblical revelation that allowed for a "theological-political" polarization of scripture in terms of a source for a secluded and sectarian community. In the Qumranites' perspective, the opponents of the "statutes of God" were both political and religious enemies.

On the contrary, Tannaitic literature intended to keep these regulations as *implicit* as possible in order to sustain the mediatory role of the Rabbinic elite and were more reluctant to manipulate scripture, although quotations from scripture in Rabbinic literature tend to differ from the so-called Masoretic text. It is evident that Tannaitic literature only nominally shared some similarities with the Qumranites who also employed hermeneutical rules for their פשר ("sectarian interpretation").

In this sense, it is plausible that the author of the *Damascus Document* reported a "manipulated" text from scripture with a precise ideological task: associating *any form* of sexual activity with a menstruating partner with the stricter category of incest. This also implied the direct assimilation of these prohibitions from males to females, while also excluding any hermeneutic negotiation but imposing only an unnegotiable "likeness" between the two of them—וכהם ("and like them"). On the other hand, Tannaitic literature rejected this assimilation between sexual activity with a menstruating partner and incest but rather pursued a complex, non-radical form of hermeneutic negotiation—even with their own ideological purposes. Which ones? For example, allowing for a more tolerant form of "blended family" that might include suppletive marriage between males and their nieces, as strongly stigmatized by the Qumranites themselves. In these terms, it is possible to interpret the difference between explicit and implicit regulations on incest as a sign for a more subtle struggle for cultural hegemony at the time of Early Judaism.

NOTES

1. See, for instance: Judith S. Antonelli, *In the Image of God: A Feminist Commentary on the Torah* (New York: Rowman, 1997). For an interesting discussion on a typology of nominal classification escaping the gender and classifier dichotomy, see: Sebastian Fedden, Jenny Audring, and Greville C. Corbett (eds.), *Non-Canonical Gender Systems* (Oxford: Oxford University Press, 2018).

2. Cf. Deborah Tannen, *Gender and Discourse* (Oxford: Oxford University Press, 1996).

3. On a discussion of "prior gender," its implicit epistemology, and gender hierarchy, see for instance: David E. S. Stein, "The Noun איש ('îš) in Biblical Hebrew: A Term of Affiliation," *The Journal of Hebrew Scriptures* 8, no. 1 (2008): 2–24.

4. For instance, see: Gen 9:20–27 and the wife-sister narratives (Gen 12, Gen 20, and Gen 26). Cf. Madeline McClenney-Sadler, *Recovering the Daughter's Nakedness: A Formal Analysis of Israelite Kinship Terminology and the Internal Logic of Leviticus 18* (London: T&T Clark, 2007), 89–90; Federico Dal Bo, *Massekhet Keritot. Text, Translation, and Commentary* (Tübingen: Mohr Siebeck, 2013), 45–50.

5. The notion of endogamy as the rejection of marrying foreign wives (Deut 7:1–4) is a fundamental legal and narrative device for the histories of Noah, Abraham, Isaac, and Jacob. As such, this notion is also correlated to the one of incest. Cf. Michael L. Satlow, *Jewish Marriage in Antiquity* (Princeton: Princeton University Press, 2001), 133–47; Dal Bo, *Massekhet Keritot*, 45–47. Cf. also Dana Edelman, "Ethnicity and Early Israel," in *Ethnicity and the Bible*, ed. Mark G. Brett (Leiden: Brill, 1996), 25–56.

6. McClenney-Sadler, *Recovering the Daughter's Nakedness*, 32–33.

7. Dal Bo, *Massekhet Keritot*, 48–50.

8. I am following here Federico Dal Bo, "Sexualities and Il/licit Relationships in Late Ancient Jewish Literatures," in *A Companion to Late Ancient Jews and Judaism: 3rd Century BCE–7th Century CE*, ed. G. Kessler and N. Koltun-Fromm (Hoboken: Wiley-Blackwell, 2020), 307–21.

9. On the authoritative status of *Jubilees* besides scripture, see: Hindy Najman, "Interpretation as Primordial Writing: Jubilees and its Authority Conferring Strategies," *Journal for the Study of Judaism in the Persian, Hellenistic, and Roman Period* 30, no. 4 (1999): 379–410. Cf. also Jacques T. A. G. M. van Ruiten, "The Book of Jubilees as Paratextual Literature," in *In the Second Degree: Paratextual Literature in Ancient Near Eastern and Ancient Mediterranean Culture and Its Reflections in Medieval Literature*, ed. Ph. Alexander, A. Lange and R. J. Pillinger (Leiden: Brill, 2010), 65–95.

10. While not explicitly stated so, differently from CD and other texts, *Jubilees* expresses its disagreement toward sexual relationship between uncle and nice by avoiding mentioning this connection in its rephrasing of biblical genealogies. See:

Betsy Halpern-Amaru, *The Empowerment of Women in the Book of Jubilees* (Leiden: Brill, 1999), 35–39. Cf. David Rothstein, "Sexual Union and Offences in 'Jubilees'," *Journal for the Study of Judaism in the Persian, Hellenistic, and Roman Period* 35, no. 4 (2004): 363–84.

11. For instance, they frequently used terms such as "shame," "disgrace," and "corruption" in a Jubilees fragment reported in 4Q222.

12. Solomon Schechter, *Documents of the Jewish Sectaries*: *Vol. I. Fragments of a Zadokite Work*, 2 vols. (Cambridge: Cambridge University Press, 1910) and Solomon Schechter, *Documents of the Jewish Sectaries*, 2 vols. (New York. KTAV Publishing House, 1970).

13. Schechter, *Documents of the Jewish Sectaries*: *Vol. I. Fragments of a Zadokite Work*, 5. The same reading is also published in Schechter, *Documents of the Jewish Sectaries*, 114 and Devorah Dimant and Donald Parry, *Dead Sea Scroll Handbook* (Leiden: Brill, 2014), 963.

14. Schechter, *Documents of the Jewish Sectaries*: *Vol. I. Fragments of a Zadokite Work*, xxxvi–xxxvii (with a few changes); cf. Schechter, *Documents of the Jewish Sectaries*,195.

15. CD 5:6–11. Text and translation from Ben Zion Wacholder, *The New Damascus Document. The Midrash on the Eschatological Torah of the Dead Sea Scrolls: Reconstruction, Translation and Commentary* (Leiden: Brill, 2006), 36–37.

16. For instance, see the very recent new edition: Steven D. Fraade, *The Damascus Document* (Oxford: Oxford University Press, 2022), 46–49. However, Fraade notes that "this is a very rare instance in the Dead Sea Scrolls of the hermeneutical logic, in multiple steps, of a law being explicitly stated" (Fraade, *The Damascus Document*, 49).

17. Israel Levy, "Un écrit sadducéen antérieur à la destruction du Temple," *Revue des études juives* 61, no. 122 (1911): 181, n. 6.

18. Cf. Eugene Urlich (ed.), *The Biblical Qumran Scroll: Transcriptions and Textual Variants* (Leiden: Brill, 2010).

19. Baesick Choi, "Leviticus and Its Reception in the Dead Sea Scrolls from Qumran" (PhD Thesis, University of Manchester, 2018), 149–50, now Baesick Choi, *Leviticus and Its Reception in the Dead Sea Scrolls from Qumran* (Eugene: Wipf and Stock Publishers, 2020).

20. I prefer treating these differences as reflected in *literature* rather than emerging from a *community* in order to avoid the anachronism of comparing two communities—the one of the Qumran and the one of the Pharisees—that do not fully overlap in time. This precaution also spares me from being involved in the controversy on the actual diversity between these social realities, as it is reflected on the dispute between Boccacini and Heger on the relationship between *Jubilees* and the Mosaic Law. See, for instance: Gabriele Boccaccini, "From a Movement of Dissent to a Distinct Form of Judaism: The Heavenly Tablets in Jubilees as the Foundation of a Competing Halakah," in *Enoch and the Mosaic Torah*, ed. Gabriele Boccaccini and Giovanni Ibba (Grand Rapids: Eedermans, 2009), 193–210; and Paul Heger, *Challenges to Conventional Opinions on Qumran and Enoch Issues* (Leiden: Brill, 2012), 172–73.

21. I am following here: Vered Noam, "Creative Interpretation and Integrative Interpretation in Qumran," in *The Dead Sea Scrolls and Contemporary Culture: Proceedings of the International Conference held at the Israel Museum, Jerusalem (July 6–8, 2008)*, ed. Adolfo D. Roitman, Lawrence H. Schiffman, and Shani Tzoref (Leiden: Brill, 2011), 363–76.

22. Martin F. Baasten, "Nominal Clauses Containing a Personal Pronoun in Qumran Hebrew," in *The Hebrew of the Dead Sea Scrolls and Ben Sira* (Leiden: Brill, 1997), 7.

23. While the marriage between aunt and nephew is forbidden by Leviticus, the Rabbis tend to consider the marriage between uncle and niece as blessed. See: tQidd 1:4, bYeb 62b and also *Derekh Eretz Rabbah* 2. The different treatment of avunculate marriage between aunt and nephew against the one between uncle and nice is obviously gender relevant. See: Reuven Klein, "Avunculate Marriage in the Bible," *Seforim Blog*, October 2015, accessible online: https://www.researchgate.net/publication/305725142_Avunculate_Marriage_in_the_Bible [Last Access August 20, 2022].

24. Literally: "like his own body."

25. Tal Ilan, *Jewish Women in Greco-Roman Palestine: An Inquiry into Image and Status* (Tübingen: Mohr Siebeck, 1995), 76–77; cf. William Loader, *The Dead Sea Scrolls on Sexuality: Attitudes Towards Sexuality in Sectarian and Related Literature at Qumran* (Grand Rapids: Eerdmans, 2009), 121–22.

26. On this subtle point, see: Aharon Shemesh, "The Laws of Incest in the Dead Sea Scrolls and the History of Halakhah," in *Halakhah in Light of Epigraphy*, ed. Albert I. Baumgarten, et al. (Göttingen: Vanderhoeck & Ruprecht, 2010), 88–89.

27. I owe this suggestion to Albert I. Baumgarten (Bar Ilan University). See also: Günther Stemberger, *Judaica Minora I* (Tübingen: Mohr Siebeck, 2010), 393–94.

28. Aharon Shemesh, "Expulsion and Exclusion in the Community Rule and the Damascus Document," *Dead Sea Discoveries* 9 (2002): 36. Cf. Dal Bo, *Massekhet Keritot*, 6.

29. Incestuous intercourses 11QTemple 66:11.

30. Gershon Brin, *Studies in Biblical Law. From the Hebrew Bible to the Dead Sea Scrolls* (London: Bloomsbury, 1994), 120 and Michael L. Satlow, *Tasting the Dish. Rabbinic Rhetorics of Sexuality* (Providence: Brown Judaic Studies, 1995), 25–42.

31. *Sifra, Aharey mot, parashah* 9: 8, *y. Git.* 8: 10, 49c, and *b. Yeb.* 76; Satlow, *Tasting the Dish*, 187–93.

32. Dal Bo, *Massekhet Keritot*, 37.

33. Hennie J. Marsman, *Women in Ugarit and Israel: Their Social and Religious Position in the Context of the Ancient Near East* (Leiden: Brill, 2021), 287.

34. William M. Schniedewind, "Qumran Hebrew as an Antilanguage," *Journal of Biblical Literature* 118, no. 2 (1999): 235–52.

35. See: Vered Noam, "Stringency in Qumran. A Reassessment," *Journal for the Study of Judaism* 40 (2009): 3.

36. See William H. Brownlee, *The Midrash Pesher of Habakkuk* (Missoula: Scholar Press, 1979), 66ss and Heinz Feltes, *Die Gattung des Habakukkommentars vom Qumran (1QpHab). Eine Studie zum fühen jüdischen Midrash* (Stuttgart: Echter Verlag, 1986),199–228.

37. See: Shani Tzoref, "'Pesher' and Periodization," *Dead Sea Discoveries* 18, no. 2 (2011): 129–54.

BIBLIOGRAPHY

Antonelli, Judith S. *In the Image of God: A Feminist Commentary on the Torah.* New York: Rowman, 1997,

Baasten, Martin F. "Nominal Clauses Containing a Personal Pronoun in Qumran Hebrew." In *The Hebrew of the Dead Sea Scrolls and Ben Sira*, edited by T. Muraoka and J. E. Elwolde, 1–17. Leiden: Brill, 1997.

Boccaccini, Gabriele. "From a Movement of Dissent to a Distinct Form of Judaism: The Heavenly Tablets in Jubilees as the Foundation of a Competing Halakah." In *Enoch and the Mosaic Torah*, edited by Gabriele Boccaccini and Giovanni Ibba, 193–210. Grand Rapids: Eedermans, 2009.

Brin, Gershon. *Studies in Biblical Law. From the Hebrew Bible to the Dead Sea Scrolls.* London: Bloomsbury, 1994.

Brownlee, Willam H. *The Midrash Pesher of Habakkuk.* Missoula: Scholar Press, 1979.

Choi, Baesick. "Leviticus and Its Reception in the Dead Sea Scrolls from Qumran." PhD Thesis, University of Manchester, 2018.

Choi, Baesick. *Leviticus and Its Reception in the Dead Sea Scrolls from Qumran.* Eugene: Wipf & Stock, 2020.

Dal Bo, Federico. *Massekhet Keritot. Text, Translation, and Commentary.* Tübingen: Mohr Siebeck, 2013.

Dal Bo, Federico. "Sexualities and Il/licit Relationships in Late Ancient Jewish Literatures." In *A Companion to Late Ancient Jews and Judaism: 3rd Century BCE – 7th Century CE*, edited by G. Kessler and N. Koltun-Fromm, 307–21. Hoboken: Wiley-Blackwell, 2020.

Dimant, Devorah and Donald Parry. *Dead Sea Scroll Handbook.* Leiden: Brill, 2014.

Edelman, Dana. "Ethnicity and Early Israel." In *Ethnicity and the Bible*, edited by Mark G. Brett, 25–56. Leiden: Brill, 1996.

Fedden, Sebastian, Jenna Audring, and Greville C. Corbett (eds.). *Non-Canonical Gender Systems.* Oxford: Oxford University Press, 2018.

Feltes, Heinz. *Die Gattung des Habakukkommentars vom Qumran (1QpHab). Eine Studie zum fühen jüdischen Midrash.* Stuttgart: Echter Verlag, 1986.

Fraade, Steven D., *The Damascus Document.* Oxford: Oxford University Press, 2022.

Halpern-Amaru, Betsy. *The Empowerment of Women in the Book of Jubilees.* Leiden: Brill, 1999.

Heger, Paul, *Challenges to Conventional Opinions on Qumran and Enoch Issues.* Leiden: Brill, 2012.

Ilan, Tal. *Jewish Women in Greco-Roman Palestine: An Inquiry into Image and Status.* Tübingen: Mohr Siebeck, 1995.

Klein, Reuven. "Avunculate Marriage in the Bible." *Seforim Blog*, October 2015. Accessible online: https://www.researchgate.net/publication/305725142_Avunculate_Marriage_in_the_Bible.
Levy, Israel. "Un écrit sadducéen antérieur à la destruction du Temple." *Revue des études juives* 61, no. 122 (1911): 161–205.
Loader, William. *The Dead Sea Scrolls on Sexuality: Attitudes Towards Sexuality in Sectarian and Related Literature at Qumran*. Grand Rapids: Eerdmans, 2009.
Marsman, Hennie J. *Women in Ugarit and Israel: Their Social and Religious Position in the Context of the Ancient Near East*. Leiden: Brill, 2021.
McClenney-Sadler, Madeline G. *Recovering the Daughter's Nakedness: A Formal Analysis of Israelite Kinship Terminology and the Internal Logic of Leviticus 18*. London: T& Clark, 2007.
Najman, Hindy. "Interpretation as Primordial Writing: Jubilees and its Authority Conferring Strategies." *Journal for the Study of Judaism in the Persian, Hellenistic, and Roman Period* 30, no. 4 (1999): 379–410.
Noram, Vered. "Stringency in Qumran. A Reassessment." *Journal for the Study of Judaism* 40 (2009): 1–14.
Noam, Vered. "Creative Interpretation and Integrative Interpretation in Qumran." In *The Dead Sea Scrolls and Contemporary Culture. Proceedings of the International Conference held at the Israel Museum, Jerusalem (July 6–8, 2008)*, edited by Adolfo D. Roitman, Lawrence H. Schiffman, and Shani Tzoref, 363–76. Leiden: Brill, 2011.
Rothstein, David. "Sexual Union and Offences in 'Jubilees'." *Journal for the Study of Judaism in the Persian, Hellenistic, and Roman Period* 35, no. 4 (2004): 363–84.
Satlow, Michael L. *Tasting the Dish. Rabbinic Rhetorics of Sexuality*. Providence: Brown Judaic Studies, 1995.
Satlow, Michael L. *Jewish Marriage in Antiquity*. Princeton: Princeton University Press, 2001.
Schechter, Solomon. *Documents of the Jewish Sectaries: Vol. I. Fragments of a Zadokite Work* 2 Vols. Cambridge: Cambridge University Press, 1910.
Schechter, Solomon. *Documents of the Jewish Sectaries*, 2 vols. New York: KTAV Publishing House, 1970.
Shemesh, Aharon. "Expulsion and Exclusion in the Community Rule and the Damascus Document." *Dead Sea Discoveries* 9 (2002): 44–74.
Shemesh, Aharon. "The Laws of Incest in the Dead Sea Scrolls and the History of Halakhah." In *Halakhah in Light of Epigraphy*, edited by Albert I. Baumgarten, 81–102. Göttingen: Vanderhoeck & Ruprecht, 2010.
Stein, David E. S. "The Noun איש ('îš) in Biblical Hebrew: A Term of Affiliation." *The Journal of Hebrew Scriptures* 8, no. 1 (2008): 2–24.
Stemberger, Günter. *Judaica Minora I*. Tübingen: Mohr Siebeck, 2010.
Tannen, Deborah. *Gender and Discourse*. Oxford: Oxford University Press, 1996.
Tzoref, Shani. "'Pesher' and Periodization." *Dead Sea Discoveries* 18, no. 2 (2011): 129–54.
Ulrich, Eugene, ed. *The Biblical Qumran Scroll: Transcriptions and Textual Variants*. Leiden: Brill, 2010.

van Ruiten, Jacques T. A. G. M. "The Book of Jubilees as Paratextual Literature." In *In the Second Degree: Paratextual Literature in Ancient Near Eastern and Ancient Mediterranean Culture and Its Reflections in Medieval Literature*, edited by Ph. Alexander, A. Lange, and R. J. Pillinger, 65–95. Leiden: Brill, 2010.

Wacholder, Ben Zion. *The New Damascus Document. The Midrash on the Eschatological Torah of the Dead Sea Scrolls: Reconstruction, Translation and Commentary*. Leiden: Brill, 2006.

5
Torah, Gender, and Rabbinic Expertise
Krista N. Dalton

INTRODUCTION

The rabbi of late ancient Roman Palestine was the singular expert of Torah and its traditions, or so rabbinic literature would have its readers believe. These texts take for granted that rabbis could uncover the true meanings of Torah through their precise hermeneutical methods and apply them to the concerns of their day. Yet those same texts provide glimpses of a reality where rabbis did not exist in social isolation. They had to work to convince other Jews to value their interpretations of Torah. For all their sense of themselves as the true experts of Torah, their fundamental engagement with other non-rabbis was dependent on their ability to persuade.

The identity of a "rabbi" was therefore an ongoing process. As rabbis did "rabbi" things they constituted their sense of themselves as experts, which was reinforced by social relationships with their peers and the perception from others that their expertise was valuable. In this way, expertise was performative, producing the identity that they claimed to possess through their habits and relationships. This performative quality of rabbinic expertise echoes the theoretical work produced by gender theorists, notably Judith Butler, since the early 1990s. Butler, drawing upon Austin's theories of speech acts, explains that a performative is "that discursive practice that enacts or produces that which it names."[1] Gender, she argues, does not exist self-evidently but is performatively constituted through both an ongoing process of speech acts, such as a doctor declaring "it's a boy!," and iterative social habits. More recently this theoretical frame has been expanded beyond gender. Saba Mahmood in *Politics of Piety* applied Butler's insight to the participation of women in the Islamic revival movement in Egypt, arguing that certain bodily habits such as wearing a hijab produced the pious subject.[2] These studies describe a pattern whereby subject formation follows discursive practice and bodily habits rather than preceding it, creating a feedback loop that constitutes a sense of self—whether a gendered self or a pious self in the case of Butler and Mahmood. Expertise, I argue, is similarly constructed.

In this chapter, I demonstrate how the production of a gendered rabbinic self was inextricably bound up in the construction of Torah expertise. I look particularly at two texts describing social relationships with a woman and a non-rabbinic Jewish man in order to trace the construction of expertise and gender enacted through these encounters. As Constance Furey argues, "Studies focused on personal relationships can expose the complexity of how body, society, and subjectivity interact through an intimate, relational process of internalization, transformation, affirmation, and rejection."[3] By looking at the personal relationships depicted in rabbinic literature, we can examine how rabbis cultivated their expertise through a relational and gendered process. Rabbinic expertise was both constituted and defended by the gendered boundaries drawn within these social relationships in order to protect rabbinic expertise from competing sources of knowledge. In short, I argue that doing masculinity and doing expertise were an integrally linked performative process that contributed to the ongoing construction of rabbis as Torah experts.

EXPERTISE THROUGH A GENDER THEORY LENS

Joan Scott writes concerning the purpose of gender analysis: "The new historical investigation is to disrupt the notion of fixity, to discover the nature of the debate or repression that leads to the appearance of timeless permanence in binary gender representation."[4] Scott's call to "disrupt fixity" stems from the scholarly consensus that gender is not an essential fact; it is discursively constructed through habitual acts that constitute the sense of gender.[5] In this way male/female, masculinity/femininity are not timeless signifiers to be uncovered in sources, but they are perceptive lenses through which to analyze their contested social meanings.[6] These meanings present themselves as natural when in fact they are socially constructed, requiring the analyst to unsettle the impression of static gender boundaries and instead ask what work they are doing in the text.

There are two such naturalized gendered impressions one would likely take away from rabbinic literature: that the sole expert of Torah was the rabbi and that the rabbinic expert must be male.[7] While there is no extended discussion of either rabbinic expertise as a profession or masculinity within the literature itself, these two "truths" are reinforced through legal rulings and stories, as well as implicitly reinforced by the fact that Torah abounds as textual proof for rabbinic teachings and only men seem to be the ones talking. This further accords with our own cultural expectation that religious experts are often men, which reinforces a sense of "naturalness" within our sources, even if we protest such patriarchal dominance. Yet rather than take these impressions as self-evident, gender theory looks beyond the *meaning* of the gendered boundary to the *work* of the discursive practice. What does it take to project and maintain these boundaries? As Scott writes, "Gender is a site of struggle about what counts as natural and what counts as social,"[8] and this struggle can reveal what is at stake in the preservation of gendered distinctions.

It is this nexus between what feels natural and what is socially constituted that particularly illuminates rabbinic expertise. There was no immediate apparatus for the rabbi within the Jewish communities of antiquity. Ancient Jews took to local courts for civic rulings and to synagogues for communal needs, the latter serving as a meeting space for public recitation of Torah, purity rituals, market transactions, and even lodging for travelers. The position of rabbi, as the self-proclaimed preserver of ancient Jewish textual traditions, did not have an automatic institutional place in the post-Temple Jewish landscape. However natural they assumed the position of Torah expert to be, rabbis had to work to validate their role as experts by cultivating social networks with other Jews. They set themselves up as judges and teachers while deploying the saturated symbols of Torah and the Second Temple past in order to solicit investment in their expertise.[9] Social recognition was a means for legitimizing the expert roles that rabbis sought to both create and fill.

This inherent instability is not just a feature of their contested place as figures of authority in ancient Jewish society. Expertise itself has been theorized as being an relational process that relies on networks of people to authenticate the expert. Take for example Stephen Turner's account of the epistemic authority of scientists:

> The cognitive authority of scientists in relation to the public is, so to speak, corporate. Scientists possess their authority when they speak as representatives of science. And the public judgments of science are of science as a corporate phenomenon, of scientists speaking as scientists.[10]

Here Turner describes the epistemic authority constituted through the collective scientific voice. The individual scientist exists as an expert because they tap into the authority of the broader scientific community. This authority is legitimated by the perception of the public that the scientific community maintains standards of competence and that the resulting advancements of science are beneficial to society. In this formulation expertise is inherently social. It is not tied to a cognitive sense of "truth" or "knowledge" but to the network of relations that reinforce the perception of expertise. Much akin to the interventions of gender theory, which set aside the biological certainty of sexed bodies in order to illuminate the socially conscribed meanings of gender, theorists of expertise set aside descriptions of experts defined by possession of knowledge in order to examine the performance required to convince others that the expert's knowledge is valuable.

Turner's formulation can apply to the ancient rabbis. Rabbis were a loose association of individual learned men who taught as "representatives" of Torah. Their expertise lay not simply in their cognitive knowledge of texts but in the "corporate phenomenon" of Torah that empowered rabbis to speak as rabbis and commanded the attention of willing Jews. As the recent work of Kendra Eshleman has shown, labels of expertise in late antiquity were not incontrovertible. She explains that the right to a label of expertise "had to be continually defended through assiduous self-presentation that in turn advanced implicit definitions of one's own field(s) and its rivals."[11] Experts were validated through the attentions of the public.[12] These attentions served to affirm and define the reputation of scholars even when those scholars might want otherwise to claim autonomy from public perception. Rabbis belonged to this ancient Mediterranean landscape of experts, whose identities were constructed through the making and remaking of relationships.

While expertise and gender share theoretical models in scholarship, they also intersect quite meaningfully in the rabbinic subject. Torah expertise is portrayed as a (almost) wholly male affair, as Michael Satlow writes, "Torah study is constructed as the masculine activity par excellence."[13] This sense of masculinity went beyond a perception of gender linked to the possession of certain genitalia. Rabbinic masculinity lodged itself in the social structures of Torah expertise by asserting Torah study as admired masculine conduct. Theorists Robert Connell and James Messerschmidt insist that

> [m]asculinity is not a fixed entity embedded in the body or personality traits of individuals. Masculinities are configurations of practice that are accomplished in social action and, therefore, can differ according to the gender relations in a particular social setting.[14]

Rabbinic work as Torah experts invoked a configuration of manliness that framed Torah expertise as social dominance. It is no surprise then that those social interactions where rabbinic expertise was questioned or at stake could invoke fierce tactics of masculinity. Rabbis responded to perceived threats to their roles as experts by deploying gendered norms as a means to reinforce their scholarly autonomy, varying in their tactics depending on the social situations at hand.

In the textual examples that follow, rabbis respond in different gendered ways based on the social encounter. In the first text a rabbi dismisses a woman who impedes on his expertise, while in the second text a rabbi engages a non-rabbinic Jewish man in an extended dialogue. While masculinity is configured differently in each textual social setting, they both present cases where gender was deployed as a tactical defense of rabbinic expertise.

THE MATRONA AND THE RICH MAN

I turn to two textual case studies from Palestinian rabbinic literature in order to illustrate the dynamics of expertise and masculinity worked out through social relationships. My first example examines the threat of a wealthy woman (lit. *matrona*) who possesses knowledge of Torah and seeks instruction from a rabbi.

> A matrona asked R. Eliezer, "How is it that, though only one sin was committed in connection with the golden calf, those who died, died by three kinds of punishments?" He said to her, "Woman has no wisdom except at the spindle," for it is written, "And all the women that were wise-hearted did spin with their hands" (Exod 35:25). Hyrcanus, his son, said to him: "So as not to answer her with a single teaching from the Torah, you have lost for us three hundred *kors* of tithe per year!" He said to him, "May they burn the words of Torah rather than deliver them to women." (Y. Sotah 3:4 19a)[15]

מטרונה שאלה את רבי לעזר: מפני מה חטיא אחת במעשה העגל והן מתים בה שלש מיתות. אמר לה: אין חכמה של אשה אלא בפילכה דכתיב (שמות לה) וכל אשה חכמת לב בידיה טוו. אמר לו הורקנוס בנו: בשביל שלא להשיבה דבר אחת מן התורה איבדתה ממנו שלש מאות כור מעשר בכל שנה. אמר ליה ישרפו דברי תורה ואל ימסרו לנשים.

I have written elsewhere about this encounter between the matrona and R. Eliezer, arguing that what is ordinarily perceived as an obvious gendered rebuke of women's access to Torah is actually encoded with the tensions of a donor expecting instruction as reciprocal exchange for her tithe.[16] Here I would like to focus on how a naturalized gender boundary, that women do not learn Torah, is deployed as a tactic to define R. Eliezer's role as expert.

The matrona asks R. Eliezer a smart question regarding the punishments that the Israelites received following their construction of a gilded calf in Exodus 32. Why three punishments if there was a singular sin? Not only does her question attend to the intricacies of the biblical narrative, but it also reflects the rabbinic hermeneutical assumption of measure for measure punishments.[17] The text continues with Rabbi Eliezer's students pressing him to answer her good question once she leaves: "Rabbi, this one you pushed away with a stick, but what would you explain to us?"[18] Different rabbinic voices weigh in with explanations to this seeming textual problem, further validating the perceptive contours of the question. Yet however astute her question may be, it triggers a visceral dismissal from R. Eliezer. On the surface, the passage would seem to suggest that her vice lies solely in her gender—women categorically should not study Torah. This binary, however, is complicated by the fact that both the matrona and Hyrcanus expected R. Eliezer to answer the question. They react as if R. Eliezer is the one out of line: the matrona breaks off her donor relationship with his family and Hyrcanus scolds his own father. These reactions suggest that the severe gendered boundary is not a natural distinction but rather an operational tactic within this encounter. I argue that if we reframe this exchange between the matrona and R. Eliezer as one where Torah expertise is at stake rather than just a misogynistic teaching, we can imagine how social relationships with women donors might have impinged upon the status of a Torah expert.

First, R. Eliezer cites a prooftext from later in the Exodus account when the Israelites began constructing the *mishkan*, or tabernacle, following the renewal of the covenant after their disastrous episode with the golden calf. Israelites brought free-will offerings of jewelry, animal skins, acacia wood, and precious metals to "be used for the tent of meeting, and for all its service, and for the sacred vestments" (Exod 35:20). Certain women with particular skill wove yarn and rich linen as a donation to this cause (Exod 35:25–16). From this passage, R. Eliezer brings the prooftext about women spinning with their hands, extrapolating that "woman has no wisdom except at the spindle." R. Eliezer's choice of prooftext is particularly illuminated by the fact that the matrona is a donor. She withdraws her yearly tithe in response to his dismissal. Not only does his message suggest that she has no part in Torah study because of her gender, but the context of the prooftext reminds her that pious donations should be given with no expectation of reciprocity. All of the gifts brought for the *mishkan*, including the women's weaving, were given by those "whose hearts made them willing to bring anything for the work that the Lord had commanded by Moses to be done" (Exod 35:29).

By contrast the matrona expects that the rabbi to whom she brings annual tithe will spend personal time on her instruction. This expectation would not have been so unheard of in the late ancient Mediterranean. Women donors played a particular role in the support of Christian scholars, for example, and received personal correspondence and instruction in exchange.[19] In this sense pious gifts, even if idyllically framed as free gifts, imposed an expectation of obligation upon the social relationship. R. Eliezer resists any sense of obligation to the matrona and in no uncertain terms tells her to stay in her lane and leave the Torah expertise to him.

Next R. Eliezer responds to his son's admonishment. The matrona canceled her annual tithe to the chagrin of Hyrcanus, who cannot understand his father's refusal to teach a single element of Torah to their wealthy donor. R. Eliezer rebukes his son with insistence that one should burn the words of Torah rather than "deliver" (ימסרו) them to women. We have reason to suspect that R. Eliezer is being hyperbolic. His wife, for example, is Imma Shalom, sister to the famed Patriarch Gamaliel II and remembered in later rabbinic traditions as a learned individual in her own right.[20] Elsewhere when R. Eliezer rules against teaching Torah to daughters, he does so in the context of the sotah ritual for suspected adultery.[21] In this mishnah, he instructs that teaching Torah to a daughter is akin to sexual immorality (*tiflut*), presumably because he thinks that it provides her a way to generate mitzvot and create an adultery loophole—her generated Torah study mitzvot would negate any adulterous sins and protect her from the ritual's curse. Here R. Eliezer's concern is not so much that a woman might study Torah but in the contextually loaded possibility that daughters might use their mitzvot to deflect the consequences of sexual immorality. His fear is not that women might come into contact with Torah but rather that Torah in the hands of women is powerful. He fears providing women the access to this power.

Further, the use of the verb מסר is notable. Rather than describe the request as instruction, he uses the language of possession. The verb denotes the sense of handing over or giving one the authority over something, such as in m. Sanhedrin 7:1 where four types of executions are given (נִמְסְרוּ) to the court or in y. Shabbat 2:7 [5b] where the three commandments of *niddah*, *challah*, and shabbat candle lighting were handed over (נִמְסְרוּ) to women. The verb is also used to describe the transmission of the Oral Law, as the famous opening of *Pirkei Avot* describes: "Moses received the Torah at Sinai and transmitted it (וּמְסָרָהּ) to Joshua." R. Eliezer understands the matrona's request not in terms of ordinary instruction but in a request to participate in a particular realm of Torah expertise that would provide her with a sense of ownership of Torah knowledge. She would embark upon the path of learning that might provide her with her own expertise that could compete with the rabbi.

When R. Eliezer speaks in universalizing terms he draws a gendered distinction upon all women, but in context he is actually speaking to the particular situation with a woman donor. The matrona physically entered rabbinic study space, attested by the spectacle of their exchange witnessed by rabbinic students, and she modeled rabbinic interpretive principles. Her presence shattered the idyllic representation of rabbinic autonomy with the reality of the rabbinic dependence upon social networks. Rabbi Eliezer constructed a rhetorical boundary between himself and the matrona on the basis of her gender so as to mask her power as a donor. The literary trope deployed by his students ("this one you pushed away with a stick") ushers the matrona's question into the safety of their scholarly circle. Thus, while the R. Eliezer admonishes transmitting Torah to women writ large, he is reacting to a specific social relationship by defending his status as Torah expert.

In the text above, R. Eliezer deployed a gendered binary in a universalizing fashion that deemed women as categorically unworthy of the transmission of Torah. But rabbis did not actually believe in this absolute gendered binary; while R. Eliezer's teaching gives the hegemonic sense that Torah belongs solely to men, what he actually means is rabbinic male experts. Non-rabbinic Jewish men posed their own threat to rabbinic expertise, as Connell and Messerschmidt explain, "[t]o sustain a given pattern of hegemony requires the policing of men as well as the exclusion or discrediting of women."[22] This policing of non-rabbinic men is illustrated by a story about R. Yannai and a wealthy Jewish householder in Leviticus Rabbah 9:3.[23] The text begins:

> It happened that R. Yannai was walking along the road and met a lavishly dressed person, and said to him: "Would my master wish to dine with us?" The man replied: "Eh, if it pleases you." He (Yannai) brought him to his house [fed him and gave him something to drink]. He (Yannai) examined him in Bible and found him wanting, in Mishnah and found him wanting, in Talmud and found him wanting, in Aggadah and found him wanting. He (Yannai) then said to him (the guest): "Recite the blessing." The guest replied: "Let Yannai bless in his own home." Whereupon he (Yannai) said: "Can you repeat what I say?" The man replied, "Yes." He (Yannai) said, "Say, a dog has eaten Yannai's bread." He (the guest) arose]and grabbed him[saying: "What is this? My inheritance is in your possession, which you are withholding from me!" He (Yannai) replied: ["And what is your inheritance that I have?" He said: One time I was passing by a school and I heard the voices of children reciting,] children recite, 'The Torah that Moses commanded us is the inheritance of the Congregation of Jacob' (Deut. 33:4). It is not written 'of the congregation of Yannai,' but rather 'of the congregation of Jacob'." When they had appeased one another, Yannai asked: "By what right did you merit eating at my table?" The man replied: "I never heard nor repeated an evil report, nor have I ever seen two people fighting without making peace between them." He (Yannai) said to him: "You have such *derech eretz*, and I called you a dog!" (Lev Rabbah 9:3)

מעשה ברבי ינאי שהיה מהלך בדרך פגע בו אדם אחד שהיה משופע ביותר. אמר לו משגח רבי לאיתקבלא גבן. אמר לו מה דהני לך. הכניסו לתוך ביתו [האכילו והשקהו].[24] בדקו במקרא ולא מצאו, במשנה ולא מצאו, בתלמוד ולא מצאו, באגדה ולא מצאו. אמר ליה בריך. אמר לה יברך ינאי בביתיה. אמר ליה אית בך אמר מה דאנא אמר לך. אמר ליה אין. אמר ליה אמר "אכול כלבא פסתיא דינאי." קם צריה [תפסיה].[25] אמר ליה מה ירותתי גבך דאת מוני לי. אמר ליה דמינוקייה.] ומה ירתותך גבי, אמר ליה חד זמן הוינא עבר קמי בית ספרא, ושמעית קלהון דמניקיא אמרין[26] (דברים לג, ד): תורה צוה לנו משה מורשה קהלת יעקב. מורשה קהלת ינאי אין כתיב כאן אלא קהלת יעקב.

מן דאיתפיסין דין לדין אמר ליה למה זכית למיכל על פתורי? אמר ליה מן יומיי לא שמעית מילא בישא וחיזרתי למריה, ולא חמית תרין דמיתכתשין דין עם דין ולא יהבית שלמא ביניהון. אמר ליה כל הדא דרך ארץ גבך וקריתך כלבא.[27]

R. Yannai was a first generation amora in the early third century CE residing in Upper Galilee. Rabbinic legend suggests that he was extremely wealthy, stating that he founded a school in Akbarah and possessed an extensive estate his own students would manage.[28] In this account, R. Yannai happens upon a rich man, "lavishly dressed" as a signifier of the man's wealth and status. R. Yannai seizes upon the opportunity to invite him into his home.[29] To invite a guest for a meal was a specific mode of hospitality that fueled social relationships.[30] These were often formal occasions with rich food and entertainment, as well as socially coded events—from the expected welcome, comfortable setting, and even the food itself.[31] The narrative suggests that while a stranger, the man's association with a particular class of wealthy elites made him a worthy dining companion and potential expansion of the rabbinic social network.

The rich man's lackluster response to R. Yannai's invitation (מה דהני לך "eh, if it pleases you") suggests initially that the rich man is the one doing R. Yannai a favor. However, soon the tables turn with R. Yannai's intense probing. He examines the guest's knowledge of Torah and types of rabbinic literature and is disgusted with his guest's ignorance. But why would R. Yannai expect a non-rabbi to be versed in the breadth of rabbinic interpretation in the first place? I suggest that R. Yannai did not actually expect his guest to have such knowledge; rather, he wanted to expose his guest's ignorance in order to showcase his own expertise. This dynamic between rabbis and hosts or guests at dining parties appears elsewhere in rabbinic texts. In T. Ma'aser Sheni 3:18, for example, a group of rabbis enter a householder's house, presumably for a meal, and immediately worry that his produce has been improperly tithed—though one would think that if the status of the produce was in question, the rabbis would have inquired before arriving! But the story unfolds in such a way that the rabbis display their expertise in dubiously tithed food stuffs in the middle of the social gathering, with the host parading the rabbis off to another room to show them his chest of golden dinars as evidence of his first fruits tithe.[32] In these examples the performance of rabbinic expertise asserts authority over the wealthy householder, reframing their social relationship so that the knowledge of rabbinic hermeneutics gives the rabbi the upper hand.

R. Yannai's probing further shares resonances with the habits of the Greco-Roman symposium table, where those reclining around the table became temporarily a self-contained community.[33] Ancient Jews adopted this convivium model, descriptions of which appear in *The Letter to Aristeas*, Ben Sira, and rabbinic literature.[34] The Hellenistic Jewish scribe Ben Sira (second century BCE) offers a useful lens through which to understand R. Yannai's examination. Ben Sira warns that during formal banquets a host might test the sage's wisdom, writing "Do not try to treat him as an equal, or trust his lengthy conversations; for he will test you by prolonged talk, and while he smiles he will be examining you" (Sirach 13:11). Here we see how banquets were occasions for the performance of aristocratic self-representation. Guests scrutinized each other as the meal was encoded with socially understood cues. How guests and the host performed at the dinner table would reflect upon their social standing. Further, members of a household or attendants of invited guests could also view the meal without participating. The meal at R. Yannai's estate could very well be imagined to include a number of witnesses, including his students—described as overseers of his vineyards—and other members of the household. These optics changed the dynamic of a meal into a spectacle.

Following his extensive probing, R. Yannai instructs his guest to give the benediction over the meal. This invitation was a formal request from the host as a sign of honor. In another rabbinic account a King invites R. Shimon to lead the benediction and R. Shimon sarcastically refuses as a sign of disrespect.[35] It is unclear whether we are to understand the guest's refusal as an insult to R. Yannai or as a sign that he in fact did not know how to recite the proper benediction, but in either case Yannai calls the man a dog in response to his refusal.[36] Cristiana Franco, historian of Greek literature, explains the power dynamics of such an insult:

> When you insult someone by calling them a dog, you are asserting that they stand in your consideration *in loco canis*, at the very bottom of the scale of honor. It is an intimidation and a demand for subordination. It is a claim to treat the insulted person as one would a dog, toward which superiority is taken for granted and exercised in constant commands and regular calls for subjection.[37]

R. Yannai's use of such an insult is a direct attempt to assert superiority over his wealthy guest in conjunction with his displays of Torah expertise.

This insult also served to deeply shame his guest. As Roman historian John D'Arms explains, "Being subjected to the ridicule of a host or another powerful man was perhaps the most common source of embarrassment for guests of lower rank."[38] Given the guest's demonstrable wealth, R. Yannai's shaming insult positions his guest into a diminished rank. The dinner table therefore becomes the setting for these two men to battle for social dominance. At stake for R. Yannai was the recognition of his expertise, that while the guest may have wealth, his proper posture toward the rabbi should be one of deference to a Torah expert. The guest should be honored to eat at R. Yannai's table. Instead, throughout the textual sequence the guest fails to be impressed by R. Yannai, requiring the tactic of shame on R. Yannai's part to elicit the desired social relationship.

This tactic of shame is informed by the gendered dynamics of the banquet table. Typically comprising men, the interactions between host and guest during dinner staged a performance of their social roles and gendered expectations. Idealized hegemonic masculinity prized dominance and was wielded against other men who were unable to perform with appropriate vigor.[39] Such manliness was expressed in relationships through verbal contest, bodily cues, and in the production of power in social roles. To shame a guest at a dinner table was to emasculate them. While some would question shame as a strategic tactic—is it really smart to shame and insult someone you hope to form a beneficial relationship with?—the point is to frame Torah expertise as the dominant form of manliness. R. Yannai conducts himself in a socially understood posture of dominance at the dinner table in order to prove that Torah scholars are worth social respect and deference.

But the wealthy guest does not take the insult lying down. The guest claims his own authority of Torah—he accesses Torah as a timeless Israelite inheritance, regardless of whether he can actually recite biblical texts, rabbinic teachings, or even the dinner benediction. The wealthy man goes on to display his facility in *derech eretz*, that is proper Jewish conduct, which satisfies R. Yannai's inquest. This neat ending to the text, likely added by a later redactor, rings false with the demonstrative tenor of the table up until this point. The redactors of this story bring the heat levels down and resolve the tension with both parties appreciating each other's expertise. This reveals a deep vulnerability on the part of rabbinic experts. While specialized Torah knowledge remained an exclusive rabbinic ideal, the participation of the Jewish public in the more general ethics of Jewish piety was the more practical rabbinic goal. This principle is articulated in Pirkei Avot: "the sages declared, 'If there is no *derech eretz* there is no Torah, and if there is no Torah there is no *derech eretz*'" (3:17). A synergetic relationship is struck between R. Yannai and the wealthy guest—R. Yannai's authority is reaffirmed while the wealthy guest's status is recognized and validated by R. Yannai's expert pronouncement of his valuable *derech eretz*.

Similar to the matrona account, this text represents a different competing claim to Torah. R. Yannai claims authority in Torah based on expertise. His knowledge throughout the examination of the guest marks him as an expert. But the wealthy elite does not appear impressed, and instead he claims his own expertise in Torah based on the timeless claim of Israel's inheritance. The wealthy guest exposes the instability of rabbinic claims to expertise because the biblical text in fact supports the guest's interpretation that Torah can be claimed by every Jew and does not once mention the need for a rabbi. Rabbis had to claim and defend the boundaries of their expertise to be seen as an expert. The gendered tactic of social shame serves in this example as a means of redefining the rabbi's social relationship with a non-rabbinic Jewish man and presenting the ideal hierarchical relationship between the two.

CONCLUSION

It was not self-evident that a scholar's knowledge should be regarded as legitimate or worthy of support. Instead, scholastic expertise was continually rehearsed. Through the cultivation of social relationships rabbis could garner the respect of the public, as Lee Levine suggests, "the extent of rabbinic influence was directly dependent upon the majority of the people's acceptance of their authority."[40] While scholars across the Mediterranean operated with their own contextual motivations and concerns, the instability of continually rehearsing expertise fueled scholastic culture.

These social relationships, however, did not always follow ideal rabbinic standards. As much as they were needed to validate rabbinic expertise, they posed threats to the rabbinic expert. Whether a woman donor intruding upon rabbinic autonomy with her expectations of reciprocal exchange or a non-rabbinic Jewish man who resisted playing by rabbinic standards of knowledge altogether, rabbinic expertise was contingent upon these types of social relationships. This very instability of the identity of expert was also enmeshed in notions of rabbinic masculinity. Both facets of identity were produced through bodily habits and "performative events" that named the boundaries of the rabbinic subject. These two textual examples demonstrate the discursive work required to maintain the ideal sense of the rabbinic man as the natural Torah expert.

NOTES

1. Judith Butler, *Bodies That Matter: On the Discursive Limits of Sex* (Abington: Routledge, 2011), 13.
2. Saba Mahmood, *Politics of Piety* (Princeton: Princeton University Press, 2011).
3. Constance M. Furey, "Body, Society, and Subjectivity in Religious Studies," *Journal of the American Academy of Religion* 80, no. 1 (2012): 25.
4. Joan Scott, "Gender: A Useful Category of Historical Analysis," *The American Historical Review* 91, no. 5 (1986): 1068.
5. Judith Butler, *Gender Trouble* (New York: Routledge, 1990).
6. "Does being female (or male for that matter) constitute a 'natural fact' or a cultural performance, or is 'naturalness' constituted through discursively constrained performative acts that produce the body through and within the categories of sex?" (Butler, *Gender Trouble*, viii).

7. Michael L. Satlow, "'Try to Be a Man': The Rabbinic Construction of Masculinity," *Harvard Theological Review* 89, no. 1 (1996): 27.

8. Joan W. Scott, "The Uses and Abuses of Gender," *Tijdschrift voor Genderstudies* 16, no. 1 (2013): 73.

9. This investment could take the form of patronage, gifts of food, or tithes, as well as the cultural capital gained from the acknowledgement of their Torah knowledge gleaned through rabbinic hermeneutical methods.

10. Stephen P. Turner, *The Politics of Expertise* (New York: Routledge, 2013), 23.

11. Kendra Eshleman, *The Social World of Intellectuals in the Roman Empire: Sophists, Philosophers, and Christians* (Cambridge: Cambridge University Press, 2012), 1.

12. For the performance of knowledge among freelance experts, see Heidi Wendt, *At the Temple Gates: The Religion of Freelance Experts in the Roman Empire* (Oxford: Oxford University Press, 2016).

13. Satlow, "Try to Be a Man," 27.

14. Robert W. Connell and James W. Messerschmidt, "Hegemonic Masculinity: Rethinking the Concept," *Gender & Society* 19, no. 6 (2005): 836.

15. I rely on the Leiden manuscript, as published in Y. Sussmann, *Talmud Yerushalmi* (Jerusalem: Academy of the Hebrew Language, 2016), column 920.

16. Krista Dalton, "Teaching for the Tithe: Donor Expectations and the Matrona's Tithe," *AJS Review* 44, no. 1 (2020): 49–73.

17. As an example of this principle, see Pirkei Avot 2:6: "Moreover he saw a skull floating on the face of the water. He said to it: because you drowned others, they drowned you. And in the end, they that drowned you will be drowned." On this principle in tannatitic literature, see Ishay Rosen-Zvi, "Measure for Measure as a Hermeneutical Tool in Early Rabbinic Literature: The Case of Tosefta Sotah," *Journal of Jewish Studies* 57, no. 2 (2006): 269.

18. רבי לזר דחיתה בקנה לנו מה אתה משיב.

On the use of this phrase in rabbinic literature, see Jenny R. Labendz, *Socratic Torah: Non-Jews in Rabbinic Intellectual Culture* (Oxford University Press, 2013), 101–20.

19. See Elizabeth A. Clark, "Patrons, Not Priests: Gender and Power in Late Ancient Christianity," *Gender & History* 2, no. 3 (1990): 253–74; Kimberly Bowes, *Private Worship, Public Values, and Religious Change in Late Antiquity* (Cambridge University Press, 2008); Mathew Kuefler, "The Merry Widows of Late Roman Antiquity: The Evidence of the Theodosian Code," *Gender & History* 27, no. 1 (April 2015): 28–52.

20. See B. Nedarim 20a, Eruvin 63a, Bava Metziah 59b, and Shabbat 116a.

21. M. Sotah 3:4.

22. Connell and Messerschmidt, "Hegemonic masculinity," 844.

23. This fifth-century midrashic compilation offers a commentary on the biblical book of Leviticus.

24. Included in *Sefer Rabbot* Constantinople 1512 manuscript most likely to qualify what it meant to invite someone to their home.

25. Included in *Sefer Rabbot* Constantinople 1512, Munich 117, London 169, and Oxford, Bodleian Opp. Add. fol. 51 manuscripts as a description of rising in anger.

26. Included in *Sefer Rabbot* Constantinople 1512 manuscript as an explanatory statement.

27. M. Margulies, *Midrash Wayyikra Rabbah: A Critical Edition Based on Manuscripts and Genizah Fragments with Variants and Notes*, 5 vols. (Jerusalem 1953–60).

28. Y. Eruvin 8:4, 24a describes *beit Yannai*, and Y. Shevi'it 6:4 suggests that R. Yannai had an extensive estate that his own students worked and shared in the profits from. B. Baba Bathra 14a states that he planted 400 vineyards.

29. See Kristi Upson-Saia, Carly Daniel-Hughes, and Alicia J. Batten (eds.), *Dressing Judeans and Christians in Antiquity* (London/New York: Routledge, 2016) for the dynamics of class and dress.

30. Inge Nielsen and Hanne Sigismund Nielsen (eds.), *Meals in a Social Context: Aspects of the Communal Meal in the Hellenistic and Roman world* (Aarhus: Aarhus Universitetsforlag, 2001) and Susan Marks and Hal Taussig, *Meals in Early Judaism* (New York: Palgrave Macmillan, 2014).

31. For thinking about meals in late/antiquity, see Dennis E. Smith, *From Symposium to Eucharist: The Banquet in the Early Christian World* (Minneapolis: Fortress Press, 2003); Patrick Faas, *Around the Roman Table: Food and Feasting in Ancient Rome* (Chicago: University of Chicago Press, 2005), Matthew B. Roller, *Dining Posture in Ancient Rome: Bodies, Values, and Status* (Princeton: Princeton University Press, 2006); and Jordan Rosenblum, *Food and Identity in Early Rabbinic Judaism* (Cambridge: Cambridge University Press, 2010).

32. Also in Avot d' Rabbi Natan A 6 and Avot d' Rabbi Natan B 11. Compare with T. Shab. 2:5, T. Sotah 13:3, T. Pes 10:12.

33. Jason König, *Saints and Symposiasts: The Literature of Food and the Symposium in Greco-Roman and Early Christian Culture* (Cambridge: Cambridge University Press, 2012).

34. For examples, see Seth Schwartz, "No Dialogue at the Symposium? Conviviality in Ben Sira and the Palestinian Talmud," in *The End of Dialogue in Antiquity*, ed. Simon Goldhill (Cambridge: Cambridge University Press, 2008), 193–216. On the *convivium* and patronage, see John D'Arms, "Control, Companionship, and Clientelia: Some Social Functions of the Roman Communal Meal," *Echos Du Monde Classique* 28, no. 3 (1984): 327–48 and "Performing Culture: Roman Spectacle and the Banquets of the Powerful," *Studies in the History of Art* 56 (1999): 300–19.

35. See M. Ber 7.1 and Gen Rab 91:3. Susan Marks argues that these blessings were part of the culture of "table talk" similar to the libation rituals in Roman homes (Susan Marks, "In the Place of Libation: Birkat Hamazon Navigates New Ground," in *Meals in Early Judaism*, ed. Susan Marks and Hal Taussig, 71–97 [New York: Palgrave Macmillan, 2014], 82).

36. For a survey of cultural perceptions of dogs in rabbinic literature, see Joshua Schwartz, "Dogs in Jewish Society in the Second Temple Period and in the Time of the Mishnah and Talmud," *Journal of Jewish studies* 55, no. 2 (2004): 273.

37. Cristiana Franco, *Shameless: The Canine and the Feminine in Ancient Greece* (University of California Press, 2014), 77.
38. D'Arms, "Performing Culture," 313.
39. For comparison with manliness and masculinity in the late ancient Christian context, see Mathew Kuefler, *The Manly Eunuch: Masculinity, Gender Ambiguity, and Christian Ideology in Late Antiquity* (Chicago: University of Chicago Press, 2001) and Colleen Conway, *Behold the Man: Jesus and Greco-Roman Masculinity* (Oxford: Oxford University Press, 2008).
40. Lee I. Levine, *Rabbinic Class of Roman Palestine in Late Antiquity* (Jerusalem/ New York: Yad Izhak Ben-Zvi/Jewish Theological Seminary of America, 1990), 131.

BIBLIOGRAPHY

Butler, Judith. *Gender Trouble*. New York: Routledge, 1990.

Butler, Judith. *Bodies that Matter: On the Discursive Limits of Sex*. Abington: Routledge, 2011.

Bowes, Kimberly Diane. *Private Worship, Public Values, and Religious Change in Late Antiquity*. Cambridge: Cambridge University Press, 2008.

Clark, Elizabeth A. "Patrons, Not Priests: Gender and Power in Late Ancient Christianity." *Gender & History* 2, no. 3 (1990): 253–74.

Connell, Robert W. and James W. Messerschmidt. "Hegemonic masculinity: Rethinking the concept." *Gender & Society* 19, no. 6 (2005): 829–59.

Conway, Colleen. *Behold the Man: Jesus and Greco-Roman Masculinity*. Oxford: Oxford University Press, 2008.

Dalton, Krista. "Teaching for the Tithe: Donor Expectations and the Matrona's Tithe." *AJS Review* 44, no. 1 (2020): 49–73.

D'Arms, John H. "Control Companionship, and Clientele: Some Functions of the Roman Communal Meal." *Echos Du Monde Classique* 28, no. 3 (1984): 327–48.

D'Arms, John H. "Performing Culture: Roman Spectacle and the Banquets of the Powerful." *Studies in the History of Art* 56 (1999): 300–19.

Eshleman, Kendra. *The Social World of Intellectuals in the Roman Empire: Sophists, Philosophers, and Christians*. Cambridge: Cambridge University Press, 2012.

Faas, Patrick. *Around the Roman Table: Food and Feasting in Ancient Rome*. Chicago: University of Chicago Press, 2005.

Franco, Cristiana. *Shameless: The Canine and the Feminine in Ancient Greece*. Oakland: University of California Press, 2014.

Furey, Constance M. "Body, Society, and Subjectivity in Religious Studies." *Journal of the American Academy of Religion* 80, no. 1 (2012): 7–33.

König, Jason. *Saints and Symposiasts: The Literature of Food and the Symposium in Greco-Roman and Early Christian Culture*. Cambridge: Cambridge University Press, 2012.

Kuefler, Mathew. *The Manly Eunuch: Masculinity, Gender Ambiguity, and Christian Ideology in Late Antiquity*. Chicago: University of Chicago Press, 2001.

Kuefler, Mathew. "The Merry Widows of Late Roman Antiquity: The Evidence of the Theodosian Code." *Gender & History* 27, no. 1 (2015): 28–52.

Labendz, Jenny R. *Socratic Torah: Non-Jews in Rabbinic Intellectual Culture.* Oxford: Oxford University Press, 2013.

Levine, Lee I. *Rabbinic Class of Roman Palestine in Late Antiquity.* Jerusalem/New York: Yad Izhak Ben-Zvi/Jewish Theological Seminary of America, 1990.

Mahmood, Saba. *Politics of Piety.* Princeton: Princeton University Press, 2011.

Marks, Susan. "In the Place of Libation: Birkat Hamazon Navigates New Ground." In *Meals in Early Judaism*, edited by Susan Marks and Hal Taussig, 71–97. New York: Palgrave Macmillan, 2014.

Marks, Susan and Hal Taussig (eds.). *Meals in Early Judaism: Social Formation at the Table.* New York: Palgrave MacMillan, 2014.

Nielsen, Inge and Hanne Sigismund Nielsen (eds.). *Meals in a Social Context: Aspects of the Communal Meal in the Hellenistic and Roman world.* Aarhus: Aarhus Universitetsforlag, 2001.

Roller, Matthew B. *Dining Posture in Ancient Rome: Bodies, Values, and Status.* Princeton: Princeton University Press, 2006.

Rosenblum, Jordan. *Food and Identity in Early Rabbinic Judaism.* Cambridge: Cambridge University Press, 2010.

Rosen-Zvi, Ishay. "Measure for measure as a hermeneutical tool in early rabbinic literature: The Case of Tosefta Sotah." *Journal of Jewish studies* 57, no. 2 (2006): 269–86.

Satlow, Michael L. "'Try to Be a Man': The Rabbinic Construction of Masculinity." *Harvard Theological Review* 89, no. 1 (1996): 19–40.

Schwartz, Joshua. "Dogs in Jewish Society in the Second Temple Period and in the Time of the Mishnah and Talmud." *Journal of Jewish studies* 55, no. 2 (2004): 246–277.

Schwartz, Seth. "No Dialogue at the Symposium? Conviviality in Ben Sira and the Palestinian Talmud", in S. Goldhill, ed., *The End of Dialogue in Antiquity*, Cambridge: Cambridge University Press, 2008, 193–216.

Scott, Joan Wallach. "Gender as a Useful Category of Historical Analysis." *The American Historical Review* 91, no. 5 (1986): 1053–76.

Scott, Joan Wallach. "The Uses and Abuses of Gender." *Tijdschrift voor Genderstudies* 16, no. 1 (2013): 63–77.

Smith, Dennis Edwin. *From Symposium to Eucharist: The Banquet in the Early Christian World.* Minneapolis: Fortress Press, 2003.

Turner, Stephen P. *The Politics of Expertise.* New York: Routledge, 2013.

Upson-Saia, Kristi, Carly Daniel-Hughes, and Alicia J. Batten (eds.). *Dressing Judeans and Christians in Antiquity.* London/New York: Routledge, 2016.

Wendt, Heidi. *At the Temple Gates: The Religion of Freelance Experts in the Roman Empire.* Oxford: Oxford University Press, 2016.

6

Constructions of Gender in Origen of Alexandria

Ilaria L.E. Ramelli

I shall examine the conception that Origen had of women, both in practice, with the presence of women at his school, and in theory. I shall therefore investigate his reflections on women's relation to God and Christ and the divine transcendence of gender categories, the destiny of gender differences in the other world, as well as Origen's reflections on the role of women in the church and their presence in the orders of the diaconate and presbyterate.

THEORETICAL PREMISES

Origen, a prominent Christian Platonist, was a disciple of Ammonius Saccas in Alexandria, like Plotinus, and may have been the same Origen, usually called "the Neoplatonist," of whom Porphyry, Hierocles, and Proclus speak. Origen's anthropology, protology, and eschatology helped him to attach scarce importance to gender differences; Gregory Nyssen—the brother of a female deacon or presbyter, as we shall see—will follow in his footsteps in this respect as in many others.

Gender differences, which arose after sin, will vanish at the resurrection, as Jesus already taught: humans will be like angels and will not marry (Matthew 22:29–30). Mindful of Jesus's statement, Origen claims that "those raised from the dead will be like angels in heaven, and like these, they neither marry nor are given into marriage. So are the risen ones. Their bodies will become heavenly and luminous, like the angelic bodies" (*C.Matt.* 17.30).[1] Instead of metensomatosis (supported by "pagan" philosophers and possibly Philo, at least esoterically, according to Sami Yli-Karjanmaa[2]), Origen proposed ἐνσωμάτωσις or "embodiment/incorporation."[3] In his perspective, souls do not enter a sequence of different bodies, as envisaged by the theory of metensomatosis, but rational creatures have only one body, which is transformed in accord with that creature's spiritual progress. This body initially was non-gendered, and will no longer be gendered in the end. Rational creatures were provided from the beginning with a body similar to the spiritual, non-gendered, angelic body of the resurrection. After the fall, their fine, immortal body was changed into a perishable and gendered body, in the case of human beings; but these will eschatologically recover their immortal, angelic body. Even the resurrected body will have different qualities than those of the mortal body, but it will be the same as the mortal one, not another body.

From the theological viewpoint, Origen insisted on the genderless nature of the Divinity, which, in its transcendence (theorized within a solid Platonic framework[4]), lies beyond any gender distinction. This removed the temptation to think about God as a male entity and model. Qua Christian, Origen identified the divine Logos with Christ, but, notwithstanding the gender of the incarnate Christ (Jesus of Nazareth), qua Christian Platonist he emphasized the genderlessness of Christ-Logos-God, who can be described in either female or male terms, as Bardaisan, Clement, and Origen did—Clement even depicted God the Father in female terms, as the Mother of Christ and of human beings, as will be pointed out. Thus, Christ is neither male nor female, since qua God Christ transcends genders and qua human Christ has assumed all humanity, and not only men, and is a model of humanity. Therefore, the grounds for an anthropological hierarchy that privileges men over women cannot subsist. Origen's theological anthropology is modeled on Christ-Logos-Sophia and firmly grounded in his protological and eschatological view of the human being as primarily a rational creature or λογικόν. Gender differentiation arose only as a result of, or in anticipation of, the fall, and will not endure in the end, just as it does not exist in Christ. As Paul stated, "in Christ there is neither male nor female," within a sentence that reverses Aristotle's categories of discrimination (Gal 3:28).[5] Since Christ-Logos is the paradigm of humanity and the end (τέλος) is ethically normative according to Origen, the male superiority model in the church is at least theoretically challenged.

ANTECEDENTS IN BARDAISAN AND CLEMENT OF ALEXANDRIA

Bardaisan of Edessa († 222 CE) in a suggestive image reported by Porphyry represents the human being, both man and woman, and the cosmos as subsumed in Christ (as the shape of the cross indicates). Bardaisan represents Christ as Logos-Wisdom/Sophia, male (Logos) and female (Sophia), just as

Origen noted that Christ, being Wisdom, is female no less than male, and as God exceeds both genders.[6]

Clement of Alexandria, a Christian imperial Platonist who was an older contemporary of Origen and influenced him, displays a remarkable view of Christ as feminine as well as masculine, common to his semi-contemporary Bardaisan. This concept will be taken over by Origen, who will also insist that Christ, being both Logos and Wisdom, is both male and female, or better transcends genders. Christ represents a paradigm for humans, and this for Clement is not only masculine. This is why Clement insists, following the Stoic Musonius, that virtue must be pursued by men and women alike, who must receive the same philosophical education. For Clement, indeed, the true "Gnostic," his ideal Christian sage, can well be a woman.[7] Also basing himself on Gal 3:28, Clement stated that "both slaves and free should philosophise, whether they happen to be a man or a woman" (*Strom.* 4.1.1). Christ and God are often described by Clement in feminine terms. For instance, Clement represents Christ's blood, shed for the salvation of humanity, as a mother's blood in childbirth (*Paed.* 1.42.2; 35.2–3), or as a mother's blood transformed into milk for the nourishment of her infant (*Paed.* 1.40.1). The Logos is the breast of God the Father, providing God's children with milk: the food is the milk of the Father, from whom the babies suckle; they rush to the care-soothing breast of the Father, the Logos. He alone provides the infants with the milk of love, and only those who suckle this breast are really blessed.[8] Clement again attaches maternal breasts to the Father in *Paed.* 1.46.1, where he claims that the Father's nipples of love supply milk to babies who seek the Logos. As in Clement, in the *Odes of Solomon* 19, too, the Son is the cup, the Father is the one who is milked, and the Holy Spirit is "she, who milked him."[9]

Clement overtly states that God is Mother as well as Father in *Div.* 37.2. As he explains, the ineffable part of God is Father, but the part that has sympathy toward creatures is Mother. By loving, the Father "became female" (ἐθηλύνθη), and the evidence is the child whom God brought forth. Clement probably had also in mind a biblical foundation for the maternal generation of the Son by God in Psalm 109.3 [LXX]: ἐκ γαστρὸς πρὸ ἑωσφόρου ἐγέννησά σε ("From the womb, before Morning-star, I [God] brought you forth"). If God gave birth to the Son from the womb, God is obviously Mother, not just Father.

This point will be taken over in the fourth century by Macarius: Christ "gives birth" to the children of God "'by some mystical principle" and "wraps them in ineffable swaddling clothes"; "She who gives birth to them is none other than the Wisdom of God . . . abundantly pouring out the two Testaments as if from two breasts" (*Apocriticus*, 3.23.8–9). We shall again encounter Christ-Wisdom as feminine in Origen. Angelomorphic

Christology, too, in patristic theology contributed to a gender-neuter image of Christ.[10]

Like Clement, the *Acts of Thomas* also describe God, and specifically the Holy Spirit, in feminine terms, possibly because of the feminine gender of the Syriac name for "Spirit," *ruḥa*. This is why Syriac theology is rich in feminine descriptions of the Holy Spirit.[11] Most scholars think that the original redaction of these *Acts* was Syriac, although Lautaro Roig Lanzillotta deems them originally composed in Greek.[12] In the Greek *Acts of Thomas*, 2.27, the Spirit is invoked as "compassionate Mother" and "Mother of the Seven Houses." And in 5.50 the Spirit is again invoked as "hidden Mother" and "Holy Dove, who bears the twin young." The same image of the Spirit as a Mother Dove who incubates two chicks appears in fragments of Bardaisan reported by Ephrem.[13]

In the time of Bardaisan and Clement, "Gnostics" also tended to represent God, including the Father, as feminine,[14] and their views were well known to Bardaisan and Clement, as well as Origen. Later, the Christian Neoplatonist Synesius, a disciple of the philosopher and mathematician Hypatia,[15] put forward in Hymn 3 a Platonizing account of the Christian Trinity, in which the Son is the "hidden root" (Hymn 4.21) to whom "the center of the Son, *both Mother and Daughter*," gives birth. To emphasize the feminine nature of the Holy Spirit, Synesius, for instance in Hymn 4.98, calls it *pnoia* (grammatically feminine, just as *ruḥa* is in Syriac). Even a contemporary of Clement such as Tertullian, who cannot be considered a supporter of women by any standard, described the generation of the Son from the Father as a childbirth: the Father-Mother brought forth the Son "from the womb of his own heart" (*Adv.Prax.* 7.1). Tertullian, like Clement, was probably thinking of the above-mentioned Psalm 109.3 [LXX].[16]

WOMEN AT ORIGEN'S SCHOOL AND HIS CONCEPTION OF MARRIAGE

Origen also taught women at his school,[17] as did philosophers such as Socrates, the Stoics, Cynics, Pythagoreans, Epicureans, and (many) Platonists, who also counted women as philosophers and heads of schools (see Hypatia).[18] Porphyry traced back this practice to Pythagoras: "Pythagoras had many disciples, not only men but also women, among whom Theano" (*VP* 19). Justin had also taught women (*Mart.Iust.* 3–4) and Origen's admirer Pamphilus also did. According to Eusebius, the presence of female students even brought about Origen's famous self-mutilation, aimed as it was at preventing gossip about relations with these women (*HE* 6.8.1–3). Epiphanius acknowledged that Origen's great holiness, chastity, and exceptional learning engendered "huge envy" against him (πλεῖστον φθόνον, *AH* 64.2), which caused his denunciation as a Christian; he was forced to perform an act of "pagan" worship under the threat of being publicly violated by a black slave; this disgraced him and forced him to move to Palestine (*AH* 64.2). Origen's self-mutilation (reported in *AH* 64.3 as excessive gossip [φασί], with hypotheses on its precise modality) also made the object of defamation by his critics, and is prolonged into Epiphanius's calumny about Origen's monastic followers as onanists (*AH* 63.1).[19]

Concerning the historicity of Origen's self-mutilation, Jacob Neusner and Bruce Chilton suspend judgment.[20] This is accepted, for instance, by Peter Brown and Chris De Wet.[21] According to Elizabeth Digeser, Origen's mutilation is historical;[22] Ronald Heine, Christoph Markschies, and, probabilistically, Rowan Williams and John Behr deny it.[23] I deem rather improbable that Eusebius (and Pamphilus) invented an embarrassing tradition, which he tried hard to justify (*HE* 6.8.1–3) by stating that Origen observed Matt 19:12 "too literally and excessively," in order to avoid gossip owing to his teaching female students as well.

This saying about Origen's self-mutilation may merely have been his opponents' slander, aimed at denying Origen's fitness for priesthood and generally at denigrating him. Still in *C.Cant.* 2.1.48, Origen reports Matt 19:12 without any kind of warning or disagreement, but he strongly approves of those who make themselves eunuchs for the Kingdom. In *C.Matt.* 15.3, however, Origen quotes *Sentences of Sextus* 13 and 273 and Philo *Det.* 176: both passages favored the practice of men's self-mutilation for the sake of chastity. Although he usually agrees with Sextus and Philo,[24] Origen disagrees with both for misinterpreting Scripture's spiritual meaning. Matt 19:12 refers to *spiritual* self-neutering, Origen maintains, and this point was misinterpreted by Sextus and those who nurture "an inordinate love for chastity" (*C.Matt.* 15.1). Origen adduces both medical reasons against self-mutilation and a biblical proof: "whoever is emasculated or has his private parts cut off shall not enter into the Lord's assembly" (Deut 23:1). Now this may well have been what his opponents likely adduced against his ordination into the presbyterate.

In *Cels.* 7.48, too, also a late work like the Commentary on Matthew, Origen praises the chastity of many Christians, who voluntarily master their desires, "in that the λόγος drives out lust from their minds," as opposed to those involved in the "pagan" Eleusinian mysteries, who rather relied on hemlock.[25] Ambrose remembered Origen's condemnation of a literal exegesis of Matt 19:12 when he remarked that those who mutilate themselves with a knife act out of weakness, because it is not impotence that makes a man continent, but it is his own will (*Vid.* 13.75–77). If Origen was initially "pagan" (a hypothesis which is impossible to prove with any certainty), his possible mutilation might have been part of the Serapis cult, which Egyptian Christians tolerated, even taking on elements of it.[26] Perhaps Origen was named "Son of Horus" from the cult of Horus and Serapis—like the four gods Sons of Horus.[27] Later, to justify the information about his self-mutilation, Christians found the explanation of a literal reading of Matthew about the blessing of "becoming eunuch" and Origen's desire to avoid gossip about the female students in his classroom—unless one supposes that the accusation of being a eunuch arose from a misunderstanding of Origen's ascetic lifestyle as a "spiritual eunuch," without any factual mutilation whatsoever.[28] That Origen understood Matt 19:12 literally clashes, as Szram observes, with his allegorical exegesis of the Bible; however, we may think of a very early deed, before he began to deploy allegoresis systematically. If the charge, instead, was entirely fabricated, in order for opponents to deny Origen's suitability for the priesthood and destroy his reputation, this would attest once again to the role of slander against Origen's figure. Irrespective of this charge or calumny, Origen remained single all of his life because he was an ascetic.[29]

In his mature *Commentary on Romans*, Origen speaks of "all those who, according to the evangelical precept, castrated themselves for the sake of the Kingdom of God, having as a model the one who instituted this norm: the Lord Jesus Christ himself, along with many other saints."[30] Jesus is the paradigm of all those Christians who "castrated themselves" for the Kingdom of God. This does not mean an act of self-emasculation on Jesus's or Origen's part, but an exhortation to observe virginity.

Origen as an ascetic did not choose marriage, but he regarded it as an institution founded by God. He observed that marriage is useful, and established by God, for a world subject to birth and corruption, but it will not be retained in the state of beatitude (ἐν τῇ μακαριότητι): "if everything is made new in the eschaton, then all the really blessed goods of life must be of a different type there."[31] Origen insisted that husbands must not deem themselves superior to their wives, since spouses have reciprocal "similarity and equality."[32] Origen did not understand "equality" as modern feminists do; nevertheless, his use of the term, all the more in reference to marriage—which in his day was anything but "equal"—is remarkable.

Origen praises asceticism over married life, as Paul did. Commenting on Matthew 19:8,[33] he cites Jesus's words: "Moses allowed you to divorce your wife, but from the beginning it was not like that." Then he refers to 1 Cor 7:2–3: each man should have his wife and each woman her husband to avoid adultery (*propter fornicationem* / διὰ τῆς πορνείας). The wife must give her husband what is due to him and the husband give his wife what is due to her. But Origen quotes Paul's remark in 1 Cor 7:6: "I say this by way of concession [κατὰ συγγνώμην], not by way of command [κατ' ἐπιταγήν]." Immediately afterward, Origen cites 1 Cor 7:30—he builds a patchwork of

Jesus's and Paul's citations—: A woman is bound to her husband for all the time he lives; if he dies, she is free, and can marry whomever she wants, only, in the Lord.

At this point Origen recalls 1 Cor 12:31, "be zealous for the better gifts," and observes that, because of the hardness of our heart and our weakness (σκληροκαρδίαν καὶ ἀσθένειαν), Paul tells this to those of us who don't want to seek more important gifts and become more blessed (τὰ χαρίσματα τὰ μείζονα καὶ μακαριωτέροις γενέσθαι). This refers to asceticism as preferable to marriage and is what Origen himself did. Then comes Origen's own remark that a second marriage while the former spouse is still alive is antibiblical (Origen speaks of women because this is the Gospel's sentence, but it is clear everywhere that he conceives the same for men too):

> Now, some of those who lead the churches, against Scripture [παρὰ γεγραμμένα], allowed a woman to marry again [ἐπέτρεψεν γαμεῖσθαι] while her husband is alive—acting against Scripture: "A woman is bond to her husband as long as he is alive" and "A wife will be called adulterous if she lives with another man while her husband is alive." This is not completely unreasonable. [πάντη ἀλόγως]

Origen remarks here that the second marriage while one's spouse is alive is contrary to Scripture, so he condemns it theoretically, although he admits that this is not a totally irrational choice: "it is likely [εἰκός, *verisimile*] that they permit this kind of intercourse [συμπεριφοράν] against the law established from the beginning in Scripture [περὶ τὰ ἀπ᾽ ἀρχῆς νενομοθετημένα καὶ γεγραμμένα] in order to avoid worse behaviour [συγκρίσει χειρόνων / *ad vitanda peiora*]," namely to avoid that a woman divorced may fall into multiple relationships or even prostitution. Origen's judgment on the Christian pastors who had permitted remarriage after divorce is that their concession is not good per se, but it is a lesser evil in front of worse outcomes. In the very next section,[34] Origen observes that the Lord does not allow to divorce one's spouse for anything else than fornication: in all other cases, one exposes one's wife to adultery. A husband often is responsible for vices which grow in his wife.

After this discussion on marriage and divorce, Origen's own preference for ascetic life over marriage or even adultery is clear from what immediately follows:[35] he cites the apostle's words: "it is not convenient to marry," glossing that "not marrying is easier and more useful" (εὐχερέστερον τὴν ἀγαμίαν), and Jesus's reply in Matt 19:10–11 that this grace has been given to those who can live in complete chastity (τὴν παντελῆ καθάρευσιν). This, Origen adds, can be achieved through ascetic exercise (ἀσκήσει) and prayers (μετ᾽ εὐχῶν), as it can be granted by God through human prayers (μετ εὐχῶν ὑπὸ θεοῦ διδόμενον). A selection of Jesus's sayings follows about prayer and about praying incessantly[36] and asking God for graces even *importune*, in order to underscore the importance of prayer in the reception of God's graces.

Thus, Origen exhorts people to pray for ascetic life and not marriage. Origen even transforms a quotation of Plato in this sense:[37] while Plato denounced that flattery "makes minds like wax" (τοὺς θυμοὺς ποιοῦσιν κηρίνους, *Leg.* 633D), Origen quotes this sentence but applying it to carnal pleasures (ἀφροδίσια), which "make minds like wax" (ποιήσασαν τοὺς θυμοὺς κηρίνους, *Cels.* 4.26). Hence also his valuing of Mary: Origen rejects some Ebionites' claim that Jesus was not born from a virgin (*Cels.* 5.61) and the Jewish insinuation that he was born from adultery.[38] He stresses Isaiah 7:14(LXX) on Christ's virginal birth (*Cels.* 1.34–35) and claims that Mary had no other children after Jesus (*C.Io.* 1.4.23: οὐδεὶς υἱὸς Μαρίας ἢ Ἰησοῦς). Mary is a prophet because of the Spirit in her (*H.Luc.* 8.1), an apostle in that she brings Jesus,[39] and a model for the study and meditation of Scripture.[40] He attests to the interpretation of Jesus's siblings and children of Joseph from a first marriage, based on the *Gospel of Peter* and *Protoevangelium Iacobi*, "to keep Mary's virginal dignity until the end" (τὸ ἀξίωμα τῆς Μαρίας ἐν παρθενίᾳ τηρεῖν μέχρι τέλους) and considers Mary's virginity "the first-fruits of virginity" for women as Jesus is for men,[41] and for all Christians a model of the generation of Christ in one's soul (*H.Luc.* 22.3). In Egypt, Mary seems to have been invoked as protector of a celibate marriage in papyri.[42]

Origen praises virginity like Ambrose and Jerome, who knew, and were indebted to, his work; they also appealed to Cyprian's *De habitu virginum*.[43] He declared that virgins "have in this world the glory of the resurrection" and "are equal to the angels of God" (*HV* 22). Here, the notion of ἰσαγγελία surfaces again, which we have seen in Clement and Origen in relation to virginity and would become prominent in Gregory of Nyssa.

Even within marriage, according to Origen, the union and concord of the spouses is more important than carnal union, on the basis of a Scriptural interpretation and probably of imperial Stoic ideas of marriage. Commenting on Gen 2:24, Origen notes that God states that the two spouses become "one flesh" after the woman is created in Paradise and well before the carnal "knowledge" of the spouses, whereas the sexual union of Adam and Eve happened only much later, in Gen 4:1, after their expulsion from Paradise because of their sin (*Fr. 1 Cor.* 29). Following Philo (whose attitude toward women is ambivalent[44]), Origen allegorized the Genesis account about Adam and Eve by interpreting the man as rationality, intellect, and virtue, and the woman as flesh, bodily matter, vice, and pleasure;[45] therefore, the Genesis fall story is not about differences between men and women, but about the effects of virtue and vice on every soul, irrespective of gender. According to Origen, marriage is made by "concord, agreement, and harmony" before intercourse and procreation (*C.Matth.* 14.16). This is in perfect line with the notion of marriage in imperial Stoicism.[46]

According to Origen, who vigorously rejected traducianism, Adam's sin—not Eve's: Origen insists on the sin of Adam and, even more seriously, the sin of satan and all demons[47]—is a paradigm; it symbolizes human sin, but it is not an inherited sin (*Cels.* 4.40; *H.Ex.* 9.1). The notion of an inherited sin in his view seems to clash against the theory of freewill, which never abandons rational creatures (*Or.* 29.13; *C.Rom.* 5.10[48]). Only concupiscence in the reproductive act of the protoplasts and of all parents seems to leave some impurity (ῥύπος, *sordes*) in the human being, which makes it advisable to baptize children, although they have not yet committed any sin of their own.[49] Origen, who was an ascetic, is negative about the carnal union in many places, although he recognizes that marriage was instituted by God; in *Pascha* 36, where he comments on the Paschal command of "being pure from any corporeal union" (καθαροὶ γενέσθαι ἀπὸ συνελεύσεως σωματικῆς) and "repress the impulsions towards the intercourse" (ἐμφράξαι τὰ τῆς μίξεως κινήματα); an example was John the Baptist, another ascetic, who "mortified every genetic impulse in himself" (νενέκρωσεν πᾶσαν τὴν κίνησιν αὐτοῦ τὴν σπερματικήν). In *H.Luc.* 6.1–2 Origen notes that Elizabeth, when she conceived John the Baptist, remained hidden for five months, since her union with her husband, although ordered by God's economy, was "disgraceful" also because of their old age and she was "embarrassed"; even younger married people are prescribed to abstain from unions in given times (cf. *Pascha* 36). Although Jesus was conceived without concupiscence, nevertheless, having taken up a human body, he needed a purification in the Temple (Luke 2:22). For "no one is free from impurity, not even if he has lived just one day" (Job 14:4–5 [LXX]). This is not sin inherited through generations, but it is a universal state of sinfulness—linked, I suspect, to the fact that humans, and all rational creatures (perhaps apart from angels) fell. Thus, although sin is not inherited, nevertheless a human being can hardly escape sinning.[50] What spares one from sinning is ethics—the exercise of virtues—and Christ who is all virtues and who saves humans through his Crucifixion.[51] The church itself is made of people who, even after baptism, are still sinners and therefore are in need of penitence.[52] Origen counts himself among the sinners, even after baptism, and waits for the baptism of martyrdom (indeed, he seems to have died as a confessor) or the other-worldly baptism of suffering for purification: "Although I have been washed once and for all, I need the baptism about which the Lord says: I have another baptism in which I must be baptized" (*H.Is.* 5.2).

WOMEN IN THE CHURCH: ORIGEN'S EXEGESIS IN SUPPORT OF WOMEN'S ORDAINED MINISTRY

Origen relied on scribes, who included women, for his homilies and commentaries on Scripture: "He had at his disposal more than seven tachygraphs, who succeeded one another at fixed times, and no fewer copyists, as well as girls skilled in calligraphy."[53] All three groups can include women. As Angela Standhartinger notes,[54] this function has been overlooked in many fields until very recently. It is debatable whether this can be regarded as a church office or ministry, but it is certainly inclusive. Origen had women among his tachygraphs, among his disciples at his school, and, as we are going to see, he included them among deacons and presbyters in the church.

Indeed, Origen seems to have advocated a degree of inclusivity in church offices such as the diaconate and the episcopate. He overtly claimed that St. Paul "teaches with apostolic authority that women too are constituted in the ecclesiastical ministry, and must be assumed into office."[55] He is commenting on Rom 16:1, about Phoebe, an ecclesiastical deacon (διάκονος) and president (προστάτις—the feminine of προστάτης, the title of Jesus himself), a phrase that already in Paul indicated "a recognised ministry" or a "position of responsibility within the congregation."[56] He remarks on her being constituted in the church ministry and stresses her *officium* and ecclesiastical *ministerium*, which he considers to be extended to other women too. These *ministrae in Ecclesia*, established on the basis of Paul's authority, hold an office that is not restricted to material cares, but consists in spiritual ministry. Therefore, Origen claims that the women invested with this ministry deserve to, and must, be honored.[57]

Origen describes as ecclesiastical *ministerium* the episcopate, presbyterate, diaconate, and the orders of widows and virgins, *without any distinction in terminology or prescriptions* between feminine and masculine orders.[58] He lists the orders of the church without distinction between male and female ministries: "anyone who has married twice may not be bishop, presbyter, deacon, or widow."[59] Origen is indeed clear that widows, if worthy and holy (ἁγίαν χήραν), are "ordained to an ecclesiastical honour or rank" (κατατετάχθαι εἰς ἐκκλησιαστικὴν τιμήν, *C.Io.* 32.12.131). The verb κατατάσσω is used exactly for an ecclesiastical ordination in Cyril, *C.Io.* 2.1.

Origen's above-mentioned parallel between male and female ministries will be found again in Modestus, the seventh-century patriarch of Jerusalem: he calls Mary Magdalene "the leader of the female disciples" (ἀρχηγὸς τῶν μαθητριῶν) and attributes to her and to all female disciples the "apostolic mission" (τὸν δρόμον τὸν ἀποστολικόν).[60] The Gospel of Mary, probably in the second century, was devoted to her as an excellent disciple.[61] Her epithet Magdalene likely derives from Semitic *migdal-migdol*, which points to her being magnified, made great (by Jesus). Origen cites Mary Magdalene with the Hebrew etymology of her name: "the women who were more contemplative and served and followed Jesus include Mary, surnamed the Woman Made Great, the Woman Exalted by Jesus, as Magdala means the action of making great, exalting," μεγαλυσμός.[62] Likewise in Latin: *Maria Magdalena de magnificatione*.[63] In Hebrew, indeed, *gadal* means "great," and one of the forms of the relevant verb means "make great." *Migdol* is interpreted by Origen as *magnificentia*, in *Hom.Num.* 16.9.[64]

Origen also reflects on Deborah, the prophetess and judge of Israel, and on the gift of prophecy bestowed on women, explicitly claiming that there is no gender diversity in matter of spiritual gifts. For they come "from purity of mind, not from gender difference."[65] Anna, who exulted for Jesus's birth at the Temple in Jerusalem, was "a holy woman" and "rightly deserved to receive the spirit of prophecy, having ascended to this peak through long chastity and long fasting," namely through the practice of asceticism.[66]

Origen interprets Tit 2:3–4 in reference to women presbyters' ministry and ascribes them the office of teaching. First, commenting on 1 Cor 14:34–35, he repeats that, as Paul attests, women can be prophets and teach other Christians, only—he adds—not in assemblies of men.[67] Was this a move inspired by modesty or a way of diminishing women's authority? Women can teach "wonderful and holy things"; only, they should not teach men, at least not at church. Immediately after, Origen interprets Tit 2:3–4 (about πρεσβύτιδες who are in a consecrated state: "female elders") as a reference to the ecclesiastical office of women presbyters. Origen read this passage in his manuscripts in the following form: "In the same way, the πρεσβύτιδες, being in a consecrated state [ἐν καταστήματι ἱεροπρεπεῖ],[68] must not be slanderers or wine addicts, but good teachers, and so on." Origen highlights that the women mentioned in Tit 2:3 are found "in a consecrated state" and therefore should certainly teach, only, not in a public assembly of men, since in that context there are men who also can announce God's word: "For women too must be teachers, and *teach good and beautiful things* [καλοδιδάσκαλοι]; only, it is not that men should sit down and listen to women, as though there were not men equally capable of *proclaiming the Word of God* [πρεσβεύειν τὸν τοῦ Θεοῦ λόγον]." Origen is obsequious to the societal topos of women who should escape notice—so prominent even in Stoic philosophers who thought that women had the same virtues as men, such as Seneca.[69] However, it is clear that, Origen regarded these πρεσβύτιδες as announcers of the Word of God: this is the office of presbyters, not of "old women." Origen regarded the πρεσβύτιδες in Tit 2:3–4 as women presbyters, not simply aged ladies; therefore, he says that they are "in a consecrated state."

A confirmation comes from Origen's Commentary on John, preserved in Greek, and not in a fragment, but in a fully preserved section. Here, he remarks that men and women presbyters, πρεσβύτεροι and πρεσβύτιδες, are prescribed the same thing in an analogous way (κελεύονται ἀνάλογον): to be καλοδιδάσκαλοι or "teachers of noble things" (*C.Io.* 32.12.132–33). This is, again, the office of presbyters, which is applied to men and women alike.

Theodore of Mopsuestia may have had Origen in mind when observing that "some people thought" that Tit 2:3 testified to "the ordination [χειροτονία] of presbyters among women."[70] He knew Origen's works and thought, and even embraced the doctrine of apokatastasis (a cornerstone of Origen's theology), as I argued elsewhere.[71] Others too interpreted Tit 2:3 in reference to women presbyters, also because the variant reading known to Origen was widespread—and might even be original.

Additionally, Tit 2:2 is constructed by Origen as an exact parallel to v. 3, as is stressed by the adverb ὡσαύτως (v. 3: "*exactly in the same way*, women presbyters in a consecrated position . . ."), and probably refers to "presbyters," rather than "old men." Origen interpreted it precisely in this way: "But you say what is apt to the *salutary teaching*: *presbyters* [πρεσβυτέρους] must be abstemious, dignified, self-controlled, healthy in their faith, in love and patience." Some manuscripts indeed read πρεσβυτέρους as a variant of πρεσβύτας. The "salutary teaching" (v. 2) belonged to the tasks of presbyters. That Origen read πρεσβυτέρους instead of πρεσβύτας—the former may well be the original reading—is confirmed by a passage preserved in Greek and whose authorship is beyond doubt (*C.Io.* 32.12.132–133). Here Origen draws a parallel between the recommendations addressed to πρεσβύτεροι and those addressed to πρεσβύτιδες in Tit 2:2–4: "women presbyters [πρεσβύτιδες] are ordered to be also *teachers of good things* [καλοδιδάσκαλοι], *exactly in the same way* as men presbyters [ἀνάλογον τοῖς πρεσβυτέροις]." The parallel drawn by Origen focuses precisely on the task of teaching, common to both men and women presbyters.

Thus, Tit 2:3–4 in Origen's view contemplated women's presbyterate and teaching ministry as parallel to men's presbyterate and teaching. Likewise, not only Rom 16:1 concerning Phoebe, but also 1 Tim 3:11 indicated women deacons, with the same parallelism between women and men as in Tit 2:2–4. Indeed, 1 Tim 3:11 parallels 1 Tim 3:8: "men deacons should be *dignified*, not *double* in their words . . . keeping the mystery of *faith*" (3:8); "*in the same way*, women (deacons) should be *dignified*, not *slanderers* . . . full of *faith* in everything" (3:11).

Origen reversed the attitude of the Pastoral Epistles, as it is reconstructed by most scholars:[72] the Pastorals, especially 1 Timothy, were composed against "Gnostics"—alluded to in the phrase "knowledge, falsely so called"—and Marcionites, who prohibited marriage and procreation and permitted women's leadership. Titus and 1 Timothy intended to reverse such trends. They contrast Paul's asceticism and appreciation of women as church leaders. An adaptation to the Hellenistic cultural context is found in the prohibition against women teaching in 1 Tim 2:12 and in the restrictions imposed on widows, which Benjamin Fiore considers aimed at excluding women from public ministries under the influence of cultural prejudices,[73] in contrast to Paul's praxis. In Pauline communities, indeed, women were leaders, involved in teaching, and had positions of responsibility; the Pastorals' household codes "domesticated" Paul's views along the lines of traditional Hellenistic households. Elisabeth Schüssler Fiorenza thinks that the injunction in 1 Tim 2:12 develops the argument in 1 Cor 14:34–6;[74] the author of the Pastorals was concerned with showing that Christians did not disrupt the Graeco-Roman order of patriarchal houses and states.[75] Indeed, impressive parallels have been detected between 1 Timothy and Titus and Hellenistic moral philosophy, including with Hierocles the Stoic's doctrines of *oikeiōsis* ("appropriation/familiarization"), *kathēkonta* ("duties/appropriate acts"), and the "contraction of circles."[76] Origen, however, also using a different text of Titus, read in both Titus and 1 Timothy—which he deemed written by Paul—as well as in 1 Corinthians and Romans the confirmation, grounded in "apostolic authority," that "women too are constituted in the ecclesiastical ministry."

Further, Origen's use of biblical allegoresis ruled out a misogynist interpretation of passages that could be read as prohibitions against women's ecclesiastical leadership. For example, Origen allegorizes the statement in 1 Tim 2:15 that women will be saved through childbearing: like Paul,[77] as seen, Origen valued virginity as the highest way of life and even spoke against remarriage after the death of one's spouse as excluding people from God's kingdom,[78] and the literal sense of v. 15 sounded absurd to him. He rather interprets "women" as souls and "childbearing" as the birth of Christ and all virtues—which are Christ-Logos, as mentioned—in one's heart,[79] since Jesus was born uselessly if he is not born in each one's heart as well.[80] In the same vein, Origen remarked that his father's death as a martyr is useless to him, Origen, if he does not live in a way worthy of Leonidas's nobility (*H. Ez.* 4.8). Therefore, according to Origen, 1 Tim 2:15 says nothing about what women should or should not do, but indicates what all human beings must do in order to be saved.

Similarly, Origen reads the first transgression of the woman (1 Tim 2:14) in reference to the bride of Canticles, who in his exegesis represents, not a woman, but each soul and the church, gathered from among pagans ("transgressors," *C.Cant.* 2.1). Similarly, under Philo's influence,[81] Origen allegorizes the creation account in Genesis by interpreting "man" as rationality, intellect, and virtue, and "woman" as flesh, bodily matter, vice, and pleasure.[82] Thus, the Genesis story of the fall is all about the effects of virtue and vice on every soul, not about the supposed different conducts of men and women. Origen refused to draw from the Genesis myth consequences concerning possible restrictions or prohibitions of women's ecclesiastical ministries.

Moreover, Origen interpreted Phil 4:3 in reference to women apostles. In Phil 4:3, Paul asks a "faithful/noble colleague" (γνήσιε σύζυγε) to help the women apostles Euodia and Syntyche, because they fought for the Gospel together with Paul. Now, clearly Origen interpreted the "noble colleague" of Paul in the apostolate as a woman, because he identifies this colleague with Persis, mentioned in Rom 16:12 as an apostle: "This woman [Persis], whom Paul also calls 'faithful/genuine/noble,' has labored a great deal in the Lord" (*C.Rom.* 10.29). So, according to Origen a woman, Persis, was a colleague of Paul in the apostolate, and highly praised by Paul himself. Another woman apostle, whom Origen knew and mentioned, was Junia, praised by Paul as "prominent/outstanding [ἐπίσημος] among the apostles" (*C.Rom.* 10.26;39).[83] Paul may indicate that she was among the apostles sent out by Jesus himself and surely calls her not only apostle, but preeminent among the apostles. Moreover, Origen regards the Samaritan woman[84] and other women as apostles (*C.Io.* 13.28.169).

WOMEN HEADS OF HOUSE CHURCHES AND PRESBYTERS IN THE DAY OF ORIGEN

Women actually taught as presbyters in Origen's time, and may still have been heads of house churches. For instance, the wealthy lady who acted as a patroness to Origen is regarded by Ronald Heine as a head of a house church.[85] Surely, many Christians, both "heretics" and "orthodox," gathered to listen to Origen preaching there according to Eusebius (*HE* 6.2.13–14). Also, Origen very probably criticized the Montanists,[86] without naming them, in *Princ.* 2.7.3 (since they assimilated the Holy Spirit to common spirits in their prophecies, were deceived by spirits of error, disturbed the churches, and prohibited marriage and meat) and detested their millenarian ideas, but significantly did *not* denigrate them, or anyone else, for ordaining women presbyters and bishops.[87]

Roughly in the time of Origen, Tertullian attests that women presbyters taught, baptized, and offered the Eucharistic sacrifice within the priestly office (*sacerdotale officium, ministerium leviticum*).[88] In the first half of the third century, Ammion, a female presbyter (πρεσβυτέρα), performed her ecclesiastical ministry in Phrygia. She was no wife of any presbyter, but a member of the clergy herself, since her epitaph was dedicated by her bishop, Dioga. Likewise, between the second and third centuries, in Egypt *Artemidora presbytera* was an ordained presbyter and not a presbyter's wife, since her inscription does not mention a husband priest, but only her parents. She probably was a consecrated virgin and presbyter, like Theosebia, the sister of Nyssen and Basil, whom I shall treat briefly below. In Museo Pio Cristiano's third-century-onward sarcophagi, initially, men and women were equally portrayed as teachers and figures of authority. Crispina, on a sarcophagus, is centrally placed in a scene that included over sixteen men; she reads a codex, bearing a Christogram, and is enclosed in a central arch with columns, which separates her from the men.[89] Other important examples of women's ecclesiastical leadership are recently analyzed by Ally Kateusz[90] and in *Patterns of Women's Leadership*.

Firmilian of Caesarea attests that in Cappadocia a woman consecrated the Eucharist and baptized, performing the priestly office.[91] The *Didascalia Apostolorum*, early in the third century, listed virgins, widows, and πρεσβύτιδες as ecclesiastical orders, and regarded women deacons as an ecclesiastical order as well as male deacons. Women deacons are there said to be worthy of honor as the symbol (τύπος) of the Holy Spirit; their relation to their bishop is the same as that of Christ-God is to the Father.[92] Women too, like male deacons and presbyters, were ordained by the bishop by hand imposition, and belonged to the clergy.[93] Their ecclesiastical office included spiritual and material support of women, pastoral visits to women, the administration of baptism, especially to women, teaching the baptized, the proclamation of the Word, ministry, and travel. Some decades before Origen, Pliny the Younger and Apuleius also attest to the presence of female ministers in the church; *ministrae* in Pliny, early in the second century, refers to women deacons or presbyters.[94] Clearly, in Origen's day there existed women in ecclesiastical orders.

This situation also seems to be reflected in some "apostolic novels" such as the *Acts of Thecla* and the *Acts of Philip*.[95] The former describes Thecla's apostolic role in terms similar to those that Origen in the same period ascribed to women presbyters. In the original version, stemming around 180–200 CE according to Jan Bremmer, Thecla, after joining Paul again, tells him that she wants to go back to Iconium, to which Paul replies: "Go and teach the word of God" (δίδασκε τὸν λόγον τοῦ Θεοῦ, *ATh* 41.6), which is a presbyterial task. After Iconium, Thecla moves to Seleucia to teach women the Gospel and finally passes away in peace (ATh 43.7). Thecla, therefore, is attributed the task of teaching (διδάσκειν) the word of God, both in general (ATh 41.6) and especially to women, as is clear from ATh 43.7, with Thecla's teaching women in Seleucia, and 39, where she is said to have spent eight days teaching the women of Tryphaena's household. Even in the later version in ms. G,[96] Thecla is said to have spent all of her time in Seleucia teaching noblewomen Christianity and healing (45.6–14). And even in ms. G Thecla is still called "apostle" (ἀπόστολος, 45.58).

Origen is a contemporary of the *Acts of Thecla*—later absorbed in the *Acts of Paul and Thecla*[97]—and like this work not only admitted the existence of women apostles and ministers in the church but more specifically described the task of women presbyters as teaching and announcing the Word of God, especially to women, more in a private than in a public context. This is the same task performed by Thecla. It is meaningful that Nyssen, who—as I shall show—seems to have shared Origen's ecclesiology and openness to women's ministry, was an admirer of Thecla. His eldest sister, Macrina, whom he held in very high regard, had Thecla as her second name.[98] Perrin also emphasizes the role of women in debates on the faith from the time of Origen to late antiquity: their involvement seemed influenced by their social standing[99]—and their ecclesiastical one.

Origen was aware not only of Christian female presbyters in his day, but also of female priestesses such as the Vestals,[100] who were "pagan" ascetics, virgins, and celebrated in epigraphs especially from Septimius Severus to the whole third century; they had the option of leaving the priesthood and marry after thirty years of service, but none is recorded to have made such a choice.[101]

ORIGEN'S "DOUBLE" ECCLESIOLOGY AND RELATIVIZATIONS

Another factor that bears on Origen's recognition of women's ecclesiastical ministry is that, consistently with the importance he attached to the spiritual exegesis of Scripture, and to the intellectual dimension vis-à-vis the material, he regarded ordained ministries, sacraments, and liturgy as both physical/historical and spiritual/symbolical. Thus, baptism can be either visible or invisible; each church has a visible bishop and an invisible one.[102] The church is double: one earthly and one spiritual/heavenly—an idea already maintained by Clement: "The ecclesiastical ranks of bishop, presbyter, and deacon are imitations of the angelic glory and of the economy that, Scripture says, awaits those who have lived in perfection of righteousness according to the Gospel" (*Strom.* 6.13.107). The Eucharist, according to Origen, is not only the sacramental bread consecrated by a presbyter,[103] but also the reading, listening to, and meditation of Scripture, "the body of Christ."[104] Consistently, the nourishment of the soul is not only the Eucharistic sacrament—which in its material aspect ends up into the belly and the toilet, and is beneficial only through the prayer upon it (*C.Matt.*11.14), since the Logos is more important than its body (*H.Ex.* 13.3)—but reading the Bible.[105] The intellectual aspect prevails over the liturgical-sacramental. Indeed, I regard Ambrose's notion of *mysterium* as "the rationale of the sacraments," *ratio sacramentorum*,[106] to be indebted to Origen (especially *C.Rom.* 5.8.102–108: *typus mysteriorum . . . uirtus eorum ac ratio*, in reference to baptism). Origen's scarce interest in ritual parallels Plotinus's famous attitude: "When Amelius became a lover of sacrifices [φιλοθύτου] and took to going round visiting the temples . . ., and asked whether he could take Plotinus along, Plotinus said: 'They ought to come to me, not I to them'" (Porphyry *V.Plot.* 10).

All Christians share the priestly office, according to Origen; a non-ordained person can be worthier of priesthood than one ordained. Only those who have an understanding of God are worthy of being called priests,[107] and not those who observe merely physical pureness.[108] Humans can be high priests according to the order of Aaron, but according to the order of Melchisedek only Christ is. All Christians share in the priestly office; a non-ordained person can be worthier of ordination than one ordained. Only those who have an understanding of God are worthy of being called priests,[109] and this applies to men and women alike. The true priest is a person who "knows and understands one's own sins" and should be chosen on account of one's eminence in every virtue.[110] A bishop should be a teacher and have dialectical skills (*Cels.* 3.68)—as Origen had.

Bishops and ecclesiastical ministers should lack any pride or arrogance (*superbia, arrogantia, elatio*),[111] but rather be examples of humility—this also reminds us of Origen's vicissitudes with his own bishop. Origen remembered Clement's claim that whoever "lives perfectly and gnostically" is "a real presbyter of the church" albeit being "not ordained by humans" (*Strom.* 6.13.106.1–2). Nyssen in turn would follow Origen: those who wish to be priests must contemplate virtue and become a sacrifice by bringing their bodies to the altar (*V.Mos.* 2.191)—as his sister Macrina had done in his own representation of her asceticism, illness, and death.[112] Under Philip the Arab, Origen criticized presbyters and bishops who sought prominence: given the increasing number of Christians, rich, noble, and powerful people regarded the Christians favorably, and therefore "some become leader of the Christian teaching for the sake of a little prestige" (*Cels.* 3.9, trans. Chadwick).[113] Only those sound in doctrine and life, who do not love power and are humble and reluctant, should take up church office, being "forced" to do so (*Cels.* 8.75). Hilary, inspired by Origen,[114] wrote under "Arian" emperors that those *sacerdotes* who accepted imperial honors were unworthy of continuing as bishops (*episcopi, Adv.Const.* 11).

To prioritize knowledge and holiness over ordination, Origen explicitly took over the Stoic paradoxes, especially "only the sage is priest," because only the sage has the worship coming from the knowledge of God (*C.Io.* 2.16.112–113). Indeed, true Levites and priests are those who, independently of ordination, "devote themselves to the divine Word and truly exist for the service of God alone" (*C.Io.* 1.10–11). Everyone can be a high priest, provided that she dons the high-priestly garments, which are described in Exodus and were allegorized by Josephus cosmologically, but were interpreted by Origen as virtues.[115] Vice-versa, among those ordained, the worthy are few: "anyone can perform the religious ministry, but few are adorned with morals, instructed in doctrines, educated in wisdom."[116]

In Origen's view, ordained ministry is found not only in the earthly church, but primarily in the heavenly/spiritual church. For instance, some deacons, presbyters, and bishops who belong to the former but are unworthy do not belong to the latter; some who are not ordained in the former but are worthy are in fact presbyters and bishops in the latter.[117] Such a dichotomous ecclesiology counters that supported by Ignatius's middle recension, especially in *Magn.* 3, where being disobedient to one's earthly bishop is equated to being disobedient to God: "you should obey your bishop and contradict him in nothing . . . whoever deceives the visible bishop, in fact mocks the One who is invisible." Some church officeholders are worthy, but some are unworthy and idle—always a serious vice to Origen's mind—while others, no officeholders, are more active (*Cels.* 3.30). True teachers are not necessarily churchmen; some ecclesiastical ministers are in fact not teachers, because they do not possess Jesus, God's Logos, and Wisdom (*H.Luc.* 18). In many churches, especially in large cities, bishops allow no one to speak with them on equal terms, not even the noblest disciples (*C.Matth.* 16.25;8), as Origen experienced personally. An ecclesiastical person can have authority over one who is much better gifted, "as Jesus was subject to Joseph" (*H.Luc.* 20); an autobiographical echo is likely.[118]

Christian tradition does not necessarily coincide with ecclesiastical institutional succession (an idea that finds a parallel in the succession of philosophers celebrated in that period by Diogenes Laertius[119]): here Origen proves closer to his adversary Marcion[120] than to Irenaeus, who influenced him in other ways. Christ teaches through the Spirit, not only by means of Paul and Peter, but also of "other saints" (*H.Ier.* 10.1). Not only bishops and presbyters, but especially teachers, theologians, and saints constitute the apostolic succession:[121] "Whenever the Savior sends someone for the salvation of humans, the messenger is an apostle of Jesus Christ" (*C.Io.* 32.17.204). One should aspire to be old as to spiritual maturity rather than age; likewise, one should aspire to be called a presbyter/elder (*presbyteri et seniores*) by virtue of the spiritual perfection of "the inner human being" (*pro interioris hominis perfecto sensu et gravitate constantiae*) rather than of ordained office (*pro officio presbyterii, H.*4. *Ps.36.*3), and perfection is not conferred on a person by an ecclesiastical ministry (*H.Ier.* 11.3). It is to be remarked that the "inner human being" is not gendered and thus it applies to both men and women.[122] It is a Platonic (ἐντὸς ἄνθρωπος, *Rep.* 9.598A7), Pauline, and Philonic heritage taken over not only by Origen, but also by Plotinus[123] and Augustine.[124]

Now, the inner human is neither male nor female. Relying on Gal 3:28, which proclaims that in Christ there is neither male nor female,[125] Origen remarks that the church, and every soul, is beyond gender,[126] like Christ himself, who can be called both Bride and Bridegroom.[127] We have seen that this characterization of Christ as male and female, or better beyond gender, was already present in Bardaisan and Clement. Indeed, according to Origen, Christ is represented as a male (ἄρρεν) lamb, which the Hebrews used to sacrifice, not because Christ is male, but because he is, etymologically, courageous (ἀνδρεῖον, *Pascha* 22.6–7). Again, drawing a parallel between the sacrificial lamb and Jesus, Origen describes Jesus as a human being (ἄνθρωπος) and not as a male (ἀνήρ) in *Pascha* 42.2–3. The Son of God took over "a human being," not a man as opposed to a woman.[128]

Within this theoretical framework, also in light of the fact that Christ's in-humanation took up all of humanity, not half thereof, it makes no sense to reserve ecclesiastical ministries for just one gender. The church rests not only on Peter but on a number of Peters (etymologically "rocks"), who can be women.[129] Therefore, Jesus gives "the keys of the Kingdom" and the relevant faculty of binding and loosing, not only to Peter, but also to these other Peters; conversely, an ordained bishop who judges unrighteously does not possess "the power of the keys" (*C.Matth.* 12.14).

THE INFLUENCE OF ORIGEN'S ECCLESIOLOGY AND IDEAS ABOUT WOMEN'S MINISTRY ON GREGORY OF NYSSA

Origen's ecclesiology—and his ideas in general[130]—deeply influenced Gregory of Nyssa, Origen's most insightful heir, who best understood and took over his thought. Not only was Gregory the brother of a woman deacon or presbyter (see below), but he refrained from reading 1 Cor 14:34–35, and any biblical passage, as forbidding women to teach or speak in churches. He provides a remarkably reductive exegesis of that passage and thus eliminates its ecclesiological implications.[131] In addition, he omits v. 34b, the most misogynist. He explains v. 35 as follows: if some women want to learn something they do not know, they should do so at home, since at church the explanations would disturb and distract the others. In Gregory's view, Paul's recommendation does not extend to all Christian women, nor establishes norms against women's ecclesiastical teaching, preaching, and presbyterate. Gregory actually encouraged this and probably ordained women, as I shall mention. He never refers to 1 Cor 14:34–35 anywhere else, nor does he ever cite 1 Tim 2:11–15. Only in *C.Eun.* 3.10.16 (GNO 2.295.9) does he refers to v. 14—not, however, to impose bans on women as ordained ecclesiastical ministers, but to claim that, since a woman was the first transgressor, a woman had to be the first apostle of Christ's resurrection. Gregory, like Origen, acknowledges the existence of women apostles.

The two other Cappadocians compiled, according to tradition, the *Philocalia*,[132] which denotes a profound knowledge and love of Origen's works. All of the Cappadocians were acquainted with Origen's ideas about material and spiritual ministries and sacraments, and women's ordination and ecclesiastical offices. They still read all of Origen's works in Greek, and in the light of their own, late fourth-century ecclesiastical context, when ordained women are well documented.[133]

In the second half of the fourth century, the Council of Laodicaea, Canon 11, testifies to the diffusion of women presbyters (πρεσβύτιδες) who presided over (προκαθημέναι) churches. In the *Martyrdom of Matthew* 28, a converted king is ordained πρεσβύτερος, his wife πρεσβύτις, his son διάκονος, and his son's wife διακόνισσα. Here neither πρεσβύτις nor διακόνισσα mean "wife of a presbyter/deacon," since both these women and men are expressly incorporated in the "priestly dignity" (ἱεροσύνη). The *Acts of Philip*, in the late fourth to early fifth century, also includes both πρεσβύτιδες and πρεσβύτεροι, and both διακόνισσαι and διάκονοι, in the clergy. Thus, here πρεσβύτιδες means neither "old women" nor "wives of presbyters," but "women presbyters." Indeed, the *Acts of Philip* presents Mariamme, the sister of the apostle Philip, as a better apostle than her brother.[134]

The Synod of Nîmes (394), Canon 2, attests that women were enrolled *in ministerium leviticum*, the priestly office. Epigraphical confirmations include a *Laeta praesbytera*, who in the fourth/fifth century was not the wife of any presbyter—her husband, the dedicator of her epitaph, was no presbyter—but a presbyter herself.[135] In the same period, near Poitiers in Gaul, a *Martia presbyteria* made or brought the oblations with Olybrius and Nepos "in the very same way" as they did (*pariter*).[136] This refers to the presbyteral ministry and the celebration of the Eucharist. Further iconographic and historical evidence along these lines has been brought to attention by Gary Macy, Mary Schäfer,[137] and the contributors to *Patterns of Women's Leadership*.

Theosebia, a sister of Basil and Nyssen, is also likely to have been a presbyter, as I have thoroughly argued.[138] She was highly praised by Nazianzen,[139] a friend of Basil, Nyssen, and their family. She was a presbyter, not in churches such as those of Montanists and other groups, who regularly ordained women presbyters, but in Cappadocia's "orthodox" church. She was not Gregory Nyssen's wife, as is often assumed, but his ordained colleague (σύζυγος)[140] in the ecclesiastical office. Nazianzen indeed describes Theosebia, among else, as "truly sacred and *truly colleague of a priest*, endowed with a *dignity equal to his*, and worthy of the celebration of the *great Mysteries*." Theosebia's ministry entailed participation in the celebration of the

Mass, supporting pious women, including the "choir of virgins" she presided over at Nyssa, and leading the Divine Office. She filled those women with confidence and pride, as Nazianzen states. He identifies the ministerial functions of a presbyter or bishop (ἱερεύς) with the celebration of the Mass and the care of souls[141]—the same functions as he attaches to Theosebia, the colleague and ὁμότιμος of a presbyter. Notably, ὁμότιμος was repeatedly used by both Nazianzen and Basil in reference to the equal dignity of male and female church ministers and of men and women in general,[142] by Nyssen in reference to the equal dignity of former master and slaves in the same house monastery (Macrina's),[143] and by Basil in reference to the same dignity of the three persons of the Trinity.[144]

Nyssen's attitude toward his ordained sister Theosebia and his consecrated sister Macrina seems to confirm his dependence on Origen's ideas on ecclesiology and women's ministry. Nyssen, unlike Nazianzen, does not mention Theosebia, who lived close to him and collaborated with him,[145] but extols Macrina, the consecrated virgin and leader of a house monastery, both in her bio-hagiography and in the dialogue *On the Soul and the Resurrection*, *De anima et resurrectione*. In the latter, Macrina is the main speaker, like Socrates in Plato's *Phaedo*—of which Gregory's dialogue is the Christian philosophical remake.[146] Just as Plato's *Phaedo* "may be considered the swan song of Socrates," not sorrowful but joyful in expectation of the blessed contemplation in the other world (*Phaed.* 85AB),[147] so is also *De anima* Macrina's joyful expectation of the other-worldly resurrection and restoration or apokatastasis. One reason for this difference between Nyssen's attitude toward Theosebia and Macrina is that Gregory venerated his eldest sister Macrina, who transmitted to him Christianity in the form of Origen's own thought, through Macrina the Elder and Gregory Thaumaturgus. The second reason is that Gregory was not interested in celebrating Theosebia's ecclesiastical rank. He preferred to represent, not Theosebia, but Macrina—albeit not ordained—as a presbyter,[148] invested with priesthood and its tasks: (1) the offering of the Eucharistic sacrifice in Macrina's bio-hagiography, as her self-sacrifice, and (2) the teaching of the Christian doctrine (*Origen*'s doctrine, including apokatastasis) in *Vita Macrinae* and *De anima*.

In Nyssen's view, as in Origen's, spiritual ministry is more important than officially ordained ministry. Nazianzen seems to have attached more eminence to ordained office; moreover, he knew Theosebia in Nyssa better than Macrina in her monastery. Nyssen, instead, venerated monastic ascetic ideals more, and distinguished ordained from lay people less, like Origen. Thus, at the beginning of Homily 3 *On the Lord's Prayer*, Nyssen, commenting on the law's rules for the high priest before he entered the Holy of Holies, remarks that Christ, the new Lawgiver, allows *every human to be a priest* by virtue of the mystical sacrifice of herself. This is in continuity with

Origen's ecclesiology and this is how Nyssen regarded Macrina and represented her in her biography. She and her fellow ascetics imitated the life of angels with their philosophical-ascetic life (the above-mentioned ἰσαγγελία). Thus they anticipated the life of the resurrection and the *telos,* which will be characterized—for Gregory just as for Origen—by apokatastasis, when all humans, through spiritual growth and purification, will return to angelic life.[149] The ministry of Macrina and her nuns, according to Nyssen, was not inferior to that of ordained ministers.[150] Macrina's self-offering, as a host, according to the Theology of the Cross, also derived from her suffering, illness, and death. Nyssen followed Origen in relativizing gender differences as a postlapsarian condition,[151] which were absent from God's initial plan, are absent in Christ, and will be absent from the eschatological scenario. The logical consequence is that they should not be taken into account in ecclesiastical ordination.

Origen influenced Gregory in the endorsement of women's ecclesiastical offices, in the twofold conception of earthly liturgy and ordained ministries and spiritual liturgy and ministries, as well as in the orientation of theology, anthropology, ethics, and ecclesiology to eschatology.[152] Indeed, for them the ideal, to be pursued already in this life by individuals and the church, is that of the *telos*. Then, gender differences and discriminations will vanish, along with all evil. The *telos* is normative for Origen and Gregory because it coincides with God's eternal plan for humanity, where there is no discrimination against women, just as there should be none "in Christ" (Gal 3:28) already on earth.[153] "In Christ" means "in the church," which is Christ's body, for both Gregory and Origen. And the body of Christ eschatologically extends to all humans or *logika*. In Paul's letter itself, the statement in Gal 3:28, according to some critics, applied not only to spiritual relationships, but also to social ones.[154]

THE ESCHATOLOGICAL RESURRECTION-RESTORATION OF CHRIST'S BODY, ALL HUMANITY AND ALL LOGIKA

The exemplaristic concept of Christ as subsuming all things through their *logoi*,[155] and more specifically all humans (because he has assumed humanity) and all rational creatures or *logika*, qua Logos, underlies Origen's glorious idea of Christ's resurrection as the resurrection of all humanity (i.e., of Christ's body, the church, composed by men and women) and the spiritual resurrection of all *logika*, which implies their salvation. For Christ's resurrection was not only that which occurred historically, but also the general, eschatological resurrection of humanity, which in turn will be both physical and spiritual. Humans, who are now "scattered" in death and perdition, will be brought to unity by, and in, Christ-Logos.

This theme is further connected by Origen with the motif of Jesus's action of gathering God's scattered children into one (ἕν),[156] which repeatedly occurs in his *Commentary on John*, where the theme of unity in Christ is pivotal, based on John 17:21. Origen claims that Christ's body—the Temple of living stones (λίθοι ζῶντες) erected upon the basement of prophets and apostles which represents the church[157]—will rise again when all humans will be resurrected. For Christ's resurrection from his death on the cross, which occurred in the past, encompasses "the mystery of the *resurrection of Christ's entire body*," that is, as mentioned, all humanity and all *logika*: the eschatological church.[158] Indeed, Christ's body has not yet risen in the final, hoped-for resurrection, a "grand and baffling mystery." Then, the bones of his body, scattered in hell, will gather together again: "At the resurrection of *Christ's true and most perfect body*, Christ's limbs and bones, now dry[159] . . . will be reassembled, up to the perfect human being."[160]

The eschatological rebuilding of Christ's body will depend on the unity of spirit—the human component that is in communication with God[161]—assured by *agapē*, when the church is glued together by love: "The unity of spirit is kept when love binds *together* those who are unified according to the spirit, and gathers them together into one and the same body, that of Christ" (*C.Eph.* fr.16.15). That the eventual unity is guaranteed by love is argued in detail in *C.Rom.* 5.10.195–226.[162] Origen refers this theme of the church as Christ's body and totality to 1 Cor 15:24–28: God "constituted Christ as the head over all beings, for *the church, which is his body, the perfect totality* of the One who perfectly accomplishes and completes all in all" (*C.Io.* 9.65ff.).

The eschatological reconstitution of Christ's body is thus related to the interpretation of 1 Cor 15:28 and Origen's typical equation between eventual universal submission to Christ—and through Christ to God—and universal salvation. Nyssen drew exactly on these ideas in *In Illud*.[163] Christ will have finished his "work" (John 17:4) only after making the last sinner righteous. If just one rational creature remains outside Christ's body and the submission to him, Christ will be unable to submit to God and complete his "work." This will be accomplished in the totality of the *logika*—Christ's body, the church—perfected by Christ; no one will remain outside. As a result, "God will be all in all" (*H.Lev.* 7.2.6). This can be only because Christ-Logos is the transcendent unity of all humans and all *logika* together, "all in One," as I have indicated, and his eventual submission to the Father is tantamount to the submission of all *logika*—all the church—to God. This will enable God, who is One and simply One, to be "in all," through Christ, and for each of these "all" to be "all," that is, all goods on Origen's interpretation. Now, this conception of God as the supreme *One* in whom *all* will be in the end, owes much to Christ-Logos's characterization as unity of all humans, men and women (qua human) and of all *logika* (qua Logos) and of all creatures (qua subsuming their Forms/Ideas/*logoi*): "All in One" and "One in All," as becomes the Middle Platonic Logos, a shown, but also Plotinus's Nous as one-many. Certainly the "body of Christ" is made by both men and women on earth, and humans transfigured in the end.

BY WAY OF CONCLUSION

The anthropology of Origen is based on their protological and eschatological view of the human being as rational creature (λογικόν). Now, the rational nature is common to men and women alike. Within this framework, the differentiation of humans into male and female arose as a result, or in prevision, of the fall, and will not endure in the ultimate end. This perspective is underpinned by the above-mentioned saying of Jesus that in the resurrection humans will be like angels and will take neither wives nor husbands,[164] as well as by Paul in Gal 3:28, which proclaims that there is neither man nor woman "in Christ." Now, the church must reflect Christ, since it is Christ's body. But Christ's body eschatologically extends to all humans or all rational creatures, and Christ's body does not include only men, but all humans and even all *logika*, as Origen insisted. What has been said of Jesus's mother Mary, "she represents the humanity that belongs to all human beings, both men and women,"[165] even more so should be said of Christ, who took up the whole of humanity, not one half of it, and qua divine transcends it, as Origen warned.

NOTES

1. The notion of similarity to angels, ἰσαγγελία, derives from Luke 20:36 (ἰσάγγελοι, of women and men in heaven, cf. Matt 22:30 and Mark 12:25), and was used already by Clement (*Strom.* 5.6.105.1) in the characterization of the perfect Christian, or "gnostic," and a great deal by Nyssen. The latter also applied it, modified, to the equality of dignity between humans and angels: "Prayer is . . . equality of dignity with the angels" (τῶν ἀγγέλων ὁμοτιμία, *Or.dom.* 1, SC 596.308.4); "Because of sin, we were thrown out from the equality of dignity with the angels" (ἀπὸ τῆς ἀγγελικῆς ὁμοτιμίας, *Hom.op.* 17, PG 44.189). But humans will be restored (ἀποκατάστασις) to a condition similar to angels (ὅμοιον ἐκείνοις), which also means "without marriage" (γάμου χωρίς, ibid.).

2. Sami Yli-Karjanmaa, *Reincarnation in Philo of Alexandria* (Atlanta: SBL, 2015), 216–48.

3. As I argued in "Origen," in *A History of Mind and Body in Late Antiquity*, ed. Anna Marmodoro (Cambridge: Cambridge University Press, 2018), 245–66.

4. Argument in my "Origen, Patristic Philosophy, and Christian Platonism: Re-Thinking the Christianisation of Hellenism," *Vigiliae Christianae* 63 (2009): 217–63; "Gregory of Nyssa on the Soul (and the Restoration): From Plato to Origen," in *Gregory of Nyssa: Historical and Philosophical Perspectives*, ed. Anna Marmodoro and Neil McLynn (Oxford: Oxford University Press, 2018), 110–41.

5. As I argued in "Gal 3:28 and Aristotelian (and Jewish) Categories of Inferiority," *Eirene* 55 (2019): 275–310.

6. My *Bardaiṣan of Edessa: A Reassessment of the Evidence and a New Interpretation. Also in the Light of Origen and the Original Fragments from Porphyry* (Piscataway, 2009; Berlin: DeGruyter, 2019); "Bardaisan of Edessa, Origen, and Imperial Philosophy: A Middle Platonic Context?," *Aram* 30, no. 1–2 (2018): 337–53.

7. See, e.g., R. Edwards, "Clement of Alexandria's 'Gnostic' Exposition of the Decalogue," *JECS* 23, no. 4 (2015): 501–28, esp. 505–06.

8. *Paed.* 1.43.2–4. See also Verna Harrison, "The Care-Banishing Breast of the Father: Feminine Images of the Divine in Clement of Alexandria's *Paedagogus* I," *StPatr* 31 (1997): 401–05.

9. See Sebastian Brock, "The Holy Spirit as Feminine," in *After Eve: Women, Theology, and the Christian Tradition*, ed. Janet Soskice (London: Collins, 1990), 73–88; Kathleen McVey, "Ephrem the Syrian's Use of Female Metaphors to Describe the Deity," *ZAC* 5, no. 2 (2001): 261–88; Judith Kovacs, "Becoming the Perfect Man: Clement on the Philosophical Life of Women," in *Women and Gender in Ancient Religions*, ed. S. Ahearne-Kroll (Tübingen: Mohr Siebeck, 2010), 289–413.

10. See Charles Gieschen, *Angelomorphic Christology: Antecedents and Early Evidence* (Waco: Baylor University, 2017).

11. See Susan Harvey, "Feminine Imagery for the Divine," *SVTQ* 37 (2004): 1–29; Sebastian Brock, "Come, Compassionate Mother, Come, Holy Spirit," *Aram* 3 (1991): 249–57; Susan Myers, "The Spirit as Mother in Early Syriac-Speaking Christianity," in *Women and Gender in Ancient Religions*, ed. James Kellhoffer et al. (Tübingen: Mohr Siebeck, 2010), 427–62.

12. Lautaro Roig Lanzillotta, "A Syriac Original for the Acts of Thomas?," in *Early Christian and Jewish Narrative: The Role of Religion in Shaping Narrative Forms*, ed. I. L. E. Ramelli and J. Perkins (Tübingen: Mohr Siebeck, 2015), 105–34.

13. Full analysis of this fragment in Ramelli, *Bardaisan of Edessa*.

14. See, e.g., the detailed analysis by M. Troiano, "Padre femenino: el Dios-Madre de los gnósticos," in *Gnose et manichéisme. Hommage à Jean-Daniel Dubois*, ed. A. van den Kerchove and Lucia Soares Santoprete (Turnhout: Brepols, 2016), 27–159; John Turner, "The Virgin That Became Male: Feminine Principles in Platonic and Gnostic Texts," in *Women and Knowledge in Early Christianity*, ed. Ulla Tervahauta et al. (Leiden: Brill, 2017), 291–324, who, after accurate analysis, finds that "those behind the first traces of the so-called Barbeloite speculation display the highest estimation of the feminine principle" (323).

15. On whom see now Edward Watts, *Hypatia: The Life and Legend of an Ancient Philosopher* (New York: Oxford University Press, 2017).

16. See my "Paul on Apokatastasis: 1 Cor 15:24–28 and the Use of Scripture," in *Paul and Scripture*, ed. Stanley Porter and Christopher Land (Leiden: Brill, 2019), 212–32.

17. On the education of women in imperial times see Emily Hemelrijk, "The Education of Women in Ancient Rome," in *A Companion to Ancient Education*, ed. Martin Bloomer (Oxford: Wiley-Blackwell, 2015), 292–304; on Socrates: Benjamin McCloskey, "On Xenophontic Friendship," *TAPA* 149 (2019): 261–86.

18. Kathleen Wider, "Women Philosophers in the Ancient Greek World: Donning the Mantle," *Hypatia* 1, no. 1 (1986): 21–62, esp. on women Pythagoreans, Epicureans, and Hypatia; Sarah Pomeroy, *Pythagorean Women: Their History and Writings* (Baltimore: Johns Hopkins University 2015); Dorota Dutsch, *Pythagorean Women Philosophers* (Oxford: Oxford University Press, 2020).

19. See Blossom Stefaniw, "Shame and the Normal in Epiphanius' Polemic against Origen," *JECS* 21 (2013): 413–35. Panayiotis Tzamalikos, *Anaxagoras, Origen, and Neoplatonism* (Berlin: de Gruyter, 2016), 5 surmises that Origen died at 80; Eusebius maintained he died at 69 "to conceal events that Epiphanius did non care to suppress," although Epiphanius was no less biased (see my *The Christian Doctrine of Apokatastasis: A Critical Assessment from the New Testament to Eriugena* [Leiden: Brill, 2013], 578–84) and mentions events back still in Alexandria.

20. "Conducting Dialectical Argument in Origen," in *The Intellectual Foundation of Christian and Jewish Discourse*, ed. James Kellhoffer et al. (New York: Routledge, 1997), 70–86: 76.

21. *The Body and Society* (New York: Columbia, 1988), 158–59; *Preaching Bondage* (Oakland: University of California, 2015), 258.

22. *A Threat to Public Piety: Christian, Platonists, and the Great Persecution* (Ithaca: Cornell, 2012), 54.

23. Markschies, *Origenes und sein Erbe* (Berlin: de Gruyter, 2007), 15–34; John Behr, Origen: First Principles (Oxford: OUP, 2017), xvii; Rowan Williams, "Origen," in The First Christian Theologians, ed. G.R. Evans, Oxford: Blackwell, 2004), 132–142: 33: 133: "its historicity is highly suspect."

24. *Social Justice and the Legitimacy of Slavery: The Role of Philosophical Asceticism from Ancient Judaism to Late Antiquity* (Oxford: Oxford University Press, 2016), Introduction; ch.1.

25. Richard Gordon, 'Mysteries', *OCD* March 2016, doi:10.1093/acrefore/9780 199381135.013.4318.

26. On the slow process of Christianization of Egypt, see at least David Frankfurter, *Christianizing Egypt: Syncretism and Local Worlds in Late Antiquity* (Princeton: Princeton University, 2017), with special attention to "lived religion."

27. Addresses to Horus's four sons are found, e.g., in the ritual described in P. Princeton Pharaonic Roll 10 (Ptolemaic period), ed. Sandrine Vuilleumier, *Un rituel osirien en faveur de particuliers à l'époque ptolémaïque* (Wiesbaden: Harrassowitz, 2016).

28. Mariusz Szram, "Origen's Castration. Solely a Spiritual Phenomenon?" *Gregorianum* 101 (2020): 23–36.

29. On singleness in the Roman world, see: *The Single Life in the Roman and Later Roman World*, ed. Sabine Huebner and Christian Laes (Cambridge: Cambridge

University Press, 2019), esp. Part IV on late antique Christianity, but later than Origen's day, esp. Raffaela Cribiore, "Different Ways of Life: Being Single in the Fourth Century CE," ch. 12; Ville Vuolanto, "Single life in Late Antiquity? Virgins Between the Earthly and the Heavenly Family," ch.13; Geoffrey Nathan, "Being a Bachelor in Late Antiquity—Desire and Social Norms in the Experience of Augustine," ch. 14.

30. *Omnes qui secundum euangelii leges semet ipsos castrauerunt propter regnum Dei, habentes exempli huius auctorem cum multos alios sanctorum tum etiam ipsum Dominum Iesum:* C.Rom. 2.9, 173 Bammel.

31. *C.Matt.* 17.33.26–58 GCS Origenes 10.2.688–89.

32. *Fr. ICor.* 33.47–49.

33. *C.Matth.* 14.23–25, PG 13.1244–50.

34. *C.Matth.* 14.24, PG 13.1245.

35. *C.Matt.* 14.25, PG 13.1250.

36. See Andrei Timotin, *La prière dans la tradition platonicienne, de Platon à Proclus* (Turnhout: Brepols, 2017), and my review BMCR 17 April 2020, https://bmcr.brynmawr.edu/2020/2020.04.32/

37. The superiority of virginity over marriage was still proclaimed at the Council of Trent, DS 1810, but not at Vatican II in the Constitution, *Gaudium et Spes.*

38. *Cels.* 1.28–33; *C.Io.* 20.16.

39. *C.Io.* 6.49; *H.Luc.* 1.3.

40. *H.Luc.* 6.7; *H.Jer.* 5.13.

41. *C.Matt.* 10.17; cf. *H.Luc.* 7.4.

42. P.Rosicr.Mag.Copt.: see Lincoln Blumell and Korshi Dosoo, "A Coptic Magical Text for Virginity in Marriage: A Witness to 'Celibate Marriage' from Christian Egypt," *HTR* 114 (2021): 118–42. On Mary's virginity before and after Jesus's birth, see Julia Kelto Lillis, "No Hymen Required: Reconstructing Origen's View on Mary's Virginity," *Church History* 89 (2020): 249–67.

43. Ed. Laura Ciccolini, *Cypriani De habitu virginum* (Turnhout: Brepols, 2016).

44. He identified the female pole as passivity and sense-perception vs. male as activity and intellection, e.g. in *Leg.All.* 2.23–24, *Opif.* 165, and *De Deo* or *De visione trium angelorum ad Abraham* 3, but he also portrays women, especially virgins, such as the Therapeutrides, very positively, capable of philosophy and the vision of God, in *De vita contemplativa*; *QG* 1.8, and *Cher.* 50. See my "Philosophical Allegoresis of Scripture in Philo and Its Legacy," *Studia Philonica Annual* 20 (2008): 55–99 and Friederike Oertelt, "Gender, Religion und Politik bei Philon von Alexandria," in *Doing Gender, Doing Religion: Case Studies on Intersectionality in Early Judaism, Christianity and Islam*, ed. Ute Eisen and Angela Standhartinger (Tübingen: Mohr Siebeck, 2013), 227–50; Kathy Ehrensperger and Shayna Sheinfeld (eds.), *Gender and Second-Temple Judaism* (Lanham: Lexington/Fortress Academic, 2020).

45. *Hom. Ex.* 2.2–3; cf. *Hom. Gen.* 4.4; 5.2. Philo also allegorized Adam as earth, though. See Sami Yli-Karjanmaa, "Call Him Earth: On Philo's Allegorisation of Adam in *Legum Allegoriae*," in *The Adam and Eve Story in the Hebrew Bible and in Ancient Jewish Writings*, ed. Antti Laato and Lotta Valve (Turku: SRHB, 2016), 253–93.

46. Examined in my "Transformations of the Household and Marriage Theory Between Neo-Stoicism, Middle Platonism, and Early Christianity," *RFN* 100 (2008): 369–96; "Hiéroclès: extraits du traité Sur le mariage de Stobée," in *L'éthique du stoïcien Hiéroclès*, ed. Jean-Baptiste Gourinat (Lille: Presses Universitaires du Septentrion, 2016), 157–67.

47. Ilaria L. E. Ramelli, "Conceptualities of Angels in Late Antiquity: Degrees of Corporeality, Bodies of Angels, and Comparative Angelologies/Daemonologies in 'Pagan' and Christian Platonism," in *Inventer les anges de l'Antiquité à Byzance: conception, représentation, perception*, ed. Delphine Lauritzen (Paris: CNRS–Centre d'Histoire et Civilisation de Byzance, 2021), 115–72.

48. See my *Apokatastasis*, 152–55.

49. *C.Rom.* 5.9; *H.Luc.* 14.3: 149; *H.Lev.* 8.3; *C.Matth.* 15.23.

50. *Fr.Ps.* 21; *H.Is.* 3.2.

51. *Ab ira ventura etiam si fides nostra nos salvet, etiam si opera iustitiae, super haec tamen amnia multo magis sanguis Christi salvos nos faciet* (*C.Rom.* 4.11.73–75).

52. *H.Luc.* 38; *H.Ios.* 10.1; *H.Is.* 3.2; 5.2; *H.Num.* 20.1; *H.Ios.N.* 10.11; *C.Matth.* 12.23.

53. Ταχυγράφοι γὰρ αὐτῷ πλείους ἢ ἑπτὰ τὸν ἀριθμὸν παρῆσαν ὑπαγορεύοντα χρόνοις τεταγμένοις ἀλλήλους ἀμείβοντες, βιβλιογράφοι τε οὐχ ἥττους, ἅμα καὶ κόραις ἐπὶ τὸ καλλιγραφεῖν ἠσκημέναις, Eusebius *HE* 6.23.1–2 (PG 20.257; GCS 2.2.568–69).

54. In her intervention after my 2021 Enoch–Nangeroni lecture. I thank her very much.

55. *Apostolica auctoritate docet etiam feminas in ministerio ecclesiae constitui . . . et tales deberi assumi* (*C.Rom.* 10.17).

56. James Dunn, *Romans 9–16* (Dallas: Word Books, 1988), 886–87. On *diakonia* in Origen see my "Diakonia in Origen: From Christ and the Angels to Men and Women," in *Deacons and Diakonia in Christianity from the Third to the Sixth Century*, Bart Koet, Edwina Murphy, and Esko Ryökas, (WUNT I, Tübingen: Mohr Siebeck, 2024), 11–30.

57. *"Commendo autem uobis Foeben sororem uestram, quae est in ministerio ecclesiae quae est Cenchris, ut eam suscipiatis in Domino digne sanctis et adsistatis ei in quibuscumque indiguerit uestri. Nam ipsa quoque adstitit multis et mihi ipsi." Et hic locus apostolica auctoritate docet etiam feminas in ministerio Ecclesiae constitui. In quo officio positam Foeben apud ecclesiam quae est Cenchris Paulus magna cum laude et commendatione prosequitur, enumerans etiam gesta ipsius praeclara . . . Et ideo locus hic duo pariter docet: et haberi, ut diximus, feminas ministras in Ecclesia, et tales deberi assumi in ministerium quae adstiterint multis et per bona officia usque ad apostolicam laudem meruerint peruenire. Hortatur etiam illud ut hi qui bonis operibus in ecclesiis dant operam uicem recipiant a fratribus et honorem, ut in quibuscumque necessarium fuerit siue spiritalibus siue etiam carnalibus officiis honorifice habeantur* (*C.Rom.* 10.17). See also my 'Theosebia'.

58. *C.Rom.* 8.9: *Exornat autem et inlustrat ministerium qui bene ministrat . . . in ministerio Ecclesiae <u>diaconus qui bene ministraverit</u> bonum gradum sibi acquirit . . . Similiter autem et si qui presbyterii gradus suscepit in Ecclesia satis agat <u>inlustrare</u>

<u>ministerium presbyterii</u> . . . *et* <u>episcopus inlustrat ministerium suum</u> *in episcopato si sit secundum quod describit apostolus . . . qui talis est* <u>inlustrat ministerium episcopatus</u> . . . *et vidua si permanet in orationibus et obsecrationibus nocte ac die inlustrat* <u>ministerium viduitatis suae</u>. *Si vero sit talis quales apostolus notat, otiosa et verbosa et non solum verbosa sed et curiosa, loquens quae non oportet, aut sit in deliciis degens et vivens mortua, haec dehonoravit et non inlustravit* <u>ministerium viduitatis suae</u>. *Eodem modo etiam virgo consecrata Deo inlustrat* <u>ministerium virginitatis suae</u> *si sit sancta corpore et spiritu et non cogitet quae hominum sunt sed quae Dei quomodo placet Deo. Si vero aliter agat . . . non inlustrat* <u>ministerium virginitatis suae</u>.

59. *H.Luc.* 17.10: *neque enim episcopus nec presbyter nec diaconus nec vidua possunt esse digami.*

60. *De myrophorois, ap.* Photius, *Bibl.* Cod. 275.

61. Karen King, *The Gospel of Mary of Magdala: Jesus and the First Woman Apostle* (Santa Rosa: Polebridge, 2003); Sarah Parkhouse, *Eschatology and the Saviour: The 'Gospel of Mary' among Early Christian Dialogue Gospels* (Cambridge: Cambridge University Press, 2019).

62. Αἱ μᾶλλον θεωροῦσαι καὶ διακονοῦσαι καὶ κρεῖττον ἀκολουθοῦσαι· ἡ ἀπὸ τοῦ μεγαλυσμοῦ Μαρία· Μάγδαλα γὰρ ΜΕΓΑΛΥΣΜΟΣ ἑρμηνεύεται, *Comm.Matth. Ser.* on Matt 22:34–27:63, 293.33–294.1.

63. *Comm.Matth.Ser.* 141.

64. On *migdol*: Nicholas De Lange, *Origen and the Jews* (Cambridge: Cambridge University Press, 1976), 120–21. Against the meaning of Magdala as toponymic: Maria-Luisa Rigato, "Maria la Maddalena: ancora riflessioni su colei che fu chiamata la Resa-grande," *Studia Patavina* 50 (2003): 727–52; Eadem, *Discepole di Gesù* (Bologna: Dehoniane, 2011), and my review *Exemplaria Classica* 16 (2012): 309–12; Elizabeth Schrader and Joan Taylor, "The Meaning of Magdalene: A Review of Literary Evidence," *JBL* 140, no. 4 (2021): 751–73.

65. *H.Iud.* 5.2: *Cum plurimi iudices viri in Istrahel fuisse referantur, de nullo illorum dicitur quia propheta fuerit nisi de Debbora muliere. Praestat et in hoc consolationem non minimam mulierum sexui . . . nequaquam pro infirmitate sexus desperent etiam prophetiae gratiae capaces se fieri possent, sed intelligant et credant quod meretur hanc gratiam* <u>puritas mentis, non diversitas sexus</u>. On prophecy see my "Prophecy in Origen: Between Scripture and Philosophy," *Journal of Early Christian History* 7, no. 2 (2017): 17–39.

66. *H.Luc.* 17.6: *et iuste sancta mulier spiritum prophetandi meruit accipere, quia longa castitate longisque ieiuniis ad hoc culmen adscenderat.*

67. *Cat. in Cor.* A74. Several scholars have hypothesised that 1Cor 14:33b, and 34–35, is an interpolation of a Pauline editor. See my "Theosebia" and "Syzygoi" and Aļesja Lavrinoviča, "The Syntactic Flexibility of 1 Corinthians 14:33b," *Journal of Biblical Literature* 141 (2022): 157–75.

68. Instead of: ἐν καταστήματι ἱεροπρεπεῖς. The variant known to Origen is attested by many manuscripts and ancient authors such as Clement of Alexandria—who used the same text as Origen did—and Basil in Cappadocia, and the Syriac translations: the Peshitta, the Palestinian, and the Harklean version.

69. Seneca regards as a "most perfect woman" (*perfecthssima femina*) his aunt, who, when her husband was the governor of Egypt, spent sixteen years there without "ever being seen in public," without "granting access to her home to any local person," and "always escaping the notice" of that province (*Cons.Helv.* 19.4–6).

70. Χειροτονία ἐν γυναιξὶν πρεσβυτέρων (*C.Tit.* 2.3a).

71. See Ramelli, *Apokatastasis*, section on Theodore and Diodore of Tarsus.

72. Adela Yarbro Collins, "The Female Body as Social Space in 1 Timothy," *NTS* 57 (2011): 155–75; my "The Pastoral Epistles and Hellenistic Philosophy: 1 Tim 5:1–2, Hierocles, and the Contraction of Circles," *CBQ* 73 (2011): 562–81; Dillon T. Thornton, *Hostility in the House of God: An Investigation of the Opponents in 1 and 2 Timothy* (Winona Lake: Eisenbrauns, 2016); Fergus J. King and Dorothy A. Lee, "Lost in Translation: Rethinking Words About Women in 1–2 Timothy," *Scottish Journal of Theology* 74 (2021): 52–66; Harry Maier, "The Entrepreneurial Widows of 1 Timothy," in *Patterns of Women Leadership and Authority in Ancient Christianity and Judaism*, ed. Joan Taylor and Ilaria Ramelli (Oxford: Oxford University Press, 2021), 59–73.

73. *The Pastoral Epistles* (Collegeville: Liturgical Press, 2007), esp. 71–9.

74. She does not deem these verses interpolated, unlike other scholars such as Jerome Murphy-O'Connor, Cettina Militello, and Maria-Luisa Rigato, *Paolo e le donne* (Assisi: Cittadella, 2006), 9–57; Eldon Jay Epp, *Junia: The First Woman Apostle* (Minneapolis: Fortress, 2005), 14–20; Pauline Nigh Hogan, "Paul and Seneca on Women," in *Paul and Seneca in Dialogue*, ed. Joseph Dodson and David Briones (Leiden: Brill, 2017), 208–31: 226. Yet others put these verses between quotation marks, as representing the ideas of Paul's interlocutors.

75. Schüssler Fiorenza, *In Memory of Her* (New York: Crossroads, 1992), 233, 266 and *passim*.

76. On *oikeiōsis* and *kathēkonta*: my "The Stoic Doctrine of Oikeiosis and its Transformation in Christian Platonism," *Apeiron* 47 (2014): 116–40 and "Ierocle Neostoico in Stobeo: I καθήκοντα e l'evoluzione dell'etica stoica," in *Thinking Through Excerpts: Studies on Stobaeus*, ed. Gretchen Reydams-Schils (Turnhout: Brepols, 2011), 537–75; on the "contraction of circles": "The Pastoral Epistles and Hellenistic Philosophy."

77. See my *Social Justice*, ch. 1; David Wheeler-Reed, *Regulating Sex in the Roman Empire: Ideology, the Bible, and the Early Christians* (New Haven: Yale University Press, 2017), 66–68; *Patterns of Women's Leadership*. On a history of virginity as value from the ancient to the Patristic world, see Sissel Undheim, *Borderline Virginities: Sacred and Secular Virginities in Late Antiquity* (London: Routledge, 2018): While *virgo*/παρθένος was also used for men (since Justin, I would say), female virgins were the majority and were sometimes seen with suspicion for fear that they presumed to overcome sexual boundaries and the traditional inferiority of women (Undheim, *Virginities*, 127;133). Indeed, there are examples of patristic thinkers who stressed that virgins still remained in their "inferior" status of women (see *More Than Female Disciples: Women Leaders and Teachers. A Background of their Authority in Ancient Christianity*, ed. Anelyia Barnes and Roberta Franchi, forthcoming in Turnhout: Brepols).

78. See above and *H.Luc.* 17.10: he recommends that widows remain widows (*vidua perseveret*). He complains that "now in the Church we can find second, third,

and fourth marriages, let alone more, and we know all too well that such marriages will throw us out of the Kingdom of God" (*nunc vero et secundae et tertiae et quartae nuptiae, ut de pluribus taceam, in ecclesia reperiantur, et non ignoramus quod tale coniugium eiciet nos de regno Dei*: ibid.).

79. *C.Rom.* 4.6.160; *H.Ier.* 4.5; *Fr.Luc.*32 Rauer.

80. This point will be taken over by Eckhart and is reflected in Origen's definition of the Gospel as "preparation for Christ's coming [παρουσίαν] and effecting [ἐμποιοῦντα] it in the souls of those who are willing to receive God's Logos" (*C.Io.* 1.26; cf. 13.392).

81. *Leg.* 3.3 and 243; *QE* 1.8.

82. *H.Ex.* 2.2–3 cf. *H.Gen.* 4.4; 5.2.

83. On Luther's and others' attempts to transform her into a man because of her apostolic identity, see Epp, *Junia*, and my review in *Rivista Biblica* 55, no. 2 (2007): 245–49. See also Bruce Winter, *Roman Wives, Roman Widows: The Appearance of New Women and the Pauline Communities* (Grand Rapids: Eerdmans, 2003), 200–04.

84. On how Samaritans were perceived in early Christianity: Reinhard Pummer, *Early Christian Authors on Samaritans and Samaritanism* (Tübingen: Mohr Siebeck, 2002).

85. "Origen's hostess appears to have had a church that met in her home" (*Origen: An Introduction to His Life and Thought* [Eugene: Wipf and Stock, 2019], 25).

86. On other criticisms of Montanism, see William Tabbernee, *Fake Prophecy and Polluted Sacraments: Ecclesiastical and Imperial Reactions to Montanism* (VCS 84, Leiden: Brill, 2007). Origen's passage should probably be included in these criticisms.

87. Women were also admitted into their hierarchy, and they assumed clerical functions, as bishops and priests (see Epiphanius *Haer.* 49.2) and deacons (see Ambrosiaster *Comm.1 Tim.* 3.11). See also Christine Trevett, *Montanism: Gender, Authority and the New Prophecy* (Cambridge: Cambridge University Press, 1996), esp. 185–86 on Montanist women in clergy; Josef Lössl, "A Clash Between Paideia and Pneuma? Ecstatic Women Prophets and Theological Education in the Second-century Church," *SCH* 57 (2021): 32–53; William Tabbernee, "Women Officeholders in Montanism," in *Patterns of Women's Leadership*. On their prophecies inspired by the Spirit, see my "Prophecy"; Vera-Elisabeth Hirschmann, *Horrenda Secta: Untersuchungen zum frühchristlichen Montanismus und seinen Verbindungen zur paganen Religion Phrygiens* (Stuttgart: Steiner, 2005); Christoph Markschies, "Montanismus," *RAC* 26 (2012): 1197–220. They left a collection of sayings and prophetical revelations attributed to Montanus (see Epiphanius *Haer.* 48.11.1; 48.11.9; 48.4.1; 48.10.3), Maximilla (Eusebius *HE* 5.16.17; Epiphanius *Haer.* 48.10.3; 48.12.4; 48.13.1) and Prisca (see Tertullian *Res.* 11.2) or Quintilla or Priscilla (Epiphanius *Haer.* 49.1.1–3), or an anonymous follower of Montanus (Tertullian *Pud.* 21.7; *Fug.* 9.4). They claimed that they alone possessed the Holy Spirit (Firmilian *ap.* Cyprian *Ep.* 75.7), and named "psychic" those who rejected their prophecies (Clement *Strom.* 4.93.1).

88. See *Virg. vel.* 9.1; *Pr. haer.* 41.5; *Bapt.* 17.4.

89. Schenk, *Crispina and Her Sisters: Women and Authority in Early Christianity* (Minneapolis: Fortress, 2017).

90. Kateusz, *Mary and Early Christian Women: Hidden Leadership* (New York: Palgrave Macmillan, 2019).

91. In a letter to Cyprian of Carthage (*Ep.* 75). On ecclesiology in Cyprian and his time: Benjamin Safranski, *St. Cyprian of Carthage and the College of Bishops* (Lanham: Lexington, 2018).

92. Interestingly, a Zayton relief represents a bishop and a female leader of consecrated women as equal in rank, specular, and with identical characteristics, the same head covering, the same pectoral cross, the same stole. See Pierre Perrier, *L'apôtre Thomas et le prince Ying* (Paris: Jubilé, 2012), 82.

93. See, e.g., my "Diakonia, Diakonos," in *Encyclopedia of Ancient Christianity*, ed. Angelo Di Berardino (Downers Grove: InterVarsity 2014), 1: 703–04.

94. Pliny, *Ep.*10.96[97].7, to Trajan; Apuleius, *Met.*9.14–15. See my *I romanzi antichi e il Cristianesimo: contesto e contatti*, pref. Brian Reardon (new edition Eugene: Cascade, 2012), Ch. 9; further proofs in Eadem, "Apuleius and Christianity: The Novelist-Philosopher in Front of a New Religion," in *Intende, Lector—Echoes of Myth, Religion and Ritual in the Ancient Novel*, ed. Marília Futre Pinheiro, Anton Bierl, and Roger Beck (Berlin: de Gruyter, 2013), 145–73.

95. For the latter see my "Mansuetudine, grazia e salvezza negli *Acta Philippi* (ed. Bovon)," *InvLuc* 29 (2007): 215–28; "Colleagues of Apostles, Presbyters, and Bishops: Women *Syzygoi* in Ancient Christianities," in *Patterns of Women's Ministry*, 26–58. On animals in the Acts of Philip, see Patricia Cox Miller, *In the Eye of the Animal: Zoological Imagination in Early* Christianity (Philadelphia: University of Pennsylvania, 2018), esp. 79–93. On Thecla, literature is growing; see, e.g., Kate Cooper, *Band of Angels: The Forgotten World of Early Christian Women* (London: Atlantic, 2013), 92–94; Rosie Ratcliffe, "The Acts of Paul and Thecla: Violating the Inviolate Body—Thecla Uncut," in *The Body in Biblical, Christian and Jewish Texts*, ed. Joan Taylor (London: T&T Clark, 2014), 184–209.

96. Codex Baroccianus, reflecting a longer conclusion from the fourth or fifth century, ending with Thecla's martyrdom.

97. On which see, inter alia, Rosie Andrious, *Saint Thecla: Body Politics and Masculine Rhetoric* (London: T&T Clark, 2020), on the Acts of Paul and Thecla and Thecla as the image of the persecuted but triumphant church.

98. See my "The Life of Macrina," in *Stories of erotic love and desire in late antique and early medieval hagiography, ERC project Novel Saints. Ancient Novelistic Heroism in Late Antique and Early Medieval Hagiography* (Gent University): https://dev.novelsaints.ugent.be/node/1045/; "The Life of Macrina and the Life of Evagrius," forthcoming; "Gregory of Nyssa on the Soul (and the Restoration)."

99. *Civitas confusionis*, ch. 3, 244–52; I studies examples of this involvement in "Theosebia: A Presbyter of the Catholic Church," *JFSR* 26, no. 2 (2010): 79–102; "Teosebia *in ministerio Ecclesiae*," in *Diakonia, Diaconiae, Diaconato. Semantica e storia nei Padri della Chiesa*, International Conference, Rome, Augustinianum, 7–9 May 2009, ed. Vittorino Grossi (Rome: Augustinianum, 2010), 217–31; "I 'cori' di consacrate e Gregorio di Nissa: il canto liturgico riflesso e anticipazione dell'armonia escatologica," in *Ascoltare gli Dèi / Divos Audire: Costruzione e Percezione della*

Dimensione Sonora nelle Religioni del Mediterraneo Antico, 2, ed. Igor Baglioni (Rome: Quasar, 2015), 207–18.

100. Early Christian claimed that Christian virginity was a free choice, as opposed to the Vestals' virginity; however, Undheim, *Virginities*, shows that often Christian virgins were socially constrained (but not always: see, e.g., Virginia Burrus, *Chastity as Autonomy* [Lewiston: Mellen, 1987]). On the Vestals see Meghan DiLuzio, *A Place at the Altar: Priestesses in Republican Rome* (Princeton: Princeton University Press, 2016).

101. Morgan Palmer, "Time and Eternity: The Vestal Virgins and the Crisis of the Third Century," *TAPA* 150 (2020): 473–97.

102. *H.Lev.* 24.1; 13.5.

103. *Cels.* 8.33; cf. 8.57: the bread as a symbol of thanksgiving to God.

104. *Pasch.* 26.5–8; 33.20–32; Ilaria Ramelli, "Origen and the Stoic Allegorical Tradition," *InvLuc* 28 (2006): 195–226.

105. *H.Lev.* 9.7; *H.Ier.* 4.6.18; *H.Num.* 27.1; *H.Gen.* 10.3.

106. *Myst.*1.2; my "Mysterium come *ratio sacramentorum* in Ambrogio," in *Contributi su Mysterion e Sacramentum nei primi secoli cristiani*, ed. Angela Mazzanti (Castel Bolognese: Itaca, 2003), 105–16.

107. *Soli sunt qui intelligent Deum et capaces sint scientiae Dei* (*H.Lev.* 1.5).

108. *Sola carnis continentia ad altare dominicum non potest perveniri, si reliquis virtutibus et sacerdotalibus ministeriis deseratur.*

109. *Hom. Lev.* 1.5.

110. *H.Lev.* 2.1; 6.3.

111. *H.Iud.* 3.2: *morbus iste superbiae penetrat non solum pauperes plebis, verum etiam ipsum sacerdotalem et leviticum ordinem . . . qui ad exemplum humilitatis positi sumus . . . arrogantiae vitium fetet . . . odor taeterrimus superbiae et elationis . . .*

112. See my "Life of Macrina" and "Theosebia."

113. On the development of offices and officeholders in early Christianity see, e.g., Mark Edwards, "The Development of Office in the Early Church," in *The Early Christian World*, ed. Philip Esler, 2nd ed. (London: Routledge, 2017), Ch. 13; *Patterns of Women's Leadership*. On crypto-Christianity in the highest social ranks still in the early time of Origen, see my "Cristiani e vita politica: il cripto-Cristianesimo nelle classi dirigenti romane nel II secolo," *Aevum* 77, no. 1 (2003): 35–51; Emiliano Urciuoli, *Servire due padroni: Una genealogia dell'uomo politico cristiano (50–313)* (Brescia: Morcelliana, 2018), Part 2.

114. See Janet Sidaway, *The Human Factor: "Deification" as Transformation in the Theology of Hilary* (Louvain: Peeters, 2016); Isabella Image, *The Human Condition in Hilary of Poitiers: The Will and Original Sin between Origen and Augustine* (Oxford: Oxford University Press, 2018); my review in *Reading Religion* 2018: http://readingreligion.org/books/human-condition-hilary-poitiers.

115. *AI* 3.151–80;184–87; Joabson Xavier Pena, "Wearing the Cosmos: The High Priestly Attire in Josephus' *Judean Antiquities*," *JSJ* 52 (2021): 1–29; Origen, *H.Lev.* 6.5.2; *H.Ex.* 9.4.

116. *H.Lev.* 6.6.1. On Origen's view about all believers' priesthood see also Theo Hermans, *Origène et la théologie sacrificielle du sacerdoce des chrétiens* (Paris: Beauchesne, 1996).

117. *C.Matth.* 16.20–23; *C.Matth.S.* 12; cf. *H.Num.* 3.3.

118. See my "Autobiographical Self-Fashioning in Origen," invited chapter in *Self, Self-Fashioning and Individuality in Late Antiquity: New Perspectives*, ed. Maren Niehoff and Joshua Levinson (Tübingen: Mohr Siebeck, 2019), 273–92.

119. See my introduction: "Successioni di filosofi," in *Diogene Laerzio*, ed. Giovanni Reale and Eadem (Milan: Bompiani, 2005), XXXIII-CXXXVIII; André Laks, in Miller-Mensch, *Diogenes*, 593: "Diogenes' continuity boils down to institutional succession: from a conceptual point of view, there is no discernible system at all"; for a comparison between Diogenes and Philodemus' Σύνταξις τῶν φιλοσόφων (probably including the *Index Academicorum*), both based on the institutional successions of philosophers (διαδοχαί), see Kilian Fleischer, "Structuring the 'History of Philosophy': A Comparison Between Philodemus and Diogenes Laertius in the Light of New Evidence," *CQ* 69, no. 2 (2020): 684–99, who deems it improbable that Diogenes was inspired by Philodemus for his succession-scheme.

120. And even the Montanists, called "Cataphrygians" (Jerome *VI* 40; Augustine *Haer.* 26) or "Phrygians" (e.g. Clem. *Strom.* 4.93.1; Epiph. *Haer.* 48.1.1; 48.1.3; 49.1), or "Pepuzenes" (Basil *Ep.* 188.1) and self-proclaimed "new prophecy" (Clement *Strom.* 4.93.1; Eusebius *HE.* 5.16.4; Tertullian *Marc.* 3.24.4; 4.22.4, etc.). But these seem to have rejected the earthly ecclesiastical institution more strongly. Probably they did so because they expected the new Jerusalem to descend upon earth soon (Epiphanius *Pan.* 48.14.1–2; 49.1). See my "Κατὰ ψιλὴν παράταξιν: Montanismo e Impero Romano nel giudizio di Marco Aurelio," in *Fazioni e congiure nel mondo antico*, ed. Marta Sordi (Milan: Vita e Pensiero, 1999), CISA 25, 81–97; "Tracce di Montanismo nel *Peregrinus* di Luciano?" *Aevum* 79 (2005): 79–94; "Lucian, Celsus, Origen and Montanism," in *"Montanism" in the Roman World: The New Prophecy Movement in Historical, Sociological, and Ecclesiological Context. FS William Tabbernee*, ed. Peter Lampe (Leiden: Brill, 2024).

121. On this see Fred Ledegang, "Origen's View of the Apostolic Tradition," in *The Apostolic Age in Patristic Thought*, ed. Anton Hilhorst (Leiden: Brill, 2004), 130–38; *Mysterium Ecclesiae. Images of the Church and its Members in Origen* (Leuven: Peeters, 2001).

122. See my "The Reception of Paul's Nous in the Christian Platonism of Origen and Evagrius," in *Der νοῦς bei Paulus im Horizont griechischer und hellenistisch-jüdischer Anthropologie*, ed. Jörg Frey and Manuel Nägele (WUNT I 464, Tübingen: Mohr Siebeck, 2021), 279–316.

123. Plotinus distinguished the inner human, the intellect, from the outer (*Enn.* 1.1.10.5–15) and criticized Aristotle's definition of a human as rational animal because "animal" is a compound of body and soul (*Enn.* 6.7.4.10–8), which in Plotinus' view only designates the "outer human." In Philo, the inner and outer human represent the two (non-chronological) phases of the "double creation," the first human created in God's image, intellectual and non-gendered, the second molded from the earth, fleshly and gendered (see my "Creation, Double," in *Brill Encyclopedia of Early Christianity*, ed. Paul van Geest et al. (Leiden: Brill, 2018), http://dx.doi.org/10.1163/2589-7993_EECO_SIM_00000793). Origen took this distinction over, e.g. *C.Cant.* prol. 2.4: *In principio verborum Moysei, ubi de mundi conditione conscribitur, duos*

invenimus homines creatos referri, primum ad imaginem et similitudinem Dei factum, secundum e limo terrae fictum; *Cels.* 6.63: the human "in God's image" is the inner human; *Princ.* 1.1.9. Clement had adopted Philo's idea, stating that "the true human," the *nous*, is the one created in God's image and likeness, while the earthly, visible human is the material one (*Protr.* 10.98.4). Basil, relying on Origen, stated: "We are intellectual souls, in which we are in the Creator's image" (*Observe Yourself* 26.17–18). See also Christoph Markschies, "Die platonische Metapher vom 'inneren Menschen,'" *ZKG* 105 (1994): 1–17; George van Kooten, *Paul's Anthropology in Context* (Tübingen: Mohr Siebeck, 2008), 358–74; Karl-Wilhelm Niebuhr, "Jakobus und Paulus über das Innere des Menschen," *NTS* 62 (2016): 1–30: 22–30, esp. on Romans 6–8.

124. The absolute novelty of Augustine in this respect is questionable. See Philippe Cary, *Augustine's Invention of the Inner Self* (Oxford: Oxford University Press, 2000).

125. For the philosophical antecedents and patristic aftermath, see Ramelli, "Gal 3:28."

126. *Super masculinum tandem et neutrum ac femininum genus et super omne omnino quod ad haec respicit esse cogitanda sunt ista de quibus sermo est, et non solum Verbum Dei, sed et ecclesia eius atque anima perfecta. Sic enim et Apostolus dicit: In Christo enim neque masculus neque femina* (*C.Cant.* 3.9.3–4).

127. *C.Cant.* 1.6.14; *H.Gen.* 14.1: "Qua God's Logos he is called Bridegroom, and qua God's Wisdom [Σοφία] he is called Bride."

128. Τὸν ἄνθρωπον τοῦ υἱοῦ τοῦ θεοῦ, *C.Io.* 1.32.236.

129. "All those against whom the gates of hell will not prevail, who have in themselves a work called Peter ('rock'), are also Peters" (*C.Matth.* 12.10–11; cf. *C.Matth.S.* 139).

130. Examples in Ilaria Ramelli, *Gregorio di Nissa: Sull'anima e la resurrezione* (Milan: Bompiani-Catholic University, 2007), reviewed by Panayiotis Tzamalikos, *VigChr* 62 (2008): 515–23; Mark Edwards, *JEH* 60 (2009): 764–65; Miguel Herrero, '*Ilu* 13 (2008): 334–36; Giulio Maspero, *ZAC* 15 (2011): 592–94. One of the most prominent cases, besides the apokatastasis doctrine, is Origen's anti-subordinationism: see my "Origen's Anti-Subordinationism."

131. *In Eccl.*7 GNO 5.409.15–21.

132. See Neil McLynn, "'What was the 'Philocalia of Origen'?," *Meddelanden Collegium Patristicum Lundense* 19 (2004): 32–43; Eric Junod, "Questions au sujet de l'anthologie origénienne," in *Lire en extraits*, ed. Sébastien Morlet (Paris, 2015), 149–66; Samuel Fernández (ed., trans.), Orígenes: Los Principios (Madrid: Ciudad Nueva, 2015), 58; and Behr, *First Principles*, xxiv sensibly accept the Cappadocians' authorship, as well as John A. McGuckin, *Origen: Master Theologian of the Early Church* (Lanham: Rowman and Littlefield, Lexington Books, Fortress Academic, 2022), ch. 3.

133. See Ramelli, "Theosebia: A Presbyter?" On the Cappadocians' ideas about the equal dignity of men and women see Verna Harrison, "Male and Female in Cappadocian Theology," *JThS* 41 (1990): 441–71.

134. See my "Mansuetudine negli *Acta Philippi*."

135. *CIL* 10.8079.

136. *CIL* 13.1183. See Kevin Madigan and Carolyn Osiek, *Ordained Women in the Early Church* (Baltimore: Johns Hopkins, 2005), 196, my review *Orpheus* 28 (2007): 338–46.

137. Gary Macy, *The Hidden History of Women's Ordination* (Oxford: Oxford University Press, 2008), my review *SMSR* 74 (2008): 347–53; Mary Schäfer, *Women in Pastoral Office: The Story of Santa Prassede* (Oxford: Oxford University Press, 2013), my review *Gnomon* 89 (2017): 42–46.

138. See Ramelli, "Theosebia."

139. Letter 197 and Epigrams 161 and 164.

140. This refers not to a spouse—Theosebia was Gregory's sister—but to a colleague. To the rich evidence in "Theosebia" I add Theodore of Mopsuestia, *C.Philipp.* 4.3a: σύζυγος in Scripture never refers to marriage, but to people of the same faith. Theodoret is likely to have been inspired by Theodore when, commenting on Phil 4:3, he remarks that σύζυγος must be interpreted as "colleague, collaborator," and not "wife," as other exegetes thought, thus originating the belief, already found in Clement, that Paul was married. The same misunderstanding generated the conviction that Theosebia was Gregory's wife. On women σύζυγοι of male colleagues in ecclesiastical offices see my "Colleagues of Apostles, Presbyters, and Bishops."

141. *Carm.* 2.1.13.1–4 PG 37.1227A. The former is also identified by Basil as a task of a presbyter in *Ep.* 93 (PG 32.485A).

142. E.g. Basil, *Hom.Jul.* 241A. Full documentation in my "Theosebia." See also Anna Silvas, "Basil of Caesarea and His View of Women in a Christian Anthropology," in *Men and Women in the Early Christian Centuries,* ed. Wendy Mayer (Strathfield: St Paul, 2014), 149–59.

143. Analysis in my *Social Justice*, 163–65; 190–91 and *passim.*

144. Τὸ τῆς φύσεως ὁμότιμον, *Ep.* 52.2, Courtonne, *Lettres*, 1.135.

145. Though Gregory in a letter mentions the "choir of virgins" at Nyssa, whom Theosebia led, and omits to mention several others of his numerous sisters and brothers.

146. See Ramelli, *Gregorio sull'anima*, with critical essays, edition, translation, and commentary; "Gregory of Nyssa on the Soul (and the Restoration)."

147. Radcliffe Edmonds, "The Song of the Nightingale: World Play on the Road to Hades in Plato's *Phaedo*," *TAPA* 150 (2020): 65–83: 66.

148. Macrina's last prayer in *Vita S. Macrinae* teems with liturgical turns of phrases, especially the Eucharistic anaphoral ritual. Macrina is identified with Christ; she offers herself as a sacrifice and participates in Christ's passion. See Derek Krueger, "Writing and the Liturgy of Memory in Gregory of Nyssa's *Life of Macrina*," *JECS* 8 (2000): 483–510, esp. 508–09; my "Life of Macrina," in *Novel Saints.*

149. Ramelli, *Apokatastasis*, 372–440. On angelic life, anticipated by ascetics especially according to Nyssen, see Ellen Muehlberger, *Angels in Late Ancient Christianity* (Oxford: Oxford University Press, 2013), ch.5.

150. One of these nuns was an ordained deacon: Lampadion, the leader of the Divine Office. Macrina was not. Though, she was the head of the double monastery. Cf. *VM* 37; Anna Silvas, *Macrina the Younger. Philosopher of God* (Turnhout: Brepols, 2008).

151. Raphael A. Cadenhead, *The Body and Desire: Gregory of Nyssa's Ascetical Theology* (Oakland: University of California Press, 2018), esp. Part 3, analyses Gregory's understanding of virginity, but claims that Gregory's relativization of maleness and femaleness does not erase sexual hierarchy in this life. This is true up to a certain point; the eschatological *telos* is an ethical ideal to follow already on earth. See my "The Legacy of Origen in Gregory of Nyssa's Theology of Freedom," *Modern Theology* 38 (2022): 363–88, http://doi.org/10.1111/moth.12777, 1–26.

152. On the application of the eschatological orientation to ethics in Gregory see Ilaria L.E. Ramelli, "Gregory Nyssen's Position in Late-Antique Debates on Slavery and Poverty and the Role of Ascetics," *Journal of Late Antiquity* 5 (2012): 87–118. On the eschatological orientation of Gregory's thought, and its dependence on Origen's, see Ramelli, *Gregorio di Nissa*, first Integrative Essay.

153. My "Gal 3:28"; and George Karamanolis, *The Philosophy of Early Christianity*, second ed. (Oxford: Routledge, 2021), 199 and 269.

154. E.g. Hogan, "Paul and Seneca on Women," 223.

155. Analysed in Ilaria L. E. Ramelli, "The Logos/Nous One-Many between 'Pagan' and Christian Platonism: Bardaisan, Clement, Origen, Plotinus, and Gregory of Nyssa," *Studia Patristica* 102 (2021): 11–44.

156. In *C.Io.* 28.21.185 Origen even joins these two motifs.

157. Origen conflates the Temple-Christ's body (*Cels.* 8.20: a *logikon* is "a precious stone of God's whole temple") with Revelations' City of God of precious stones (*C. Rom.* 8.8.10) and with the "living stone" of 1Peter 2:4–5, which he alludes to in *Princ.* 2.11.1–3, again in an eschatological context: in the next life, in the Jerusalem city of saints, those not yet perfected in this life will be educated and become an elect and precious living stone. Note that a parallel to this situation in the *telos* is attested in the *arkhē*: Eve in Eden was adorned by "every precious stone" (*Genesis Rabbah* 18.1, trans. Jacob Neusner [Atlanta: Scholars, 1985], 1, 190). On Temple imagery in early Christianity see now Eyal Regev, *The Temple in Early Christianity: Experiencing the Sacred* (New Haven: Yale University Press, 2019), esp. ch. 6 on John and 8 on Hebrew.

158. *C.Io.* 10.35–36.225–38; 275–76. On the church-Christ's body-humanity as a temple see my 'Clement's notion of the Logos' and Ledegang, *Mysterium Ecclesiae*.

159. Reference to Ez 37. On its reception in Patristics, including Origen's *C.Io.* 10, see Nicolas Bossu, *Une prophétie au fil de la tradition* (Paris: Gabalda, 2015).

160. Ibidem 233–36. The scriptural reference is to Eph 4:13.

161. See my "The Spirit as Paraclete in 3rd to 5th-Century Debates and the Use of John 14–17 in the Pneumatology of That Time," in *Receptions of the Fourth Gospel in Antiquity*, ed. Jörg Frey et al. (Tübingen: Mohr Siebeck, forthcoming). Origen sticks to Paul's trichotomic anthropology of body, soul, and spirit (σῶμα, ψυχή, πνεῦμα, *Princ.* 4.2.4; *Heracl.* 6), which he also attaches to Christ (ibid., 7); he also has the body, soul and intellect tripartition (σῶμα, ψυχή, νοῦς). See my 'Tricotomia', in *Enciclopedia Filosofica*, ed. Virgilio Melchiorre (Milan: Bompiani, 2006), 11772–76; Kooten, *Paul's Anthropology in Context*. Some scholars detect an influence of the Stoic doctrine of material *pneuma* (present in Paul according to Engberg-Pedersen, *Cosmology and Self in Paul*) in Origen's notion of *pneuma*: Gitte Buch-Hansen, "The Spirit in Origen's Commentary on St. John's Gospel. The Stoic Foundation of

Origen's Theory of Universal Restoration," in Engberg-Pedersen–Gregersen, *Essays in Naturalism and Christian Semantics*, 119–52; That Origen knew the Stoic *pneuma* is out of question; that he embraced its materialism, however, is less probable, given his transcendental, Platonic perspective (which he also uses when he insists that God is *pneuma, nous*, and immaterial). See also my "Reception of Paul's Nous in the Christian Platonism of Origen."

162. as I pointed out in *Apokatastasis*, 170–76.
163. See my "*In Illud*"; further "Anti-Subordinationism."
164. Matthew 22:30; Mark 12:25.
165. John Paul II, *Mulieris dignitatem* (Rome: LEV, 1988), 4.

BIBLIOGRAPHY

Andrious, Rosie. *Saint Thecla: Body Politics and Masculine Rhetoric*. London: T&T Clark, 2020.

Blumell, Lincoln and Korshi Dosoo. "A Coptic Magical Text for Virginity in Marriage: A Witness to 'Celibate Marriage' from Christian Egypt." *HTR* 114 (2021): 118–42.

Bossu, Nicolas. *Une prophétie au fil de la tradition*. Paris: Gabalda, 2015.

Brakke, David. "The Lady Appears: Materializations of 'Woman' in Early Monastic Literature." *Journal of Medieval and Early Modern Studies* 33 (2003): 387–402.

Brock, Sebastian. "The Holy Spirit as Feminine." In *After Eve: Women, Theology, and the Christian Tradition*, edited by Janet Soskice, 73–88. London: Collins, 1990.

Brock, Sebastian. "Come, Compassionate Mother, Come, Holy Spirit." *Aram* 3 (1991): 249–57.

Brown, Peter. *The Body and Society*. New York: Columbia, 1988.

Burrus, Virginia. *Chastity as Autonomy*. Lewiston: Mellen, 1987.

Cadenhead, Raphael A. *The Body and Desire: Gregory of Nyssa's Ascetical Theology*. Oakland: University of California Press, 2018.

Cary, Philippe. *Augustine's Invention of the Inner Self*. Oxford: Oxford University Press, 2000.

Ciccolini, Laura. *Cypriani De habitu virginum*. Turnhout: Brepols, 2016.

Cooper, Kate. *Band of Angels: The Forgotten World of Early Christian Women*. London: Atlantic, 2013.

Cox Miller, Patricia. *In the Eye of the Animal: Zoological Imagination in Early Christianity*. Philadelphia: University of Pennsylvania, 2018.

De Lange, Nicholas. *Origen and the Jews*. Cambridge: Cambridge University Press, 1976.

De Wet, Chris. *Preaching Bondage*. Oakland: University of California, 2015.

Digeser, Elizabeth DePalma. *A Threat to Public Piety: Christian, Platonists, and the Great Persecutio*. Ithaca: Cornell, 2012.

DiLuzio, Meghan. *A Place at the Altar: Priestesses in Republican Rome*. Princeton: Princeton University Press, 2016.

Dunn, James. *Romans 9-16*. Dallas: Word Books, 1988.
Dutsch, Dorota. *Pythagorean Women Philosophers*. Oxford: Oxford University Press, 2020.
Edmonds, Radcliffe. "The Song of the Nightingale: World Play on the Road to Hades in Plato's *Phaedo*." *TAPA* 150 (2020): 65–83.
Edwards, Mark. "The Development of Office in the Early Church." In *The Early Christian World*, 2nd ed., edited by Philip Esler, ch. 13. London: Routledge, 2017.
Edwards, Robert. "Clement of Alexandria's 'Gnostic' Exposition of the Decalogue." *Journal of Early Christian Studies* 23 (2015): 501–28.
Ehrensperger, Kathy and Shayna Sheinfeld (eds.). *Gender and Second-Temple Judaism*. Lanham: Lexington/Fortress Academic, 2020.
Epp, Eldon Jay. *Junia: The First Woman Apostle*. Minneapolis: Fortress, 2005.
Fernández, Samuel, editor and translator. Orígenes: Los Principios. Madrid: Ciudad Nueva, 2015.
Fiore, Benjamin. *The Pastoral Epistles*. Collegeville: Liturgical, 2007.
Fleischer, Kilian. "Structuring the 'History of Philosophy': A Comparison Between Philodemus and Diogenes Laertius in the Light of New Evidence." *Classical Quarterly* 69 (2020): 684–99.
Frankfurter, David. *Christianizing Egypt: Syncretism and Local Worlds in Late Antiquity*. Princeton: Princeton University, 2017.
Gieschen, Charles. *Angelomorphic Christology: Antecedents an Early Evidence*. Waco: Baylor University, 2017.
Gordon, Richard. "Mysteries." *Oxford Classical Dictionary*, March 2016. doi:10.109 3/acrefore/9780199381135.013.4318.
Harrison, Verna. "The Care-Banishing Breast of the Father: Feminine Images of the Divine in Clement of Alexandria's Paedagogus I." *Studia Patristica* 31 (1997): 401–05.
Harvey, Susan. "Feminine Imagery for the Divine." *St Vladimir Theological Quarterly* 37 (2004): 1–29.
Heine, Ronald. *Origen: An Introduction to His Life and Thought*. Eugene: Wipf and Stock, 2019.
Hemelrijk, Emily. "The Education of Women in Ancient Rome." In *A Companion to Ancient Education*, edited by Martin Bloomer, 292–304. Oxford: Wiley-Blackwell, 2015.
Hermans, Theo. *Origène et la théologie sacrificielle du sacerdoce des chrétiens*. Paris: Beauchesne, 1996.
Hirschmann, Vera-Elisabeth. *Horrenda Secta: Untersuchungen zum frühchristlichen Montanismus und seinen Verbindungen zur paganen Religion Phrygiens*. Stuttgart: Steiner, 2005.
Hogan, Pauline N. "Paul and Seneca on Women." In *Paul and Seneca in Dialogue*, edited by Joseph Dodson and David Briones, 208–31. Leiden: Brill, 2017.
Huebner, Sabine and Christian Laes (eds.). *The Single Life in the Roman and Later Roman World*. Cambridge: Cambridge University Press, 2019.
Image, Isabella. *The Human Condition in Hilary of Poitiers: The Will and Original Sin between Origen and Augustine*. Oxford: Oxford University Press, 2018.

John Paul II. *Mulieris dignitatem*. Rome: LEV, 1988.
Junod, Eric. "Questions au sujet de l'anthologie origénienne." In *Lire en extraits*, edited by Sébastien Morlet, 149–66. Paris: CNRS, 2015.
Karamanolis, George. *The Philosophy of Early Christianity*, 2nd ed. Oxford: Routledge, 2021.
Kateusz, Ally. *Mary and Early Christian Women: Hidden Leadership*. New York: Palgrave Macmillan, 2019.
King, Karen. *The Gospel of Mary of Magdala: Jesus and the First Woman Apostle*. Santa Rosa: Polebridge, 2003.
KeltoLillis, Julia. "No Hymen Required: Reconstructing Origen's View on Mary's Virginity." *Church History* 89 (2020): 249–67.
Kooten, George van. *Paul's Anthropology in Context*. Tübingen: Mohr Siebeck, 2008.
Kovacs, Judith. "Becoming the Perfect Man: Clement on the Philosophical Life of Women." In *Women and Gender in Ancient Religions*, edited by Susan Ahearne-Kroll, 289–413. Tübingen: Mohr Siebeck, 2010.
Krueger, Derek. "Writing and the Liturgy of Memory in Gregory of Nyssa's *Life of Macrina*." *Journal of Early Christian Studies* 8 (2000): 483–510.
Lavrinoviča, Alesja. "The Syntactic Flexibility of 1 Corinthians 14:33b." *Journal of Biblical Literature* 141 (2022): 157–75. https://doi.org/10.15699/jbl.1411.2022.9.
Lee, Dorothy A. "Lost in translation: rethinking words about women in 1–2 Timothy." *Scottish Journal of Theology* 74 (2021): 52–66.
Lössl, Josef. "A Clash Between Paideia and Pneuma? Ecstatic Women Prophets and Theological Education in the Second-century Church." *Studies in Church History* 57 (2021): 32–53.
Macy, Gary. *The Hidden History of Women's Ordination*. Oxford: Oxford University Press, 2008.
Madigan, Kevin and Carolyn Osiek. *Ordained Women in the Early Church*. Baltimore: Johns Hopkins, 2005.
Maier, Harry. "The Entrepreneurial Widows of 1 Timothy." In *Patterns of Women Leadership and Authority in Ancient Christianity and Judaism,* edited by Joan Taylor and Ilaria Ramelli, 59–73. Oxford: Oxford University Press, 2021.
Markschies, Christoph. "Die platonische Metapher vom 'Inneren Menschen'." *ZKG* 105 (1994): 1–17.
Markschies, Christoph. *Origenes und sein Erbe*. Berlin: de Gruyter, 2007.
Markschies, Christoph. "Montanismus." *Reallexikon für Antike und Christentum* 26 (2012): 1197–220.
McCloskey, Benjamin. "On Xenophontic Friendship." *TAPA* 149 (2019): 261–86.
McLynn, Neil. "What was the Philocalia of Origen?" *Collegium Patristicum Lundense* 19 (2004): 32–43.
McVey, Kathleen. "Ephrem the Syrian's Use of Female Metaphors to Describe the Deity." *Zeitschrift für Antikes Christentum* 5, no. 2 (2001): 261–88.
Muehlberger, Ellen. *Angels in Late Ancient Christianity*. Oxford: Oxford University Press, 2013.
Murphy-O'Connor, Jerome, Cettina Militello, and Maria-Luisa Rigato. *Paolo e le donne*. Assisi: Cittadella, 2006.

Myers, Susan. "The Spirit as Mother in Early Syriac-Speaking Christianity." In *Women and Gender in Ancient Religions*, edited by James Kellhoffer et al., 427–62. Tübingen: Mohr Siebeck, 2010.
Neusner, Jacob and Bruce Chilton. "Conducting Dialectical Argument in Origen." In *The Intellectual Foundation of Christian and Jewish Discourse*, edited by James Kellhoffer et al., 70–86. New York: Routledge, 1997.
Niebuhr, Karl-Wilhelm. "Jakobus und Paulus über das Innere des Menschen." *New Testament Studies* 62 (2016): 1–30.
Oertelt, Friederike. "Gender, Religion und Politik bei Philon von Alexandria." In *Doing Gender, Doing Religion: Case Studies on Intersectionality in Early Judaism, Christianity and Islam*, edited by Ute Eisen and Angela Standhartinger, 227–50. Tübingen: Mohr Siebeck, 2013.
Palmer, Morgan. "Time and Eternity: The Vestal Virgins and the Crisis of the Third Century." *Transactions and Proceedings of the American Philological Association* 150 (2020): 473–97.
Parkhouse, Sarah. *Eschatology and the Saviour: The 'Gospel of Mary' among Early Christian Dialogue Gospels*. Cambridge: Cambridge University Press, 2019.
Parks, Sara, Sheinfeld, Shayna, and Warren, Meredith. *Jewish and Christian Women in the Ancient Mediterranean*. London: Routledge, 2022.
Perrier, Pierre. *L'apôtre Thomas et le prince Ying*. Paris: Jubilé, 2012.
Pomeroy, Sarah. *Pythagorean Women: Their History and Writings*. Baltimore: Johns Hopkins University, 2015.
Pummer, Reinhard. *Early Christian Authors on Samaritans and Samaritanism*. Tübingen: Mohr Siebeck, 2002.
Ramelli, Ilaria L. E. "Κατὰ ψιλὴν παράταξιν: Montanismo e Impero Romano nel giudizio di Marco Aurelio." In *Fazioni e congiure nel mondo antico*, edited by Marta Sordi, 81–97. Milan: Vita e Pensiero, 1999.
Ramelli, Ilaria L. E. "*Mysterium* come *ratio sacramentorum* in Ambrogio." In *Contributi su Mysterion e Sacramentum nei primi secoli cristiani*, edited by Angela Mazzanti, 105–16. Castel Bolognese: Itaca, 2003a.
Ramelli, Ilaria L. E. "Cristiani e vita politica: il cripto-Cristianesimo nelle classi dirigenti romane nel II secolo." *Aevum* 77 (2003b): 35–51.
Ramelli, Ilaria L. E. "Tracce di Montanismo nel *Peregrinus* di Luciano?" *Aevum* 79 (2005a): 79–94.
Ramelli, Ilaria L. E. "Successioni di filosofi." In *Diogene Laerzio*, edited by Giovanni Reale and Ilaria Ramelli, XXXIII–CXXXVIII. Milan: Bompiani, 2005b.
Ramelli, Ilaria L. E. "Tricotomia." In *Enciclopedia Filosofica*, edited by Virgilio Melchiorre, 11772–76. Milan: Bompiani, 2006.
Ramelli, Ilaria L. E. *Gregorio di Nissa: Sull'anima e la resurrezione*. Milan: Bompiani–Catholic University, 2007a.
Ramelli, Ilaria L. E. "Mansuetudine, grazia e salvezza negli *Acta Philippi* (ed. Bovon)." *Invigilata Lucerne's* 29 (2007b): 215–28.
Ramelli, Ilaria L. E. "Philosophical Allegoresis of Scripture in Philo and Its Legacy." *Studia Philonica Annual* 20 (2008a): 55–99.

Ramelli, Ilaria L. E. "Transformations of the Household and Marriage Theory Between Neo-Stoicism, Middle Platonism, and Early Christianity." *RFN* 100 (2008b): 369–96.

Ramelli, Ilaria L. E. "Origen, Patristic Philosophy, and Christian Platonism: Re-Thinking the Christianisation of Hellenism." *Vigiliae Christianae* 63 (2009): 217–63.

Ramelli, Ilaria L. E. "Teosebia *in ministerio Ecclesiae*." In *Diakonia, Diaconiae, Diaconato. Semantica e storia nei Padri della Chiesa*. Rome, Augustinianum, May 7–9, 2009, 217–31. Rome: Augustinianum, 2010.

Ramelli, Ilaria L. E. "Theosebia: A Presbyter of the Catholic Church." *Journal of Feminist Studies in Religion* 26, no. 2 (2010): 79–102.

Ramelli, Ilaria L. E. "The Pastoral Epistles and Hellenistic Philosophy: 1Tim 5:1-2, Hierocles, and the Contraction of Circles." *Catholic Biblical Quarterly* 73 (2011): 562–81.

Ramelli, Ilaria L. E. *I romanzi antichi e il Cristianesimo: contesto e contatti*, pref. Brian Reardon, new ed. Eugene: Cascade, 2012.

Ramelli, Ilaria L.E. "Gregory Nyssen's Position in Late-Antique Debates on Slavery and Poverty and the Role of Ascetics." *Journal of Late Antiquity* 5 (2012): 87–118.

Ramelli, Ilaria L. E. *The Christian Doctrine of Apokatastasis: A Critical Assessment form the New Testament to Eriugena*. Vigiliae Christianae Supplements 120. Leiden: Brill, 2013a.

Ramelli, Ilaria L. E. "Apuleius and Christianity: The Novelist-Philosopher in Front of a New Religion." In *Intende, Lector—Echoes of Myth, Religion and Ritual in the Ancient Novel*, edited by Marília Futre Pinheiro, Anton Bierl, and Roger Beck, 145–73. Berlin: De Gruyter, 2013b.

Ramelli, Ilaria L. E. "Diakonia, Diakonos." In *Encyclopedia of Ancient Christianity*, edited byAngelo Di Berardino, 703–04. Downers Grove: InterVarsity, 2014.

Ramelli, Ilaria L. E. "I 'cori' di consacrate e Gregorio di Nissa: il canto liturgico riflesso e anticipazione dell'armonia escatologica." In *Ascoltare gli Dèi / Divos Audire: Costruzione e Percezione della Dimensione Sonora nelle Religioni del Mediterraneo Antico*, 2, edited by Igor Baglioni, 207–18. Rome: Quasar, 2015.

Ramelli, Ilaria L. E. *Social Justice and the Legitimacy of Slavery: The Role of Philosophical Asceticism from Ancient Judaism to Late Antiquity*. Oxford: Oxford University Press, 2016a.

Ramelli, Ilaria L. E. "Hiéroclès: extraits du traité Sur le mariage de Stobée." In *L'éthique du stoïcien Hiéroclès*, edited by Jean-Baptiste Gourinat, 157–67. Lille: Presses Universitaires du Septentrion, 2016b.

Ramelli, Ilaria L. E. "Prophecy in Origen: Between Scripture and Philosophy." *Journal of Early Christian History* 7, no. 2 (2017): 17–39.

Ramelli, Ilaria L. E. "Gregory of Nyssa on the Soul (and the Restoration): From Plato to Origen." In *Gregory of Nyssa: Historical and Philosophical Perspectives*, edited by Anna Marmodoro and Neil McLynn, 110–41. Oxford: Oxford University Press, 2018a.

Ramelli, Ilaria L. E. "Bardaisan of Edessa, Origen, and Imperial Philosophy: A Middle Platonic Context?" *Aram* 30 (2018b): 337–53.

Ramelli, Ilaria L. E. "Origen." In *A History of Mind and Body in Late Antiquity*, edited by Anna Marmodoro and Sophie Cartwright, 245–66. Cambridge: Cambridge University Press, 2018c.

Ramelli, Ilaria L. E. "Creation, Double." In *Brill Encyclopedia of Early Christianity*, edited by Paul van Geest et al., Leiden: Brill, 2018c. http://dx.doi.org/10.1163/2589-7993_EECO_SIM_00000793.

Ramelli, Ilaria L. E. "Review of Image 2018." *Reading Religion*, 2018d: http://readingreligion.org/books/human-condition-hilary-poitiers.

Ramelli, Ilaria L. E. *Bardaiṣan of Edessa: A Reassessment of the Evidence and a New Interpretation. Also in the Light of Origen and the Original Fragments from Porphyry*. Piscataway: Gorgias; Berlin: DeGruyter, 2009–2019.

Ramelli, Ilaria L. E. "Paul on Apokatastasis: 1 Cor 15:24-28 and the Use of Scripture." In *Paul and Scripture,* edited by Stanley Porter and Christopher Land, 212–32. Leiden: Brill, 2019a.

Ramelli, Ilaria L. E. "Gal 3:28 and Aristotelian (and Jewish) Categories of Inferiority." *Eirene* 55 (2019): 275–310, 2019b.

Ramelli, Ilaria L. E. "Autobiographical Self-Fashioning in Origen." Invited chapter in *Self, Self-Fashioning and Individuality in Late Antiquity: New Perspectives*, edited by Maren Niehoff and Joshua Levinson, 273–92. Tübingen: Mohr Siebeck, 2019c.

Ramelli, Ilaria L. E. "The Logos/Nous One-Many between 'Pagan' and Christian Platonism: Bardaisan, Clement, Origen, Plotinus, and Gregory of Nyssa." *Studia Patristica* 102 (2021a): 11–44.

Ramelli, Ilaria L. E. "The Reception of Paul's Nous in the Christian Platonism of Origen and Evagrius." In *Der νοῦς bei Paulus im Horizont griechischer und hellenistisch-jüdischer Anthropologie*, edited by Jörg Frey and Manuel Nägele, WUNT I 464, 279–316. Tübingen: Mohr Siebeck, 2021b.

Ramelli, Ilaria L. E. "Conceptualities of Angels in Late Antiquity: Degrees of Corporeality, Bodies of Angels, and Comparative Angelologies/Daemonologies in 'Pagan' and Christian Platonism." In *Inventer les anges de l'Antiquité à Byzance: Conception, Représentation, Perception*, edited by Delphine Lauritzen, 115–72. Paris: CNRS–Collège de France, Centre d'Histoire et Civilisation de Byzance, 2021c.

Ramelli, Ilaria L.E "Colleagues of Apostles, Presbyters, and Bishops: Women Syzygoi in Ancient Christian Communities." In *Patterns of Women Leadership and Authority in Ancient Christianity and Judaism,* edited by Joan E. Taylor and Ilaria L. E. Ramelli, 26–58. Oxford: Oxford University Press, 2021d.

Ramelli, Ilaria L. E. "The Legacy of Origen in Gregory of Nyssa's Theology of Freedom." *Modern Theology* 38 (2022): 363–88.

Ramelli, Ilaria L. E. "Diakonia in Origen: From Christ and the Angels to Men and Women." In *Deacons and Diakonia in Christianity from the Third to the Sixth Century*, edited by Bart Koet, 11–30. Tübingen: Mohr Siebeck, 2024.

Ramelli, Ilaria L. E. "Biography, Hagiography, and Philosophy in Late Antiquity: *The Eroticism–Asceticism Relation and Late Antique Platonism in the Lives of Macrina and Evagrius,*" forthcoming.

Ratcliffe, Rosie. "The Acts of Paul and Thecla: Violating the Inviolate Body—Thecla Uncut." In *The Body in Biblical, Christian and Jewish Texts*, edited by Joan Taylor, 184–209. London: T&T Clark, 2014.

Regev, Eyal. *The Temple in Early Christianity: Experiencing the Sacred*. New Haven: Yale, 2019.
Rigato, Maria-Luisa. "Maria la Maddalena: ancora riflessioni su colei che fu chiamata la Resa-grande." *Studia Patavina* 50 (2003): 727–52.
Rigato, Maria-Luisa, *Discepole di Gesù*. Bologna: Dehoniane, 2011.
Roig Lanzillotta, Lautaro. "A Syriac Original for the Acts of Thomas?." In *Early Christian and Jewish Narrative: The Role of Religion in Shaping Narrative Forms*, edited by I. L. E. Ramelli and J. Perkins, 105–34. Tübingen: Mohr Siebeck, 2015.
Safranski, Benjamin. *St. Cyprian of Carthage and the College of Bishops*. Lanham: Lexington, 2018.
Schäfer, Mary. *Women in Pastoral Office: The Story of Santa Prassede*. Oxford: Oxford University Press, 2013.
Schenk, Christine. *Crispina and Her Sisters: Women and Authority in Early Christianity*. Minneapolis: Fortress, 2017.
Schrader, Elizabeth and Joan Taylor. "The Meaning of Magdalene: A Review of Literary Evidence." *Journal of Biblical Literature* 140, no. 4 (2021): 751–73.
Schüssler Fiorenza, Elizabeth. *In Memory of Her*. New York: Crossroads, 1992.
Sidaway, Janet. *The Human Factor: "Deification" as Transformation in the Theology of Hilary*. Louvain: Peeters, 2016.
Silvas, Anna. *Macrina the Younger. Philosopher of God*. Turnhout: Brepols, 2008.
Silvas, Anna. "Basil of Caesarea and His View of Women in a Christian Anthropology." In *Men and Women in the Early Christian Centuries*, edited by Wendy Mayer, 149–59. Strathfield: St Paul, 2014.
Stefaniw, Blossom. "Shame and the Normal in in Epiphanius' Polemic against Origen." *Journal of Early Christian Studies* 21 (2013): 413–35.
Szram, Mariusz. "Origen's Castration. Solely a Spiritual Phenomenon?" *Gregorianum* 101 (2020): 23–36.
Tabbernee, William. *Fake Prophecy and Polluted Sacraments: Ecclesiastical and Imperial Reactions to Montanism*. VCS 84. Leiden: Brill, 2007.
Taylor, Joan E., and Ramelli, Ilaria L. E. (eds.). *Patterns of Women's Leadership in Early Christianity*. Oxford: Oxford University Press, 2021.
Thornton, Dillon T. *Hostility in the House of God: An Investigation of the Opponents in 1 and 2 Timothy*. Winona Lake: Eisenbrauns, 2016.
Timotin, Andrei. *La prière dans la tradition platonicienne, de Platon à Proclus*. Turnhout: Brepols, 2017.
Trevett, Christine. *Montanism: Gender, Authority and the New Prophecy*. Cambridge: Cambridge University Press, 1996.
Troiano, Mariano. "Padre femenino: el Dios-Madre de los gnósticos." In *Gnose et manichéïsme, Hommage à Jean-Daniel Dubois*, edited by A. van den Kerchove and Lucia Gabriela Soares Santoprete, 27-159. Turnhout: Brepols, 2016.
Turner, John. "The Virgin That Became Male: Feminine Principles in Platonic and Gnostic Texts." In *Women and Knowledge in Early Christianity*, edited by Ulla Tervahauta et al., 291–324. Leiden: Brill, 2017.

Tzamalikos, Panayiotis. *Anaxagoras, Origen, and Neoplatonism.* Berlin: De Gruyter, 2016.
Undheim, Sissel. *Borderline Virginities: Sacred and Secular Virginities in Late Antiquity.* London: Routledge, 2018.
Urciuoli, Emiliano. *Servire due padroni: Una genealogia dell'uomo politico cristiano (50-313).* Brescia: Morcelliana, 2018.
Vuilleumier, Sandrine. *Un rituel osirien en faveur de particuliers à l'époque ptolémaïque.* Wiesbaden: Harrassowitz, 2016.
Watts, Edward. *Hypatia: The Life and Legend of an Ancient Philosopher.* New York: Oxford University Press, 2017.
Wheeler-Reed. David. *Regulating Sex in the Roman Empire: Ideology, the Bible, and the Early Christians.* New Haven: Yale, 2017.
Wider, Kathtleen. "Women Philosophers in the Ancient Greek World: Donning the Mantle." *Hypatia* 1 (1986): 21–62.
Winter, Bruce. *Roman Wives, Roman Widows: The Appearance of New Women and the Pauline Communities.* Grand Rapids: Eerdmans, 2003.
Xavier Pena, Joabson. "Wearing the Cosmos: The High Priestly Attire in Josephus' *Judean Antiquities*." *Journal for the Study of Judaism* 52 (2021): 1–29.
Yarbro Collins, Adela. "The Female Body as Social Space in 1 Timothy." *NTS* 57 (2011): 155–75.
Yli-Karjanmaa, Sami. *Reincarnation in Philo of Alexandria,* Atlanta: SBL, 2015.
Yli-Karjanmaa, Sami. "Call Him Earth: On Philo's Allegorisation of Adam in *Legum Allegoriae*." In *The Adam and Eve Story in the Hebrew Bible and in Ancient Jewish Writings*, edited by Antti Laato and Lotta Valve, 253–93. Turku: SRHB, 2016.

7

One of the Boys
Jerome's Fabulous Frontier Masculinity
Matthew R. Anderson

Figure 7.1 Mistatim Awâsis (Horsechild) and Cameron, 1885. *Source*: Public Domain.

The story is a plain one and it will be told plainly. And if the dramatic setting, the romantic atmosphere of a wild and lonely land, the smoke of teepees and the native eloquence of men, naked and brown as leaves in autumn, do not invite the seeker of the sensational and melodramatic in literature, the tale is not for him.

—William Bleasdell Cameron.[1]

Figure 7.2   St. Jerome the Penitent. *Source*: Vincenzo Foppa, fifteenth century.

Come, and come quickly. Do not think of old ties—the desert loves the naked—do not be deterred by the hardships. . . . The day will come later when you shall return in triumph to your true country, when, crowned as a man of might, you shall walk the streets of the heavenly Jerusalem. Then you shall share with Paul the franchise of that city. . . . Yes, and for me also you shall intercede, who urged you on to victory. (Jerome)[2]

INTRODUCTION

At the dawn of imperial Roman Christianity, Jerome was a "man on the make."[3] Jerome portrayed himself to potential patrons as an ascetic, a desert-dweller, a biblical exegete, a conduit of the Greek Christian tradition, a fluent Hebrew speaker, and a Holy Land monk. His self-promotion relied on declarations of identities considered frontier and exotic by the fourth-century imperial center of power. This chapter employs a decolonizing, aware-settler hermeneutic[4] to analyze these claims as specific strategies by which Jerome tried to cement his influence and establish his authority as a Roman elite male.[5]

I first proposed an aware-settler lens to examine biblical texts and their reception (for instance, in re-reading the so-called "Great Commission" of Matthew 28:25–28).[6] In reading Jerome's letters, however, it soon became clear that an aware-settler hermeneutic also offered insights into his attempts to stake claims from a "frontier periphery" to perform virility for, and seek recognition and patronage from, an imperial audience.

Aware-settler approaches listen to and learn from Indigenous scholarship.[7] The above photograph (Figure 7.1) taken in 1885 in the Canadian west, even without the text with which I paired it, aptly illustrates how settler identity is worked out in a complex mutuality with and dependence on Indigeneity, despite the settler goal of displacing Indigenous people and presence.[8] An aware-settler lens also identifies and analyzes settler attempts to construct narratives of heroic virtue, evident in the "wild west" costumes of Cameron's photograph. Applied to Jerome, this lens helps us focus on his physical and literary location in an ancient "contact zone."[9] Jerome used literary narratives and images typical of frontier masculinity to advance himself,[10] despite frontier masculinity being a form of what Homi Bhabha has called "fetishized colonial culture,"[11] with its attendant queer undertones.[12] The eventual acceptance and reification of Jerome's self-promotion in his reception is witnessed by the common representation of him and his setting we see in Vincenzo Foppa's fifteenth-century painting (the second image). In Jerome beating his breast outside a cave, history reproduces what Burrus has called "the queerly feminized and darkly exoticized literary persona of his [Jerome's] own construction."[13]

Important queer examinations of Jerome's masculinity have contributed to our understanding by focusing on his fascinating non-normative behaviors.[14] However, Jerome's "queer failure,"[15] that is, his inability in his lifetime to achieve the esteem and influence necessary to obtain the coveted position of the Roman imperial *vir*, or male, arises directly from his seeking such normative status.[16] Jerome was not unique in the ways in which his "rhetorical praxis and gender identity [were] parts of an interconnected whole."[17] In his letters, hagiographies, commentaries, and other writings, Jerome wanted to be seen as exemplifying the masculine traits of *virtus* (a reputation for authoritative moral valor and virtue) and *imperium* (domination, or control). He did this by declaring his mastery over textual, ecclesiastical, and physical territory, with an eye to securing and maintaining patronage, especially from a powerful network of elite Roman Christian women.

It is only in recent decades, and under the influence of feminist thinkers, that masculinity as a construction of "cultural representations and social practices" has received much attention.[18] Since then, there have been many examinations of masculine identity construction through literary self-presentation in early texts such as Paul's letters,[19] and in later Christian writings such as the Church Fathers. In her work *"Begotten, Not Made": Conceiving Manhood in Late Antiquity*, Virginia Burrus focused on the construction of elite Christian masculinity in the context of the great theological debates of the Christianizing empire. She concludes that the "fourth-century doctrine of a transcendent God who is Father, Son, and Holy Spirit was inextricably intertwined with the particular late-antique claims for masculinity."[20] Jerome's carnal asceticism represented an extreme position in that development. Here I argue that his marginal position and his attempts to profit from that position by casting himself in his writings as master of a frontier both alluring and potentially deadly, form an important part of the evolution of elite masculine identity construction in late antiquity. "So I read, so I am written, so I write, reluctant to make an end of it."[21] Burrus's words were not specifically about Jerome but could easily form his epitaph.

I want to identify four actions typical of a settler colonist[22] in Jerome's work: (1) a declaration of *terra nullius* or "empty land" in certain key areas where he wished to assert ownership, (2) a proclamation of precedence by which he stated himself to be the first from the imperial center to assert sovereignty over those domains, (3) the commodification and trading of the resources of the physical or reputational territory, which necessarily meant the suppression and further delegitimization of those who first "inhabited" those territories, and finally (4) the construction and retelling of a settler imaginary, a mythic narrative of heroic labor and pioneer virtue which reinforced his *virtus* and *imperium*.

Maud Gleason writes of the first century CE orator Favorinus that "Like every great sophist, [he] lived his life in fierce pursuit of international recognition and immortal fame."[23] Jerome's works show that he likewise intended his self-promotion to extend to his legacy.[24] Through his preserved works, his "queer failure" was overcome, and he achieved the reputation he had so desired. As evidenced in the painting by Foppa (figure 7.2), Christian tradition eventually incorporated, mythologized, and even celebrated aspects of Jerome's non-normative masculinity. That reception finally gave him the pride of place he had worked diligently to obtain in the narrative of Western Christianity's history.[25]

JEROME'S IDENTITY PERFORMANCE AS SETTLER COLONIALISM

Jerome's standing in the shifting theatre of early imperial Christianity was always contested. His posthumous status as an authoritative translator and scholar of scripture, a champion of Nicene orthodoxy, and a heroic ascetic was never granted in his own lifetime. Instead, Jerome's writings show him competing for aristocratic patronage hampered by a reputation often in doubt and occasionally in tatters. He preferred to present his travails as the sufferings of the unjustly persecuted: "it is not surprising," he wrote, "if we . . . offend very many when we try to strip away their vices."[26]

Through his writings from Antioch and Bethlehem, Jerome performed his identity for an elite audience in his "true country," patrician Christian Rome, "a city where the people once was the world."[27] Jerome sought to insert himself as a key player in the evolving state church.[28] He took part in what has been called the late fourth century's "ascetic transformation of the imperial elite,"[29] led by a group of patrician Christian women and their clients. After initial successes, including a likely stint as a secretary to Pope Damasus,[30] Jerome experienced significant setbacks. Mid-career, he left Italy in haste following an episcopal court's verdict against him on charges of "clerical misconduct stemming from allegations of legacy hunting and sexual impropriety."[31] In his correspondence, he presented himself as one of Judah's exiles, dragged from Jerusalem to Babylon. He begged for prayers he might soon return to his "Mount Sion."[32] His bitterness, but also his tactics, are evident: "Let Rome keep her bustle for herself, the fury of the arena, the madness of the circus, the profligacy of the theatre, and—for I must not forget our Christian friends—the daily meetings of the matron's senate."[33]

Given that almost all of what we know about Jerome comes from his self-presentations, it's easy to become distracted by their thickets of gossip, reproach, fantasy, sexuality, appropriation, and erudition. There we encounter the full queerness of Jerome's masculinity. The importance he attached to celibacy, virginity, and chastity as superior to sexual relations, marriage, and child raising was typical of the Church Fathers.[34] Jerome, however, went further. Even in his day, he was judged for how he took Christian celibate eros[35] to a fever pitch.[36] For instance, he portrays one of his fictional Christian martyrs tortured by burning metal. When the young man overcomes that, he is tormented instead by garlands of flowers and the embraces of a beautiful woman:

Her arms [were] around his neck in tender embraces, and then-oh, sinful even to relate-[she] began to caress him wantonly, in order that she might force him to yield to her shameless advances. What should a soldier of Christ do? Where could he turn? Lust was on the point of overcoming him whom torture could not conquer. At last, inspired from heaven, he bit off a piece of his tongue and spat it into her face as she kissed him. Ensuing pain prevailed over lustful passion.[37]

It is easy to be distracted by the scandal and strangeness of such a piece. If we are, we lose sight of the competitive literary goals Jerome sought by writing such scenes: to upstage Athanasius and the public success of his *Life of Anthony*, and to seduce certain readers—the elite Christian women of Rome.[38] Perhaps distraction was a part of Jerome's strategy, but in this he was not successful. Such saintly erotica, together with Jerome's extreme views on asceticism,[39] and his dubious actions regarding the noblewoman ascetic Paula and her family, kept him in exile. What Burrus calls his "all-too-carnal theologizing" and the sister-wife pairing he cultivated with Paula—or she with him—led to his disgrace.[40] Typically, however, Jerome turns his readers' attention away through gossip: "It wearies me to tell how many virgins fall daily," he sighs.[41]

Simmering scandals, hyperbolic attacks, fantastic creativities, and queer sexualities all tend to blind us to how Jerome's actions were in many ways *typical* of a Roman seeking to prove his manliness. With his aristocratic patrons firmly in mind, Jerome sought to turn his marginalized location to his benefit. I make the following arguments: firstly, that an aware-settler lens applied to Jerome's masculinity helps explain his particular use of the empire's margins to display Roman male values of *virtus* and *imperium*.[42] Second, Jerome's moves to declare *terra nullius,* to establish sovereignty claims against other Latin Christian writers, to commodify and traffic in the resources of the frontier for the purpose of seeking patrons and patronage, and finally to invent for himself a narrative of pioneer *virtus*, or virtue, are all evidence of what I am here calling a frontier masculinity.

I am not the first to suggest a decolonizing lens. While not specifically applying this to Jerome, Virginia Burrus has pointed to and problematized a colonial and post-colonial perspective for examining ancient conceptions of virginity.[43] Andrew S. Jacobs noted Jerome's extractive interactions with Palestinian Jews and his attempts to exercise control over the burgeoning practice of Christian pilgrimage to the Holy Land.[44] Here I add to their work by pointing out how Jerome sought to build his aspirational identity and his reputation in ways typical of frontier men.

Jerome's first "desert" sojourn near Syrian Antioch and his later permanent move to Bethlehem, were both prompted by some sort of expulsion, first from Aquileia and later from Rome.[45] In both cases Jerome's writings show him trying to turn exile to his advantage. My contention is that Jerome's method of appropriating the resources of the places to which he had taken flight show that he was not just an agent of an imperial religion (the more typical focus of decolonizing approaches). Additionally, Jerome was a settler.[46] Like his character Malchus the Monk, Jerome built a life and a literature at the edge of empire, in Pratt's "contact zone."[47]

For Christians and Jews, the desert is a particular *kind* of contact zone, rich in biblical narrative and image. Not only biblical characters, but angels, saints, and fantastical creatures make it home.[48] From his first time in the east in the early 370s, Jerome began to extract value from this notional desert. Even while enjoying the richness of Syrian Antioch, residence of the emperor Valens and known for its urban pleasures, Jerome peppered his letters with references to solitude, desert, and wilderness (*eremus*). He depicted himself to Rome as a Jacob, a Moses, and true-life incarnation of his fictional Malchus.[49] He writes himself to be near-naked, persecuted, a shepherd in intent if not profession, virtuous although troubled by the presence of women, and living in solitude.[50] After a brief illness during his stint in the Antiochian suburbs, he writes that he himself

> was caught up in the spirit and dragged before the Judge's judgement seat: and here the light was so dazzling, and the brightness shining from those who stood around so radiant, that I flung myself on the ground and did not dare to look up.[51]

Thus he added mystic to his other exotic qualifications. As Burrus notes, in Jerome "ascetic fantasy quickly overwhelms historical description."[52]

The desert life, and asceticism in general, had developed remarkable caché among the literate elite of Christian Rome because of the recently translated *Life of Anthony*. Jerome took advantage of the trend, writing hagiographies almost as autobiographical fictions that placed him firmly in a notional wilderness. In them, he blurred the lines between himself, the monk Paul of Thebes, the apostle Paul, Isaiah, and John of Revelation. "All of a sudden, riders on horses and camels, Ishmaelites, rushed up with hairy and beribboned heads and half-naked bodies," he writes in the novelistic *Vita Malchi*.[53]

I refer to the zones Jerome occupied by the term "frontiers." Frontier is a value-laden and imperial word. Just as "civilized" requires its opposite in "savage," the word frontier is given meaning by the colonizing center behind it, and the wilderness depicted beyond. Jerome takes his place among those border people—almost entirely men—who as much in the Roman empire as in the Victorian age traded narratives of "frontier" experience for reputation and authority, *virtus* and *imperium*.[54] From his stint in Syrian Antioch to his final days in Bethlehem, from Paul the Monk to Malchus, Jerome is obsessed with periphery and center. "[Your] letter was handed to me by the saintly Evagrius in that part of the desert which forms a broad boundary line between the Syrians and the Saracens," Jerome wrote in one of his earliest letters.[55]

Performed self-identity must, of course, be performed for some*one* or a group of someones. The fourth-century Roman equivalent of investors were the Christian elite, whose patronage meant success or failure for ambitious clerics such as Jerome, Rufinus, Damasus, Augustine, and Evagrius.[56] "You send us gifts," Jerome wrote unselfconsciously in 385 to Marcella, and "we send you back letters of thanks."[57] Jerome's memory of his first encounters with his patrons is telling:

> When the needs of the Church brought me also to Rome, in company with the holy pontiffs Paulinus and Epiphanius . . . I in my modesty was inclined to avoid the gaze of ladies of rank. But Marcella was so urgent both in season and out of season, as the apostle says, that her persistence overcame my timidity. At the time I had some repute as a student of the Scriptures.[58]

Narrative was a particularly powerful tool in the hands of a rhetorician, hagiographer, letter writer, biblical commentator, and spinner of romances like Jerome.[59] However, while the ascetic may have promiscuously employed and even invented different literary forms,[60] he remained remarkably constant in his literary *goals*. In service of his *virtus*, Jerome employed the same techniques he describes in his letter eulogizing Nepotianus: "The rhetorician's rule," Jerome wrote, "is [to] go back to the ancestors of the man you have to praise, and first recount their glorious deeds. Then gradually you will come to your hero, making him the more illustrious by the virtues of his forefathers."[61] It explains why Jerome made himself the climax of his *Lives of Illustrious Men*.

POSITIONALITY, PLACE, AND FRONTIER LANGUAGE

Nêhiyaw (Cree) scholar Margaret Kovach writes that "our knowledges are bound to place."[62] She goes on to note that "introducing Indigenous knowledges into any form of academic discourse (research or otherwise) must ethically include the influence of the colonial relationships."[63] Kovach and other Indigenous scholars emphasize the importance of land, story, relation, and community good, to the researcher's position and inquiry.[64] For that reason I turn to my own place and positionality.

There is a reason I recognize the settler in Jerome. I am a second-generation European-background Canadian. My paternal grandfather emigrated from Norway to take up the so-called free land. The area where both my paternal and maternal families took root had been cleared of its millennia-long presence of Lakota, Nakota, Anihšināpēk (Saulteaux), nêhiyawak (Cree), and Niisitapi peoples only fifty years or so before my grandparents' arrival. That clearing took place through government facilitated starvation and cynical treaty-making.[65] As a Canadian, and the grandchild of homesteaders on Indigenous land, I recognize familiar narratives in Jerome's writing. Many settlers were ill-fitted or unsuccessful in their countries of origin.[66] Not a few, reminiscent of Jerome in 385, fled scandal. Most carried their "old countries" with them. Despite the substantial differences between fourth-century Rome's borders and settler colonialism fifteen centuries later, I grew up surrounded by often-repeated narratives of self-described heroism. There were men's self-congratulatory tales of arriving in a harsh and unwelcoming wilderness with nothing in their pockets and yet somehow "making good." Such stories, like Jerome's, often work to hide or diminish the significant financial resources invested by others to ensure success.[67]

Both William Bleasdell Cameron and Jerome came from marginal positions within the empires they represented, making them what Bhabha calls "mimic men."[68] Bleasdell Cameron was in fact a lowly clerk in the Hudson's Bay Company, a chartered British corporation which—without consultation with Indigenous peoples—was for a time "granted" by the English crown much of the territory of modern-day Canada. Cameron gained a certain stardom when he survived being taken captive during the calamitous 1885 Métis resistance in what became western Canada. Because of this he went on to write a book about his adventures and was briefly editor of the American magazine *Field and Stream*. The photo at the outset of the article was taken in 1885 of a twenty-six-year-old William Bleasdell Cameron together with the twelve-year-old Mistatim Awâsis (the nêhiyawak or Cree name for "Horse Child"). Mistatim Awâsis was the son of the nêhiyaw leader Mistahi-maskwa (Big Bear). It is not a mistake that Cameron's most famous photo is with Mistatim Awâsis. It was Cameron's relationship to the boy's father that gave him his limited fame.[69]

Jerome's birthplace Stridon was a provincial town, and while Jerome was not poor, neither was he among the empire's elite.[70] Like Cameron, it was Jerome's self-storied encounters with Indigenous spaces and peoples (Eastern Greek Christians, ascetic hermits, and Palestinian Jews) that he used in service of his notoriety. "Oh, how often," Jerome wrote, "when I was living in the desert, in that lonely waste, scorched by the burning sun, which affords to hermits a savage dwelling place, how often did I fancy myself surrounded by the pleasures of Rome!"[71] Estimates as to the factual truth of Jerome's account vary. Perhaps influenced by art such as Foppa's, his biographer Kelly proposed that Jerome found a cleft in the rock and stayed a couple of years.[72] Contemporary scholars believe Jerome simply camped out at a country estate called *Maronia*.[73] The point is that both men built their reputations on exaggerations of "frontier" experiences. "Filled with stiff anger against myself," wrote Jerome,

> I would make my way alone into the desert; and when I came upon some hollow valley or rough mountain or precipitous cliff, there I would set up my oratory, and make that spot a place of torture for my unhappy flesh.[74]

Aware-settler approaches see such compelling *stories*, or myths, as an ideological mechanism, a tool by which settlers both suppress and perform Indigeneity, performing their "mastery" of the frontier.[75]

VIRTUS, IMPERIUM, AND FRONTIER MASCULINITY

A migrant joins an existing society intending to adapt themselves to that society—a colonist intends to supplant it. Settlement is permanent. It displaces. In Aileen Moreton-Robinson's *The White Possessive*, she notes that "possession is the foundation of property; it requires physical occupation and the will and desire to possess."[76] Whatever his actual successes in hagiography, orthodoxy, ascetic authority, translation, and exegesis, they were inscribed by Jerome himself not only as triumphs, but as *firsts*, accomplishments allowing him to claim ownership: "I have therefore determined to write a few words about the beginning of Paul's eremitical life and about his death . . . because the account has never been written."[77] Just as he takes pains to make Athanasius's Anthony bow before his literary Paul of Thebes (whom critics even in his own day doubted was ever a real person),[78] Jerome defines the exegetical, ecclesiastical, ascetic, and other reputational territories he wishes to claim as empty of meaningful, that is, *Latin*, precedent.[79]

The reputations of both the frontiersman and the ancient Roman man depended on the shaky foundation of public opinion. Jerome knew very well how in such arenas, as Maude Gleason has pointed out, "rhetoric was a calisthenics of manhood."[80] He wrote and compiled his letters accordingly. Because ancient masculinity was competitively performed rather than biologically assumed, the public status of a Roman man was rare, contested and constantly in danger of being lost.[81] One man's masculinity could be gained, or held, at the expense of another's.[82] The purpose of a public insult was to emasculate the other; thus Jerome snidely compares Rufinus's education to his own: "If you had studied letters, the jar of your little genius would still have the odor."[83] Unfortunately for him, Jerome was more often on the receiving end. Shortly after his flight from Rome he wrote:

I a scandal, I a slippery turncoat, I a liar using Satan's art to deceive! Which shows the greater subtlety, I wonder, to believe these charges (perhaps even to invent them about an innocent man), or to say: "I do not wish to believe them even though he is guilty?"

Here Jerome publicly challenges, taunts, and defends; but typically, leaves the crucial questions unanswered.

To combat the inevitable parries of others, elite Roman men sought to display *vir* and *virtus*, the traits of valor and virtue.[84] "*Virtus*," writes Craig Williams, "is an eminently praiseworthy quality, whether in a male (who should naturally have it), or a female (who may, exceptionally, attain to it)."[85] Readers of Jerome will recognize how his rhetorical constructions, for instance his eulogy for Paula (*Letters* 108), are structured to emphasize just this type of *virtus*.[86] As elsewhere in the ancient world, the greatest honor Jerome gave a woman was that she somehow "overcame" her gender, and became a man.[87] Nevertheless, Jerome reserved his highest praise for himself:

Before I became acquainted with the households of the saintly Paula, all Rome was enthusiastic about me. Almost everyone concurred in judging me worthy of the highest office in the Church. My words were always on the lips of Damasus of blessed memory. Men called me saintly; men called me humble, and eloquent.[88]

Virtus worked best to support masculinity when paired with the other performative characteristic of elite Roman manliness: *imperium*. *Imperium* was defined as control, over oneself at the least—which is where stoicism helped attenuate it[89]—but ideally also over others.[90] Here it is worth noting that Jerome's often-noted cantankerousness has been shown to be related more often to his epistolary rhetoric than to his personality.[91] Nonetheless, Jerome often seemed to fail to demonstrate control, whether over his own reactions, or more importantly, over the theological and political winds of late-antique Rome. His attempts led him to adopt four strategies characteristic of settler colonial frontiersmen. I turn to these now.

JEROME'S DECLARATIONS OF TERRA NULLIUS

In the Americas, settler colonial states declared the places they wished to exploit as *terra nullius*, that is, legally unoccupied territory. That such territories were manifestly *not* unoccupied was the reason they needed a declaration.[92]

Ultimately, European powers decided that it was enough to declare a lack of legal occupation if existing inhabitants could be declared as not human, or at least, not *worthily* human. In speaking of how this legality was applied in North America, Mackey shows how settlers redefined the land as "empty of people and societies *that mattered* (emphasis added)."[93] Applied to an anchorite cave in Syria or a pre-existing commentary on Ephesians, Jerome's various claims of *terra nullius* likewise depended on precedents being considered savage, insufficient, or in a particularly useful fourth-century twist, heretical. Foucault speaks of place being fundamental to any exercise of power.[94] Like other male settlers, Jerome must be understood by the use he made of place, and how he tried to demonstrate mastery while negotiating with Indigenous precedence.

The first recorded European on the North American plains was Henry Kelsey, an early seventeeth-century trader. He was guided every step by nêhiyawak, Nakota, and others who made sure the young Englishman lost neither his way nor his life. Yet Kelsey's journals make little mention of the locals. Where he does, he characterizes the very people on whom he depended as perverse, uncivilized, and unreliable—terms that could almost be lifted from some of Jerome's letters from the east.[95] Kelsey—and Jerome—illustrate the attitude of the settler colonist. For the purpose of dispossession and/or assimilation, frontier epistemology either delegitimizes existing inhabitants and their work, or valorizes and romanticizes them, but places them firmly in the past. While he of course never uses the phrase, Jerome makes the *terra nullius* argument throughout his writing. He *over*writes earlier accounts, both hagiographical and exegetical. For instance, he begins his introduction to the Galatians commentary: "I shall undertake a work that no Latin writer before me has attempted and that hardly any among the Greeks have executed in a manner worthy of the exalted nature of the subject matter."[96]

Jerome's adoption of a *terra nullius* strategy is particularly evident in his about-face on Origen's orthodoxy, even while making extensive use of Origen's work.[97] It was well known that Jerome owed much to Origen.[98] Jerome's advocacy of asceticism, the way he tied ascetic life to the translation of scripture from its original languages, especially Hebrew, and his time in Palestine—all were strategies seemingly adapted from the earlier Greek Church Father.[99] Origen also provided significant source material that Jerome sometimes translated nearly verbatim into his own Latin commentaries.[100] This was not necessarily unusual in the ancient world. However, that Jerome should then pronounce Origen heretical owes both to the power politics of the moment and to Jerome's convoluted relationship with his one-time intimate Rufinus, who had embarked on much the same settler-colonial path with Origen, but earlier, and with more success.[101]

Jerome and Rufinus were engaged in rival efforts to exploit the resources of the long-Christian Greek east for the imperial audiences of a newly attentive Catholic west. Jerome's turn on Origen, what Vessey calls his "panicky sale of stock," is proof that to Jerome the resources of the Christian east were just that:

resources. Similarly, Jerome's contacts among the rabbis appear in his rhetoric as little more to him than living reference manuals for translation.[102] It must be remembered that the fourth-century imperial Christian building of shrines in Palestine was also a displacement of whatever Jewish population was in those centers, and a monumentalizing of supersessionism.[103] In terms of Jerome's practice, a focus on *resource* over *relation* is settler colonialism distilled to its essence.

We can picture both Jerome and his contemporary Rufinus in the settler-colonial garb of competing traders like William Bleasdell Cameron (figure 7.1). "In your old age," Jerome writes against Rufinus, "you concoct stories about another old man which a cutthroat would not tell about a thief,"[104] and relates that Rufinus has accused him of bribing scribes to obtain Rufinus's rough drafts.[105] We are so often distracted by the late fourth-century intricacies of Nicene theology that we don't recognize settler colonialism during this period. From its angle, the battle of letters between Jerome and Rufinus essentially marked a trade war.[106]

Jerome's working principle of *terra nullius* is also evident in his treatment of the Syrian anchorites. He ended his time in Antioch complaining bitterly about the hermits whom he groused would not leave him "so much as a corner of the desert."[107] However, he realized his claims to ascetic authority required that he appear no less rigorous. He had to present himself to his Roman interlocutors as the very "model of eremitic holiness."[108] Although Jerome intimated that he was constantly hungry and alone, his "limbs worn away with fasting on the bare ground,"[109] Rebenich points out how he "must have lived in quite a spacious hollow to store his expanding collection of codices and to supervise young assistants, or protégés, who were copying manuscripts there."[110] Typically, Jerome forestalled criticism by leveling accusations at others:

I myself have seen some men who after they had renounced the world—in garb, at least . . . but not in reality—changed nothing of their former mode of life. [Meanwhile] . . . amidst crowds of servants swarming round them they claim the name of hermit.[111] Were Jerome's cancellations of his predecessors and his *terra nullius* claims successful? Not in his lifetime. Yet the image of Jerome alone in a cave is typical of how he was eventually remembered. In most visual representations, as in his own fictive hagiographies, Jerome enjoys a virtuous solitude, having tamed the "savage," the lion so symbolic of the frontier "other," sleeping peacefully at his feet (figure 7.2).[112]

JEROME'S FLAG-PLANTING: CLAIMS OF SOVEREIGNTY

Tightly bound with declaring physical or expert territories as *terra nullius*, and their inhabitants as savage or heretical, is a parallel move intrinsic to frontier masculinity: proclaiming ownership. *Terra nullius* always works in tandem with some sort of "planting of the flag." This is where settler-colonial behavior meets Roman *imperium*. Where *terra nullius* is aimed at existing inhabitants, "flag-planting" is undertaken with an eye to competition from the imperial center. Throughout his writing we see how often Jerome mentions his competition and posits his precedence. In the last section we saw how competition helps explain his correspondence with Rufinus. Jerome wrote: "he who is now my enemy, cannot call me a heretic, whom he declared a short while ago not to be at variance with his own faith."[113] In the fourth century, the borders of heresy moved fast.

Jerome's life, as well as his hagiographies, are remarkable for the frequent reporting of pairs. Even the lions who dig Paul of Thebes's grave in Jerome's hagiography are paired. In his youth, Jerome did not go to Trier alone to make his fortune, but with Bonosius. In Aquileia if not before, Jerome's fast friend Rufinus was attracted to asceticism with him. Melania the Elder, of Roman senatorial class, became the female patron of Rufinus, while Jerome sought out the patronage of Paula. Melania and Rufinus set up a Latin Christian monastic community at the Mount of Olives; a few years later Jerome and Paula set up a Latin Christian monastic community in Bethlehem. Rufinus translated Origen; so did Jerome.

Despite the often-clear evidence to the contrary, in each case Jerome presented himself as the greater member of the pair. Bonosius may have gone to an island in the Adriatic as a hermit, but later he, Jerome, was the first to embrace asceticism; while he "sits in the safe retreat of his island . . . I lie in the tomb of my sins."[114] The *Life of Anthony* may have been popular, but Jerome's hagiography concerned the greater hermit. Gregory of Nyssa wrote possibly the first female *Vita* in the *Life of Macrina*, but Jerome's *Vita* for Paula was better, and about a more worthy subject.[115] Gaius Marius Victorinus may have produced commentaries, but somehow Jerome in *his* commentary on Paul still undertook "a work . . . no Latin writer before me has attempted."[116]

This one-upmanship has long been recognized. I propose that such a concern with status is typical of a frontier man. Jerome stated in his *Vita* that Hilarion was the first monk of Palestine, neatly displacing Rufinus, since he himself couldn't.[117] Or perhaps he could: "Which one of us fulfilled all that is expected of him in the name of the monk?" he taunted Rufinus later.[118] Burrus describes Jerome's sleight of hand in claiming his *Life of Paul* (written about 374) as the first hagiography, when clearly the *Life of Anthony* had been written some fifteen years earlier by Athanasius, and was already immensely popular in the Latin version translated by the same Evagrius whose patronage Jerome enjoyed in Antioch.[119] Burrus argues that Jerome tried to void Athanasius's (and Evagrius's) priority in two ways: firstly by claiming that his subject, Paul, was in fact the first but *secret* desert hermit. Secondly, Jerome stated that the *Life of Anthony* was not really a hagiography, but a "source," making his own book the first of the genre.[120]

JEROME'S COMMODIFICATION AND TRADE OF THE "EXOTIC"

The third move of settler colonialism is its real goal: the commodification and advantageous trading of the resources (in this case, the reputation, writings, and languages) of the colonized periphery to the imperial center. As a displaced settler in the east, Jerome sought to trade ideas and texts from those colonized areas toward the center of Roman Christian power in exchange for support and status. Whether seeking the sponsorship of Valerian, Damasus, Marcellus, or Paula, Jerome's letters illustrate the extent to which, in Curran's words, the "major theological disputes of the period were themselves coloured by an upper-class social agenda" behind which sat the undeniable levers of patronage.[121]

The type of capital sought by an ambitious Christian like Jerome aspiring to *vir*-hood included the ecclesiastical patronage of bishops, popes, and occasionally emperors, especially during the battle for power between Nicene and other groups. Jerome's patrons came from a group of more informal powerbrokers. Especially important in Jerome's lifetime were elite Christian ascetic widows including the notables Marcella,[122] Melania, Asella,[123] Fabiola,[124] and Paula.[125] "Why should I go back to ancient times and quote instances of female virtue from books?" Jerome writes to Furia, "Before your own eyes in Rome . . . you have many women whom you might well choose for your model."[126] Model for *her*, patron for *him*. "Was I ever attracted by silk dresses, flashing jewels, painted faces, display of gold?" he writes. "No other matron in Rome could dominate my mind but one who mourned and fasted, who was squalid with dirt, almost blinded by weeping."[127]

Like ancient masculinity, and in relation to it, Jerome's access to elite Christian female patronage was constantly under negotiation and threat.[128] To hold it, Jerome marshaled resources such as, firstly, the claim to speak for the explosive new-to-the-west monastic and ascetic movements, secondly, the claim to own the heritage of the apostles, especially Paul, via new Latin commentaries, third, the claim to privileged access to more ancient Christian and Jewish tradition via Greek Christian interpreters and the ability to read and translate Hebrew,[129] and finally, but not least, the claim to manage the increasingly fashionable travel of elite persons to the holy sites in Palestine.[130]

Jerome's voluminous attempts to correspond with elite Roman Christian women are echoed in his criticism of others who, as he complained, "devote their whole life and all their energies to finding out about the names, the households, and the characters of married ladies."[131] Jerome warned his letters' recipients constantly against the ecclesiastical flatterers with curled hair that "still shows traces of the tongs," whom he depicted as scurrying from house to house.[132] Stuck in Bethlehem, it was a circumambulation *he* was forced to make via his correspondence.

Elite Latin women like Melania, Marcellus, Paula, and others had begun to Christianize patrician society via a movement of courtly monasticism, characterized by chastity, charity, intense biblical studies, and theological debate. Jerome saw himself as their "natural" mentor. He wrote: "I praise wedlock, I praise marriage; but it is because they produce me virgins. I gather the rose from the thorn, the gold from the earth, the pearl from the oyster."[133]

Jerome knew his "brand" depended on location. Just as Syrian Antioch was his claim to ascetic authority, Bethlehem, Jerusalem, and their environs supported his claims (parallel to Origen's, earlier) to proper biblical translation and commentary. Cain notes how Jerome

> recalibrated how excellence in biblical scholarship was to be measured in the west and obtruded himself as being better equipped than any of his Latin forebears or contemporaries to unlock the mysteries of the Bible and especially of the Old Testament.[134]

Being "on site" was all-important.[135] As with so many of his identity claims, Jerome's job description for the ideal exegete of scriptures happened to line up precisely with himself.[136]

The criterion of location also helps explain Jerome's oft-noted grumpiness to the fashion of elite Latin pilgrimage to the Holy Land: if exotic location was for him a type of currency, it was devalued by so many visitors.[137] This was true unless Jerome himself could orchestrate the travel of potential elite patrons and the associated benefits that arrived with them.[138] "Blessed Jesus," he brags of Fabiola's brief visit,

> with what fervour and zeal did she study the sacred volumes! In her eagerness to satisfy her hunger, she ran through the prophets, the gospels, and the psalms; she suggested questions and stored up my answers in her heart's repository.[139]

As I demonstrate in "Aware-Settler Biblical Studies: Breaking Claims of Textual Ownership," one's position as a settler-descended academic can encourage certain readings of ancient text.[140] My position makes me particularly aware of another dynamic of Jerome's writing. Specifically, Jerome linked the real Holy Land of his residence and the fictive Holy Land of his correspondence with a real and fictive frontier territory. He did so to stake his claim during the renewed interest in the Christian sites that began with Helena and gathered momentum throughout the fourth century.

During a much later European expansion this strong linking of biblical territory, imperial interest, and frontier would become an important ideological rationalization for colonialism, with each new "frontier" of settlement declared a repristinated Holy Land. Examples abound, but those that touched my family in particular were the immigration posters from the very early twentieth century for the Canadian west that call it a "land of milk and honey." As with the accounts of Joshua, a local population was seen to stand in the way of each new "Holy Land" reaching its full potential.[141] And as with Jerome, literary and epistolary images from the scriptures served to sanctify the drive toward commodification of each new Holy Land.

JEROME'S PIONEER NARRATIVE: THE INVENTION OF A SETTLER IMAGINARY

The fourth settler-colonial strategy I identify in Jerome is his construction of an ideological narrative, or a settler imaginary.[142] This is where Jerome excels.[143] Cain has called Jerome's earliest letter collection "a tightly knit bundle of interlocking propagandistic pieces."[144] Jerome's entire oeuvre can be seen through this lens. Certainly, his letters, his disputations with Rufinus and others, his *Lives of Illustrious Men,* and even tangential comments in his biblical commentaries work to bolster his self-presentation. Cain points out the "often underappreciated but fundamentally propagandistic nature" of Jerome's letters.[145] The sheer volume of Jerome's correspondence contradicts his complaint that "Every stroke of my secretary's pen is so much loss of life for me."[146] Rather, those pen-strokes ended up constituting his life, as he clearly hoped they would.

Jerome's pioneer narrative was complicated by his own multiple, nested identities. In part, this is what Jacobs and others refer to as his "imperial hybridity."[147] Jerome was not from the capital. He was an ambitious provincial from Stridon, first seeking his fortune in Trier.[148] Cameron, the Hudson's Bay clerk (figure 7.1), was also a provincial, raised in small-town Ontario before heading west. Frontier masculinity is always a nuanced, messy affair: we need to question hard-edged polarities, especially when the settler colonist is themselves from the imperial margin.[149] Jerome's settlement took place during a time when the Roman empire was convulsed by migration, refugee movements, and settlement from those outside its boundaries.

In any case, it is not actual historical individuals, such as the Jewish convert in Antioch whom Jerome mentions as his tutor,[150] nor the Syrian hermits with whom he argued, or even Origen or Athanasius, who are most important to this analysis. What was functionally crucial for Jerome's stories were the identities he appropriated. Asceticism interested Jerome, but always asceticism in its links to ecclesiastical and exegetical authority. Similarly, Jerome does not foreground Hebrew speakers or texts, but *his* translations. We are dealing in Jerome's writings with "idealized reifications rather than self-evident subjectivities."[151]

The colonized do not represent a simple, oppressed, mirror to the colonizer.[152] Such distinctions deny them agency.[153] Jerome is evidence of what Jacobs calls "the double-faced, hybrid quality of imperial identity."[154] Nowhere is this more evident than in Jerome's self-descriptions, especially his hagiographies. In Jacobs's work on Simeon Stylites, in which he applies contemporary celebrity theory to ancient hagiography, he observes: "the writing of a saint's life transforms a person into a sign, which can then be interpreted, circulated, and recapitulated in multiple forms."[155] Jerome used his semi-autobiographical hagiographies[156] to seek celebrity. Coon lists among hagiographies' purposes "biblical *topoi*, literary invention, and moral imperative."[157] Jerome shows how conveniently they also worked as settler imaginaries of self-promotion.

At the same time, Jerome's epistolary abilities allowed him to make up for what may have been a less-than-commanding physical presence. Here we must exercise double caution: added to the usual dangers of taking Jerome's rhetorical self-descriptions at face value are the ways in which this particular dichotomy of "weak in body, strong in written word" lines up so neatly with similar expressions in Paul's letters. In any case, once he was established in Bethlehem, Jerome's impressive letter writing allowed him to practice what Cain has termed his "textual presence-in-absence"[158] among the elite circle of women he ascetically courted.

CONCLUSION: FRONTIER MASCULINITY AND JEROME'S SUCCESSFUL AFTERLIVES

I have shown how an aware-settler lens reveals four interlocking rhetorical maneuvers Jerome employed: first, a declaration of *terra nullius* in certain key territories where he wished to assert ownership; second, a proclamation of precedence claiming he was the first from the imperial center to assert sovereignty or masculine *imperium* over a certain domain; third, a typically settler-colonial commerce in the resources of the colonized territory; and finally, the construction and retelling of a settler imaginary, a masculine myth of heroic labor and pioneer virtue which reinforced his *virtus*.

An aware-settler approach also helps solve the recurring problem of the "reality-rhetoric divide" in Jerome's writings.[159] From the hippocentaurs and she-wolves "panting with thirst" with which he populates the desert of his *Life of Paul*, to the sexual double-entendres of some of his letters,[160] it is a risk to take Jerome too literally. If we have to impose contemporary categories, Jerome was more novelist than historical autobiographer. Some biographies, especially Kelly's,[161] and Steinmann's[162] works, but even Rebenich's,[163] fail to resolve this tension. Faced with the problem of having to say something about the historical Jerome, these biographers tend to report many of his embellished or invented details as fact, even while noting his inventiveness.

In his study *Settler Colonialism: A Theoretical Overview*, Lorenzo Varacini repeats an observation that might help explain why Jerome's greatest triumph is to forever be pictured as a gaunt and naked ascetic in a Bethlehem cave (figure 7.2). Varacini notes that the goal of settler colonialism has always been two-fold. The first goal, ably accomplished by a self-styled ascetic exegete, is to suppress actual locals.[164] Compare Jerome, writing about his time in the desert, to the very real but fractious Syrian anchorites whom he anathemizes as quarrelsome, pretentious, and gluttonous.[165] Meanwhile, the local rabbis, and an unnamed Jewish convert, whose language he disdains as full of "hissing and breath-demanding words,"[166] he dismisses in the same breath with which he claims Hebrew as his own new tongue,[167] and champions the exegetical principle of *Hebraica veritas*.[168] Jerome's supersessionism is in curious contrast to the importance he attaches to the sources, until we understand his concerns as motivated by a commodification of Hebrew:

> I put myself in the hands of one of the brethren who had been a Hebrew before his conversion, and asked him to teach me his language. Thus, after having studied the pointed style of Quintilian, the fluency of Cicero, the weightiness of Fronto, and the gentleness of Pliny, I now began to learn the alphabet again and practice harsh and guttural words.[169]

Like Origen, Jerome was quick both to appropriate and to subvert Jewish learning from the location of the Holy Land.[170] (By so doing, he replicated in Christian literary tradition the physical appropriation of Jewish space that Constantine's building program had begun.)

This leads to Varacini's second goal of settler colonialism, which is the performance of one's own indigenization.[171] Witness Jerome's fanciful self-descriptions of desert living. During his short stay in a semi-urban estate, Jerome rhapsodizes the "wilderness bright with Christ's spring flowers," and the "desert rejoicing in God's familiar presence."[172] He allows that his skin "through long neglect had become rough and black as an Ethiopian's." In whatever brief time he actually had as an anchorite, he states his only companions were "scorpions and wild beasts."[173] He fails to include the numerous secretaries whom he complains about elsewhere, wrinkling their brows and fidgeting when he slows his dictation.[174] Jerome even claims he has nearly forgotten his native Latin because of his familiarity with the "barbarous jargon"[175] of eastern lands. In his famous but much-doubted Ciceronian conversion account he states that doctors pronounced him near death from his fasting: "It may sound incredible," he pretends to confide, "but the ravages . . . brought on my unhappy frame were so persistent that . . . my bones scarcely held together."[176] Burrus remarks that "Jerome is . . . a master of romance but a lousy historian."[177]

Contemporary scholarship varies from those who guardedly take some of Jerome's self-descriptions as fact, through to Burrus who writes of "dancing" or "playing" with him.[178] It seems obvious that Jerome's rhetoric clearly trumps historical reality. However, the aware-settler lens asks a different historical question. What was the historical *effect* Jerome's rhetoric intended? That is, what was the history his writing *created*? Were what Burrus calls the "genre-shattering repetitions"[179] of his hagiographies also *gender*-shattering instances of imaginative writing and self-promotion?

The fact is that Jerome never permanently returned to Rome. This alone should remind us that in his lifetime he was not successful at his goal of exercising *imperium* at the center of imperial Christianity. Despite his relative gains, in his lifetime Jerome never achieved the reputational status his writings so clearly portray him as seeking.[180] However, he did succeed at other goals: "Jerome, the Christian *litteratus*, wanted to make himself the spiritual leader of wealthy Christian intellectuals, who in their turn were able to support Jerome's ambitious literary projects and ascetic community in Bethlehem."[181] In these more modest goals he succeeded.

But Jerome was never modest.

> Many years ago for the sake of the kingdom of heaven I cut myself off from home, parents, sister, relations, and, what was harder, from the dainty food to which I had been used. But even when I was on my way to Jerusalem to fight the good fight there, I could not bring myself to forego the library which with great care and labour I had got together at Rome.[182]

The basic ingredients of Jerome's self-presentation mirror ancient masculinity: virtues exemplified by asceticism, while never leaving behind the *imperium* gained by impeccable classical learning. Through them Jerome sought his status in a hierarchy of holiness and reward that he believed existed both in this life and in the hereafter.[183]

Over the longer term, then, was Jerome's performance of masculine *virtus* and *imperium* successful? His ascetic approach, while never fully embraced, marked the borders of the west's future practice. His emphasis on texts and original languages set the course of biblical studies to this day.[184] Most certainly he would have approved of his biographer Steinmann's description of his legacy, written in prose almost as florid as his own: "In the days when the savages swept all before them, [Jerome] saved the heritage of faith and of learning."[185] Like most paintings of Jerome (figure 7.2), that is the fabulous story taken at face value. Frontiersman Jerome would have been proud.

NOTES

1. William Bleasdell Cameron, *Blood Red the Sun* (Calgary: Kenway Publishing, 1970. 1st edition 1927), xi.

2. *Letters* XIV, 29, 33. All English translations of Jerome's *Letters* are from F. A. Wright, *Select Letters of St. Jerome*. The Loeb Classical Library (London: William Heinemann Ltd., 1933).

3. This piece first appeared in *The Bible and Critical Theory* 18, no. 2 (2022) and reappears here with permission. I would like to thank the *B&CT* anonymous reviewers for their time and scholarly attention. Their thoughtful and constructive comments on structure and resources greatly improved the piece.

4. Matthew R. Anderson, "'Aware-Settler' Biblical Studies: Breaking Claims of Textual Ownership," *JIBS* 1, no. 1 (2019): 42–68.

5. For a summary, see Colleen M. Conway, "Masculinity Studies," in *The Oxford Handbook of New Testament, Gender, and Sexuality*, ed. Benjamin H. Dunning (Oxford: Oxford University Press, 2019), 77–93. Also Maud W. Gleason, *Making Men: Sophists and Self-Presentation in Ancient Rome* (Princeton: Princeton University Press, 1995).

6. Anderson, "Aware-Settler," 56–60.

7. Among the many Indigenous scholars who have influenced my work are Margaret Kovach, *Indigenous Methodologies: Characteristics, Conversations, and Contexts* (Toronto: University of Toronto Press, 2009); Leanne Betasamosake Simpson, *As We Have Always Done: Indigenous Freedom through Radical Resistance* (Minneapolis: University of Minnesota Press, 2017); Linda Tuhiwai Smith, *Decolonizing Methodologies*, 2nd ed. (London, Zed Books, 2012); Chris Andersen, "Critical Indigenous Studies: From Difference to Density," *Cultural Studies Review* 15, no. 2 (2009): 80–100; and Aileen Moreton-Robinson, *The White Possessive: Property, Power, and Indigenous Sovereignty* (Minneapolis: University of Minnesota Press, 2015).

8. Avril Bell, *Relating Indigenous and Settler Identities: Beyond Domination* (New York: Palgrave Macmillan, 2014), 3.

9. Mary Louise Pratt, *Imperial Eyes: Travel Writing and Transculturation* (London: Routledge, 1992), 6–7. For Indigenous perspectives on contact zones, see Laura E. Donaldson, "Native Women's Double-Cross: Christology from the Contact Zone," *Feminist Theology* 10, no. 29 (2002): 96–117, esp. 97–98 and Betasamosake Simpson, *As We Have Always Done*, chapter 9.

10. I use the term "frontier masculinity" as shorthand for the hypermasculinity of many first-person colonial narratives (and the later myths where such "pioneers" are portrayed). These stories often cast the land itself as an othered, female, presence that "requires" control, domination, or "civilizing." See Daniel Coleman, *White Civility: The Literary Project of English Canada* (Toronto: University of Toronto Press, 2006).

11. Homi Bhabha, "Of Mimicry and Man: The Ambivalence of Colonial Discourse," *October* 28 (1984): 131.

12. On queerness and positionality, Chris Greenough's *Queer Theology: The Basics* (London: Routledge, 2020), 25–26 is helpful.

13. Virginia Burrus, "Queer Lives of Saints: Jerome's Hagiography," *Journal of the History of Sexuality* 10, no. 3–4 (2001): 443–44.

14. In addition to the above: Virginia Burrus, *The Sex Lives of Saints: An Erotics of Ancient Hagiography* (Philadelphia: University of Pennsylvania Press, 2004); Patricia Cox Miller, "The Blazing Body: Ascetic Desire in Jerome's Letter to Eustochium," *JECS* 1, no. 1 (1993): 21–45; and Patricia Cox Miller, "Jerome's Centaur: A Hyper-Icon of the Desert," *JECS* 4, no. 2 (1996): 209–33.

15. Jack Halberstam, *The Queer Art of Failure* (Durham: Duke University Press, 2011), 87–88. Note that unlike Halberstam's prototype, Jerome never "quietly lost" his cause on his way to imagining "other goals for life, for love, for art, and for being" (88). For another example of queer failure, see Favorinus in Gleason, *Making Men*, 20.

16. The fact that ancient masculinity was performed did not necessarily mean either that the individual had free agency in choosing what to perform, or that their performances were successful, as Jerome is example. See Nikki Sullivan, *A Critical Introduction to Queer Theory* (New York: New York University Press, 2003), 89.

17. Gleason, *Making Men*, xxvi.

18. Joseph A. Marchal, "Queer Studies and Critical Masculinity Studies in Feminist Biblical Studies," in *Feminist Biblical Studies in the Twentieth Century: Scholarship and Movement*, ed. Elisabeth Schüssler Fiorenza (Atlanta: Society of Biblical Literature, 2014), 267.

19. For example: Kathy Ehrensperger, "Paul the Man: Enigmatic Images," in *Gender and Second-Temple Judaism*, ed. Kathy Ehrensperger and Shayna Sheinfeld (Lanham: Lexington/Fortress, 2020), 65–84; Jennifer Larson, "Paul's Masculinity," *JBL* 123, no. 1 (2004): 85–97; and Grace Emmett, "The Apostle Paul's Maternal Masculinity," *Journal of Early Christian History* 11, no. 1 (2021): 15–37.

20. Virginia Burrus, *"Begotten, Not Made": Conceiving Manhood in Late Antiquity* (Stanford: Stanford University Press, 2000).

21. Burrus, *"Begotten, Not Made,"* 193.

22. On the field of settler colonialism see Lorenzo Veracini, *Settler Colonialism: A Theoretical Overview*, Cambridge Imperial and Post-Colonial Studies Series (Houndmills, Basingstoke: Palgrave Macmillan, 2010).

23. Gleason, *Making Men*, 8.

24. Andrew Cain, *The Letters of Jerome: Asceticism, Biblical Exegesis, and the Construction of Christian Authority in Late Antiquity* (Oxford: Oxford University Press, 2009), 3.

25. Mark Vessey, "Jerome and the *Jeromonesque*," in *Jerome of Stridon: His Life, Writings and Legacy*, ed. Josef Lössl (Abingdon, Oxon: Taylor & Francis, 2009), 235.

26. *Letters* XL, 2, 169.

27. *Letters* CXXVII, 3, 443.

28. Cain, *The Letters of Jerome*, 198, notes that "Jerome notoriously went to great lengths to create the impression that he was the spiritual and scholarly centre of gravity of the late antique church."

29. Lynda L. Coon, *Sacred Fictions: Holy Women and Hagiography in Late Antiquity* (Philadelphia: University of Pennsylvania Press, 1997), 96.

30. Stefan Rebenich, *Jerome*. The Early Church Fathers (London: Routledge, 2002), 31–33.

31. Andrew Cain, "Jerome's *Epitaphium Paulae*: Hagiography, Pilgrimage, and the Cult of Saint Paula," *JECS* 19 (2010): 108. Also Cain, *The Letters of Jerome*, 99. See also *Letters* XLV, 2, 181: "Nothing is laid to my charge except my sex, and that only when Paula is likely to set out for Jerusalem." This was possibly the second time Jerome was forced to leave his home because of scandal, per Jean Steinmann, *Saint Jerome*, trans. Ronald Matthews (London: Geoffrey Chapman, 1959), 30–31 and J. N. D. Kelly, *Jerome: His Life, Writings, and Controversies* (London: Duckworth, 1975), 34.

32. *Letters* XLV, 6, 187.

33. *Letters* XLIII, 3, 175–76.

34. Mathew Kuefler, "Desire and Body in the Patristic Period," *The Oxford Handbook of Theology, Sexuality, and Gender*, ed. Adrian Thatcher (Oxford: Oxford University Press, 2015), 244.

35. See Elizabeth A. Clark, "The Celibate Bridegroom and His Virginal Brides: Metaphor and the Marriage of Jesus in Early Christian Ascetic Exegesis," *CH* 77, no. 1 (2008): 9.

36. Cox Miller, "The Blazing Body," 26: Cox Miller notes Jerome's valuation of desire in the act of his devaluation of body, and how his writings constitute "an erotics of asceticism that will be applicable not only to women but also to men."

37. Roy J. Deferrari (trans.), "The Life of Paul the Hermit," in *Early Christian Biographies: Lives of St. Cyprian, St. Ambrose, St. Augustine, St. Anthony, St. Paul the First Hermit, St. Hilarion, Malchus, St. Epiphanius* (Washington, DC: The Catholic University of America Press, 1952), 226–27. For a reading of this story from the woman's point of view, see Burrus, *The Sex Lives of Saints*, 50–51.

38. Burrus, "Queer Lives of Saints," 451.

39. Elizabeth A. Clark, "Theory and Practice in Late Ancient Asceticism: Jerome, Chrysostom, and Augustine," *JFSR* 5, no. 2 (1989): 31–32.

40. Burrus, *The Sex Lives of Saints*, 67.

41. *Letters*, XXII, 13, 79.

42. On the importance of specific land, see Anderson, "Aware-Settler," 53.

43. Virginia Burrus, "Mimicking Virgins: Colonial Ambivalence and the Ancient Romance." *Arethusa* 38, no. 1 (2005): 49–88.

44. Andrew S. Jacobs, "The Lion and the Lamb: Reconsidering Jewish-Christian Relations in Antiquity," in *The Ways That Never Parted: Jews and Christians in Late*

Antiquity and the Early Middle Ages, ed. Adam H. Becker and Annette Yoshiko Reed (Minneapolis: Fortress, 2007), 112–15.

45. Rebenich, *Jerome*, 12.

46. On the utility of using colonialism as a lens to study the ancient world see Geraldine Heng, "Reinventing Race, Colonization, and Globalisms Across Deep Time: Lessons from the 'Longue Durée'," *PMLA: Publications of the Modern Language Association of America* 130, no. 2 (2015): 358–66.

47. Pratt, *Imperial Eyes,* 6–7.

48. Aline Canellis, "Désert et Ville Dans La Correspondance De Saint Jérôme." *VC* 67, no. 1 (2013): 27 notes Jerome considered it «un endroit dépeuplé d'habitants mais assiégé par les troupes de saints» ("a place empty of inhabitants but besieged by saints," translation mine). On the desert and its mythical creatures see Cox Miller, "Jerome's Centaur," 221.

49. See Rebenich, *Jerome*, 16.

50. See especially chapter 5, "Malchus' Life Among the Saracens," in Jerome, *Vita Malchi*, trans. Christa Gray, 185. Halberstam, *The Queer Art of Failure*, 120, was not thinking of Jerome's novelistic hagiographies, but her observations on the characteristics of queer fairy tales nonetheless seem applicable here.

51. *Letters*, XXII, 30, 127.

52. Burrus, *The Sex Lives of Saints*, 19.

53. *Vita Malchi*, 83.

54. Cameron's autobiographical *Blood Red the Sun* is only one example among very many in this genre.

55. *Letters* VII, 1, 19.

56. Considerable variation existed in the relations between elite women and their client men within this grouping. See Clark, "Theory and Practice in Late Ancient Asceticism," 29–30, 43. Page 34: "Whereas 34 percent of Jerome's letters and 23 percent of Chrysostom's are addressed to women, only 7 percent of Augustine's are so designated."

57. *Letters*, XLIV, 177. On Roman women's patronage see Carolyn Osiek, "*Diakonos* and *Prostates*: Women's Patronage in Early Christianity," *HTS: Theological Studies* 61, no. 1–2 (2005): 347–70, especially 352–54.

58. *Letters*, CXXVII, 7, 453.

59. Mark Vessey notes that "generic inventiveness is the keynote of Jerome's writings" on p. 321 of Vessey, "Jerome and Rufinus," in *The Cambridge History of Early Christian Literature*, ed. Frances M. Young, Lewis Ayres, and Andrew Louth (Cambridge: Cambridge University Press, 2004).

60. On Jerome's invention of the Christian genre of "illustrious biographies" see Jamie Wood, "Playing the Fame Game: Bibliography, Celebrity, and Primacy in Late Antique Spain," *JECS* 20, no. 4 (2012): 615–16.

61. *Letters*, LX, 8, 279. See also Wood, "Fame Game," 617: Wood points out how Jerome used his literary invention of biography, his *Lives of Illustrious Men*, for declaring which of his predecessors really "counted."

62. Kovach, *Indigenous Methodologies,* 37.

63. Kovach, *Indigenous Methodologies,* 30.

64. Kovach, *Indigenous Methodologies*, 48.

65. Perhaps the best-researched study of this to date is James Daschuk, *Clearing the Plains: Disease, Politics of Starvation, and the Loss of Aboriginal Life* (Regina: University of Regina Press, 2013).

66. Bhabha, "Of Mimicry and Man," 128.

67. See Sheela McLain, "'We Built a Life from Nothing': White Settler Colonialism and the Myth of Meritocracy," *Policy Alternatives* 27, no. 12 (2017): 32–33.

68. Bhabha, "Of Mimicry and Man," 128.

69. The photo was taken in Regina Saskatchewan during the trial of Mistahi-Maskwa and others. Remarkably (and showing the "entanglements" typical of colonialism), there is another photo of Cameron and Mistatim Awâsis, taken sixty-two years later in 1947: http://digital.scaa.sk.ca/ourlegacy/solr?query=ID%3A28301&start=0&rows=10&mode=view&pos=0&page=1.

70. In *Letters*, LII, 6, 207, Jerome is as usual exaggerating when he writes that he "was born in a humble home . . . and once could scarcely get enough millet and course bread to satisfy the howlings of [his] stomach."

71. *Letters* XXII, 7, 67.

72. Kelly, *Jerome*, 48.

73. Rebenich, *Jerome*, 16.

74. *Letters*, XXII, 7, 69.

75. See Gina Starblanket and Dallas Hunt, *Storying Violence: Unravelling Colonial Narratives in the Stanley Trial* (Winnipeg: ARP Books, 2020); Anderson, "Aware-Settler," 42–68; Bell, *Relating Indigenous and Settler Identities,* 11; Bhabha, "Of Mimicry and Man," 132.

76. Moreton-Robinson, *The White Possessive,* 132.

77. "The Life of Paul the Hermit," 225–26. See also Vessey, "Jerome and Rufinus," 321–22.

78. Kelly, *Jerome*, 61.

79. For a narrative analysis using Jerome's hagiographical Life of Paul, see Charles Goldberg, "Jerome's She-Wolf," *JECS* 21, no. 4 (2013): 625–28.

80. Gleason, *Making Men,* xx.

81. Ehrensperger, "Paul the Man," 67–69.

82. Gleason, *Making Men,* 61, states that Ambrose refused to "receive a priest whose gait showed signs of arrogance." In this context note that Jerome defends his walk, which he says others criticized. *Letters* XLV, 2, 181.

83. Jerome, *Against Rufinus,* 100. All English translations of Against Rufinus are from John N. Hritzu (trans.), *Saint Jerome: Dogmatic and Polemical Works*. The Fathers of the Church: A New Translation 53 (Washington, DC: The Catholic University of America Press, 1965).

84. Craig A. Williams, *Roman Homosexuality*, 2nd ed. (Oxford: Oxford University Press, 2010), 145.

85. Williams, *Roman Homosexuality*, 146.

86. See Johanna C. Lamprecht, "Jerome's Letter 108 to Eustochium: Contemporary Biography in Service of Ascetic Ideology?" *HTS Teologiese Studies/Theological Studies* 73, no. 3 (2017): 1–10.

87. For other ancient examples, see Origen *Homily on Joshua* 9:69; *Gospel of Thomas Logion* 114; Nag Hammadi Codex 8.1; 1 Clement 55:3; Josephus, *War*, 159; Porphyry *Letter to Marcella* 33.

88. *Letters*, XLV, 3, 183.

89. Jennifer Glancy, *Corporal Knowledge: Early Christian Bodies* (Oxford: Oxford University Press, 2010), 28.

90. Williams, *Roman Homosexuality*, 148, notes: "The status of being a Roman man is associated with dominion or imperium (*"ut tibi imperes"*), and the incarnations of the opposing principles are slaves and women."

91. Andrew Cain, "*Vox Clamantis in deserto*: Rhetoric, Reproach, and the Forging of Ascetic Authority in Jerome's Letters from the Syrian Desert," *JTS* 57 (2006): 503.

92. See Eva Mackey, *Unsettled Expectations: Uncertainty, Land, and Settler Decolonization* (Winnipeg: Fernwood, 2016), 47–49.

93. Mackey, *Unsettled Expectations*, 48.

94. Michel Foucault, *Power/Knowledge: Selected Interviews and Other Writings, 1972–1977* (New York: Pantheon Books, 1980), 63.

95. See Kelly, *Jerome*, 55.

96. *Commentary on Galatians*, Book 1, 56. All translations of Jerome's Commentary on Galatians are from Andrew Cain (trans.), *Commentary on Galatians*, The Fathers of the Church: A New Translation 121 (Washington, DC: The Catholic University of America Press, 2010).

97. For an alternate view that gives more weight to Jerome's theology of asceticism, see Elizabeth A. Clark, "The Place of Jerome's Commentary on Ephesians in the Origenist Controversy: The Apokatastasis and Ascetic Ideals," *VC* 41, no. 2 (1987): 154–71.

98. Peter Brown, *The Body and Society: Men, Women and Sexual Renunciation in Early Christianity* (London: Faber & Faber, 1989), 42.

99. Megan Hale Williams, *The Monk and the Book: Jerome and the Making of Christian Scholarship* (Chicago: University of Chicago Press, 2006), 29; Vessey, "Jerome and Rufinus," 321.

100. Cain, "Introduction," *Commentary on Galatians*, 27.

101. Vessey, "Jerome and Rufinus," 323. Also Lewis Ayres, "Articulating Identity," *The Cambridge History of Early Christian Literature*, ed. Frances Young, Lewis Ayres, and Andrew Louth (Cambridge: Cambridge University Press, 2004), 454. See Jerome, in *Against Rufinus,* 159: "Your Origen, and (lest perchance you complain that you have been touched keenly by this fictive praise) our Origen (I call him ours for the excellence of his genius, not for the truth of his doctrines) explains and expounds in all his books the translations of the Jews."

102. Jacobs, "The Lion and the Lamb," 112.

103. Oded Irshai, "Book Review: Christians and the Holy Places: The Myth of Jewish-Christian Origins." *JRS* 84 (1994): 265.

104. *Against Rufinus*, 155–56.

105. *Against Rufinus*, 156.

106. See Brown, *The Body and Society,* 380.

107. Cain, *The Letters of Jerome,* 31.

108. Cain, *The Letters of Jerome*, 25.
109. *Letters*, XIV, 10, 51.
110. Rebenich, *Jerome*, 14.
111. *Letters*, CXXV, 16, 427.
112. On Jerome's use of real or fantastical animal imagery in his writings, see Cox Miller, "Jerome's Centaur," 209–33. While there is not space here to pursue this inquiry, it seems suggestive that in Jerome's fantastical *Life of Paul*, Anthony encounters a centaur and a satyr in the desert. As Cox Miller points out, both creatures represented hyper-sexuality, fluid gender, and uncontrolled desire. As elsewhere in this article, I suggest these symbols and their representations are intersectional. The centaur, with its "barbarous sounds rather than lucid speech" also represents the barbarian. Given that Jerome was in the process of extracting value from a frontier area peopled by "barbarians" and Jews, it may be that his image of the satyr is his anti-Judaic or perhaps anti-Nazorean caricature of people from whom he was learning Hebrew and borrowing ancient texts. This identification would underline Cox Miller's point that "the satyr was, like the centaur, a guardian of undeciphered secrets (223)." See also Goldberg, "Jerome's She-Wolf," 626. On Jerome and the Nazoreans see Martinus C. de Boer, "The Nazoreans: Living at the Boundary of Judaism and Christianity," *Tolerance and Intolerance in early Judaism and Christianity*, ed. Graham N. Stanton and Guy G. Stroumsa (Cambridge: Cambridge University Press, 1998), 239–62.
113. *Against Rufinus*, 63.
114. *Letters*, VII, 3, 23.
115. Burrus, *The Sex Lives of Saints*, 12, 65.
116. *Commentary on Galatians*, Book One, 56.
117. Andrew Cain, "Rethinking Jerome's Portraits of Holy Women," in *Jerome of Stridon*, ed. Cain, A. and J. Lössl (Aldershot: Ashgate, 2009), 56, n 59.
118. *Against Rufinus*, 103.
119. For more on Jerome and Evagrius see Williams, *The Monk and the Book*, 39.
120. Burrus, *The Sex Lives of Saints*, 22–23.
121. John Curran, "Jerome and the Sham Christians of Rome," *JEH* 48, no. 2 (1997): 218.
122. *Letters* CXXVII is Jerome's encomium of Marcella.
123. On Jerome's rhetorical use of both Marcella and Asella, see Cain, "Rethinking Jerome's Portraits of Holy Women," 47–57.
124. *Letters* LXXVII, 7, 325–27.
125. See Cain, "Jerome's *Epitaphium Paulae*."
126. *Letters* LIV, 18, 263.
127. *Letters* XLV, 3, 183.
128. On ancient elite women's patronage (and differences between patronage and commerce) see Shelly Matthews, "Ladies' Aid: Gentile Noblewomen as Saviors and Benefactors in the Antiquities." *HTR* 92, no. 2 (1999): 213.
129. On the unlikely facticity of the claim to have learned Hebrew as a youth: Williams, *The Monk and the Book*, 27.
130. Kelly, *Jerome*, 225–26 reads into Jerome's later writings that Jerome was anxious to gain financial support for the monasteries from travelers. Jas Elsner writes:

"the monasteries provided the principal tour guides, hostels, and in some cases even the central attractions (in the form of living saints or the relics of departed ones) for the practice of Palestinian pilgrimage": Jas Elsner and Ian Rutherford, *Pilgrimage in Graeco-Roman & Early Christian Antiquity: Seeing the Gods* (Oxford: Oxford University Press, 2010), 429.

131. *Letters*, XXII, 28, 119.
132. *Letters* XXII, 28, 119–21.
133. *Letters*, XXII, 20, 95.
134. Cain, *The Letters of Jerome*, 198.
135. Vessey, "Jerome and Rufinus," 322, notes: "astonishingly, [Jerome was] able for a time to make the town of Christ's nativity the centre of the Latin-reading Christian world."
136. Burrus, *The Sex Lives of Saints*, 22.
137. Rebecca Stephens Falcasantos, "Wandering Wombs, Inspired Intellects: Christian Religious Travel in Late Antiquity," *JECS* 25, no. 1 (2017): 107–08. Also Rebenich, *Jerome*, 41.
138. Cain, "Jerome's *Epitaphium Paulae*," 113.
139. *Letters*, LXXVII, 7, 327.
140. Anderson, "Aware-Settler," 57.
141. For an Indigenous perspective: Robert Allen Warrior, "Canaanites, Cowboys, and Indians: Deliverance, Conquest, and Liberation Theology Today," *Christianity and Crisis* 49, no. 12 (1989): 261–65.
142. Bell, *Relating Indigenous and Settler Identities*, 11.
143. Although Heng, "Lessons from the 'Longue Durée'," 360, does not include Jerome in her list of "early literatures of colonization," I believe his letters have all the earmarks of this genre.
144. Cain, *The Letters of Jerome,* 17.
145. Cain, *The Letters of Jerome*, 6.
146. *Letters* LX, 19, 309.
147. Jacobs, "The Lion and the Lamb," 112–14.
148. Reading Jerome's letters I was reminded of Stendhal's *The Red and the Black*, where the protagonist chooses a career in the church over the army after evaluating which might better reward his ambition.
149. Tim Whitmarsh, *Greek Literature and the Roman Empire: The Politics of Imitation* (Oxford: Oxford University Press, 2002), 20.
150. *Letters*, CXXV, 12, 419.
151. Whitmarsh, *Greek Literature and the Roman Empire,* 20.
152. Burrus, "Mimicking Virgins," 49, reminds us to look for "diverse intertextual strategies of appropriation, fragmentation, recombination, and parody."
153. In terms of Indigenous peoples see Tuhiwai Smith, *Decolonizing Methodologies,* 24.
154. Jacobs, "The Lion and the Lamb," 114. See also Bhabha, "Of Mimicry and Man," 132.
155. Andrew S. Jacobs, "'I Want to Be Alone' Ascetic Celebrity and the Splendid Isolation of Simon Stylites," in *The Garb of Being: Embodiment and the Pursuit*

of Holiness in Late Ancient Christianity, ed. Georgia Frank, Susan R. Holman, and Andrew S. Jacobs (New York: Fordham University Press, 2020), 161.

156. Beginning with his novelistic hagiography of an unnamed women in his earliest letters. See Steff Coppieters, Danny Praet, Annelies Bossu, and Maarten Taveime, "Martyrdom, Literary Experiment and Church Politics in Jerome's Epistula Prima, to Innocentius, on the Septies Percussa," *VC* 68, no. 4 (November 2014): 384–408.

157. Coon, *Sacred Fictions,* 143.

158. Cain, *The Letters of Jerome,* 10.

159. Jacobs, "The Lion and the Lamb," 105.

160. There certainly may be not-so-hidden penile references in *Letters* XIV, 9, 49.

161. For instance, in an older biography from 1975, Kelly reports as fact Jerome's regular and friendly correspondence with Marcella in Rome. See Kelly, *Jerome,* 179. This, despite the evidence for this detail existing only in Jerome's letters, and despite ample reason for him to exaggerate such a point.

162. Steinmann, *Saint Jerome.*

163. Rebenich, *Jerome,* calls his first chapter "Between Career and Conversion," masking over the fact that for Jerome these two were the same.

164. Veracini, *Settler Colonialism,* 95.

165. *Letters,* XXII, 34, 137.

166. Rebenich, *Jerome,* 15.

167. *Against Rufinus,* 170.

168. Cain, *Commentary on Galatians,* translator's Introduction, 36. See also Stefan Rebenich, "Jerome: The 'Vir Trilinguis' and the 'Hebraica Veritas,'" *VC* 47, no. 1 (March 1993): 50–77 and Jacobs, "The Lion and the Lamb," 112.

169. *Letters,* CXXV, 12, 419.

170. Jacobs, "The Lion and the Lamb," 111.

171. Veracini, *Settler Colonialism,* 95.

172. *Letters,* XIV, 10, 49.

173. *Letters,* XXII, 7, 67.

174. *Commentary on Galatians,* Book Three, 205.

175. *Letters,* VII, 2, 21, and CXXV, 12, 419.

176. *Letters,* XXII, 30, 127.

177. Burrus, "Queer Lives of Saints," 445.

178. See Burrus, *The Sex Lives of Saints,* 49–52.

179. Burrus, *The Sex Lives of Saints,* 48.

180. On Jerome's posthumous rise in reputation see Vessey, "Jerome and the *Jeromonesque,*" 235 and Cain, "Rethinking Jerome's Portraits of Holy Women," 47–49.

181. Rebenich, "Jerome: The 'Vir Trilinguis,'" 60.

182. *Letters,* XXII, 30, 125. Megan Williams, *The Monk and the Book,* 31, notes that Jerome's "attraction seems to have been more to the ascetic idea than to the ascetic life," at least during his time in Syrian Antioch in the mid 370s.

183. Clark, "The Place of Jerome's Commentary on Ephesians," 166.

184. Cain, "Introduction," *Commentary on Galatians,* 37.

185. Steinmann, *Saint Jerome,* 321.

BIBLIOGRAPHY

Primary Sources

Photograph of twelve-year-old Mistatim Awâsis (Horsechild) and William Bleasdell Cameron. Public Domain. http://digital.scaa.sk.ca/ourlegacy/permalink/28300.

Saint Jerome, penitent. Painting by Vincenzo Foppa (1427–1515). Wikimedia Commons.

Jerome

Cain, Andrew (trans.). *Commentary on Galatians.* The Fathers of the Church: A New Translation 121. Washington, DC: The Catholic University of America Press, 2010.

Deferrari, Roy J. (trans.). "The Life of Paul the Hermit." In *Early Christian Biographies: Lives of St. Cyprian, St. Ambrose, St. Augustine, St. Anthony, St. Paul the First Hermit, St. Hilarion, Malchus, St. Epiphanius.* Washington, DC: The Catholic University of America Press, 1952.

Gray, Christa (trans.). *Vita Malchi: Introduction, Text, Translation, and Commentary.* Oxford Classical Monographs. Oxford: Oxford University Press, 2015.

Hritzu, John N. (trans.). *Saint Jerome: Dogmatic and Polemical Works.* The Fathers of the Church: A New Translation 53. Washington, DC: The Catholic University of America Press, 1965.

Wright, F. A. (trans.). *Select Letters of St. Jerome.* The Loeb Classical Library. London: William Heinemann Ltd., 1933.

Secondary Works

Andersen, Chris. "Critical Indigenous Studies: From Difference to Density." *Cultural Studies Review* 15, no. 2 (2009): 80–100.

Anderson, Matthew R. "'Aware-Settler' Biblical Studies: Breaking Claims of Textual Ownership." *Journal for Interdisciplinary Biblical Studies* 1, no. 1 (2019): 42–68.

Ayres, Lewis. "Articulating Identity." In *The Cambridge History of Early Christian Literature,* edited by Frances Young, Lewis Ayres, and Andrew Louth, 414–63. Cambridge: Cambridge University Press, 2004.

Bell, Avril. *Relating Indigenous and Settler Identities: Beyond Domination.* Identity Studies in the Social Sciences. New York: Palgrave Macmillan, 2014.

Bhabha, Homi. "Of Mimicry and Man: The Ambivalence of Colonial Discourse." *October* 28 (1984): 125–33.

Boer, Martinus C. de. "The Nazoreans: Living at the Boundary of Judaism and Christianity." In *Tolerance and Intolerance in early Judaism and Christianity*, edited by Graham N. Stanton and Guy G. Stroumsa, 239–62. Cambridge: Cambridge University Press, 1998.

Brown, Peter. *The Body and Society: Men, Women and Sexual Renunciation in Early Christianity.* London: Faber & Faber, 1989.

Burrus, Virginia. *"Begotten, Not Made": Conceiving Manhood in Late Antiquity.* Stanford CA: Stanford University Press, 2000.
Burrus, Virginia. "Queer Lives of Saints: Jerome's Hagiography." *Journal of the History of Sexuality* 10, no. 3–4 (2001): 442–79.
Burrus, Virginia. *The Sex Lives of Saints: An Erotics of Ancient Hagiography.* Philadelphia: University of Pennsylvania Press, 2004.
Burrus, Virginia. "Mimicking Virgins: Colonial Ambivalence and the Ancient Romance." *Arethusa* 38, no. 1 (2005): 49–88.
Cain, Andrew. "*Vox Clamantis in deserto*: Rhetoric, Reproach, and the Forging of Ascetic Authority in Jerome's Letters from the Syrian Desert." *Journal of Theological Studies* 57 (2006): 500–25.
Cain, Andrew. *The Letters of Jerome: Asceticism, Biblical Exegesis, and the Construction of Christian Authority in Late Antiquity.* Oxford: Oxford University Press, 2009.
Cain, Andrew. "Rethinking Jerome's Portraits of Holy Women." In *Jerome of Stridon,* edited by A. Cain and J. Lössl, 47–57. Aldershot: Ashgate, 2009.
Cain, Andrew. "Jerome's *Epitaphium Paulae*: Hagiography, Pilgrimage, and the Cult of Saint Paula." *Journal of Early Christian Studies* 19 (2010): 105–39.
Cain, Andrew and J. Lössl (eds.). *Jerome of Stridon.* Aldershot: Ashgate, 2009.
Cameron, William Bleasdell. *Blood Red the Sun.* Calgary: Kenway Publishing, 1970. 1st edition 1927.
Canellis, Aline. "Désert et Ville Dans La Correspondance De Saint Jérôme." *Vigiliae Christianae* 67, no. 1 (2013): 22–48.
Clark, Elizabeth A. "The Place of Jerome's Commentary on Ephesians in the Origenist Controversy: The Apokatastasis and Ascetic Ideals." *Vigiliae Christianae* 41, no. 2 (1987): 154–71.
Clark, Elizabeth A. "Theory and Practice in Late Ancient Asceticism: Jerome, Chrysostom, and Augustine." *Journal of Feminist Studies in Religion* 5, no. 2 (1989): 25–46.
Clark, Elizabeth A. "The Celibate Bridegroom and His Virginal Brides: Metaphor and the Marriage of Jesus in Early Christian Ascetic Exegesis." *Church History* 77, no. 1 (2008): 1–25.
Coleman, Daniel. *White Civility: The Literary Project of English Canada.* Toronto: University of Toronto Press, 2006.
Conway, Colleen M. "Masculinity Studies." In *The Oxford Handbook of New Testament, Gender, and* Sexuality, edited by Benjamin H. Dunning, 77–93. Oxford: Oxford University Press, 2019.
Coon, Lynda L. *Sacred Fictions: Holy Women and Hagiography in Late Antiquity.* Philadelphia: University of Pennsylvania Press, 1997.
Coppieters, Steff, Danny Praet, Annelies Bossu, and Maarten Taveime. "Martyrdom, Literary Experiment and Church Politics in Jerome's Epistula Prima, to Innocentius, on the Septies Percussa." *Vigiliae Christianae* 68, no. 4 (November 2014): 384–408.
Curran, John. "Jerome and the Sham Christians of Rome." *The Journal of Ecclesiastical History* 48, no. 2 (1997): 213–29.

Daschuk, James. *Clearing the Plains: Disease, Politics of Starvation, and the Loss of Aboriginal Life*. Regina: University of Regina Press, 2013.

Donaldson, Laura E. "Native Women's Double Cross: Christology from the Contact Zone." *Feminist Theology* 10, no. 29 (2002): 96–117.

Ehrensperger, Kathy. "Paul the Man: Enigmatic Images." In *Gender and Second-Temple Judaism*, edited by Kathy Ehrensperger and Shayna Sheinfeld, 65–84. Lanham: Lexington/Fortress, 2020.

Elsner, Jaś and Ian Rutherford. *Pilgrimage in Graeco-Roman & Early Christian Antiquity: Seeing the Gods*. Oxford: Oxford University Press, 2010.

Emmett, Grace. "The Apostle Paul's Maternal Masculinity." *Journal of Early Christian History* 11, no. 1 (2021): 15–37.

Falcasantos Rebecca Stephens. "Wandering Wombs, Inspired Intellects: Christian Religious Travel in Late Antiquity." *Journal of Early Christian Studies* 25, no. 1 (2017): 89–117.

Foucault, Michel and Colin Gordon. *Power/Knowledge: Selected Interviews and Other Writings, 1972–1977*. New York: Pantheon Books, 1980.

Glancy, Jennifer. *Corporal Knowledge: Early Christian Bodies*. Oxford: Oxford University Press, 2010.

Gleason, Maude W. *Making Men: Sophists and Self-Presentation in Ancient Rome*. Princeton: Princeton University Press, 1995.

Goldberg, Charles. "Jerome's She-Wolf." *Journal of Early Christian Studies* 21, no. 4 (2013): 625–28.

Greenough, Chris. *Queer Theology: The Basics*. London: Routledge, 2020.

Halberstam, Judith. *The Queer Art of Failure*. Durham: Duke University Press, 2011.

Heng, Geraldine. "Reinventing Race, Colonization, and Globalisms Across Deep Time: Lessons from the 'Longue Durée'." *PMLA: Publications of the Modern Language Association of America* 130, no. 2 (2015): 358–66.

Irshai, Oded. "Book Review: Christians and the Holy Places: The Myth of Jewish-Christian Origins." *The Journal of Roman Studies* 84 (1994): 264–65.

Jacobs, Andrew S. "The Lion and the Lamb: Reconsidering Jewish-Christian Relations in Antiquity." In *The Ways That Never Parted: Jews and Christians in Late Antiquity and the Early Middle Ages*, edited by Adam H. Becker and Annette Yoshiko Reed, 95–118. Minneapolis: Fortress, 2007.

Jacobs, Andrew S. "'I Want to Be Alone' Ascetic Celebrity and the Splendid Isolation of Simon Stylites." In *The Garb of Being: Embodiment and the Pursuit of Holiness in Late Ancient Christianity*, edited by Georgia Frank, Susan R. Holman, and Andrew S. Jacobs, 145–68. New York: Fordham University Press, 2020.

Kelly, J. N. D. *Jerome: His Life, Writings, and Controversies*. London: Duckworth, 1975.

Kovach, Margaret. *Indigenous Methodologies: Characteristics, Conversations, and Contexts*. Toronto: University of Toronto Press, 2009.

Kuefler, Mathew. "Desire and Body in the Patristic Period." In *The Oxford Handbook of Theology, Sexuality, and Gender*, edited by Adrian Thatcher, 241–54. Oxford: Oxford University Press, 2015.

Lamprecht Johanna C. "Jerome's Letter 108 to Eustochium: Contemporary Biography in Service of Ascetic Ideology?" *HTS Teologiese Studies/Theological Studies* 73, no. 3 (2017): 1–10.

Larson, Jennifer. "Paul's Masculinity." *Journal of Biblical Literature* 123, no. 1 (2004): 85–97.

Mackey, Eva. *Unsettled Expectations: Uncertainty, Land, and Settler Decolonization*. Winnipeg: Fernwood, 2016.

Marchal, Joseph A. "Queer Studies and Critical Masculinity Studies in Feminist Biblical Studies." In *Feminist Biblical Studies in the Twentieth Century: Scholarship and Movement,* edited by Elisabeth Schüssler Fiorenza, 261–80. Atlanta: Society of Biblical Literature, 2014.

Matthews, Shelly. "Ladies' Aid: Gentile Noblewomen as Saviors and Benefactors in the Antiquities." *Harvard Theological Review* 92, no. 2 (1999): 199–218.

McLain, Sheela. "'We Built a Life from Nothing': White Settler Colonialism and the Myth of Meritocracy." *Policy Alternatives* 27, no. 12 (2017): 32–33.

Miller, Patricia Cox. "The Blazing Body: Ascetic Desire in Jerome's Letter to Eustochium." *Journal of Early Christian Studies* 1, no. 1 (1993): 21–45.

Miller, Patricia Cox. "Jerome's Centaur: A Hyper-Icon of the Desert." *Journal of Early Christian Studies* 4, no. 2 (1996): 209–33.

Moreton-Robinson, Eileen. *The White Possessive: Property, Power, and Indigenous Sovereignty*. Minneapolis: University of Minnesota Press, 2015.

Osiek, Carolyn. "*Diakonos* and *Prostates*: Women's Patronage in Early Christianity." *HTS: Theological Studies* 61, no. 1–2 (2005): 347–70.

Pratt, Mary Louise. *Imperial Eyes: Travel Writing and Transculturation*. London: Routledge, 1992.

Rebenich, Stefan. "Jerome: The 'Vir Trilinguis' and the 'Hebraica Veritas'." *Vigiliae Christianae* 47, no. 1 (1993): 50–77.

Rebenich, Stefan. *Jerome*. The Early Church Fathers. London: Routledge, 2002.

Simpson, Leanne Betasamosake. *As We Have Always Done: Indigenous Freedom through Radical Resistance*. Minneapolis: University of Minnesota Press, 2017.

Smith, Linda Tuhiwai. *Decolonizing Methodologies*, 2nd ed. London: Zed Books, 2012.

Starblanket, Gina and Dallas Hunt. *Storying Violence: Unravelling Colonial Narratives in the Stanley Trial*. Winnipeg: ARP Books, 2020.

Steinmann, Jean. *Saint Jerome*. Translated by Ronald Matthews. London: Geoffrey Chapman, 1959.

Sullivan, Nikki. *A Critical Introduction to Queer Theory*. New York: New York University Press, 2003.

Veracini, Lorenzo. *Settler Colonialism: A Theoretical Overview*. Cambridge Imperial and Post-Colonial Studies Series. Houndmills, Basingstoke: Palgrave Macmillan, 2010.

Vessey, Mark. "Jerome and Rufinus." In *The Cambridge History of Early Christian Literature*, edited by Frances M. Young, Lewis Ayres, and Andrew Louth, 318–27. Cambridge: Cambridge University Press, 2004.

Vessey, Mark. "Jerome and the Jeromesque." In *Jerome of Stridon: His Life, Writings and Legacy,* edited by Josef Lössl, 225–35. Abingdon, Oxon: Taylor and Francis, 2009.

Warrior, Robert Allen. "Canaanites, Cowboys, and Indians: Deliverance, Conquest, and Liberation Theology Today." *Christianity and Crisis* 49, no. 12 (1989): 261–65.

Whitmarsh, Tim. *Greek Literature and the Roman Empire: The Politics of Imitation.* Oxford: Oxford University Press, 2002.

Williams, Craig A. *Roman Homosexuality,* 2nd ed. Oxford: Oxford University Press, 2010.

Williams, Megan Hale. *The Monk and the Book: Jerome and the Making of Christian Scholarship.* Chicago: University of Chicago Press, 2006.

Wood, Jamie. "Playing the Fame Game: Bibliography, Celebrity, and Primacy in Late Antique Spain." *Journal of Early Christian Studies* 20, no. 4 (2012): 613–40.

8

Queen Helena of Adiabene through the Centuries

Sarit Kattan Gribetz

WHO WAS HELENA OF ADIABENE?

According to the first-century historian Josephus, Queen Helena of Adiabene traveled to Jerusalem because she loved the Jewish God and wished to worship in the temple; she stayed because she fell in love with the city and its people. Helena became a beloved patron of Jerusalem, feeding its residents during famine and erecting monumental buildings, including a palace and a mausoleum. She died in Adiabene, but her son returned her remains to Jerusalem so that she could be buried in the holy city.[1]

Josephus, who grew up in Jerusalem in the final decade or two of Queen Helena's life, refers a number of times to Helena's buildings in his early writings—they serve as recognizable landmarks when he describes his hometown and the battles that ensued there during the Jewish revolt against Rome.[2] In his later work, Josephus tells Helena's story of conversion, pilgrimage, and patronage.[3] Scholars have studied Josephus's portrayal of Helena of Adiabene quite extensively.[4] Josephus composed his writings several decades after Helena's death, and he likely did not author the section on the royal house of Adiabene himself: the unit about Helena and her sons embedded into Josephus's *Antiquities* is probably based on earlier literary sources (themselves composed of multiple distinct sources) to which we no longer have access save through Josephus's text.[5] We therefore cannot directly answer the question "who was Helena of Adiabene?" for our earliest source about her is already a retrospective and composite one, as so many historical accounts are.

We can, however, wonder how Helena of Adiabene was remembered in antiquity and thereafter. In this study, I turn to Helena's legacy as it developed after Josephus's account. I ask: what did Queen Helena of Adiabene, so prominent a figure in first-century Jerusalem, represent to different individuals and communities in the centuries thereafter, both in Jerusalem and elsewhere?

I trace portrayals of and references to Helena in select late ancient and medieval sources, including Christian texts from the fourth and fifth centuries that promote the memory of Helena as a model for contemporary women's patronage of Jerusalem, and some of which portray Helena as one of Jesus's earliest followers; rabbinic texts that emphasize Helena's connection with the temple and temple-oriented rituals; and versions of Toledot Yeshu in which she is remembered as the ruler of Jerusalem and the figure who saved Judaism from Jesus. These sources are quite different from one another, and yet in each one Helena is remembered as a prominent figure in Jerusalem. Such memories of Helena of Adiabene persisted for centuries. Why?

I start my analysis of the sources with a brief passage from Pausanias, who tells a fantastic tale about Helena's tomb—a perfect place to begin a journey into Helena's afterlife. I then examine Jerome's Letter to Eustochium, in which he mourns his patron Paula's death and recounts Paula's travels in the Holy Land, mentioning Helena's tomb on the way. I read Jerome's account alongside those of Eusebius and Rufinus, with whom Jerome was undoubtedly in conversation and competition. Then, I turn to several passages in rabbinic sources in which Helena features as a benefactor of the temple, a performer of rabbinic rituals, a builder of an enormous Sukkah, and a pious Nazirite. Even though the Christian texts I discuss date to periods later than the earliest rabbinic sources, I deliberately begin with them both because they are based on Josephus's account and also because they are helpful in de-centering rabbinic sources about Helena. Reading rabbinic depictions of Helena in light of those by Jerome, Eusebius, and Rufinus highlights how rabbinic traditions forged an altogether different but not inevitable path in their memory of Helena. The comparison also allows us to offer a reason for the contrast between the two corpora's portrayals of Helena's relationship to the city of Jerusalem. Next, I analyze two sources that explicitly claim Helena as an early Christian: Orosius's *Historiae adversus paganos*, which identifies Helena as a follower of Christ, and Moses of Khorene's *History of Armenia*, in which Abgar of Edessa, an early Christian king, is said to be married to Helena. I conclude with a look at the significantly later Helena manuscripts of Toledot Yeshu, in which Helena stars as queen of Jerusalem during the time of Jesus. This medieval narrative tradition credits Helena with exposing Jesus as a charlatan and saving Jerusalem's Jewish community from the threat of Christianity. In addition to being a fascinating corpus in its own right, it is also a surprisingly helpful set of sources for revisiting earlier depictions of Helena with new perspective.

Tessa Rajak notes that even though Helena was "the more famous figure in the world at large," in part because of her well-known tomb in Jerusalem, Josephus's focus remains on the birth and life of Helena's son Izates; Josephus consistently presents Helena as Izates's mother, and her actions in relation to her son's, rather than as an important figure of authority herself.[6] I argue that later sources, for the most part, flip the narrative focus, placing Helena at the center and her sons, if mentioned, as secondary characters (with the exception of some rabbinic passages that replace Helena altogether with one of her sons). Wittingly or not, these later memories matriarchalize the Adiabene narrative.

In the course of analysis, I demonstrate that Helena's tomb's inclusion in Christian descriptions of Jerusalem and on Christian pilgrimage routes, her presence in rabbinic accounts of the temple, her surprising insertion into Latin and Armenian Christian history, and her centrality in one prominent strand of Toledot Yeshu traditions suggest that Helena was not only prominent in her lifetime, but also that through her tomb's grandiosity in Jerusalem's urban landscape, the wide circulation of Josephus's writings about her, and a set of traditions found exclusively in rabbinic narratives, her memory grew even more prominent after her death—so much so that, by the medieval period, some Jews imagined her to be the ruler of Jerusalem during the time of Jesus! Importantly, there is not just one tradition of remembering Helena: there are several different, and even sometimes distinct, traditions of remembering Helena in late antique and medieval sources, each with their own trajectories.

Helena is not merely remembered, however: in all of these later sources, she also comes to be promoted as an exemplary figure, not only someone whose memory is worth preserving but also whose actions (generous material patronage, ritual and legal practices, beliefs and piety, communal and even national allegiances) ought to be emulated. Especially for rabbinic and patristic authors, Helena represents a particular form of female piety that they depict as worthy of emulation. It is perhaps for this reason that modern historiography and archaeology took particular interest in re-narrating and reframing the story of Helena and her family in light of pressing political and religious concerns in the nineteenth and twentieth centuries, and why debates about Helena's legacy persist to this day (a full treatment of this later history is beyond the scope of this chapter but one I am pursuing in my current book project). I argue that Helena's foreign origins, conversion, travels, patronage, gender, and motherhood allowed disparate communities and causes to imagine her as their own ancestor or advocate for a wide variety of reasons. Much of Helena's malleability as a figure after her death, I suggest, results precisely from her multiple positions of alterity, a theme explored in more detail in the conclusion.

PAUSANIAS'S HELENA

Following Josephus's *Antiquities*, the earliest source that mentions Helena of Adiabene appears in the second-century Greek geographer Pausanias's *Description of Greece*. Pausanias declares that he knows "many marvelous graves" (τάφους δὲ ἀξίους θαύματος), and tells a magical story about Helena's tomb:

> The Hebrews have a grave, that of Helen, a native woman, in the city of Jerusalem, which the Roman Emperor razed to the ground. There is a contrivance in the grave whereby the door, which like all the grave is of stone, does not open until the year brings back the same day and the same hour. Then the mechanism, unaided, opens the door, which, after a short interval, shuts itself. This happens at that time, but should you at any other [time] try to open the door you cannot do so; force will not open it, but only break it down.[7]

A number of dimensions of Pausanias's description are striking. First, Pausanias pairs his discussion of Helena's tomb with that of Mausolus, king of Halicarnassus, whose tomb was so large and glorious that, apparently, Romans decided to call all large tombs "Mausolea," in reference to Mausolus's tomb. The comparison of Mausolus's and Helena's tomb, moreover, presents Helena's tomb as a well-known landmark—one that Pausanius associates with the "land of the Hebrews."

Second, in Pausanias's account, Helena is a native Jerusalemite, rather than a foreign woman. She *represents* the Jewish locals. This portrayal of Helena as a local figure might stem from Pausanias's own foreignness or status as an outsider in Jerusalem: as a visitor to the region, he regarded those already there (or buried there), regardless of their origins, as local.

Third, Pausanias explains that the stone door to Helena's tomb only opens once a year at the very same day and hour, at which point the door opens on its own for a short period of time. Pausanias seems to attribute this strange phenomenon not to a divine miracle, but rather to a specific (technical?) mechanism that was perhaps triggered by an astronomical phenomenon (as it only happened once a year at the very same day and time annually), magic, or human intervention—he does not specify.[8] Pausanias also does not mention in which season or on which date the tomb door opens; the annual occurrence brings to mind the entry of the high priest into the Holy of Holies in the Jerusalem temple, which was likewise limited to a single day, the Day of Atonement (that Helena of Adiabene is associated, in rabbinic sources, with the temple is an interesting though probably coincidental connection).[9] At other times of the year, the only way to enter the tomb would have been to break the door down. According to Pausanius, Helena's tomb is virtually inaccessible, but at particular moments it becomes entirely accessible—the doors open on their own, without requiring any effort to pry them open. The time-telling dimension of Helena's tomb is also fascinating (the door only opens once a year, on the same day and hour), especially in light of a later rabbinic tradition, found in the Babylonian Talmud (discussed below), that Helena donated some sort of chandelier to the temple that, because of the particular way in which sunlight reflected off of it, was used to tell the correct timing of the morning Shema. For Pausanias, Helena's tomb is a magical, mysterious place.

Fourth, Pausanias juxtaposes Helena's tomb, which still stands, with the city of Jerusalem, which he emphasizes had been destroyed by the Romans. This contrast between that which has survived war and that which has been razed further glorifies Helena as an important figure whose monument has withstood violence and destruction. The city might be in shambles, but her memory, embedded into the city's topography and architecture, persists.

JEROME'S HELENA

While Josephus notes, in his account of Jerusalem's destruction, the locations of Helena's monumental tomb and palace to orient his readers within the city, Pausanius presents Helena's tomb as an impressive structure to be admired by visitors who came from afar, its sophisticated and mysterious mechanisms worthy of marvel. These two dimensions of Helena's tomb, as a noteworthy city landmark and a beautiful site to visit, continue to resonate in later sources as well, including in the writings of the theologian and translator Jerome. In 404 CE, Jerome composed a letter eulogizing his patron, Paula; Jerome addressed his letter to Paula's daughter Eustochium.[10] Helena of Adiabene plays an important role in this epistle.

Jerome begins his message to Eustochium with hyperbolic praise of Paula, and the tone of his opening words carries through to the end of the letter:

> If all the members of my body were to be converted into tongues, and if each of my limbs were to be gifted with a human voice, I could still do no justice to the virtues of the holy and venerable Paula.[11]

Jerome also notes Paula's wealth and lauds her for using it for pious purposes:

> Noble in family, she was nobler still in holiness; rich formerly in this world's goods, she is now more distinguished by the poverty that she has embraced for

Christ . . . she preferred Bethlehem to Rome, and left her palace glittering with gold to dwell in a mud cabin.[12]

Jerome then recounts Paula's life story—her illustrious familial roots (her mother a descendant of the Scipios and the Gracchi, her father from Greek aristocracy), her marriage to an equally elite man, her decision upon entering widowhood to leave Rome for the Holy Land (settling eventually in Bethlehem), her praiseworthy ascetic practices, and her extreme generosity. Jerome explains that "one [Paula] who while she lived at Rome was known by no one outside it has by hiding herself at Bethlehem become the admiration of all lands Roman and barbarian."[13] According to Jerome, leaving Rome, embracing Christianity, settling in Bethlehem, and funding local Christian institutions catapulted Paula into fame and praise far beyond her local community and long after her lifetime.

Jerome describes Paula's time in Jerusalem, and especially her experiences at Jesus's tomb, as a turning point in her life, and it is in this section of his epistle that he evokes Helena of Adiabene. Jerome recalls that when Paula made her pilgrimage to the Holy Land in the late fourth century, the last place she passed before entering Jerusalem was Helena of Adiabene's mausoleum, which stood on her way to the holy city (whether or not Paula stopped to visit Helena's tomb will be discussed shortly). When Jerome mentions Helena's tomb, he identifies Helena as the woman who "helped the people with grain in their famine."[14] Here, Jerome recalls a tradition about Helena mentioned in Josephus and elsewhere, that Helena arrived in Jerusalem during a famine, and that her first act in the city entailed importing grain and figs from Alexandria and Cyprus to feed the starving residents of the city.

Jerome's mention of Helena's tomb and his description of her benefaction fit well in his letter praising Paula. Both women were widows who came to the region from afar, enthusiastically embraced a religious life, served as patrons of local life, and built important institutions (in Helena's case a palace and tomb in Jerusalem, while in Paula's case a convent and monastery in Bethlehem). The opening words of Jerome's letter compare Paula to God in her acts of benefaction to the poor,[15] and his subsequent description of Paula's time in Jerusalem mirrors his praise of Helena: "Then, after distributing money to the poor and her fellow servants so far as her means allowed, she [Paula] proceeded to Bethlehem, stopping only on the right side of the road to visit Rachel's tomb."[16] Helena serves, in Jerome's letter, as a precursor figure to Paula, and it is therefore fitting that Jerome chooses to mention her tomb as he narrates Paula's entry into Jerusalem.

The language Jerome uses to describe what Paula did when she reached Helena's tomb is ambiguous. Jerome writes: "Quid diu moror? ad laeuam mausoleo Helenae derelicto, quae Adiabenorum regina in fame populum frumento iuuauerat, ingressa est Hierosolymam, urbem τριώνυμον: Iebus, Salem, Hierosolymam . . ." The passage can be translated as follows:

> Why do I delay any longer? Having left behind / neglecting on the left the tomb of Helena, the queen of Adiabene who helped the people with grain in their famine, she [Paula] entered Jerusalem, the city of three names: Jebus, Salem, and Jerusalem.

The operative word in this passage is "derelicto."[17] The verb has several meanings, including "to leave behind" (in a neutral sense) and "to neglect or abandon" (in a negative sense), such that the passage could be translated in a few different ways: that Paula visited the tomb (i.e., that she deliberately stopped by to see it) and then left it for Jerusalem; that Paula passed by it (i.e., that she noticed it on her way from the road but did not stop at it) on her way to Jerusalem; or that Paula deliberately neglected to visit Helena's tomb even though she saw it from the road (i.e., that she passed it on her left but decided not to stop at it, likely due to her excitement to get to Jerusalem as quickly as possible). Because *derelicto* modifies *mausoleo*, it could also mean that the tomb itself was neglected (as in, poorly maintained), and some scholars have translated the passage in this way as well.[18] In other passages in this very epistle as well as in his broader corpus of writings, Jerome uses the verb "derelicto" in both senses.[19] The former reading, in which Paula stops at the tomb, suggests that Jerome found it important to include Paula's visit to or view of Helena's mausoleum in his epistle. The latter reading suggests that Helena's mausoleum was such a recognizable landmark that Jerome mentions it even though Paula didn't (or didn't necessarily) visit it, and perhaps even though it was not well maintained. In short, Paula either visited the tomb or passed by it. Jerome does not list every landmark or monument that Paula passed on her trip from Rome to Jerusalem, so the fact that he mentions Helena's tomb is itself significant, regardless of what he meant precisely to describe. What is important is that Jerome mentions Helena's tomb in connection with Paula, not whether she visited it or even knew about it.

According to any of the readings proposed above, Jerome's reference to Helena plays a narrative role in the epistle, linking Paula's to Helena's legacies. Helena's tomb and legacy were well-known or significant enough in Jerome's context or useful for his presentation of Paula that he chose to mention them, an especially interesting choice given that Jerome generally only includes biblical figures and places associated with biblical narratives in this pilgrimage account.

If Jerome pointed out or visited Helena's tomb with Paula on their pilgrimage, Jerome might have capitalized on the memory of this past patron of the city as a fundraising strategy, urging Paula to be a similarly generous patron.[20] By praising the queen of Adiabene's acts of patronage, Jerome might have forecast the praise that his current patron Paula, who also financially contributed to the people of the region, might expect in the future. Moreover, noting this tomb on Paula's journey would have sent a powerful message: your place of burial, too, could be marked onto the city's geography and included on a future iteration of such a pilgrimage if you follow in Helena's generous footsteps.

But whether or not Jerome evoked Helena in his trip with Paula, the reference to Helena's tomb is particularly apt in an encomium written in the aftermath of Paula's death, and it thus plays a powerful rhetorical function in the epistle. Noting Helena's tomb on Paula's way to Jerusalem and praising both women's charity links the two women and their legacies. Jerome might be suggesting that Paula's tomb ought to be likewise venerated and her memory preserved, serving as an example for future patrons (including the recipient of Jerome's letter, Eustochium, and other wealthy Christian women of the period), as Helena's tomb did for Paula.[21] In other words, Jerome might have used Helena's example as part of his strategy of cultivating Paula as a donor, and/or he could have used the coupling of Helena and Paula to promote further patronage by other contemporary wealthy Christian women who would do well to follow in the long tradition of women's patronage in the region.[22] Thus noting Helena's tomb was not merely part of a recollection of a pilgrimage route, but a strategic, rhetorical choice that cast one woman in light of another.

We learn from Jerome's letter that some Christians in the fourth and fifth centuries remembered Helena of Adiabene's patronage of the poor in Jerusalem and that some pilgrims (whether or not Paula was among them) might have visited her tomb as part of their pilgrimage to the Holy Land, imagining her as a woman who used her vast financial resources to care for the poor. Helena seems to have been regarded—or strategically employed—by such Christians as a role model for wealthy women who likewise sought to leave their mark through acts of charity and patronage.[23]

EUSEBIUS'S AND RUFINUS'S HELENA

Jerome might have learned about Helena from local memory, through her mausoleum and the stories that were told about the queen who built it and the family interred there. He could also have read about her in Josephus's *Antiquities*, or in other works that transmitted some of the traditions Josephus preserves in his writings. For example, Jerome might have read about Helena in Book 2 of Eusebius's *Ecclesiastical History*, a book dedicated to recording "events which took place after his [Jesus's] ascension." Eusebius's description suggests knowledge of the tomb's placement at the outskirts of the city—perhaps Eusebius had even visited the tomb during one of his travels to town.

Eusebius probably relied on Josephus's text but he also added his own interpretation and historical contextualization in his description of Helena and her tomb:

> And at this time it came to pass that the great famine took place in Judea, in which the queen, Helena, having purchased grain from Egypt with large sums, distributed it to the needy. You will find this statement also in agreement with the Acts of the Apostles, where it is said that the disciples at Antioch, each according to his ability, determined to send relief to the brethren that dwelt in Judea; which also they did, and sent it to the elders by the hands of Barnabas and Paul. But splendid monuments of this Helena, of whom the historian has made mention, are still shown in the suburbs of the city which is now called Aelia. But she is said to have been queen of the Adiabeni.[24]

Eusebius largely relies on one part of Josephus's narrative, about Helena's distribution of food for the needy, and connects it with a story in the book of Acts that references the same period of famine in the region of Judea. Doing so allows Eusebius to link Helena with Jesus and the apostles, including Paul, thereby recasting Helena as a figure associated with the early Jesus movement and its sacred history. According to Eusebius, Helena's actions mirror the activities of Jesus's disciples, who aided the people in Judea at a time of need. In his passing reference to Helena's tomb, Jerome might have had these associations in mind as well.

Rufinus, Jerome's contemporary in Jerusalem, translated Eusebius's text into Latin, sticking quite closely to Eusebius's description of Helena.[25] Unlike Eusebius, who lived in Caesarea and had a complicated relationship with Jerusalem, Rufinus lived and worked on the Mount of Olives, not far from Helena's tomb.[26] Like Eusebius, he probably had first-hand experience visiting or passing the tomb.

Eusebius calls the city Aelia, the name given to it when it was transformed into a Roman colony by Hadrian in the mid-second century; Rufinus refers to it as Jerusalem, living as he does in a Christianized city. Otherwise, Rufinus does not veer far from Eusebius's text. Eusebius, Rufinus, and Jerome all seem to rely on Josephus's text or on a tradition based on Josephus as well as local knowledge of the city, remembering Helena as a patron of the city whose tomb graced its landscape.

As I explore in more detail below, Helena of Adiabene's memory is employed in the writings of fourth- and fifth-century Christians in conjunction with their deployment of the figure of Helena mother of Constantine. This is especially true of Eusebius and Rufinus, who each wrote effusively about the latter Helena, Eusebius in his *Life of Constantine* (which details Helena's trip to Jerusalem and her imprint on the city) and Rufinus in his *Ecclesiastical History* (in which he develops one of the earliest versions of the Legend of the Finding of the True Cross, in which Helena discovers Jesus's tomb and builds the Anastasis above it).[27] Eusebius might have even modeled his portrayal of Helena mother of Constantine upon Josephus' depiction of Helena of Adiabene. Portraying these two Helenas—Helena of Adiabene during Jesus's lifetime, and Helena mother of Constantine shortly before and during their own lifetimes—as patrons of Jerusalem allowed Eusebius, Jerome, and Rufinus to use them as models for Christian women in their own day, from whom they sought benefaction in their efforts to Christianize Jerusalem. This observation aligns with the broader cultural context of late antique women's patronage of synagogues, churches, monasteries, and libraries, in which attracting wealthy women from beyond the city to one's community was deemed strategically important.[28]

THE RABBIS'S HELENA

For Jerome, Eusebius, and Rufinus, Helena was a patron of the poor in the region of Jerusalem, whose example they harnessed to inspire women such as Paula. Rabbinic sources mention Helena several times as well.[29] What is unique about the classical rabbinic Helena, and what might this tell us about how and to what ends rabbinic texts employed the memory of Helena in a cultural context in which there were multiple ways of appropriating her? How does the Helena found in rabbinic sources align and contrast with depictions of Helena in other contemporaneous and later sources from the broader region?

Classical rabbinic sources about Queen Helena of Adiabene, similar to their Christian counterparts, celebrate her contributions to the city of Jerusalem and its residents. But, instead of describing her conversion to Judaism or the landmarks that she constructed within the city as Josephus does, and rather than emphasizing her patronage of the poor, as Eusebius, Jerome, and Rufinus do (and which rabbinic sources attribute to her sons instead), rabbinic sources present Helena's building and benefaction in ritual and cultic terms, connected with specifically Jewish practices and even with the temple in Jerusalem. They recast Helena's character and her contributions to the ritual life of the city of Jerusalem.

There are three main rabbinic traditions about Helena: she became a Nazirite; she built a large sukkah, in which she and her seven sons sat; and she made significant contributions to the temple. *M. Nazir* 3:6 recounts that Helena committed to live as a Nazirite for many years, in exchange for her son's safe return home from war.[30] After fulfilling her seven-year vow in Adiabene, Helena arrives in Jerusalem and lives, upon rabbinic guidance, as a Nazirite for another seven years.[31] The doubling of seven years recalls Jacob's work for Laban for multiples of seven years in Genesis 29; in Jacob's case, his long years of labor function to express his deep devotion to his beloved wife Rachel, while for Helena these years of living a Nazirite vow demonstrate her abiding love of God and her son. Because Helena becomes ritually defiled at the end of her second set of seven years, she commits herself to a third round of being a Nazirite, for a total of twenty-one years, outdoing the patriarch Jacob himself. (Rabbi Judah disagrees and suggests she was a Nazirite for a total of fourteen years.) This tradition about Helena is unique to the Mishnah, and presents Helena as exceptionally pious, even ascetic—a person who not only practices piety but also embodies it.

In *t. Sukkah* 1:1, Helena builds an enormous sukkah, itself loosely associated with the temple (the holiday is one of three pilgrimage festivals and the first and second temples were both dedicated on Sukkot).[32] Her sukkah is invoked in a halakhic discussion about the height of such structures: can a sukkah's height exceed twenty cubits? Helena's sukkah is used to resolve this rabbinic dispute. Rabbi Judah recollects that Helena's sukkah did indeed reach higher than twenty cubits, and yet elders visited her in it, suggesting that a sukkah that reached above twenty cubits must compromise a kosher sukkah. The rabbis dismiss Rabbi Judah's story by saying that it did not matter that Helena sat in a non-kosher sukkah, because as a woman she is not obligated to observe the positive time-bound commandment of sitting in a sukkah. Rabbi Judah has the last halakhic word when he elaborates that Helena did not sit in the sukkah alone, but had her seven sons—all Torah scholars—to keep her company, and as Jewish men they would have been obligated to sit in a kosher sukkah.[33]

The Babylonian Talmud, in *b. Sukkah* 2b–3a, expands upon this narrative, adding that the sukkah was built in the city of Lod. The extended halakhic discussion addresses many other dimensions of kosher sukkot. The first debate revolves around whether Helena's sons were minors at the time, and thus not obligated to sit in a sukkah; the rabbis debate the age at which boys become obligated, and conclude that at least some of the seven must have been old enough to be obligated—and thus that Helena's sukkah must have been kosher. The text emphasizes that Helena always performed all of her deeds in accordance with the words of the Sages (ת"ש ועוד כל מעשיה לא עשתה

אלא ע"פ חכמים), emphasizing that her actions ought to be considered not only halakhically appropriate but to even carry weight as halakhic precedents. The pericope then discusses other aspects of the sukkah's construction and their halakhic permissibility, including whether the walls were connected to the roof and whether it is possible that Helena's sukkah was very small (i.e., too small to be kosher), and suggests that perhaps it was a large sukkah made up of different sub-sukkot for each of her sons and one for her. In each case, Helena's sukkah is ultimately deemed halakhically kosher and used to teach various rules about proper sukkah construction. Her building project, in this set of narratives, was not only impressive in its size and height and grandeur, but also pedagogically important for teaching rabbinic halakhah. Through her ritual actions, Helena becomes a generator and transmitter of halakhic knowledge.

In *m. Yoma* 3:10, Helena donates a golden candelabrum (נברשת של זהב), placed at the opening of the temple's sanctuary, along with a golden tablet (טבלא של זהב) with the text of the Sotah ritual engraved upon it.[34] These items are both made of pure gold, in contrast to all of the other temple donations listed in the Mishnah, including Ben Qatin's spigots and Monbaz's vessels with gold handles. *T. Yoma* 2:3 adds that the candelabrum shone in the morning sun, emphasizing how glistening the gold was. In *b.* Yoma 37a–38a, Helena's candelabrum is explicitly interpreted as functioning as a sundial or some other type of timekeeping device for determining the proper time for the recitation of the morning Shema. Helena's gift is identified as helping the city's people keep time, a reference to the opening discussions of *b. Berakhot*, in which priestly time is contrasted with other people's time, including the time of the poor.[35] That Helena's gifts to the temple appear in a tractate devoted to temple rituals (specifically those associated with the Day of Atonement) and in a list of temple benefactors rather than, for example, the tractate about the Sotah ritual (into which Helena's Sotah slab could also have been inserted), further places the memory of Helena in the context of Jerusalem, the temple, and its cultic rituals. Unlike in Jerome's letter, which seems to use Helena's patronage as an example for women's philanthropy and care of the poor and hungry, here the discussion of her gifts functions differently, highlighting Helena's dedication to the temple and the proper observance of rituals within it.

Why do rabbinic sources reframe Helena's relationship to the city of Jerusalem and its institutions in such ways? In contrast to Jerome, and as we'll see in the next section also in other sources, most of these rabbinic sources (and in particular the traditions found in tannaitic sources) do not obviously rely on Josephus, but rather on alternative traditions about Helena that must have circulated within rabbinic communities in the centuries thereafter. Rabbinic sources (with the exception of a story about her sons' circumcision in Genesis Rabbah) do not discuss Helena's conversion, her patronage of the poor, the building of her tomb and palace—the central aspects of Josephus's narratives. They mention her son as a patron of the poor during famine instead. The other aspects of Josephus's narrative are largely omitted. Rabbinic knowledge about Helena likely stemmed from communal memory or local knowledge, rather than a particular text, Josephus or otherwise. Rabbinic sources represent their own version of traditions about Helena, and their version places Helena comfortably within a rabbinic framework, and in particular a rabbinic view of the past when the temple still stood in Jerusalem. Helena becomes a nostalgic figure of a bygone era. The rabbis' Helena commits herself as a Nazir, builds a sukkah, and donates to the temple.

Helena's dedication of the Sotah tablet in particular evokes discussions of women's roles in the study and transmission of text, knowledge, and expertise.[36] Helena, as the rabbis imagine her, wants to ensure that the Sotah ritual—a brutal ritual in which a woman accused of adultery undergoes a humiliating, potentially painful, and seemingly arbitrary process to determine her innocence or guilt—is performed correctly, and so she commissions the instructions to be engraved on gold and hung in the temple precinct. This is a rare example in rabbinic sources of a woman producing a text and transmitting it, in the context of the temple no less (that the biblical Sotah passages are constructed in these same rabbinic sources as the only portion of the Torah permissible for a father to teach his daughters is integral to understanding Helena's role in sustaining the Sotah ritual and transmitting these biblical passages about it).[37] In the Babylonian Talmud, even Helena's candelabrum is presented as a halakhic object rather than as merely decorative (adorning the temple) or utilitarian (lighting the space)—it is used to determine the correct time for the recitation of the Shema on a daily basis, even though women themselves are not obligated in the daily recitation of the Shema just as they are not obligated to sit in a sukkah. Indeed, Helena is also associated with the proper observance of sukkah building, and it is the physical dimensions of *her* sukkah that Rabbi Judah uses (and upon which the Babylonian Talmud later elaborates) to resolve a rabbinic dispute about sukkah height. Again, Helena—in this instance through her actions rather than her donations—transmits halakhic knowledge. As a Nazirite, she does not only observe rituals but she embodies them, and as a mother of seven Torah scholars she also passes Torah knowledge on to the next (male) generation.

The rabbis use Helena in part to celebrate and promote the role of women as gatekeepers and enforcers of rabbinic Judaism, transmitters in line with rabbinic knowledge and norms—rather than those who subvert or challenge it, as some other rabbinic women do. In presenting her in such ways, donating to the temple and transmitting rabbinic Torah, they neutralize the power and the potentially dangerous influence she might otherwise wield, as a royal figure and a benefactor, to challenge their own rabbinic authority.[38] That Helena is a figure from the second temple past, rather than a contemporary woman, seems central to this portrayal as well; perhaps the rabbis express implicit nostalgia for a past era in which they imagine women to have upheld communal practices (even those that harmed them), rather than speaking out against or wittingly undermining them as they might have sensed some contemporary women in their own lives to have done (as Beruriah, Rabbi Meir's wife, does in several rabbinic narratives, for example).[39] Helena's temporality—a venerated woman of the past—is not incidental. Just as Jerome's Helena, a woman from the lifetime of Jesus, is used as a model for contemporary (fourth- and fifth-century) Christian women's piety, the rabbinic Helena, who hails from the templed past, serves as a model for contemporary (third-, fourth-, and fifth-century) rabbinic women's piety.

A final thought. Each of these rabbinic narratives does not only present Helena's practice of ritual as proper; they emphasize that she goes above and beyond the requirement or custom—even to absurd degrees. She isn't a Nazirite for a short period of thirty days, she is a Nazirite for twenty-one years! She doesn't just build a sukkah, she builds the tallest and largest sukkah that causes the rabbis to debate whether it's a sukkah at all. Her donations to the temple are not just made of precious metals, they are fully gold; she doesn't only donate peripheral objects but a chandelier that provides light and a tablet that contains a passage from scripture and serves as a ritual aid. We might explain Helena's golden donations as related to Helena's royalty and wealth; as a queen, her temple contributions are over the top. This is certainly part of the rabbinic portrayal. But her royal background does not explain the extreme religious enthusiasm that lies behind her Nazirite vow nor her large sukkah. These traditions navigate between celebrating Helena as a committed rabbinic Jew (portraying her even as a transmitter of rabbinic norms), and gently poking fun at her for her oversized enthusiasm to fulfill rituals and make lasting and noticeable contributions to the Jewish community.

PAULUS OROSIUS AND MOSES OF KHORENE'S HELENA

Jerome, Eusebius, and Rufinus were not the only Christians to remember Helena of Adiabene. Following the sack of Rome in 410 CE, Augustine of Hippo requested that Paulus Orosius record the world's natural disasters, in order to demonstrate that natural disasters befell the world long before Christianity (and therefore that Christianity was not the cause of such disasters, as some people seemed to believe). Nestled in Book 7 of his *Historiae adversus paganos*, completed in 416–417 CE, Orosius writes that in the fourth year of Emperor Claudius's rule "there was a terrible famine throughout Syria. The needs of the Christians at Jerusalem, however, were bountifully supplied with grain that Helena, the queen of Adiabene and a convert to the faith of Christ, had imported from Egypt."[40] Here, Orosius follows the tradition found in Josephus and Jerome, that Helena provided grain during famine, but he also follows Eusebius and Rufinus by associating her with the early Jesus movement. While Jerome's mention of Helena's tomb on Paula's journey to Jerusalem might have suggested that late fourth-century Christians identified Helena as a Christian, Orosius explicitly presents Helena as a devoted follower of Christ who ensured that those in Jesus's circle were well-fed during times of famine.

The dating of Moses of Khorene's *History of Armenia* is a matter of considerable scholarly discussion.[41] The text was long assumed to originate in the fifth century, as its author claims, but a study of its use of sources suggests that it could have been composed as late as the eighth century, though the text's precise date does not matter for our discussion of its portrayal of Helena of Adiabene.[42] The work relies on earlier sources, including extensive reliance on both Eusebius and Josephus.[43] It, too, mentions Helena, albeit in a different context (Robert Thomson has noted that Moses relies, in this section, on the Armenian version of Eusebius's *Ecclesiastical History*).[44] The author of this text strategically identifies Helena as the chief wife of Abgar V, king of Osroene in Edessa. He writes that when Sanadroug (ruler of Armenia), a figure the text associates with idolatrous worship, waged war against the sons of Abgar (ruler at Edessa), considered pious Christians, the inhabitants of the region were eager to sign a treaty with Sanadroug that would allow them to continue practicing their Christian faith even under a non-Christian ruler. Sanadroug does not keep his word. In the course of the violent slaughter of the house of Abgar that follows (the sons killed, the daughters expelled), Sanadroug takes Helena, Abgar's chief wife, captive during his military offensive:

> Likewise the chief of Abgar's wives, who was called Helena, he sent to dwell in his own city Harran, leaving her the throne of all Mesopotamia in return for the benefits that he had gained from Abgar through her.[45]

Helena, widowed and captured by an invading ruler, seeks to find an escape. The text describes how she therefore plotted to visit Jerusalem during the reign of Claudius, arriving at the city during times of famine, which her late husband Abgar had predicted:

This Helena, pious like her husband Abgar, could not bear to live among idolators but went to Jerusalem in the days of Claudius, during the famine that Abgar had predicted. Spending all her treasures in Egypt, she bought a great quantity of wheat and distributed it to all the needy, to which Josephus bears witness.[46]

The narrative ends by remarking that "Her famous mausoleum stands before the gate at Jerusalem to this very day."[47] Moses of Khorene mentions the same acts of charity—feeding Jerusalemites during a time of famine—and the prominence of the site of her burial, immediately outside Jerusalem's gate, as Jerome and Josephus do, but he also includes an additional story line of war and conquest.

To be clear, this text is unique—it alone connects Helena of Adiabene with Abgar. What is interesting about it is not the history it proposes (which is almost certainly not historically accurate) but rather that the author employs the memory of Helena in his telling of this narrative. Helena is used to reflect on her late husband Abgar's piety, and on the piety of the broader Armenian Christian population who suddenly found themselves, according to this narrative, in a challenging situation under unsympathetic rule. As royalty from Adiabene, she also serves, in the text, as a bridge between Jerusalem and Armenia.

TOLEDOT YESHU'S HELENA

Helena's memory is revived in a significant number of medieval Toledot Yeshu manuscripts that date to no later than the thirteenth century, and possibly as early as the tenth (and might preserve yet older traditions).[48] These versions of Toledot Yeshu portray Queen Helena as having ruled over the region of Judea, and she plays a leading role in the narratives. Galit Hasan-Rokem, in her study of the figure of Helena in Toledot Yeshu, summarizes the various ways in which the manuscripts describe her role in Jerusalem: in Strasbourg BnU 3974 she "held sway over the Land of Israel"; Cod. Hebr. 2240, Cod. Hebr. B.H. 17, and Cod. Hebr. 2178 specify that the events of the narrative transpire "in the fifth year" of Queen Helena; the *tam u-mu'ad* version identifies Queen Helena with the Hasmonean dynasty (perhaps a conflation with Salome Alexandra or Berenice, both of whom were or had ties to the Hasmoneans) and explicitly states that Helena "reigns over Israel and Jerusalem"; Wagenseil (Cambridge MA Harvard Houghton Lib. 57) identifies Helena as King Yannai's wife, again conflating this queen with Salome Alexandra, as does a Yiddish manuscript (Ms. Jerusalem NLI Heb. 8 5622).[49] One Judeao-Arabic manuscript (CUL, T.-S. NS 298.57) identifies Helena as a "Byzantine woman who was ruling at that time and her name was Helena."[50] Another Judeo-Arabic manuscript (RNL Evr.-Arab. II:1993) describes Helena as follows: "At that time in Jerusalem, a queen ruled and her name was Helena, from the land of the Byzantines, ruling over all the people."[51]

Helena of Adiabene indeed lived in Jerusalem and served as patron of the city during Jesus's lifetime, though she never ruled the city. Her debates with her son about circumcision, described at length in Josephus, fit comfortably with similar debates between Paul and his followers recorded in Paul's epistles, including Paul's Letter to the Galatians; though rabbinic sources such as *Genesis Rabbah* 46:11 mention these debates about circumcision (in reference to Helena's son, not mentioning the queen), they do not appear in early Christian sources.[52] In other words, Josephus's Helena is remembered as engaging in a debate that Paul also entered, and that became a defining discussion in constructions of Jewish-Christian difference in the decades and centuries thereafter, but Josephus never connects Helena with Jesus.[53]

In the Toledot Yeshu narratives, Helena is initially drawn to Jesus's miracles. She is eventually convinced, however, that he is a charlatan and hands him over to the Romans, affirming her faith in the (rabbinic) community that has rejected Jesus. This story aligns well with the legacy of the rabbinic Helena, whose conversion story from Josephus and her devout adherence to rabbinic Judaism, a prominent theme in rabbinic sources, are both evoked in the Toledot Yeshu text. It even works against Christian traditions that claim Helena to be one of the earliest of Jesus's followers and a devout Christian. Moreover, in some versions (such as the Strasbourg manuscript, noted as a widespread representative of the "Helena" version of Toledot Yeshu, though it is late), Helena asks the Jews whether scripture teaches about Jesus, her eagerness for religious and exegetical truth on full display. An important scene occurs in the temple when Judah enters the Holy of Holies and places a small piece of parchment with God's name on it (copied from the foundation stone that has God's name engraved into it) into his thigh in order to obtain the ability to perform miracles.[54] Helena questions Jesus's burial and, through messengers, discovers that his tomb is empty, a role played by women (but not Helena) in the canonical Gospels. By the end of the narrative, she condemns Jesus. The Toledot Yeshu narratives that incorporate the figure of Helena employ a foreign woman who has converted to Judaism as the person who ultimately rejects Jesus and seeks to exclude him from the Jewish community. While the narratives differ substantially in many ways, they are fairly uniform in their portrayal of Helena and her role in the story of Jesus's life.

Whether Toledot Yeshu's Helena refers exclusively to the queen of Adiabene or also embeds within the Helena character a version of the mother of Constantine is left ambiguous, what Hasan-Rokem calls "a hermeneutical palimpsest in the heart of the text."[55] Indeed, certain versions of Toledot Yeshu explicitly evoke the figure of Helena mother of Constantine; one manuscript glosses her name, identifying her as the "wife of Constantine" even though Constantine's mother lived in the fourth century rather than the first.[56] The conflation of these two Helena is not as surprising as it first seems, for the two women are portrayed similarly in ancient sources. They were both foreign queens drawn to a religious tradition to which they converted, they both mothered powerful sons who became kings, they visited Jerusalem and became patrons and builders in the city. Despite the appearance of this conflation only in medieval Toledot Yeshu manuscripts, the tradition of associating these two queens might not be an exclusively medieval development. Some of our earliest depictions of Helena, mother of Constantine, might themselves have had Helena of Adiabene in mind as a model or precursor, and this connection between the two figures would have then been sustained in later historical memory. It is possible, for example, that Helena, mother of Constantine might have modeled herself after Helena of Adiabene in some way, as an earlier patron of Jerusalem, or that contemporary or later figures, such as Eusebius, drew such connections between the two women in their depictions of them.[57] We have established, in our earlier survey of the sources, that Helena of Adiabene was a prominent figure, especially in Jerusalem and in the Galilee among rabbis and Christians, and it is therefore not surprising that Helena of Adiabene could have served as a model for the later Helena, mother of Constantine. Helena of Adiabene's tomb would have been visible to Helena, mother of Constantine, when she arrived in Jerusalem on pilgrimage. But if Helena, mother of Constantine, herself did not consider Helena of Adiabene a model, then those who wrote about her after her death might nonetheless have implicitly made the connection between the two Helenas, presenting the latter Helena in terms similar to those of the former Helena, constructing the fourth-century Helena in the image of the first-century Helena. Eusebius, for instance, mentions Helena of Adiabene's tomb in his *Ecclesiastical History*, and in his *Life of Constantine* he discusses Helena mother of Constantine at some length, in ways that resemble Josephus's descriptions of Helena of Adiabene in *Antiquities*. He seems to have modeled his portrayal of Helena, mother of Constantine, on the figure of Helena of Adiabene. Likewise, Rufinus, Socrates, Sozomen, Theodoret, Ambrose, Paulinus of Nola, and Sulpicius Severus told versions of the Legend of the Finding of the True Cross, some of which present Helena mother of Constantine as a convert to Christianity who visited Jerusalem and, as a pious promoter of the Christianization of the region, found the True Cross, commissioned the building of the Anastasis in the place of Jesus's tomb, established the feast of the Finding of the True Cross (which interestingly is celebrated in the same season as Sukkot, a holiday associated in rabbinic sources with Helena of Adiabene), and exported relics of the True Cross across the empire.[58] We know from Jerome and Orosius—contemporaries of Rufinus from the late fourth and early fifth centuries—that Helena of Adiabene was a legendary figure at that time, revered for her patronage of the city in the same vein as Helena, mother of Constantine.

In one strand of later manuscripts, Toledot Yeshu conflates Helena of Adiabene and Helena, mother of Constantine, more extensively and explicitly by retelling the Legend of the Finding of the True Cross.[59] In this narrative, appended to the end of the "Long Italian" version of Toledot Yeshu, Helena is motivated to find the True Cross because her husband Constantine falls ill and the True Cross is his only hope for recovery.[60] The Jews of Rome direct her to Jerusalem, where local wise Jewish elders, led by Rabbi Judah, fabricate crosses that they then pretend to discover and deliver to Helena.[61] Rabbi Judah uses God's Ineffable Name to perform miracles that he attributes to the wood of the cross, so that Helena believes that it is in fact the True Cross. Rabbi Judah ends up praised by the Christians for facilitating this discovery, and joins other undercover agents, including Paul, who appear to be helping the Jesus-following Christians but are actually working for the Jews.

Rufinus is one of our earliest sources to feature Helena in the Legend of the Finding of the True Cross (Ambrose also incorporates a version of this legend into his funeral oration on the occasion of the death of Emperor Theodosius in 395 CE), and Rufinus likely does so with his patron Melania in mind—such a presentation of Helena, mother of Constantine, as patron of the city and its Christianization would have been helpful to develop as a model for Melania. Indeed, apparently it was Melania who told Paulinus of Nola one version of this legend about Helena and the True Cross![62] Jerome does something similar, but with another, earlier Helena. He uses the memory of Helena of Adiabene as a patron of the city as a model for his patron Paula. The two Helenas both therefore functioned, in the later fourth and through the fifth and sixth centuries and beyond, as models for wealthy Christian women whose patronage Church fathers and bishops sought. Jews were likely aware of the Legend of the Finding of the True Cross in some version (not only in the version of Toledot Yeshu that explicitly retells the legend), given how widespread it was in both narrative and iconography, and perhaps also in the appropriation of Helena of Adiabene into the figure of Helena, mother of Constantine. That connection between the two Helenas is exploited in Toledot Yeshu, both in versions that contain the Legend of the True Cross narrative as well as those that do not.[63] They present a figure named Helena who is at once meant to reclaim the memory of Helena of Adiabene for the Jews and subvert the memory of Helena, mother of Constantine, who becomes, in Toledot Yeshu, a figure who disproves Jesus's identity by uncovering the true story of his death and crucifixion, rather than a person celebrated for popularizing Christianity across the entire empire, and especially in Jerusalem.[64]

Reading Toledot Yeshu in the context of Helena of Adiabene's reception not only provides a fascinating example of how far memory of her traveled in later sources and allows us to reexamine earlier sources with new insights. It might also help us to date and place the "Helena" strand of Toledot Yeshu traditions, the origins of which have been notoriously difficult to contextualize.[65] In what historical and geographical context were Jews most likely to have celebrated Helena as a central figure in Jewish history or sought to claim her as a convert to and proponent of Judaism rather than Christianity? Research on the Helena manuscripts of Toledot Yeshu is ongoing, especially with efforts to integrate the Judeo-Arabic manuscripts into studies that have largely relied, until now, on Hebrew and Aramaic manuscripts.[66] Among the earliest Helena versions of Toledot Yeshu are Judeo-Arabic manuscripts that might have originated in Egypt, Palestine, Syria, or Babylonia.[67] Contextualizing Toledot Yeshu's portrayal of Helena might make it possible, for example, to pinpoint where the figure of Helena was celebrated, and to wonder if Jewish reappropriations of this queen emerged from those contexts.

CONCLUSIONS

How important was Helena of Adiabene in antiquity? Josephus mentions Helena several times in his two most important works. He suggests that she was a prominent figure in Jerusalem in the second quarter of the first century, mentioning her conversion to Judaism, her pilgrimage to worship the Jewish God in the temple in Jerusalem, her patronage of the people during famine upon her arrival in the city, her building of monumental buildings in and around the city, and her interment just outside the city in the tomb that she constructed. In his account of the fighting in Jerusalem during the Jewish revolt against Rome, Josephus mentions both Helena's palace and tomb as known landmarks; he must have imagined that his readers would have known of them and been familiar with their location—otherwise his mention of them to describe the whereabouts of fighting would have been pointless. Josephus's account indicates that in the decades after her death, Helena's tomb and palace were associated with her. It is therefore reasonable to assume that during and shortly after her lifetime Helena was a known and well-respected figure both in Jerusalem and, through the circulation and impact of Josephus's writings, in the broader region as well.

What did Helena symbolize in later sources, after the first century CE? In the second century, Pausanias describes her tomb as a magical place, famous for its beauty and mystery. Tannaitic sources about Helena are likewise important, because they confirm that in the second and third centuries, when the Mishnah and Tosefta were composed and compiled, Helena was still a known figure in the region, remembered as a benefactor of the temple, a Nazirite, and a pious observer of Jewish rituals. Later rabbinic texts, including the Palestinian and Babylonian Talmuds and Genesis Rabbah, expand upon these early rabbinic traditions, embellishing Helena's contributions to the temple and their significance—and indicating that, rather than her memory waning, Helena's prominence persisted in later rabbinic texts. Whereas Palestinian sources regarded Helena as a local figure, the Babylonian Talmud's interest in Helena is at least in part related to her place of origin, and the connections she drew between Mesopotamia and Jerusalem, connections that those in Babylonia were likewise eager to cultivate.

At around the same time as these later rabbinic sources, a set of early Christian figures, all intertwined with one another, also incorporated Helena into their writings. First, Eusebius includes a reference to Helena in his *Ecclesiastical History*, which Rufinus translates. Jerome and Orosius both include similar references in their texts. Eusebius, Jerome, Rufinus, and Orosius all had strong Jerusalem connections—Rufinus and Jerome spent years in and around the city and played key roles in its Christianization. Although Eusebius hailed from Caesarea and spent most of his life there, he too had deep ties to Jerusalem and saw it as a rival city before embracing its centrality. Orosius, originally not from the Mediterranean, traveled to Jerusalem in 415 CE upon Augustine's insistence, where he met with Jerome, participated in the Synod of Diospolis in Lydda, and took relics of St. Stephen from Jerusalem back to Braga. Their texts focus on Helena's tomb and often note its location within the city suburbs, suggesting that local knowledge—not only of local traditions but also of local sites and geography—played a role in what and how they wrote about Helena, even when they rely on Josephus's and on each other's writings as well.

Jerome mentions Helena's tomb in his letter about Paula's pilgrimage. It is a short reference, only a single sentence long. But the briefness of Jerome's mention of Helena does not mean that she was unimportant. Recall that Jerome mentions Helena's tomb because it is a landmark on Paula's pilgrimage that, presumably, other pilgrims would also have visited—even if Jerome's letter does not indicate that Paula stopped at Helena's tomb, Jerome's letter suggests that she might have, and thus that other pilgrims, perhaps those not in as much a rush to enter Jerusalem as Paula, did. Helena's tomb is the last landmark before pilgrims' entry into the city of Jerusalem, the epicenter of Paula's pilgrimage. Helena must have been quite a prominent figure in Jerusalem and in Christian pilgrimage imagination during this period of rapid Christianization of the Holy Land in the fourth and fifth centuries because of the prominent landmark that marked her memory— perhaps even more prominent in the centuries after her death than during or immediately after her lifetime—despite only brief references to her in written sources.[68] Her memory was embedded in Jerusalem's topography through the prominence of her tomb as a monumental building and its veneration on pilgrimages. That her memory persisted not only in texts but also in the topography is key: her tomb promoted her memory, as it was likely intended to do. Helena's tomb served to perpetuate traditions about her role in the city, and so the tomb and texts together form the sum of traditions about her.

One key difference between rabbinic sources and late antique Christian texts is that rabbinic passages do not mention Helena's construction of permanent, monumental buildings in Jerusalem; they only list Helena's golden donations to the Jerusalem temple. There might be a historical reason for this. During the period in which these rabbinic texts were composed, after 135 CE, Jews might not have been permitted to live in or visit Jerusalem, which had since been re-founded as a Roman colony by Hadrian and renamed Aelia Capitolina. Tertullian, Justin Martyr, and Eusebius note that Hadrian formally banned Jews from living in or visiting Jerusalem save on the Ninth of Av, to mourn the temple's destruction, though whether such a residency restriction was enforced after Hadrian's reign is a less settled matter (some sources suggest that even if enforcement of this ban waned, it might have been reinstated by Constantine in the fourth century, though the evidence is complicated, suggesting some continued Jewish, including rabbinic, presence in Jerusalem also then).[69] Regardless, even if some Jews lived in the city, it would have been a modest number. Rabbinic communities mainly settled in the Mediterranean coastal region to the west, the Galilee to the north, and Babylonia to the east thrived in those regions instead. The situation of rabbinic Jews as outsiders—those without (for the most part) first-hand experience of Jerusalem as a contemporary, material city—is particularly relevant, for they would not have frequented Helena's tomb nor regarded it as an integral part of Jerusalem's topography. For them, the figure of Helena existed independently of her presence in Jerusalem's landscape, and their Helena is thus not a product of that landscape. Rabbinic ideas about Helena thus stand strikingly in contrast to the late antique Christian figures who mention Helena, all of whom spent significant time in Jerusalem, and some of whom even wrote their texts *in* Jerusalem. Whereas rabbinic texts do not mention Helena's tomb (did they not know about it or was it just not relevant to their experience of the world?), the early Christian texts focus almost exclusively on Helena's tomb and its impact on the city's topography (is it all they know about Helena or how they first learned about Helena?). The Christian texts focus on Helena in contemporary Jerusalem, which they know well, while the rabbinic sources focus on Helena from an imagined or past Jerusalem (a Helena who donated to the temple, and whose candelabrum still tells the right time within the temple)

Queen Helena of Adiabene through the Centuries 217

because that is the only Jerusalem that they know. The rabbis' Jerusalem has a temple with Helena's candelabrum, while the Christian Jerusalem has Helena's tomb, situated not far from Jesus's tomb. The rabbis' Jerusalem is frozen in time—it is a city in which Helena's donations to the temple are still relevant and persist despite the temple's destruction.

Each of these depictions of Helena serves a different purpose: to cultivate Christian female piety and patronage in the environs of a rapidly Christianizing Holy Land or a rabbinic female piety in the Galilee or in Babylon; to inspire national and religious pride and identity in an Armenian historiographical tradition; and to polemicize against Christianity within a prominent Jewish literary tradition by showing readers that Helena of Adiabene had not converted to Jesus's Judaism, but had in fact rejected Jesus in favor of a rabbinically inflected Judaism. In rabbinic and patristic traditions, Helena's piety plays a supporting role, reinforcing patristic and rabbinic authority rather than challenging it. Within this constellation, each version of Helena seems less inevitable and far stranger than we might first have expected.

There are also similarities. In some sources, Helena is presented as a paradigmatic mother, as in Josephus, in which her relationship to her two sons and her role in her son's conversion constitute the heart of the tale, and in rabbinic texts, which refer repeatedly to her place as a mother of many sons. In other sources that do not discuss Helena's role as a mother, she often still appears in the specter of motherhood. Jerome does not present her as a mother but mentions her in a eulogy he writes to a daughter about her mother, and in various late antique and medieval texts, including the Toledot Yeshu narratives, her character evokes that of Constantine's mother. Depictions of Helena as the sustainer of Jerusalem—someone who feeds its starving population—present her as the city's nourishing mother feeding her children.

Sources also present Helena as an example of piety while never depicting her as too powerful to be threatening. She was a queen, but of a faraway land. She often represents the positions of the authors who wrote about her: Josephus presents her as an advocate of Judaism and conversion; rabbinic sources insist that she observes rabbinic practices, tows the rabbinic party line, and donates to the central Jewish institution; late antique Christian writers remember her as a patron of the city in the vein of Helena, mother of Constantine, a staunch proponent of Christianization and of the empire; Armenian texts credit her with spreading Christianity; and in Toledot Yeshu she is a defiant defendant of Judaism in the face of Jesus and an emerging Christian community.

In first-century Jerusalem, Helena was, in contemporary parlance, an intersectional figure: she was a woman, she was a foreigner, she was single (presumably widowed), she was older, and she was a convert.[70] That is, she occupied a liminal position with respect to her gender, ethnicity, familial status, age, and religion. Her status was both as one who is part of the community but also someone outside of it: she was from Adiabene but buried in Jerusalem; she came from far away but became a local figure; she was not born Jewish but converted to Judaism (and in other sources, an example of an early Jesus follower); she was a newcomer to the faith but also a staunch advocate for and defender of it; she was imagined as a Jew but because she was a woman she was of lower status and not obligated in all Jewish practices; she was a woman but she wielded economic and political power; she was a mother but because she was widowed she was far more independent, relying on her sons but not bound to a husband. Her religious, ethnic, and gendered identities are all woven together, each inextricably linked and co-constituted, in traditions about her. This liminality became central to how later sources imagined and appropriated memory of her. Helena thus proved particularly useful for those grappling with the intersections of communities, such as in Toledot Yeshu and the History of Armenia, but also for those committed to the project of recording ecclesial history, Christianizing Jerusalem and the Holy Land, and asserting rabbinic authority not only in the present but also back into the pre-Christian or pre-rabbinic past.

Helena's mausoleum—described by Josephus as a monumental structure of three pyramids, by Pausanias in fantastical terms, and by Eusebius, Jerome, and Rufinus as a place of pilgrimage and local importance—was located not far from the city gates; it apparently housed not only Helena's bones but also those of her son Izates and likely others from her family as well.[71] I have argued that, at least in part, Helena's ancient and medieval legacy was tied to this monumental tomb. It was hard to miss, and anyone who passed it likely wondered who built it and who was buried inside. The tomb is what reinforced Helena's memory: she was remembered *because* her tomb was so prominent in the city. Her tomb sustained her memory. (Over time, Jerusalem's landscape became peppered with women's tombs to which people came to worship; these sites, too, sustained local memories of women.)[72] Memory of Helena thus had a local and regional dimension as well. Indeed, for centuries, pilgrims and other visitors to the city stopped at the tomb or noted its presence along the road on their way to the city center. In the medieval period, they likewise came to pay respects to Helena of Adiabene. These visits played a role in sustaining and transmitting stories about her. This monument, moreover, was one of the few monumental buildings in Jerusalem to survive the Roman destruction of the city, and we might imagine that had it been destroyed along with the temple and its surroundings, local traditions associated with the place of Helena's burial might not have persisted, and her legacy as an important figure in Jerusalem would likely have been quite different. A few centuries later, though her tomb was not destroyed, its association with her was muddied: while it was not entirely forgotten, the tomb became associated with other figures as well, and memories of Helena waned.

Sometime in the medieval period, the tomb was misidentified by some visitors as belonging to Israelite kings imagined to rest there: it became known, in some medieval, early modern, and modern sources as the Tomb of the Kings, rather than the tomb of Queen Helena (though Helena's memory was never fully forgotten, as some maps of Jerusalem and other sources, beyond the scope of this chapter, indicate). Pilgrims began visiting the site believing that they were venerating Kings David and Solomon, who conquered the city from the Jebusites, made it the capital of the kingdom, and built a royal palace and the temple, or other later kings, rather than a place built to commemorate a foreign queen whose love of the city and its residents sustained them through famine almost a thousand years thereafter. Once the monument that commemorated Helena was misidentified, local memories of her in Jerusalem diminished as well, though sources that circulated primarily beyond Jerusalem (such as Josephus and Toledot Yeshu) remembered her with no less zeal.

In the long nineteenth and the first half of the twentieth centuries, with increased travel to the region and interest in the region's biblical past, Helena's tomb was excavated and eventually re-identified as belonging to her.[73] In 1863, archaeologist Louis Félicien Joseph Caignart de Saulcy excavated the "Tomb of the Kings."[74] While doing so, he found, in one of the tomb's side rooms, a sarcophagus with human remains in it.[75] The inscription on this sarcophagus reads, in two different Aramaic scripts (the first Seleucid Aramaic script and the second formal Jewish script), "מלכתא צדן" on one line and "מלכתה צדה" on the other, meaning "Sadan the Queen" or "Sadah the Queen."[76] This inscription indicates that the sarcophagus belonged to a queen, and indeed a woman's remains were found inside. De Saulcy, unwilling to part with the idea that the tomb did not contain biblical royalty, insisted that it housed the remains of one of the wives of the kings of Judea, and could not be persuaded otherwise. But other archaeologists agree that the tomb complex was most likely built by Helena and housed her remains alongside her relatives' remains. Scholars rely upon Josephus's writings about Helena's mausoleum to locate and identify the tomb in the contemporary Jerusalem landscape, three to four furlongs from one of the city gates.[77] The inscription was eventually interpreted as possibly belonging to one of the women of the Adiabene dynasty. Some disagreement surrounded whether the found sarcophagus with the inscription was Helena's or belonged to another member of her family; scholarly consensus now largely agrees, based on the inscription and the bones within, that it likely housed the body of one of the younger royal women of the Adiabene family, though not to Queen Helena herself.[78] De Saulcy absconded with the sarcophagus from Helena's tomb to France in 1863, where it remained hidden in a storeroom at the Louvre for over a century, and where it is prominently displayed today.

The tomb structure still stands, currently hidden from view behind a tall stone fence under French governmental control and accessible to the public only during limited visiting hours: the words "Tombeau des rois" continue to obscure Helena's presence in the city. Yet a street—"Heleni Ha-Malka"— not too far from there is named after her and so her memory has been reinscribed into the city streets as it has been back into the archaeological and historical record.[79] (At least two other streets, in Herzliya and Lod, are also named after her, indicating that her memory is once again being revived not only in Jerusalem but more broadly in Israel, again through associating places and spaces with her.) A royal palace discovered in 2007 on the other side of town has been identified by some archaeologists as built and inhabited by Helena, and personal material affects, such as jewelry, found nearby has been imagined to belong to the queen herself, even though such identifications of this jewelry are wishful historical thinking (given that the earrings date to the later Roman period).[80] In 2010, the Louvre agreed to loan the sarcophagus from the tomb to the Israel Museum in Jerusalem for a few months for an exhibition titled "Breaking Ground: Pioneers of Biblical Archaeology," which ran from July 2010 through April 2011; Israeli media celebrated the occasion, declaring it "A Royal Return."[81] Today, replicas of the jewelry discovered near the palace are sold under the name "Queen Helene's Jewelry," and a veil named in her memory can be purchased in a bridal boutique all the way in Philadelphia.[82] On occasion pilgrims gather again at these sites—violence erupted when her tomb first re-opened to the public in 2019, prompting a temporary closure, but as of the writing of this chapter, it is welcoming visitors again, though the neighborhood in which it is located is the site of ongoing political tension.[83] Helena's memory is now actively revived through archaeological visits, commercial endeavors, naming practices, and in some cases religious devotional practices. Her legacy is actively being reimagined, to serve particular ideological and communal ends, as it always has been in each context in which her story has been told and her memory preserved.

The figure of Helena has not only captured popular interest. Her story has also become the subject of recent scholarly work interested in constructions of gender and ethnicity, conversion, national identity, patronage, and poverty in antiquity. This chapter itself joins this renewed interest in the figure of Helena, the house of Adiabene, and its legacy.

NOTES

1. I shared some of these materials at the 2020 Association for Jewish Studies Annual Meeting; I thank Gregg Gardner, Marjorie Lehman, and M Tong for being excellent conversation partners during that session, and Daniel Schwartz who went above and beyond as a respondent to my paper. I had the opportunity of workshopping a draft at the Tauber Institute's Jewish Studies Colloquium at Brandeis University, and thank Lynn Kaye, Sylvia Fuks Fried, and David Briand for the kind invitation and participants in the workshop, especially Eugene Sheppard and ChaeRan Freeze, for helpful questions. I also thank René Bloch and Ranon Katzoff who answered a Latin translation question about Jerome. I am grateful to have discussed this essay further at the Enoch Seminar's conference "Constructions of Gender" in July 2021, and I thank Kathy Ehrensperger, Shayna Sheinfeld, Joshua Scott, and Juni Hoppe for organizing the conference and editing this volume, and Magdalena Díaz Araujo for her response. Finally, I thank Yevgeniy Safronov for reading a full draft and offering feedback. All remaining errors and shortcomings are mine. I am currently writing a book about Helena of Adiabene; this essay represents my early research into the history of this figure.

2. Josephus, *Jewish War* 5.119 and 5.147 mention Helena's tomb, and *Jewish War* 5.253–254 and 6.355 mention Helena's palace.

3. Josephus discusses Helena of Adiabene's conversion to Judaism, pilgrimage to Jerusalem, benefaction during famine, death and burial in *Antiquities* 20.34–53, 92–96.

4. Geo Widengren, "Quelques rapports entre juifs et iraniens àl'époque des Parthes," Supplements to *Vetus Testamentum* 4 (1957): 197–241; Jacob Neusner, "The Conversion of Adiabene to Judaism: A New Perspective," *Journal of Biblical Literature* 83 (1964): 60–66; Lawrence H. Schiffman, "The Conversion of the Royal House of Adiabene in Josephus and Rabbinic Sources," in *Josephus, Judaism, and Christianity*, ed. Feldman and Hata (Detroit: Wayne State University Press, 1987), 294–98; Marco Frenschkowski, "Iranische Königslegende in der Adiabene: zur Vorgeschichte von Josephus, 'Antiquitates' XX, 17–33," *Zeitschrift der Deutschen Morgenländischen Gesellschaft* 140, no. 2 (1990): 213–33; Daniel Schwartz, "God, Gentiles, and Jewish Law: On Acts 15 and Josephus' Adiabene Narrative," in *Geschichte - Tradition - Reflexion: Festschrift für Martin Hengel zum 70. Geburtstag*, ed. Hubert Cancik, Hermann Lichtenberger, and Peter Schäfer (Tübingen: Mohr Siebeck, 1996), 263–82; Tessa Rajak, "The Parthians in Josephus," in *The Jewish Dialogue with Greece and Rome: Studies in Cultural and Social Interaction*, ed. Tessa Rajak (Leiden: Brill, 2001), 273–97; Michal Marciak, "Biblical Allusions in the Adiabene Narrative (Antiquitates Judaicae 20:17–96)," *Polish Journal of Biblical Research* 10, no. 1–2 (2011): 63–84; Lawrence M. Wills, *The Jewish Novel in the Ancient World* (Eugene: Wipf and Stock, 2015), 206–11; Anthony Rabin, "The Adiabene Narrative in the Jewish Antiquities of Josephus" (Ph.D. diss., Wolfson College, Oxford, 2017); Etka Liebowitz, "A New Perspective on Two Jewish Queens in the Second Temple Period: Alexandra of Judaea and Helene of Adiabene," in *Sources and Interpretation in Ancient Judaism: Studies for Tal Ilan at Sixty*, ed. Meron M. Piotrkowski (Leiden: Brill, 2018): 41–65. Simcha Gross, "Hopeful Rebels and Anxious Romans: Jewish Interconnectivity in the Great Revolt and Beyond," *Historia: Zeitschrift*

für Alte Geschichte 72 (2023): 479-513. Michal Marciak, *Izates, Helena, and Monobazos of Adiabene: A Study on Literary Traditions and History* (Wiesbaden: Harrassowitz, 2014) and David A. Barish, *Adiabene: Royal Converts to Judaism in the First Century C.E.: A Study of Sources* (Ph.D. diss. Hebrew Union College, 1983) discuss Josephus, rabbinic literature, and archaeological sources; additional publications focus on the region of Adiabene as well, e.g. Michal Marciak, *Sophene, Gordyene, and Adiabene: Three Regna Minora of Northern Mesopotamia Between East and West* (Leiden: Brill, 2017); "The Cultural Environment of Adiabene in the Hellenistic, Parthian, and Sasanian Period," *Parthica: Incontri di culture nel mondo antico* (2014): 11–150.

5. Discussion of the royal house of Adiabene, which contains within it the story of Helena's conversion and trip to Jerusalem, appears in *Antiquities* 20.17–96; the textual history is explained in detail in Schiffman, "The Conversion of the Royal House of Adiabene," 294–98, who himself relies on the work of Abraham Schalit, "Evidence of an Aramaic Source in Josephus' 'Antiquities of the Jews'," *Annual of the Swedish Theological Institute* 4 (1975): 163–88, and Rajak, "The Parthians in Josephus," 319–22, who argues that even if Josephus adapted his narrative from existing sources, "there is no reason to think that Josephus copied from them verbatim" (321). Rajak explains that while previous studies argued that Josephus drew on Parthian royal annals or chronicles as well as Jewish sources, the more likely genre is that of the popular royal biography, which likely focused on the life of Izates (322). Worth noting as well is that Josephus does not mention Helena at the end of book 3 of *Wars*, where she would fit chronologically in his account of Jerusalem in the early first century, further suggesting that Josephus's later inclusion of the Adiabenaan history does not represent his own writing but rather is based on an independent source. I note that the account told in Josephus itself has several interesting gendered dimensions. For instance, while Izates is in Charax Spasini, he marries Symmacho, the daughter of the local king. We later learn that, while in Charax Spasini, Izates meets a Jew named Ananias, who has already convinced the kingdom's royal women to embrace Judaism before he convinces Izates to do so as well. When Izates returns to Adiabene, he finds that his mother has already converted to Judaism, thanks to another Jew, and decides to fully convert himself, including to undergo circumcision. As the story unfolds, the dynamics between mother and son are particularly interesting. The role of pregnancy, gender, travel, conversion, and boundary-crossing are thus already deeply bound up with the story of Helena and the house of Adiabene in Josephus's *Antiquities*.

6. Josephus's focus on Izates seems to stem from the sources upon which he relies, which tell a life of Izates from birth to death.

7. Pausanias, *Description of Greece* 8.16.5; trans. W. H. S. Jones in Pausanias, *Description of Greece*, Vol. III (Loeb Classical Library 272; Cambridge, MA: Harvard University Press, 1933), 426–27.

8. A study of the tomb's mechanism is provided in Maximilian Kon, *Tombs of the Kings [Kivre Ha-Melachim]* (Tel Aviv: Dvir, 1947) [Hebrew].

9. I thank Yevgeniy Safronov for making this suggestion.

10. Jerome, Letter 108; *Sancti Eusebii Hieronymi Epistulae*, ed. Isidorus Hilberg, 3 v. (New York: Johnson, 1970, repr. CSEL, 1910–18), 2.306–51, ep.108; translation with adaptation from https://epistolae.ctl.columbia.edu/letter/445.html.

11. Jerome, Letter 108.1.
12. Jerome, Letter 108.1.
13. Jerome, Letter 108.3.
14. So too Eusebius of Caesarea, relying on Josephus, mentions Helena in his *Ecclesiastical History* II.12.
15. The passage perhaps references Psalm 35:10, "All my bones shall say, O Lord, who is like you? You deliver the weak from those too strong for them, the weak and needy from those who despoil them."
16. Later in the letter, Jerome elaborates: "She gave her money to each according as each had need, not ministering to self-indulgence but relieving want. No poor person went away from her empty handed. And all this she was enabled to do not by the greatness of her wealth but by her careful management of it."
17. The word functions as a participle in an ablative absolute: *mausoleo derelicto* = "the tomb having been left behind." I thank Danny Schwartz and Paola Tartakoff for helping me understand this passage.
18. Susan Weingarten, *The Saint's Saints: Hagiography and Geography in Jerome* (Leiden: Brill, 2005), 240, takes the passage to mean that Paula looked at Helena's (neglected) tomb on her left on her way to Jerusalem.
19. In Letter 108.8, Jerome uses the term to refer to leaving (not abandoning or neglecting) the Roman colony of Berytus and the ancient city of Sidon, and in 108.14, Jerome uses it to describe going past or around the country of the Horites and Gittites, Mareshah, Edom, and Lachish (rather than "visiting and then departing"). See also Jerome, *Chron.* S.a. 374, discussed in Alan D. Booth, "The Chronology of Jerome's Early Years," *Phoenix* 35, no. 3 (1981): 237–59, at 248–49, who takes "unico praetore tunc urbano filio derelicto" to mean "whose only-surviving son, whom she had left formerly, was at that time urban praetor" (249).
20. Peter Brown, *Through the Eye of a Needle: Wealth, the Fall of Rome, and the Making of Christianity in the West, 350–550 AD* (Princeton: Princeton University Press, 2012), esp. 383–412, discusses both Jerome's letter about Paula and Christian women's patronage more generally. See also Elizabeth Clark, "Patrons, Not Priests: Gender and Power in Late Antique Christianity," *Gender & History* 2, no. 3 (1990): 253–73. On women's patronage in the Roman world, see Emily Ann Hemelrijk, *Hidden Lives, Public Personae: Women and Civic Life in the Roman West* (Oxford: Oxford University Press, 2015).
21. Jerome alludes at several points in his letter to Paula's accumulation of treasure in heaven, a theme associated with the house of Adiabene in rabbinic sources as well, e.g., *t. Peah* 4:18, and a theme in much early Christian literature.
22. We know that Jerome and Rufinus were persistent fundraisers, and that they targeted wealthy widows in particular, on which see e.g., Krista Dalton, "Teaching for the Tithe: Donor Expectations and the Matrona's Tithe," *AJS Review* 44, no. 1 (2020): 68–72; Mathew Kuefler, "The Merry Widows of Late Roman Antiquity: The Evidence of the Theodosian Code," *Gender & History* 27, no. 1 (2015): 28–52.
23. Helena's patronage of Jerusalem can be placed into a long history of women's patronage and philanthropy. On women's patronage in antiquity, especially in synagogue settings, see Bernadette Brooten, *Women Leaders in the Ancient Synagogue:*

Inscriptional Evidence and Background Issues (Brown Judaic Studies, 1982), including discussion of both Julia Severa and Tation; on women's patronage in rabbinic sources, see Dalton, "Teaching for the Tithe," 49–73; on women's roles in the creation of Jewish museums in the American context see Ariel Paige Cohen, "The Ethical Will, Embodied: American Jewish Museums and the Women Who Created Them," *Fordham Center for Jewish Studies Blog* (29 November 2020): https://jewishstudies.ace.fordham.edu/2020/11/29/ariel-paige-cohen-american-jewish-museums/; on women's philanthropy and volunteering often going unnoticed, uncompensated, or undervalued, see Arlene Kaplan Daniels, "Invisible Work," *Social Problems* 34, no. 5 (1987): 403–15; a recent example of gendered forms of giving appears in Valeriya Safronova, "How Women Are Changing the Philanthropy Game," *New York Times* (31 January 2021): https://www.nytimes.com/2021/01/30/style/mackenzie-scott-prisclila-chan-zuckerberg-melinda-gates-philanthropy.html?action=click&module=Editors%20Picks&pgtype=Homepage.

24. Eusebius, *Ecclesiastical History* 2.12.1–3.

25. On Rufinus's translations, see J. E. L. Oulton, "Rufinus's Translation of the Church History of Eusebius," *The Journal of Theological Studies* 30, no. 118 (1929): 150–74.

26. On Eusebius's vexed relationship with Jerusalem, see Oded Irshai, "Fourth Century Christian Palestinian Politics: A Glimpse at Eusebius of Caesarea's Local Political Career and its Nachleben in Christian Memory," in *Reconsidering Eusebius: A Fresh Look at His Life, Work, and Thought*, ed. Sabrina Inowlocki-Meister and Claudio Zamagni (Leiden: Brill, 2011), 25–38.

27. Eusebius, *Life of Constantine* 41–43; Rufinus, *Ecclesiastical History* 10.7–8.

28. I thank Bernadette Brooten for articulating this point so clearly in her comments to our panel on Helena of Adiabene at the 2020 Association for Jewish Studies Conference.

29. Helena is mentioned in *t. Nazir* 3:6; *t. Sukkah* 1:1; *m. Yoma* 3:10; *t. Kippurim [Yoma]* 2:3; and in parallels in the talmudim; other sources, e.g., *t. Peah* 4:18, *t. Megillah* 3(4):30; *Genesis Rabbah* 46:11, mention Monobaz but not Helena, even though Josephus's version of some of these narratives do mention Helena. On rabbinic portrayals of the house of Adiabene, see Isaiah M. Gafni, "The Conversion of the Rulers of Adiabene in Light of Talmudic Literature (Hebrew)," *Niv Ha-Midrashiah*, 1971, 204–12; Schiffman, "The Conversion of the Royal House of Adiabene," 298–308; Tal Ilan, *Mine and Yours Are Hers: Retrieving Women's History from Rabbinic Literature* (Tübingen: Mohr Siebeck, 1997): 280–82; *Integrating Women into Second Temple History* (Tübingen: Mohr Siebeck, 1997): 25–26, 66–71; Richard Kalmin, "The Adiabenian Royal Family in Rabbinic Literature of Late Antiquity," in *Tiferet leYisrael: Jubilee Volume in Honor of Israel Francus*, ed. J. Roth, et al. (New York: Jewish Theological Seminary, 2010), 61–77; Malka Simkovich, "Queen Helena of Adiabene and Her Sons in Midrash and History," *TheTorah.com* (2018): https://thetorah.com/article/queen-helena-of-adiabene-and-her-sons-in-midrash-and-history; Tal Ilan and Vered Noam, *Josephus and the Rabbis* (Leiden: Brill, 2019), 508–20; Gregg Gardner, "Giving, Receiving, and Reception: Rabbinic Depictions of Adiabene's Benefactions," Association for Jewish Studies Conference paper (December 2020); Gregg E. Gardner, *Wealth, Poverty, and Charity in Jewish Antiquity* (Oakland: University of California Press, 2022), 1–2, 117–139.

30. Simkovich, "Queen Helena of Adiabene and Her Sons in Midrash and History," suggests that rabbinic sources might be confusing Helena, who does not make a Nazirite vow in Josephus' account, and Berenice, whom Josephus describes as having made one in *Wars* 2.15.1, on which see also Christophe Batsch, "Reines et nazaréennes: deux femmes de pouvoir à l'époque du deuxième Temple: Hélène d'Adiabèn et Bérénice de Chalcis," *Tsafon: Revue d'études juives du Nord* 54 (2007–8): 67–78. On Berenice in rabbinic sources, see Tal Ilan, *Queen Berenice: A Jewish Female Icon of the First Century* (Leiden: Brill, 2022).

31. The text intimates that she fulfills her first Nazirite vow in Adiabene without saying so explicitly.

32. On which see Cynthia M. Baker, "The Queen, the Apostate, and the Women Between: (Dis)Placement of Women in Tosefta Sukkah," in *A Feminist Commentary on the Babylonian Talmud: Introduction and Studies*, ed. Tal Ilan, et al. (Tübingen: Mohr Siebeck, 2007), 169–81; Galit Hasan-Rokem, "Material Mobility Versus Concentric Cosmology in the Sukkah: The House of the Wandering Jew of a Ubiquitous Temple?" *Things: Religion and the Question of Materiality*, ed. Dick Houtman and Birgit Meyer (New York: Fordham University Press, 2012), 153–79, at 160–64.

33. The reference to Helena's seven sons alludes to the biblically significant number seven and relates to Josephus, *Antiquities* 20.70, in which Izates fathers twenty-four sons and twenty-four daughters, five of whom he sends to study Hebrew and learn Jewish wisdom in Palestine, on which see Schiffman, "The Conversion of the Royal House of Adiabene," 299; Rajak, "The Parthians in Josephus," 321. That Helena had specifically seven sons might also allude to the narrative of the mother of seven sons, all of whom are martyred, which is told in various versions in 2 Maccabees 7, Lamentations Rabbah 1:50, *b. Gittin* 57b, and other sources. As with the tradition of Helena's Nazirite vow, Helena's seven sons in this rabbinic source might highlight, through allusion to other traditions about mothers and their seven sons, Helena's unparalleled dedication to teaching her sons devotion to God, and in turn her own fidelity to God.

34. On this passage, see Miriam B. Peskowitz, *Spinning Fantasies: Rabbis, Gender, and History* (Berkeley: University of California Press, 1997), 136–39; Ishay Rosen-Zvi, *The Mishnaic Sotah Ritual: Temple, Gender and Midrash* (Leiden: Brill, 2012), 158–60; a broader analysis of the pericope is found in Nathan Schumer, "The Memory of the Temple in Palestinian Rabbinic Literature" (Ph.D. diss, Columbia University, 2017), 89–93. I discuss this text in "Consuming Texts: Women as Recipients and Transmitters of Ancient Texts," in *Rethinking 'Authority' in Late Antiquity: Authorship, Law, and Transmission in Jewish and Christian Tradition*, ed. Abraham J. Berkovitz and Mark Letteney (London: Routledge, 2018), 178–206. On women's pilgrimage and piety in rabbinic sources, with particular attention to temple donations, see Jane L. Kanarek, "Pilgrimage and Piety: Rabbinic Women and Vows of Valuation, Mishnah 'Arakhin 5:1, Tosefta 'Arakhin 3:1, BT 'Arakhin 19a," *Nashim: A Journal of Jewish Women's Studies & Gender Issues* 28 (2015): 61–74.

35. *b. Berakhot* 2b, which asks whether the "time when the priests come home to eat their terumah" is the same as the "time when the poor come home to eat dinner" (and the time when "the people return to eat their shabbat meal"). There is an

extended discussion in this text about whether these three times (which all appear in tannaitic sources and/or are beraitot in the Babylonian Talmud) are the same or different times. The sugya ultimately concludes that they each represent a different time. This discussion relates to the discussion about Helena's temple object, the reflection of which helped local people in Jerusalem (as the text says) tell the time for the morning Shema, but which wasn't relevant for priests who woke up earlier to accomplish their tasks in the temple. I discuss this text in *Time and Difference in Rabbinic Judaism* (Princeton University Press, 2020), 196. This sugya is also at the center of analysis in Marjorie Lehman, "Transmitting Ritual, Rearing Sons: The Role of Helene in Bavli Yoma," Association for Jewish Studies Conference paper (December 2020), and Marjorie Lehman, *Bringing Down the Temple House: Engendering Tractate Yoma* (Waltham: Brandeis University Press, 2023), 55–70.

36. Gribetz, "Consuming Texts," 183–84. The case of Helena is one of several in which rabbis interact with wealthy women patrons; another example from the same tractate is analyzed in Dalton, "Teaching for the Tithe." The comparison of narratives about Helena and Matrona in tractate Sotah is especially interesting, as both women function as liminal figures, wealthy and yet their belonging within the rabbinic community is complicated not only because of their gender but also their status as foreign or imperial women.

37. On which see my "Consuming Texts."

38. I thank Krista Dalton for this observation.

39. Much as they do in their portrayal of the Hasmonean queen Salome Alexandra, whom they remember in Sifre Deuteronomy 42 as a beloved ruler during whose reign the kingdom prospered, and in contrast, for example, to rabbinic portrayals of Beruriah, who presents a contrarian woman's voice within rabbinic tradition. See e.g., *t. Kelim Baba Metzia* 1:6, *b. Eruvin* 53b, *b. Berakhot* 10a; *b. Pesahim* 62b, and the discussion in Daniel Boyarin, *Carnal Israel: Reading Sex in Talmudic Culture* (Berkeley: University of California Press, 1993), 181–96. Another female character who expresses interest in studying biblical texts and their rabbinic interpretations within rabbinic narratives is Matrona, on which see Tal Ilan, "Matrona and Rabbi Jose: An Alternative Interpretation," *Journal for the Study of Judaism* 25 (1994): 18–51, and the sources and scholarship discussed there.

40. Orosius, *Historiae adversus paganos* 7.6.12, discussed in Aimee Turner, "'She Acted with Arrogance': Orosius on Women," *Studies in Late Antiquity* 4, no. 2 (2020): 203–27: "Eodem anno imperii eius fames grauissima per Syriam facta est, quam etiam prophetae praenuntiauerant; sed Christianorum necessitatibus apud Hierosolymam conuectis ab Aegypto frumentis Helena Adiabenorum regina conuersa ad fidem Christi largissime ministrauit."

41. For the text and an extensive discussion of its dating and use of sources, see Movsēs Xorenacʻi, *History of the Armenians*, edited and translated by Robert W. Thomson (Cambridge, MA: Harvard University Press, 1978; Ann Arbor: Caravan Books, 2006). On the text and its sources, see Nina Garsoïan, "L'Histoire attribuée à Movsēs Xorenacʻi: que reste-t-il à en dire?" *Revue des Études Arméniennes* 29 (2003–2004): 29–48; Aram Topchyan, *The Problems of the Greek Sources of Movsēs Xorenacʻi's 'History of Armenia'* (Peeters: Leuven, 2006).

42. I assume that what scholars of this text mean by "unreliable" is that the history that it tells is unreliable, as is its early dating; I treat it here as a late text and read it in that context. See A. O. Sarkissian, "On the Authenticity of Moses of Khoren's History," *Journal of the American Oriental Society* 60, no. 1 (1940): 73–81; Robert H. Hewson, "'The Primary History of Armenia': An Examination of the Validity of an Immemorially Transmitted Historical Tradition," *History of Africa* 2 (1975): 91–100.

43. For an extensive discussion, see Thomson, *History of the Armenians*, 13–56.

44. Thomson, *History of the Armenians*, 26, 35. See also Jacob Neusner, "The Conversion of Adiabene to Christianity," *Numen* 13, no. 2 (1966): 144–50; Ilaria L. E. Ramelli, "Possible Historical Traces in the *Doctrina Addai*," *Hugoye: Journal of Syriac Studies* 9, no. 1 (2006 [2009]): 51–127, at 96–104, who connects Helena of Adiabene with the Doctrina Addai more generally as well.

45. Thomson, *History of the Armenians*, 176, notes that Moses's identification of Helena as having a throne in Mesopotamia accords with the Armenian translation of Eusebius, which identifies Helena as being from Mesopotamia, rather than the Greek text, which refers to her as being from Adiabene. See also *ANF* 8, X.3301; Moses of Chorene, *History of Armenia*, trans. R. P. Pratten (Dalcassian Publishing Company, 2020), 22.

46. Thomson, *History of the Armenians*, 177.

47. Thomson, *History of the Armenians*, 22.

48. On Toledot Yeshu (including texts, translations, and introductions), see most recently Peter Schäfer and Michael Meerson (eds. and trans.), *Toledot Yeshu: The Life Story of Jesus*, 2 vol. and database (Tübingen: Mohr Siebeck, 2014), as well as two important collections of essays, Peter Schäfer, Michael Meerson, and Yaacov Deutsch (eds.), *Toledot Yeshu ("The Life Story of Jesus") Revisited: A Princeton Conference* (Tübingen: Mohr Siebeck, 2011), and Daniel Barbu and Yaacov Deutsch (eds.), *Toledot Yeshu in Context: Jewish-Christian Polemics in Ancient, Medieval, and Modern History* (Tübingen: Mohr Siebeck, 2020). Miriam Goldstein, *A Judeo-Arabic Parody of the Life of Jesus: The Toledot Yeshu Helene Narrative* (Tübingen: Mohr Siebeck, 2023), published after this essay was written, is now a crucial resource and will inform my future analysis of these sources.

49. Galit Hasan-Rokem, "Polymorphic Helena: *Toledot Yeshu* as a Palimpsest of Religious Narratives and Identities," in *Toledot Yeshu Revisited*, 247–82; Gavin McDowell, "The Alternative Chronology: Dating the Events of the Wagenseil Version of *Toledot Yeshu*," in *Toledot Yeshu in Context*, ed. Daniel Barbu and Yaacov Deutsch (Tübingen: Mohr Siebeck, 2020), 74; Claudia Rosenzweig, "The 'History of the Life of Jesus' in a Yiddish Manuscript from the Eighteenth Century (Ms. Jerusalem, NLI, Heb. 8 5622)," in *Toledot Yeshu in Context*, ed. Daniel Barbu and Yaacov Deutsch (Tübingen: Mohr Siebeck, 2020), 300.

50. Editions and translation of this text can be found in Alexandra Cuffel, "*Toledot Yeshu* in the Context of Polemic and Sīra Literature in the Middle East from the Fatimid to the Mamluk Era," in *Toledot Yeshu in Context*, ed. Daniel Barbu and Yaacov Deutsch (Tübingen: Mohr Siebeck, 2020), 162–64; and Goldstein, *A Judeo-Arabic Parody of the Life of Jesus*; I rely on Goldstein for the translation, Goldstein translates רומיה as "Byzantine" while Cuffel uses "Roman." Immediately after

introducing Helena the text describes the stone in the temple, interesting in light of the Sotah stone associated with Helen in *m. Yoma* 3:10. Additional Judeo-Arabic manuscripts of Toledot Yeshu have now been compiled in Goldstein, *A Judeo-Arabic Parody of the Life of Jesus*.

51. Goldstein, *A Judeo-Arabic Parody*.

52. On which see, e. g. Schwartz, "God, Gentiles, and Jewish Law," 263–83.

53. On which see M Adryael Tong, "'Given as a Sign': Circumcision and Bodily Discourse in Late Antique Judaism and Christianity" (Ph.D. diss, Fordham University, 2019).

54. Perhaps the name of God engraved on the foundation stone recalls Helena's gift of a golden tablet inscribed with the Sotah passages upon it.

55. Hasan-Rokem, "Polymorphic Helena," 257.

56. Meerson and Schäfer, *Toledot Yeshu*, Vol. 1:123–24.

57. This is an argument that I also found in Adolf von Harnack, *The Mission and Expansion of Christianity in the First Three Centuries*, Vol. 1 (Williams and Norgate, 1908), 2: "A striking parallel, a century and a half later, is afforded by the conversion of the royal house of Edessa in Christianity. Renan (*Les Apôtres*, ch. xiv) is not wrong when he remarks, in his own way, that 'the royal family of Adiabene belongs to the history of Christianity.' He does not mean to say, with Orosius (vii. 6) and Moses of Chorene (ii. 35), that they actually became Christians, but simply that 'in embracing Judaism, they obeyed a sentiment which was destined to bring over the entire pagan world to Christianity.' A further and striking parallel to the efforts of Queen Helena of Adiabene (cp. Jos. *Antiq.*, xx. 2 f.; *B.J.*, v. 2–4, v. 6. I, vi. 6. 3) is to be found in the charitable activity of Constantine's mother, Queen Helena, in Jerusalem. Possibly the latter took the Jewish queen as her model, for Helena of Adiabene's philanthropy was still remembered in Jerusalem and by Jews in general (cp. Eus. *H.E.*, ii. 12, and the Talmudic tradition)." Hasan-Rokem also elaborates on the similarities between both Helenas in "Material Mobility," 161–62 and "Polymorphic Helena," 247–82, and discusses the complex ways in which portrayals of the figures mutually impacted one another. A similar connection is made in Michael Thomas, "The Conversions of Adiabene and Edessa in Syriac Christianity and Judaism: The Relations of Jews and Christian in Northern Mesopotamia in Antiquity," *Concordia Theological Journal* 7, no. 1 (2020): 10–33.

58. On this textual tradition, see Jan Willem Drijvers, *Helena Augusta: The Mother of Constantine the Great and the Legend of Her Finding of the True Cross* (Leiden: Brill, 1992); Stephan Borgehammer, *How the Holy Cross Was Found: From Event to Medieval Legend* (Stockholm: Almqvist & Wiksell, 1991).

59. On this portion of the text and the precise version of the legend on which it is based, see Schäfer and Meerson, *Toledot Yeshu*, Vol. 1, 120–24; Galit Hasan-Rokem, "Polymorphic Helena," 264–68; Ora Limor and Israel Jacob Yuval, "Judas Iscariot: Revealer of the Hidden Truth," in *Toledot Yeshu . . . Revisited*, 208–18; Sarit Kattan Gribetz, "The Mothers in the Manuscripts: Gender, Motherhood and Power in the *Toledot Yeshu* Narratives," in *Toledot Yeshu in Context: The Jewish "Life of Jesus" in Ancient, Medieval, and Modern History*, ed. Daniel Barbu and Yaacov Deutsch (Tübingen: Mohr Siebeck, 2020), 99–129.

60. It also appears in some Judaeo-Arabic versions, as Goldstein, *A Judeo-Arabic Parody of the Life of Jesus*, demonstrates.

61. Whereas in Christian tradition Judas betrays Jesus, in Toledot Yeshu the Judas character pretends to assist the Christians but in fact betrays them as well, becoming a Jewish hero.

62. Schäfer and Meerson, *Toledot Yeshu*, Vol. 1, 121.

63. Schäfer and Meerson, *Toledot Yeshu*, Vol. 1, 124 note: "It is therefore not impossible that *Toledot Yeshu* was inspired by these motifs in the Christian legends of the Holy Cross and responded to them long before the actual composition of the Cyriacus parody and its attachment to *Toledot Yeshu* took place."

64. I explain this dynamic at length in Gribetz, "The Mothers in the Manuscripts," 99–129.

65. The distinctions between the various versions of Toledot Yeshu were outlined in Riccardo di Segni, *Il vangelo del ghetto* (Rome: Newton Compton, 1985), and modified only slightly in Schäfer and Meerson, *Toledot Yeshu*. The question of the origins and earliest manuscripts of this recension have most recently been discussed in Goldstein, *A Judeo-Arabic Parody*.

66. On which see, e.g., Miriam Goldstein, "Judeo-Arabic Versions of *Toledot Yeshu*," *Ginzei Qedem* 6 (2010): 9–42; "A Polemical Tale and its Function in the Jewish Communities of the Mediterranean and the Near East," *Intellectual History of the Islamicate World* 7 (2019): 192–227; "Jesus in Arabic, Jesus in Judeo-Arabic: The Origins of the Helene Version of the Jewish 'Life of Jesus' (*Toledot Yeshu*)," *Jewish Quarterly Review* 111, no. 1 (2021): 83–104; Cuffel, "*Toledot Yeshu* in the Context of Polemic and Sīra Literature," 131–68; Daniel Stökl Ben Ezra, "On Some Early Traditions in *Toledot Yeshu* and the Antiquity of the 'Helena' Recension," in *Toledot Yeshu in Context*, ed. Daniel Barbu and Yaacov Deutsch (Tübingen: Mohr Siebeck 2020), 43–58. Also important for dating the Helena versions of Toledot Yeshu is Yaacov Deutsch, "New Evidence of Early Versions of *Toldot Yeshu*," *Tarbiz* 69 (2000): 177–97. In my forthcoming book, I analyze and contextualize the early Judaeo-Arabic manuscripts of Toledot Yeshu within the broader history of Helena's reception.

67. Stökl Ben Ezra, "On Some Early Traditions," 48.

68. On the role of burial sites and sacred topography in remembering biblical matriarchs in late antique Palestine, see my article, "Topographies of Mother Absence in Late Antique Palestine: A View from Jewish Sources," in *Missing Mothers: Maternal Absence in Antiquity*, ed. Sabine R. Huebner and David Ratzan (Leuven: Peeters, 2021), 276–320.

69. Tertullian, *Adv. Jud.* 13; Justin Martyr, *Dialogue* 16, 1 *Apol.* 77; Eusebius, *Hist. Eccl.* 5.6.3; these sources and extensive scholarship on the question of Hadrian's ban and Jewish residency in Jerusalem in the second through fourth centuries are discussed in Dayna S. Kalleres, *City of Demons: Violence, Ritual, and Christian Power in Late Antiquity* (Berkeley: University of California Press, 2015), 125–27, 292–93.

70. On applying this conceptual framework to historical figures, see Roland Betancourt, *Byzantine Intersectionality: Sexuality, Gender, and Race in the Middle Ages* (Princeton: Princeton University Press, 2020).

71. Josephus, *Antiquities* 20.4.3. On the archaeology of the tomb, see Kon, *Tombs of the Kings*; Abraham Ezra Millgram, *Jerusalem Curiosities* (Philadelphia: Jewish Publication Society, 1990), 125–27; Ruth Jacoby, "The Decoration and Plan of Queen Helena's Tomb in Jerusalem," in *The Real and Ideal Jerusalem in Jewish, Christian, and Islamic Art* (Jerusalem: Hebrew University, Center for Jewish Art, 1998), 460–62; Lee I. Levine, *Jerusalem: Portrait of the City in the Second Temple Period: 538 BCE–70 CE* (Philadelphia: Jewish Publication Society, 2002), 211–12, and various other references between 313–50; Omri Abadi and Boaz Zissu, "The Purpose of the Ritual Baths in the Tombs of the Kings: A New Proposal," *Electrum* 26 (2019): 97–108.

72. See, e.g., Jon Seligman and Rafa Abu Raya, "A Shrine of Three Religions on the Mount of Olives: Tomb of Hulda the Prophetess, Grotto of Saint Pelagia, Tomb of Rabi'a al-'Adawiyya," *'Atiqot* 42 (2001): 221–36. On local traditions and women's piety at other cultic places of worship, see e.g., Stephen J. Davis, *The Cult of St Thecla: A Tradition of Women's Piety in Late Antiquity* (Oxford: Oxford University Press, 2001); Susan Starr Sered, "Rachel's Tomb: The Development of a Cult," *Jewish Studies Quarterly* 2 (1995): 103–48.

73. Even before such archaeological excavations, François-René de Chateaubriand, *Itinéraire de Paris à Jérusalem et de Jérusalem a Paris, n allant par la Grèce, et revenant par l'Égypte, la B arbarie et l'Espagne* (Paris: Le Normant, Imprimeur-Libraire, 1811) raises the possibility that the tomb belonged to Helena of Adiabene. I explore the modern history of this tomb in detail in my forthcoming book.

74. On his excavation of the Tomb of the Kings, see Louis Félicien Joseph Caignart de Saulcy, *Voyage en Terre Sainte* 1 (Paris: Didier, 1865), 345–410.

75. Museum of the Louvre, Paris, inv. no. AO 5029.

76. Hannah M. Cotton, Leah Di Segni, Werner Eck, Benjamin Isaac, Alla Kushnir-Stein, Haggai Misgav, Jonathan Price, Israel Roll, and Ada Yardeni, eds., *Corpus Inscriptionum Iudaeae/Palaestinae, Volume I: Jerusalem: 1–704, A Multi-lingual Corpus of the Inscriptions from Alexander to Muhammad* (Berlin: de Gruyter, 2014), 165–67, no.123.

77. Archaeological reports that regard this tomb as that of Helena of Adiabene include, as representative samples, Donald T. Ariel and Alon De Groot, "Excavations at the City of David 1978–1985, Directed by Yigal Shiloh: Volume IV, Various Reports," *Qedem* 35 (1996), 1–x, 1–342, at 10; Orit Peleg-Barkat, "The Temple Mount Excavations in Jerusalem 1968–1978, Directed by Benjamin Mazar; Final Reports Volume V: Herodian Architectural Decoration and King Herod's Royal Portico," *Qedem* 57 (2017): 1–249, at 18.

78. Megan Sauter, "The Tomb of Queen Helena of Adiabene: Which is the Queen's Sarcophagus?" *Biblical Archaeology* (2014): https://www.biblicalarchaeology.org/daily/ancient-cultures/ancient-israel/the-tomb-of-queen-helena-of-adiabene/, outlines this debate and makes a persuasive case that one of the coffin lids may have belonged to Helena's sarcophagus, while the sarcophagus itself likely belonged to a younger relative. She identifies Charles S. Clermont-Ganneau, "Le temple de Baal Marcod à Deir el-Kala'a," *Recueil d'archéologie orientale* 1 (1886): 107–08 as the earliest work suggesting the sarcophagus belonged to the queen herself. The inscription was

published in Ada Yardeni, Jonathan Price, and Haggai Misgav, "123. Sarcophagus of Queen Sadan from the 'Tomb of the Kings' with Aramaic Inscription," in *Corpus Inscriptionum Iudaeae/Palaestinae* 11, ed. Hannah Cotton et al. (Berlin: de Gruyter, 2010), 165–67. Michal Marciak, "Royal Converts from Adiabene and the Archaeology of Jerusalem," *Göttinger Forum für Altertumswissenschaft* (2018): 29–58 offers a comprehensive study of both the tomb and the palace, coming to many of the same conclusions about the tomb and sarcophagus.

79. I also explore the history of this street and its name in my forthcoming book.

80. Doron Ben-Ami and Yana Tchekhanovets, "Has the Adiabene Royal Family 'Palace' been Found in the City of David?" in *Unearthing Jerusalem: 150 Years of Archaeological Research in the Holy City*, ed. Katharina Galor and Gideon Avni (Winona Lake: Eisenbrauns, 2011); R. Steven Notley and Jeffrey P. García, "Queen Helena's Jerusalem Palace—In a Parking Lot?" *Biblical Archaeology Review* (May/June 2014): 28ff.

81. Ran Shapira, "A Royal Return," *Haaretz* (1 October 2020): https://www.haaretz.com/1.5119727.

82. "City of David: Earrings Fit for a Queen (Helena)," https://www.travelujah.com/stories/city-david-earrings-fit-queen-helena; the jewelry collection can be seen here: https://store.cityofdavid.org.il/collections/queen-helene. The "Helena Veil," sold by Nilah & Company can be viewed here: https://nilah.com/wordpress1/product/helena-veil.

83. On the initial reopening, see Ilan Ben Zion, "France Reopens Contested Jewish Tomb in East Jerusalem," *abcNews* (8 November 2019), https://abcnews.go.com/International/wireStory/france-reopens-contested-jewish-tomb-east-jerusalem-66842218; on its current state, see Krystal V. L. Pierce, "Tomb of the Kings Now Open!," *Biblical Archaeology, Biblical History Daily* (1 June 2020), https://www.biblicalarchaeology.org/daily/biblical-sites-places/biblical-archaeology-sites/tomb-of-kings-now-open/.

BIBLIOGRAPHY

Abadi, Omri and Boaz Zissu. "The Purpose of the Ritual Baths in the Tombs of the Kings: A New Proposal." *Electrum* 26 (2019): 97–108.

Baker, Cynthia M. "The Queen, the Apostate, and the Women Between: (Dis)Placement of Women in Tosefta Sukkah." In *A Feminist Commentary on the Babylonian Talmud: Introduction and Studies*, edited by Tal Ilan et al., 169–81. Tübingen: Mohr Siebeck, 2007.

Barbu, Daniel and Yaacov Deutsch (eds.). *Toledot Yeshu in Context: Jewish-Christian Polemics in Ancient, Medieval, and Modern History.* Tübingen: Mohr Siebeck, 2020.

Barish, David A. *Adiabene: Royal Converts to Judaism in the First Century C.E.: A Study of Sources.* Ph.D. Dissertation. Hebrew Union College, 1983.

Batsch, Christophe. "Reines et nazaréennes: deux femmes de pouvoir à l'époque du deuxième Temple: Hélène d'Adiabèn et Bérénice de Chalcis." *Tsafon: Revue d'études juivees du Nord* 54 (2007–8): 67–78.

Ben-Ami, Doron and Yana Tchekhanovets. "Has the Adiabene Royal Family 'Palace' been Found in the City of David?" In *Unearthing Jerusalem: 150 Years of Archaeological Research in the Holy City*, edited by Katharina Galor and Gideon Avni, 231–240. Winona Lake: Eisenbrauns, 2011.

Ben Zion, Ilan. "France Reopens Contested Jewish Tomb in East Jerusalem." *abcNews*, November 8, 2019. https://abcnews.go.com/International/wireStory/france-reopens-contested-jewish-tomb-east-jerusalem-66842218.

Betancourt, Roland. *Byzantine Intersectionality: Sexuality, Gender, and Race in the Middle Ages*. Princeton: Princeton University Press, 2020.

Booth, Alan D. "The Chronology of Jerome's Early Years." *Phoenix* 35, no. 3 (1981): 237–59.

Borgehammer, Stephan. *How the Holy Cross Was Found: From Event to Medieval Legend*. Stockholm: Almqvist & Wiksell, 1991.

Boyarin, Daniel. *Carnal Israel: Reading Sex in Talmudic Culture*. Berkeley: University of California Press, 1993.

Brooten, Bernadette. *Women Leaders in the Ancient Synagogue: Inscriptional Evidence and Background Issues*. Brown Judaic Studies, 1982.

Brown, Peter. *Through the Eye of a Needle: Wealth, the Fall of Rome, and the Making of Christianity in the West, 350–550 AD*. Princeton: Princeton University Press, 2012.

Clark, Elizabeth. "Patrons, Not Priests: Gender and Power in Late Antique Christianity." *Gender & History* 2, no. 3 (1990): 253–73.

Clermont-Ganneau, Charles S. "Le temple de Baal Marcod à Deir el-Kala'a." *Recueil d'archéologie orientale* 1 (1886): 107–08.

Cotton, Hannah M., Leah Di Segni, Werner Eck, Benjamin Isaac, Alla Kushnir-Stein, Haggai Misgav, Jonathan Price, Israel Roll, and Ada Yardeni (eds.). *Corpus Inscriptionum Iudaeae/Palaestinae, Volume I: Jerusalem: 1–704, A Multi-lingual Corpus of the Inscriptions from Alexander to Muhammad*. Berlin: de Gruyter, 2014.

Cuffel, Alexandra. "*Toledot Yeshu* in the Context of Polemic and Sīra Literature in the Middle East from the Fatimid to the Mamluk Era." In *Toledot Yeshu in Context*, edited by Daniel Barbu and Yaacov Deutsch, 162–64. Tübingen: Mohr Siebeck, 2020.

Dalton, Krista. "Teaching for the Tithe: Donor Expectations and the Matrona's Tithe." *AJS Review* 44, no. 1 (2020): 68–72.

Deutsch, Yaacov. "New Evidence of Early Versions of *Toldot Yeshu*." *Tarbiz* 69 (2000): 177–97.

Drijvers, Jan Willem. *Helena Augusta: The Mother of Constantine the Great and the Legend of Her Finding of the True Cross*. Leiden: Brill, 1992.

Frenschkowski, Marc. "Iranische Königslegende in der Adiabene: zur Vorgeschichte von Josephus, 'Antiquitates' XX, 17–33." *Zeitschrift der Deutschen Morgenländischen Gesellschaft* 140, no. 2 (1990): 213–33.

Gafni, Isaiah M. "The Conversion of the Rulers of Adiabene in Light of Talmudic Literature (Hebrew)." *Niv Ha-Midrashiah* (1971): 204–12.

Gardner, Gregg E. "Giving, Receiving, and Reception: Rabbinic Depictions of Adiabene's Benefactions." *Association for Jewish Studies Conference Paper*, December 2020.

Gardner, Gregg E. *Wealth, Poverty, and Charity in Jewish Antiquity*. Oakland: University of California Press, 2022.

Garsoïan, Nina. "L'Histoire attribuée à Movsēs Xorenac'i: que reste-t-il à en dire?" *Revue des Études Arméniennes* 29 (2003–2004): 29–48.

Goldstein, Miriam. "Judeo-Arabic Versions of *Toledot Yeshu*." *Ginzei Qedem* 6 (2010): 9–42.

Goldstein, Miriam. "A Polemical Tale and its Function in the Jewish Communities of the Mediterranean and the Near East." *Intellectual History of the Islamicate World* 7 (2019): 192–27.

Goldstein, Miriam. "Jesus in Arabic, Jesus in Judeo-Arabic: The Origins of the Helene Version of the Jewish 'Life of Jesus' (*Toledot Yeshu*)." *Jewish Quarterly Review* 111, no. 1 (2021): 83–104.

Goldstein, Miriam. *A Judeo-Arabic Parody of the Life of Jesus: The Toledot Yeshu Helene Narrative*. Tübingen: Mohr Siebeck, 2023.

Gross, Simcha. "Hopeful Rebels and Anxious Romans: Jewish Interconnectivity in the Great Revolt and Beyond." *Historia: Zeitschrift für Alte Geschichte* 72 (2023): 479–513.

Harnack, Adolf von. *The Mission and Expansion of Christianity in the First Three Centuries*, Vol. 1. Williams and Norgate, 1908.

Hasan-Rokem, Galit. "Polymorphic Helena: *Toledot Yeshu* as a Palimpsest of Religious Narratives and Identities." In *Toledot Yeshu Revisited,* edited by Peter Schäfer, Michael Meerson, and Yaacov Deutsch, 247–82. Tübingen: Mohr Siebeck, 2011.

Hasan-Rokem, Galit. "Material Mobility Versus Concentric Cosmology in the Sukkah: The House of the Wandering Jew of a Ubiquitous Temple?" In *Things: Religion and the Question of Materiality*, edited by Dick Houtman and Birgit Meyer, 153–79. New York: Fordham University Press, 2012.

Hemelrijk, Emily Ann. *Hidden Lives, Public Personae: Women and Civic Life in the Roman West*. Oxford: Oxford University Press, 2015.

Hewson, Robert H. "'The Primary History of Armenia': An Examination of the Validity of an Immemorially Transmitted Historical Tradition." *History of Africa* 2 (1975): 91–100.

Ilan, Tal. "Matrona and Rabbi Jose: An Alternative Interpretation." *Journal for the Study of Judaism* 25 (1994): 18–51.

Ilan, Tal. *Integrating Women into Second Temple History*. Tübingen: Mohr Siebeck, 1997.

Ilan, Tal. *Mine and Yours Are Hers: Retrieving Women's History from Rabbinic Literature*. Tübingen: Mohr Siebeck, 1997.

Ilan, Tal, and Vered Noam. *Josephus and the Rabbis*. Leiden: Brill, 2019.

Ilan, Tal. *Queen Berenice: A Jewish Female Icon of the First Century*. Leiden: Brill, 2022.

Irshai, Oded. "Fourth Century Christian Palestinian Politics: A Glimpse at Eusebius of Caesarea's Local Political Career and its Nachleben in Christian Memory." In *Reconsidering Eusebius: A Fresh Look at His Life, Work, and Thought*, 25–38. Leiden: Brill, 2011.

Jacoby, Ruth. "The Decoration and Plan of Queen Helena's Tomb in Jerusalem." In *The Real and Ideal Jerusalem in Jewish, Christian, and Islamic Art*, 460–62. Jerusalem: Hebrew University, Center for Jewish Art, 1998.

Kalleres, Dayna S. *City of Demons: Violence, Ritual, and Christian Power in Late Antiquity*. Berkeley: University of California Press, 2015.

Kalmin, Richard. "The Adiabenian Royal Family in Rabbinic Literature of Late Antiquity." In *Tiferet leYisrael: Jubilee Volume in Honor of Israel Francus*, edited by J. Roth et al., 61–77. New York: Jewish Theological Seminary, 2010.

Kanarek, Jane L. "Pilgrimage and Piety: Rabbinic Women and Vows of Valuation, Mishnah *'Arakhin* 5:1, Tosefta *'Arakhin*3:1, BT *'Arakhin* 19a." *Nashim: A Journal of Jewish Women's Studies & Gender Issues* 28 (2015): 61–74.

Kaplan Daniels, Arlene. "Invisible Work." *Social Problems* 34, no. 5 (1987): 403–15.

Kattan Gribetz, Sarit. "Consuming Texts: Women as Recipients and Transmitters of Ancient Texts." In *Rethinking 'Authority' in Late Antiquity: Authorship, Law, and Transmission in Jewish and Christian Tradition*, edited by Abraham J. Berkovitz and Mark Letteney, 178–206. London: Routledge, 2018.

Kattan Gribetz, Sarit. "The Mothers in the Manuscripts: Gender, Motherhood and Power in the *Toledot Yeshu* Narratives." In *Toledot Yeshu in Context: The Jewish "Life of Jesus" in Ancient, Medieval, and Modern History*, edited by Daniel Barbu and Yaacov Deutsch, 99–129. Tübingen: Mohr Siebeck, 2020.

Kattan Gribetz, Sarit. *Time and Difference in Rabbinic Judaism*. Princeton: Princeton University Press, 2020.

Kon, Maximilian. *Tombs of the Kings [Kivre Ha-Melachim]*. Tel Aviv: Dvir, 1947 [Hebrew].

Kuefler, Mathew. "The Merry Widows of Late Roman Antiquity: The Evidence of the Theodosian Code." *Gender & History* 27, no. 1 (2015): 28–52.

Lehman, Marjorie. "Transmitting Ritual, Rearing Sons: The Role of Helene in Bavli Yoma." *Association for Jewish Studies Conference Paper*, December 2020.

Lehman, Marjorie. *Bringing Down the Temple House: Engendering Tractate Yoma*. Waltham: Brandeis University Press, 2023.

Levine, Lee I. *Jerusalem: Portrait of the City in the Second Temple Period: 538 BCE – 70 CE*. Philadelphia: Jewish Publication Society, 2002.

Liebowitz, Etka. "A New Perspective on Two Jewish Queens in the Second Temple Period: Alexandra of Judaea and Helene of Adiabene." In *Sources and Interpretation in Ancient Judaism: Studies for Tal Ilan at Sixty*, edited by Meron M. Piotrkowski et al., 41–65. Leiden: Brill, 2018.

Marciak, Michal. "Biblical Allusions in the Adiabene Narrative (Antiquitates Judaicae 20:17–96)." *Polish Journal of Biblical Research* 10, no. 1–2 (2011): 63–84.

Marciak, Michal. "The Cultural Environment of Adiabene in the Hellenistic, Parthian, and Sasanian Period." *Parthica: Incontri di culture nel mondo antico* (2014): 11–150.

Marciak, Michal. *Izates, Helena, and Monobazos of Adiabene: A Study on Literary Traditions and History*. Wiesbaden: Harrassowitz, 2014.

Marciak, Micha. *Sophene, Gordyene, and Adiabene: Three Regna Minora of Northern Mesopotamia Between East and West*. Leiden: Brill, 2017.

Marciak, Michal. "Royal Converts from Adiabene and the Archaeology of Jerusalem." *Göttinger Forum für Altertumswissenschaft* (2018): 29–58.

McDowell, Gavin. "The Alternative Chronology: Dating the Events of the Wagenseil Version of *Toledot Yeshu*." In *Toledot Yeshu in Context*, edited by Daniel Barbu and Yaacov Deutsch, 74. Tübingen: Mohr Siebeck, 2020.

Millgram, Abraham Ezra. *Jerusalem Curiosities*. Philadelphia: Jewish Publication Society, 1990.

Neusner, Jacob. "The Conversion of Adiabene to Judaism: A New Perspective." *Journal of Biblical Literature* 83 (1964): 60–66.

Neusner, Jacob. "The Conversion of Adiabene to Christianity." *Numen* 13, no. 2 (1966): 144–50.

Notley, R. Steven, and Jeffrey P. García. "Queen Helena's Jerusalem Palace—In a Parking Lot?" *Biblical Archaeology Review*, May/June 2014: 28ff.

Paige Cohen, Ariel. "The Ethical Will, Embodied: American Jewish Museums and the Women Who Created Them." *Fordham Center for Jewish Studies Blog*, November 29, 2020. https://jewishstudies.ace.fordham.edu/2020/11/29/ariel-paige-cohen-american-jewish-museums/.

Pausanias. *Description of Greece* 8.16.5. Translated by W. H. S. Jones. In Pausanias, *Description of Greece*, Vol. III (Loeb Classical Library 272; Cambridge, MA: Harvard University Press, 1933), 426–27.

Peleg-Barkat, Orit. "The Temple Mount Excavations in Jerusalem 1968–1978, Directed by Benjamin Mazar; Final Reports Volume V: Herodian Architectural Decoration and King Herod's Royal Portico." *Qedem* 57 (2017): 1–249.

Peskowitz, Miriam B. *Spinning Fantasies: Rabbis, Gender, and History*. Berkeley: University of California Press, 1997.

Pierce, Krystal V. L. "Tomb of the Kings Now Open!" *Biblical Archaeology, Biblical History Daily*, June 1, 2020. https://www.biblicalarchaeology.org/daily/biblical-sites-places/biblical-archaeology-sites/tomb-of-kings-now-open/.

Rabin, Anthony. "The Adiabene Narrative in the *Jewish Antiquities* of Josephus." Ph.D. Dissertation. Wolfson College, Oxford, 2017.

Rajak, Tessa. "The Parthians in Josephus." In *The Jewish Dialogue with Greece and Rome: Studies in Cultural and Social Interaction*, edited by Tessa Rajak, 273–97. Leiden: Brill, 2001.

Ramelli, Ilaria L. E. "Possible Historical Traces in the *Doctrina Addai*." *Hugoye: Journal of Syriac Studies* 9, no. 1 (2006 [2009]): 51–127.

Rosen-Zvi, Ishay. *The Mishnaic Sotah Ritual: Temple, Gender and Midrash*. Leiden: Brill, 2012.

Rosenzweig, Claudia. "The 'History of the Life of Jesus' in a Yiddish Manuscript from the Eighteenth Century (Ms. Jerusalem, NLI, Heb. 8 5622)." In *Toledot Yeshu in Context*, edited by Daniel Barbu and Yaacov Deutsch, 300. Tübingen: Mohr Siebeck, 2020.

Safronova, Valeriya. "How Women Are Changing the Philanthropy Game." *New York Times*, January 31, 2021. https://www.nytimes.com/2021/01/30/style/mackenzie-scott-prisclila-chan-zuckerberg-melinda-gates-philanthropy.html?action=click&module=Editors%20Picks&pgtype=Homepage.

Sarkissian, A. O. "On the Authenticity of Moses of Khoren's History." *Journal of the American Oriental Society* 60, no. 1 (1940): 73–81.

Sauter, Megan. "The Tomb of Queen Helena of Adiabene: Which is the Queen's Sarcophagus?" *Biblical Archaeology*, 2014. https://www.biblicalarchaeology.org/daily/ancient-cultures/ancient-israel/the-tomb-of-queen-helena-of-adiabene/.

Schäfer, Peter and Michael Meerson (eds. and trans.). *Toledot Yeshu: The Life Story of Jesus*, 2 vol. and database. Tübingen: Mohr Siebeck, 2014.

Schäfer, Peter, Michael Meerson, and Yaacov Deutsch (eds.). *Toledot Yeshu ("The Life Story of Jesus") Revisited: A Princeton Conference.* Tübingen: Mohr Siebeck, 2011.
Schalit, Abraham. "Evidence of an Aramaic Source in Josephus' 'Antiquities of the Jews'." *Annual of the Swedish Theological Institute* 4 (1975): 163–88.
Schiffman, Lawrence H. "The Conversion of the Royal House of Adiabene in Josephus and Rabbinic Sources." In *Josephus, Judaism, and Christianity*, edited by Feldman and Hata, 294–98. Detroit: Wayne State University Press, 1987.
Schumer, Nathan. *The Memory of the Temple in Palestinian Rabbinic Literature.* Ph.D. Dissertation. Columbia University, 2017.
Schwartz, Daniel. "God, Gentiles, and Jewish Law: On Acts 15 and Josephus' Adiabene Narrative." In *Geschichte - Tradition - Reflexion: Festschrift für Martin Hengel zum 70. Geburtstag*, edited by Hubert Cancik, Hermann Lichtenberger, and Peter Schäfer, 263–82. Tübingen: Mohr Siebeck, 1996.
Shapira, Ran. "A Royal Return." *Haaretz*, October 1, 2020. https://www.haaretz.com/1.5119727.
Simkovich, Malka. "Queen Helena of Adiabene and Her Sons in Midrash and History." *TheTorah.com*, 2018. https://thetorah.com/article/queen-helena-of-adiabene-and-her-sons-in-midrash-and-history.
Stökl Ben Ezra, Daniel. "On Some Early Traditions in *Toledot Yeshu* and the Antiquity of the 'Helena' Recension." In *Toledot Yeshu in Context*, edited by Daniel Barbu and Yaacov Deutsch, 43–58. Tübingen: Mohr Siebeck, 2020.
Thomas, Michael. "The Conversions of Adiabene and Edessa in Syriac Christianity and Judaism: The Relations of Jews and Christians in Northern Mesopotamia in Antiquity." *Concordia Theological Journal* 7, no. 1 (2020): 10–33.
Tong, M Adryael. *'Given as a Sign': Circumcision and Bodily Discourse in Late Antique Judaism and Christianity.* Ph.D. Dissertation. Fordham University, 2019.
Topchyan, Aram. *The Problems of the Greek Sources of Movsēs Xorenacʻi's 'History of Armenia'.* Peeters: Leuven, 2006.
Turner, Aimee. "'She Acted with Arrogance': Orosius on Women." *Studies in Late Antiquity* 4, no. 2 (2020): 203–27.
Weingarten, Susan. *The Saint's Saints: Hagiography and Geography in Jerome.* Leiden: Brill, 2005.
Widengren, Geo. "Quelques rapports entre juifs et iraniens àl'époque des Parthes." *Supplements to Vetus Testamentum* 4 (1957): 197–241.
Wills, Lawrence M. *The Jewish Novel in the Ancient World.* Eugene: Wipf and Stock, 2015.
Xorenacʻi, Movsēs. *History of the Armenians.* Edited and translated by Robert W. Thomson. Cambridge, MA: Harvard University Press, 1978; Ann Arbor: Caravan Books, 2006.
Yardeni, Ada, Jonathan Price, and Haggai Misgav. "123. Sarcophagus of Queen Sadan from the 'Tomb of the Kings' with Aramaic Inscription." In *Corpus Inscriptionum Iudaeae/Palaestinae* 11, edited by Hannah Cotton et al, 165–67. Berlin: de Gruyter, 2010.

9

"For Rachel I Will Return the Israelites"

Maternal Grief and Loss in the Early Jewish Imagination

Sari Fein

INTRODUCTION

In the so-called "rewritten Bible" texts that proliferated in Jewish communities during the first few centuries of the Common Era, authors deployed biblical narratives and figures for their own social, political, and intellectual purposes. Biblical mothers proved to be a particularly rich site to mine for creative expression.[1] In retelling the stories of biblical mothers, these authors revealed their beliefs and values about concepts such as gender, family, and communal identity.[2] In this article, which is part of a larger project on retold narratives of biblical mothers in early Jewish art and literature, I investigate a phenomenon which reveals itself in some early Jewish texts: a conception of the figure of a mother mourning her children as endowed with increased powers or abilities. Certain writings conceived of mourning mothers as able to "stand in the breach" between the divine and human realms. In this literature, a grieving mother's voice of lament was understood to be able to "challenge the divine force or forces"[3] in ways that were not accessible to others, precisely because of her experience with grief.

This contribution examines an early Jewish rabbinic text, *Lamentations Rabbah*, which presents the figure of Rachel as capable of interceding with God because of the power of her maternal grief. In an introductory "proem" (*petiḥta*) to the midrash, number 24, Rachel is described as castigating God for sending her children into exile and allowing them to suffer and die, all for the sake of divine jealousy toward idols. I argue that the authors of this midrash understood Rachel's success in interceding with God as a result of how Rachel leverages her maternal grief to challenge divine decree.[4] Situating Rachel in a midrash to Lamentations, which mourns the violent exile of the Jewish people from their holy land, demonstrates that mourning mothers were sometimes imagined as a tool of political community formation for the Jewish people in times of national crisis.

I compare this text with other early Jewish literature which similarly recognized the power contained in the voices of grieving mothers, especially at moments of communal crisis. *Lamentations Rabbah, petiḥta* 24 distinguishes itself, however, as it constructs Rachel as eloquently and forcefully making a case against God, effectively making her an intercessor between God and the Jewish people. Rachel's grief becomes the impetus for her speech which convinces God to bring the Israelites back to their land, as God promises בשבילך רחל אני מחזיר את ישראל למקומן/*beshvilekh Rakhel 'ani makhazir 'et yisra'el limkoman*: "For you, Rachel, I will return the Israelites to their land."[5] This reading of maternal grief illuminates an underappreciated facet of early Jewish motherhood as understood by the rabbis and other early Jewish authors: mourning mothers, instead of being passive objects of pity, were reframed as empowered to challenge and advocate even to God on behalf of their communities. In the early Jewish imagination, Rachel represents the possibility of redemption for the people of Israel at a time when they are defeated, dispersed, and exiled from their land.

RACHEL IN RABBINIC MIDRASH

Lamentations Rabbah is a rabbinic midrash whose composition scholarly consensus places in the land of Israel and dates to the fourth through sixth centuries CE, making it one of the earliest midrashic collections.[6] The text takes as its inspiration the book of Lamentations, part of the historical writings of the Hebrew Bible. The biblical book is a collection of laments traditionally attributed to the prophet Jeremiah, written in response to the destruction of Jerusalem by the Babylonian empire in 586 BCE. *Lamentations Rabbah* is an example of exegetical midrash, providing a systematic chapter by chapter, verse by verse, and sometimes even word by word commentary on the "source text" material of the biblical book of Lamentations.[7] This commentary consists of more than twenty introductory *petiḥta'ot*, or proems, as well as exegesis on each verse of Lamentations, from 1:1 through 5:22. As midrash, *Lam. Rab.* can be understood to be seeking to "fill the gaps" left by scripture—to answer questions, add details, and "smooth out" inconsistencies in the text.[8] In our narrative in *Lam. Rab.*, the rabbis attempt to answer questions about theodicy, grief, and community which are implied throughout the book of Lamentations.

Tod Linafelt notes that much of *Lamentations Rabbah* is motivated by the need to address "the . . . looming 'gap' left by the absence of God's voice in the book of Lamentations."[9] In *petiḥta* 24, the text attempts to address this gap by exploring God's response to the destruction of Jerusalem and the Second Temple by the Romans in 70 CE. The book of Lamentations, which addressed the destruction of the *first* Temple in 586 BCE, provided the perfect venue in which to work through the existential questions raised by the tragedy of 70 CE. While much can be said about the theological worldview the rabbis construct in *petiḥta* 24,[10] I focus upon the issues of child loss and maternal mourning that are raised along the way. This text, perhaps inadvertently, constructs a model of maternal grief that is at once both moving and powerful.

petiḥta 24 can be divided into two sections, which both explore the theme of parental grief. The first section interprets Isaiah 22:12: "The Lord God of Hosts called, on that day/to weeping and lamenting/to baldness and putting on sackcloth."[11] This section of the *petiḥta* focuses mainly on God the "parent," who experiences great grief at the suffering and loss of God's children, the people of Israel, in the destruction of Jerusalem. Linafelt notes that this midrash has picked up one of the major themes of the book of Lamentations as a whole; that is, "the concern for threatened children . . . it is of course the loss of children (or a child) that has engendered [God's] response and brought God to the state of emotional breakdown and halakhic liminality."[12] The second section of *petiḥta* 24 continues the theme of "the concern for threatened children," although it approaches this theme from a very different angle.

Section 2 shifts the locus of the pathos from God to human beings and focuses more on human mourning for one's children. In this section, the patriarch Abraham first appears, weeping and mourning, and begs God for an explanation of his "shame and humiliation." Abraham is followed by Isaac, Jacob, and even Moses, who attempt to move God to show mercy for the exiled people of Israel. Mimicking God in the first section of the *petiḥta*, the patriarchs are stirred to action by parental grief—by the compassion they feel for the "battered children" of Israel.[13] After Moses describes to Abraham, Isaac, and Jacob the terrible fate that has befallen their "children," the patriarchs "weep and lament lamentations: 'Woe for what has happened to our children [ווי על דמטא לבנן /*way 'al dimt'a livnan*]! How you have become orphans without a father!'" God, however, is utterly unmoved. The deity is "largely silent, and when he does speak (with the exception of the climax) he speaks as Israel's accuser."[14] Against all the patriarchs' heartfelt pleas, "[God's] obduracy and lack of feeling become almost painful to observe."[15] The patriarchs, despite their great show of paternal grief, have failed to stir mercy in the divine. Moses has the final word in this section of the *petiḥta*. He describes a heart-wrenching scene in which the Chaldeans force a father to kill his son in front of the child's mother, and how the mother "wept, her tears flowing over [her son]" (בכיא אימה, ונתרין דמעתא עלוהי /*bakhi'a 'imah wenatrin dimat'a 'alohi*), and the father "hung his head" (ואבוהי תלה ליה רישיה /*we 'avuhi telah leh resheh*). Moses chastises God for letting this atrocity occur, accusing God of allowing a child to be killed along with its mother on the same day, as is expressly forbidden in the Torah (cf. Lev. 22:28).

At some point, whether upon the initial composition of the *petiḥta* or upon later redaction, the author of this text found this particular ending unsatisfying.[16] Linafelt ascribes this to the narrative's "drive for survival"; the story cannot end on a note of defeat and despair. In its quest for survival, the authors of the text make a particular choice. They take the image of parental grief as their jumping-off point to construct a more satisfactory conclusion. Because grieving fathers have failed to arouse compassion in the deity, the text turns now to an examination of *maternal* grief.

This choice coheres with the findings of Ekaterina Kozlova in her book *Maternal Grief in the Hebrew Bible*. Maternal grief is unique, Kozlova argues, because while it is shaped by many factors that may vary widely cross-culturally, published findings suggest that almost universally, "mothers . . . are more likely to directly connect to their raw feelings, responding to the death [of their children] through the experience and expression of strong emotions."[17] The recognition of this behavior has resulted in a "cross-cultural tendency to encode great distress in gender/mother-specific terms regardless of the gender of the distressed."[18] This does not mean that maternal grief looks identical cross-culturally, but rather that there is a near-universal recognition of the strong response of mothers to the death of their children which is deployed in literature for a community's unique rhetorical purposes.

Appearing out of nowhere, the text states באותה שעה קפצה רחל אמנו לפני הקב״ה /*be'otah sha'ah qufṣah Rakhel 'imenu lifne Ha Kadosh Barukh Hu* (in Neusner's poetic translation, "Then Rachel, our mother, *leapt into the fray* before the Holy One, Blessed be He," XXIV.ii.3.LLL, emphasis mine).[19] Rachel addresses God directly as רבש״ע/*Rabsh'a* ("Master of the Universe"), and describes how she overcame her jealousy of her sister Leah when she was given to Jacob as a bride in Rachel's stead, going so far as to hide under Leah and Jacob's marriage bed and answer Jacob in her own voice so her sister would not be discovered and shamed. Rachel then demands God account for God's actions: "Why are you jealous of idolatry [lit. '*avodah zarah*], in which there is nothing, and sent my children into exile, allowed them to be killed by the sword, and let their enemies do to them whatever they desired?!" Somewhat shockingly, God relents, and says "For you, Rachel, I will return the Israelites to their land." Stern attributes the power of this scene to the "sight of God yielding to Rachel, of His masculine hardness submitting to the compassionate softness of the matriarch's plea."[20] God does indeed yield, but Rachel is anything but soft; her compassion, I argue, makes her fierce.

While Rachel argues her merit on the basis of her lack of jealousy and compassion for her sister Leah, the climax of her argument seems to be the line with which she concludes: "Why are you jealous of idolatry, in which there is nothing, and sent my children into exile, allowed them to be killed by the sword, and let their enemies do to them whatever they desired?!" The invocation of Rachel's children hearkens back to the patriarch's emphasis on their own children in the first section of the *petiḥta*. It forms a bridge between the two parts of the narrative, which both address the themes of parental love and grief for lost children. Rachel's speech is efficacious—it causes God to change God's mind and bring Israel back from exile, reversing the plight in which they had found themselves. It also leads to the ultimate proof text that the narrative brings at the final conclusion of the *petiḥta*, from Jer. 31:15–17:

> Thus says the LORD:
> A voice is heard in Ramah,
> > lamentation and bitter weeping.
> Rachel is weeping for her children;
> > she refuses to be comforted for her children,
> > because they are not.
> Thus says the LORD:
> Keep your voice from weeping,
> > and your eyes from tears;
> for there is a reward for your work, says the LORD:
> > [they] shall return from the land of the enemy.

The retelling of Rachel's narrative in *Lamentations Rabbah, petiḥta* 24 demonstrates the pivotal role mourning mothers played in the early Jewish imagination as an intercessor with the divine, which could sometimes serve as a tool of political communal formation for the nation in times of crisis. An examination of other retold narratives about biblical mothers in Late Antiquity reveals how *petiḥta* 24 belonged to an established trope and simultaneously distinguished itself from it.

OTHER MOURNING MOTHERS IN EARLY JEWISH LITERATURE

Putting the narrative of Rachel in *Lamentations Rabbah, petiḥta* 24 in conversation with other early Jewish texts such as Sisera's mother in *Talmud Rosh HaShanah* 33b, Sarah in *Leviticus Rabbah* 20:2, the mourning woman in *4 Ezra* 9:38–47, and Rachel in Matthew 2 demonstrates the existence of a literary trope in Jewish antiquity in which the figure of a mourning mother was viewed as endowed with unique capabilities to intercede on behalf of the vulnerable. In this trope, mothers are typically depicted as expressing their grief by wordlessly weeping in despair at the death of their child(ren). The figure Rachel as depicted in *Lam. Rab.* is part of this trope, yet the text distinguishes itself: instead of weeping, Rachel articulates her grief with words and argues with God. It is this direct speech that enables her to successfully convince God to reverse God's punishment of the Israelites and allow them to return to their land.

An example of this trope can be found in some rabbinic literature which preserves a tradition of associating the sound of the shofar with a mother's cry uttered upon the loss of her child. In the fourth- or fifth-century Talmudic tractate Rosh HaShanah 33b,[21] the sages seek to understand Numbers 29:1, which states that Rosh Hashanah will be "a day of תרואה/*teruʿah*" which they translate as "a day of יבבא/*yabava*." Understanding יבב/*yabav* is thus key to understanding the meaning of the verse. To explain this term, the sages turn to Judges 5, the only place in the Hebrew Bible where this root appears, in reference to the cries of Sisera's mother as she waits for her son's return. Judges 5:28 explains how the mother of the Canaanite general Sisera, himself recently slain by Jael, peers through the window to await his return from battle. His mother ותיבב/*teyabev* (NRSV: "wailed," BDB: "cry shrilly") as she waits and wonders why he is taking so long to return to her.[22] Of course, the reader knows that he will not be returning at all.

The sages disagree about which sound of the shofar, exactly, corresponds to Sisera's mother's cries. The text states: "One sage holds that ותיבב/*vateyabev* means גנוחי גנח /*genukhe ganakh* ['moanings'], as in the blasts of *shevarim*. And one sage holds that ותיבב/*vateyabev* is 'wailing,' as in the short blasts of the *yelule yelel*/ ילולי יליל [*'teruot'*]."[23] In their attempt to define the sounds of the shofar, the sages inadvertently reveal an early Jewish perspective on maternal grief. Maternal grief, they seem to say, transcends the limits of human speech; a mother's grief for her son is best expressed in a wordless utterance, which may take the form of moaning or wailing. The sound of this grief is understood to be so universally recognizable that the rabbis assume their audience would be familiar with it, and do not bother to describe it any further. Additionally, even a mother of a sworn enemy of the Jewish people, the Canaanite general Sisera, is humanized to the point that it is accepted that she would mourn for her child just as much as an Israelite or Jewish mother.

A similar tradition about maternal grief is found about Sarah, the mother of Isaac, in Midrash Tanchuma, Vayera 23; Vayikra Rabbah 20:2; and Pirkei deRabbi Eliezer 32:8. In this tradition, Sarah, upon hearing that Abraham took their son to sacrifice him upon Mount Moriah, immediately dies. In Vayikra Rabbah 20:2 and Pirkei deRabbi Eliezer 32:8, Sarah cries out before she dies, which the sages associate with the sounds of the shofar. Vayikra Rabbah 20:2 (compiled around the fifth century CE) explains that when Isaac returns from the *aqedah*, he describes to his mother how his father bound and nearly slaughtered him. Sarah confirms, "If an angel had not appeared, you would have been slaughtered?" to which Isaac replies, "Yes." At this news, Sarah lets out six קולות/ *qolot* which the sages explain correspond to the six תקיעות / *tekiot* of the shofar, and promptly dies. The sages use this to parse the verse in Gen. 23:2, "Abraham came to mourn for Sarah and to weep for her," thus relocating the focus of the narrative to Sarah's grief and at the same time explaining Sarah's death. A later tradition found in Pirkei de Rabbi Eliezer 32:8 (ninth century CE) has the angel Sammael misleadingly inform Sarah that Abraham has successfully slaughtered Isaac, whereupon Sarah began to בכתה שלש בכיות/*bakhtah shelosh bekhiot* ("cry out . . . three cries"), which correspond to the תקיעות / *tekiot* of the shofar, and בכתה. . . שלש יללות/ *bakhtah . . . shelosh yelelot* ("cry out . . . three wails"), which correspond to the יבבות/*yebavot* of the shofar. As in Vayikra Rabbah, after uttering these wordless sounds of despair, Sarah dies. This text, like Rosh Hashanah 33b, constructs an image of a mourning mother who is rendered speechless at the mere suggestion of her child's death. Indeed, the force of maternal grief is so powerful that it is understood that it could even cause the mother's own death. Together, these rabbinic texts conceive of a motherhood that is so deeply connected to one's children that the loss of a child can cause the mother to lose her capacity for speech, or even her own life.

However, that the mourning voices of Sarah and of Sisera's mother are compared to the sound of the shofar offers insight into the power of mourning mothers as understood by early rabbinic authorities. A Talmudic text establishes the importance of God's hearing of the shofar. In Rosh Hashanah 16a, the rabbis describe how God instructs the people to sound the ram's horn (the shofar) so that God can think of the *aqedah* and remember it on the people's behalf:

> R. Abbahu said: Why does one sound a shofar from a ram['s horn on Rosh HaShanah]? The Holy One, blessed be He said: Sound before Me a shofar from a ram['s horn] so that I will remember you for the binding of Isaac, the son of Abraham, and to account it to you as if you had bound yourselves before me.[24]

The text implies that the sound of the shofar has the power to reach God and influence God's thinking and behavior, as God will "remember" and "account [the merit of the *aqedah*]" to the one who sounds the shofar. Thus, texts which associate the sounds of mourning mothers' wails with the shofar suggest that the rabbis understood the voices of mourning mothers to have the same ability to bridge the human-divine divide and, potentially, to sway God to experience certain emotions or take certain actions.

An alternative perspective on mourning motherhood, and particularly the use of the mother's voice, is presented in the text of 4 Ezra, a first/second century CE apocalyptic text in which Ezra (of the biblical book) is described as having seven visions. In Ezra's fourth vision, Ezra encounters a woman who at first is said to be ܀‏ܪ‎ ܀‏ܪ‎ ܀‏ܪ‎ ܀‏ܪ‎ ܀‏ܪ‎ /*mrqd' hwt wbky' bkl' rm'* ("mourning and lamenting in a loud voice," 9:38).[25] The author of this text emphasizes the noises the grieving mother makes, adding that ܀‏ܪ‎ ܀‏ܪ‎ ܀‏ܪ‎/*bnfšh mttnḥ' hwt wm'q' sgy* ("in her soul, she was sighing very much").[26] It is revealed to Ezra that the cause of the woman's grief is the loss of her son, whom she had conceived after being "barren" (*'qrt'*/܀‏ܪ‎) for thirty years. Much like other mothers in the Hebrew Bible, this woman conceives after fervent prayer to God, who finally hears her voice (܀‏ܪ‎/*ql*) and grants her a child.[27] The woman describes how she is given a son, rejoices over him, and brings him up with much care, including arranging a marriage for him. Tragically, when the son enters his wedding chamber, he "fell down and died" (܀‏ܪ‎ ܀‏ܪ‎/*nfly wmyt*). Typically, this narrative is read as an extended metaphorical description of the destruction and rebirth of the city of Jerusalem.[28] Uriel the angel explains this to Ezra in 10:44–48:

> This woman whom you saw, whom you now behold as an established city, is Zion. And as for her telling you that she was barren for thirty years, [it is] because there were three thousand years in the world before any offering was offered in it. And after 3000 years, Solomon built the city, and offered offerings; then it was that the barren woman bore a son. And as for her telling you that she brought him up with much care, that was the period of residence in Jerusalem. And as for her saying to you "When my son entered his wedding chamber, he died"; that was the destruction that befell Jerusalem.[29]

The woman's description of her response to the loss of her son in 4 Ezra differs remarkably from the responses of Sarah and of Sisera's mother in rabbinic literature, whose weeping and groaning the rabbis compare to the sounds of the shofar. The mourning woman relates to Ezra that after her son dies, she ܀‏ܪ‎ /*šlyt* ("remains quiet").[30] She flees to the wilderness, ceases eating and drinking, and vows to mourn (܀‏ܪ‎/*mt'ḥl'*) and fast until she dies. Her explanation to Ezra is clear and lucid, almost detached; she gives a detailed recounting of her past actions and plan for her future ones. This is distinct from Sarah and from Sisera's mother, who offer few words, if any, in response to their grief. The introduction of the woman's extensive speech and emphasis on her silence as an immediate response to her son's death distinguishes her from these other responses (though by the time Ezra encounters her, she has commenced "mourning and lamenting in a loud voice," as described above). Kindalee Pfremmer deLong argues that it is indeed her voice which compels the transformation in Ezra's understanding of his visionary journey; I contend that her voice also contributes to the audience's understanding of the voice of the mourning mother.[31] The mother figure in 4 Ezra offers multiple possible models of maternal mourning: one which results in complete silence, one which is so full of grief that it can only be expressed in wordless wails, and one which is characterized by speech and action.

While the mother plans her journey to culminate in her own death (due to fasting), this does not end up being the case. As chapter 10 describes, after her conversation with Ezra, the woman utters "a loud and fearful cry" (10:26) and transforms into a city, which the angel Uriel identifies as Zion. Notably, it is only at the sound of her voice that she is reborn as "an established city," as Ezra relates:

> Her face suddenly shone exceedingly, and her countenance flashed like lightning . . . behold, she suddenly uttered a loud and fearful cry, so that the earth shook at her voice . . . the woman was no longer visible to me, but there was an established city, and a place of huge foundations showed itself. (10:25–10:27)[32]

Unlike Sarah, who cries out and then dies, or Sisera's mother, who disappears from the narrative after she wails at the window, the mourning woman in 4 Ezra is transformed into something glorious and eternal. I submit that it is her speech, her thoughtfulness with which she expressed herself to Ezra, which enables her extraordinary end—to continue living as eschatological Zion.[33]

Finally, we must consider the two texts that form the basis for interpretation laid out in *Lamentations Rabbah, petiḥta* 24: Lamentations, especially chapters 1–2, and Jeremiah 31. Both of these texts conceive of a mourning mother's voice as key to her power to communicate with human and divine audiences, especially in times of communal crisis. In the first two chapters of the book of Lamentations, weeping plays an important role for personified Zion. Zion explains in her own words in 1:16: עַל־אֵלֶּה אֲנִי בוֹכִיָּה עֵינִי ׀ עֵינִי יֹרְדָה מַּיִם כִּי־רָחַק מִמֶּנִּי מְנַחֵם מֵשִׁיב נַפְשִׁי הָיוּ בָנַי שׁוֹמֵמִים כִּי גָבַר אוֹיֵב / *'al 'eleh 'ani bokhiyah 'eni / yordah mayim ki-rakheq mimeni menakhem meshiv nafshi hayu banay shomemim ki gavar 'oyev* ("For these things I weep; my eyes, my eyes flow with tears; my children are desolate, for the enemy has prevailed"). In his article "Daughter Zion and Weeping in Lamentations 1–2," David A. Bosworth notes that Zion's weeping is inextricably tied to the death of her "children," the inhabitants of the land: "In Lamentations 1, Zion is depicted as weeping twice (1.2, 16). In Lamentations 2, the narrator weeps (2.11) and calls on the wall of Zion (i.e., Zion) to weep (2.18). All these instances of weeping are connected to the death of children."[34] That Zion is a mother is key to the rhetorical power of her weeping. Bosworth argues that Zion's weeping in these verses "draws on the pathos of child death . . . her maternal perspective draws forth her own tears (1.2, 16; 2.18–20) and the empathetic tears of the narrator (2.11–12)."[35] Instead of words, her tears are used to convey her suffering, as they "communicate intense pain and the need for assistance."[36]

Even though they are wordless, her tears have much to say. The implied addressee of her expressions of grief is God; the speaker in Lamentations asks the Lord to look upon her sorry state in 1:9 and 1:11. The audience, too, is asked to look upon Zion with pity: "The text employs both the miserable state of the children and the pitiable weeping of mother Zion to intensify the presentation of Zion's pain and draw empathy from divine and human audiences."[37] Zion's laments have another purpose: to confront God for the divine choice to create such a desperate situation in the city that mothers are forced to eat their own children (2:20). Maier observes that Zion's outcry is meant to suggest that this cannibalism is "outrageous" and that God's behavior "cannot be justified by any cause."[38] As Ekaterina Kozlova observed, mourning mothers have an "unrivalled energy for intercessions" with the divine, which we see biblical authors harnessing in these chapters. And yet, Zion's confrontation is not fruitful. God is unmoved by her words, Lamentations 2 ends in despair, and the literary figure of "Daughter Zion" disappears from the narrative.[39]

This narrative context serves as the background for the scene of maternal intercession which takes place in *petiḥta* 24. In the second section of this *petiḥta*, Zion is ever-present in the background. The "ministering angels" accuse God of "despising" Jerusalem and Zion, and quote Jer. 14:19, "Have you completely rejected Judah? Does your soul loathe Zion?" The destruction of the Temple in Jerusalem and the suffering and death of Zion's inhabitants (i.e., her children) form the basis of the patriarchs' accusations against God. It seems fitting, then, for the authors to turn to the figure of a mourning mother, the ultimate symbol of both pathos and strength, as their savior, in order to make the greatest emotional impact on and serve as a rhetorical tool of political community formation for their audience.

Thus at the end of the *petiḥta*, the rabbis bring in Jer. 31:15–17, which they explicitly cite as the proof-text explaining why God ultimately agrees to "return Israel to their land." Jeremiah 31 describes the conquest and destruction of Jerusalem, which results in the Israelites—the children of Rachel—exiled in a foreign land, which is Rachel's "ground for weeping."[40] Rachel here is presented as "the symbolic mother of the nation: defeated, exiled, and suffering."[41] This text is aligned with the tradition of presenting mourning mothers as weeping, especially in times of communal crisis, as seen also in Lam. 1–2. Indeed, it explicitly states that Rachel is "weeping for her children" (רָחֵל מְבַכָּה עַל־בָּנֶיהָ/*Rakhel mevakah ʿal-baneha*). These verses may contain the seeds of the interpretation that Rachel speaks to God directly, in her own voice, in *Lamentations Rabbah*. Bob Becking and Phyllis Trible identify a hint of Rachel's direct speech in Jer. 31:15–17. Becking notes that the "discrepancy between the plural, 'her sons,' in 15d.f and the singular, 'there is no one left,' in 15g" can be explained by understanding 15g as "the wording of the complaint of Rachel in direct speech."[42] Becking's reading is based on Phyllis Trible's analysis of the verse, which understands "there is no one here" (כִּי אֵינֶנּוּ /ki ʾenenu) to be Rachel's own words, as the particle *ki* is known to introduce direct speech.[43] Though Rachel's words are few, Trible notes, their impact is powerful:

> [T]his fading speech belongs to an enduring voice. Directed to no one in particular and hence to all who may hear, the voice of Rachel travels across the land and through the ages to permeate existence with a suffering that not even death can relieve.[44]

God responds directly to Rachel's words in Jer. 31:15–17. In verse 17, God promises Rachel that וְשָׁבוּ מֵאֶרֶץ אוֹיֵב /weshavu meʾerets ʾoyev ("they [her children, the Israelites] will return from the land of the enemy"). That Rachel's words of grief for her children have the power to sway God here might have provided the basis for the rabbis to expand her speech and make it just as efficacious in *petiḥta* 24, where Rachel's accusation of "You sent my children into exile, allowed them to be killed by the sword, and let their enemies do to them whatever they desired" stirs God's mercy and changes the divine mind, allowing the Israelites to return from exile to their land.

petiḥta 24 was not the only text to pick up on the powerful image of Rachel as a mourning mother and deploy it for its own political purposes. The New Testament gospel of Matthew (first century CE) describes the "slaughter of the innocents," in which King Herod kills all the children in and around Bethlehem, out of fear of a prophecy that foretells that one of them will be the Messiah. Matthew 2:17 explicitly states that this event "fulfills" (ἐπληρώθη/*eplērothe*) the words of the prophet Jeremiah in Jer. 31:15. Ancient audiences would have heard the intertextual echoes of Jer. 31:15–17 in Matthew. The mention of Bethlehem would have triggered an association with Rachel, who died on the road to Bethlehem (Gen. 35:19; the verse specifies that Ephrath is another name for Bethlehem). The author of Matthew would have made this allusion intentionally; Sébastian Doane argues that its purpose is to harness the "affective impact" of the Jeremiah narrative.[45] He calls the quote from Jer. 31:15 "an emotional poetic text that evokes multiple layers of biblical allusions."[46] Doane notes the addition of the word πολύς/*polus* (much, many, or more) in Matt. 2:18: κλαυθμὸς καὶ ὀδυρμὸς πολύς /*klauthmos kai odermos polus* ("weeping and loud lamentation") in Matthew's quotation of Jeremiah 31:15. He argues that the addition of πολύς/*polus* is the means by which "Matthew indicates that there are *several* complaints and tears [emphasis mine]. We can see in this word a reference to various biblical narratives connected with Rachel's suffering."[47] These "several complaints and tears" included the tragedies of Rachel's life in Genesis, the explicitly cited laments of Jeremiah, and the thematic parallel of the slaughter of young Hebrew boys in Exodus.[48] These layers of intertextual references serve to build up the figure of Rachel in the imagination of Matthew's audience. They emphasize her role as a mourning mother, which connects her to the immediate context of mourning mothers in Matthew's own time. As Wainwright states, "the voice of Rachel weeping uncovers another silence in the text—the mothers of Bethlehem weeping for their children . . . slaughtered at the hands of a tyrant king."[49] Rachel's grieving voice, here as elsewhere, is her power. Though it is wordless, her voice "pierces the male world of power, of slaughter and of divine favour. [Rachel] stands in the place of the erased women, but she also stands in the place of divine compassion likewise erased."[50] For Matthew's audience, as for the audience of *Lamentations Rabbah*, the figure of the mourning mother stood in the breach between divine and human and called God to account.

Putting *petiḥta* 24 in conversation with these other texts featuring mourning mothers reveals how *petiḥta* 24 distinguishes itself from the others. In rabbinic literature, Sisera's mother and Sarah both express their grief in powerful sounds that the rabbis compare to the shofar, and, I argue, have a similar power to capture divine attention. In 4 Ezra, the "mourning woman" provides a thematic bridge from the grief-sounds of these two mothers to the rational speech of Rachel in *Lam. Rab.*, by modeling both of these in response to her son's death. Matthew 2 picks up on Rachel's potential power to speak to contemporary audiences by placing Jer. 31:17 in the narrative of the slaughter of the innocents, but does not expand Rachel's role in any significant way. Finally, in *petiḥta* 24, Rachel's grief moves her beyond wordless weeping or wailing and is the impetus for her to clearly and decisively argue with God on behalf of her metaphorical children, the people of Israel. This response is based in the source texts of Genesis, which describes the tragedies of Rachel's life, including her own death; Lamentations, in which personified Zion acts as a mourning mother; and Jeremiah, which first configures Rachel as a mourning mother. The *petiḥta* uses Rachel's grief to transform her into a tool of political community formation who has the power to compel their deity to return the scattered Israelites to their sacred homeland.

CONCLUSION

The diverse, dynamic world of Late Antiquity meant an explosion of creative literary production in Jewish communities. As Jews sought to find their place in this new world, they turned to their holy scriptures for guidance. Retelling their sacred stories in new cultural contexts helped them re-articulate their values about issues such as gender, family, and communal identity. Retold stories about mourning mothers reveal a belief that mothers who lost their children were endowed with particular powers and had the ability to reach the divine in a way that others could not. Sometimes, these powers were imagined as a tool of political formation for the displaced and dispersed Israelite community, as in 4 Ezra, when the mourning woman becomes eschatological Zion, or in *Lam. Rab. petiḥta* 24, when Rachel convinces God to return the people of Israel to their land, and God relents: "For you, Rachel, I will return the Israelites to their land." In the early Jewish imagination, a mother's grief was not the end of her story, but could perhaps be the beginning of a new one for her people.

NOTES

1. I am grateful for the many voices that helped shape the final form of this paper: Dr. Meghan Henning, who responded to its first iteration at the 2019 Society of Biblical Literature Annual Meeting; the Hadassah-Brandeis Institute, whose support allowed me to develop this paper further in the Spring of 2021; my advisors at Brandeis, who supported the work of my dissertation, of which this essay is a part; and finally, the organizers and participants of the Nangeroni meeting of the Enoch Seminar in July 2021, entitled "Constructions of Gender in Late Antiquity," at which this paper was presented.

2. Emily Olmstead Gravett's 2013 dissertation from the University of Virginia, "The Literary Phenomenon of Narrative Biblical Retellings," usefully synthesizes the scholarship of biblical reception history. Reception history has been conceived by various scholars as the study of allusions, intertextuality, inner-biblical discourse, *midrash*, afterlife/*nachleben*, renarration, and transfiguration (pp. 10–31). Inspired by Lesleigh Cushing Stahlberg (*Sustaining Fictions: Intertextuality, Midrash, Translation, and the Literary Afterlife of the Bible*, Library of Hebrew Bible/Old Testament Studies, 486 [London; New York: T&T Clark International, 2008]). Gravett suggests that the best term to describe this phenomenon is "retelling." She finds this term preferable for a number of reasons. Most significantly, it is

> neutral . . . suggests that a complete story is being retold . . . implies the dynamism, the incompleteness in the act of storytelling . . . suggests the presence of an origin and implies causality and directionality . . . without prioritizing one of the works over the other . . . [and] highlights the presence of multiple "texts" within one work. (32–33)

I shall follow Gravett in referring to the postbiblical texts upon which I focus as "biblical retellings." Emily Olmstead Gravett, "The Literary Phenomenon of Narrative Biblical Retellings" (PhD diss., University of Virginia, 2013).

3. Galit Hasan-Rokem, "Bodies Performing in Ruins: The Lamenting Mother in Ancient Hebrew Texts," in *Lament in Jewish Thought: Philosophical, Theological, and Literary Perspectives*, eds. Ilit Ferber and Paula Schwebel (Berlin: De Gruyter, 2014), 48.

4. Hasan-Rokem argues that the rabbis make "a comprehensive theological and emotional move . . . seeking a mother figure with a greater potential for compassion."

"The Rhetoric of Intimacy, the Rhetoric of the Sacred," *Temenos* 23 (1987): 45–57. See also *Web of Life: Folklore and Midrash in Rabbinic Literature*, trans. Batya Stein (Stanford: Stanford University Press, 2000), especially ch. 6, "The Social Context of Folk Narratives in the Aggadic Midrash: The Feminine Power of Laments, Tales, and Love," 108–29.

5. These translations and those that follow are my own, based on Solomon Buber, ed., *Midrasch Echa Rabbati* (Vilna: Press of Widow and Brothers Romm, 1899). Perhaps because of its somewhat difficult redactional history, there exists no critical edition of *Lamentations Rabbah*. Buber's version, which was published in Vilna in 1899 and re-issued in 1964, is the closest we have to a scholarly edition. For the *petiḥtaot*, Buber used the "printed edition" of *Lam. Rab.*, which is the Venice recension (1545), which was based in turn on the Pesaro recension (1519) and the Constantinople recension (1520), with emendations from a manuscript from the British Museum, 1076.4 Add. 27089. Carl N. Astor, "The *Petihta'ot* of Eicha Rabbah" (PhD Diss., Jewish Theological Seminary, 1995), 74 n. 1 and 90 n. 1. Because Buber's is the closest to a critical edition that we have, and it is used by most scholars as the basis for their analysis, I will also use it in this chapter. See also Michel G. Distefano, "The Inner-Midrashic Introduction in Lamentations Rabbah," in *Inner-Midrashic Introductions and Their Influence on Introductions to Medieval Rabbinic Bible Commentaries* (Berlin: De Gruyter, 2009), 85–125. For more on the manuscript history of *Lamentations Rabbah*, see Paul Mandel, "Between Byzantium and Islam: The Transmission of a Jewish Book in the Byzantine and Early Islamic Periods," in *Transmitting Jewish Tradition: Orality, Textuality, and Cultural Diffusion*, ed. Yaakov Elman and Israel Gershoni (New Haven: Yale University Press, 2000), 74–103.

6. "We can see a consensus which has developed claiming it to be one of the earliest of midrashic collections from which many others have borrowed. It would have to have been compiled sometime between the late fourth and early sixth century in the land of Israel. I would lean towards the earlier period mainly due to the large amount of original material and the fact that no sages are mentioned who were later than that time." Astor, "Petihta'ot," quote from 88; see pp. 83–8. On the numbering and ordering of the *petiḥtaot*, see pp. 74–83. David Stern proposes that the story of Rachel in *petiḥta* 24 is a later addition to *Lam. Rab.*, and of Babylonian origin. David Stern, *Midrash and Theory: Ancient Jewish Exegesis and Contemporary Literary Studies* (Evanston: Northwestern University Press, 1996), 112 n. 26.

7. Moshe Herr, "Midrash," in *Encyclopedia Judaica*, ed. Michael Berenbaum and Fred Skolnik, 2nd ed., vol. 14 (Detroit, MI: Macmillan Reference USA, 2007), 183.

8. Tod Linafelt offers an alternative view of midrash, that instead of "filling the gaps," it instead *widens* them: "Midrash opens the biblical text out to the vast multiplicity of (often conflicting) interpretive avenues available." (Linafelt, *Surviving Lamentations: Catastrophe, Lament, and Protest in the Afterlife of a Biblical Book* [Chicago: University of Chicago Press, 2000], 104). Midrash is polysemic: it speaks with many voices which do not always cohere with one another. Multiple meanings are possible depending on the particular exegetical strategies of the interpreter and the socio-historical context of the audience, which conditions their response.

9. Linafelt, *Surviving*, 104.

10. See, for example, Julia Watts Belser, *Rabbinic Tales of Destruction: Gender, Sex, and Disability in the Ruins of Jerusalem* (New York: Oxford University Press, 2018); David Kraemer, *Responses to Suffering in Classical Rabbinic Literature* (Cary: Oxford University Press, Incorporated, 1994).

11. These and subsequent translations are my own.

12. Linafelt, *Surviving*, 107–8.

13. "Overcome by pathos for the battered children of Israel, the patriarchs intercede before God on their behalf." Alan Mintz, *Hurban: Responses to Catastrophe in Jewish Literature* (New York: Columbia University Press, 1984), 82.

14. Paul M. Joyce and Diana Lipton, *Lamentations through the Centuries*, 1st ed., Wiley Blackwell Bible Commentaries (New York: Wiley, 2013), 89.

15. David Stern, "Imitatio Hominis: Anthropomorphism and the Character(s) of God in Rabbinic Literature," *Prooftexts* 12, no. 2 (1992): 162.

16. David Stern notes that the anonymous author of proem 24 seems to have joined two separate narratives together "because they share a common subject, God's behavior in the aftermath of the Destruction of the Second Temple." Stern, "Imitatio Hominis," 158. Alternatively, Neusner divides the midrash into three parts: the first, a "clause-by-clause amplification" of a biblical verse, perhaps Lam. 5:18; the second, "another interpretation" of Isaiah 22:12; and the third, the interpretation of Samuel bar Nahman. Jacob Neusner, *Lamentations Rabbah: An Analytical Translation* (Atlanta, GA: Scholars Press, 1989), 79.

17. Ruth Malkinson and Liora Bar Tur, "Long Term Bereavement Processes of Older Parents: The Three Stages of Grief," *Om* 50 (2005): 105; in Ekaterina Kozlova, *Maternal Grief in the Hebrew Bible* (Oxford: Oxford University Press, 2017), 11–12.

18. Kozlova, *Maternal Grief*, 16.

19. Neusner, *Lamentations Rabbah*.

20. Stern, "*Imitatio Hominis*," 163.

21. On the dating of this tractate, see Marcus Mordecai Schwartz, *Rewriting the Talmud: The Fourth-Century Origins of Bavli Rosh HaShanah* (Tübingen: Mohr Siebeck, 2019).

22. תיבב /*teyabev* is from יבב /*yabav*, which is a *hapax legomenon* and only appears in Judges 5:28.

On critical feminist readings of the book of Judges, see Athalya Brenner-Idan, ed., *The Feminist Companion to Judges* (Sheffield: JSOT Press, 1993); and *Judges: A Feminist Companion to the Bible* (Sheffield: Sheffield Academic Press, 1999); on the reception history of Judges 4–5 in particular, see Colleen M. Conway, *Sex and Slaughter in the Tent of Jael: A Cultural History of a Biblical Story* (Oxford University Press, 2017).

23. Different manuscripts present these arguments in a different order. Here I have replicated the order of Oxford Opp. Add. Folio 23, London BL Harl 5508 (400), NY-JTS Rab. 1608 (ENA 850), Vatican 134, the Pesaro Print (1514), the Venice Print (1521), and Vilna (1899) which place *teruot* before *shevarim*. Munich 140 and Rosh HaShanah G134 reverse the order, placing *shevarim* before *teruot*. There is no significant difference in meaning between these two traditions. Manuscripts accessed through The Saul and Evelyn Henkind Talmud Text Databank.

24. My translation, from the William Davidson digital edition of the Koren Noé Talmud Bavli.

25. The Syriac text is taken from R. J. Bidawid, *The Old Testament in Syriac According to the Peshitta Version, Part IV, fasc. 3, 4 Esdras* (Leiden: Brill, 1973).

26. The verb here ܡܬܬܢܚ/*mttnḥ*' is in passive participle singular feminine ittaphel form, from ܐܢܚ/*'nḥ* or ܬܢܚ/*tnḥ*. It suggests "sighing" (תנח / *t-n-ḥ* "to sigh" in ithpaal and ithpeal (Marcus Jastrow, *A Dictionary of the Targumim, the Talmud Babli and Yerushalmi, and the Midrashic Literature*, s.v. "תנח," (London: Luzac & Co., 1903), 1681 and אנח / *'-n-ḥ* "to sigh" in hithpael (Jastrow, Dictionary, s.v. "אנח"). In the Hebrew Bible, אנח / *'-n-ḥ* is used, significantly, several times in Lamentations ch. 1: to describe the groaning of Zion's priests (associated with the mourning of her roads, because there is no one on them) (v. 4), Zion's groaning when others see her nakedness (v. 8), the groaning of the people when they search for bread (v. 11), and the groaning of Zion herself, when no one comforts her (v. 21). It is also used in Jer. 22:23 to suggest the groaning of childbirth: מַה־נֵּחַנְתְּ בְּבֹא־לָךְ חֲבָלִים חִיל כַּיֹּלֵדָה/*mah nekhant bevo'-lakh khavalim khyl kayoledah* ("How you [inhabitant of Lebanon] will groan when labor pains come upon you, pains like a woman in labor!"). The use of this verb in connection with Lamentations, in which Zion is personified as a woman and often as mother and explicitly in connection with a woman in childbirth, suggests that this verb would have evoked associations of particularly maternal grief for ancient audiences.

27. In the Hebrew Bible, God "hearing the voice" (שמע בקל/*shema' beqol*) of a petitioner is a standard phrase to indicate receptive listening.

28. Stone suggests that a miracle à la the resurrection of the Shunammite woman's son might be intended here. He cites Gunkel's claim that elements in this story indicate that it may have arisen from a folk tale. Michael Edward Stone, *Fourth Ezra: A Commentary on the Book of Fourth Ezra*, Hermeneia: A Critical and Historical Commentary on the Bible (Minneapolis: Fortress Press, 1990), 323. See Hermann Gunkel, *Das Vierte Buch Esra* (Freiburg: J.C.B. Mohr (P. Siebeck), 1899).

29. 4 Ezra 10:44–48. Translation by Michael E. Stone and Matthias Henze, *4 Ezra and 2 Baruch: Translations, Introductions, and Notes* (Minneapolis, MN: Fortress Press, 2013), Kindle locations 1127–1134.

30. "Gunkel had remarked on the contrast between the woman's quiet or silence and the usual expressions of maternal grief." Stone, *Fourth Ezra*, 312. "Sonst zeigt sich doch mütterlicher Schmerz in Jammern und Klagen; sie aber ist vor Schmerz stumm." ("Usually maternal pain shows itself in wailing and lamenting; but she is mute with pain." My translation.) Gunkel, *Das Vierte Buch Esra*, 386 n. r.

It is worth noting the possible relationship between ܫܠܝܬ/ *šlyt* (from ܫܠܐ/ *šl'*/ *šly*, to be at ease, quiet, unconcerned; see Jastrow, *Dictionary, s.v.* "שלי" *šly*) and ܫܠܝܗ/ܫܠܝܐ *šlyh*/*šly*' (afterbirth, placenta; see Jastrow, Dictionary, s.v. שיליא/ שליא *šly'*/ *šyly*', which cites: Niddah 3:4, Tosefta ib. 4:9, Niddah 26a, Leviticus Rabbah s. 35, Yerushalmi Berakhot I, 3b, Avot d' Rabbi Natan ch. 29, Yerushalmi Ma'aser Sheni II, 53c; see also Jastrow p. 1584 s.v. *šlyt*/' שליתא, which cites: Targum Yerushalmi Deut. 28:57, Berakhot 6a, BT Shabbat 134a. The usage is also attested in The Aphorisms of Hippocrates 23 (1), the Mandaic magic bowl 2364 1:21, and the Mandaic amulet 16:b6). I venture that the choice of word to describe the woman's quietude is intentional here to emphasize the maternal nature of the woman's emotional state, that is, her grief.

31. Kindalee Pfremmer de Long, "'Ask a Woman': Childbearing and Ezra's Transformation in 4 Ezra," *Journal for the Study of the Pseudepigrapha* 22, no. 2 (2012): 138.

32. Stone and Henze, *4 Ezra*, Kindle Locations 1111–1114. Uriel explains this event as the woman transforming into eschatological Zion in 10:44 above.

33. My analysis concurs with de Long's, who in her examination of the childbearing motifs throughout 4 Ezra finds that "the childbearing motif prepares the audience to see the woman's speech as climactically instructive for Ezra because it moves him to join her lament, which in turn sets in motion her transformation and the remainder of the narrative." de Long, "'Ask a Woman,'" 143.

34. David A. Bosworth, "Daughter Zion and Weeping in Lamentations 1–2," *Journal for the Study of the Old Testament* 38, no. 2 (2013): 230.

35. Bosworth, "Daughter Zion," 236.

36. Bosworth, "Daughter Zion," 218.

37. Bosworth, "Daughter Zion," 237.

38. Christl M. Maier, *Daughter Zion, Mother Zion: Gender, Space, and the Sacred in Ancient Israel* (Minneapolis: Fortress Press, 2008), 156.

39. Maier, *Daughter Zion*, 156.

40. Bob Becking, "A Voice was Heard in Ramah: Some Remarks on Structure and Meaning of Jeremiah 31, 15–17," *Biblische Zeitschrift* 38, no. 2 (1994): 236.

41. Sébastien Doane, "Rachel Weeping: Intertextuality as a Means of Transforming a Reader's Worldview," *Journal of Biblical Reception* 4, no. 1 (2017): 7.

42. Becking, "A Voice Was Heard in Ramah," 234.

43. Becking, "A Voice Was Heard in Ramah," 234 n.14. On *kî* as introduction of the direct speech see: HALOT (1994) 471, sv *ki* II,7, and A. Schoors, "The Particle 'kî,'" in *Remembering All the Way* (Leiden: Brill, 1981), 258: "Kî introducing direct speech . . . has the emphatic force of the original deictic particle."

44. Phyllis Trible, *God and the Rhetoric of Sexuality* (Minneapolis: Fortress Press, 1978), 40.

45. Doane, "Rachel Weeping," 3.

46. Doane, "Rachel Weeping," 6.

47. Doane, "Rachel Weeping," 6. "For Krister Stendahl, this quote is a version of the Hebrew text, see *The School of St Matthew and Its Use of the Old Testament* (Uppsala: Almquist & Wiksells, 1954). For Ulrich Luz, it comes from a fusion between the Greek and Hebrew texts, see *Matthew 1–7: A Commentary*, Hermeneia (Minneapolis: Fortress Press, 2007), 118–9. There is a comparison between Matt 2:18 and Jer 31:15 in its different versions in Michael Knowles, *Jeremiah in Matthew's Gospel: The Rejected Prophet Motif in Matthaean Redaction* (Sheffield: JSOT, 1993), 36–8 and Raymond E. Brown, *The Birth of the Messiah: A Commentary on the Infancy Narratives in the Gospels of Matthew and Luke* (New York: Doubleday, 1993), 223–5." P.6 n. 20.

48. See Doane, "Rachel Weeping," 6–9.

49. Elaine Wainwright, "Rachel Weeping for Her Children: Intertextuality and the Biblical Testaments—A Feminist Approach," in *A Feminist Companion to Reading the Bible*, ed. Athalya Brenner-Idan and Carol Fontaine (Sheffield: Sheffield Academic Press, 1997), 467.

50. Wainwright, "Rachel Weeping," 467.

BIBLIOGRAPHY

Astor, Carl N. *The* Petihta'ot *of Eicha Rabbah*. Ph.D. Dissertation. Jewish Theological Seminary, 1995.

Becking, Bob. "'A Voice Was Heared in Ramah': Some Remarks on Structure and Meaning of Jeremiah 31, 15-17." *Biblische Zeitschrift* 38, no. 2 (September 22, 1994): 229–42. https://doi.org/10.1163/25890468-03802005.

Belser, Julia Watts. *Rabbinic Tales of Destruction: Gender, Sex and Disability in the Ruins of Jerusalem*. New York: Oxford University Press, 2018.

Bidawid, R. J. *The Old Testament in Syriac According to the Peshitta Version*. Part IV, fasc. 3, *4 Esdras*. Leiden: Brill, 1973.

Bosworth, David A. "Daughter Zion and Weeping in Lamentations 1–2." *Journal for the Study of the Old Testament* 38, no. 2 (December 2013): 217–37. https://doi.org/10.1177/0309089213511752.

Brenner-Idan, Athalya (ed.). *A Feminist Companion to Judges*. The Feminist Companion to the Bible, Vol. 4. Sheffield: Sheffield Academic Press, 1993.

Brenner-Idan, Athalya (ed.). *Judges: A Feminist Companion to the Bible*. The Feminist Companion to the Bible (Second Series), Vol. 4. Sheffield: Sheffield Academic Press, 1999.

Buber, Solomon (ed.). *Midrasch Echa Rabbati*. Vilna: Press of Widow and Brothers Romm, 1899.

Conway, Colleen M. *Sex and Slaughter in the Tent of Jael: A Cultural History of a Biblical Story*. New York: Oxford University Press, 2017.

de Long, Kindalee Pfremmer. "'Ask a Woman': Childbearing and Ezra's Transformation in 4 Ezra." *Journal for the Study of the Pseudepigrapha* 22, no. 2 (December 2012): 114–45. https://doi.org/10.1177/0951820712467887.

Distefano, Michel G. *Inner-Midrashic Introductions and Their Influence on Introductions to Medieval Rabbinic Bible Commentaries*. Berlin: De Gruyter, 2009.

Doane, Sébastien. "Rachel Weeping: Intertextuality as a Means of Transforming the Readers' Worldview." *Journal of the Bible and Its Reception* 4, no. 1 (April 25, 2017): 1–20. https://doi.org/10.1515/jbr-2017-2000.

Ferber, Ilit, Paula Schwebel, and Gershom Scholem (eds.). *Lament in Jewish Thought: Philosophical, Theological, and Literary Perspectives*. Perspectives on Jewish Texts and Contexts, Vol. 2. Berlin: De Gruyter, 2014.

Gravett, Emily Olmstead. *The Literary Phenomenon of Narrative Biblical Retellings*. Ph.D. Dissertation. University of Virginia, 2013. UMI 3572776.

Gunkel, Hermann. *Das Vierte Buch Esra*. Freiburg: J. C. B. Mohr (P. Siebeck), 1899.

Hasan-Rokem, Galit. "The Rhetoric of Intimacy - the Rhetoric of the Sacred." *Temenos - Nordic Journal of Comparative Religion* 23 (January 1, 1987). https://doi.org/10.33356/temenos.6169.

Hasan-Rokem, Galit. *Web of Life: Folklore and Midrash in Rabbinic Literature.* Contraversions. Stanford: Stanford University Press, 2000.

Hasan-Rokem, Galit. "Bodies Performing in Ruins: The Lamenting Mother in Ancient Hebrew Texts." In *Lament in Jewish Thought: Philosophical, Theological, and Literary Perspectives*, edited by Ilit Ferber and Paula Schwebel, 33–63. Berlin: De Gruyter, 2014.

Herr, Moshe. "Midrash." In *Encyclopedia Judaica*, 2nd ed., Vol. 14, edited by Michael Berenbaum and Fred Skolnik, 182–185. MacMillan Reference, 2007.

Jastrow, Marcus. *A Dictionary of the Targumim, the Talmud Babli and Yerushalmi, and the Midrashic Literature.* London: Luzac & Co., 1903.

Joyce, Paul M. and Diana Lipton. *Lamentations Through the Centuries.* Wiley-Blackwell Bible Commentaries. Chichester: Wiley-Blackwell, 2013.

Kozlova, Ekaterina E. *Maternal Grief in the Hebrew Bible*, 1st ed. Oxford Theology and Religion Monographs. Oxford: Oxford University Press, 2017.

Kraemer, David Charles. *Responses to Suffering in Classical Rabbinic Literature.* New York: Oxford University Press, 1995.

Linafelt, Tod. *Surviving Lamentations: Catastrophe, Lament, and Protest in the Afterlife of a Biblical Book.* Chicago: University of Chicago Press, 2000.

Maier, Christl M. *Daughter Zion, Mother Zion: Gender, Space, and the Sacred in Ancient Israel.* Minneapolis: Fortress Press, 2008.

Malkinson, Ruth, and Liora Bar-Tur. "Long Term Bereavement Processes of Older Parents: The Three Phases of Grief." *OMEGA - Journal of Death and Dying* 50, no. 2 (March 2005): 103–29. https://doi.org/10.2190/W346-UP8T-RER6-BBD1.

Mandel, Paul. "Between Byzantium and Islam: The Transmission of a Jewish Book in the Byzantine and Early Islamic Periods." In *Transmitting Jewish Tradition: Orality, Textuality, and Cultural Diffusion*, edited by Yaakov Elman and Israel Gershoni, 74–103. New Haven: Yale University Press, 2000.

Mintz, Alan L. *Ḥurban: Responses to Catastrophe in Hebrew Literature.* New York: Columbia University Press, 1984.

Neusner, Jacob (ed.). *Lamentations Rabbah: An Analytical Translation.* Brown Judaic Studies 193. Atlanta: Scholars Press, 1989.

Schoors, A. "The Particle 'kî.'" In *Remembering All the Way: A Collection of Old Testament Studies Published on the Occasion of the Fortieth Anniversary of the Oudtestamentisch Werkgezelschap in Nederland*, edited by B. Albrektson, 240–76. Leiden: Brill, 1981.

Schwartz, Marcus Mordecai. *Rewriting the Talmud: The Fourth Century Origins of Bavli Rosh Hashanah.* Texte Und Studien Zum Antiken Judentum 175. Tübingen: Mohr Siebeck, 2019.

Stahlberg, Lesleigh Cushing. *Sustaining Fictions: Intertextuality, Midrash, Translation, and the Literary Afterlife of the Bible.* Library of Hebrew Bible/Old Testament Studies 486. New York: T & T Clark, 2008.

Stern, David. "Imitatio Hominis: Anthropomorphism and the Character(s) of God in Rabbinic Literature." *Prooftexts* 12, no. 2 (May 1992): 151–74.

Stern, David. *Midrash and Theory: Ancient Jewish Exegesis and Contemporary Literary Studies*. Rethinking Theory. Evanston: Northwestern University Press, 1996.

Stone, Michael E. and Frank Moore Cross. *Fourth Ezra: A Commentary on the Book of Fourth Ezra*. Hermeneia–a Critical and Historical Commentary on the Bible. Minneapolis: Fortress Press, 1990.

Stone, Michael E. and Matthias Henze (eds.). *4 Ezra and 2 Baruch*. Minneapolis: Fortress Press, 2013.

Trible, Phyllis. *God and the Rhetoric of Sexuality*. Overtures to Biblical Theology 2. Philadelphia: Fortress Press, 1978.

Wainwright, Elaine. "Rachel Weeping for Her Children: Intertextuality and the Biblical Testaments—A Feminist Approach." In *A Feminist Companion to Reading the Bible: Approaches, Methods, and Strategies,* edited by Athalya Brenner-Idan and Carole Fontaine, 453–69. Sheffield: Sheffield Academic Press, 1997.

10

The Body as a Wonderland

Rabbinic Talk of the Human Body as a Sex/Gender Construction

Daniel Vorpahl

The interdisciplinary achievements and modes of knowledge provided by queer and gender studies have profoundly influenced the academic discourse of Jewish and religious studies over the past decades. Whenever feminist research approaches or gender-related topics are chosen, there is no getting around without referring at least to the groundbreaking theories of Judith Butler,[1] although this does not mean that these obtain general acceptance. Some scholars continue to follow the basic assumption of a binary conception of man, uncritically adhering to the two categories "male" and "female."[2] A distinction between a biological sex and a social gender identity is also implicitly maintained, inasmuch as the human body is regarded as an object "which only bears cultural constructions and, therefore, cannot be a construction"[3] itself.[4] Contrary to this, Judith Butler and the gender/queer studies that have been built on their theories recognize the idea of a biological sex that exists prior to a social gender identity as deficient.[5] Because the material human body cannot be excluded from discourses of gender and sexuality,[6] and neither can the talk of the human body.

It should be noted up front that the idea of only two sexes can be regarded as overly simplistic, as it remains unclear whether biological sex is meant to be based on a person's anatomy, hormones, chromosomes, or genes, whose interaction might be construed by a majority society as inconsistent sex assignments.[7] Expecting the complex biology of a human being to be either "female" or "male," is like playing music on a stereo system that has one button for "loud" and one for "soft" instead of a volume regulator with a variety of loudness levels. Socio-cultural gender norms are not independent thereof, but belong to the same category of knowledge,[8] obviously if gender identity is limited to the same binary frame as the biological sex.[9] Moreover, within many socio-cultural fields of relevance gender identities are not generally awarded to any person independent from their attributed sex. Accordingly, cultural constructions of gender rather imply or even start with the cultural construction of biological sex. In line with this, the "body reappears even in the writing of those who would turn attention to language, power, and culture,"[10] as Thomas Laqueur exposes with exemplary reference to Michel Foucault.

The talk of the human body within each field of a society, including its literature,[11] thus makes a major contribution to the construction of sex/gender as a category of knowledge. In the present chapter I will explain how the talk of the human body functions as an anatomical and biological argumentation for the construction of social gender roles, norms, and identities within rabbinic literature of the Amoraic period. I will illustrate this along a few selected examples, primarily taken from the intertextually tradition-bound Babylonian Talmud, which shall demonstrate that the construction of sex/gender through the talk of the human body is a prominently appearing phenomenon within rabbinic tradition. This chapter is far less than an exhaustive study of the rabbinic talk of the human body, but reveals why such a study is worthwhile. My primary aim is to draw attention to this special aspect of rabbinic literature in light of gender studies and to encourage further research in this field.

To clarify therefore the close relation between the human body's sex and gender I will explicate both terms operatively at the end of this introductory part. I take Judith Butler's theories as a starting point to deconstruct sex-gender relations as being reciprocal instead of dichotomous. I proceed on the assumption that sex/gender affiliations and attributions as well as the underlying binary classification system, with all its dichotomies, are no natural precepts but the result of social processes.[12] To analyze these processes within rabbinic literature it is conducive to cast off the limitations of "binary structures that appear as the language of universal rationality."[13] Therefore, I will consider additional theoretical approaches by the French sociologist Pierre Bourdieu that supplement Judith Butler's general critique of a universal binarity. Arguing with Bourdieu, "conceptual dualisms"[14] like the notion that rabbinic laws "help define what it means to be male and female"[15] should be overcome by focusing instead on the "active and creative relation[s]"[16] of different sex/gender identities. If "binary oppositions provide insight into the way meaning is constructed," as the historian Joan Scott elucidates, "then analyses of meaning cannot take binary oppositions at face value but rather must 'deconstruct' them for the processes they embody."[17]

Taking a deconstructivist approach to analyze rabbinic talk of the human body is, in my eyes, not only legitimate,[18] but highly suitable. Charlotte Fonrobert claimed that Butler's critique does "hardly apply to the case of rabbinic legal thinking," since the rabbis do not constitute their "gender dimorphism by taking recourse to nature" but with reference to the Jewish tradition, "a cultural construct to begin with, albeit one with divine authority."[19] But the Jewish tradition that accredits the founding of human existence to divine authority, as in the narrative of Genesis 1–2, explains the very same origination that Western societies construct and frame—under the cultural influence of *Jewish-Christian* myths of creation—as "nature." The rabbis' "clear distinction between the sexes"[20] is by implication as much a cultural construct as is the naturalization of two biological sexes.[21] Both tradition and nature are fields of discourse in which knowledge of sex/gender is culturally constructed through processes that the deconstructivist approach aims to expound by certain strategies of reading.

I will follow this aim along distinct forms of rabbinic talk of the human body, based on exemplary texts from the Babylonian Talmud. Beginning with the next subsection, I seek to gain insights into the halakhic significance and rating of the human body. Subsequently, I would like to take a look at the metaphorical talk of the body. Following this, in the final subsection I will examine examples of the Amoraim's narrative talk of the body in aggadic fables about transformation and metamorphosis. Insights from these analyses will hopefully illustrate the variety of literary manifestations of the human body and convey the relevance of the body-gender-relation within rabbinic fields of discourses. This might complement previous scientific approaches and inspire further ones.

While I begin my survey from a non-binary perspective, it is consensus to the greatest extent that the rabbinic gender-discourse is oriented along the assumption of two biological sexes, resulting in a hierarchical dichotomy of femininity and masculinity, with the latter being anticipated as the normative human prototype.[22] Pierre Bourdieu denotes such a preconsciousness as a *doxa*, a truth that is taken for granted to the extent that it is beyond conscious perception.[23] The cultural act of biologizing gender in accordance with a "natural sex" becomes manifest within categorical knowledge of sex/gender and finally appears as indisputable justification for gender-specific differences that have actually been constructed by this cultural act.[24] As a result, a program of perception, valuation, and action is imprinted into each subject's body, as Bourdieu emphasizes.[25]

The perception that the rabbinic distinction between female and male bodies is accompanied by the hierarchical upvaluation of a normative masculinity opposite a devalued, substandard femininity, is challenged by Charlotte Fonrobert in her monograph *Menstrual Purity*.[26] Therein Fonrobert concludes that "the rabbinic configuration of the female body corresponds more to the Hippocratic model [. . .] of the woman as a completely different creature and not simply a substandard man."[27] But precisely the idea of "the woman" as a "completely different creature" does not mean that the "female body" is defined by its own parameters. Following Jacques Derrida's linguistic concept of *différance*, the functionality of meaning of a "female body" (significate) as a "woman" (signifier) is solely based on its perception as being different from other bodily creatures, above all by being different from a "male body," for whom the same linguistic logic applies.[28] The perceived difference of a masculinized body toward a feminized body, and vice versa, is not an expression of independence but of relation.[29] Fonrobert is nevertheless right that within the rabbinic discourse "the woman" is not only a variation of "the man" but its opposite, as the latter is presumed as a human prototype.[30]

The understanding of a male human being as "male" because it is not female, and vice versa, is most prominently expressed in Gen 2:23, when the first woman (אשה/*išâ*) is separated from the first man (איש/*iš*). Before this event, *the human being* is exactly called like that, *ha-adam* (האדם). In other words, according to this biblical tradition the earthling did not become a man until they became a woman. But since according to tradition the woman was made out of the man (Gen 2:22), a solidifying *doxa* was established in the following, imparting that these human beings were facing one another not reciprocally but hierarchically. This concept is manifest in the man's sovereignty over women according to Gen 3:16 and strengthens the creation myth of Adam as the primary (hu)man. Emerging from this tradition and being further influenced by similar ones,[31] the rabbinic discourse on human fetal growth for example proceeds on the assumption that the development of a male fetus is completed prior to a female fetus (m. Nid. 3:7 and b. Nid. 30a–31b).

Indeed, it seems absurd to deduce enormous social, legal, political, and cultural consequences during centuries of daily life situations from relatively small physical differences such as having a penis or a vagina, whose development and functionality are beyond themselves so dependent upon hormones, chromosomes, and genes, and which are not even visible but just assumed in the moments that their existence becomes relevant.[32] In the end it is not vaginas or penises that induce binary differentiations. These concomitant anatomical effects are only taken as indicators to model a synergic bodily construct, composed of idealized forms and proportions, size, body tension, skin texture, posture, and so on. According to social and legal standards currently in force, the gendered parts of the human body are expected to look, to be felt, to move, and act in a certain way. To do justice to these processes of doing gender, I would like to explicate the terms for biological sex and social gender, as already noted. I consider it necessary to make both terms more explicit to elucidate that these are not two random words to describe independent circumstances (sex and gender), but two closely interrelated problems (sex/gender), justifying the same solution: a binary categorization of human beings in each and every area of their life.

In line with this, I will use here the term *sex-skeleton* to express my understanding of sex as a multi-part inner scaffold, which is upholding and embodying a fitted outer shell. This outer shell in turn I will call *gender-bodice*,[33] which is on the one hand formed according to its assumed underlying sex-skeleton and on the other hand constricts and shapes a person's identity according to the socially established norms of this exact form. The term *gender-bodice* shall express my understanding of gender as actively shaping identity, while being passively dependent from the form uphold by the sex-skeleton. Gender is never perceived fully independent from sex insofar as sex culturally presets the gender's basic form. Both are related to the human body, one based on something coming from the inside naturally/biologically, one based on something coming from the outside culturally/socially. Both together are upholding (sex-skeleton) and shaping (gender-bodice) an identity, which would not exist without both of them and which is constantly judged along the (binary) norms of a social environment.

INTO THE HALAHKIC FIELD: RABBINIC TALK OF BODIES IN THE BODY OF LAW

The complex halakhic discourse, which rabbis in Palestine and the Sassanid Empire spawned over several centuries and through multi-branched editorial processes, is marked, as noted, by the binary *doxa* of two opposing sexes/genders and a male human prototype.[34] "The binary is simply the air that the rabbis breathe,"[35] as Sarra Lev emphasizes. In the following I will give an exemplarily insight into the halakhic significance and rating of the human body by reference to sugyot of the Babylonian Talmud. Thereby, it should be taken into account that the halakhic pleadings from the Tannaitic Mishnah (second century CE) have been adopted, recontextualized, and upgraded by the Babylonian Amoraim in a much later timescale (fifth to eighth century CE),[36] within a different cultural context, and with an apparent tendency to more misogynistic viewpoints.[37]

Accordingly, the general impression that the halakhic body of law is intended to be inhabited and accessed primarily by "men" pertains all the more to the Babylonian Talmud. There the study of Torah is described as a physical experience (b. ʽErub. 54a), which requires the virtue of self-restraint, which is exclusively ascribed to men, while women are considered to be less self-disciplinary.[38] This standpoint assumes that everybody knows what exactly men and women are, while both sex/gender identities are actually created through the halakhic discourse. The study of Torah is thus "constructed as the masculine activity *par excellence*," as Michael Satlow underscores, which has to be fulfilled "through constant exercise of discipline."[39] This idea of physical practice involves the performance of controlled penetrative, heterosexual intercourse as an expression of self-control,[40] which interrelates this idealistic element of the male gender-bodice directly to a male sex-skeleton. Claiming that men are able to study Torah because of their "natural" self-restraint is in fact constructing the idea of a "masculine" body with "natural" self-restraint. A declared attribute of the male gender-bodice is here forming the masculinized body, assuming that its underlying sex-skeleton features exactly the same attribute. By contrast, this male gender-bodice is not provided for persons with a female sex-skeleton, for one thing because of the lack of a penis, for another thing because women are denied to have sexual self-control.[41] This dualistic assumption results in an implicit deprivation of women's sexual self-determination and in a hierarchical embodiment of intellectual capabilities, leading to a restricted access to the study of Torah. It becomes apparent that this rabbinic construction of the male gender-bodice encodes a power relation into the human body[42] and is in this way constructing a sex-skeleton. Pierre Bourdieu labels such structural domination as symbolic violence:[43] By reserving the control over the Torah solely to a male gender-bodice all other gender identities are excluded from this social field, which is a violent act of discrimination against them. As this exclusive ascription to a male gender-bodice is justified by the construction of a male sex-skeleton in opposition to a female sex-skeleton, their bodies themselves become symbolic surrogates for this social violence.

The majority of body-related laws that can be found in the Torah affect "men" in particular. The twenty-four laws that determine inappropriate partners for penetrative intercourse in Lev 18:7–22, for example, are addressed to people with a masculinized sex-skeleton, wherein the biblical *doxa* of heteronormative penetration as the normative form of sexual intercourse is manifested.[44] This is shared by the Babylonian Amoraim, then culminating in the extent of heterosexualizing the intellectual act of studying the Torah (b. 'Erub. 54b).[45]

In the Mishnah the Tannaim elaborate the Torah's body of law into a wide variety of specific regulations, focusing recognizably on issues concerning the human body.[46] Thereby, feminized bodies become disproportionately more often objects of the halakhic discourse than in the Hebrew Bible.[47] Female virginity, for example, is of utmost interest for the rabbis, whereby the ordinary biblical myth about the hymen's intactness indicating virginity[48] is explicated to an understanding of virginity as "physical integrity" of the feminized body, with enormous relevance for the legal status of the female gender-bodice.[49] The underlying cause for this is the rabbis' binary worldview, which distinguishes the feminized sex-skeleton and all its biological attributes as something that is not normal. Taken the masculinized sex-skeleton as the norm, any deviations of its biological processes, like menstruation or the hymen, are classified as strange, endangering, or destabilizing the masculine norm.[50]

Masculinized bodies again are treated in much less detail in the halakhic field of discourse, but the male sex-skeleton eludes its cultural variation and deconstruction perfectly well in the hidden.[51] The Tannaim's and Amoraim's awareness of problems is instead focused on sex/gender-identifications that deviate from the normative he-man, namely female, trans- or intersexual sex-skeletons. The continual references to queer bodies within the Mishnah and the Talmudim, where the *saris* for example is mentioned more than 150 times,[52] is indeed remarkable. Leaving the historical question aside, if intersexuality's prevalence documents that it was culturally more acknowledged,[53] queer sex-skeletons are continually sorted into a binary classification system. Being declared as an insufficiently developed man (*saris*, b. Yebam. 80b), an underdeveloped woman (*aylonit*, ibid.) or suchlike (*androgynous*, *tumtum*),[54] any queer sex-skeleton is determined along a binary raster of feminized and masculinized body-references.[55] As Charlotte Fonrobert formulates, they were integrated into a "legal system with a dual-gender grid."[56] But the necessity of "integration" means that there is no matching gender-bodice for any queer sex-skeleton, but only occasion-related partial ascriptions along either a male or female gender-bodice.

The halakhic status of a gender-bodice is thus subject to the underlying sex-skeleton in accordance with its current measure of completeness, which includes a body's process of growing. According to b. Nid. 45b (cf. m. Nid. 5:6) a girl becomes contractually capable with reservations at the age of eleven, and fully legally competent when she turns twelve,[57] while for a boy the same is true with one-year delay. In the subsequent Gemara and the following mishnayot, these indications of age turn out to rather mark the physical beginning of puberty (b. Nid. 45b–46b; 47a). This is further illustrated by comparing the growing of the feminized body metaphorically to the three degrees of ripeness of a fig (b. Nid. 47a; cf. m. Nid. 5:7–9). The girl child is thereby compared to an unripe fig and the pubescent girl to a ripening one, both staying under the legal guardianship of the girl's father (b. Nid. 47a). Becoming capable of bearing children, a woman is pictured as a ripe fig, being legally independent (m. Nid. 5:7). The Babylonian Amoraim add that at this stage of bodily development the protuberance above the vagina, called "a swollen place" (probably the mons veneris), is softening, while the two previous stages of development are characterized by the lack of growth of pubic hair in the same body area (b. Nid. 47b).

While in analogous cases male adolescents are identified primarily by the growing of pubic hair (b. Sanh. 68b; m. Nid. 5:9; m. Sanh. 8:1), we find the development of the feminized body to be considered in more detail. In b. Nid. 47a–b the feminized sex-skeleton is linguistically modeled by the body-descriptive fig-imagery. This metaphorical use of a domesticated fruit-plant, which is cultivated to become a product for consumption, objectifies the feminized body itself into a product for consumption. Subsequently the discourse is further extended into a rabbinical debate about additional or visible indications of a prolific female adolescent:

> Rabbi Yosei HaGelili says: Who gets a fold [appearing] below the breast. Rabbi Akiva says: Whose breasts sag. Ben Azzai says: Whose areola darkens. Rabbi Yosei says: When a [person's] hand is placed on the nipple and it sinks in and slows to return. (b. Nid. 47a)

Beside further variations it is even considered that residency and social setting might influence if the growing of breasts or of pubic hair begins earlier or later (b. Ned. 48b).[58] There is no certainty in how far these suggestions have ever been applied to judicial practice.[59] But looking at b. Nid. 47a–b as a theoretical debate, the constructed chat of sages appears to be a form of verbal voyeurism, disguised as intellectual effusion of legal relevance.[60] The rabbis empower themselves here by fulfilling two operations in one: They inscribe a power relation into the feminized body, which they construct at the same time as embodiment of a biologized sex-skeleton.[61] This talk of the human body thus generates a female sex-skeleton to use it at once as measurement device for the halakhic status and rights of the female gender-bodice.

As similar but less detailed halakhic classifications are generated from debates about the masculinized human body, it can be stated so far that the halakhic status of binary gender-bodices is likewise established and derived along the dual construction of feminized and masculinized sex-skeletons. Accordingly, the question about the "difference between a man and a woman" in b. Soṭah 23a is there answered by a list of binarily ascribed halakhic provisions, whose justification as "natural" consequences have already become a *doxa*. But in fact, these binarily ascribed halakhic provisions are instruments for the construction of gender-bodices, that are keeping a person's sex/gender identity in the exact form that their constructed sex-skeleton designates it for.[62] Within the halakhic field of discourse, the Amoraim's talk of the human body verbally constructs binary sex-skeletons in order to use these as ontological substantiations for the legal status and the rights of access ascribed to female and male gender-bodices.

BUILDING AND REBUILDING THE BODY: MAPPING THE SEX-SKELETON IN METAPHORICAL ROOMS

The way we talk about things has a performative impact on the way these things are handled in daily routines, which immediately affects the way we live and consequently influences how we shape our surrounding world, while it is shaping us.[63] A popular performative instrument of such cultural influencing and imprint can be found in metaphorical language, which is much more than a verbal illustration. The metaphor is not only a stylistic device, but it becomes part of knowledge categories, including estimations and everyday behavior derived thereof.[64] As George Lakoff and Mark Johnson have prominently pointed out: "Our ordinary conceptual system, in terms of which we both think and act, is fundamentally metaphorical."[65]

To talk of the human body in metaphors makes it more readable, as Charlotte Fonrobert puts it.[66] It enriches the capabilities of signification within such talk, but likewise it eases the appropriation of the interpretational sovereignty over other human beings' bodies. Furthermore, the cultural phenomenon of body-metaphorical language spreads out retroactively and leads to an embodiment of the language itself. In this regard, as Juliana Goschler points out, embodiment "means that parts of our conceptual system and therefore some aspects of our language are structured by the features of our bodies and the functioning of our bodies in everyday life."[67]

The description of bodies or body parts as containers, for example, is common in many cultures; for instance, biblical texts like Job 32:18, 1 Kgs 7:14, or Deut 34:9, where we find phrases about people being *filled* with words or wisdom. It is worth bearing in mind that according to Gen 2:7 the human being was actually created out of the soil's dust and formed like clay, just as pottery.[68] The other way around, containers are often anthropomorphized, talking of bottlenecks, bellied vases, or the arms, shoulders, or feet of jugs, pots, or other vessels.[69] The historico-cultural correlation of these metaphors might be identified in the early conception of the human body as being filled with and dropping out liquids.[70] This was especially problematized concerning feminized bodies, whose breasts were supposed to give milk, and whose wombs were supposed to carry blood.[71] Biblical descriptions of body parts in a spatial manner also reveal a sex/gender dichotomy, as God opens mainly men's organs of perception (2 Kgs 6:17.20; Isa 50:5; Num 22), but women's organs of reproduction (Gen 29:31; 30:22; 1 Sam 1:19–20).

Within the halakhic context of purity laws, the spatial fragmentation of the human body into several parts appears consistently, mostly separating temporary body parts, such as nails, hairs, or saliva.[72] Accordingly, the human body cannot be considered here as a "fixed, unified, and monolithic entity" alone, as Mira Balberg points out. Especially "when it comes to the contraction and conveyance of impurity [...] it is seen as consisting of various parts, and its different constituents are subject to different rules."[73]

A crude rabbinical case study, carrying the destruction of the human body into its pieces to extremes, is recorded in b. Bek. 45a and requires a content warning concerning the following depiction of violence. The text reports about students of Rabbi Yehuda who boiled the corpse of a sex worker, which was burned to death at the king's instigation. In the end the students found 252 limbs of the sex worker's corpse and demanded an explanation, as the tradition tells that the human body has only 248 limbs.[74] Up to that point the text has already erected a hierarchical dichotomy regarding the scope of gender-bodices: the masculinized protagonists (rabbi, students, king) are all figured as intellectually active when they talk about, examine, and judge the sex worker's body. By way of contrast the feminized sex worker is depicted as a passive object of masculinized violence by being sentenced to death, burned, cooked, autopsied, and fragmented.

As the result of the men's investigation the four limbs proved to be additional are lastly identified as "two hinges" and "two doors," accounted for by a Baraita's speech acts attributed to Rabbi Elazar and Rabbi Yehoshua saying that a "woman" has hinges and doors similar to a house (b. Bek. 45a). The consulted scriptural proofs (1 Sam 4:19 and Job 3:10) tell in no uncertain terms that this door-metaphor stands for the vagina, which is taken as entrance and exit of the feminized womb. The uterus is thereby not only construed as a container, but as a house which, as a dwelling, has a tradition-steeped social function and religious meaning in Jewish perspective.[75] A following quote by Rabbi Akiva embellishes the house-metaphor, saying that there is a key to a woman as there is a key to a house, with reference to the opening of Rachel's womb in Gen 30:22. The key holder within this rabbinically widespread house-metaphor is never the woman themself but their groom. Although in Rachel's case as in other biblical examples God opened the uterus for conception, the masculinized sex/gender finally gains access there through the vagina. As if the groom's gender-bodice includes a keychain, the Amoraim take the married man for an owner of the woman/house by the symbolic opening of the vagina "for his exclusive habitation."[76] Accordingly, the term "open door" is used in the Babylonian Talmud for metaphorical descriptions of a putative physical "losing" of a woman's virginity (b. Ketub. 10a–b).[77] Thereby the penis functions symbolically as the key or phallic door opener to the vagina, which is seen as the entrance to the groom's homestead (woman/house). Viewed in this light, the house-metaphor is used to define a certain relation of binary gender-bodices by inscribing metaphorical functions into the feminized and masculinized sex-skeletons in a strictly heteronormative orientation.

In the whole Talmudic literature, the metaphorical understanding of a sex-skeleton as a house is broadly established for the feminized body alone.[78]

This makes it easier to cherish the practice and understanding of marriage as a change of ownership of a woman from father to husband. Beyond that the metaphor represents a linguistic embodiment that initiates a wife's identification with "her household" as a social obligation. The female gender-bodice is seen as being chained up to the real house, which enables a spatialization of the feminized sex-skeleton into a set of functionalized rooms, until the "woman herself has become 'house'."[79]

Although the house-metaphor refers to a dynamic place of multiple dimensions instead of a static container,[80] it is also used to construe the feminized body as a "storage bin"[81] whenever it is associated with menstruation, pregnancy, and birth to define the female sex-skeleton as a room for maternity. This way, both male and female gender-bodices are determined by the function of their binary sex-skeletons, based on the *doxa* of heteronormative penetration. The social consequences of correlating body images affect male and female gender-bodices likewise, but not equally.[82]

A spatialized bodily process that causes, as previously mentioned, a lot of attention within the halakhic discourse is menstruation.[83] In b. Nid. 17b it is drawn on the house-metaphor to identify the source of menstrual blood in distinction from exceptional bleedings. In a quote from an anonymous group of sages the uterus is thereby described as a room, the vaginal canal as a corridor, and the bladder as an upper story (b. Nid. 17b).[84] The architecture of this metaphorical dwelling is especially interesting in terms of the organs' anatomical location. In order to describe the bladder as an upper story, being located above the uterus, the human body must be observed in a horizontally lying position. Only then the description of the vaginal canal as an entry corridor becomes more visual as well. I assume that this perspective is another component of the metaphorical construction of the feminized body as a horizontally placed disposition of rooms, to be opened by a male key holder's penis in a heteronormative act of penetration.

According to the rabbis' anatomical insight the procreation of human life comes to pass by the confluence of male and female seed, as respective emissions of moisture were understood.[85] Consequently, the blood flow of menstruation was "considered to be a loss of a potential new life,"[86] causing ritual impurity according to Lev 15:19–24.[87] Accordingly, established cleaning rituals were nevertheless practiced even after the discontinuation of the temple cult.[88] There is a good case to believe that one's own state of (im)purity related to menstruation was a matter of personal responsibility from ancient times (m. Nid. 1:1). It became part of the female gender-bodice very early, not least to the extent that the individual caretaking led to forms of social suppression (expulsion, isolation, mystification). The socio-cultural handling of menstruation inscribed thus a power-related stigmatization into the feminized sex-skeleton, whose internalization Pierre Bourdieu would identify as the symbolic violence of self-suppression.[89] Along menstruation, conception, pregnancy, or childbirth the way the rabbis talk about the human body constructs the feminized sex-skeleton in relation to the practical arrangement of everyday living, whereas the ascriptions to the masculinized sex-skeleton with reference to priests for example remained mostly theoretical.[90]

The rabbinic talk of masculinized body parts within the Babylonian Talmud can occasionally be identified as emblematic instead of metaphorical, representing certain qualities. In b. Sanh. 101b and b. Mo'ed Qaṭ. 18a for example, a penis is taken as a transmitter for signs of a leader's power and contributes thereby to the construction of a hegemonial male gender-bodice. So, while the masculinized sex-skeleton refers to attributes of a male gender-bodice according to the rabbinic talk of body, the feminized sex-skeleton becomes a metaphor for sacral architecture and objects. In the Babylonian Talmud the staves of the Ark of the Covenant, protruding through the curtain, are compared to a woman's breasts becoming apparent through their cloth, with reference to Song 1:13 (b. Yoma 54a; cf. b. Menaḥ. 98b). For another example, the biblical line "my breasts are like towers" (Song 8:10) is interpreted in b. B. Bat. 8a as representing synagogues and study halls (see also b. Pesaḥ. 87a). These examples illustrate that while the Amoraim consider masculine body parts as symbolically representing social qualities of a male gender-bodice, they adopt a biblical text's direct speech of female breasts as metaphorical language, interpreting it according to sacral architecture, thereby silencing the described biblical woman. Furthermore, the Torah is compared to a female breast in a manner of feeding (b. 'Erub. 54b), and so is the taste of the biblical *manna* compared to the taste of breastmilk (b. Yoma 75a). Such metaphorization of direct talk of the feminized body reinforces the impression that the Babylonian Amoraim mystified the female sex-skeleton. The linguistic modeling of both masculinized and feminized bodies have an impact on the male and female gender-bodices and their social relation. But the formation of this impact is exclusively under the control of those who have the sovereignty of composition of post-biblical law, the prerogative of interpretation over biblical texts, and finally the cultural power of telling stories.

THE BODY AS A WONDERLAND: AGGADIC TRANSFORMATIONS AND METAMORPHOSES OF SEX/GENDER

It should be made clear so far that the Babylonian Amoraim established a sovereignty over the linguistic modeling of sex-skeletons and the construction of gender-bodices in many ways by the talk of the human body. As "the subjection of one's body to another person's gaze is a quintessential way of asserting the power of the one looking over the one being looked at,"[91] the rabbis assert their hegemonial power mainly over non-male sexes/genders, especially by the aid of halakhic debates. Within aggadic traditions this approach was built up to a power of narration, establishing further scopes of action for the construction of sex/gender. I will conclude my observations on the rabbinic talk of the human body in the following with narrative examples of transformations and metamorphoses in the Babylonian Talmud with parallel traditions in the likewise Amoraic, but Palestinian aggadic Midrash *Genesis Rabbah* (fifth century CE).

In both sources a productive reception of Gen 30:10 is recorded, narrating about pregnant Leah's concern, her sister Rachel might be embarrassed if she would give birth to another male child, whereupon the fetus inside her womb was metamorphosed from male into female, then being born as Dinah (b. Ber. 60a and Gen. Rab. 72:6). This aggadic tradition conforms the previously mentioned rabbinic assumption of a prior development of masculine fetuses (b. Nid. 30a–31b). Likewise, the tradition expresses the higher renown of a male gender-bodice and therefore represents the rabbinic *doxa* of a sex/gender binarity, with the male considered as the human prototype. Based on this sex/gender dualism, the *niph'al*-form of the root הפך (*hāpak*) in b. Ber. 60a, to be translated as "being changed" into the opposite of something, indicates the prenatal metamorphosis of the fetus inside Leah's womb. Thereby, the child's gender-bodice is pronounced biologically, dependent on its sex-skeleton, even though these circumstances are obscured by the story's miraculous punch line. This becomes necessary as for the rabbis solely the origin of the fetal sex-skeleton is debatable, but not the prerogatives of its associated gender-bodice.

Corresponding narrative constructions of human bodies may help to establish the self-evidence of an anticipated male normativity and to legitimize sex/gender-related dichotomies within the halakhic discourse. The associated metaphorization and mystification of feminized bodies revealed here in the Babylonian Talmud[92] enabled its male authors[93] to establish a narrative prerogative of interpretation over feminized bodily procedures such as conception, childbirth, and breastfeeding.[94] Carried to the extremes, this leads to aggadic traditions of transforming men, who developed female breasts to become able to nurse a child (b. Shab. 53b) or were just enabled to lactate, as told in Gen. Rab. 30:8 about Mordechai breastfeeding Esther. These miracles appeared out of necessity, as in spite of every effort, a wet nurse was not available. In any case, the male characters have neither been metamorphosed into a feminized sex-skeleton nor being regarded as queer sex-skeletons. The aggadic freedom of narration allows to add the ability of breastfeeding to a male sex/gender identity like an additionally acquired feature, without questioning the male gender-bodice or discussing the masculinized body. In Gen. Rab. 30:8 this occurrence is even halakhically safeguarded, as the milk of a male is declared as clean.

Especially female breasts are often functionalized in aggadic traditions into a vessel that works as a liquid dispenser. A narrative in b. B. Meṣ. 87a for example talks about Abraham and Sarah inviting people who did not believe that they became birth parents at a great age. As their guests brought their own children with them but not their wet nurses, and the children suddenly became hungry, Sarah's breasts were "opened like two springs" (b. B. Meṣ. 87a) and she nursed all of the children, proving her motherhood to the community. The described transformation of Sarah's body, leading to an extensive milk ejection reflex, consolidates her social status as a mother. But the doubts about Abraham's biological fatherhood are then resolved when Isaac's face transforms into the image of Abraham's face (b. B. Meṣ. 87a). Accordingly, Abraham's body needs no transformation to prove his fatherhood, but it is his offspring's face that adjusts to resemble the face of Abraham and thereby confirms his fatherly gender-bodice.[95]

These narrative examples shed additional light on the rabbinic talk of the human body and in how far it functions as an instrument for the construction of a normative system of binary sex-skeletons to form and establish ipso facto a socio-cultural dichotomy of male and female gender-bodices. I have identified this so far for the Babylonian Talmud, where halakhic and aggadic traditions are extensively recorded. But based on the intertextual relations to many further rabbinic texts that I have already referred to on several occasions within this chapter, I have demonstrated the additional heuristic value by following this specific aspect of gender studies and expanding it to further research within the field of rabbinic literature. As it became apparent so far, the talk of the human body is of enormous relevance for the construction of sex/gender identities, as a person's social status is always bound to its gender-bodice, which is in turn constantly tied to a person's sex-skeleton. Both are constructed culturally, then as now. If we acknowledge this for the rabbinic tradition and encourage further research in this field, we should be able to unlock the universal binary rationality in our minds in order to accept and internalize the reciprocal interrelation of sex and gender. This way we could start to follow new, non-binary approaches in research that might help us to understand the world and us within not alone along the terms and conditions of our academic framing but also according to the reality of their irrational complexity.

NOTES

1. See for examples from the field of rabbinic literature Charlotte E. Fonrobert, "Regulating the Human Body: Rabbinic Legal Discourse and the Making of Jewish

Gender," in *The Cambridge Companion to the Talmud and Rabbinic Literature*, ed. idem and Martin S. Jaffee (New York: Cambridge University Press, 2007), 270–94, here 272 and Sarra Lev, "Inside/Outside. The Rabbinic Negotiation of Binaries BT *Me'ilah* 15b–16a," *Nashim: A Journal of Jewish Women's Studies and Gender Issues* 28 (2015): 106–19, here 107–08. Most of these publications are referring to Judith Butler, *Gender Trouble. Feminism and the Subversion of Identity* (New York: Routledge, 1990).

2. A continual use of the undefinedly distinguished categories 'men' and 'women' for instance is found in Elizabeth Shanks Alexander, *Gender and Timebound Commandments in Judaism* (New York: Cambridge University Press, 2013), 44, 60, 62 et al. Judith Hauptman, *Rereading the Rabbis. A Woman's Voice* (Boulder/Oxford: Westview Press, 1998), 30–31 et al. and Fonrobert, "Regulating," 271.

3. Judith Butler, *Bodies That Matter. On the Discursive Limits of "Sex"* (New York: Routledge, 1993 [Reprint 2014]), 28.

4. According to Elizabeth Shanks Alexander the rabbis did not construct different sexes, but they construct gender as "*knowledge* about sexual difference" (emphasis in original). Alexander, *Gender*, 45.

5. See Butler, *Gender Trouble. Feminism and the Subversion of Identity*, 11–13 and Anne Fausto-Sterling, *Sexing the Body. Gender Politics and the Construction of Sexuality* (New York: Basic Books, 2000), 21–22.

6. See Butler, *Bodies That Matter*, 29.

7. See Fausto-Sterling, *Sexing the Body*, 3–5, 46 and Claire Ainsworth, "Sex Redefined," *Nature* 518 (February 15, 2015): 288–91.

8. About the understanding of sex/gender as a category of knowledge see Ulrike E. Auga, *An Epistemology of Religion and Gender. Biopolitics—Performativity—Agency* (New York: Routledge, 2020), 35.

9. See Butler, *Gender Trouble*, 30–34.

10. Thomas Laqueur, *Making Sex. Body and Gender from the Greeks to Freud*, 10th ed. (Cambridge/London: Harvard University Press, 2003), 13. See also Cynthia M. Baker, *Rebuilding the House of Israel. Architectures of Gender in Jewish Antiquity* (Stanford: Stanford University Press, 2002), 75.

11. This is vindicable by an adopted structuralist linguistic understanding of literature as a system "through which meaning is constructed and cultural practices organized and by which, accordingly, people represent and understand their world, including who they are and how they relate to others" (Joan W. Scott, "Deconstructing Equality-Versus-Difference: Or, the Uses of Poststructuralist Theory for Feminism," in *The Postmodern Turn. New Perspectives on Social Theory*, ed. Steven Seidman [New York: Cambridge University Press, 1995], 282–98, here 283) which formulates essential cultural functions of rabbinic literature.

12. See Anna Babka, *Gender(-Forschung) und Dekonstruktion. Vorläufige Überlegungen zu den Zusammenhängen zweier Reflexionsräume* (Wien, 2007), 2.

13. Butler, *Gender Trouble*, 13. "Indeed, if structuralism has taught us anything it is that humans impose their sense of opposition onto a world of continuous shades of difference and similarity." Lacqueur, *Making Sex*, 19. Such dichotomies are never value-neutral but (re)establish hierarchies of norms and deficient abnormalities.

See Anna Babka and Gerald Posselt, *Gender und Dekonstruktion* (Wien: Facultas, 2016), 29.

14. Pierre Bourdieu and Loïc J. D. Wacquant, *An Invitation to Reflexive Sociology* (Cambridge: Polity Press, 1992), 122.

15. Alexander, *Gender*, 60. The quotation expresses the underlying conception of exactly two naturally and obviously existing biological sexes that have to be identified unalterably. Likewise, Charlotte Fonrobert is admittedly correct by saying that "different cultures inscribe" the reality of different bodies "with their specific ways of differentiating between genders," but she is limiting "this reality" by saying that the difference of natural bodies is constituted of the difference between "male and female." Fonrobert, "Regulating," 271.

16. Bourdieu and Wacquant, *An Invitation*, 122.

17. Scott, "Deconstructing," 286.

18. See Frederico Dal Bo, *Deconstructing the Talmud: The Absolute Book* (New York: Routledge, 2020), 1.

19. Fonrobert, "Regulating," 272. Reservations about the applicability of Western feminist theory on "the reading of gender differences in Talmudic literature" are already formulated in Charlotte Fonrobert, *Menstrual Purity. Rabbinic and Christian Reconstructions of Biblical Gender* (Stanford: Stanford University Press, 2000), 43.

20. Fonrobert, "Regulating," 271.

21. Any talk of nature inevitably implies an idea of culture as its opposition. Concerning the naturalization of sex/gender see Nina Degele, *Gender/Queer Studies* (Paderborn: Wilhelm Fink, 2008), 60–62.

22. See Michael L. Satlow, "'Try to Be a Man'. The Rabbinic Construction of Masculinity," *Harvard Theological Review* 89, no. 1 (1996): 19–40, here 28, Judith R. Baskin, *Midrashic Women. Formations of the Feminine in Rabbinic Literature* (Hanover: Brandeis University Press, 2002), 47 and Hauptman, *Rereading the Rabbis*, 30.

23. See Pierre Bourdieu, *Outline of a Theory of Practice*, trans. Richard Nice (Cambridge: Cambridge University Press, 2005), 16. For examples of expressions of a consequently established gender *doxa* see Penelope Eckert and Sally McConnel-Ginet, *Language and Gender* (Cambridge: Cambridge University Press, 2003), 9.

24. See Pierre Bourdieu, "Die männliche Herrschaft," in *Ein alltägliches Spiel: Geschlechterkonstruktion in der sozialen Praxis*, ed. Irene Dölling and Beate Krais (Frankfurt am Main: Suhrkamp, 1997), 153–217, here 169. "Because the social principle of vision constructs the anatomical difference and because this socially constructed difference becomes the basis and apparently natural justification of the social vision which founds it, there is thus a relationship of circular causality which confines thought within the self-evidence of relations of domination." Pierre Bourdieu, *Masculine Domination*, trans. Richard Nice (Stanford: Stanford University Press, 2001), 11.

25. See Bourdieu, "Herrschaft," 168 and also Butler, *Gender Trouble*, 175–76. The objection concerning frequent occurrences of non-binary sex/gender identities (*androgynos, tumtum, saris,* or *aylonit*) within the halakhic literature can be invalidated by the notice that these are nevertheless physically and legally located within

binary sex/gender categories. See Lev, "Inside/Outside," 118 and cf. Fonrobert, "Regulating," 289.

26. See Fonrobert, *Menstrual Purity*, 44. In her argumentation Fonrobert is proceeding from the halakhic discourse around Lev 15:2 and 9, although the biblical text differentiates not between male and female bodies but between their discharges, based on the manifested *doxa* of a distinction between feminized and masculinized bodies.

27. Fonrobert, *Menstrual Purity*, 63.

28. "The play of differences supposes, in effect, syntheses and referrals which forbid at any moment, or in any sense, that a simple element be present in and of itself, referring only to itself. Whether in the order of spoken or written discourse, no element can function as a sign without referring to another element which itself is not simply present." Jacques Derrida, "Semiology and Grammatology. Interview with Julia Kristeva," in idem. *Positions*, trans. Alan Bass (Chicago: The University of Chicago Press, 1981), 15–35, here 26.

29. See Bourdieu and Wacquant, *An Invitation*, 122. According to Derrida, there exists any number of non-human/non-male/non-female entities that differ from the human male/female. Correspondingly, rabbinic comparisons explain a woman's breast being located near the heart, at a "more beautiful" or "honorable place" than most animals' breasts (b. Ber. 10a; Lev. Rab. 14:3). The binary coding of male-female-oppositions is nevertheless primarily established within biblical traditions and rabbinical discourses, based on the androcentric worldview of the humans' rise into a cultural creature in opposition to nature. See Daniel Vorpahl, "A Donkey That Speaks Is a Donkey No Less: Talking Animals in the Hebrew Bible and Its Early Jewish Reception," in *Talking Animals in Ancient Literature*, ed. Hedwig Schmalzgruber (Heidelberg: Universitätsverlag Winter, 2020), 509–25, here 509–10, 516.

30. Elsewhere, Fonrobert states the same concerning the Mishnah. See Fonrobert, *Menstrual Purity*, 58.

31. See Michael Segal, *The Book of Jubilees. Rewritten Bible, Redaction, Ideology and Theology* (Leiden/Boston: Brill, 2007), 50–51.

32. About the social phenomenon of "cultural genitals" see Suzanne J. Kessler and Wendy McKenna, *Gender. An Ethnomethodological Approach* (New York: Wiley, 1978), 154.

33. A bodice is a laced garment similar to a corset. I have chosen this archaic term for two reasons. For one thing because it is less frequently known nowadays and thus easier to adapt, and for a second thing because it is etymologically related to the term bodies.

34. See Hauptman, *Rereading the Rabbis*, 4.

35. Lev, "Inside/Outside," 115.

36. See David Weiss Halivni, *The Formation of the Babylonian Talmud* (New York: Oxford University Press, 2013), xxvii and Richard Kalmin, *Jewish Babylonia Between Persia and Roman Palestine* (New York: Oxford University Press, 2006), vii.

37. See Tal Ilan, Lorena Miralles-Maciá and Ronit Nikolsky, "Die Bibel und die Frauen—Rabbinische Literatur Einleitung," in *Rabbinische Literatur*, ed. idem (Stuttgart: Kohlhammer, 2021), 9–48, here 28.

38. See Hauptman, *Rereading the Rabbis*, 30–31 and Satlow, "'Try to Be a Man'," 27, 32.
39. Satlow, "'Try to Be a Man'," 27.
40. See Satlow, "'Try to Be a Man'," 29. According to b. Nid. 31a–b, "a woman will conceive a male child if she 'emits her seed' first", which presumably refers to the female orgasm. This male-heteronormative sexualization does furthermore discredit any other forms of sexuality, which according to b. Ned. 20a–b will lead to nonconforming children, which depreciates persons with disabilities (dumb, deaf, blind). See ibid., 31.
41. See Satlow, "'Try to Be a Man'," 28–29. In b. Ketub. 65a it is stated that after four cups of wine women would even request intercourse from "a donkey in the marketplace."
42. See Bourdieu, "Herrschaft," 170.
43. See Bourdieu, *Masculine Domination*, 34–35.
44. Lev 18:22 adds the prohibition of homosexual penetration. The patriarchal aspiration for the procreation of 'the man' is hereof only one aspect of heteronormativity, insofar as any other forms of non-penetrative intercourse, or lesbian intercourse for example, are also not considered in the Torah.
45. See Satlow, "'Try to Be a Man'," 32.
46. See Daniel Boyarin, *Carnal Israel. Reading Sex in Talmudic Culture* (Berkely/Los Angeles: University of California Press, 1993), 5.
47. See Fonrobert, *Menstrual Purity*, 40 and Ilan, Miralles-Maciá and Nikolsky, "Die Bibel," 17.
48. See M. J. H. M. Poorthuis, "Rebekah as a Virgin on her Way to Marriage: A Study in Midrash," *JSJ* 29, no. 4 (1998): 438–62, here 438. That virginity was principally measured by the alleged intactness of the hymen (vaginal corona) can also be seen as being affirmed when later single rabbinic traditions back away from that criterion. See ibid., 443–44 and 455–56. About the myth-making of the vaginal corona as a maidenhead see Anna Knöfel Magnusson, *Vaginal Corona. Myths Surrounding Virginity—Your Questions Answered*, ed. RFSU (Stockholm: Brommatryck & Brolins, 2009) [https://www.rfsu.se/globalassets/pdf/vaginal-corona-english.pdf]. I want to emphasize that I am using the term myth here in a colloquial context and not exactly according to its understanding in cultural sciences.
49. See m. Ketub. 1:1–3.6–10; 3:1 and its constructive reception in b. Ketub. 2a; 10a; 11a–b; 12b–13a.
50. See Shai Secunda, *The Talmud's Red Fence. Menstrual Impurity and Difference in Babylonian Judaism and Its Sasanian Context* (Oxford: Oxford University Press, 2020), 177 and Babka, *Gender(-Forschung)*, 16.
51. "Because masculinity can often function as an invisible norm, it might be harder to locate normalized masculinity in a given discourse", says Todd W. Reeser, *Masculinities in Theory. An Introduction* (Oxford: Wiley-Blackwell, 2010), 32.
52. The statistics of the term's appearances were taken from Rabbi Elliot Kukla, "Terms for Gender Diversity in Classical Jewish Texts," TransTorah, last modified June 11, 2021, http://www.transtorah.org/PDFs/Classical_Jewish_Terms_for_Gender_Diversity.pdf.

53. Anne Fausto-Sterling considers that intersexual newborn in modern times "disappear from view" because they may pass through surgical transition, while in the past they were generally accepted as they were born. Fausto-Sterling, *Sexing the Body*, 31.

54. For an overview about the queer sex-skeletons described within the Talmudic literature and the special halakhic regulations that are applied to them see Sarra Lev, "They Treat Him As a Man and See Him As a Woman: The Tannaitic Understanding of the Congenital Eunuch," *JSQ* 17, no. 3 (2010): 213–43. An extensive example of special halakhic regulations for an *androgynus* can be found in the appendix of m. Bik. 4.

55. See Sarra Lev, "How the *'Aylonit* Got Her Sex," *AJS Review* 31, no. 1 (2007): 297–316, here 310–16.

56. Fonrobert, "Regulating," 289.

57. Examples of the practical consequences of this legal age scaling become apparent in b. Nid. 45a concerning marriage or in m. Ketub. 3:8 concerning cases of rape and enslavement.

58. Within a Baraita it is assumed that the frequent use of urban bathhouses favored the growth of hair, while the grinding with mills, commonly outside of cities, might have favored the development of breasts (b. Nid. 48b).

59. See Fonrobert, "Regulating," 277–78. In b. Nid. 48b it is regulated in which cases the physical examination shall be carried out by women.

60. See Fonrobert, "Regulating," 276–77 and idem, *Menstrual Purity*, 54. See also Mira Balberg, *Purity, Body, and Self in Early Rabbinic Literature* (Berkeley/Los Angeles: University of California Press, 2014), 62 about the construction of the equation of the human body and the self.

61. See Bourdieu, "Herrschaft," 175.

62. The human body is thereby as well constructed and valued according to normative provisions of its form. By b. Ketub. 75a for example, it was considered to be a blemish when the space between female breasts was a hand wide, while the ideal space should be of a three-finger-size. Also, a woman's breasts should not be 'too big' (ibid.).

63. See Butler, *Gender Trouble*, 156–60 and Maja Suderland, "Habitus und Literatur. Literarische Texte in Bourdieus Soziologie," in *Pierre Bourdieus Konzeption des Habitus. Grundlagen, Zugänge, Forschungsperspektiven*, ed. Alexander Lenger et al. (Wiesbaden: Springer, 2013), 325–45, here 331–32.

64. See Christian Hoffstadt, *Denkräume und Denkbewegungen. Untersuchungen zum metaphorischen Gebrauch der Sprache der Räumlichkeit* (Karlsruhe: KIT Scientific Publishing, 2009), 63.

65. George Lakoff and Mark Johnson, *Metaphors We Live By* (Chicago/London: The University of Chicago Press, 1980), 3.

66. See Fonrobert, *Menstrual Purity*, 40.

67. Julia Goschler, "Embodiment and Body Metaphors," *metaphoric.de* 9 (2005): 33–52, here 35.

68. See Sara Kipfer and Silvia Schroer, "Der Körper als Gefäß. Eine Studie zur visuellen Anthropologie des Alten Orients," *lectio difficilior* 1 (2015): 1–26, here 2–5.

69. See Kipfer and Schroer, "Körper als Gefäß," 3.
70. See Kipfer and Schroer, "Körper als Gefäß," 15.
71. "Menstrual blood was imagined as having a permanent source in the womb, the womb imagined as an organ continually being full of blood." Ida Fröhlich, "The Female Body in Second Temple Literature," in *Religion and Female Body in Ancient Judaism and Its Environment*, ed. Géza Xeravits (Berlin/Boston: De Gruyter, 2015), 109–27, here 123. See also Kipfer and Schroer, "Körper als Gefäß," 15.
72. See Balberg, *Purity*, 59–62 and Fröhlich, "Female Body," 124.
73. Balberg, *Purity*, 59.
74. See also Fonrobert, *Menstrual Purity*, 58.
75. See Baker, *Rebuilding*, 56–57.
76. Fonrobert, *Menstrual Purity*, 60. See also See Baker, *Rebuilding*, 56.
77. See Fonrobert, *Menstrual Purity*, 59.
78. Similar in b. Moʿed Qaṭ. 7b a woman is identified with a tent. Nevertheless, in Gen. Rab. 18:3 for example it is mentioned that women's bodies are constructed with more storage rooms to receive embryos, which suggests that masculinized bodies are constructed with less storage rooms, but still with rooms. But such an idea is, to the best of my knowledge, not further explained within the rabbinic literature.
79. Fonrobert, *Menstrual Purity*, 63. See Baker, *Rebuilding*, 54.
80. See Baker, *Rebuilding*, 57.
81. Fonrobert, *Menstrual Purity*, 58.
82. The social consequences of halakhic norms and instructions have to be ascertained in proportion to local historical circumstances, as the law written down is not identical to the social reality it describes or regulates. See Hauptman, *Rereading the Rabbis*, 6, 35 and Ilan, Miralles-Maciá and Nikolsky, "Die Bibel," 14.
83. See Thomas Hieke, "Menstruation and Impurity. Regular Abstention from the Cult According to Leviticus 15:19–24 and Some Examples for the Reception of the Biblical Text in Early Judaism," in *Religion and Female Body in Ancient Judaism and Its Environment*, ed. Géza Xeravits (Berlin/Boston: De Gruyter, 2015), 54–70, here 65–67.
84. See also b. Nid. 41b; 65b and m. Nid. 2:5. Charlotte Fonrobert states furthermore that the body-related house-metaphor was inspired by the Greco-Roman medical literature. See Fonrobert, *Menstrual Purity*, 61–63.
85. See Fröhlich, "Female Body," 121–23.
86. Fröhlich, "Female Body," 123.
87. The same consequence applies to male seminal emission (Lev 15:16–18), but without any metaphorical ascriptions.
88. See Hieke, "Menstruation," 55.
89. See Bourdieu, "Herrschaft," 170.
90. Theoretical considerations demand, for example, an unimpaired penis and testicles (m. Yebam. 8:1–2), symmetrical body proportions, and a non-female breast (m. Bek. 7) for the ability to execute priestly service. A priest was declared invalid when having breasts the "size of woman's" or a swollen belly (b. Bek. 44b).
91. Mira Balberg, "Rabbinic Authority, Medical Rhetoric, and Body Hermeneutics in Mishnah Nega'im," *AJS Review* 35, no. 2 (November 2011): 323–46, here 330.

92. See b. Pesaḥ. 87a; b. B. Bat. 8a; b. Bek. 45a; b. Nid. 17b.41b and 65b.
93. See Secunda, *Talmud's Red Fence*, 177 and Hauptman, *Rereading the Rabbis*, 31.
94. See b. 'Erub. 54b; b. Yoma 75a and cf. m. Nid. 1–2 and Sipre Num. 89:1.
95. It can be assumed that the Babylonian Amoraim responsible for this aggadic tradition were familiar with the story's version recorded in Gen. Rab. 53:9. See Susanne Plietzsch, "Übernatürliche Schönheit, universale Mutter und Evastochter. Sara in Bereshit Rabba und im Babylonischen Talmud," in *Rabbinische Literatur*, ed. Tal Ilan, Lorena Miralles-Maciá, and Ronit Nikolsky (Stuttgart: Kohlhammer, 2021), 219–45, here 238–42.

BIBLIOGRAPHY

Primary Literature

Bereshit Rabbah / מדרש בראשית רבא. 3 Vol. Edited by Julius Theodor and Chanoch Albek. Jerusalem: Shalem Books, 1996.
Biblia Hebraica Stuttgartensia. Edited by Rudolph Kittel et al. Stuttgart: Deutsche Bibelgesellschaft, 1997.
Die Mischna / משניות. Vol.: *Sanhedrin / סנהדרין*. Edited by Michael Krupp et al. Jerusalem: Lee Achim Sefarim, 2006.
Die Mischna / משניות. Vol.: *Nidda / נידה*. Edited by Melanie Mordhorst-Mayer and Haim Mayer. Jerusalem: Lee Achim Sefarim, 2016.
Talmud Bavli. 44 Vol. Edited by Adin Steinsaltz. Jerusalem: Koren, 1982–2009.

Secondary Literature

Ainsworth, Claire. "Sex Redefined." *Nature* 518 (February 15, 2015): 288–91.
Alexander, Elizabeth Shanks. *Gender and Timebound Commandments in Judaism*. New York: Cambridge University Press, 2013.
Auga, Ulrike E. *An Epistemology of Religion and Gender. Biopolitics—Performativity—Agency*. New York: Routledge, 2020.
Babka, Anna. *Gender(-Forschung) und Dekonstruktion. Vorläufige Überlegungen zu den Zusammenhängen zweier Reflexionsräume*. Wien, 2007.
Babka, Anna and Gerald Posselt. *Gender und Dekonstruktion*. Wien: Facultas, 2016.
Baker, Cynthia M. *Rebuilding the House of Israel. Architectures of Gender in Jewish Antiquity*. Stanford: Stanford University Press, 2002.
Balberg, Mira. "Rabbinic Authority, Medical Rhetoric, and Body Hermeneutics in Mishnah Nega'im." *AJS Review* 35, no. 2 (November 2011): 323–46.
Balberg, Mira. *Purity, Body, and Self in Early Rabbinic Literature*. Berkeley/Los Angeles: University of California Press, 2014.
Baskin, Judith R. *Midrashic Women. Formations of the Feminine in Rabbinic Literature*. Hanover: Brandeis University Press, 2002.

Bourdieu, Pierre. "Die männliche Herrschaft." In *Ein alltägliches Spiel: Geschlechterkonstruktion in der sozialen Praxis*, edited by Irene Dölling and Beate Krais, 153–217. Frankfurt am Main: Suhrkamp, 1997.
Bourdieu, Pierre. *Masculine Domination*. Translated by Richard Nice. Stanford: Stanford University Press, 2001.
Bourdieu, Pierre. *Outline of a Theory of Practice*. Translated by Richard Nice. Cambridge: Cambridge University Press, 2005.
Bourdieu, Pierre and Loïc J. D. Wacquant. *An Invitation to Reflexive Sociology*. Cambridge: Polity Press, 1992.
Boyarin, Daniel. *Carnal Israel. Reading Sex in Talmudic Culture*. Berkeley/Los Angeles: University of California Press, 1993.
Butler, Judith. *Gender Trouble. Feminism and the Subversion of Identity*. New York: Routledge, 1990 (Reprint 2008).
Butler, Judith. *Bodies That Matter. On the Discursive Limits of "Sex."* New York: Routledge, 1993 (Reprint 2014).
Dal Bo, Frederico. *Deconstructing the Talmud. The Absolute Book*. New York: Routledge, 2020.
Degele, Nina. *Gender/Queer Studies*. Paderborn: Wilhelm Fink, 2008.
Derrida, Jacques. "Semiology and Grammatology. Interview with Julia Kristeva." In *Positions*, translated by Alan Bass, 15–35. Chicago: The University of Chicago Press, 1981.
Eckert, Penelope and Sally McConnel-Ginet. *Language and Gender*. Cambridge: Cambridge University Press, 2003.
Fausto-Sterling, Anne. *Sexing the Body. Gender Politics and the Construction of Sexuality*. New York: Basic Books, 2000.
Fonrobert, Charlotte E. *Menstrual Purity. Rabbinic and Christian Reconstructions of Biblical Gender*. Stanford: Stanford University Press, 2000.
Fonrobert, Charlotte E. "Regulating the Human Body: Rabbinic Legal Discourse and the Making of Jewish Gender." In *The Cambridge Companion to the Talmud and Rabbinic Literature*, edited by idem and Martin S. Jaffee, 270–94. New York: Cambridge University Press, 2007.
Fröhlich, Ida. "The Female Body in Second Temple Literature." In *Religion and Female Body in Ancient Judaism and Its Environment*, edited by Géza Xeravits, 109–27. Berlin/Boston: De Gruyter, 2015.
Goschler, Juliana. "Embodiment and Body Metaphors." *metaphoric.de* 9 (2005): 33–52.
Halivni, David Weiss. *The Formation of the Babylonian Talmud*. New York: Oxford University Press, 2013.
Hauptman, Judith. *Rereading the Rabbis. A Woman's Voice*. Boulder/Oxford: Westview Press, 1998.
Hieke, Thomas. "Menstruation and Impurity. Regular Abstention from the Cult According to Leviticus 15:19–24 and Some Examples for the Reception of the Biblical Text in Early Judaism." In *Religion and Female Body in Ancient Judaism and Its Environment*, edited by Géza Xeravits, 54–70. Berlin/Boston: De Gruyter, 2015.

Hoffstadt, Christian. *Denkräume und Denkbewegungen. Untersuchungen zum metaphorischen Gebrauch der Sprache der Räumlichkeit.* Karlsruhe: KIT Scientific Publishing, 2009.

Kalmin, Richard. *Jewish Babylonia Between Persia and Roman Palestine.* New York: Oxford University Press, 2006.

Kessler, Suzanne J. and Wendy McKenna. *Gender: An Ethnomethodological Approach.* New York: Wiley, 1978.

Kipfer, Sara and Silvia Schroer. "Der Körper als Gefäß. Eine Studie zur visuellen Anthropologie des Alten Orients." *lectio difficilior* 1 (2015): 1–26.

Knöfel Magnusson, Anna. *Vaginal Corona. Myths Surrounding Virginity—Your Questions Answered*, edited by RFSU. Stockholm: Brommatryck & Brolins, 2009.

Koller, Andreas. "Doxa (doxa)." In *Bourdieu-Handbuch*, edited by Gerhard Fröhlich and Boike Rehbein, 79–80. Stuttgart: J. B. Metzler, 2014.

Kukla, Elliot. "Terms for Gender Diversity in Classical Jewish Texts." *TransTorah*, last modified June 11, 2021. http://www.transtorah.org/PDFs/Classical_Jewish_Terms_for_Gender_Diversity.pdf.

Lakoff, George and Mark Johnson. *Metaphors We Live By.* Chicago/London: The University of Chicago Press, 1980.

Lev, Sarra. "How the *'Aylonit* Got Her Sex." *AJS Review* 31, no. 1 (2007): 297–316.

Lev, Sarra. "They Treat Him as a Man and See Him As a Woman: The Tannaitic Understanding of the Congenital Eunuch." *JSQ* 17, no. 3 (2010): 213–43.

Lev, Sarra. "Inside/Outside. The Rabbinic Negotiation of Binaries BT *Me'ilah* 15b–16a." *Nashim: A Journal of Jewish Women's Studies and Gender Issues* 28 (2015): 106–19.

Plietzsch, Susanne. "Übernatürliche Schönheit, universale Mutter und Evastochter. Sara in Bereshit Rabba und im Babylonischen Talmud." In *Rabbinische Literatur*, edited by Tal Ilan, Lorena Miralles-Maciá, and Ronit Nikolsky, 219–45. Stuttgart: Kohlhammer, 2021.

Poorthuis, Marcel J. H. M. "Rebekah as a Virgin on her Way to Marriage: A Study in Midrash." *JSJ* 29, no. 4 (1998): 438–62.

Reeser, Todd W. *Masculinities in Theory. An Introduction.* Oxford: Wiley-Blackwell, 2010.

Satlow, Michael L. "'Try to Be a Man': The Rabbinic Construction Of Masculinity." *HTR* 89, no. 1 (1996): 19–40.

Scott, Joan W. "Deconstructing Equality-Versus-Difference: Or, the Uses of Poststructuralist Theory for Feminism." In *The Postmodern Turn. New Perspectives on Social Theory*, edited by Steven Seidman, 282–98. New York: Cambridge University Press, 1995.

Secunda, Shai. *The Talmud's Red Fence. Menstrual Impurity and Difference in Babylonian Judaism and Its Sasanian Context.* Oxford: Oxford University Press, 2020.

Segal, Michael. *The Book of Jubilees. Rewritten Bible, Redaction, Ideology and Theology.* Leiden/Boston: Brill, 2007.

Suderland, Maja. "Habitus und Literatur. Literarische Texte in Bourdieus Soziologie." In *Pierre Bourdieus Konzeption des Habitus. Grundlagen, Zugänge,*

Forschungsperspektiven, edited by Alexander Lenger et al., 325–45. Wiesbaden: Springer, 2013.

Vorpahl, Daniel. "A Donkey That Speaks Is a Donkey No Less: Talking Animals in the Hebrew Bible and Its Early Jewish Reception." In *Talking Animals in Ancient Literature*, edited by Hedwig Schmalzgruber, 509–25. Heidelberg: Universitätsverlag Winter, 2020.

11

Shush Shelamzion, Your Brother Shimon Is Speaking!

A Peculiar Pattern of Palestinian Passivation

Andrew W. Higginbotham

Rabbinic literature in the Talmudic period mainly voice the concerns of men. As such, its internal debates are voiced by the male rabbis and are oriented to the male gaze on the world in which its readers dwell. The rabbis and their disciples are shown in their literature to be the true power center, with both the monarchy and the priesthood functioning as biblically mandated but practically sidelined entities. Women in particular play a marginal—and marginalized—role and their contributions to the discussion are often re-attributed to men. Tal Ilan discusses this phenomenon in three ways: women quoting scripture—who are anonymized, women asking about difficult verses—who become generic characters, and women who reference biblical narratives generally—who likewise remain nameless.[1] The episodes reviewed in this study may then constitute a fourth way, how women enter into halakhic discussions and how they are marginalized. If we read the five parallels of the "Shimon deceives Yannai and then prays at his banquet" narrative, we see a progressive erasure of Queen Shelamzion (141–67 BCE) from the scene. I will argue in this study that the Yerushalmi, more proximate in time to Shelamzion, erases her power or even her presence from its version of the rabbinic episodes that occurred ostensibly during her reign, while the Babylonian and midrashic sources restore her identity and agency.

METHOD, AFTER TAL ILAN

Tal Ilan, in her book *Silencing the Queen* (2006), demonstrated the effacement that Shelamzion (Alexandra), as well as other early Jewish women, underwent when their deeds of influence were recorded in male-authored texts. However her focus is on the earlier texts of Josephus and Qumran.[2] She does reference and analyze later rabbinic texts as part of her survey, laying a foundation for the work I do here, but she truncates a fuller reading of the later texts. For instance, Ilan begins to compare the variant readings between Sifre Devarim 42 and b.Taan 23a, but does not explore why the name "Shelamzion" is removed in the latter but present in the former beyond using it as an example of "paling and elimination."[3] Later, Ilan, in her study of Sifre Devarim, focuses on the treatment of women between the (putative) schools of Ishmael and Akiva more generally, even signaling, "the program of the present chapter ... has much to do with *Sifre Deuteronomy* itself, and little to do with Shelamzion Alexandra."[4] This study will complete the circle that Ilan began, exploring the literary techniques of erasure used to remove Shelamzion from the events remembered in the rabbinic texts.[5]

Utilizing Ilan's work as a guide, I will also employ some modal analysis of the literary tropes employed in the various appearances of Shelamzion. Northrop Frye's literary models help identify the genre markers of certain features of narrative discourse that shape the perception of the reader as to the positioning of the characters within the plot.[6] In other words, how Shelamzion is characterized—a central figure, an auxiliary sharing the scene, or a silent observer— communicates to the reader both the rabbis' view of Shelamzion in history and their relative view of the other characters in the scene. Ilan herself already saw the potential of such analysis when she characterized the portrayal by Nicolaus of Damascus of Mariamne as "an ideal tragic heroine," even invoking Shakespeare as a model.[7] This method derived from Frye is used in my larger research program to study the silencing and exclusion of (male) outsiders to the rabbinic enterprise, such as Elisha ben Abuyah and Jacob of Kefar Sekhania.

YERUSHALMI ERASURE VERSUS AGGADIC/BABYLONIAN VOICING

One of the longest episodes in which both Shelamzion and Shimon ben Shetach appear is the story of the three hundred Nazirites, in which Shimon bests Yannai by use of his knowledge of Torah. In four versions (Table 11.1)—y.Ber 7:2 (11b), y.Naz 5:3 (54b), Genesis Rabbah 91:3, and Qohelet Rabbah 7:12.1—the tale opens with near-identical language: "Three hundred

Nazirites went up [to fulfill their vows] in the time of Shimon ben Shetach." Shimon's wisdom then allows him to release half (150) of the Nazirites without sacrifices, but the other half still require their 450 offerings. Shimon goes to Yannai and asks the king if he will provide the sacrifices—"We have here 300 Nazirites who must offer 900 sacrifices. If you donate half, I will donate half"—neglecting to mention that the king will be the only one giving since Shimon's half have all been released without cost. Word then comes to Yannai of Shimon's deception and the king becomes enraged.[8] Later, when eminent guests from Persia are dining with Yannai and Shelamzion, they ask about Shimon: "We remember that a certain elder used to be here and used to speak words of wisdom to us," and then they request that he return to court.

At this point, the versions divide in how the request scene proceeds. In y.Ber 7:2 and y.Naz 5:3, the guests speak directly to Yannai.[9] In GenRab 91:3 and QohRab 7:12.1, Yannai asks for Shelamzion, referred to as "his [Shimon's] sister," to send for him. In these four versions, Shimon enters the banquet and "seats himself between the king and the queen"—which, in the two Yerushalmi versions, is the only mention, elliptical as it is, of Shelamzion. In b.Ber 48a, the central element of Shelamzion's persuasion of Yannai anchors this recounting of the need for Shimon to bless the meal. Here the king and queen are eating after Yannai has killed the rabbis, but they need someone to bless the food. Yannai asks Shelamzion where he might find "a man to say the blessing for us," and she makes him take an oath not to harm the one she will bring.

In four versions,[10] Yannai then questions Shimon's behavior during the deception about the Nazirite sacrifices, the flight from Yannai, and Shimon's present posturing in a place of honor (Table 11.2). Shimon responds to each question with a short midrash on biblical verses that explain his behavior as allowable, perhaps even authorized.[11] This then leads into an extended scene in which Shimon protests having to bless food or drink that he has not consumed himself, but which do not involve Shelamzion.

In b.Ber 48a, when the king and queen are eating after Yannai has killed the rabbis, Shelamzion has made Yannai swear his oath of security and has Shimon seated between Yannai and herself. Yannai then says to Shimon, "Do you see how I pay you respect?" to which Shimon replies, "It is Torah that honors me, as it is written, 'Extol her and she will exalt you'."[12] Yannai protests this affront, saying "Do you see how he does not accept my authority?!" What is also interesting here is that the rabbis avoid what I see as a potential name-midrash on Shelamzion as the one who brings peace to Zion/Jerusalem by restoring Shimon the rabbi to the court of King Yannai. As all five versions have no mention of this play-on-words, there is not much we can say other than perhaps that the femininity of Shelamzion prevented the rabbis from elevating her status with such a notice.

Table 11.1 Comparison of Three Hundred Nazirites Narrative in b.Ber 48a, GenRab 91:3, y.Naz 5:3, y.Ber 7:2, and QohRab 7:12.1

b.Ber 48a[a]	GenRab 91:3[b]	y.Naz 5:3[c]	y.Ber 7:2[d]	QohRab 7:12.1[e]
Three hundred Nazirites came up in the days of Shimon b. Shetah. For one hundred and fifty he found grounds for absolution, but for the other hundred and fifty he could find no grounds.	Three hundred Nazirites came up [to Jerusalem] in the days of R. Shimon b. Shetah. For one hundred fifty of them he found grounds for absolution, and for one hundred fifty of them he did not find grounds for absolution.	It was taught: Three hundred Nazirites went up to Jerusalem to have their vows annulled] in the time of R. Shimon b. Shetah. [Shimon] found a way out of the vows for one hundred and fifty of them. But he could not find a way out of the vows for [the remaining] one hundred and fifty.	Three hundred Nazirites went up to offer nine hundred sacrifices in the days of Shimon b. Shetah. In the case of one hundred and fifty he found a way out but not with the rest.
Accordingly he repaired to King Yannai and said to him, "Three hundred Nazirites have come up and they need nine hundred sacrifices. Do you give half and I will give half." Yannai did so,	He came to Yannai the king. [Shimon] said to him, "There are here three hundred Nazirites who require nine hundred offerings. You give half from your [property] and I shall give half from mine." [Yannai] sent him four hundred and fifty [sacrifices].	He went to Yannai the king and said to him, "We have here three hundred Nazirites who must offer nine hundred sacrifices [to fulfill their vows.] If you donate half, I will donate half." [Yannai] sent him four hundred and fifty [animals].	Shimon b. Shetah went to King Yannai and said to him, "There are three hundred Nazirites who wish to offer nine hundred sacrifices, but they have not the means. You give a half from your resources and I will give half from mine, so that they may go and sacrifice."

Shush Shelamzion, Your Brother Shimon Is Speaking! 285

King Yannai and the queen broke bread together. It was after he had killed the rabbis, so there was no one around to recite the blessing for them. He said to his wife, "Who will bring us a man to say the blessing for us?" She said to him, "Take an oath to me that if I bring you someone, you will not give him any trouble."

Some time after certain Persian dignitaries were dining at King Yannai's table, and they observed, "We remember that there used to be an old man here who spoke to us words of wisdom." [Yannai] said to [Shimon's] sister, "Send for him to come here." "Give him your promise [of safety]," she returned, "and he will come."

After [some] days, important men came up from the kingdom of Persia to Yannai the king. When they were sitting and eating, they said to him, "We recall that there was here a certain old man who said before us words of wisdom. Let him teach us something." They said to him, "Send and bring him."

But a tale-bearer went and informed him that Shimon had given nothing. When Shimon learned this, he fled.

An evil rumor came to [Yannai], "He gave nothing of his own." Yannai the king heard and was angered. Shimon b. Shetah was frightened and fled.

One tale-bearer then went and told Yannai that [Shimon] did not contribute any of his own. Yannai, the king, heard this and became angry. Shimon ben Shetah feared the consequences and fled.

People came and slandered Shimon b Shetah to King Yannai, telling him, "All that the Nazirites offered was provided by you, and Shimon b. Shetah has contributed nothing." When he heard this, he was enraged against Shimon b. Shetah and when the latter heard it he fled.

Some time later certain men from the kingdom of Persia were there, sitting at the table of King Yannai. While at the meal they said to Yannai, "Your Majesty, we remember that there was an old man here who expounded to us the words of the Torah." He said to Shelamzion, [Shimon's] sister, the wife of Yannai, "Send and fetch him." She replied, "Give me your word [that you will not harm him] and send him your ring [as a sign of goodwill]; then he will come."

(continued)

Table 11.1 Continued

b.Ber 48a[a]	GenRab 91:3[b]	y.Naz 5:3[c]	y.Ber 7:2[d]	QohRab 7:12.1[e]
He took the oath for her. She brought him Shimon b. Shetah, her brother, seating [Shimon] between [Yannai] and her.	The promise having been given, he came and sat between the king and the queen.	[Yannai] sent and gave [Shimon] his word, and he came. He seated him[self] between the king and the queen.	He sent for him with assurance [that no harm would befall him]. And Shimon came back and took his place of honor between the king and the queen.	He gave her his word and Shimon came. On his arrival he sat between the king and the queen.

[a] Jacob Neusner, trans., *Bavli Tractate Berakhot*, volume I, number 24, *The Talmud of Babylonia: An Academic Commentary* (Atlanta,GA: Scholars Press, 1996): 319–320, modified to read "Shimon" instead of "Simeon."

[b] Harry Freedman, trans., *Genesis*, volume two, *Midrash Rabbah*, third edition (London/New York, NY: Soncino Press, 1983): 836, modified to read "Shimon" instead of "Simeon" and "Yannai" for "Jannai."

[c] Jacob Neusner, trans., *Nazir*, vol. 24 in *The Talmud of the Land of Israel: A Preliminary Translation and Explanation* (Chicago,IL: University Chicago Press, 1985): 123–124, modified to read "Shimon" instead of "Simeon."

[d] Tzvee Zahavy, trans., *Berakhot*, vol. 1 in *The Talmud of the Land of Israel: A Preliminary Translation and Explanation* (Chicago,IL: University Chicago Press, 1989): 264, modified to read "Shimon" instead of "Simeon."

[e] Abraham Cohen, trans., *Ecclesiastes*, Midrash Rabbah, third edition (London/New York, NY: Soncino Press, 1983): 190–191, modified to read "Shimon"instead of "Simeon," "Yannai" for "Jannaeus," and "Shelamzion" for "Salome."

Thus far I have treated the five versions of the "Shimon deceives Yannai and then prays at his banquet" narrative in an approximate chronological order (Table 11.3). But now I will venture into a stylometric reading-order so that I can elucidate how the effacement of Shelamzion occurs textually.[13] I argue, under the principle of *lectio brevior potior*, that the version behind b.Ber 48a is the generative text that allows for the expansion and concatenation that creates the Shelamzion and Shimon versions found in the other four texts discussed. The singular question and response between Yannai and Shimeon is the anchor point that scribes used to expand the scene in their transferal of narrative emphasis from Shelamzion to Shimon. Additionally, the *Sitz im Leben* of needing Shimon to bless the food explains why all four versions also move from the deception-redemption narrative directly into a discussion of blessing food which the supplicant has not eaten, even in contexts where the blessings are not immediately in view.

Based on the sequencing of the narrative's development across the four versions, GenRab 91:3 preserves the expansion to three questions in their initial redactional order (1. Why did you seat yourself here? 2. Why did you deceive me? 3. Why did you flee?). The 300 Nazir conflict that sends Shimon into exile is thus added directly before the dinner scene found in b.Ber 48a, which is transformed to be a larger banquet of court guests, sidelining or de-emphasizing Shelamzion's status from equal to attendant. We can also see the Proverbs 4:8 quotation, "Cherish her and she will exalt you," and Yannai's protestation, "Why must you persist in stubbornness?" as the bracketing elements surrounding the redactional insert of the two new questions and responses. The first noteworthy change is the conflation of Ben Sira 11:1 with Prov 4:8 as the prooftext-response to the first question, "Why did you seat yourself here?" The atypical mixing of rabbinically canonical and extramural texts also occurs in y.Naz 5:3, indicating an early origin for this heterogeneous element.[14] The second noteworthy change is the shift of the agency from Shelamzion to Shimon. While the queen is the one who requests the presence of her rabbi-brother in the narrative, it is Shimon who positions himself in the place of honor, unlike how it is depicted in b.Ber 48a. A third element supporting the relative position of GenRab 91:3 in the sequence of redaction is the inclusion of the explanatory element, "If I had told you what I would do, you would not have given the offerings." This revealing of why the treachery was conducted belies an early stage of development of the narrative since such transparent comment indicates that the connection between the question-responses and the two scenes is not immediately clear.

The two Yerushalmi versions, y.Naz 5:3 and y.Ber 7:2, are the end of the redactional sequence and also display the most severe silencing of Shelamzion. The first noteworthy change is the re-sequencing of the three questions (now, 1. Why did you deceive me? 2. Why did you flee? 3. Why

Table 11.2 Comparison of Yannai/Shimon Dinner Scene in b.Ber 48a, GenRab 91:3, y.Naz 5:3, y.Ber 7:2, and QohRab 7:12.1

b.Ber 48a[a]	GenRab 91:3[b]	y.Naz 5:3[c]	y.Ber 7:2[d]	QohRab 7:12.1[e]
[Yannai] said to [Shimon], "Do you see how much I honor you?" [Shimon] said to him, "You are not the one who honors me, but it is the Torah that honors me,[f] for it is written, 'Exalt her and she will promote you.'" [Prv 4:8] [Yannai] said to [his wife], "Don't you see that he does not accept [my] authority!"	"What is the meaning of this [that you sit between the king and queen]?" [Yannai] demanded. "[I do this] because it is written in the book of Ben Sira, 'Esteem her,[g] so shall she exalt you and seat you between princes.'" [Prv 4:8/Ben Sira 11:1] [Shimon] replied.	[Yannai] said to him, "Why did you deceive me?" [Shimon] said to him, "I did not deceive you. You [gave] of your money and I [gave] of my [Torah], as it is written, 'For wisdom is a defense even as money is a defense.'" [Qoh 7:12]	Yannai said to [Shimon], "Why did you deceive me?" Shimon said to him, "I did not deceive you. You gave your part out of your wealth. And I gave my part out of my knowledge of the Torah [by finding a way out of their vows], as it is written, 'For the protection of wisdom is like the protection of money.'" [Qoh 7:12]	Yannai asked [Shimon], "Why did you flee?" He answered, " I heard that you were angry with me and I was afraid of you lest you should kill me, so I fled and fulfilled this verse, 'Hide yourself for a little moment, until the anger is past.'" [Isa 27:20]
	"Why did you fool me?" [Yannai] asked. [Shimon said,] "Heaven forbid! I did not fool you, but you gave of yours [money] while I gave of mine [knowledge], for it is written, 'For wisdom is a defense, even as money is a defense.'" [Qoh 7:12] "Then why did you not tell me this?" [Yannai] asked. "Had I told you, you would not have done so," [Shimon] retorted.	[Yannai] said to him, "Why did you flee?" [Shimon] said to him, "I heard that my lord was angry against me, and I wanted to carry out this Scripture, 'Hide yourself for a little moment, until the anger be past.' [Isa 26:20] And [Yannai][h] cited concerning him, "The advantage of knowledge of wisdom will give life to those who possess it." [Qoh 7:12]	Yannai said to him, "Why then did you flee?" [Shimon] said to him, "I heard that my master was angry at me and I wanted to fulfill this verse, 'Hide yourselves for a little while until the wrath is past' [Isa 26:20] And it was said concerning me, 'And the advantage of knowledge is that wisdom preserves the life of him who has it.'" [Qoh 7:12]	"Why did you deceive me?" the king asked. "Heaven forbid!" [Shimon] replied, "I did not deceive you; but [you paid] with your money and I with my learning, as it is written, 'For wisdom is a defense, even as money is a defense.'" [Qoh 7:12]

Shush Shelamzion, Your Brother Shimon Is Speaking! 289

"And why did you flee?" [Yannai] pursued. "Because it is written, 'Hide yourself for a little moment, until the anger is past.'" [Isa 26:20].	[Yannai] said to him, "And why did you sit down between the king and the queen?" [Shimon] said to him, "In the book of Ben Sira, it is written, 'Esteem her, so she shall exalt you and seat you between princes.'" [Prv 4:8/Ben Sira 11:1]	Yannai said to him, "Why did you take a seat between the king and the queen?" [Shimon] said to him, "In the book of Ben Sira it written, 'The wisdom of a humble man will lift up his head and will seat him among the great.'" [Ben Sira 11:1]	"Why did you seat yourself between the king and the queen?" [Yannai asked] [Shimon] replied, "It is thus written in the book of Ben Sira, 'Extol her,[i] and she shall exalt you and make you to sit between princes.'" [Prv 4:8/Ben Sira 11:1] The king said to him, "Do you see how I pay you respect?" [Shimon] replied, "Not you, but my learning gains me respect, as it is written, 'Extol her and she shall exalt you.'"
They gave him a cup for the recitation of a blessing. [Shimon] said, "How shall I say a blessing? 'Blessed be what Yannai and his fellows have eaten of His.'"	[Yannai] filled a glass for him and bid him recite Grace, whereupon [Shimon] said, "Let us say Grace for the food which Yannai and his companions have eaten."	[Yannai] said, "Give him the cup so that he may say the blessing." [Shimon] took the cup and said, "Let us bless the food that Yannai and his companions have eaten."	[Yannai] said, "Bring him the cup so that he may recite the blessing." They brought Shimon the cup and he said, "Let us recite a blessing for the food that Yannai and his associates have eaten."	The king told his attendants, "Mix a cup of wine for him that he may say Grace." [Shimon] asked, "What formula shall I use in the Grace? Shall I say, 'Blessed be He of whose bounty Yannai has eaten?'"

(continued)

Table 11.2 Continued

b.Ber 48a[a]	GenRab 91:3[b]	y.Naz 5:3[c]	y.Ber 7:2[d]	QohRab 7:12.1[e]
He drank that cup and they gave him another and he said a blessing.	"I have never heard you recite it thus!" [Yannai] exclaimed. "What do you want," [Shimon] said, "that I should say, 'Let us say grace for the food which I have not eaten?'" A second glass was then filled for him and he recited, "Let us say Grace for the food that we have eaten."	[Yannai] said to him, "Are you stubborn even to such an extent?" [Shimon] said to him, "What shall we say, 'For the food that we have not eaten'?" [Yannai] said, "Give him something to eat." They gave [Shimon] and he ate and said, "Let us bless the food that we have eaten."	Yannai said to him, "Must you persist in your stubbornness?" Shimon said to him, "What then should I say, 'Let us recite the blessing for the food that we have not eaten?'" Yannai said, "Bring him food so that he may eat." So they brought out the food. He ate and then he said, "Let us recite the blessing for the food that we have eaten."	The king exclaimed, "You still remain obstinate! Never have I heard Yannai mentioned in the Grace!" [Shimon] retorted, "Am I to say, 'Blessed be He of whose bounty we have eaten' when I have not eaten?" [Yannai] ordered, "Bring him something to eat" adn after his meal, [Shimon] said, "Blessed be He of whose bounty we have eaten."

[a] Neusner, *The Talmud of Babylonia: An Academic Commentary*, 320, modified to read "Shimon" instead of "Simeon."
[b] Freeman, *Genesis*, 836–837, modified to read "Shimon" instead of "Simeon" and "Yannai" for "Jannai."
[c] Neusner, *Nazir*, 124–125, modified to read "Shimon" instead of "Simeon."
[d] Zahavy, *Berakhot*, 264–265, modified to read "Shimon" instead of "Simeon."
[e] Cohen, *Ecclesiastes*, 191–192, modified to read "Shimon" instead of "Simeon" and "Yannai" for "Jannaeus."
[f] Yet, narratively, it is Shelamzion that put Shimon in the place of honor.
[g] Freeman opts for "knowledge" as intended by "her," but the ambiguity could also include Shelamzion.
[h] The text is ambiguous—"he." Neusner opted for Yannai, while I think that this is reflexive, "And [Shimon] cited concerning him[self] . . ." I have retained Neusner's translation so as not to privilege my own argument.
[i] Cohen opts for "Torah" as intended by "her."—"Shelamzion" is not an option because of how both Yannai and Shimon continue the discussion.

did you seat yourself here?) to align them with the order of the deception and the banquet scenes. Both Yerushalmi versions also include both parts of Qohelet 7:12 ("For the protection of wisdom is like the protection of money, and the advantage of knowledge is that wisdom gives life to the one who possesses it") as Shimon's responses to the two questions about the deception. This sequence is most likely what generates the deception scene as a *mashal* for the halakhic decision to invalidate the offerings of the Nazir. However, the lack of an independent instance of the ruling outside of the banquet-scene framing and the "interruption" of the Isa 26:20 quotation, found in the two versions that do not include Qoh 7:12b, makes this assertion tentative. Finally, the redactional sequencing between y.Naz 5:3 and y.Ber 7:2 cannot be clarified because y.Ber 7:2 removes the Prov 4:8 quote and restores the beginning of Ben Sira 11:1. Whether y.Ber 7:2 is later due to the loss of Prov 4:8 or whether y.Naz 5:3 (and the source for GenRab 91:3) is later due to conflation of the two prooftexts cannot be definitively answered, though I lean toward the former hypothesis and place y.Naz 5:3 between the version found in GenRab and the one found in y.Ber. The close literary relationship between Talmud Yerushalmi and Genesis Rabbah also implies that they should be understood as "neighbors" in the redactional sequence.[15] Ilan has recently made the point that Yerushalmi silences the female voices that Genesis Rabbah permits.[16]

QohRab 7:12.1 represents, in my opinion, the final stage of redaction and harmonization. This is based on the complete lack of correspondence between the three questions and the two narrative scenes. While QohRab opens with the 300 Nazir and then proceeds to the banquet scene, the three questions are inverted (1. Why did you flee? 2. Why did you deceive? 3. Why did you seat yourself here?). The QohRab version also adds Shelamzion's request for the signet-ring of Yannai as collateral for the promise of safety and repeats the use of Prov 4:8 as a prooftext following Yannai's assertion that he is being disrespected. Also any ambiguity concerning the referent of "Extol her" in Ben Sira 11:1 is effaced in QohRab 7:12.1, in which Shimon pointedly mentions that "My learning gains me respect."[17] These variants indicate that QohRab 7:12.2 is a harmonization of the b.Ber 48a and GenRab 91:3 versions, placing it both redactionally and chronologically late.

If we read the five versions of the "Shimon deceives Yannai and then prays at his banquet" narrative in the order I have described, we see a progressive erasure of Shelamzion from the scene. In b.Ber 48a, she is an active agent, able to argue with her husband the king and exert her will in both protecting her brother and bending the opinion of the king. In GenRab 91:3, Shelamzion is moved into a subordinate place, both to the authority of Yannai to recall Shimon to court and to the power of Shimon to seat himself in the place of honor. In the Yerushalmi versions, Shelamzion is removed, her role as requesting Shimon's return taken up by the Persian guests, and the oath of peace given by Yannai in his own stead. Though the versions appear in the opposite order historically, it is clear that their underlying textual development indicates a desire in Eretz-Israel to suppress Shelamzion's power, while the Babylonian (or later) writers were more tolerant of her presence as a powerful queen.

SHIMON VERSUS SHELAMZION IN HALAKHIC DISPUTE

Ilan has noticed that women rarely engage in halakhic discussion with the rabbis in Talmudic literature.[18] However, Shelamzion appears as one of the few who are involved in the development of religious practice in the Yerushalmi, albeit in an obscured way. In y.Ket 8:11 (32c), we find that "Shimon ben Shetah made three decrees: that a man may do business with the [money of the] marriage contract of his wife; that children should go to school, [and] that glassware is susceptible to becoming unclean."[19] This ruling is then discussed by the compiler as to whether it was Judah ben Tabbi, or Judah and Shimon together as a pair, that decreed this interpretation, as well as whether the ruling is for glass vessels or for metal vessels. The text then resolves the ambiguity with the statement by Yose ben Bun in the name of R. Levi, "That was the law as they had received it, but they had forgotten it, and then the pairs went and [reasoned the law and so] came to the conclusion again as did their predecessors."[20] In the context of Ketubot, this brief interlude into the compositional theory of rulings seems a diversion.

However, I will argue that the ambiguity has to do with the erasure of the one who promulgated the ruling in the first place. In other words, the ruling made by Shimon points to an erroneous practice, which we will soon see is done by Shelamzion, that he is correcting. Daniel Boyarin has argued, "It seems . . . that our Babylonian texts were at much greater pains to simply eliminate the possibility that women would be considered candidates for study of Torah."[21] However, we have seen in this study that the Babylonian sources seem to (re)insert Shelamzion back into the (now halakhic) conversation whereas the Yerushalmi sources make an effort to efface her presence entirely by using Shimon ben Shetach as the rabbinic mouthpiece.

In b.Shab 16b, a lengthy discussion (15b–16a) of the susceptibility of glassware to become unclean is punctuated with the following interaction between Shelamzion and Shimon:

> Shimon ben Shatah ordained the requirement of a marriage settlement for a wife and made a decree concerning the uncleanness for metal utensils.

But the fact that metal utensils are subject to uncleanness derives from the Torah! For it is written, "the gold and silver—anything that can stand in fire—you shall pass through fire and it shall be clean." [Num 31:22]

It was necessary to make such a decree with respect to the prior uncleanness [that when they are repaired they revert to their prior status], for R. Judah said that Rab said, "There was the incident involving <u>Shelamzion, the queen</u>, who made a banquet for her son, but all her utensils were made unclean, so she had them broken and gave them to the goldsmith. He melted them down and made new utensils of them." Then the sages said, "They revert to their prior status of uncleanness."

How come? They wanted to establish a protective fence to make sure that the rite of purification through the water of separation [described in Num 19] would not fall into disuse.[22]

Two things are noteworthy here. First, the enduring connection between the marriage contract and the uncleanness of vessels in both the Yerushalmi and Bavli versions of the episode may indicate that the banquet by Shelamzion is the generative event that induced the rulings. Second, the valence of metal versus glass utensils is set in parallel with the valence between purification by fire and purification by water, the latter which is used for utensils that cannot endure fire while both metal and glass do survive heating. This tension is striking, given that water-purification is subordinate to fire-purification in the Torah. In other words, the goldsmith's remelting of the utensils has been negated and seen as invalid because of both its lack of rabbinic oversight and the rabbinic subordination of fire/Torah to water/rabbinic precedence.

This fantasy is most apparent in a passage like b.Shab 16b, where the redactors set the stage as a direct conflict between the rabbinic and monarchic authorities, with the male rabbi achieving dominance. Ilan has noted that the rabbinic sources

> have chosen, with the passage of time, to stress the queen's contemporary—the sage Shimeon ben Shatah—as responsible for important social and legal innovations of his time. Yet, this is obviously a rabbinic fantasy, since the real power at the time was in the hands of the queen, and she must have been the power behind these developments.[23]

In y.Ket 8:11, the dominance erases even the presence of the queen from the discussion, rendering her and all women as silent subordinates to male power over valuables.

Another interesting text that centers the male/female equality in light of the precedence of honor established in Torah is b.Ker 28a–28b. The passage opens with three equivalences derived from the Torah: that of lambs and goats as choice sacrifices, turtle-doves and pigeons as bird sacrifices, and father and mother as deserving of honor. This is immediately undercut by both the (re)precedence of father over mother, as "both [the son] and his mother are liable to pay honor to his father," and by the precedence of rabbi over father, as "both the son and his father are liable to pay honor to his master."[24] The dual eclipsing of the female mother by male father and male rabbi is then endorsed by a chiastic set of proclamations that were supposedly given in the Temple courtyard. The outer pair of negative pronouncements links the removal of Hophni and Phineas, sons of Eli, from the Temple to the expulsion of Issachar of Kfar Barqai from his role as high priest because of their contempt of the Holy Things of heaven.[25] The inner pair of positive announcements link Yohanan ben Nidbai, disciple of Pinqai, with Elishama ben Pikai, disciple of Phineas. Worth noting here is the sustained emphasis of a master–student relationship in addition to, if not over, a father–son relationship: the displacement of Hophni and Phineas enables the "priest-ification" of Samuel as heir to Eli, while both Yohanan and Elishama are identified as disciples and as sons.

Issachar's contempt is then described as fastidiousness, in that, "he would wrap silk over his hands and thus carry out the sacrifice."[26] He treated the sacred meat offerings as if they would defile his hands. This linkage to the equivalent sacrifices that opened the section is itself paired with a subtle link to proper and improper fastidiousness—Yohanan ben Nidbai is praised in his mention because he would eat all of the leftover remnant meat in the courtyard.

Issachar's punishment is what brings to the stage both Yannai and Shelamzion. The king and queen are discussing whether lambs or goats are the better sacrifice, the question opening this passage. They decide to consult Issachar as he in his role as high priest would know the proper ritual decision. Issachar tragically favors the queen's ruling and is punished for his insolence, characterized in the account as dismissively waving his hand in the presence of the king, by having his hands cut off. The account then closes with the opening ruling of lamb and goat equivalence and a scathing critique of Issachar as being ignorant even of the biblical text itself.

We can now return to Ilan's observation that the rabbis choose to displace halakhic authority away from Shelamzion. In one illustrative story concatenated with a pronouncement of sacrificial equivalence, the redactors manage to discount three loci of power that threaten their own predominance. Yannai, the monarch, portrayed as impulsive and violent, is shown to be unworthy to rule justly. Issachar, the high priest, portrayed as foolish and impudent, is equally disqualified to interpret the Torah. Most importantly for this study, Shelamzion, the queen, who rules halakhically, but "incorrectly" so, implicitly dismissed as subordinate female and subordinated monarch. The rabbis and their disciples are then shown to be the true hierarchy-dynasty in this account, with both the monarchy and the priesthood serving only as negative examples of less-than-adequate decision making.

CONCLUSIONS, IN LIGHT OF RABBINIC OUTSIDERS AND BOUNDARY TRANSGRESSION

In this study, I have argued that the Yerushlami sources, more proximate in time to Shelamzion, erase her power or even her presence from rabbinic episodes that occurred ostensibly during her reign, while the Babylonian and later midrashic sources restore her identity and agency. In y.Ket 8:11, b.Shab 16b, and b.Ker 28a-28b, we found that the rabbinic authorial hand manages to dismiss or downplay the halakhic authority of the Hasmonean queen. In this, we again recognize, as Charlotte Elisheva Fonrobert states, "women's overwhelming silence in the Talmud itself, as well as in the last one thousand years of talmudic scholarship."[27] These brief examples speak to the hegemony of gaze that incorporates gender-neutral issues, such as ritual object cleanliness, into the male prerogative, which then renders gendered cleanliness, such as *niddah*, as also the province of male authority and oversight.

In y.Ber 7:2 and y.Naz 5:3, Shelamzion is completely removed from the narrative, though she is active and central to the story in GenRab 91:3, QohRab 7:12.1, and b.Ber 48a. If we fail to notice her displacement, we also fail to notice her presence in each version.[28] Shelamzion is originally thought of as co-equal with her husband and then as the true monarch after his death.[29] Yet the rabbinic sources replace her with her contemporary (brother?) Shimeon ben Shetach, whose role as male and as rabbinic forebear is more comfortable for them.[30] It is beyond the scope of this study to elaborate how the rhetorical move connects to the intervening Herodian and post-Destruction history of early rabbinic literature, but this case study shows that the rabbis perceive Shelamzion less favorably than the earlier historians and authors.

The rabbinic silencing of Shelamzion is a species of the larger genus of silencing of (usually male) outsiders in rabbinic texts. Such silencing, once fronted, reveals that the authors of the rabbinic corpus distanced themselves from the achievements, even the positive and laudatory ones, of those who did not align with them halakhically or interpretationally. Similar, sidelining can be seen in the use of the *minim* as interlocutors and opponents, especially when the rabbinic enterprise moves too close to the boundary line of orthodoxy. It is then that the reader is redirected to a new standard of belief or conduct and the normal pattern of multiple opinions voiced in the text is absent.

Table 11.3 The Redactional Sequence of the Five Versions of the Three Hundred Nazirites + Yannai/Shimon Dinner Narrative in b.Ber 48a, GenRab 91:3, y.Naz 5:3, y.Ber 7:2, and QohRab 7:12.1

b.Ber 48a	GenRab 91:3	y.Naz 5:3	y.Ber 7:2	QohRab 7:12.1
	300 Nazir **Shimon flees**	300 Nazir Shimon flees	300 Nazir Shimon flees	300 Nazir Shimon flees
Blessing food	**Banquet**	Banquet	Banquet	Banquet
Oath of peace: **Shelamzion requests**	Oath of peace: Shelamzion requests	Oath of peace: **Yannai himself**	Oath of peace: Yannai himself	Oath of peace: **Shelamzion requests + ring**
1. Do you see how I honor you?	1.Why did you seat yourself here?	2. Why did you deceive? (now derives from story)	2. Why did you deceive?	3. Why did you flee? (harmonizing b.Ber and GenRab?)
Proverbs 4:8	Proverbs 4:8 **Ben Sira 11:1**	Qoh 7:12a	Qoh 7:12a	Isa 26:20
	2. Why did you deceive me? Qoh 7:12(a)	3. Why did you flee? Isa 26:20 **Qoh 7:12b**	3. Why did you flee? Isa 26:20 Qoh 7:12b	2. Why did you deceive? Qoh 7:12a
	You would not have given the sacrifices if told			
	3. Why did you flee?	1.Why did you seat yourself here?	1.Why did you seat yourself here?	1.Why did you seat yourself here?
	Isa 26:20	Proverbs 4:8 Ben Sira 11:1	Ben Sira 11:1	Proverbs 4:8 Ben Sira 11:1
2. No respect for my authority!				2. No respect for my authority
				Proverbs 4:8 (again)
	Blessing over uneaten food—why must you persist in stubbornness?	Blessing over uneaten food—why must you persist in stubbornness?		Blessing over uneaten food—why must you persist in stubbornness?

---------- **BOLD** = new material ---------- *Italics* = material moved to a new position.

I also hope that I have accomplished what Ilan has proposed when she stated, "Each and every one of the sources, which hint at the queen and her story, should be read with suspicion and caution. All should be suspected of reworking, editing, and silencing."[31] I also hope that, in some small way, this study engages the challenge of Sara Parks to produce "scholarship on women and gender *by men for men.*"[32] That is to say, the study of the silencing of powerful women in rabbinic texts also speaks to the negotiation of power between the men in those same texts.

NOTES

1. Tal Ilan, "Women Quoting Scripture in Rabbinic Literature," in Tal Ilan, Lorena Miralles-Maciá, and Ronit Nikolsky, eds., *Rabbinic Literature*, Volume 4.1 in *The Bible and Women: An Encyclopaedia of Exegesis and Cultural History* (Atlanta, GA: SBL Press, 2022): 45–72.

2. Tal Ilan, *Silencing the Queen: The Literary Histories of Shelamzion and Other Jewish Women* (Tübingen: Mohr Siebeck, 2006): 56–60, 73.

3. *Ibid.*, 36–37.

4. *Ibid.*, 125.

5. After this paper was presented (July 22, 2021), Ilan published more on the silencing of women in rabbinic literature in her recent chapter, "Women Quoting Scripture in Rabbinic Literature." She includes Shelamzion in her list of notable women who appear in the Babylonian Talmud (p. 52, note 12), but Ilan does not address Shelamzion in the article itself.

6. Space does not permit me to fully elucidate how Northrop Frye understands plot and character, but one quote will have to suffice. Northrop Frye, *Anatomy of Criticism: Four Essays* (Princeton University Press, 1957, reprint New York: Atheneum, 1968): 33, 35, argues that

> fictions, therefore, may be classified, not morally, but by the hero's power of action, which may be greater than ours, less, or roughly the same. . . . Also there is a general distinction between fictions in which the hero becomes isolated from his society and fictions in which he is incorporated into it. This distinction is expressed by the words "tragic" and "comic" when they refer to aspects of plot in general."

The markers of plot and character are explained by Frye in his Third Essay, "Archetypal Criticism: Theory of Myths" (pp. 131–239 in *Anatomy of Criticism*), which should be read in conjunction with Robert D. Denham, *Northrop Frye and Critical Method* (University Park, PA/London: Pennsylvania State University Press, 1978): 58–87 as both systemizer and critic of Frye.

7. Tal Ilan, *Integrating Women into Second Temple History* (Tübingen: Mohr Siebeck, 1999): 111.

8. GenRab 91:3 omits an explicit statement of Yannai's anger.

9. Yannai explains Shimon's absence in the y.Ber version, while the y.Naz version has both the question and the request follow without interruption.

10. y.Ber 7:2 (11b), y.Naz 5:3 (54b), Genesis Rabbah 91:3, and Qohelet Rabbah 7:12.1.

11. This sequence of questions and answers will be explored in greater detail below.

12. Proverbs 4:8.

13. Please also see the table at the end for a graphical presentation of what I describe here.

14. However, b.Ber 48a retains only the Prv 4:8 portion, which also supports my hypothesis that the Bavli version retains an earlier form.

15. *cf.* Hans-Jürgen Becker, "Texts and History: The Dynamic Relationship between Talmud Yershalmi and Genesis Rabbah," chapter 6, pp. 145–158 in Shaye J.D. Cohen, ed., *The Synoptic Problem in Rabbinic Literature*, Brown Judaic Studies 326 (Providence, RI: Brown University Press, 2020).

16. Ilan, "Women Quoting Scripture in Rabbinic Literature," 58.

17. Cf. notes 23-24 and 26 above for my thoughts concerning how the texts and translators understand the reference of Prv 4:8/Ben Sira 11:1.

18. Ilan, "Women Quoting Scripture in Rabbinic Literature," 55–67.

19. Jacob Neusner, trans., *Ketubot*, volume 22, *The Talmud of the Land of Israel: A Preliminary Translation and Explanation* (Chicago, IL: University of Chicago Press, 1985): 264, modified to read "Shimon" instead of "Simeon."

20. *Ibid.*

21. Daniel Boyarin, *Carnal Israel: Reading Sex in Talmudic Culture*, The New Historicism: Studies in Cultural Poetics 25 (Berkeley, CA/Los Angeles CA/London: University California Press, 1993): 177.

22. Jacob Neusner, trans., *Bavli Tractate Shabbat*, volume II.A - chapters I through XII, number 32, *The Talmud of Babylonia: An Academic Commentary* (Atlanta, GA: Scholars Press, 1996): 60–61, modified to read "Shimon" instead of "Simeon" and "Shelamzion" instead of "Shalsion." Neusner's italics have been removed and the underline is mine.

23. Ilan, *Silencing the Queen*, 279.

24. Jacob Neusner, trans., *Bavli Tractate Keritot*, volume XXXIV, number 2, *The Talmud of Babylonia: An Academic Commentary* (Atlanta, GA: Scholars Press, 1996): 198–199.

25. *cf.* 1Sam 2, which describes their "contempt for the Lord's offerings."

26. Neusner, *The Talmud of Babylonia: An Academic Commentary*, 199.

27. Charlotte Elisheva Fonrobert, "Feminist Interpretations of Rabbinic Literature: Two Views," *Nashim: A Journal of Jewish Women's Studies & Gender Issues*, 4: Feminist Interpretations of Rabbinic Literature (Fall 5762/2001): 7.

28. Ilan, *Integrating Women into Second Temple History*, 278: "If we fail to note the silencing we will also fail to note what is being silenced."

29. Ilan, *Integrating Women into Second Temple History*, 278–279.

30. *Ibid.*, 279.

31. Ilan, *Silencing the Queen*, 279–280.

32. Sara Parks, "'The Brooten Phenomenon': Moving Women from the Margins in Second-Temple and New Testament Scholarship," *The Bible & Critical Theory* 15, no. 1 (2019): 51, but see also p. 61.

BIBLIOGRAPHY

Becker, Hans-Jürgen. "Texts and History: The Dynamic Relationship between Talmud Yershalmi and Genesis Rabbah." chapter 6 In *The Synoptic Problem in Rabbinic Literature*, edited by Shaye J.D Cohen, 145–58 . Brown Judaic Studies 326. Providence: Brown University Press, 2020.

Boyarin, Daniel. *Carnal Israel: Reading Sex in Talmudic Culture*. The New Historicism: Studies in Cultural Poetics 25. Berkeley/Los Angeles/London: University of California Press, 1993.

Cohen, Abraham (trans.). *Ecclesiastes*. Midrash Rabbah, 3rd ed. London/New York: Soncino Press, 1983.

Denham, Robert D. *Northrop Frye and Critical Method*. University Park/London: Pennsylvania State University of Press, 1978.

Elisheva Fonrobert, Charlotte. "Feminist Interpretations of Rabbinic Literature: Two Views." *Nashim: A Journal of Jewish Women's Studies & Gender Issues. 4: Feminist Interpretations of Rabbinic Literature* Fall 5762 (2001): 7–14.

Freedman, Harry (trans.). *Genesis*, Vol. 2, Midrash Rabbah, 3rd ed. London/New York: Soncino Press, 1983.

Frye, Northrop. *Anatomy of Criticism: Four Essays*. Princeton University of Press, 1957, reprint New York: Atheneum, 1968.

Ilan, Tal. *Integrating Women into Second Temple History*. Tübingen: Mohr Siebeck, 1999.

Ilan, Tal. *Silencing the Queen: The Literary Histories of Shelamzion and Other Jewish Women*. Tübingen: Mohr Siebeck, 2006.

Ilan, Tal. "Women Quoting Scripture in Rabbinic Literature." In *Rabbinic Literature*, Vol. 4.1 in *The Bible and Women: An Encyclopaedia of Exegesis and Cultural History*, edited by Tal Ilan, Lorena Miralles-Maciá, and Ronit Nikolsky, 45–72. Atlanta: SBL Press, 2022.

Neusner, Jacob (trans.). *Ketubot*, Vol. 22, *The Talmud of the Land of Israel: A Preliminary Translation and Explanation*. Chicago: University of Chicago Press, 1985.

Neusner, Jacob (trans.). *Nazir*, Vol. 24, *The Talmud of the Land of Israel: A Preliminary Translation and Explanation*. Chicago: University of Chicago Press, 1985.

Neusner, Jacob (trans.). *Bavli Tractate Berakhot*, Vol. I, number 24, *The Talmud of Babylonia: An Academic Commentary*. Atlanta: Scholars Press, 1996.

Neusner, Jacob (trans.). *Bavli Tractate Shabbat*, Vol. II.A - chapters I through XII, number 32, *The Talmud of Babylonia: An Academic Commentary*. Atlanta: Scholars Press, 1996.

Neusner, Jacob (trans.). *Bavli Tractate Keritot*, Vol. XXXIV, number 2, *The Talmud of Babylonia: An Academic Commentary*. Atlanta: Scholars Press, 1996.

Parks, Sara. "'The Brooten Phenomenon': Moving Women from the Margins in Second-Temple and New Testament Scholarship." *The Bible & Critical Theory* 15, no. 1 (2019): 46–64.

Zahavy, Tzvee (trans.). *Berakhot*, Vol. 1, *The Talmud of the Land of Israel: A Preliminary Translation and Explanation*. Chicago: University of Chicago Press, 1989.

12

Eve in Early Christian Armenian Tradition

David Zakarian

INTRODUCTION

The Armenian narrative texts on Eve and Adam, composed between the fifth and eighteenth centuries, have extensively been examined by Michael Stone,[1] whose prolific scholarship on this subject has focused on the transmission of the texts within the Armenian context, their theological interpretations and implications, and their rewriting and appropriation throughout centuries.[2] As a result, we now possess an invaluable corpus of texts related to the Eden story, which enables us to extend our understanding of the significance of these narratives in the Armenian tradition. However, the representation of Eve (and Adam) has yet to be explored from the perspective of gender studies, and this contribution intends to fill, albeit partially, this lacuna. More specifically, I shall examine how the Armenian church interpreted the Eden story in late antiquity and how much the representation of Eve influenced the church's discourse on women's role in society.

In the present chapter, the discussion will be limited to the Armenian texts of the fifth century, for this century marked the onset of Armenian written tradition that played a crucial role in the formation of Christian Armenian identity.[3] In particular, I will examine Agat'angełos's *History of the Armenians* (*ca* 460s), Ełišē's *History of Vardan and the Armenian War* (second half of the fifth century) and the *Commentary on Genesis* attributed to him, Łazar P'arpec'i's *Letter* in his *History of Armenia* (end of fifth–beginning of the sixth century), the homilies attributed to St.Gregory the Illuminator (recorded in the fifth century), and the homilies believed to have been composed by the Armenian Catholicos Yovhan Mandakuni (r. 478–490).

A comparative study of the Armenian, Greek, and Syriac traditions[4] on Eve will allow us to identify the similarities but, most importantly, the differences of these traditions, revealing the interesting tendencies in the process of the construction of gender identities in early Christian Armenian literature.[5] Through a carefully chosen language,[6] the authors of the texts moralized the historical events they were relating and promoted specific Christian role models which largely relied on biblical motives. While in neighboring Christian traditions Eve's figure was deployed for the symbolic construction of "woman" as God's creation who is inferior to man, the Armenian church adopted a relatively neuter stance toward her.

EVE AND THE GRECO-LATIN AND SYRIAN CHURCH FATHERS

The theological thinking of the fifth-century Armenian authors was largely dependent on the works of Greek and Syrian Fathers. The invention of the Armenian alphabet in *ca* 405 marked not only the birth of the Armenian written tradition but also became a century of copious translations of influential Christian texts originally composed in Greek and Syriac. These translations were sponsored by the Armenian ecclesiastical authorities and could not but have a direct impact on the thinking of Armenian authors, all of whom are believed to belong to the circle of translators. One might therefore expect that the representation of Eve would also largely follow the approaches found in the works of John Chrysostom, Basil Caesarea, Ephrem, Aphrahat, and others.[7] It is, therefore, essential to include the Greek and Syriac traditions in the discussion on the topic of the depiction of Eve before embarking on the exploration of the differences and similarities we find in the Armenian interpretation.

The representation of Eve in the Testaments and early Christian texts has been addressed from various methodological perspectives in several recent studies.[8] They allow us to draw a relatively comprehensive picture of how the early Church Fathers interpreted Eve's representation in sacred texts to construct and promote certain gender norms, which, albeit reflecting the social conventions of their times, proved extraordinarily persistent for many centuries to come. As pointed out by Elizabeth Clark in connection with the universalizing tendency of ideology,[9] "nowhere is this more obvious in patristic literature than in the amalgamation of all women to 'woman' and the identification of 'woman' with Eve."[10] Despite the plurality of social, cultural, and political contexts within which the discourse on women developed, scholars have identified several common typologies that emerge from the works of the Church Fathers in connection with the first woman. Since it is beyond the scope of this chapter to discuss them in detail, I shall limit myself to a brief overview of the main tendencies.

One of the most common typological interpretations relates to Eve's creation after Adam and from his rib (Gen 2:21–22), which gave rise to a hierarchical understanding of the sexes, with women occupying the second and, therefore, inferior position to men.[11] In this respect, the frequently cited verses from 1 Tim 2:11–14 gave this typology an apostolic blessing, making it a convenient means for developing and reinforcing a discourse that disparaged women.

A general theme that runs through many works of the Church Fathers is the blame put on Eve for the Fall. A selective reading of various passages from the Testaments, such as Gen 3:6 and 3:17, and 1 Tim 2:14, was deployed by the Church Fathers to attribute responsibility for the Paradise lost and introduction of the sin into this world primarily to Eve and, by extension, to all women.[12] This approach was often deployed to justify and corroborate women's secondariness in society and the church and their subordinate position in relation to men.[13] In John Chrysostom's words, "the first dominance and servitude was that in which men ruled over women. After the original sin, a need arose for this arrangement; before the sin, the woman was like the man."[14] For Aphrahat, the first woman has become "a way for the Adversary to gain access to people, and until the end he will [continue to] accomplish this"; she is "the weapon of Satan," through whom "he fights against the [spiritual] athletes."[15] In the same place, Aphrahat also identifies all women with Eve, blaming her for the curse that was put on the world, but he does not elaborate on the hierarchical division between men and women. Furthermore, within a different context, Aphrahat also highlights Adam's defiance of the Lord's commandment without recalling Eve.[16]

The typological understanding of the Virgin Mary as the second Eve is closely linked to this theme.[17] As the Mother of God, she came to rectify Eve's mistake, and as John Chrysostom points out in his comment on Psalm 44: "A virgin expelled us from paradise; through a virgin we found eternal life."[18] This juxtaposition of Eve and Mary is also extensively explored in the early Syriac tradition, especially in the works of St Ephrem.[19] Mary comes to reverse all the tribulations caused by Eve: the "leaves of shame" that Eve put on in her virginity are replaced by Mary's "robe of glory,"[20] and, instead of the "bitter fruit / which Eve had plucked from the tree," she provides "a sweet Fruit for humanity."[21] Aphrahat, in turn, claims that

> by the coming of the child of the blessed Mary, the thistles are uprooted, the sweat is wiped away, the fig tree is cursed, the dust is made salty, the curse is nailed to the Cross, the point of the sword is removed from before the tree of life (which is given as food to the faithful), and paradise is promised to the blessed and the virgins and the holy ones.[22]

In the same way, albeit much less commonly, Eve was also compared to Mary Magdalene. This juxtaposition was built on the understanding that, unlike Eve, Mary Magdalene was a source of redemption as the one who witnessed Christ's resurrection.[23] Another theme developed mainly by the Latin Church Fathers related to the identification of Eve with the church, which gave rise to the typology of Eve as the sacraments.[24]

Finally, in the early church much ink was spent on the discussion of Eve's nature.[25] In particular, her creation in the image of God, her rationality, her role in relation to Adam, and the traits of her character were debated.[26] As pointed out by John Flood,[27] in his Homily 15 on Genesis John Chrysostom stresses the idea that the woman is created as a helper for Adam, but "like man in every detail—rational, capable of rendering him what would be of assistance in times of need and the pressing necessities of life."[28] Despite this, Chrysostom turns to Paul's authority to support the view that woman should be in a subservient position because Adam "constituted God's image and glory, whereas woman is man's glory."[29]

Clark has already pointed out the ambivalence with which the Church Fathers approached the creation narrative,[30] whereas Flood has underscored the importance of considering the typologies of Eve "in the context of the *oeuvres* of the writers in which they appear, as an individual writer using a common image may vary its nuance or the tone of his treatment of the theme."[31]

There were many interpretations and points of contention in the approaches adopted by the early Church Fathers, but the recurring motif that emerged in these elaborations was the inferiority of women in relation to men, for the female sex descended from the first transgressor. By introducing sin into this world, Eve contributed to the immense amount of suffering that hounded the human race since its onset. The consequences of Eve's transgression were redressed by the Virgin Mary, but even that was not sufficient to cleanse women from the sin of the first woman and to grant them equal status to men. Thus, as an archetypal figure, Eve was to occupy a prominent role in the process of construction of gender stereotypes in the early Greek and Syriac (and Latin) churches, but the Armenian church, as we shall see below, did not fully follow this lead.

EVE AND THE ARMENIAN CHURCH IN THE FIFTH CENTURY

In the fifth century, the Armenian church leaders, the *vardapet*s (doctors of the church), and the educated clergy, in general, were undoubtedly familiar with the Church Fathers' discussions of biblical passages that featured Eve.

They could access them either in the original Greek or Syriac or via the translations into Armenian that proliferated after the creation of the Armenian alphabet, and, as was the case with other theological issues, the Armenian church had to take a stance on this matter. The subsequent discussion focuses on the texts from the beginning of Armenian written tradition, which contain references to the typologies of Eve. It attempts to reveal the prevalent views in the country's ecclesiastical circles that sponsored the first translations of the works of the Church Fathers and significantly contributed to the creation of Christian Armenian theological, literary, and historiographical traditions.

Historiographical Texts

Agat'angełos's History of the Armenians

Agat'angełos's *History of the Armenians,*[32] which came from the Greek strand of Armenian Christianity, was perhaps the most influential text produced in the fifth century. It contains the received tradition of Armenia's Christianization that has been promoted by the church throughout centuries until this day. The story of the conversion of the Armenian King Trdat III (IV) and the entire land of Armenia by Gregory the Illuminator (Grigor Lusaworič') after the martyrdom of the Roman virgin Hřip'simē and her companions on the Armenian soil consists of various layers, most of which are legendary. In spite of that, this story was extremely popular not only in Armenia but also beyond its borders, as the existence of various recensions of this text preserved in multiple languages evinces.

Eve is mentioned several times in the narrative, either by her name or by the author referring to her as "the first woman." The first instance is in the episode when St. Gregory remembers Eve in his prayer addressed to God pronounced while he is being tortured by King Trdat's men after having refused to worship the Zoroastrian Goddess Anahit(a):

> For as through the first virgin, Eve, death entered the world, so through this virgin [i.e. Mary] life will enter the world. As through Eve's giving birth, Cain's curse and sweat and toil and agitation and troubles entered the world; so through the birth of your Son from the virgin, rest and life and blessings will enter the world.[33]

The typological juxtaposition of Eve and the Virgin Mary is referred to in this passage with the description of the consequences of Eve's transgression and the redemptive power of the Mother of God. No further evaluation or any other additional comment is made by St. Gregory.

The second reference to Eve appears in the passage, which describes the predicament of the consecrated virgin Hřip'simē, whom Emperor Diocletian wishes to marry. Agat'angełos deploys an extended metaphor to compare the emperor with the serpent and Eve with Hṙipʻsimē: like the serpent in the garden Diocletian has become a means by which Satan threatens to destroy God's church, whereas Hṙipʻsimē overcomes the temptation and with the support of her companion nuns rejects the advancements of the emperor:

> But when the virtuous women saw the hidden arrows of the enemy, who is accustomed to shoot secretly at the saints who love Christ, they found that the Emperor (had become) a vessel of evil. Just as in the garden he had used the snake as a vehicle for causing the forgetting of the commandment, entering into the senseless ear of the first woman, so here too he had used the lawless emperor as a mask through which he could fight the church built by God.[34]

The reference to ear is borrowed from the Syriac tradition, in which not only was Eve deceived by listening to the serpent, but also "Mary conceived by the Word entering her by the ear."[35] Here, Agatʻangełos replaces Mary with Hṙipʻsimē, one of the most celebrated saints in Armenian Christianity, and it is Hṙipʻsimē who is to "transcender la faiblesse de la première femme"[36] and bring blessings to the Armenian people.

The next reference to the creation story features only Adam, as he is mentioned in the *Teaching of St Gregory*, a long homily written in the form of "catechetical instruction."[37] It is pronounced by St.Gregory's in front of the Armenian populace of the capital Vałaršapat after the conversion and constitutes a large section of Agatʻangełos's *History* (§§259–715). While explicating the creation of the world, St.Gregory emphasizes Adam's creation in the image of God.[38] In relation to Eve, he points at Gen 2:23–24, Mt 19:5–6, and Mk 10:7–8, and mentions the creation of Eve from Adam's rib[39] but without any elaboration on the hierarchy of creation. More importantly, St Gregory underscores the unity of woman and man by reciting twice from Gen 2:24: "a man will leave his father and his mother and will cleave to his wife, and they two will become one flesh."[40]

The homily then continues with an elaboration on the Fall, where only Adam's responsibility for the lost paradise is discussed.[41] St. Gregory stresses that Adam "had freedom and free will and wisdom from God,"[42] which he failed to deploy to fight the adversary and "they, deceived because of his sophistry, tasted, and transgressing the commandment were stripped of divine glory."[43] This approach to the Fall is reiterated again in §347 and §350, with reference to Rom 5:12–14, where again only Adam appears in the context of the first sin.

In the subsequent elaborations on the significant aspects of the Christian faith, St. Gregory again mentions the Virgin Mary. He presents her as the recipient of divine grace, who "conceived by the Holy Spirit the son of God in her chaste and pure womb in a manner that passes comprehension."[44] This participation of the Holy Virgin in the divine plan paves the way to salvation for all women, for in St.Gregory's words, "women also were blessed on account of the virgin birth which was from among them."[45]

These passages testify to Agatʻangełos's acquaintance with the aforementioned common typologies found in Greco-Syriac patristic literature. There is, however, a conspicuous absence of an attempt to generalize Eve's transgression and extend it to all women. On the contrary, Agatʻangełos seems to corroborate the view that advocates women's complete absolution from Eve's sin thanks to the Virgin Mary.

Other historiographical texts from the fifth century, which are discussed below, mention the creation narrative only briefly, and their approach largely concurs with the approach we find in Agatʻangełos.

Ełišē's *History of Vardan and the Armenian War*

Ełišē in his *History of Vardan and the Armenian War*,[46] which discusses the uprising of the Armenian nobles against the oppressive religious policies of the Sasanian king Yazdegerd II (*r*. 439–57 CE), in 450–451, mentions the Fall in a very generic manner:

> One of the host of immortal angels left heaven in revolt. Coming to our world, with treacherous words and false promise, he proffered an unrealizable hope to the untested, inexperienced, and newly created man, as to a child, turning his mind upwards so that by eating of the fruit of the tree—which he had been commanded not to approach—he might become god. So he forgot God's command, was tricked into following that erring deceit, and lost the glory of immortality that he possessed; nor did he gain the dream of his hope. Therefore, expelled from the place of life, he was cast into this corruptible world, in which you too now dwell and senselessly err following the new counsellor—no longer by eating of the forbidden tree but by calling creatures god, worshipping the dumb elements, offering food to demons who have no stomachs, and neglecting the Creator of all.[47]

As Armenian does not distinguish grammatical gender, it is not immediately evident whether the personal pronoun *na* (third person singular), translated by Thomson as "he," refers here to Adam or Eve. However, the use of the word *mard* (man) to speak about the one who "was tricked into following that erring deceit, and lost the glory of immortality that he possessed" points in the direction of Adam, for the first human being is repeatedly referred to as *mard* in the creation narrative.[48]

And yet, not calling him by name prompts that Ełišē implies the culpability of humankind in general, without laying the blame exclusively at the door of Adam. This understanding is reflected in an earlier passage too. Ełišē ascribes the Fall in general to the "man" or, more precisely, the "creation" or "created being" (*araracn*), without making any reference to the gender of the culprit:

> He [God] who is himself incorruptible begat creatures without corruption; but the latter fell of his own will and was rendered corruptible, and by himself was no longer able to stand on his feet. Because he was from earth and had acted for and by himself, he returned to the same nature.[49]

Ełišē, thus, appears not to be interested in exploiting the disobedience of the humans in the Garden of Eden as a tool to construct and promote gender norms or hierarchies.

Łazar P'arpec'i's Letter

Łazar P'arpec'i's *History of the Armenians*[50] presents a slightly different interpretation of the Armenian revolt against the Sasanians in 450–451 with an additional portrayal of the subsequent hostilities that took place in 482–484. Appended to the *History* we find Łazar's *Letter* to his patron Vahan Mamikonian, in which, *inter alia*, he speaks of envy that other clerics feel for him, comparing it to the devil's envy at the beginning of the time. In Łazar's words, "the devil brought down the first created [man] through envy and turned him into dust."[51] He then goes on to mention Adam and his offspring, Cain and Abel, but Eve's name does not appear in it. Like Ełišē, Łazar evinces no interest in Eve's transgression and only focuses on the deadly sin of envy.

Homiletic and Exegetical Texts

Homilies Attributed to Yovhan Mandakuni

There are several theological treatises attributed to the Armenian patriarch Yovhan Mandakuni, who lived and reigned in the fifth century. However, very little is known about his life and work, and there is no scholarly consensus about the authorship of the collection of homilies discussed here.[52] I shall nevertheless consider the content of some of the homilies as they seem to fit well with the Armenian Church Fathers' aforementioned approach to the representation of Eve and Adam. In fact, Eve is not mentioned at all in these homilies, whereas Adam appears quite often and always as the main culprit responsible for the Fall.

Homily 25, which discusses virtues and vices, uses the creation narrative to explain why there are vices in humans:

> God created the man and put *him* in the softness of the Paradise, with all *his* senses alive in *his* nature. Now when *he* listened to the one who deceived *him*,

he then took all vices and was immediately deprived of *his* great and wonderful glory, so that the man would know that there are vices which push *him* away from God.[53]

The use of masculine pronouns in my English translation of the text is arbitrary here because the author refers to humankind in general. The end of the homily, nevertheless, indicates that the author had Adam in mind: the enumeration and definition of the vices is concluded by stating that all of them "Adam took upon himself when he ate the fruit of the tree and fell under the feet of death."[54]

In the homily *On Love, Grudge, and Envy*, only Adam is remembered in relation to the lost Paradise: "Because the beginning of vices is envy and malevolence. For through them Satan fell from glory, through them Adam [fell] from Paradise. And curse and sweat, thorn and thistle, death and sin reigned over the offspring of Adam."[55]

The same approach can be observed in other homilies too.[56] This allows us to see clear parallels with Ełišē's understanding of the Fall. A close reading of these passages shows that when pronouncing Adam's name, the author of the homilies refers to "humankind" in general, in the original meaning of the word *adam* in Hebrew. What happened in the Garden of Eden is the fault of humankind, and they all must bear full responsibility for the Fall.

Homilies Attributed to St Gregory the Illuminator

St Gregory the Illuminator is one of the most important figures of Armenian Christianity and is considered to be the evangelizer of Armenia. Despite the fact that he died long before the invention of the Armenian alphabet, a collection of twenty-three dogmatic homilies known as *Yačaxapatum* bears his name as the author of this important theological work. The date of its composition remains unclear. Some scholars believe it was originally composed in Greek and then translated into Armenian, thus confirming St Gregory's authorship;[57] others attribute it to the inventor of the Armenian alphabet Mesrop Maštocʻ,[58] whereas the second half of the fifth century seems to be the most plausible date of the composition.[59]

There is only one mention of Eve and Adam together in the homily dedicated to fasting. According to it, "as lack of restraint brought a curse and death upon Eve and Adam, so those who were born from them and had the same lack of restraint were deprived of kindness through gluttony."[60] We can see that no distinction is drawn between Adam and Eve, as they are both accountable for the Fall. The author of the homilies does not attempt to use the transgression of the first humans to "fix" their representation by producing or reinforcing stereotypes.[61]

Commentary on Genesis Attributed to Ełišē

Finally, it is worth including a brief discussion on the *Commentary on Genesis* attributed to Ełišē, which has not been preserved in full.[62] The biggest fragments were incorporated into the work of Vardan Arewelc'i (*ca* 1200–1271), and it is not clear how much of the original text of the *Commentary* has been amended.[63] It contains a verse-by-verse commentary of the biblical text and differs from the aforementioned texts in its interpretation of the creation of humankind, but agrees on the understanding of the Fall and the relation of Eve to the Virgin Mary. A noticeable inconsistency that is discussed below, however, may be a sign of interpolation that happened during its adaptation in the thirteenth century, which may provide an additional argument in favor of a later date of composition of this text or of different authorship.

The representation of Eve and Adam in the *Commentary* largely concurs with the predominant discourse of the Greek and Syrian Fathers. When commenting on the creation of Eve from the rib of Adam, the commentator unequivocally states that

> she will not be of equal honor, as also she is not contemporary or of the same stature, but rather is younger and second, so that she will be obedient to Adam and silent. For speaking belongs to the head and silence to the rib.[64]

This hierarchical division, however, is not consistent with the assertion that follows later in the text when the commentator speaks of the Fall: "For at first they were equals, and she wished to have authority over the man."[65] This is an unequivocal statement that Eve and Adam were created equal, but later Eve attempted to overturn the established order by eating the fruit from the Tree of Knowledge and thus lost her position and was removed "from political rule, and the governance of cities, and power and all honorable positions from (by?) the man."[66]

This passage is summarized by a chastisement directed toward Adam. He is not acquitted of the transgression despite his excuse that he was coerced to eat the fruit by the woman, who was in her turn deceived by the snake. Since Adam listened to his woman and not to God, he brought a curse upon the earth.[67]

The commentary also draws a parallel between Eve and the Virgin Mary:

> Adam gave his wife the name "life." The one who named all of the animals called his wife "Eve" because he knew prophetically that she, who became the mother of death, is also the mother of all men who ought to come into the world. He took the fruit from her hands and not from the tree so that he would die with her in compassion, in the manner of the Lord, who chose to die with the mortals in his mercy. And now, he calls her life, to comfort her in the hope

of her daughter, Mary, who truly became the mother of the one who said "I am life" (John 14:6). She is the mother of all living things.[68]

This commentary echoes the Church Fathers' interpretation that Mary became the source of life for the living by giving birth to Christ. There is, however, no mention of the expiation of Eve's transgression through the agency of the Mother of God.

As it becomes apparent, the representation of Eve in this *Commentary on Genesis* does not fully accord with the approach adopted in other fifth-century Armenian texts, includingEłišē's *History*. This detail may serve as another piece of evidence supporting different authorship of the *Commentary*, though a more thorough and nuanced investigation of various aspects of the text should be carried out for a more definitive conclusion.

CONCLUSION

The discussed passages from the historiographical and theological texts composed in Armenian in the fifth century demonstrate that the Armenian Church Fathers did not exploit the Creation and the Garden of Eden stories to construct "woman" as an inferior creation to "man," as was the tendency in the Greek and Syriac traditions. In most texts, the Fall was presented as a transgression of humankind that disobeyed God's commandment, without specifically putting the blame on Eve or Adam. In other cases, when the culprit was pointed out, then it was Adam, rather than Eve, who was chastised for failing to comply with the will of God. The Virgin's immaculate conception and giving birth to God's son was believed to be more than sufficient to cleanse women from the sin of the first woman as described in the biblical texts.

This approach, as I have argued elsewhere,[69] was most likely determined by the pre-Christian beliefs of the Armenians, which was a local variant of Zoroastrianism with various elements from Indo-European, Sumero-Akkadian, and Urartian religious traditions.[70] Despite Armenia's society being largely patriarchal, the religious beliefs of the Armenians before the introduction of Christianity played a minor role in the construction and perpetuation of gender stereotypes. Women played an essential role in the domestic economy[71] and the education of the younger generations,[72] and downgrading them to a secondary role would have jeopardized the efforts of the ecclesiastical authorities to spread Christianity to the larger masses. Thus, contrary to their counterparts in the Greek and Syrian churches, the fifth-century Armenian authors adopted a less discriminatory and relatively more empowering discourse on women that would enable them to achieve their goals.

NOTES

1. See, for example, Michael E. Stone, *Adam and Eve in the Armenian Traditions: Fifth through Seventeenth Centuries* (Atlanta: Society of Biblical Literature, 2013); idem, "Satan and the Serpent in the Armenian Tradition," in *Beyond Eden: The Biblical Story of Paradise (Genesis 2–3) and Its Reception History*, ed. Konrad Schmid and Christoph Riedweg (Tübingen: Mohr Siebeck, 2008), 141–86; idem, *Adamgirkʻ: The Adam Book of Aṙakʻel of Siwnikʻ* (New York: Oxford University Press, 2007); idem, "Adam and Eve Traditions in Fifth Century Armenian Literature," *Le Muséon* 119, no. 1–2 (2006): 89–120; idem, *The Penitence of Adam*. 2 vols. *CSCO* 40–41, *Scriptores Armeniaci* 14 (Leuven: Peeters, 1981); idem, "The Death of Adam: An Armenian Adam Book," *Harvard Theological Review* 59 (1973): 283–91.

2. Stone, *Adam and Eve*, xix.

3. See Theo M. Van Lint, "The Formation of Armenian Identity in the First Millennium," *Church History and Religious Culture* 89, nos. 1–3 (2009): 251–78, especially 269–75.

4. Latin Christianity had no direct influence on the development of Armenian theological thought in Late Antiquity, which is why the discussion of Eve's representation in Latin sources is barely included here.

5. These tendencies have briefly been discussed in my recent book *Women, Too, Were Blessed: The Portrayal of Women in Early Christian Armenian Texts* (Leiden: Brill, 2021), which explores the portrayal of women in fifth-century Armenian historiographical texts. The present chapter considerably expands some of the points made in the book.

6. Here, I follow Averil Cameron's approach that "[l]anguage is one of the first and most fundamental elements in the construction of sexual identity." Averil Cameron, "Sacred and Profane Love: Thoughts on Byzantine Gender," in *Women, Men and Eunuchs: Gender in Byzantium,* ed. Liz James (London: Routledge, 1997), 1–23, here 17.

7. For specific details, see, for instance, Emilio Bonfiglio, "The Armenian Translations of John Chrysostom: The Issues of Selection," in *Caught in Translation: Studies on Versions of Late Antique Christian Literature*, ed. Madalina Toca and Dan Batovici (Leiden: Brill, 2020), 35–63; Ervand G. Ter-Minasyan, *Hayocʻ Ekełecʻu Yaraberutʻiwnnerə Asorwocʻ Ekełecʻineri het (Haykakan ew Asorakan Ałbiwrneri hamajayn)* (The Relations between the Armenian Church and the Syrian Churches (according to Armenian and Syriac Sources)), 2nd ed. (Ējmiacin: Mayr Atʻoṙ S. Ējmiacni Hratarakčʻutʻyun, 2009), 13–58; Edward G. Mathews, "Early Armenian and Syrian Contact: Reflections on Koriwn's *Life of Maštocʻ*," *St. Nersess Theological Review* 7 (2002): 5–27; Levon Ter-Petrosyan, "La plus ancienne traduction arménienne des *Chroniques* : Étude préliminaire," *Revue des Études Arméniennes* 18 (1984): 215–25; Robert W. Thomson, "The Fathers in Early Armenian Literature," *Studia Patristica* 12 (1975): 457–70, here 460–6.

8. See, for instance, Bob Becking, "Once in a Garden: Some Remarks on the Construction of the Identity of Woman and Man in Genesis 2–3," in *Out of Paradise:*

Eve and Adam and Their Interpreters, ed. Bob Becking and Susanne Hennecke (Sheffield: Sheffield Phoenix Press, 2011), 1–13, here 1–11; Geert Van Oyen, "The Character of Eve in the New Testament: 2 Corinthians 11.3 and 1 Timothy 2.13–14," in *Out of Paradise: Eve and Adam and Their Interpreters*, ed. Bob Becking and Susanne Hennecke (Sheffield: Sheffield Phoenix Press, 2011), 14–28; van Oyen, "The Character of Eve," 14–28; Willemien Otten, "The Long Shadow of Human Sin: Augustine on Adam, Eve and the Fall," in *Out of Paradise: Eve and Adam and Their Interpreters*, ed. Bob Becking and Susanne Hennecke (Sheffield: Sheffield Phoenix Press, 2011), 29–49; John Flood, *Representations of Eve in Antiquity and the English Middle Ages* (London: Routledge, 2011), 7–48; Kristen E. Kvam, Linda S. Schearing, and Valarie H. Ziegler, eds., *Eve and Adam: Jewish, Christian, and Muslim Readings on Genesis and Gender* (Bloomington, IN: Indiana University Press, 1999), 108–55.

9. In the discussion of the construction of "woman" in Late Antiquity, Clark extensively draws on the writings of John B. Thompson, Anthony Giddens, and Terry Eagleton on ideology and identifies four operations that enable those who control discourse "to 'fix' representation of the self: through stereotyping, naturalizing, universalizing, and de-historicizing of the self. Certain types of narrative writing and intertextual writing practices also serve as carriers of ideological meaning." Elizabeth A. Clark, "Ideology, History, and the Construction of 'Woman' in Late Ancient Christianity," *Journal of Early Christian Studies* 2, no. 2 (1994): 155–84, here 155.

10. Ibid., 168.

11. See the discussions in Elizabeth A. Clark, "Devil's Gateway and Bride of Christ: Women in the Early Christian World," in *Ascetic Piety and Women's Faith: Essays on Late Ancient Christianity*, ed. Elizabeth A. Clark (Lewiston, NY: Edwin Mellen Press, 1986), 23–60, here 31; Deborah F. Sawyer, *Women and Religion in the First Christian Centuries* (London: Routledge, 1996), 149–53; and Kvam, Schearing, and Ziegler, *Eve and Adam*, 110 and 112.

12. Clark, "Ideology," 156 and Clark, *Women*, 15–16. See also Rosemary Radford Ruether, "Misogynism and Virginal Feminism in the Fathers of the Church," in *Religion and Sexism: Images of Women in the Jewish and Christian Traditions*, ed. Rosemary Radford Ruether (Eugene, OR: Wipf and Stock, 1998), 150–83, here 157.

13. See, for instance, Clark, "Devil's Gateway," 30–3; Clark, "Ideology," 168–9; Sawyer, *Women and Religion*, 153–6; Flood, *Representations of Eve*, 13.

14. Clark, *Women*, 34; John Chrysostom, "In Genesim: Sermo IV," *PG* 54, 594: Ἔστι τοίνυν ἀρχὴ καὶ δουλεία πρώτη, καθ' ἣν καὶ γυναικῶν οἱ ἄνδρες κρατοῦσι· μετὰ γὰρ τὴν ἁμαρτίαν ἡ ταύτης ἐγένετο χρεία. Πρὸ γὰρ τῆς παρακοῆς ὁμότιμος ἦν τῷ ἀνδρί. Even scholars who attempt to rationalise and justify Chrysostom's condescending, to say the least, tone and remarks regarding women and their role in society agree that for Chrysostom Eve, who is the main culprit of the Fall, the one who misled Adam and the one who was created second, is the reason for women's submission to men. See David C. Ford, *Women and Men in the Early Church: The Full Views of St. John Chrysostom* (South Canaan, PA: St. Tikhon's Seminary Press, 1996), 90–2; Valerie Karras, "Male Domination of Woman in the Writings of Saint John Chrysostom," *The Greek Orthodox Theological Review* 36, no. 2 (1991): 131–40, here 138–9; and

Theodoros Zissis, Ἄνθρωπος καὶ κόσμος ἐν τῇ οἰκονομίᾳ τοῦ Θεοῦ: Κατά τον Ἱερόν Χρυσόστομον (Man and Word in the History of Salvation: According to John Chrysostom). *Analekta Vlataoōn* 9 (Thessaloniki: Patriarchikon Idryma Paterikōn Meletōn, 1971), 80–1.

15. Aphrahat, *Demonstration* VI:6, 181 (all references to Aphrahat's *Demonstrations* and the cited translations are from Lehto, *The Demonstrations of Aphrahat*).

16. Aphrahat, *Demonstration* IX:14, 250: "The condition of Adam was earthy; he was from the ground. His Lord gave him a command to keep; if he had kept what was commanded him, his Lord would have brought him to an exalted position. But because he wanted to receive exaltation, which was not part of his original condition, his Lord made him return to his former condition of abasement"; XIV:37, 341: "But the transgression of the Law is found with Adam. From the first day and forever, he transgresses the Law."

17. Flood, *Representations of Eve*, 16; Sawyer, *Women and Religion*, 155–7.

18. John Chrysostom, "Expositio in Psalmum XLIV," *PG* 55, 193: Παρθένος ἡμᾶς ἐξέβαλε παραδείσου, διὰ παρθένου ζωὴν εὕρομεν αἰωνίαν. For similar ideas, see also Proclus, Archbishop of Constantinople, "Oratio de Laudibus S. Mariae," in *Patrologiae Cursus Completus: Series Graeca*, ed. Jacques Paul Migne, col. 715–758, v. 65. Paris, 1864; and Irenaeus, *Contra Haereses*, *PG* 7, 3.22, 958–60.

19. See Sebastian Brock, *The Luminous Eye: The Spiritual World Vision of Saint Ephrem*. Rev. ed. Cistercian Studies Series, no. 124 (Kalamazoo, MI: Cistercian Publications, 1992), 71–3, 126–7; and idem, *Brides of Light: Hymns on Mary from the Syriac Churches* (Kerala: St. Ephrem Ecumenical Research Institute, 1994), 3, 6, 25, 31–2, 34.

20. Ibid., 25.

21. Ibid., 34.

22. Aphrahat, *Demonstration* VI:6, 181.

23. Flood, *Representations of Eve*, 16.

24. Ibid., 14.

25. Ruether, "Misogynism," 150–7.

26. Flood, *Representations of Eve*, 21–4; Sawyer, *Women and Religion*, 151.

27. Flood, *Representations of Eve*, 22.

28. John Chrysostom, *Homilies on Genesis 1–17*, 200; "In Genesim: Homilia XV," *PG* 53, 122: κατά πάντα τῷ ἀνθρώπῳ ὅμοιον, ἀντὶ τοῦ, λογικόν, δυνάμενον ἐν τοῖς καιρίοις αὐτῷ καὶ τοῖς ἀναγκαίοις καὶ συνέχουσι τὴν ζωὴν τὰ τῆς βοηθείας εἰσφέρειν.

29. John Chrysostom, *Homilies on Genesis 1–17*, 111; "In Genesim: Homilia VIII," *PG* 53, 73: Ἐπειδὴ γὰρ κατὰ τὸν τῆς ἀρχῆς λόγον τὸ τῆς εἰκόνος παρείληφε, καὶ οὐ κατὰ τὴν μορφήν, ὁ δὲ ἄνθρωπος ἀρχὴ πάντων, ἡ δὲ γυνὴ ὑποτέτακται, διὰ τοῦτο φησι περὶ τοῦ ἀνδρός ὁ Παῦλος, ὅτι εἰκὼν καὶ δόξα Θεοῦ ὑπάρχει, ἡ δὲ γυνὴ δόξα ἀνδρός ἐστιν.

30. Clark, *Women*, 27. See also ibid., 27–76 for extracts from Greek and Latin Fathers discussing the creation narrative.

31. Flood, *Representations of Eve*, 16.

32. The Armenian text and English translation of Agat'angełos's *History*, including the *Teaching of Saint Gregory*, will be referred to as *Aa*: for the Armenian text, see Agat'angełos, *Patmut'iwn Hayoc'*; for the English translation of the *History*, see Thomson, *The Lives of Saint Gregory*, and for the English translation of the *Teaching*, see Thomson, *The Teaching*.

33. *Aa* §79: Չի զոր օրինակ ի ձեռն կուսին առաջնոյ Եւայի մահ եմուտ յաշխարհ՝ սոյն օրինակ եւ ի ձեռն այսր կուսի կեանք մտցեն յաշխարհ: Չի զոր օրինակ ի ձեռն ծնընդեան Եւայի՝ Կահելի անէծք եւ բրտունք եւ աշխատութիւնք եւ երերմունք եւ տատանմունք մտին յաշխարհ՝ սոյն օրինակ եւ ծնանելով Որդւոյ քոյ ի կուսէն հանգիստք եւ կեանք եւ օրհնութիւնք մտցեն յաշխարհ·

34. Ibid., §141: Իսկ իբրեւ տեսին առաքինիքն զզաղտածիզ նեստ բշնամւոյն, որ ի ծածուկն սովոր էր ձգել ի սուրբսն քրիստոսասէրսն, աման չարի զտեալ զթագաւորն. որպէս ի դրախտի անդ զօձն անդրունար արարեալ, առ ի պատուիրանէն մոոանալոյ, մտեալ յանզզամ յունկն կնոջն առաջնոյ. սոյնպէս եւ ասա զթագաւորն անօրէն իբրեւ զվահանակ երեսաց զտեալ՝ նովաւ մարտուցեալ ընդ աստուածաշէն եկեղեցիս.

35. As pointed out by Robert Murray ("Mary, the Second Eve in Syriac Tradition," *Eastern Churches Review* 3 (1971): 372–84, here 374): "[t]he reference to ears is a peculiarity of Syriac tradition," according to which not only was Eve deceived by listening to the serpent, but also "Mary conceived by the Word entering her by the ear."

36. Valentina Calzolari, "Le sang des femmes et le plan de Dieu: Réflexions à partir de l'historiographie arménienne ancienne (Ve siècle ap. J.-C.)," in *Victimes au féminin: Actes du colloque de l'Université de Genève, 8–9 mars 2010*, ed. Agnes A. Nagy and Francesca Prescendi (Genève: Georg, 2011), 178–94, here 187.

37. Thomson, *The Lives*, 13–15.

38. *Aa* §§263–264, 271, 273, 275, and 350.

39. *Aa* §275: Այս այժմ ոսկր յոսկերաց իմոց եւ մարմին ի մարմնոյ իմմէ. սա կոչեսցի կին, զի յառնէ իւրմէ առաւ; "This bone now is from my bone, and this flesh from my flesh; she will be called woman, because she was taken from her husband."

40. *Aa* §§275–276.

41. Ibid., §§279–281.

42. *Aa* §279: ունէր ազատութիւն Ադամ եւ անձնիշխան կամս եւ իմաստութիւն յԱստուծոյ. On Adam's free will in fifth-century texts, see Stone, *Adam and Eve*, 19–21.

43. *Aa* §280: նորա վասն նորին պատճառանաց խաբեալք՝ ճաշակեցին, եւ անցեալ զպատուիրանաւն՝ յաստուածակերպ փառացն մերկացան.

44. *Aa* §392: Եւ յղացեալ այնուհետեւ ի Հոգւոյն սրբոյ շնորհագիւտ կուսին յանարատ յանապական արգանդին զորդին Աստուծոյ՝ անհասական պայմանաւ. Cf. John Chrysostom, "In Matthaeum: Homilia IV," *PG* 57, 42: Καὶ πῶς τὸ Πνεῦμα εἰργάσατο τοῦτο ἐκ παρθένου; Εἰ γὰρ τῆς φύσεως ἐργαζομένης ἀδύνατον ἑρμηνεῦσαι τῆς διαπλάσεως τὸν τρόπον, πῶς τοῦ Πνεύματος θαυματουργοῦντος δυνησόμεθα ταῦτα εἰπεῖν; "'But how was it that the Spirit wrought this of a virgin?' For if, when nature is at work, it is impossible to explain the manner of the formation; how, when the Spirit is working miracles, shall we be able to express these?" (John Chrysostom, "Epistle of St Paul," 22).

45. *Aa* §684: եւ կանայք օրհնեցան վասն կուսանին ծննդեանն որ ի նոցանէն.
46. For the Armenian text, see Ełišē, *Ełišēi Vardapeti vasn Vardanac'* and for the English translation – Ełišē, *History of Vardan*. For the sake of convenience, both texts of the *History* are referred to as Ełišē, followed by the page number of the English translation and in square brackets by the page number of the Armenian original. Whereas for the bilingual (Classical Armenian and English) *Commentary of Genesis* attributed to Ełišē and cited below, I shall use Ełišē, *Meknut'iwn Araracoc'*.
47. Ełišē, 89 [37]: Ո՜ւն ի հրեշտակաց յանսահիցն զնդէն ստամբակեալ եւ ի բաց զնացեալ յերկնից, եւ ի մեր աշխարհս եկալ՝ պատիր բանիւք եւ սուտ խոստմամբ զանվնեալի յոյսն առաջի դնէր՝ իբրեւ տղայ մանկան՝ անփորձ եւ անկիրթ նորաթեք մարդոյն, ի վեր հայեցուցանելով զմիտս նորա, ուտելով ի պտղոյ ծառոյն, - յոր հուպն չիրամայեաց երթալ, - զի լիցի աստուած: Իսկ նորա մոռացեալ զպատուիրանն Աստուծոյ, խաբեցաւ զկնի մոլար խաբէութեանն, կորոյս զոր ունէր զիաստ անմահութեանն, եւ չեհաս երազայոյս կարծեացն: Վասն որոյ եւ մէրժեալ ի կենաց տեղւոյն, ընկեցաւ յայսականելի աշխարհս, յորում եւ դուք էք բնակեալ այժմ, եւ ցնորեալ մոլորիք զկնի նորին խրատատու. ոչ եւս ուտելով ի պատուիրեալ ծառոյն, այլ զարարածս աստուած ասելով, եւ անիսա տարերցս երկիր պագանելով, եւ անդրովայն դիւաց կերակուր մատուցանելով, եւ յարարիչն բոլորեցունց ի բաց լինելով.
48. See, for example, Gen 1:26–27 and Gen 2:18.
49. Ełišē, 86 [32]: Զի որ ինքն [Աստուած] անապական է, եւ զարարածս առանց ապականութեան ծնաւ. իսկ սա կամօք զլորեալ ապականեցաւ, եւ անձամբ եւս ոչ կարէր կանզնել կալ ի վերայ ոտից: Վասն զի էր ի հողոյ, անձամբ անձին արարեալ՝ անդրէն ի նոյն բնութիւն դարձաւ.
50. For the Armenian text, see Łazar P'arpec'i, *Patmut'iwn Hayoc' ew T'ułt'*; for the English translation, see Łazar P'arpec'i, *History of Łazar P'arpec'i*. For the sake of convenience, both texts are referred to as *ŁP*, followed by the page number of the English translation and in square brackets by the page number of the Armenian original.
51. *ŁP*, 251 [188]: ի սկզբանն զնախաստեղծն ընկճեալ նախանձու բանսարկուին՝ դարձոյց զնա ի հող.
52. Some scholars attribute the collection to the Armenian theologian Yovhan Mayragomec'i (ca 575 – 650). See, e.g., Aram Mardirossian, *Le Livre des Canons Arméniens (Kanonagirk' Hayoc') de Yovhannēs Awjnec'i: Église, Droit et Société en Arménie du IVe au VIIIe Siècle* (Lovanii: Peeters, 2004), 260–3; and Hambarjum M. K'enderyan, *Hovhan Mayragomec'i: Kyank'ə ew Gorcuneut'yunə* (Yerevan: Haykakan SSH GA Hratarakč'ut'yun, 1973), 63–133. However, Mandakuni's authorship seems equally possible, as advocated by Hrant T'amrazyan, "Erku Hayac'k' Ašxarhik Arvesti masin ew Hovhan Mandakunu Čaṙə" (Two Perspectives on Secular Art and the Homily by Yovhan Mandakuni), in *Hay K'nnadatut'yun: Grakan Mtk'i Akunk'nerə ew Jewavorumə: V Dar* (Armenian Criticism: The Origins and Formation of Literary Thinking: V Century), ed. Hrant T'amrazyan (v. I. Yerevan: Sovetakan Groł, 1983), 183–221, here 183–205.
53. Yovhan Mandakuni, *Teaṙn Yovhannu*, 188: Արար Աստուած զմարդն, եւ եդ զնա ի դրախտին փափկութեան, զամենայն զզայութիւնս ողջունելով ի բնութեան իւրում: Արդ իբրեւ լուաւ այնմ՝ որ խաբեացն զնա, յայնժամ էառ

զախտս ամենայն, եւ իսկույն ընկեցեալ եղեւ արտաքս ի մեծ եւ շքնաղ փառաց իւրոց. Չի ծանիցէ մարդ՝ թէ զոն ախտր որ մերժեն զնա յԱստուծոյ.

54. Ibid., 189: Այս է զոր երարձն Ադամ՝ յորժամ եկերն ի պտղոյ ծառոյն, եւ անկաւ ընդ ոտիւք մահուն.

55. Ibid., 100: Քանզի ընկիզրն ախտից է նախանծ եւ շառակնութիւն. զի նովաւ անկաւ սատանայ ի փառացն, նովաւ եւ Ադամ ի դրախտէն. եւ անէծք եւ բրտուունք, փուշ եւ տատասկ, մահ եւ մերք ի վերայ ամենայն ծնընդոց Ադամայ տիրեցին.

56. In *On A Small Theft about Which They Do Not Confess*, Mandakuni provides the example of Adam, who "did not steal much but cut a certain fruit. And now behold a multitude of punishments, curses, and death, not only upon Adam but also upon all Adam's offspring. For he was not guilty of stealing the fruit, but of [breaking] the Creator's commandments and word that came out of his mouth"; եւ Ադամայ ոչ եթէ մեծ էին գողացնք, այլ հատումն մի յնչ մրգոյ. եւ արդ տես զբազում հոյլք պատուհասիցն, զանիծիցն եւ զմահուցն, ոչ միայն ի վերայ Ադամայ, այլեւ ամենայն ծնընդոց Ադամայ. զի ոչ եթէ գողուն մրգոցն եղեւ պարտապան, այլ հրամանացն արարչին եւ բանի բերանոյ նորա (ibid., 115). In the homily *On Steadfastness in Fasting*, Mandakuni refers to Adam by saying that he "abandoned the steadfast fasting and left the Paradise for the land that produces thorns"; Ահա Ադամ հեռացաւ ի պահոցն ալնդուէթենէ, եւ ել ի դրախտէն յերկիր փշաբեր (ibid., 33).

57. Nelli Petrosyan, "'Hačaxapatum čaṙk'i' kaṙuc'vack'n u žanrayin bnuyt'ə" (The Structure and the Genre of the 'Hačaxapatum čaṙk''), *Kant'eł* 2 (2016): 118–23.

58. A. N. Srapyan, "'Yačaxapatum' čaṙeri hełinaki harc'ə" (On the Authorship of the 'Yačaxapatum' homilies), *Tełekagir Hasarakakan Gitut'yunneri* 5 (1962): 25–38.

59. See Vardan Hac'uni, "Erb šaradruac en 'Yačaxapatum čaṙk'" (When Were 'Yačaxapatum čaṙk'' Composed?), *Bazmavēp* 10 (1930): 401–6; and Kiwreł K'iparean, "'Yačaxapatum' čaṙeru hełinaki harc'ə" (The Question of the Author of the 'Yačaxapatum' Homilies), *Bazmavēp* 9–12 (1962): 237–42.

60. Grigor Lusaworič', *Srboy Hōrn Meroy Grigori Lusaworč'i Yačaxapatum Čaṙk' ew Ałōt'k'* (Venice: I Tparani Srboyn Łazaru, 1954), Homily IX, 101: Չի որպէս անձունկալութիւնն Եւայի եւ Ադամայ անէծս ի վերայ էած եւ մահ, նոյնպէս ծնելոցս ի նոցանէ որ զնոյն անձունժութիւնն ունին՝ արտաքոյ բարւոյն որդւայնամոյութեամբն անկանիցին.

61. See footnote 9.

62. With regard to the authorship and date of the *Commentary* no scholarly consensus has been reached yet. For the fifth-century date and Ełišē's authorship, see, for example, Boghos Levon Zekiyan, "Quelques observations critiques sur le 'Corpus Elisaeanum'," in *The Armenian Christian Tradition: Scholarly Symposium in Honor of the Visit to the Pontifical Oriental Institute, Rome of His Holiness Karekin I, Supreme Patriarch and Catholicos of all Armenians, December 12, 1996*, ed. Robert F. Taft (Roma: Pontificio Instituto Orientale, 1997), 71–123, here 107–15. Robert W. Thomson, "Is There an Armenian Tradition of Exegesis?" in Papers Presented at the Fourteenth International Conference on Patristic Studies Held in Oxford 2003, ed. Frances M. Young, Mark J. Edwards, and Paul M. Parvis (Leuven: Peeters, 2006), 97–113 here 101–2, on the other hand, expressed doubts about this attribution and date. Levon Xač'ikyan produced a critical edition of the surviving fragments of the text preserved in a few manuscripts,

which was published posthumously in 1992 and then reproduced with an English translation in 2004. For details, see Ełišē, *Meknut'iwn Araracoc'* (Commentary on Genesis), ed. Levon Xač'ikyan, Hakob Kyoseyan, and translated by Michael Papazian (Yerevan: Magaghat Publishing House, 2004), 8–13.

63. Thomson, "Is There an Armenian Tradition of Exegesis?," 102.

64. Ełišē, *Meknut'iwn Araracoc'*, 51; [. . .] մի համապատիւ իցէ, որպէս եւ ոչ հանգէտումանակ եւ ոչ համահասակ, այլ կրսեր եւ երկրորդ, զի հնազանդ լիցի Ադամայ եւ լուռ: Զի որպէս խաւպէն զլխոյն է եւ լութիւնն կողին (ibid., 50).

65. Ibid., 67; Զի նախ հաւասարք էին, եւ զի կամեցաւ ճոխանալ քան զայրն (ibid., 66).

66. Ibid., 67; յիշխանութենէ, եւ ի քաղաքավարութենէ, եւ առնէ տերութիւն եւ ամենայն աստիճանք պատուականք.

67. Ibid.: Նախ աւձն խաբեաց, ապա կինն պատրեալ եկեր, եւ, ապա Ադամ առաւ ի կնոջէն եկեր «փոխանակ զի լուար ձայնի կնոջ քո»: Յայտ արարեալ թէ ոչ վճարէ ինչ պատճառէն զայլս, որք խաբեցինն զայս եւ սկիզբն եղեն մեղացն. փոխանակ զի լուար ձայնի կնոջդ եւ ոչ Աստուծոյ ՝ անիծեալ լիցի երկիր ի գործու քո; First, the snake tricked the woman, the woman was deceived and ate, and then Adam took the fruit from the woman and ate "because you listened to the voice of your wife." He makes clear that he does not acquit the blaming of others, who tricked and became the origin of sin. Because you listened to the voice of your wife and not God, the earth is cursed because of your deeds (ibid.).

68. Ibid., 73; Եւ կոչեաց Ադամ զանուն կնոջ իւրոյ կեանս: Նա որ զամենայն կենդանեացն անուն կոչեաց եւ զկնոջն՝ Եւայ, զի մարգարէաբար գիտաց, թէ նա, որ մայր եղեւ մահու, լինի եւ մայր ամենայն մարդոյ, որ գալոց են յաշխարհ: Այն որ առ ի ձեռաց նորա զպտուղն եւ ոչ ի ծառոյն զի մեղքն ընդ նմա գթովք. յարինակ Տեառն, որ ընդ մեղաւորացս ընտրեաց մեռանիլ ողորմութեամբ իւրով : 22 Եւ արդ, կոչէ զնա կեանք՝ մխիթարել զնա ի յոյս դստեր նորա՝ Մարիամու, որ ստուգապէս մայր եղեւ այնմ, որ ասացն ՝ «Ես եմ կեանք»: Նա է մայր ամենայն կենդանեաց (ibid., 72).

69. See Zakarian, *Women, Too, Were Blessed*, Armenian Texts and Studies Series, vol. 4, especially 41–66.

70. James R. Russell, *Zoroastrianism in Armenia* (Cambridge, MA: Harvard University, Department of Near Eastern Languages and Civilizations; National Association for Armenian Studies and Research, 1987), 15.

71. See Zakarian, *Women, Too, Were Blessed*, 50–1 and 152–4.

72. See Zaroui Pogossian, "Women at the Beginning of Christianity in Armenia," *Orientalia Christiana Periodica* 69 (2003): 355–80, here 373–5; and Zakarian, *Women, Too, Were Blessed*, 143–51.

BIBLIOGRAPHY

Agat'angełos. *Patmut'iwn Hayoc'* (History of the Armenians), edited by Galust Tēr-Mkrtč'ean and Step'an Kanayeanc'. Introduction by Robert W. Thomson. Facs. reprod. 1909 Tiflis edition. Delmar: Caravan Books, 1979.

Becking, Bob. "Once in a Garden: Some Remarks on the Construction of the Identity of Woman and Man in Genesis 2–3." In *Out of Paradise: Eve and Adam and Their Interpreters*, edited by Bob Becking and Susanne Hennecke, 1–13. Sheffield: Sheffield Phoenix Press, 2011.

Bonfiglio, Emilio. "The Armenian Translations of John Chrysostom: The Issues of Selection." In *Caught in Translation: Studies on Versions of Late Antique Christian Literature,* edited by Madalina Toca and Dan Batovici, 35–63. Leiden: Brill, 2020. https://doi.org/10.1163/9789004417182_004.

Brock, Sebastian. *The Luminous Eye: The Spiritual World Vision of Saint Ephrem.* Rev. ed. Cistercian Studies Series, no. 124. Kalamazoo: Cistercian Publications, 1992.

Brock, Sebastian (ed. and trans.). *Brides of Light: Hymns on Mary from the Syriac Churches*. Kerala: St. Ephrem Ecumenical Research Institute, 1994.

Calzolari, Valentina. "Le sang des femmes et le plan de Dieu: Réflexions à partir de l'historiographie arménienne ancienne (Ve siècle ap. J.-C.)." In *Victimes au féminin: Actes du colloque de l'Université de Genève, 8–9 mars 2010*, edited by Agnes A. Nagy and Francesca Prescendi, 178–94. Genève: Georg, 2011.

Cameron, Averil. "Sacred and Profane Love: Thoughts on Byzantine Gender." In *Women, Men and Eunuchs: Gender in Byzantium*, edited by Liz James, 1–23. London: Routledge, 1997.

Clark, Elizabeth A. *Women in the Early Church*. Message of the Fathers of the Church, v. 13. Wilmington: M. Glazier, 1983.

Clark, Elizabeth A. "Devil's Gateway and Bride of Christ: Women in the Early Christian World." In *Ascetic Piety and Women's Faith: Essays on Late Ancient Christianity*, edited by Elizabeth A. Clark, 23–60. Women and Religion 20. Lewiston: Edwin Mellen Press, 1986.

Clark, Elizabeth A. "Ideology, History, and the Construction of 'Woman' in Late Ancient Christianity." *Journal of Early Christian Studies* 2, no. 2 (1994): 155–84.

Ełišē. *Ełišēi Vardapeti vasn Vardanac' ew Hayoc' Paterazmin* (On Vardan and His Men, and on the War of the Armenians). Jerusalem: I Tparani Srboc' Yakovbeanc', 1865.

Ełišē. *History of Vardan and the Armenian War*. Translated and edited by Robert W. Thomson. Cambridge, MA: Harvard University Press, 1982.

Ełišē. *Meknut'iwn Araracoc'* (Commentary on Genesis). Edited by Levon Xač'ikyan, Hakob Kyoseyan, and translated by Michael Papazian. Yerevan: Magaghat Publishing House, 2004.

Flood, John. *Representations of Eve in Antiquity and the English Middle Ages*. Routledge Studies in Medieval Religion and Culture. London: Routledge, 2011.

Ford, David C. *Women and Men in the Early Church: The Full Views of St. John Chrysostom*. South Canaan: St. Tikhon's Seminary Press, 1996.

Grigor Lusaworič'. *Srboy Hōrn Meroy Grigori Lusaworč'i Yačaxapatum Čaṙk' ew Ałōt'k'* (Dogmatic Homilies and Prayers of Our Holy Father Grigor Lusaworč'). Venice: I Tparani Srboyn Łazaru, 1954.

Hac'uni, Vardan. "Erb šaradruac en 'Yačaxapatum čaṙk'"" (When Were 'Yačaxapatum čaṙk'' Composed?). *Bazmavēp* 10 (1930): 401–06.

Irenaeus. *Contra Haereses*. In *Patrologiae Cursus Completus: Series Graeca*, Vol. 7, edited by Jacques Paul Migne. Paris, 1857.
John Chrysostom. "In Genesim: Homilia VIII." In *Patrologiae Cursus Completus: Series Graeca*, edited by Jacques Paul Migne, col. 69–76, Vol. 53. Paris, 1862.
John Chrysostom. "In Genesim: Homilia XV." In *Patrologiae Cursus Completus: Series Graeca*, edited by Jacques Paul Migne, col. 118–125, Vol. 53. Paris, 1862.
John Chrysostom. "In Genesim: Sermo IV." In *Patrologiae Cursus Completus: Series Graeca*, edited by Jacques Paul Migne, col. 593–598, Vol. 54. Paris, 1862.
John Chrysostom. "Expositio in Psalmum XLIV." In *Patrologiae Cursus Completus: Series Graeca*, edited by Jacques Paul Migne, col. 182–203, Vol. 55. Paris, 1862.
John Chrysostom. "In Matthaeum: Homilia IV." In *Patrologiae Cursus Completus: Series Graeca*, edited by Jacques Paul Migne, col. 39–54, Vol. 57. Paris, 1862.
John Chrysostom. *Homilies on Genesis 1–17*. Translated by Robert C. Hill. Washington, DC: The Catholic University of America Press, 1986.
John Chrysostom. "Epistle of St Paul the Apostle to the Ephesians." In *Homilies on Galatians, Ephesians, Philippians, Colossians, Thessalonians, Timothy, Titus, and Philemon*, edited by Philip Schaff and translated by Alexander Gross, 49–172. Nicene and Post-Nicene Fathers. Series 1, Vol. 13. Peabody: Hendrickson Publishers, 1994.
Karras, Valerie. "Male Domination of Woman in the Writings of Saint John Chrysostom." *The Greek Orthodox Theological Review* 36, no. 2 (1991): 131–40.
Kʻenderyan, Hambarjum M. *Hovhan Mayragomecʻi: Kyankʻə ew Gorcuneutʻyunə* (Yovhan Mayragomecʻi: Life and Work). Yerevan: Haykakan SSH GA Hratarakčʻutʻyun, 1973.
Kʻiparean, Kiwreł. "'Yačaxapatum' čaṙeru hełinaki harcʻə" (The Question of the Author of the 'Yačaxapatum' Homilies). *Bazmavēp* 9–12 (1962): 237–42.
Kvam, Kristen E., Linda S. Schearing, and Valarie H. Ziegler, eds. *Eve and Adam: Jewish, Christian, and Muslim Readings on Genesis and Gender*. Bloomington: Indiana University Press, 1999. https://doi.org/10.2307/j.ctt2050vqm.
Łazar Pʻarpecʻi. *Patmutʻiwn Hayocʻ ew Tʻułtʻ aṙ Vahan Mamikonean* (History of Armenia and Letter to Vahan Mamikonean). Edited by Galust Tēr-Mkrtčʻean and Stepʻanos Malxasean. Tʻiflis: Tparan Mnacʻakan Martiroseancʻi, 1904.
Łazar Pʻarpecʻi. *History of Łazar Pʻarpecʻi*. Translated by Robert W. Thomson. Atlanta: Scholars Press, 1991.
Lehto, Adam (trans. and ed.). *The Demonstrations of Aphrahat, the Persian Sage*. Gorgias Eastern Christianity Studies 27. Piscataway: Gorgias Press, 2010.
Mardirossian, Aram. *Le Livre des Canons Arméniens (Kanonagirkʻ Hayocʻ) de Yovhannēs Awjnecʻi: Église, Droit et Société en Arménie du IVe au VIIIe Siècle*. Lovanii: Peeters, 2004.
Mathews, Edward G. Jr. "Early Armenian and Syrian Contact: Reflections on Koriwn's *Life of Maštocʻ*." *St. Nersess Theological Review* 7 (2002): 5–27.
Murray, Robert. "Mary, the Second Eve in Syriac Tradition." *Eastern Churches Review* 3 (1971): 372–84.

Otten, Willemien. "The Long Shadow of Human Sin: Augustine on Adam, Eve and the Fall." In *Out of Paradise: Eve and Adam and Their Interpreters*, edited by Bob Becking and Susanne Hennecke, 29–49. Sheffield: Sheffield Phoenix Press, 2011.

Petrosyan, Nelli. "'Hačaxapatum čaṙk'i' kaṙuc'vack'n u žanrayin bnuyt'ə" (The Structure and the Genre of the 'Hačaxapatum čaṙk'"). *Kant'eł* 2 (2016): 118–23.

Pogossian, Zaroui. "Women at the Beginning of Christianity in Armenia." *Orientalia Christiana Periodica* 69 (2003): 355–80.

Proclus, Archbishop of Constantinople. "Oratio de Laudibus S. Mariae." In *Patrologiae Cursus Completus: Series Graeca*, edited by Jacques Paul Migne, col. 715–758, Vol. 65. Paris, 1864.

Ruether, Rosemary Radford. "Misogynism and Virginal Feminism in the Fathers of the Church." In *Religion and Sexism: Images of Women in the Jewish and Christian Traditions*, edited by Rosemary Radford Ruether, 150–83. Eugene: Wipf and Stock, 1998.

Russell, James R. *Zoroastrianism in Armenia*. Cambridge, MA: Harvard University, Department of Near Eastern Languages and Civilizations; National Association for Armenian Studies and Research, 1987.

Sawyer, Deborah F. *Women and Religion in the First Christian Centuries*. London: Routledge, 1996.

Srapyan, A. N. "'Yačaxapatum' čaṙeri hełinaki harc'ə" (On the Authorship of the 'Yačaxapatum' homilies). *Tełekagir Hasarakakan Gitut'yunneri* 5 (1962): 25–38.

Stone, Michael E. "The Death of Adam: An Armenian Adam Book." *Harvard Theological Review* 59 (1973): 283–91.

Stone, Michael E. *The Penitence of Adam*. 2 vols. *CSCO* 40–41, *Scriptores Armeniaci* 14. Leuven: Peeters, 1981.

Stone, Michael E. "Adam and Eve Traditions in Fifth Century Armenian Literature." *Le Muséon* 119, no. 1–2 (2006): 89–120. https://doi.org/10.2143/MUS.119.1.2011770.

Stone, Michael E. *Adamgirk': The Adam Book of Aṙak'el of Siwnik'*. New York: Oxford University Press, 2007.

Stone, Michael E. "Satan and the Serpent in the Armenian Tradition." In *Beyond Eden: The Biblical Story of Paradise (Genesis 2–3) and Its Reception History*, edited by Konrad Schmid and Christoph Riedweg, 141–86. Tübingen: Mohr Siebeck, 2008.

Stone, Michael E. *Adam and Eve in the Armenian Traditions: Fifth through Seventeenth Centuries*. Atlanta: Society of Biblical Literature, 2013.

T'amrazyan, Hrant. "Erku Hayac'k' Ašxarhik Arvesti masin ew Hovhan Mandakunu Čaṙə" (Two Perspectives on Secular Art and the Homily by Yovhan Mandakuni). In *Hay K'nnadatut'yun: Grakan Mtk'i Akunk'nerə ew Jewavorumə: V Dar* (Armenian Criticism: The Origins and Formation of Literary Thinking: V Century), edited by Hrant T'amrazyan, 183–221, Vol. I. Yerevan: Sovetakan Groł, 1983.

Ter-Minasyan, Ervand G. *Hayoc' Ekełec'u Yaraberut'iwnnerə Asorwoc' Ekełec'ineri het (Haykakan ew Asorakan Ałbiwrneri hamajayn)* (The Relations between the

Armenian Church and the Syrian Churches [according to Armenian and Syriac Sources]), 2nd ed. Ējmiacin: Mayr At'oṙ S. Ējmiacni Hratarakč'ut'yun, 2009.

Ter-Petrosyan, Levon. "La plus ancienne traduction arménienne des *Chroniques*: Étude préliminaire." *Revue des Études Arméniennes* 18 (1984): 215–25.

Thomson, Robert W. "The Fathers in Early Armenian Literature." *Studia Patristica* 12 (1975): 457–70. Berlin: Akademie Verlag GmbH. Reprinted in *Studies in Armenian Literature and Christianity* XII. Variorum, 1994.

Thomson, Robert W. (trans. and ed.). *The Teaching of Saint Gregory*. New Rochelle: St. Nersess Armenian Seminary, 2001.

Thomson, Robert W. "Is There an Armenian Tradition of Exegesis?" In *Papers Presented at the Fourteenth International Conference on Patristic Studies Held in Oxford 2003*, edited by Frances M. Young, Mark J. Edwards, and Paul M. Parvis, 97–113. *Studia Patristica*, Vol. 41. Leuven: Peeters, 2006.

Thomson, Robert W. (trans. and ed.). *The Lives of Saint Gregory: The Armenian, Greek, Arabic, and Syriac Versions of the History Attributed to Agathangelos*. Ann Arbor: Caravan Books, 2010.

Van Lint, Theo M. "The Formation of Armenian Identity in the First Millennium." *Church History and Religious Culture* 89, no. 1–3 (2009): 251–78. https://doi.org/10.1163/187124109X407925.

Van Oyen, Geert. "The Character of Eve in the New Testament: 2 Corinthians 11.3 and 1 Timothy 2.13–14." In *Out of Paradise: Eve and Adam and Their Interpreters*, edited by Bob Becking and Susanne Hennecke, 14–28. Sheffield: Sheffield Phoenix Press, 2011.

Yovhan Mandakuni. *Teaṙn Yovhannu Mandakunwoy Hayoc' Hayrapeti Čaṙk'* (Homilies of Our Lord Armenian Patriarch Yovhan Mandakuni), 2nd ed. Venice: I Tparani Srboyn Łazaru, 1860.

Zakarian, David. *Women, Too, Were Blessed: The Portrayal of Women in Early Christian Armenian Texts*. Armenian Texts and Studies Series, Vol. 4. Leiden: Brill, 2021. https://doi.org/10.1163/9789004445031.

Zekiyan, Boghos Levon. "Quelques observations critiques sur le "Corpus Elisaeanum." In *The Armenian Christian Tradition: Scholarly Symposium in Honor of the Visit to the Pontifical Oriental Institute, Rome of His Holiness Karekin I, Supreme Patriarch and Catholicos of all Armenians, December 12, 1996*, edited by Robert F. Taft, 71–123. Roma: Pontificio Instituto Orientale, 1997.

Zissis, Theodoros. Ἄνθρωπος καὶ κόσμος ἐν τῇ οἰκονομίᾳ τοῦ Θεοῦ: Κατά τον Ἱερόν Χρυσόστομον (Man and Word in the History of Salvation: According to John Chrysostom). *Analekta Vlataoōn* 9. Thessaloniki: Patriarchikon Idryma Paterikōn Meletōn, 1971.

13

The Stillborn Messiah and the Non-Viable Redeemer

Gender and Judeo-Christian Entanglement

Ruth Kara-Ivanov Kaniel

There's something preliminary about Jewish history; hence its inability to give of itself entirely. For the Messianic idea is not only consolation and hope. Every attempt to realize it tears open the abysses which lead each of its manifestations *ad absurdum*. There is something grand about living in hope, but at the same time there is something profoundly unreal about it. It diminishes the singular worth of the individual, and he can never fulfill himself, because the incompleteness of his endeavors eliminates precisely what constitutes its highest value. Thus in Judaism the Messianic idea has compelled a *life lived in deferment*, in which nothing can be done definitively, nothing can be irrevocably accomplished. One may say, perhaps, the Messianic idea is the real anti-existentialist idea.[1]

In kabbalistic literature, activity is linked to masculinity, while passivity is linked to femininity. Both divine and human masculine power are characterized by breaking through, setting in motion, breaching and inseminating. Containing, holding, bearing, and accepting the seed are on the other hand attributes of the *Bina* and the *Shekhinah*, the sublime mother and daughter, respectively, as well as emblematic of human feminine figures. Yet, the Messiah, who symbolizes the epitome of life and rebirth, surprisingly appears in midrashic and kabbalistic traditions as a "dead baby" or a hero that almost was not born. Death, suffering, deterioration, weakness, brokenness, and passiveness seem to be inappropriate symbols of the redeemer, who is naturally associated with almighty power and is considered a superhero. In the following contribution I explore the motif of a "non-viable Messiah" as a concept that reflects history-gendered collective identities and liminal cultural personalities. Utilizing the tools of mythic studies combined with gender theory, I discuss Jewish and Christian attitudes toward controversial issues pertaining to the subject of a Messiah who possesses feminine attributes. My discussion will follow the development of shared patterns of thought between the two religions, such as the positing of "two Messiahs" or the archetypal connections between Adam, David, Joseph, and Jesus, ideas that can be traced from early antiquity to the Zoharic literature in the Middle Ages, and even to Safedian kabbalah of the sixteenth century.

In recent years, I dedicated a study to the figure of King David as a feminine Messiah in the kabbalistic literature.[2] My book on this topic raised the question of why the "masculine David," warrior and conqueror, was "converted" in the Zohar into a representation of the *Shekhinah*, the major feminine configuration of the Godhead. By combining different fields of research, such as literary theories of myth and mysticism, gender studies, psychoanalysis, and theories of masculinity and sexuality, as well as of comparative religion, I have argued that this tendency to identify David with a feminine figure may be rooted in Jewish and Christian discourses, interfaith polemics, and interfaith dialogues. In addition, I have suggested that notions of the feminized Messiah reflect issues of national identity and political authority.

Consequently, I have claimed that the figure of the *Shekhinah*, or the feminine *sefirah* of *Malkhut*, represents the fragility of the Jews—who, though deprived of political and national sovereignty, derived from the noetic realm of the divine *sefirot* the invigorating power of endurance. Belief in a spiritual kingdom enhanced these feelings. While *Malkhut* ("kingdom," symbolizing the Messiah and David in the Zohar) does not equate to *melekh* ("king"), the term holds a dual meaning, which enables a gendered context which functions on both the mystical and political levels. Thus, by adhering to "David" and his mystical representation in *Malkhut* (i.e., the *Shekhinah*), the kabbalists transformed their national vulnerability into a virtue. As Gershom Scholem adds, "the magnitude of the Messianic idea corresponds to the endless powerlessness in Jewish history during all the centuries of exile, when it was unprepared to come forward onto the plane of world history."[3]

In the Jewish *mythos*, David has been viewed as a historical and epic figure, even while he simultaneously is presented as a symbol of a mythical entity, one diversely "reincarnated" in various phases of Jewish religious experience. The plethora of homilies about him and their richness in the biblical, rabbinic, kabbalistic, Sabbatean, and Hasidic corpora alike highlight the centrality of the Davidic figure in literature and mythology. In this body of writings, David reflects the faces of the homilists observing him and thus serves as an ideal case study for the gender-oriented and psychoanalytic components of Jewish mysticism. For example, midrashic literature presents David as an idealized hero, righteous judge, and *talmid chaham* (scholar).[4]

The Zohar transforms David into a feminine figure, but there are certain themes concerning him that are systematically and consistently developed over generations. Indeed, the main textual tradition stresses the themes of *sin and repentance* as the key terms for understanding the riddle of salvation and the enigma of the messianic figure. Jewish exegesis, as well as that of the Church Fathers, justified David's sins. The sages labored to present him as the model of a penitent even as they claimed that he had never sinned.[5] By transforming the historical battlefields of the Bible into the metaphorical field of Jewish law, they were able to present David as a pious rabbi. Following Irenaeus, Augustine, and others, later Christian commentators explained that the sins of David had been transformed into virtue. For example, St. Gregory and Angelomus describe David's life as an allegory for the life of Jesus, in which Bathsheba represents the Church (or the New Testament that replaces the Old Testament), and Uriah represents the Jewish nation, namely the Devil, who must be put to death. Thus, Angelomus determines "Let us love David inasmuch as he is to be loved, since he freed us from the devil by his mercy."[6]

In both medieval Jewish and Christian exegesis, David's behavior was cleansed of negative incidents like adultery and infidelity, while his other characteristics (such as his overt sexuality and physical, masculine power) were emphasized.[7] This was done to ensure his rights of ultimate sovereignty and his enduring kingdom.[8] The combination of the motifs of transgression and redemption in the figure of the Redeemer/Messiah reveals a model of chosenness that stems from sexual transgression, which in turn is vindicated through *tikkun* (reparation) and repentance.

I now turn to the motif of the Messiah "that was born dead," as it develops from the biblical narrative and rabbinic midrash through the Zohar, in order to analyze the centrality of David's figure as vulnerable and thus feminized in medieval Jewish and Christian entanglement and polemic.

DAVID AS A STILLBORN AND *BAR NAFLE*

Three main midrashic traditions explore the idea that David lacks life and struggles to survive, from his first appearance "on the stage of history."

1. The first tradition, which appears in the Talmud tractate *Sanhedrin*, designates the Messiah as "son of the fallen" (*Bar Nafle*), who was granted life as a gift:

> R. Nahman said to R. Isaac: "Have you heard when Bar Nafle will come?" "Who is Bar Nafle?" he asked. "Messiah," he answered. "Do you call Messiah Bar Nafle?"—"Even so," he rejoined, "as it is written, 'in that day I will raise up the tabernacle of David *ha-nofelet* [that is fallen].'"[9]

The term *Nafle* holds a double meaning: while it might allude to the miraculous giants or titans (*Nephilim*) and supernatural heroes to whom the chosen son belongs, it invokes at the same time completely opposite features, like weakness, vulnerability (associated with the feminine), and lack of life that are attributed both to the Davidic lineage and to his own personality. In both cases, *Bar Nafle* describes a liminal position, in which David exists between two worlds, the divine and the human.

The biblical verse which the midrash addresses is Amos 9:11: "On that day I will raise up the booth of David that is fallen and repair its breaches and raise up its ruins and rebuild it as in the days of old." The sages use this verse to refer to the unique bond between God and David. In the same manner, the book of Psalms (a composition attributed to David, although written much later) claims, "I have become a stranger to my kindred, an alien to my mother's children" (Ps. 69:9); and its author adds: "If my father and mother forsake me, the Lord will take me up" (Ps. 27:10).

David's fallen shelter or booth (*sukat David*, which has feminine attributes, resembling a womb), serves as an image both of his fragility but also of the "divine shelter" that protects him in the midst of the calamity that is described in prophecy in Amos 9. With the help and protection of God, David becomes a giant, impervious to human reality. Thus, he can overcome even death and deserves to be designated the "Messiah." Unlike other humans, he relies only upon the almighty God.

In addition, the description of David as a fallen baby resonates with maternal images and the trauma of stillbirth, which later in kabbalistic literature will be linked to the myth of the Edomite kings, who, according to the Zohar and Lurianic Kabbalah, are the basis for the development of the *sefirot*.[10] The dead kings—mentioned in Gen. 36:31: "These are the kings who reigned in the land of Edom before any king reigned over the Israelites"—symbolize the forces that did not survive and that are like "stillborns" (*nefalim*) whose death was necessary to enable the creation of the world.

God himself is depicted in the Bible as a woman in labor, and the midrash implies that He remembers the unborn worlds, as it is stated in a midrash in Genesis Rabba:

> R. Abbahu said: This proves that the Holy One, blessed be He, went on creating worlds and destroying them until He created this one and declared, "This one pleases Me; those did not please Me."[11]

This midrash implies that God weeps and remembers the worlds that were destroyed, as cosmic "miscarriages" that preceded the creation. In that sense, David as the future savior has a performative role in the process of history. He plays not only the role of death, which is linked to femininity, ("Her feet go down to death" Proverbs 5:5) but also the role of the divine mother, who suffers from postpartum depression or who wants to keep the fetus in her womb forever.

Interpreted through the lens of Jung's psychology, we may suggest that the birth of the stillborn messiah symbolizes the struggle of the ego to extricate himself from the womb of the "great mother" and from the sea of the unconscious. The Messiah as a miraculous child, the *puer aeternus*, must be in danger and survive, in order to go through the process of individuation and separation.[12]

In previous research, I have analyzed the dominant role of the motherly figure in the genealogy of the Davidic dynasty, and claimed that David became a messianic figure because of his superior maternal line. Moreover, his "feminization" alludes to the feminine plots in his lineage that include narratives of incest, seduction, and harlotry.[13] The sexual transgression that allegedly leaves an imprint on David's character and biography mirrors the history of seductions of his ancestral mothers, but it also emphasizes the miraculous births of Perez (son of Judah and Tamar); Yishai (son of Boas and Ruth); and even Moab (son of Lot and his oldest daughter). These births contribute to the emergence of the messianic dynasty. The combination of the themes of sin and supernatural birth provides the material for a significant breakthrough in the presentation of David and his personality in the kabbalistic literature. In the Zohar, David's messianic image merges feminine and masculine aspects and thus characterizes redemption also as a motherly configuration that is likened to giving birth, or to the "rebirth of the soul." Redemption is leading from sin to repentance and finally to the restoration of the self, a process which must start at the point of "falling," and with a hero who is a stillborn.

2. While the above Talmudic exegesis describes David as both son of Nephilim and as a *nefel* (stillborn) who received protection from God, in a parallel midrashic tradition the sages recount that David was born dead and that Adam granted him seventy years of life:

> "seventy shekels according to the holy shekel" (Numbers 7:13) . . . Another explanation. *Parallel to the seventy years that Adam took away from his life and gave to David ben Yishai.* It was fit that he live for a thousand years, as it says "...for on the day that you eat thereof, you shall surely die." (Genesis 2:17) And a day to the Holy One is a thousand years, as it says "For a thousand years are in Your eyes like yesterday, which passed, and a watch in the night." (Psalms 90:4) [*Numbers Rabbah* 14:11][14]

Here we encounter a new connection between Adam and David, both human beings on the one hand—yet Adam was never born of man; he is, indeed, the primal "son of God" that appears in Eden, and God "breathes" His breath into him ("breathed into his nostrils the breath of life," Gen 2:7). David is the proper non-human follower of Adam, since, according to another Talmudic *sugiya*, David is expected to "return from the dead": "The Holy One, Blessed be He, is destined *to establish another David*" (b. Sanhedrin 98b). This idea of course alludes to Jewish and Christian polemics regarding the theme of the resurrection.

In addition, David and Adam are both archetypal sinners. By generously giving his seventy years (as a parallel to the "seventy shekels" mentioned in the sacrifices and dedication offerings of the leaders in the desert [Num 7:13]), Adam compensates for his mortal sin. Had the first man not eaten from the Tree of Knowledge, all humanity might live forever, innocent of the struggle of mortality. Following the story of creation, David and Adam are responsible to "use" their own sins in order to "save" and repair humanity. However, unlike in Christian traditions, the sages believe that the Messiah need not be a perfect and "pure" figure; rather, they accept a human being who has faults and damages. The Jewish Messiah is the chosen *precisely* because he accepts the fact that he will never be perfect and "immaculate" (without any defect). He accepts the "dirtiness" and imperfection of life, and thus enables the salvation of others.

This midrash claims that David, as the future Messiah, can repair Adam's sin because he understands his motivation and the circumstances that compel all human beings to repeat it. The sages also suggest that Adam's salvation protects all future generations.[15] If Adam gives years of life to David, then it means that the Messiah cannot live forever (unlike the myth regarding the eternal life of Jesus).[16] Moreover, according to this reading, David indeed contains within himself the "compressed extract" of Adam's destiny and essence. This idea develops later in the Kabbalah, where we encounter the acronym *ADaM,* referencing the three characters that mythically reflect one another: Adam, David, and the Messiah.[17]

The denotation of the seventy years and the willingness of David to "be built by another" provide the path for restoration of the primal sin. Again, unlike in the Christian concept, here the cataclysm is not complete: the "fallen infant" is eventually rescued by his ancestors. If the Patriarch can rescue future generations, while sons can help to repair the sins and defects that occurred in the time of their predecessors, then in the eyes of the rabbis, the Messiah symbolizes the vanquishing of the temporal in favor of eternal life.

Yet death, deterioration, and weakness are unavoidable, even for David/the Messiah. Although he comes from a damaged lineage, the Messiah struggles against all obstacles and wins. He even overcomes the threat of murder that "preceded [his] life"—as we learn from a parallel midrash dealing with the wish of his father, Yishai, to kill his son who was redheaded like the foreign handmaid, since Yishai suspected his son's mother of infidelity.[18] The Messiah does not save us; rather, we aim to "save" him. This idea is expanded in the Zoharic reading that I will discuss below. The Zohar expands the task of

Adam to all the Patriarchs and to Joseph, implying that all humanity ought to support the Messiah and lend him years, since we are all his progeny.

The idea that David was granted his life by grace is transformed later in the Zohar. The well-known passage from *sabba de-mishpatim* alludes that to David's "femininity":

> Nevertheless, although the tree was enhanced, when David came he remained in the lower tree of the Female, and *had to receive life from another*. (Zohar 2, 103b; emphasis is mine)[19]

In another Zoharic reading, Adam is joined by the Patriarchs Abraham and Jacob, as well as by Joseph, each of whom granted years of his life to David:

> Rabbi Shim'on said, as already noted, before King David existed, *he had no life at all, but Adam gave him 70 years of his own*; so David's existence totaled 70 years, while Adam's came to 1000 minus 70. Thus Adam and King David shared these first 1000 years. He opened, saying, "*He asked You for life; You granted it—length of days forever and ever* (Psalms 21:5)." *He asked You for life*—King David, for when the blessed Holy One created the Garden of Eden, He cast King David's soul there and, gazing upon it, saw that it possessed no life of its own. It stood before Him all day long. Once He created Adam, He said, "Here, indeed, is his existence!" So from Adam derived the 70 years for which King David endured in the world. Further, the patriarchs bequeathed some of their life to him, each and every one. Abraham bequeathed to him, as did Jacob and Joseph; Isaac didn't bequeath anything to him because King David derived from his side. (ZOHAR 1,168b = Matt, III, 18)

Similarly to the identification of David with the sefira of *Malkhut*, Isaac (who symbolizes the sefira of *Gevurah*) also represents the powers that derive from the "dark" and feminine side. The Zohar proposes that those who dwell in the shadow are in fact capable of receiving vitality from the illuminated figures who draw their strength from the right column of the sefirotic tree, including *Hesed*, *Tiferet*, and *Yesod*, who are in turn identified with Abraham, Jacob, and Joseph, respectively. Thus David contains within him all the Patriarchs—those who are notable for their absence and those who are present in their force and vibrancy—to become the fourth leg of the Divine Chariot.

The most striking aspect of this Zoharic reading is the fact that Joseph (who takes the place of Isaac) also loans "years of life" to the Messiah. This statement contradicts another tradition which appears in the better-known discussion in the Babylonian Talmud.

3. There, in tractate Sukkah, we learn that after the terrifying vision of the slain Messiah, son of Joseph, David begs God for life. This homily is based on the statement in Psalms: "He asked you for life; you gave it to him length of days for ever and ever" (Ps. 21:5). David, in many rabbinic *derashot*,

is identified with "the Messiah *son of* David," and the words of his hymn become an archetypal foundation to the relations that later developed between the "two Messiahs."

> "The land will eulogize, each family separately; the family of the house of David separately, and their women separately, the family of the house of Nathan separately, and their women separately" (Zechariah 12:12).—what is the nature of this eulogy? R. Dosa and the Rabbis disagree concerning this matter. *One said that this eulogy is for Messiah ben Yosef who was killed*] in the war of Gog from the land of Magog prior to the ultimate redemption with the coming of Messiah ben David [, And one said that this eulogy is for the evil inclination that was killed [. . .] The Sages taught: To Messiah ben David, who is destined to be revealed swiftly in our time, the Holy One, Blessed be He, says: *Ask of Me anything and I will give you*, as it is stated: "I will tell of the decree; the Lord said unto me: You are My son, this day have I begotten you, ask of Me, and I will give the nations for your inheritance" (Psalms 2:7–8). *Once the Messiah ben David saw Messiah ben Yosef, who was killed,* he says to the Holy One: Master of the Universe, I ask of you only life; that I will not suffer the same fate. The Holy One says to him: Life? Even before you stated this request, your father, David, already prophesied about you with regard to this matter precisely, as it is stated: "*He asked life of You, You gave it to him; even length of days for ever and ever*" (Psalms 21:5) (b. Sukkah 52a, the emphasis is mine).

Since "there is no late and early" in the Zohar, Joseph, the mythical slain Messiah, symbolizes here the "life giver," instead of the dead brother.[20] This tradition, of course, reflects the transformation that both Joseph and David experience in the Zohar: David is located lower than Joseph in the *sefirotic* tree, and is identified with the feminine Malkhut, while Joseph is the masculine, stable "foundation," called Yesod.

The Yesod transforms the image of the "slain Messiah" into that of eternal life, stability, and strength. By stating that David has borrowed life from Joseph, the Zohar inverts the dependent relations between these two figures and opens up new possibilities for their relationships as reflections of the divine world. The generosity exhibited by Joseph toward David, (symbolically portrayed as Yesod "giving life" to Malkhut) intended to downplay the implicit rivalry between the two national Messiahs. This emotional "shift," vis-à-vis an imaginary power struggle for the title of Messiah, was instead transformed by the Zohar into an act of gracious giving and brotherly love.[21]

Moreover, there develops from the midrash to the kabblistic literature an expansion of the biographies of the private figures of Joseph and David, who come to symbolize the messianic heir and successor. So evolves a code for understanding the character of the follower "Son of David" viz. "Son of Joseph."

Like David, whose successor is "another David" or "son of David," so too the biblical Joseph, holds the fate of his future offspring, "the slain messiah," son of Joseph. Indeed, Joseph was the hated brother who was nearly killed by his brothers (just like David). In the eyes of his father, Joseph truly *was* dead: only after seventeen years did he see his son and his spirit return to life: "But when they told him all the words of Joseph that he had said to them, and when he saw the wagons that Joseph had sent to carry him, *the spirit of their father Jacob revived*" (Gen 45: 27).

Here we see similar motifs to Jesus's resurrection in both David's and Joseph's stories. All these heroes must overcome conditions that "contrast life," as we learn from the pattern of the hero's birth.[22] Like Jesus, both Joseph and David suffer persecution, hatred, and estrangement.

The Zoharic prism allows us to combine the image of the suffering Messiah (of Zech 9; Isa 53) with the warrior-hero and the chosen Davidic descendant (Isa 11; Ps 2). In a way, as I have suggested elsewhere, the biblical David himself unites both sides of the messianic figure, as a contradictive appearance of his persona in Psalms and Samuel. While the book of Samuel highlighted David's tyrannical and manipulative, masculine behavior, in the book of Psalms he appeared in the "feminine," weak image, lacking agency and power.[23]

In fact, following the Jewish scriptures duality of the character of David, the New Testament and the synoptic gospels demonstrate the "Jewish tendency" to unite all messianic features in one figure. Matthew 1 attributes Jesus's lineage to the Judean line of foreign messianic mothers (Tamar, Ruth, Rahab, Bathsheba, and others), and the fathers (Judah, Boaz, and others) who coupled with them in sin (through adultery, incest, prostitution, etc.).[24] By overcoming these transgressions and foreignness, Jesus presents himself as the Davidic-designated successor, "the Messiah, son of David." Yet, Jesus is also the son of Joseph, although his father never copulated with his mother Mary. In this way, Jesus is chosen twice: He is the son of God who triumphed over sin and over the circle of life and death. Moreover, Jesus symbolizes the archetype of the suffering Messiah,[25] even as he symbolizes victory over the corporeal. He is, therefore, beyond death and bodily pain, qualities that later are attributed retroactively to Jewish heroes like David and Joseph.

Moreover, in the concluding remarks to my book, *The Feminine Messiah*, I discuss Jewish and Christian entanglement regarding messianic heroes and suggest that not only does the Zoharic Messiah unite David and Joseph (Yesod and Malkhut), but he reflects also the bond between Mary and Jesus. David is, simultaneously, the "mother" (identified with the *Shechina*, as the *stabat mater* and the weeping heroine) as well as the son who is sacrificed and who will be resurrected.

Caroline Bynum has shown that many men in the late Middle Ages viewed Jesus as a feminine and motherly figure, and even described themselves with feminine imagery (even while in roles of authority—which surprisingly were identified with motherly functions). Yet, the religious experience of women reflects "traditional" feminine roles and classic identities that continue in their present condition: in their being the wife, sister, or mother of Jesus. Moreover, during mystical experiences and Eucharistic rituals, women continue to express non-liminal states, compared to the "distress" that characterizes men's model of reversal.[26]

In the same way, the Zoharic David is privileged as a male figure to be "both sexes," to use the "power of the powerless" and eventually to possess agency, which real women in both Judaism and Christianity in the Middle Ages cannot possess.

A precedent for the bond between a messianic mother and her son can be found in the book of Zerubbabel, a late midrashic apocalypse that is based on earlier traditions in Lamentation Rabbah and the Palestinian Talmud, regarding the birth of the Messiah on the ninth of Av (*Tisha b'Av*), the day of the destruction of the Temple.[27] Almost all versions of the birth of Menachem ben Ammiel make connections between birth and death, extermination and demolition, and devastation and salvation. The dead messiah also plays a role in the book of Zerubbabel through the development of the Davidic and Josephic Mmessiahs. In addition, this "counter-history" situates against the "good mother" Hefzibah, a stone idol of the mother of Armilus. According to David Biale, the "dark mother" symbolizes Mary, a polemical image reflecting both her seductive and static position in the eyes of Jewish narrators. According to Biale, the author of *Sefer Zerubavel* "sexualizes the idolatry he identifies with Christianity. In so doing, he inverts the image of Mary from virgin to harlot."[28] At the same time, Martha Himmelfarb convincingly shows that the image of Mary is split between the stone idol and Hefzibah herself, reflecting contradictory emotions toward Mary's cult.[29]

THE DEPRIVED MESSIAH

In another homily, the Zohar preserves the rabbinic tradition according to which only *Adam* bequeathed to David seventy years of his life, without the commitment by the Patriarchs and Joseph. This reading, found in Zohar *Va-Yehi*, deals with David's existential crisis: he cries to God and begs to understand why he was born lifeless, but he was not permitted to know:

> He opened, saying, "YHVH, let me know my end, what is the measure of my days" (Psalms 39:5). This verse has been established but come and see! My end—end of the right, linked with David. "What is the measure of my

days—actually empowered over his days." Rabbi Yehudah said, "I have heard from Rabbi Shim'on that this verse was uttered for those days decreed for him from Adam—namely seventy." As has been said, he had no life at all, but Adam offered David some of his own days—seventy years. This is the mystery of the heavenly curtain, performing no function at all, and the moon not shining on her own at all—illumined by seventy years on all sides, life of David, unspecified. So David sought to know this mystery—why the moon has no life of her own— and to know his essence. What is the measure of my days—upper, concealed rung, poised above all those days constituting her life, a site illumining all. That I may know how חדל (hadel), ephemeral, I am. What does this mean?" David said, 'That I may know why I am hadel, destitute, of light of my own, deprived of being like all those other supernal ones, all possessing life. And I, why am I destitute, why am I deprived? This is what David wanted to know—and was not permitted to know. "Come and see: All supernal blessings are transmitted to this rung, to bless all. Even though She has no light of Her own, all blessings, all joy, all goodness exist in Her and issue from Her; so She is called 'cup of blessing' and simply 'blessing.' Of this is written Blessing of YHVH, she enriches (Proverbs 10:22)—blessing of YHVH, truly! And similarly: Filled with blessing of YHVH, possess the west and the south (Deuteronomy 33:23). So She shares in all the others, filled by them all, partaking of them all. She is blessed by all those supernal blessings, transmitted to Her to bless." (ZOHAR 1:233b–234a, Matt, III, 413–414, emphasis is mine.)

I argue that we find in the Zohar two debating schools of thought, regarding the nature of the relations between David and Joseph. In the above quotation, David is a powerless figure unable even to garner an explanation for his bad luck and deprivations.

This homily is based on Psalms 39 and is seen through the narrative of David's own unstable life. Biblical, rabbinic, and Zoharic scenes present him in a feminine light as a "nocturnal poet," musician, and lyric writer of Psalms, who is weeping to God but cannot solve "the riddle of his life." Here we can detect David's identification with the pain of the Shekhinah, which, on the one hand, reflects the mystery of the heavenly curtain—the Vilon, which performs "no function at all." On the other hand, he is called a "cup of blessing" that contains the upper flow and then sustains and nourishes the whole world.

According to another Zoharic apocalyptic tradition, the Messiah is "sleeping" in a bird's nest (*Ken Tsipor*), until one day he will awaken in "the land of Galilee." Lurianic kabbalists explain that this is an essential stage in the development of the Messiah as a savior. As Vital states,

As someone who fell into deep sleep, until the soul of the soul (*neshama le'neshama*) would come to him and he would alert and got power of prophecy and wake up from his sleep ... and only then he will recognize himself as the Messiah.[30]

This reading maintains traditional gender roles, which associate the first stage of the lack of self-awareness, with weakness and femininity, and the second stage of alertness, with the awakening of the masculine warrior messiah who intends to take revenge on his enemies.

THE TWO MESSIAHS

We must remember that the Zoharic homilies are a product of a late medieval tradition based on annual Jewish and Christian understandings of the messianic riddle. The Zohar perceives these traditions as a mythical combination of both dialogue and polemic, mutual influences, and unsolved issues. The Zohar is not intended, then, as a chronological and historical record, but suggests a mythical, contradictive method of interpretation.

In other Zoharic traditions, we find other messianic combinations—for example, the union of Davidic and *Mosaic* (Moses) traditions in *Tiqqunei ha-Zohar*. Although the book centers on the figure of Moses and the Loyal Shepherd (*Raya Mehemana*), who resembles neither David nor Rashbi, scenes from the life of David are attributed to him as redeeming evidence of his character.[31] This text describes the hero as an expert slingshot, echoing the killing of Goliath by David.[32] In other homilies of the Zohar, we might find the union of the Messiah, son of David, with the Messiah, son of Joseph, in the figure of Rabbi Shim'on bar Yohai, who identified with the Joephic Yesod, yet symbolizes the *Shekinah* (sefira of Malkut): the beloved of God.

Following the Zoharic path, an ongoing wish to unify these two messianic figures continues to attract the attention of commentators. For example, in his mystical diary *Sefer ha-Ḥezyonot*, composed in Damascus after the death of Luria, Vital describes a dream in which R. Isaac Luria comes to R. Chaim Vital and they both share the roles of the Messiah: son of David and Son of Joseph.[33] In other texts, such as the Kabalistic composition *Sha'ar ha-Glgulim*, "Gate of Transmigration" (written after the personal diary), Vital identifies himself also with the suffering son of Joseph:

> Shmuel [Vital, his son] said, even though my father, of blessed memory, hid his words in this place, I remember that face to face, he one day revealed to me, that this verse alludes to the intimacy [*korvat*] of his soul . . . However, in the time of my father it is possible that, if Israel repents, my father will be the messiah from the line of Joseph. [intro. 36]

In other homilies, Vital treats the theme of the slain messiah, and explains the meeting between David and Saul as a return of the repressed, or "reincarnation," of the confrontation between the dynasties of Judah and of Joseph:

This is the secret of our Sages, z"l: "Had you not been David and he Saul, I would have destroyed many Davids before Saul." (Moed Katan 16b) Understand this well. Sometimes the soul of a new person is very lofty but he [still] cannot overcome his *yetzer*—if he could, he would easily be very pious. This is a powerful lesson, for it explains why sometimes a person may only transgress lightly but receive a serious punishment, while someone else may perform a terrible sin, and yet not get punished for it.[34]

Like the primal union of the Josephic and Davidic stories in the life of Jesus, here again, the combination of the two messiahs in one entity is intended to hasten the coming of salvation, and reflects the wish to "overcome death." On one level, this is the death that preceded life, the death of David as a non-viable infant; simultaneously, this is the tragic death that Jesus, the executed Josephic Messiah, encountered when he was crucified by the Romans.

In light of the above traditions, we might newly interpret the well-known statement in the Palestinian Talmud: "If the King Messiah comes from among the living, his name will be David; *if from among the dead*, his name will be David as well (y. Berkahot 2:4 [13d])."[35]

The Babylonian Talmud phrases it a bit differently:

Rav Naḥman says: If the Messiah is among the living in this generation, he is a person such as me [. . .] Rav says: If the Messiah is among the living in this generation, he is a person such as our saintly Rabbi Yehuda HaNasi, who was renowned for his sanctity, piety, and Torah knowledge. If the Messiah is among the dead he is a person such as Daniel, the beloved man. Rav says: The Holy One, Blessed be He, is destined to establish *another David* as it is stated: "And they shall serve the Lord their God, and David their king, whom I will establish for them" (Jer. 30:9). It is not stated: I established, but "I will establish." (b. Sanhedrin 98b)

This formulation indicates not only that the future king's name will be David, but that he himself may be resurrected, like Jesus, as Yuval and Liebes suggested in their studies.[36] Moreover, in the continuation of this text, David is described as "half God," the "viceroy," who is sitting to the right of the emperor:

Rav Pappa said to Abaye: But isn't it written: "And my servant David shall be their prince forever" (Ezekiel 37:25), like an emperor and a viceroy. (b. Sanhedrin 98b)

Although Rashi (R. Shlomo ben Yiṣḥaqi) explains that this image means that the Messiah, "the new David," will be king (emperor) and that David will be second-in-command (viceroy), I suggest interpreting this statement in light of the *sugiya* in b. Hagigah 14a: "Till thrones were places, and 'One that was ancient of days did sit!' (Dan. 7:9)—one throne for God (*Atik Yomin*), and one throne for David."

Emmanuel Levinas, in his reading of this interpretation, emphasizes the innovative idea of the Redeemer as "a double figure,"

> The verse quoted does not say "whom I raise up" but "whom I will raise up." The use of the future points, therefore, to the coming in the future of a new king who will be called David. From this text R. Papa extracts the idea that the David of the future is not a new David, but the old David. The conclusion (worthy of the promise!) is: an emperor and a viceroy. The new David shall be the king, and the former David shall be his viceroy. Where does the Talmud get its imagination from? A Messiah and a Vice-Messiah! This strange text defies historians because it affirms *the existence of two Davids* and, perhaps even more profoundly, *it affirms that every historical character possesses a double.*[37]

This metaphorical interpretation of the messianic doubleness and of multiplicity of the redeeming self resonates Freud's discussion of the uncanny and the threatening doppelganger.[38] The "New Messiah" has a role to redeem the "Old Messiah," and to meet his own rejected and intimidating aspects.

If we combine the midrash in b. Sanhedrin 96b, which states that Messiah was born as a non-viable infant (*bar nafle*), with David's plea for life in b. Sukkah 52a, we might conclude that David is indeed connected to the myth of resurrection, like Jesus, even as he struggles endlessly with the threat of losing his life. In Zoharic terminology, "he is coming from the side of death": at an essential level, his fate is to grapple with death, bereavement, and loss. Only if he succeeds in the battle with the Angel of Death does he deserve the title of Messiah.

CLOSING REMARKS

The paradoxical notion of the Messiah as a baby is subverted by his characterization as a dead fetus. Why does the Messiah appear as a hero that almost "was *not* born"?

On the psychoanalytic level, the stillborn baby represents an unrealized new beginning, one that never had the opportunity to develop. It might symbolize the "unlived life" and the feeling of frustration in the face of non-realized reality and a lack of self-fulfillment.[39]

On the other hand, in every human being who wants to be "his own" savior, (instead of waiting for a future, non-existent redeemer), this myth stimulates an urgent self-fulfillment and realization that arises only in the sight of death and loss.[40] Even though the Messiah died, he stayed alive. But now this life is derived from death, recognizing the preciousness of every moment of life. As the Zohar says in parashat *Huqqat*:

> So it is written "I praise the dead who have already died" these are living, yet called dead. Because they have already tasted the taste of death! (*Zohar* III, 182b; Matt vol. 9, 215)

From a gender and feminine perspective, the messiah is *of Woman Born*, and, as such, he suffers *her* death and pain at birth.[41] In addition, in the kabbalistic symbolization, Eve and all women brought punishment to this world, and are linked to "the Tree of Death" (which is opposed to the masculine "Tree of Life"). Thus, we might suggest that the savior is born "dead" in order to contain inside himself the otherness of femininity, of suffering and evil (*sitra ahra*, meaning, literally, "the other side"). Only by including the feminine and death, can he rescue all humanity.

On the one hand, the infant messiah symbolizes the eternal promise of birthing, re-birthing, and becoming, thereby emphasizing positive aspects of femininity. Yet by locating the messiah in the regressive stage of a fetus (or a stillborn), the sages reveal their unconscious "fear of the feminine" (in the terms of Erich Neumann).[42]

This model alludes to the basic power-relationship hierarchy: male is to female as divine is to human and the mother is to the child. If the messiah is an infant, he belongs to the kingdom of "the great mother." As a dead infant, he represents a frightened and "damaged male," who is still captured by the maternal womb, and thus burdened by all the threatening attributes of the Great Mother and the dark-feminine. Like her, he is flawed, yet she stands against him as a male and an enemy prisoner. He might never be rescued from the uroborotic bond and the primal dragon (the tail-eating serpent). The kabblistic numerology of the words "snake" and "Messiah," both equal to the number 358, allude to this fear.

Unlike the zoharic female messiah in the image of King David—although he "has no light of his own," yet has the power of the powerless, that is, seduction, harlotry, and antinomian deeds—the baby messiah is a helpless hero longing for life and protection. He has still *not* appeared on the stage of history, rather he only symbolizes the hope of *becoming*. Moreover, unlike the stereotypical phallic movement forward into life or the symbol of the ruler and king, the dead messiah as feminine reflection indicates the fear of being born, and thus an impossible yearning for salvation—a desire that will never come true.

In addition, as I have proposed, this myth suggests an alternative to the Christian narrative of resurrection. *We* are saving the Messiah instead of the illusion that he is rescuing us. Each one of us (as descendants of Adam, who lent years to the Redeemer), gives life to the Messiah and helps him to exist as an eternal wish.

Furthermore, it seems that the sages, who sensed the dangerous potential of trusting a false Messiah, decided to impose a defect (*p'gam*) onto his perfect figure. No human being is faultless, they claimed, even the Messiah! By preemptively attacking the idealized Messiah, and developing the paradoxical idea of the "living-dead person," they imply that we should not fall into the illusion of human saviors, and not cast all our hopes on a person who will certainly disappoint us. Instead of surrendering to a false Messiah we can continue to evolve *His Myth*.

Franz Kafka claims that "The Messiah will come only when he is no longer necessary; he will come only on the day after his arrival; he will come, not on the last day, but on the very last."[43] According to this statement, every coming messiah is a false redeemer. The Messiah is always dead, since he must remain a fantastic illusion that cannot be completely fulfilled.

NOTES

* I'm grateful to the participants of the EJCR conference (the Encyclopedia of Jewish-Christian Relations) in Potsdam, especially to Kathy Ehrensperger, Juni Hoppe, Tali Artman, and Shayna Sheinfeld.

1. Gershom Scholem, *Toward an Understanding of the Messianic Idea in Judaism* (New York: Schocken, 1971), 113 [the emphasis is mine].

2. See: Ruth Kara-Ivanov Kaniel, *The Feminine Messiah: King David in the Image of the Shekhinah in Kabbalistic Literature* (Leiden: Brill, 2021).

3. Scholem, *Messianic Idea*, 113.

4. See for example b. Berakhot 4a: "All the kings of the East and the West sit with all their pomp among their company, whereas my hands are soiled with the blood, with the fetus and the placenta, in order to declare a woman clean for her husband." Compare to b. Moed Katan 16b; b. Avodah Zarah 5a; Sanhedrin 107a.

5. Avigdor Shinan, "'Al Demuto shel ha-Melekh David be-Sifrut ḤaZaL," in *David: From Shepherd to Messiah* (Jerusalem: Ben-Zvi Institute, 1995), 181–199; Richard Kalmin, *The Sage in Jewish Society of Late Antiquity* (New York: Routledge, 1999); James Diamond, "King David of the Sages: Rabbinic Rehabilitation or Ironic Parody?" *Prooftexts* 27 (2007): 373–426; Shulamit Valler, "King David and His Women: Biblical Stories and Talmudic Discussions," in *A Feminist Companion to Samuel and Kings*, ed. Athalya Brenner (Sheffield: Sheffield Academic Press, 1994), 129–142.

6. Henri De-Lubac, *Medieval Exegesis: The Four Senses of Scripture* (Grand Rapids, MI: Eerdmans, 2000), 64–67.

7. While in the kabbalistic literature we find justification of the sexual sin, Ruth Karras claims that rabbinic literature mainly emphasizes the killing of Uriah rather than the seduction of Bathsheba. As she states:

> Medieval masculinity contained both the idea of dominance and the idea of male passion as an unstoppable force . . . David could still be important as a symbol of repentance, even

if his sin was to be blamed on a woman . . . Masculinity resided both in being subject to temptation—that is, having an appetite for women—and in being powerful enough to act.

Ruth Mazo Karras, "David and Bathsheba: Masculine Sexuality in Medieval Judaism and Christianity," in *God's Own Gender? Masculinities in World Religions*, ed. Daniel Gerster and Michael Krüggeler (Würzburg: Ergon Verlag, 2018), 201–218, here 206–207. Karras explores essential differences between Jewish and Christian exegesis in the Middle Ages: "While Christianity used David as a model of repentance putting the emphasis on humanity's free will and God's mercy, Rabbinic Judaism, ironically or not, put the emphasis on God's plan and David's obedience to it." Yet, according to her analyses, both cultures stress David's masculinity. Karras, "'Goliath Thought David Rather Boastful': Royal Masculinity in Kingless Societies," *The Haskins Society Journal* 28 (2016): 90. See also recently: Karras, *Thou Art the Man: The Masculinity of David in the Christian and Jewish Middle Ages* (Philadelphia: University of Pennsylvania Press, 2021).

8. For more on comparative aspects of the messianic language and theme, see Matthew V. Novenson, *The Grammar of Messianism* (Oxford: Oxford University Press, 2017).

9. b. Sanhedrin 96b.

10. See, for example, *Sha'ar Mamarei Rashbi, Pekudei* 33a.

11. *Genesis Rabbah* 9:1 (Albeck ed., 68).

12. Carl Gustav Jung and Carl Kerenyi, *Essays on a Science of Mythology: The Myth of the Divine Child and the Mysteries of Eleusis* (Princeton: Princeton University Press, 1973); James Hillman, *Senex and Puer, Uniform Edition,* vol. 3 (Connecticut: Spring Publications, 2006).

13. Ruth Kara-Ivanov Kaniel, *Holiness and Transgression: Mothers of the Messiah in the Jewish Myth* (New York: Academic Studies Press, 2017).

14. Liebes, "Long Live the King"; Shinan, *David*, 183; Gershom Scholem, *Sabbatai Zevi and the Sabbatean Movement during His Lifetime* (Tel Aviv: Am Oved, 1957), 134, 808; Haviva Pedaya, *Vision and Speech* (Los Angeles: Cherub Press, 2002), 216, 226; and Zohar 1:168a and 3:279a. See also I Enoch 69:12.

15. See Genesis Rabba 24: 2 "In the time that the Holy One created Adam Harishon, [as] a golem He created him and he was set up from [one] end of the world and unto its [other] end – that's what is written: "Your eyes saw my golem." And compare, *Yalkut Shimoni,* Remez 41 "The Book of Adam's Descendants was passed before him. He saw David's portion of life would be three hours. He said, "Master of the world, this should not be decreed! A thought has come to me." He [Adam] said to him, "How many are my years?" God said, "1,000 years." Adam said, "Can I give some as a gift?" God said, "Yes." Adam said, "I will give him 70 years to be his fate."

16. In the "Disputation of Barcelona" (1263), this midrash and others, such as b. Sukka 52a, are cited and discussed in the debate between the King, the convert Pablo Christiani, and Nahmanides regarding the nature of the Messiah and the question of his eternal life:

> Now you, our lord, asked a better question, raising the difficulty that it is unnatural for a man to live 1,000 years, and I shall make clearer now my answer to your question. Adam

lived for 1,000 years, *less 70*; and it is clear from Scripture that he died through his sin, and if he had not sinned, he would have lived much longer, or perhaps for ever . . . After the Messiah comes, it will be abolished from all of us, but in the case of the Messiah himself, it is totally abolished, so that it is quite fitting that the Messiah should live for 1,000 years, or 2,000 years, or even for ever, *as the Psalm says, "He asked life of Thee, Thou gavest it him"* (Psalms, 21: 5).

See: Haym Maccoby, *Judaism on Trial: Jewish-Christian Disputations in the Middle Ages* (Liverpool: Littman, 1993), 116 emphasis mine. The editor adds in his comments that "Nahmanides is not sure whether the fall of Adam brought death into the world, or whether Adam would have died eventually even if he had not eaten of the Tree of Knowledge. He also leaves open the question whether the Messiah will live forever, or will eventually die."

17. Ramdal, Secret Passover, Schocken Institute Ms.13161 93b-94a; I am grateful to Avishai bar-Asher for this reference. See also R.Menahem Recanati, Commentary on the Torah, Genesis ("naase adam"j; Vayeshev (sod halbur"j! Etc. R. isaac of Acre, Meirat Einaim (Perushei Vechiburei Talmidei Harashba al Kabbalat Harambam, Jerusalem 2021, 112.

18. "The stone that the builders rejected has become the chief cornerstone" (Psalms 118:22) Jesse abstained from sexual relations with his wife for three years, and after three years he acquired a beautiful handmaid and lusted after her. He said to her: "My daughter, prepare yourself for tonight so you can come to me and thus you will be emancipated." The handmaid went and told her mistress: "Deliver you, my soul, and my master from hell!" The mistress answered her "What is the reason?" So the handmaid told her everything. Said the mistress "My daughter, what can I do, seeing that today he has not touched me in three years?" The handmaid answered: "I will give you advice: go and prepare yourself, as will I, and tonight, when he says to close the door, you will enter and I will leave." And so that is what they did. At night, the handmaid stood and extinguished the light. She then went to close the door, and her mistress entered as she left. The mistress was with him all night and conceived David. Because of Jesse's love [lust] for the handmaid, David's "redness" stood out among his brothers. After nine months had passed, when they saw he was a redhead, her sons wished to kill her and her son David. Jesse said to them, "Leave him and he will be a servant and shepherd for us." Samuel asked Jesse: "Are these all the boys you have?" He replied: "There is still the youngest. He is tending the flock . . . Since he arrived, the oil has begun to bubble and rise." The Lord said: "Rise and anoint him, for this is the one" . . . Jesse and his sons trembled with fear, as they said "Samuel is coming to degrade us and to inform Israel that we have an illegitimate son." And David's mother was inwardly happy and outwardly sad. When Samuel took the cup of salvation, they were all happy. Samuel stood up and kissed him [David] on his head and said: "The Lord said to me, 'You are my son; today I have begotten you'" (Psalms 2:7). At that moment his mother said: "The stone that the builders rejected [has become the chief cornerstone]." It is not written—*habonim* (builders) but rather—*habanim* (the sons). The son, who was rejected by his brothers, has become the chief cornerstone and surpassed them all. His sons said to him: "This is the Lord's doing," and therefore "This is the day that the Lord

has made; let us rejoice and be glad in it" *Yalkut ha-Makhiri* on Psalms 118: 28 (ed. Buber, 214). For more on this text, see: Charlotte E. Fonrobert, "The Handmaid, the Trickster and the Birth of the Messiah," in *Current Trends in the Study of Midrash*, ed. Carol Bakhos (Leiden: Brill, 2006), 245–273; Kaniel, *The Feminine Messiah*, chapter 1.

19. Translation by Daniel Matt, *The Zohar: Pritzker Edition*, vol. 5 (Stanford, CA: Stanford University Press, 2009), 64.

20. Compare also Zohar 3:279a.

21. For more on the similarities between the two figures and on Joseph as "the true redeemer of Israel," see Tali Artman, "Messiah Son of Joseph in Genesis Rabbah" [forthcoming].

22. See: Otto Rank, *The Myth of the Birth of the Hero* (New York: Vintage Books, 1959); Alan Dundes, "The Hero Pattern and the Life of Jesus," in *Quest of the Hero*, ed. Robert A. Segal (Princeton, NJ: Princeton University Press, 1990), 179–223.

23. Moshe Halbertal and Stephen Holmes, *The Beginning of Politics: Power in the Biblical Book of Samuel* (Princeton, NJ: Princeton University Press, 2017).

24. Raymond E. Brown, *The Birth of the Messiah: A Commentary on the Infancy Narratives in the Gospels of Matthew and Luke* (Garden City: Doubleday, [1977] 1993), 71–74, 590–595.

25. See for example Isaiah 53: 4-5; Zech 9:9; Lam. 4: 20. For further discussion see Israel Knohl, *The Messiah before Jesus: The Suffering Servant of the Dead Sea Scrolls* (Berkeley: University of California Press, 2000).

26. Caroline W. Bynum, *Fragmentation and Redemption: Essays on Gender and the Human Body in Medieval Religion* (New York: Zone Books, 1992), 27–51.

27. PT Berakhot 2:4- 5:1; Lam. Rabbah 1:16 ;Lam. Zutta (second version) ch. 1: 2. See also Galit Hasan-Rokem, *Web of Life: Folklore and Midrash in Rabbinic Literature* (Stanford: Stanford University Press, 2000), 152–160.

28. David Biale, "Counter-History and Jewish Polemics Against Christianity: The *Sefer Toldot Yeshu* and the *Sefer Zerubavel*," *Jewish Social Studies* 6 (1999): 130–145, here 140.

29. Martha Himmelfarb, "The Mother of Messiah in the Talmud Yerushalmi and Sefer Zerubbabel," in *The Talmud Yerushalmi and Graeco-Roman Culture*, ed. Peter Schäfer (Tübingen: Mohr Siebeck, 2002), 369–389.

30. R. Haim Vital's commentary on the Zohar, printed in Or-haHama by Abraham Azulai. For discussion see Yehuda Liebes, "'Two Young Roes of a Doe': The Secret Sermon of Isaac Luria before his Death," *Jerusalem Studies in Jewish Thought* 10 (1992): 113–169, here from fn. 98.

31. The verse "The stone which the builders rejected has become the head stone of the corner" (Ps. 118:22), which is usually symbolically attributed to the *Shekhinah* in her attribute of David in the Zohar, we surprisingly find in Tikkun 21; while this verse is also ascribed to the *Shekhinah*, here it is in relation to Moses, her "Loyal Shepherd" and not David. Biti Roi, *Love of the Shekhinah* (Ramat Gan: Bar-Ilan University Press, 2017), 408–410. Amos Goldreich adds other examples of the appropriation of Davidic biblical and zoharic characteristics onto the figure of Moses in TZ; for example, see Tikkun 18, 36b, which deals with the image of the rainbow and calls

RM (Raya Mehemna) the Messiah, as compared to Zohar, Noah 1:72b, which speaks about David. While the verse "the spirit of God swept over the face of the waters" (Gen. 1, 2) both in the Midrash and in the Zohar is taken to refer to David, in Tikkun 26, 76b it refers to Moses and RM as the Messiah. See Amos Goldreich, "The Mystical Self-Image of the Author of Tiqqune ha-Zohar," in *Massu'ot: Studies in Kabbalistic Literature and Jewish Philosophy in Memory of Prof. Ephraim Gottlieb*, ed. Michal Oron and Amos Goldreich (Jerusalem: Bialik Institute, 1994), 468–469.

32. See *Tiqqunei ha-Zohar* (TZ), Tikkun 21, 61b–62a.

33. R. Haim Vital, *Sefer ha-Ḥezyonot*, ed. Morris M. Faierstein (Jerusalem: Ben-Zvi Institute, 2006), 5a–b, 8a. For more on the messianic idea and Vital's and Luria's relationship see Ronit Meroz, Redemption in the Lurianic Kabbalah, PhD Dissertation, Hebrew University of Jerusalem, 1988, 255–359.

34. *Sha'ar ha-gilgulim*, Introduction, no. 27.

35. The emphasis is mine. Compare b. Sanhedrin 98b: "The Holy One, blessed be He, will raise up another David for us."

36. Yehuda Liebes, "Maẓmiah Qeren Yeshu'ah," *Jerusalem Studies in Jewish Thought* 3, no. 3 (1983): 313–348; Israel J. Yuval, *Two Nations in Your Womb: Perceptions of Jews and Christians in Late Antiquity and the Middle Ages*, trans. Barbara Harshav and Jonathan Chipman (Berkeley: University of California Press, 2006).

37. Emmanuel Levinas, *Difficult Freedom* (Baltimore: Johns Hopkins University Press, [1990] 1997), 90.

38. Freud claimed that one of the strongest experiences of the "uncanny" (*Unheimlich*) is seeing a "double," that is, suddenly and unexpectedly meeting one's own image in a mirror, Sigmund Freud, "The Uncanny," in *On Creativity and the Unconscious* (New York: Harper and Row [1919] 1958), 122–162. Other thinkers conceptualized this image either as the self's wishful, positive need for a twin figure that it can admire and in light of which it can develop healthily, or as a hallucinatory, pathological state reflecting intrusive identification with the object. See: Heinz Kohut, *The Analysis of the Self* (Chicago: University of Chicago Press, 1971); Wilfred Bion, "The Imaginary Twin," in *Second Thoughts* (London: William Heineman Books, 1967), 3–22.

39. For more on the concept of mental "non-viability," see Thomas H. Ogden, *Reclaiming Unlived Life: Experiences in Psychoanalysis* (London and New York: Routledge, 2016); Adam Phillips, *Missing Out: In Praise of the Unlived Life* (New York: Picador, 2013).

40. As it is hinted in the words of Rav Naḥman: "If the Messiah is among the living —he is a person such as me!" (b. Sanhedrin 98b).

41. Cf. Ruth Kara-Ivanov Kaniel, *Birth in Kabbalah and Psychoanalysis* (Berlin: De-Gruyter, 2022).

42. Erich Neumann, *The Fear of the Feminine: And Other Essays on Feminine Psychology* (Princeton, NJ: Princeton University Press, 1994).

43. Franz Kafka, *Parables and Paradoxes* (New York: Schocken, 1971), 81.

BIBLIOGRAPHY

Biale, David. "Counter-History and Jewish Polemics Against Christianity: The *Sefer Toldot Yeshu* and the *Sefer Zerubavel.*" *Jewish Social Studies* 6 (1999): 130–45.

Bion, Wilfred R. *The Imaginary Twin*. Oxfordshire: Routledge, 1967.

Brown, Raymond E. *The Birth of the Messiah: A Commentary on the Infancy Narratives in the Gospels of Matthew and Luke*. Garden City: Doubleday, [1977] 1993.

Bynum, Caroline W. *Fragmentation and Redemption: Essays on Gender and the Human Body in Medieval Religion*. New York: Zone Books, 1992.

De-Lubac, Henri. *Medieval Exegesis: The Four Senses of Scripture*. Grand Rapids: Eerdmans, 2000.

Diamond, James. "King David of the Sages: Rabbinic Rehabilitation or Ironic Parody?" *Prooftexts* 27 (2007): 373–426.

Dundes, Alan. "The Hero Pattern and the Life of Jesus." In *Quest of the Hero*, edited by Robert A. Segal, 179–223. Princeton: Princeton University Press, 1990.

Fonrobert, Charlotte E. "The Handmaid, the Trickster and the Birth of the Messiah." In *Current Trends in the Study of Midrash*, edited by Carol Bakhos, 245–73. Leiden: Brill, 2006.

Freud, Sigmund. *On Creativity and the Unconscious*. New York: Harper and Row, [1919] 1958.

Goldreich, Amos. "The Mystical Self-Image of the Author of Tiqqune ha-Zohar," In *Massu'ot: Studies in Kabbalistic Literature and Jewish Philosophy in Memory of Prof. Ephraim Gottlieb*, edited by Michal Oron and Amos Goldreich, 468–69. Jerusalem: Bialik Institute, 1994.

Halbertal, Moshe and Stephen Holmes. *The Beginning of Politics: Power in the Biblical Book of Samuel*. Princeton: Princeton University Press, 2017.

Hasan-Rokem, Galit. *Web of Life: Folklore and Midrash in Rabbinic Literature*. Stanford: Stanford University Press, 2000.

Hillman, James. *Senex and Puer, Uniform Edition*, Vol. 3. Connecticut: Spring Publications, 2006.

Himmelfarb, Martha, "The Mother of Messiah in the Talmud Yerushalmi and Sefer Zerubbabel." In *The Talmud Yerushalmi and Graeco-Roman Culture*, edited by Peter Schäfer, 369–89. Tübingen: Mohr Siebeck, 2002.

Jung, Carl Gustav and Carl Kerenyi. *Essays on a Science of Mythology: The Myth of the Divine Child and the Mysteries of Eleusis*. Princeton: Princeton University Press, 1973.

Kafka, Franz. *Parables and Paradoxes*. New York: Schocken, 1971.

Kalmin, Richard. *The Sage in Jewish Society of Late Antiquity*. New York: Routledge, 1999.

Kara-Ivanov Kaniel, Ruth. *Holiness and Transgression: Mothers of the Messiah in the Jewish Myth*. New York: Academic Studies Press, 2017.

Kara-Ivanov Kaniel, Ruth. *The Feminine Messiah: King David in the Image of the Shekhinah in Kabbalistic Literature*. Leiden: Brill, 2021.

Kara-Ivanov Kaniel, Ruth. *Birth in Kabbalah and Psychoanalysis*. Berlin: De-Gruyter, 2022.
Karras, Ruth Mazo. "'Goliath Thought David Rather Boastful': Royal Masculinity in Kingless Societies." *The Haskins Society Journal* 28 (2016): 83–100.
Karras, Ruth Mazo. "David and Bathsheba: Masculine Sexuality in Medieval Judaism and Christianity." In *God's Own Gender? Masculinities in World Religions,* edited by Daniel Gerster and Michael Krüggeler, 201–18. Würzburg: Ergon Verlag, 2018.
Karras, Ruth Mazo. *Thou Art the Man: The Masculinity of David in the Christian and Jewish Middle Ages*. Philadelphia: University of Pennsylvania Press, 2021.
Knohl, Israel. *The Messiah before Jesus: The Suffering Servant of the Dead Sea Scrolls*. Berkeley: University of California Press 2000.
Kohut, Heinz. *The Analysis of the Self*. Chicago: University of Chicago Press, 1971.
Levinas, Emmanuel. *Difficult Freedom*. Baltimore: Johns Hopkins University Press, [1990] 1997.
Liebes, Yehuda. "Maẓmiah Qeren Yeshu'ah." *Jerusalem Studies in Jewish Thought* 3, no. 3 (1983): 313–48.
Liebes, Yehuda. "'Two Young Roes of a Doe': The Secret Sermon of Isaac Luria before his Death." *Jerusalem Studies in Jewish Thought* 10 (1992): 113–69.
Maccoby, Haym. *Judaism on Trial: Jewish-Christian Disputations in the Middle Ages*. Liverpool: Littman, 1993.
Matt, Daniel. *The Zohar: Pritzker Edition*, 12 vols. Stanford: Stanford University Press, 2006–2013.
Neumann, Erich. *The Fear of the Feminine: And Other Essays on Feminine Psychology*. Princeton: Princeton University Press 1994.
Novenson, Matthew V. *The Grammar of Messianism*. Oxford: Oxford University Press, 2017.
Pedaya, Haviva. *Vision and Speech*. Los Angeles: Cherub Press, 2002.
Philips, Adam. *Missing Out: In Praise of the Unlived Life*. New York: Picador, 2013.
Rank, Otto. *The Myth of the Birth of the Hero*. New York: Vintage Books, 1959.
Roi, Biti. *Love of the Shekhinah*. Ramat Gan: Bar-Ilan University Press, 2017.
Scholem, Gershom. *Sabbatai Zevi and the Sabbatean Movement during His Lifetime*. Tel Aviv: Am Oved, 1957.
Scholem, Gershom. *Toward an Understanding of the Messianic Idea in Judaism*. New York: Schocken, 1971.
Shinan, Avigdor. "'Al Demuto shel ha-Melekh David be-Sifrut ḤaZaL." In *David: From Shepherd to Messiah,* 181–99. Jerusalem: Ben-Zvi Institute, 1995.
Valler, Shulamit. "King David and His Women: Biblical Stories and Talmudic Discussions." In *A Feminist Companion to Samuel and Kings*, edited by Athalya Brenner, 129–42. Sheffield: Sheffield Academic Press, 1994.
Vital, R. Haim. *Sefer ha-Ḥezyonot*, edited by Morris M. Faierstein. Jerusalem: Ben-Zvi Institute, 2006.
Yuval, Israel J. *Two Nations in Your Womb: Perceptions of Jews and Christians in Late Antiquity and the Middle Ages*. Translated by Barbara Harshav and Jonathan Chipman. Berkeley: University of California Press, 2006.

14

Tying Knots of Fortitude to Withstand Your Beauty

Women as Temptresses and Tests of Fortitude in Sufi Literature

Matthew R. Hotham

INTRODUCTION

The scholarship on women's roles in Sufism has shifted immensely over the past few decades. From an early focus on Sufism as a gender-egalitarian expression of Islam, more contemporary works have incorporated feminist scholarship and critiqued the earlier, rosier assessments of Sufism and women.[1] Rabi'a al-Adawiyya takes an outsized role in this conversation as one of the few early women that later Sufi biographical dictionaries give her own entry and mention by name. In contemporary English-speaking contexts, her prominence has been bolstered by the work of Margaret Smith in the mid-twentieth century and the reinvention of Rabi'a in late twentieth and early twenty-first centuries in spiritual but not religious discourse. Rabi'a has numerous stories showing her one-upping her male counterparts and demonstrating a superior piety to them. When it comes to discussing her legacy in relation to the issue of women in Sufism, however, the line that gets cited most often comes from Farid al-Din 'Attar's introduction to her biography in his late twelfth- or early thirteenth-century collection of saintly hagiographies, the *Tadhkirat al-Awliya*. The line reads: "When a woman is a man on the path of the Lord most high, she cannot be called a woman."[2] It is sometimes cited as evidence of the gender egalitarianism inherent in Sufism, even if such egalitarianism could only be expressed in terms of gender binaries, because of the limitations of the time period.[3] If we read 'Attar as generously as possible within the larger context of his writing on women mystics, he seems to be attempting to express the potential for spiritual companionship and rivalry that transcends gender, but can only do so using the language of gender binary, privileging one side of that binary. Others take issue with this reading, problematizing the quote, but more importantly directing attention to issues of patriarchy and male privilege within the institutions that profess to foster and perpetuate the particular mode of religious engagement we mark with the term "Sufism."[4] Regardless of his views of Sufi women like Rabi'a, it is clear that women like her are the exception and not the rule. Her spiritual attainments have separated her from the category of "woman" in 'Attar's eyes. This invites the question: What does it mean to be a woman, for 'Attar? More importantly for the purposes of this chapter, what does it mean for a man on the path of the Lord when he encounters a woman who *can* be called a woman?

Several important works have been written on the role of women in the development of early Muslim ascetic and piety movements that are later claimed by Sufism.[5] These works grapple with the reasons that named women are largely absent from historical sources on early Sufism and discuss what we can nevertheless glean about their participation in and contributions to Sufism. This chapter relies on but takes a significantly different approach from these works. Rather than examine stories of pious Sufi women in the biographical accounts of early Sufis, this chapter will explore how non-Sufi women are framed as sources of temptation and tests of spiritual fortitude for early Sufi men by examining two cases: the biography of Ibn Khafif as it shifts across multiple biographical collections spanning centuries and "The Story of Sheikh San'an" in Farid al-din Attar's *The Conference of the Birds*. Ibn Khafif (d. 982 CE) was a member of Abu al-Qasim al-Junayd's circle who was renowned for both his asceticism and theological acumen. His biography is recorded in six of the most significant Sufi hagiographic collections, in both Arabic and Persian,[6] and as such is a rich site of contestation for those debating the place of asceticism, and especially celibacy, in Sufism. Farid al-din Attar was a twelfth-century poet and Sufi who composed an important collection of Sufi hagiographies, *The Memorial of God's Friends*, which contains an entry on Ibn Khafif, and *The Conference of the Birds,* an allegorical mystical poem recording the journey of numerous birds to find their king. Within the frame tale of the birds seeking their king are numerous brief stories exemplifying various Sufi principles. These stories often involve historical political and religious figures, including those cataloged in the *The Memorial of God's Friends*, and in other cases revisit common Sufi teaching tales. "The Story of Sheikh San'an" is by far the longest story in *The Conference of the Birds* and occurs right before the birds set aside their fears and embark on their journey.

In both cases, women are portrayed as both tools for and obstacles to the spiritual development of the main male characters. What later comes to be called Sufism traces its lineage through early ascetic figures like Ibn Khafif who gathered and learned together in Baghdad. Sheikh San'an is most likely an entirely fictional character, but has many of the attributes of a pious Sufi ascetic. These foundational figures, almost entirely men with one notable exception, engaged in a number of ascetic practices—from sleep deprivation to fasting, physical discomfort to abstinence.

Abstinence, in particular, was a tricky issue for these early ascetics and their later biographers. The Prophet Muhammad was not abstinent; properly regulated sexual intercourse is generally viewed positively and valued in Islamic Law; and an over-valuation of celibacy comes to smack of "monkishness" and opens up ascetics to critiques of being overly Christian in their practices. In the later biographies of early ascetic figures, we therefore see *sexual desire* as something to be avoided even if marriage and the sexual act are not.

This chapter will examine how women are framed as tempters and tests for these male ascetics. In the case of Ibn Khafif who had multiple wives but, possibly, no children, his biographers attempt to navigate this fact in various ways, but they all depict Ibn Khafif's wives as mere tools for his further spiritual development. In one common account, even his favorite wife is told she is a temptation to be resisted on par with a plate of delicious food. Likewise, in "The Story of Sheikh San'an," a Christian girl is depicted as a stumbling block for the sheikh, but one which he eventually overcomes to achieve an even higher spiritual status, even as she herself dies. Such depictions problematize some contemporary Western depictions of Sufism as gender-blind or even inherently gender-egalitarian. They also reveal how the asceticism of these early figures challenged later biographers who needed to depict them as spiritual exemplars without implying that they exceeded or contradicted the model of the Prophet Muhammad.

DEBATING SUFISM

Today Sufism is a name without a reality, but formerly it was a reality without a name.[7]

The first written historical reference to the term "Sufism" comes from the above quotation—where Sufism is defined as a term that, once coined, ceased to have a meaningful referent. On the first page of a number of introductory textbooks, authors are quick to gloss the term "Sufism" as being equivalent to and coextensive with "Islamic Mysticism."[8] The problems with this definition are manifold. The term mysticism itself, as Michel de Certeau has pointed out, is derived from a particular branch of medieval Christian theology.[9] In its scholastic formulation, it involved rituals of praise and devotion, private reflection and contemplation, as well as techniques of bodily control and ascetic denial. But as the word developed within both Western scholarly and popular discourse through the eighteenth and nineteenth centuries, it came to be purged of the external, embodied aspects of medieval practice. Leigh Eric Schmidt traces this development through European and American intellectuals, focusing particularly on William James and Unitarian Universalism as vectors for the interiorization of mystical "experience."[10] Thus, the term mysticism in its contemporary configuration excludes many of the practices, objects, and historical phenomena that might otherwise be captured by the word "Sufism." Furthermore, this exclusion works in the reverse direction. If we take for granted our inherited definition of mysticism as a form of individual contemplation of and search for proximity with the divine, associating this exclusively with Sufism in the Islamic tradition excludes a number of practices and communities that might otherwise count—such as Shi'i notions of *'irfan*. Finally, such a stark definition of Sufism as interiority within Islam concedes ground to those who wish to mark the Sunni legal tradition as historically orthodox in its normative prescriptions for structuring human relations and embodied practice.

Ibn Khafif, as with most early figures cataloged in later Sufi biographical dictionaries, probably saw themselves as ascetics more than mystics. The contours of what later comes to be called Sufism in Western scholarship, such as formal orders and set ritual practices, were not developed and formalized until several generations after Ibn Khafif and his ilk. The word Sufi itself was in circulation but often as a term of derision rather than of self-identification. Many scholars, most notably Carl Ernst, have questioned whether the English word "Sufism," and its European language analogues, coherently delineate a real-world phenomenon or if it is a term and concept conjured up by European Orientalists.[11]

For the sake of brevity, rather than revisit this debate, this chapter adopts Knysh's definition of Sufism. Knysh sees "Sufism" as a broad term that points to a complex and messy real-world phenomenon—the heterogeneous but bounded ascetic-mystical elements of Islam whose later texts and traditions see the ascetics and asceticism discussed in this chapter as foundational.[12] The later tradition's uneasiness with and attempts to navigate the asceticism of figures like Ibn Khafif is one element that impacts how women are depicted in these Sufi works.

ASCETICISM, RENUNCIATION, AND POVERTY

Developing out of early Islamic ascetic traditions, Sufism was closely tied to the notion of poverty during its formative period. Among the various etymologies proposed for the word Sufi, *ṣūf*, meaning wool and indicating the practical and unadorned wool garments of an ascetic, is the most accepted derivation of the word.[13] This woolen garment, called a *muraqqaʿa* (patched frock), was a personal symbol for the Sufi themself reminding of their renunciation of worldly desires. It also served as a public symbol, marking the Sufi as a person separate from society. Another frequently posited derivation for the word, though linguistically unlikely, comes from the Arabic *suffa* (bench), indicating a group of early Muslims who lived in the mosque at Medina and who had no possessions, relying on the Prophet's largess to sustain them in their devotion to God.[14] Thus two of the most frequently cited derivations for the term "Sufi" emphasize notions of impoverishment and unworldliness.

No biography of an early Sufi saint is complete without descriptions of his or her ascetic practices, whether it be going without food for days on end, sleeping on nothing but a reed mat, or wearing the same tattered frock for decades. Poverty was not simply an abstract concept but a lived reality for these early saints. Later commentators grappled with the practical questions surrounding how one enacts a life of poverty including questions of whether or not there should be set floors or ceilings on the personal resources of a Sufi, whether certain extremes of poverty might actually harm the aspirant in their quest for God, and whether a Sufi was required to earn enough to meet prior financial obligations or could leave these obligations behind. Often these discussions revolved around financial obligations to wives and children, seeing them as potential barriers to one's renunciation.

Definitions and stipulations regarding poverty in the early period are as diverse as are the writers addressing the topic. Although views on poverty would become more complex in later centuries, all the major early commentators agree that it is a station along the path toward God. When they disagree, it is over where this station occurs, what it leads to, and its relative value in relation to other stations. For Abu Nasr al-Sarraj, poverty comes in three forms depending upon the spiritual advancement of the practitioner. The most basic form is the poverty of one who renounces all worldly possessions, does not complain about his material want or request assistance, and vehemently refuses aid should it be offered. The second form is actually less stringent, and indicates one who meets the above criteria, but may accept assistance freely offered to them. The third form is yet more relaxed still, meeting the criteria of form two, with the added benefit of being able to ask for assistance when necessary.[15] This scale of poverty, with the strictest form actually being the lowest in spiritual attainment, indicates the way in which post-Junaydi Sufism articulates itself as being distinct from asceticism for asceticism's sake.[16] The implication is that poverty is a tool to train a Sufi to no longer desire worldly goods. Those first starting on the path require the greatest restrictions on their access to worldly temptations, whereas those who have already overcome the temptations of food and comfort may accept or even seek it out if it will benefit them in their higher spiritual pursuits, or if lack of one or the other might hinder them. For Sarraj, poverty leads to the station of patience (*sabr*) and comes relatively early along the path, just after renunciation (*zuhd*). Nevertheless, with his demarcation of three separate forms, it encompasses a great deal of spiritual development within a single station.

Other more practical discussions of material poverty are prevalent. Ghazali, attempting to demarcate the minimum bar one must meet to achieve poverty, argues that "poverty is the privation of what is essentially needed by a human being . . . privation of what is unessential to a person is not called poverty."[17] Other writers might take issue with this definition; however, since the goal of poverty is the realization that one really needs nothing but God, so approaching poverty with the understanding that one is giving up something "essentially needed" might seem contradictory to the goals of such privation.

Kalabadhi, highly concerned with minutiae of the life of poverty, discusses whether or not it is appropriate for a Sufi to acquire any earnings whatsoever, resolving that it is permissible should those earnings be used to assist others or to repress desires which might distract one from remembrance of God.[18] He goes so far as to argue that earning is compulsory for one who is responsible for dependents, so poverty is not a state that can or should be imposed upon one's family members.[19] This understanding of poverty thus sets up dependents, such as wives and children, as barriers to the full pursuit of renunciation and begins to provide a framework for seeing them as potential burdens to be avoided along the Sufi path.

Qushayri generally agrees with Kalabadhi's practical view of material poverty, but supports his arguments with a greater bulk of spiritual reasons. Among his list of spiritual stations, poverty ranks relatively high, but is *followed* by Sufism (*tasawwuf*). Like Sarraj and Kalabadhi, Qushayri engages in arguments about the physical manifestations of poverty, such as from whom, if anyone, one can accept gifts and the proper attitude the poor should demonstrate toward the wealthy.[20] He quotes al-Daqqaq approvingly, who says it is "preferable that a man be given enough to sustain himself and maintain himself within those limits."[21] The goal of poverty is not impoverishment then, but rather ridding oneself of unreasonable wants. For Qushayri, true poverty is fear of poverty and so the goal of material poverty is to free oneself from the prison of fear.[22]

With Ansari, we see a greater emphasis on the spiritual attributes of poverty and less concern for its practical attributes. Ansari places poverty relatively low among the spiritual stations, listing it as number 48 out of 100, followed by wealth (*ghani*).[23] Like Sarraj, however, he divides poverty into three kinds: compulsory, voluntary, and realized.[24] These three categories do not directly relate to Sarraj's, though there is some overlap. Whereas Sarraj concerns himself primarily with the physical actions one may or may not take and only implies the inner state to which these actions may relate, Ansari's definitions revolve around the attitude one has toward poverty rather than the characteristics of one's poverty.

Hujwiri notes that poverty has both a form (*rasm*) and essence (*haqiat*) and in his writings we see the balance between discussing spiritual and material poverty prevalent in the work of later Persian poet Farid al-Din 'Attar. Like Qushayri and Kalabadhi before him, he notes that "poverty is being empty of desire not empty of provision."[25] He addresses a debate about the relative value of the stations of poverty and wealth, as Ansari had previously, but disagrees with those who argue that wealth is superior since it is an attribute of God whereas poverty is not. He argues that material wealth is both created and a means to an end, whereas divine wealth is both uncreated and an end itself, therefore human wealth and God's wealth cannot be compared.[26] Turning this argument on its head, Hujwiri notes that wealth is not about the acquisition of "benefits, but of acquisition of the benefactor."[27] Thus true wealth is really just the opposite side of the coin of spiritual poverty, where the former focuses on the fullness of divine presence, and the latter emphasizes the absence of veils that may hinder the experience of such presence.

All this discussion of the relationship between asceticism and Sufism, especially if we understand poverty as synecdochally standing in for renunciation, comes to a head in the writings of Farid al-Din 'Attar. By 'Attar's lifetime, the notion of poverty in Sufism had developed far beyond early Islamic asceticism. Concerned with both the practical aspects of material poverty and the benefits attained through spiritual poverty, Hujwiri's notion of poverty begins to resemble the multi-faceted concept of poverty 'Attar utilizes in his *The Conference of the Birds*—a concept which seems complex and expansive enough to warrant 'Attar's placement of it right beside annihilation (*fana'*) as the final stage along the Sufi path.

In his book on the body in Sufism, Scott Kugle argues that the trials of the spiritual path are "like refining metal through intense heat: heat does not actually destroy the metal but rather burns away the impurities to create a substance that is still metal, but stronger."[28] For 'Attar this intense heat is provided by the notion of poverty, because poverty is the uniquely human condition. The primary difference between humans and angels, humans and Iblis, is that "Adam's makeup was molded of need."[29] The Qur'anic statement that humans were made in God's own image has historically been interpreted in two ways. Either it means that humans were made to meet a preexisting pattern in the mind of God, implying a system similar to the Platonic notion of Forms, or it means that humans were created in God's own image. 'Attar favors the latter of these two interpretations, seeing the human soul as actually being derived from divine essence. So how could a creature created in God's image also be a creature of need?

According to one account, when God first created humans, Iblis went to inspect the new creation and discovered Adam to be hollow, which he interpreted as a sign of weakness, not suspecting what that hollowness was meant to be filled with.[30] For 'Attar, this hollowness is filled with the divine breath which was breathed into Adam to animate him. This mystery of creation, that humans should be a frail hollow shell somehow able to contain and encompass a portion of the divine, perplexed even Iblis. Thus "Adam's need distinguishes him sharply from all other creatures, who are satisfied with what they have."[31] For Ibn Arabi, "poverty is an affair that is inherent in everything other than God," and while this may be so, it is only humans who realize their poverty because they have been created out of the combination of utter lack and overabundance, earth and divine breath, and thus feel their shortcoming.[32] Humans are only "possible being" which require the "Necessary Being" in order to actually exist.[33] It is this need that ends up being the greatest asset of humans, since it creates a space for union with the divine, a space other beings do not have. This need to cultivate one's sense of lack also undergirds a number of spiritual practices meant to induce yearning for things of this world as an analogue for yearning for God. In this way, sexual desire can function as a tool to induce one's sense of inner privation and sublimation can redirect that induced desire toward God instead of the material object of one's initial desire.

When 'Attar speaks of spiritual poverty, it is this level of ultimate need for which he aspires, though there are other elements of poverty along the path. Spiritual poverty must start as material poverty because "initially poverty is renunciation of the world and all in it; ultimately it is annihilation."[34] Material poverty clears the path for spiritual poverty, because "to the degree that people find wealth and independence in themselves and see themselves as positive and good, they will be empty of love for God."[35] But material poverty cannot be an end in itself, for one can come to pride oneself on one's asceticism, which would be another barrier separating one from God. Thus spiritual poverty must also be cultivated because "only those who possess no perfection whatsoever can truly love God, for only they have absolute, unqualified need."[36] "The Story of Sheikh San'an" exemplifies the numerous layers of poverty along the spiritual path, and how for 'Attar it is not simply a single way station near the beginning or end, but rather a constant presence along one's journey, and a necessary prerequisite to annihilation in God (*fana'*). The primary tool for attaining this spiritual poverty in this story is a Christian girl who tempts Sheikh San'an into renouncing his religion. Though his desire for her is initially a stumbling block, she ultimately serves as a tool for furthering his spiritual poverty and elevating his spiritual status, at the eventual cost of her own religion, social status, and life.

THE STORY OF SHEIKH SAN'AN

"The Story of Sheikh San'an" is the single longest vignette in *The Conference of the Birds* at 434 lines, and perhaps the most famous of the individual stories within the collection. It tells the story of a sheikh, custodian of the Ka'ba, renowned for his piety, with four hundred disciples, perfect in his ritual observations, who has made the Hajj fifty times. One night, he dreams that he is worshiping an idol in Rome, probably meaning Byzantium or a city in the Anatolian peninsula under Muslim control but with a majority Christian population. Tormented by this dream, he travels to the city in his dream with his disciples and falls in love with a wealthy Christian girl who has no idea the sheikh even exists. Throughout the story, the Christian girl is portrayed as at first indifferent and then mean-spirited and cruel. For a month, she does not notice him at all. Once it comes to her attention that there is a poor, dirty, old Muslim man living on the streets outside her house she is initially disgusted, finding his age and poverty particularly repellant. After her initial expression of disgust doesn't dissuade the sheikh, she begins to see how far she can push this old man before he breaks. Constantly promising that she will be his if he can prove himself to her, she tests his devotion to her by asking him to get drunk with her, and then to forswear Islam and burn a Qur'an. After he does all of this, she then asks him to convert to Christianity, which he does. Finally, citing her father's potential objection to their union, she asks him to win her father's favor by working as a swineherd for the family for a year. Each act further degrades the sheikh in the eyes of his students and sets the Christian girl up as the idol of the sheikh's dreams—an object of worship requiring the renunciation of all other devotions and obligations.

During this time his disciples abandon him and head back to Mecca. On their return journey, a loyal disciple and friend of the sheikh listens to their tales and nevertheless scolds them for abandoning their teacher, ordering them to return to Byzantium immediately and continue to follow their sheikh's example, even if that means herding pigs and converting to Christianity. During their return journey they pray daily until the loyal disciple is visited by Muhammad in a dream. According to tradition, the appearance of Muhammad in a dream proves the dream's veracity since Satan is said to be barred from appearing in the image of the Prophet. The dream reveals that the sheikh has been freed from his obsession over the Christian girl and absolved of wrongdoing. The sheikh leaves Byzantium and is reunited with his disciples, resuming his life as a Muslim and Sufi sheikh. But shortly after his departure, the Christian girl realizes her love for the sheikh and leaves her opulent life behind to pursue him through the desert, perishing from exhaustion just moments after catching up with the group and falling into the sheikh's arms.[37]

This story is often read through the lens of passionate love; the Christian girl interpreted as analogous to God, for whom one gives up all sense of self just for a chance at proximity.[38] It is also used to depict the importance of following one's sheikh, no matter how bizarre their requests and actions may seem. The most important lesson of the story, however, revolves around the subject of poverty, which it addresses in detail on all its various levels. The thread of poverty may not be obvious at first, because "The Story of Sheikh San'an" does not start with a main character engulfed in worldly pleasures. The sheikh is a long-time Sufi who has worn the patched frock for many years and lives at the Ka'ba in Mecca. One would assume that material poverty is not an issue for such a man. What the story reveals, however, is that though the sheikh was not weighed down by worldly goods, he was burdened with his positive reputation, adoring students, and pride in his own spiritual attainments. The story of Sheikh San'an is one in which a Sufi who has outwardly achieved a high station along the path must be humbled before he can address hidden barriers that are preventing his attainment of union with God. The agent of this humbling is of course a woman who tempts him and then torments him before being cast aside for his spiritual growth.

IBN KHAFIF

Women are not framed as barriers to men's spiritual development only in fiction. In Sufi biographical dictionaries we also see women portrayed as sexual tempters and wives depicted as barriers to achieving true renunciation. Just as in the case of Sheikh San'an, these women are not always framed as obstacles to be avoided but rather springboards to higher spiritual status. This is perhaps nowhere more explicitly clear than in the biographical entries on Ibn Khafif. Ibn Khafif was a ninth-century ascetic who was a member of al-Junayd's circle in Baghdad. He was an important transmitter of Baghdadian mystical terminology to Khorisan. He was also renowned for his asceticism—indeed his name itself, Ibn Khafif—"Son of Slimness"—indicated his avoidance of food. In one biographical account, he eats nothing but a handful of beans once per day for over a year.

Ibn Khafif's asceticism was important for later Sufis because it exemplified a key principle important to many later Sufi *tariqas*: "solitude within society." Later Sufis would frequently critique ascetic practice that required isolation and solitude.[39] Such criticism of retreat from the world is reminiscent of the prophetic hadith that states there is no monkhood in Islam. Although many of the early ascetics who proved foundational to later Sufism had positive relationships with Syriac Christian ascetics,[40] the heirs to their legacy often felt the need to defend themselves against criticism that Sufism was derived from or influenced by non-Islamic practices. To counter these criticisms, some Sufis put even greater emphasis on the Qur'anic and Prophetic origins of their practices, pointing to the Prophet Muhammad as their spiritual exemplar and occasionally choosing to bar or explain away practices that diverged from Muhammad's model. Among the early ascetic practices that troubled later Sufis, perhaps none was more vexatious than celibacy.[41]

We can trace the growing discomfort with celibacy across the four hundred years of biographical entries on Ibn Khafif. Hujwiri's biography, written in the eleventh century, contains the following account of Ibn Khafif and his wives:

> I have heard from Abu 'l-Hasan 'Ali b. Bakran of Shiraz that one day several of his wives were gathered together, and each one was telling some story about him. They all agreed *sese nunquam eum vidisse libidini obsequentem* [that he would gaze upon them but controlled his passions]. Hitherto each of them had believed that she was peculiarly treated in this respect, and when they learned that the Sheikh's behaviour was the same towards them all, they were astonished and doubted whether such was truly the case. Accordingly, they sent two of their number to question the vizier's daughter, who was his favourite, as to his dealings with her. She replied: "When the Shaykh wedded me and I was informed that he would visit me that night, I prepared a fine repast and adorned myself assiduously. As soon as he came and the food was brought, he called me to him and looked for a while first at me and then at the food.[42] Then he took my hand and drew it into his sleeve. From his breast to his navel there were fifteen knots (*'aqd*) growing out of his belly. He said, 'Ask me what these are'; so I asked him and he replied, 'They are the knots made by the tribulation and anguish of my abstinence in renouncing a face like this and viands like these.' He said not more, but departed; and that is all my intimacy with him."[43]

In this passage, celibacy is praiseworthy and comprises a substantial part of Ibn Khafif's biography. Still, celibacy is not something one pursues through isolation but is rather something one does while presumably fulfilling one's social obligation of marriage. The women here seem confused by his abstinence at first, assuming that he is merely avoiding sexual relations with some, but not all, of them. It is only when they compare notes with one another, and his "favorite" wife, that they realize the truth of the sheikh's celibacy, which he feels the need to keep concealed from even his wives apparently. Why marry at all then? The practical explanations are numerous—the marriages predate his asceticism and must be maintained, or are contracted for political expediency, or he feels the need to keep up appearances that he is not practicing celibacy. Beyond these practical reasons, there is also a spiritual reason for keeping numerous wives around and for marrying a new woman—"his favorite"—after his celibate life began. His wives, in particular the vizier's daughter, are tools to his spiritual development. Though he does this with all his wives, it seems that he most frequently summons the vizier's daughter in order to gaze upon her lustfully before sending her away. Wives are therefore turned into tools for Ibn Khafif's practice of spiritual poverty and solitude within society. In the story, their own needs are only of concern for the sake of the plot—once they question the vizier's daughter, it becomes clear that in this biography they are just objects upon which Ibn Khafif hones his self-discipline. The story even equates sexual desire with appetite, since Ibn Khafif gazes on and resists both women *and* food as *objects* to be used in the pursuit of *self-mastery*.[44]

The relative disinterest in women as human beings in Sufi discourse, since they are framed as merely one means by which a male ascetic may demonstrate self-mastery, becomes more apparent in Farid al-Din 'Attar's reappropriation of this story two hundred years later. 'Attar recounts Hujwiri's story nearly exactly, with only slight changes. For example, the women no longer talk among themselves to discover their husband's celibacy but instead respond to the questions of an unnamed "they" who asks about their husband's austerity. While little changes in this story, we can see a shifting view of the spiritual danger posed by women by the story directly preceding it in 'Attar:

> It is related that one midnight [I]bn Khafif said to his servant, "Get me a wife!"
> "Where am I supposed to go in the middle of the night?" the servant asked. "I do, however, have a daughter myself. If the sheikh permits, let me bring her."
> "Bring her," the sheikh said.
> So the servant brought his daughter. The sheikh married her at once. After seven months she gave birth to a child, but it died. The sheikh told his servant, "Tell your daughter to get a divorce, or if she wishes, to remain as she is."
> The servant asked "Sheikh, what is the secret behind this?"
> "The night when I married," Ebn Khafif said, "I saw the Prophet (peace and blessings be upon him) in a dream. There were many people, bewildered and drowning in their own sweat. All of a sudden, a child came and took his father's hand and led him over the Narrow Bridge as quick as the wind. I also wanted to have a child. Since this child has now come and gone, my aim has been achieved."[45]

Whereas in Hujwiri's tale the main danger women pose is seemingly sexual temptation; in this tale we see a different danger posed by sexual relations. At first, 'Attar leads us to believe that this is a story about sexual temptation. What else could inspire Ibn Khafif's late-night request besides the need to satisfy a sudden, overwhelming sexual urge? It seems that his servant is under the same impression but still willingly offers his daughter for the sheikh's sexual pleasure. After the woman becomes pregnant and the child dies prematurely, Ibn Khafif says that his new wife can either seek divorce or remain married but presumably, given the story immediately following this, sexually deprived for the rest of her marriage. This perplexes the woman's father, who questions Ibn Khafif's actions. Note, however, that he does not question the sheikh as a protective father or a confused servant, but as a spiritual disciple asking for the inner meaning of the sheikh's actions.

In response to this request, Ibn Khafif reveals that not only was his servant's daughter merely an object for his spiritual development, so too was the man's grandchild. Ibn Khafif recounts a prophetic dream, which as we mentioned previously confirms its divine provenance. Ibn Khafif is thus able to adhere to the Prophet's model by marrying, having sexual intercourse, and fathering a child. He is not, however, ever burdened by sexual desire or financial and familial obligations to a child that could hinder his renunciation.

By means of this dream account, which doesn't appear in any other biography of Ibn Khafif, 'Attar is able to situate Ibn Khafif's record of celibacy more comfortably within later Sufi theological positions on celibacy. Ibn Khafif holds unbroken mastery over his passions—he is celibate for his whole life, except for this one divinely inspired copulation. At the same time, however, the value of parenthood is affirmed. This story resolves a tension between two seemingly competing values in Sufism: control of the *nafs* (animal portion of the soul) on the one hand, and fatherhood on the other (as demonstrated by the prophetic model). Taken together, 'Attar's accounts of Ibn Khafif's relationship to his wives and child reveal them to be a means to an end—and the story seems to argue that it is preferable that they simply cease to burden him after they have helped him achieve his spiritual end.

CONCLUSION

Much discussion of the place of the body in Sufism has focused on ascetic practice, ranging from sleep deprivation to self-mortification. Implicit within these discussions is the notion that men are speaking to other men about resisting bodily temptation. The varied kinds of bodily transformations sleep deprivation or extreme fasting might induce are framed around the male body. The potential threats the world can offer to distract a mystic often focus upon women and children. Within this conversation, little thought is given to this elevated valuation of the male human body over other kinds of bodies.

This returns us to the 'Attar quote with which we began: "When a woman is a man on the path of the Lord most high, she cannot be called a woman." For 'Attar, anxiety about sexual temptation can be displaced and equal relations are possible if one fails to note gender difference. He quotes Hasan al-Basra, a prominent early mystic, as saying "I was with Rabeʻa for one full day and night. I was talking about the path and the truth in such a way that the thought 'I am a man' never crossed my mind, nor did 'I am a woman' ever cross hers."[46] What prevents this from being scandalous (though nevertheless makes it remarkable enough to include in a hagiography) is that neither Hasan al-Basra nor Rabiʻa thought about their *own* gender.[47] It is notable that Hasan al-Basra does not say "I did not notice she was a woman and she did not notice that I was a man"—what is threatening to propriety in this case is not objectification, seeing the *other* as a gendered being with which one can only have a physical relationship, nor is it even Rabiʻa's womanhood as a source of temptation, but rather the recognition of one's self as a gendered being. If one can forget one's own embodiment, which is inherently gendered in this context, then the threats posed by the body are negated. ʻAttar struggles to articulate this notion of a genderless transcendence, observing that "When a woman is a man on the path of the Lord most high, she cannot be called a woman," just moments after quoting the *hadith* "God does not regard your forms," which he explains by adding "it is not a matter of form but of right intention."[48] ʻAttar's account of Sufi lives attempts to resolve the essential asceticism of early Sufi men like Ibn Khafif with his own preference for instrumental asceticism. We are left, then, with a path toward transcendence that eliminates gender, but does so by effacing women.

If we read ʻAttar's struggle to articulate the licitness of some women's presence in Sufi circles as generously as possible, women themselves are still seen as a problem. Only those women who are exceptions, such as Rabi'a, do not elicit the recognition of gender binaries that would hinder spiritual development. The women most often admitted into these Sufi circles as exceptions often had something that seemingly made them sexually undesirable or off-limits—their old age, their familial relationship to the Sufi men, or "bodies ruined from fasting or weeping."[49] The concern, then, is women who might provide sexual temptation. Sexual desire and its fulfillment, however, are not themselves illicit, are rewards for the pious in the afterlife, and were valued by the Prophet Muhammad. For these Sufi men, then, it is not sexual desire itself that is the problem. As we see in the case of Ibn Khafif, inducing and then not acting on sexual desire provides him spiritual fulfillment. The problem, then, for these Sufi men, is that women might become a more long-term distraction to spiritual practice. This is especially the case if fulfillment of sexual desire leads to long-term financial obligations. When a "woman is a man on the path of the Lord" she apparently does not induce sexual desire in these Sufi men—but more importantly, her own renunciation means she will not call on them to enter into a marriage that requires financial support of her material needs or the needs of children. If one is independently wealthy, like Ibn Khafif, such material obligations are manageable. He can therefore marry a host of women while treating them like tools for his own spiritual fulfillment. Sufi men of more modest means, however, are seemingly warned to be wary of women since one moment of temptation could lead to a lifetime of obligation that might lead one off the Sufi path.

NOTES

1. Meena Sharify-Funk, "Gender and Sufism in Western Scholarship: Contemporary Constructions and Contestations," *Studies in Religion/Sciences Religieuses* 49, no. 1 (March 1, 2020): 50–72.

2. Michael Anthony Sells, *Early Islamic Mysticism: Sufi, Qur'an, Miraj, Poetic and Theological Writings* (Mahwah, NJ: Paulist Press, 1996), 155.

3. See, for example, Margaret Smith, *Muslim Women Mystics: The Life and Work of Rábi'a and Other Women Mystics in Islam* (Oxford: Oneworld, 2001), 19–21.

4. See, for example, Laury Silvers, "Early Pious, Mystic Sufi Women," in *The Cambridge Companion to Sufism*, ed. Lloyd Ridgeon, Cambridge Companions to Religion (Cambridge: Cambridge University Press, 2015), 46–47.

5. See, for example, Rkia Elaroui Cornell, *Rabi'a From Narrative to Myth: The Many Faces of Islam's Most Famous Woman Saint, Rabi'a al-'Adawiyya* (London: Oneworld Academic, 2019) or Silvers, "Early Pious."

6. Sulami's *Tabaqat al-Sufiya* (Arabic), Ansari's *Hilyat al-Awliya* (Persian), Qushayri's *Risala* (Arabic), Hujwiri's *Kashf al-Mahjub* (Persian), 'Attar's *Tadhkirat al-Awliya* (Persian), and Jami's *Nafahat al-Uns* (Persian).

7. 'Alī ibn 'Usmān Hujvīrī and Reynold Alleyne Nicholson, *Kashf Al-Maḥjūb of Al-Hujwīrī: The Revelation of the Veiled: An Early Persian Treatise on Sufism*, new ed. reprinted with corrections (Wiltshire: Aris & Phillips, 2000), 44. As cited in Annemarie Schimmel, *Mystical Dimensions of Islam* (University of North Carolina Press, 1975), 22.

8. See, for example, Arthur John Arberry, *Sufism: An Account of the Mystics of Islam* (Mineola, NY: Dover Publications, 2001); Julian Baldick, *Mystical Islam: An Introduction to Sufism* (New York: New York University Press, 1989); William C. Chittick, *Sufism: A Beginner's Guide* (Oxford: Oneworld, 2007); Martin Lings, *What Is Sufism?*, 2nd edition (Cambridge: Islamic Texts Society, 1999); Huston Smith, *Essential Sufism*, ed. Robert Frager and James Fadiman, 1 Reprint edition (San Francisco: HarperOne, 1999).

9. Michel De Certeau, "Mystic Speech," in *Heterologies: Discourse on the Other* (Minneapolis: University of Minnesota Press, 1986), 80–100.

10. Leigh Eric Schmidt, "The Making of Modern 'Mysticism,'" *Journal of the American Academy of Religion* 71 (2003): 273–302.

11. Carl W. Ernst, *The Shambhala Guide to Sufism* (Boston, MA: Shambhala, 1997), 8–18.

12. Alexander Knysh, *Sufism: A New History of Islamic Mysticism* (Princeton, NJ: Princeton University Press, 2017), 15–34.

13. "Taṣawwuf," Lewishon et al. in *Encyclopaedia of Islam*, ed. P. Bearman, Th. Bianquis, C.E. Bosworth, E. van Donzel and W.P. Heinrichs (Leiden: Brill, 2008).
14. Ernst, *Sufism*, 22.
15. John Renard, *Knowledge of God in Classical Sufism: Foundations of Islamic Mystical Theology* (New York: Paulist Press, 2004), 95.
16. Christopher Melchert, "The Transition from Asceticism to Mysticism at the Middle of the Ninth Century C.E," *Studia Islamica* 83 (1996): 51–70.
17. Javad Nurbakhsh, *Spiritual Poverty in Sufism: Faqr and Faqir* (London: Khaniqahi-Nimatullahi Publications, 1984), 36.
18. Abu Bakr al-Kalabadhi, *The Doctrines of the Sufis*, trans. Arthur John Arberry (New York: Cambridge University Press, 1977), 73.
19. Ibid., 73.
20. Abu'l-Qasim al-Qushayri, *Principles of Sufism*, trans. B.R. Con Schlegell (Oneonta, NY: Mizan Press, 1990), 294.
21. Ibid., 293.
22. Ibid., 291.
23. Ernst, *Sufism*, 104–105.
24. Nurbakhsh, *Spiritual Poverty*, 32.
25. Mawlana Ali al-Hujwiri, *Kashf al-Mahjub*, trans. Reynold Nicholson (London: Gibb Memorial Trust, 2000), 25.
26. Ibid., 21–22.
27. Ibid., 22.
28. Scott Alan Kugle, *Sufis and Saints' Bodies: Mysticism, Corporeality, and Sacred Power in Islam* (Chapel Hill: University of North Carolina Press, 2007).
29. Chittick, *Sufism*, 159. Iblis is the name of a jinn who refuses to bow before Adam at God's command and thus becomes Satan in Islamic theology.
30. Kugle, *Sufis and Saints' Bodies*, 38.
31. Chittick, *Sufism*, 159.
32. Ibid.
33. Nurbakhsh, *Spiritual Poverty*, 6.
34. Ibid., 9.
35. Chittick, *Sufism*, 158.
36. Ibid.
37. Farid ud-Din Attar, *The Conference of the Birds*, trans. Dick Davis and Afkham Darbandi (New York: Penguin Books, 2001), 57–74.
38. See, for example: Claudia Yaghoobi, *Subjectivity in 'Attār, Persian Sufism, and European Mysticism* (West Lafayette, IN: Purdue University Press, 2017), 124 or Cyrus Ali Zargar, *Polished Mirror: Storytelling and the Pursuit of Virtue in Islamic Philosophy and Sufism* (London: Oneworld Academic, 2017), 247.
39. Hamid Algar, "Jami Ii. And Sufism," *Encyclopedia Iranica*, June 23, 2008, http://www.iranica.com/articles/jami-ii.
40. See: Tor Andrae, *In the Garden of Myrtles: Studies in Early Islamic Mysticism* (Albany: State University of New York Press, 1987).
41. Cornell points out that several Qur'anic passages praise celibacy or chastity (3:39, 21:91, 66:12) (173). In the early Sufi context, "celibacy was tolerated but it

was not required as part of the ascetic lifestyle. It was not seen as fundamental to the practice of asceticism itself" (176).

42. The explicit association between sexual and gustatory pleasure in this story is perhaps unusual for early Sufis, because as Cornell notes:

> For early Christians, impurities were believed to enter the body through the sexual organs. This is one reason why celibacy was such a crucial practice for Christian ascetics. By contrast, Muslim practitioners of *wara'*, along with pagan Neo-Platonists, believed that impurities were more likely to enter the body through the mouth than through sexual activity. For this reason, early Muslim ascetics tended to be more concerned with food pollution than with sexual pollution. (Cornell, *Rabi'a*, 98)

43. Hujvīrī and Nicholson, *Kashf al-maḥjūb of al-Hujwīrī*, 247–248. The inclusion of Latin here was a common practice in Orientalist translations of passages deemed sexually explicit, under the presumption that such passages should be censored for the general reading public but accessible to non-Orientalist scholars (who presumably would know Latin).

44. Borrowing terms from Eliezer Diamond and Richard Valentasis, Cornell divides asceticism into three categories in early Sufism: instrumental, reactionary, and essential. Relevant to this passage is the distinction between instrumental and essential asceticism. This story portrays Ibn Khafif as engaged in essential asceticism, where active denial of temptations is important to his religious practice, in contrast to an instrumental asceticism which rejects the world as a distraction from God. Ibn Khafif does not merely disregard or ignore his wives, he actively puts himself in a position of temptation in order to overcome that temptation—an act of asceticism which then inscribes itself upon his body. The idea that active rejection of worldly temptation was virtuous itself was critiqued by early women Sufis, like Rabi'a, who gravitated toward instrumental rather than essential forms of asceticism.

45. Farid ud-Din 'Attar, *Memorial of God's Friends*, trans. Paul Losensky (New York: Paulist Press, 2009), 389–390. For many early Sufis, children were viewed as burdensome because they required financial support that detracted from one's spiritual practices (see Cornell, 173). In this story, Ibn Khafif gets the best of both worlds, gaining the spiritual benefits of emulating the Prophet and fathering a child without the worldly entanglements of having to raise that child.

46. 'Attar, *Memorial of God's Friends*, 104.

47. This was in no way a unique occurrence. Cornell notes that "Despite their disapproval of women in general, many celibate male ascetics—including Darani—frequently visited women ascetics such as Rabi'a al-'Adawiyya and her contemporaries. In fact, not only did they visit them but they also visited them alone and after dark" (Cornell, *Rabi'a*, 174). The problem, then, seems not to be women themselves but women who represent a sexual temptation—or even more so a potential future familial entanglement.

48. 'Attar, *Memorial of God's Friends*, 97.

49. Silvers, "Early Pious," 46.

BIBLIOGRAPHY

Algar, Hamid. "Jami ii. And Sufism." In *Encyclopedia Iranica*, June 23, 2008. http://www.iranica.com/articles/jami-ii.
Andrae, Tor. *In the Garden of Myrtles: Studies in Early Islamic Mysticism*. Albany: State University of New York Press, 1987.
Arberry, Arthur John. *Sufism: An Account of the Mystics of Islam*. Mineola: Dover Publications, 2001.
Attar, Farid ud-Din. *The Conference of the Birds*. Translated by Dick Davis and Afkham Darbandi. New York: Penguin Books, 2001.
Attar, Farid aD-Din. *Farid Ad-Din Attar's Memorial of God's Friends: Lives and Sayings of Sufis*. Translated by Paul Losensky. New York: Paulist Press, 2009.
Baldick, Julian. *Mystical Islam: An Introduction to Sufism*. New York: New York University Press, 1989.
Certeau, Michel De. "Mystic Speech." In *Heterologies: Discourse on the Other*, edited by Michel de Certeau, 80–100. Minneapolis: University of Minnesota Press, 1986.
Chittick, William C. *Sufism: A Beginner's Guide*. Oxford: Oneworld, 2007.
Cornell, Rkia Elaroui. *Rabi'a From Narrative to Myth: The Many Faces of Islam's Most Famous Woman Saint, Rabi'a al-'Adawiyya*. New York: One World, 2019.
Ernst, Carl W. *The Shambhala Guide to Sufism*. Boston, Mass: Shambhala, 1997.
Hujvīrī, 'Alī ibn 'Usmān and Reynold Alleyne Nicholson. *Kashf Al-Maḥjūb of al-Hujwīrī: The Revelation of the Veiled: An Early Persian Treatise on Sufism*. Wiltshire: Aris & Phillips, 2000.
Jāmī, 1414-1492, and Muḥammad Adīb Jādir. *Nafaḥāt Al-Uns Min Ḥaḍarāt al-Quds*. Al-Ṭab'ah 1. Bayrūt: Manshūrāt Muḥammad 'Alī Bayḍūn, Dār al-Kutub al-'Ilmīyah, 2003.
Kalabadhi, Abu Bakr al-. *The Doctrines of the Sufis*. Translated by A. J. Arberry. New York: Cambridge University Press, 1977.
Karamustafa, Ahmet T. *Sufism: The Formative Period*. Berkeley: University of California Press, 2007.
Knysh, Alexander. *Sufism: A New History of Islamic Mysticism*, 2017.
Kugle, Scott Alan. *Sufis and Saints' Bodies: Mysticism, Corporeality, and Sacred Power in Islam*. Chapel Hill: University of North Carolina Press, 2007.
Lewishon et al. "Taṣawwuf." In *Encyclopaedia of Islam*, edited by P. Bearman, Th. Bianquis, C. E. Bosworth, E. van Donzel and W. P. Heinrichs. Leiden: Brill, 2008.
Lings, Martin. *What Is Sufism?* 2nd ed. Cambridge: Islamic Texts Society, 1999.
Losensky, Paul. "The Creative Compiler: The Art of Rewriting in 'Attar's Tazkirat al-Awliya'." In *The Necklace of the Pleiades: Studies in Persian Literature Presented to Heshmat Moayyad on His 80th Birthday - 24 Essays on Persian Literature, Culture and Religion*, edited by Franklin Lewis and Sunil Sharma, 107–19. Leiden: Leiden University Press, 2010.
Melchert, Christopher. "The Transition from Asceticism to Mysticism at the Middle of the Ninth Century C.E." *Studia Islamica* 83 (1996): 51–70.

Mojaddedi, Jawid. "Jami's Re-Contextualization of Biographical Traditions: 'The Biography of Ansari' in the Framework of the Nafahat al-Uns." In *Studies in Islamic and Middle Eastern Texts and Traditions in Memory of Norman Calder*, edited by Norman Calder, G. R. (Gerald R.) Hawting, J. A. (Jawid Ahmad) Mojaddedi, and Alexander Samely, 195–211. Oxford: Oxford University Press, 2000.

Mojaddedi, Jawid. *The Biographical Tradition in Sufism: The Tabaqat Genre from al-Sulamī to Jāmī*. Richmond, Surrey: Curzon Press, 2001.

Nurbakhsh, Javad. *Spiritual Poverty in Sufism*. New York: Khaniqahi Nimatullahi Publications, 1984.

Qushayri, Abu 'l-Qasim Al-. *Al-Qusharyri's Epistle on Sufism: Al-Risala Al-Qushayriyya Fi 'ilm Al-Tasawwuf*. Translated by Alexander Knysh. Reading: Garnet Publishing, 2007.

Renard, John. *Knowledge of God in Classical Sufism: Foundations of Islamic Mystical Theology*. New York: Paulist Press, 2004.

Safi, Omid. *The Politics of Knowledge in Premodern Islam : Negotiating Ideology and Religious Inquiry*. Chapel Hill: University of North Carolina Press, 2006.

Schimmel, Annemarie. *Mystical Dimensions of Islam*. Chapel Hill: University of North Carolina Press, 1975.

Schmidt, Leigh Eric. "The Making of Modern 'Mysticism'." *Journal of the American Academy of Religion* 71 (2003): 273–302.

Sells, Michael Anthony. *Early Islamic Mysticism: Sufi, Qur'an, Miraj, Poetic and Theological Writings*. Mahwah: Paulist Press, 1996.

Sharify-Funk, Meena. "Gender and Sufism in Western Scholarship: Contemporary Constructions and Contestations." *Studies in Religion/Sciences Religieuses* 49, no. 1 (2020): 50–72.

Silvers, Laury. "Early Pious, Mystic Sufi Women." In *The Cambridge Companion to Sufism*, edited by Lloyd Ridgeon, 24–52. Cambridge: Cambridge University Press, 2015.

Smith, Huston. *Essential Sufism*, edited by Robert Frager and James Fadiman. San Francisco: HarperOne, 1999.

Smith, Margaret. *Muslim Women Mystics: The Life and Work of Rábi'a and Other Women Mystics in Islam*. Oxford: Oneworld, 2001.

Yaghoobi, Claudia. *Subjectivity in 'Attār, Persian Sufism, and European Mysticism*. West Lafayette: Purdue University Press, 2017.

Zargar, Cyrus Ali. *Polished Mirror: Storytelling and the Pursuit of Virtue in Islamic Philosophy and Sufism*. London: Oneworld Academic, 2017.

Index

Abadi, Omri, 230n71
Abu Raya, Rafa, 230n72
Ainsworth, Claire, 271n7
Alexander, Elizabeth Shanks, 271nn2, 4, 272n15
Alexander, Philip, 92n9
Algar, Hamid, 360n39
Andersen, Chris, 181n7
Andersen, Francis I., 49
Anderson, Gary A., 44n20, 47n74, 49
Anderson, Matthew, x, xix, 42n1, 161–94
Ando, Clifford, xxin8
Andrae, Tor, 360n40
Andrious, Rosie, 146n97
Antonelli, Judith S., 92n1
Arbel, Vita Daphna, 48n79, 49
Arberry, Arthur John, 359n8, 360n18
Ariel, Donald T., 230n77
Artman, Tali, 338n1, 341n21
Ashbrook Harvey, Susan, 45n4, 47n68, 49, 139n11
Astor, Carl N., 250nn5–6
Aubin, Melissa, 46n51, 49
Audring, Jenny, 92n1
Auga, Ulrike E., 271n8
Avni, Gideon, 231n80
Ayres, Lewis, 184n59, 186n101

Baasten, Martin F., 94n22
Babka, Anna, 271–72nn12–13
Baglioni, Igor, 147n99
Baker, Cynthia M., 225n32, 271n10, 276nn75–76, 79–80
Bakhos, Carol, 341n18
Bakker, Arjen F., xxi
Balberg, Mira, 265, 276nn72–73, 91
Balberg, Mira, 275n60
Balch, David L., 17n22
Baldick, Julian, 359n8
Bar-Asher Siegal, Michal, x, xxin14
Barbu, Daniel, 227nn48–49, 228n59, 229n66
Barish, David A., 222n4
Barry, Jennifer, x
Bar Tur, Liora, 251n17
Baskin, Judith R., 272n22
Bass, Alan, 273n28
Bassler, Jouette, 48n84, 49
Batovici, Dan, 312n7
Batsch, Christophe, 225n30
Batten, Alicia J., 112n29
Baumgarten, Albert, x, 94nn26–27
Bautch, Kelley, 48n79
Beck, Roger, 146n94
Becker, Adam H., 184n44
Becker, Hans-Jürgen, 298n15

Becking, Bob, 253n40, 253nn42–43, 312–13n8
Behr, John, 119, 149n132
Bell, Avril, 181n8, 185n75, 188n142
Belser, Julia Watts, 251n10
Ben-Ami, Doron, 231n80
Ben Zion, Ilan, 231n83
Berenbaum, Michael, 250n7
Betancourt, Roland, 229n70
Bhabha, Homi, 182n11, 185nn66, 68, 75, 188n154
Biale, David, 332, 341n28
Bianchi, Emanuela, 66n13, 67n24, 69n37
Bierl, Anton, 146n94
Bion, Wilfred R., 342n38
Bird, Phyllis, 28, 45n32, 49
Bloch, René, xxi, 221n1
Bloomer, Martin, 140n16
Blumell, Lincoln, 141n42
Blyth, Caroline, 33, 42n1, 46n48, 49
Boccaccini, Gabriele, x, 93n20
Bonesho, Catherine, x
Bonfiglio, Emilio, 312n7
Booth, Alan D., 223n19
Borgehammer, Stephan, 228n58
Bossu, Annelis, 189n156
Bossu, Nicolas, 151n159
Bosworth, David A., 245, 253nn34–37
Bourdieu, Pierre, 258–59, 262, 267, 272nn14, 16, 23–25, 273n29, 274nn16, 42–43, 275n61, 276n89
Bowes, Kimberly, 111n19
Boyarin, Daniel, 274n46, 292, 298n21
Brenner-Idan, Athalya, 251n22, 254n49
Brett, Mark G., 92n5
Brettler, Marc Zvi, 43n11
Briand, David, 221n1
Brin, Gershon, 94n30
Briones, David, 144n74
Brisson, Luc, 16n13, 19
Brock, Sebastian, 139n9, 314n19
Bronner, Leila Leah, 46n58, 49
Bronson, Catherine, x
Brooten, Bernadette, x, xii, xix, 1–18, 223n23, 224n28

Brown, Peter, xiii, xiv, xxin4, 43n10, 49, 119, 186nn98, 106, 223n20
Brown, Raymond E., 253n47, 341n24
Brownlee, William H., 94n36
Buber, Solomon, 250n5
Buchanan, Neil, 66n18
Buch-Hansen, Gitte, 151n161
Buckley, Jorunn J., 65n4
Burrus, Virginia, 163–64, 166–67, 182nn13–14, 20–21, 183nn37–38, 40, 43, 184n52, 187n115, 188nn136, 152, 189nn177–79
Butler, Judith, xxiin26, 99–100, 110nn1, 5–6, 257–58, 271nn1, 3, 5–6, 9, 13, 272n25, 275n63
Bynum, Caroline, 332, 341n26

Cadenhead, Raphael A., 151n151
Caignart de Saulcy, Louis Félicien, 230n74
Cain, Andrew, 182n24, 183n28, 186nn91, 100, 107, 187nn108–109, 111, 117, 188nn134, 138, 144–45, 189nn158, 168, 184
Calzolari, Valentina, 315n36
Cameron, Averil, xxn2, xxin12, 312n6
Cameron, William Bleasdell, 162, 169, 173, 181n1, 184n54
Cancik, Hubert, 221n4
Canellis, Aline, 184n48
Canone, Eugenio, 68n27
Cary, Philippe, 149n124
Castelli, Elizabeth, 47nn65–66
Cerioni, Lavinia, x, xii, xix, 48n88, 55–69
Certeau, Michel De, 359n9
Charlesworth, James H., 44n24, 49
Chilton, Bruce, 119
Chipman, Jonathan, 342n36
Chittick, William C., 359n8, 360nn29, 31, 35–36
Choi, Baesick, 81, 93n19
Ciccolini, Laura, 141n43
Clanton, Dan, 29, 43n6, 44n16, 45n36
Clark, Elizabeth, 29, 45n37, 56, 65n2, 66nn10–11, 111n19, 183nn35, 39,

184n56, 186n97, 189n183, 223n20, 302, 313nn9–14, 314n30
Clermont-Ganneau, Charles S., 230n78
Cohen, Abraham, 290
Cohen, Shaye J. D., 298n15
Coleman, Daniel, 182n10
Coleman, Roche, 46n47
Colgan, Emily, 42n1
Collar, Anna, xxin14
Connell, Robert W., 102, 106, 111nn14, 22
Conway, Colleen M., 113n39, 181n5, 251n22
Coogan, Michael D., 44n28
Coon, Lynda L., 37, 47n72, 178, 183n29, 189n157
Cooper, Kate, 146n95
Coppieters, Steff, 189n156
Corbett, Greville C., 92n1
Cornell, Rkia Elaroui, 359n5, 361nn42, 44, 47
Cotton, Hannah M., 230n76, 231n78
Cribiore, Raffaela, 141n29
Cuffel, Alexandra, 227n50, 229n66

D'Arms, John, 108, 112n34, 113n38
Dal Bo, Federico, x, xiii, xix, 73–94, 272n18
Dalton, Krista N., x, xviii, xix, 99–112, 223n22, 226n38
Daniel-Hughes, Carly, x, 112n29
Darbandi, Afkham, 360n37
Daschuk, James, 185n65
Davies, Steven L., 47n65
Davis, Dick, 360n37
Davis, Stephen J., 230n72
De Bruin, Tom, 44n15
De Certeau, Michel, xvi, xxiin17
De Chateaubriand, François-René, 230n73
De Conick, April D., 70n61
Deferrari, Roy J., 183n37
Degele, Nina, 272n21
De Groot, Alon, 230n77
De Jonge, Marinus, 46n54
De Lange, Nicholas, 143n64

De Long, Kindalee Pfremmer, 244, 253nn31, 33
De-Lubac, Henri, 338n6
Denham, Robert D., 297n6
Denzey Lewis, Nicola, 66n10
Derrida, Jacques, 260, 273nn28–29
Deryugina, Tatyana, x
De Temmerman, Koen, 146n98
Deutsch, Yaakov, 227nn48–49, 228n59, 229n66
Deutschmann, Barbara, 23–24, 28, 43nn3, 8, 13, 45n31
De Wet, Chris, 119
Diamond, Eliezer, 361n44
Diamond, James, 338n5
Díaz Araujo, Magdalena, x, 44nn17, 25, 221n1
Di Berardino, Angelo, 146n93
Digeser, Elizabeth DePalma, 119
Dijkstra, Jitse H. F., xxiin18
DiLuzio, Meghan, 147n100
Dimant, Devorah, 93n13
Di Segni, Leah, 230n76
Distefano, Michel G., 250n5
Doane, Sébastian, 247, 253nn41, 45–48
Dodson, Joseph, 144n74
Doerfler, Maria, 45n41
Dölling, Irene, 272n24
Donaldson, Laura E., 181n9
Dosoo, Korshi, 141n42
Drijvers, Jan Willem, 228n58
Dundes, Alan, 341n22
Dunn, James, 142n56
Dunning, Benjamin H., 181n5
Dutsch, Dorota, 140n18

Eagleton, Terry, 313n9
Eck, Werner, 230n76
Eckert, Penelope, 272n23
Edelman, Dana, 92n5
Edmonds, Radcliffe, 150n147
Edwards, Karen L., 46n61
Edwards, Katie B., 42n2, 46n47
Edwards, Mark, 147n113, 149n130
Edwards, Robert, 139n7

Ehrensperger, Kathy, ix–xxi, 48n87, 141n44, 182n19, 185n81, 221n1, 338n1
Eisen, Ute E., 19nn63, 65, 47n65, 141n44
Ellis, Teresa A., 45n34
Elman, Yaakov, 250n5
Elsner, Jan, 187–88n130
Emmett, Grace, 182n19
Endres, John, 48n79
Epp, Eldon Jay, 144n74
Ernst, Carl W., 348, 359n11, 360nn14, 23
Eshleman, Kendra, 102, 111n11
Esler, Philip F., 47n66, 147n113

Faas, Patrick, 112n31
Fadiman, James, 359n8
Faierstein, Morris M, 342n33
Falcasantos, Rebecca Stephens, 188n137
Fausto-Sterling, Anne, 271nn5, 7, 275n53
Fedden, Sebastian, 92n1
Fein, Sarah E. G., x, xx, 41, 48n87, 237–53
Feltes, Heinz, 94n36
Ferber, Ilit, 249n3
Fiano, Emanuel, 45n41
Fiore, Benjamin, 127
Fisch, Yael, xxi
Fleischer, Kilian, 148n119
Flood, John, 45n38, 313n8, 314nn17, 23, 26–27, 31
Fonrobert, Charlotte Elisheva, 1, 15, 16n5, 19n69, 258–59, 263, 265, 270nn1–2, 272nn15, 19–20, 273nn25–27, 30, 274n47, 275nn56, 59–60, 66, 276nn74, 76–79, 81, 84, 295, 298n27, 341n18
Fontaine, Carole, 254n49
Ford, David C., 313n14
Foucault, Michel, 74, 186n94, 258
Fowden, Garth, xiii, xiv, xxin7, xxin13
Fraade, Steven D., 93n16
Frager, Robert, 359n8
Franco, Christiana, 108, 113n37
Frank, Georgia, 189n155
Frankfurter, David, 140n26
Fredriksen, Paula, xxi
Freedman, Harry, 290
Freeze, ChaeRan, 221n1
Frenschkowski, Marco, 221n4
Freud, Sigmund, 342n38
Frey, Jörg, 148n122, 151n161
Fröhlich, Ida, 276nn71–72, 85–86
Frye, Northrop, 282, 297n6
Fuks Fried, Sylvia, 221n1
Furey, Constance, 100, 110n3
Füssel, Marian, xxiin18
Futre Pinheiro, Marília, 146n94

Gafney, Wilda C., 28, 45n31
Gafni, Isaiah M., 224n29
Galgay, Erin, x
Galor, Katharina, 231n80
García, Jeffrey P., 231n80
Gardner, Gregg, 221n1, 224n29
Garsoïan, Nina, 226n41
Gathergood, Emily, 48n85
Gerber, Christine, 19nn63, 65
Gershoni, Israel, 250n5
Gerster, Daniel, 339n7
Giddens, Anthony, 313n9
Gieschen, Charles, 139n10
Glancy, Jennifer, 39, 48n83, 186n89
Gleason, Maud W., 16n13, 164, 170, 181n5, 182nn15, 17, 23, 185nn80, 82
Goldberg, Charles, 185n79, 187n112
Goldreich, Amos, 341–42n31
Goldstein, Miriam, 227nn48, 50, 228n51, 229nn60, 66
Goodey, Chris, 17n14
Gordon, Richard, 140n25
Goschler, Juliana, 265, 275n67
Gourinat, Jean-Baptiste, 142n46
Graumann, Lutz Alexander, 16n13
Gravett, Emily Olmstaed, 249n2
Gray, Christa, 184n50
Greenough, Chris, 182n12
Grigor, Lusaworič, 317n60

Gunkel, Hermann, 252nn28, 30
Gurtner, Daniel M., 43n11, 44n21

Hac'uni, Vardan, 317n59
Halberstam, Jack, 182n15, 184n50
Halbertal, Moshe, 341n23
Halivni, David Weiss, 273n36
Halpern-Amaru, Betsy, 93n10
Halvgaard, Tilde Bak, 66n12
Hanson, Helen, 46n61
Harkings, Angela, 48n79
Harnack, Adolf, 66n18
Harper, Kyle, 19n65
Harris, William V., xxin13
Harrison, Nonna Verna, 45n43, 139n8, 149n133
Harshav, Barbara, 342n36
Hasan-Rokem, Galit, 210, 225n32, 227n49, 228nn55, 59, 249n3, 341n27
Hauptman, Judith, 271n2, 272n22, 273n34, 274n38, 276nn82, 93
Heger, Paul, 93n20
Heine, Ronald, 119, 128
Hemelrijk, Emily Ann, 140n17, 223n20
Henderson, Ian H, xxiin19
Heng, Geraldine, 184n46, 188n143
Hennecke, Susanne, 313n8
Henning, Meghan, 249n1
Henze, Matthias, 252n29, 253n32
Herr, Moshe, 250n7
Herrero, Miguel, 149n130
Heszer, Catherine, 19nn63, 65
Hewson, Robert H., 227n42
Hieke, Thomas, 276nn83, 88
Higginbotham, Andrew, x, xx, 281–98
Higgins, Jean M., 34, 46n52
Hilberg, Isidorus, 222n10
Hillman, James, 339n12
Himmelfarb, Martha, 332, 341n29
Hirschmann, Vera-Elisabeth, 145n87
Hoffmann, Alexandra, x
Hoffstadt, Christian, 275n64
Hogan, Pauline Nigh, 144n74, 151n154
Holman, Susan R., 189n155

Holmes, Steven, 341n23
Hoppe, Juni, ix–xxi, 221n1, 338n1
Hotham, Matthew, x, xiii, xviii, xx, 345–61
Houtman, Dick, 225n32
Hritzu, John N., 185n83
Huebner, Sabine, 140n29, 229n68
Hunt, Dallas, 185n75

Ilan, Tal, 44nn29, 94n25, 224n29, 225nn30, 32, 226n39, 273n37, 276nn82, 95, 281–82, 297nn1–5, 7, 298nn16, 18, 298nn23, 28–31
Image, Isabella, 147n114
Inglebert, Hervé, xxin3, xxiin22
Inowlocki-Meister, Sabrina, 224n26
Irshai, Oded, 186n103, 224n26
Isaac, Benjamin, 230n76

Jacobs, Andrew S., 166, 177–78, 183n44, 186n102, 188nn147, 189nn155, 168, 189n170
Jacoby, Ruth, 230n71
Jaffee, Martin S., 16n5, 271n1
James, Edward, xxin2
James, Liz, 312n6
James, William, 348
Jastrow, Marcus, 252nn26, 30
Jennot, Lance, 68n30
Jensen, Robin M., 47nn74–75
Johnson, Mark, 265, 275n65
Johnson, Scott F., xxin3
Johnston, Jay, 67n25
Joyce, Paul M., 251n14
Jung, Carl Gustav, 339n12
Junod, Eric, 149n132

Kiparean, Kiwrel, 317n59
Kafka, Franz, 338, 342n43
Kahlos, Maijastina, xxin5, xxin14, xxiin20
Kalleres, Dayna S., 229n69
Kalmin, Richard, 224n29, 273n36
Kanarek, Jane L., 225n34
Kanner-Botan, Allison, x

Kaplan Daniels, Arlene, 224n23
Kara-Ivanov Kaniel, Ruth, xiii, xx, 323–40
Karamanolis, George, 151n153
Karras, Ruth Mazo, 338n7, 339n7
Karras, Valerie, 313n14
Kashani-Sabet, Firoozah, 16n5
Kateusz, Ally, 146n90
Kathoff, Ranon, 221n1
Kattan Gribetz, Sarit, x, xx, 195–230
Kaye, Lynn, 15n1, 221n1
Kellhoffer, James, 139n11, 140n20
Kelly, John N. D., 179, 183n31, 185nn72, 78, 186n95, 187n130, 189n161
Kelto Lillis, Julia, 141n42
Kerenyi, Carl, 339n12
Kessler, Gwynn, 1, 15, 15n1, 16nn1, 4, 5, 19n67
Kessler, Suzanne J., 273n32
Kimelman, Reuven, 16n1
King, Fergus J., 144n72
King, Karen, 58, 65nn4–5, 68nn28, 30, 70n61, 143n61
Kipfer, Sara, 275n68, 276nn69–71
Klawans, Jonathan, 43n11
Klein, Reuven, 94n23
Knöfel Magnusson, Anna, 274n48
Knohl, Israel, 341n25
Knowles, Michael, 253n47
Knysh, Alexander, 359n12
Koet, Bart, 142n56
Kohut, Heinz, 342n38
Koltun-Fromm, Naomi, 16n4, 92n8
Kon, Maximilian, 222n8, 230n71
König, Jason, 112n33
Kosior, Wojciech, 45n42, 46n57
Kotrosits, Maia, x
Kovach, Margaret, 168, 181n7, 184nn62–63, 185n64
Kozlova, Ekaterina, 240, 246, 251nn17–18
Kraemer, David, 251n10
Kraemer, Ross S., 43n9
Krais, Beate, 272n24

Krueger, Derek, 150n148
Krüggeler, Michael, 339n7
Kuefler, Mathew, 10, 18n49, 111n19, 113n39, 183n34, 223n22
Kugle, Scott Alan, 351, 360nn28, 30
Kukla, Elliot, 274n52
Kushnir-Stein, Alla, 230n76
Kvam, Kristen E., 313nn8, 11
Kyoseyan, Hakob, 318n62

Laato, Antti, 141n45
Labendz, Jenny R., 111n18
Labovitz, Gail, 16n10
Lachs, Samuel Tobias, 45n35
Laes, Christian, 17nn14, 22, 140n29
Lakoff, George, 265, 275n65
Laks, André, 148n119
Lampe, Peter, 148n120
Lamprecht, Johanna C., 185n86
Land, Christopher, 140n16
Lapsley, Jacqueline E., 44n30
Laqueur, Thomas, 257–58, 271nn10, 13
Larson, Jennifer, 182n19
Lauritzen, Delphine, 142n47
Lavrinoviča, Alesja, 143n67
Ledegang, Fred, 148n121
Lee, Dorothy A., 144n72
Lehman, Marjorie, 221n1, 226n35
Lenger, Alexander, 275n63
Lettieri, Gaetano, 68n27
Lev, Sarra L., 1, 15n1, 16n3, 19n62, 261, 271n1, 273n35, 275nn54–55
Levinas, Emmanuel, 336, 342n37
Levine, Amy-Jill, 43nn9, 11, 45n37, 47n74, 113n40
Levine, Lee I., 110, 230n71
Levinson, Joshua, 148n118
Levison, John R., 44nn24–25, 45n34
Levi-Strauss, Claude, 43n10
Levy, Israel, 93n17
Lichtenberger, Hermann, 221n4
Lieberman, Saul, 18nn57–58
Liebes, Yehuda, 341n30, 342n36
Liebowitz, Etka, 221n4
Lillie, Celene, 36, 46n63, 47n64

Limor, Ora, 228n59
Linafelt, Tod, 238–40, 250n8, 251nn9, 12
Lings, Martin, 359n8
Lipton, Diana, 251n14
Lloyd, Janet, 16n13
Loader, William, 84, 94n25
Losensky, Paul, 361n45
Lössl, Josef, 145n87, 187n117
Louth, Andrew, 184n59, 186n101
Lundhaug, Hugo, 68n30
Luz, Ulrich, 253n47

Maccoby, Haym, 340n16
MacDonald, Margaret Y., 19n65
Mackey, Eva, 172, 186nn92–93
Macy, Gary, 150n137
Madigan, Kevin, 150n136
Mahmood, Saba, 99–100, 110n2
Maier, Christl M., 253nn38–39
Maier, Harry, 144n72
Malkinson, Ruth, 251n17
Mandel, Paul, 250n5
Marchal, Joseph A., 4, 16n13, 182n18
Marciak, Michal, 221–22n4, 231n78
Margulies, Mordecai, 112n27
Marks, Susan, 112nn30, 35
Markschies, Christoph, 68nn27, 29, 119, 140n23, 145n87, 149n123
Marmodoro, Anna, 138–39n3–4
Marsman, Hennie J., 94n33
Maspero, Giulio, 149n130
Mathews, Edward G., 312n7
Matt, Daniel, 341n19
Matthews, Ronald, 183n31
Mayer, Wendy, 150n142
McClenney-Sadler, Madeline, 75, 92nn4, 6
McCloskey, Benjamin, 140n17
McConnel-Ginet, Sally, 272n23
McDowell, Gavin, 227n49
McGuckin, John A., 149n132
McKenna, Wendy, 273n32
McLain, Sheela, 185n67
McLynn, Neil, 139n4, 149n132
McVey, Kathleen, 139n9

Meerson, Michael, 227n48, 228nn55, 59, 229nn62–63
Melchert, Christopher, 360n16
Messerschmidt, James, 102, 106, 111nn14, 22
Methuen, Charlotte, 47n65
Meyer, Birgit, 225n32
Migne, Jacques Paul, 314n18
Mikkelsen, Gunner B., 67n25
Militello, Cettina, 144n74
Miller, Patricia Cox, 146n95, 182n14, 183n36, 184n48, 187n112
Millgram, Abraham Ezra, 230n71
Mills, Lawrence M., 43n11
Mintz, Alan, 251n13
Miralles-Maciá, Lorena, 276nn82, 95, 297n1
Misgav, Haggai, 230n76, 231n78
Mitchell, Stephen, xxiin23
Moreton-Robinson, Aileen, 170, 181n7, 185n76
Morlet, Sébastien, 149n132
Morse, Holly, 23, 28, 32, 43nn4, 7, 45nn33–34, 46nn45, 50, 47n70, 48nn81, 89
Muehlberger, Ellen, 150n149
Murphy-O'Connor, Jerome, 144n74
Murray, Robert, 48n82, 315n35
Myers, Susan, 139n11

Nägele, Manuel, 148n122
Nagy, Agnes A., 315n16
Najman, Hindy, xxi, 92n9
Naples, Nancy A., 65n8
Narayanan, Vasudha, 16n4
Nathan, Geoffrey, 141n29
Neumann, Erich, 337, 342n42
Neusner, Jacob, 119, 151n157, 221n4, 227n44, 240, 251nn16, 19, 290, 298nn19, 22, 24, 26
Neuwirth, Angelika, xxi
Newsom, Carol A., 44nn30
Nice, Richard, 272nn23–24
Nicholson, Reynold, 360n25, 361n43
Niebuhr, Karl-Wilhelm, 149n123

Niehoff, Maren, 148n118
Nielsen, Inge, 112n30
Nikolsky, Ronit, 276nn82, 297n1
Noam, Vered, 94nn21, 35, 224n29
Notley, R. Steven, 231n80
Novenson, Matthew V., 339n8
Nurbakhsh, Javad, 360nn17, 24, 33–34

O'Rawe, Catherine, 46n61
Obsequens, Julius, 18n27
Oegema, Gerbern S., xxiin19, 44n24
Oertelt, Friederike, 141n44
Ogden, Thomas H., 342n39
Olyan, Sail M., 17n19
Omar, Sara, x
Orbe, Antonio, 68n27
Oron, Michal, 342n31
Osiek, Carolyn, 17n22, 150n136, 184n57
Otten, Willemien, 313n8

Pagels, Elaine, 43n6, 46n62, 65n4, 68n30
Paige Cohen, Ariel, 224n23
Palmer, Morgan, 147n101
Papazian, Michael, 318n62
Parker, Julie Faith, 24, 43n12
Parkhouse, Sarah, 143n61
Parks, Sara, x, xix, xxiin27, 23–49, 297, 298n32
Parry, Donald, 93n13
Pedaya, Haviva, 339n14
Peleg-Barkat, Orit, 230n77
Perkins, Judith, 139n12
Perkins, Pheme, 67n25
Perrier, Pierre, 146n92
Peskowitz, Miriam B., 225n34
Pétrement, Simone, 65n4
Petrosyan, Nelli, 317n57
Phillips, Adam, 342n39
Pierce, Krystal V. L., 231n83
Piotrkowski, Meron M., 221n4
Plietzsch, Susanne, 276n95
Pogossian, Zaroui, 318n72
Pomeroy, Sarah, 140n18

Poorthuis, Marcel J. H., 274n48
Pope, Michael, 48n80
Porter, Stanley, 140n16
Posselt, Gerald, 272n13
Praet, Danny, 189n156
Pratt, Mary Louise, 181n9, 184n47
Prescendi, Francesca, 315n16
Price, Jonathan, 230n76, 231n78
Pummer, Reinhard, 145n84

Radford Ruether, Rosemary, 45n32, 313n12, 314n25
Rajak, Tessa, 197, 221–22nn4–5, 225n33
Ramelli, Ilaria L.E., x, xix, 115–51, 227n44
Rank, Otto, 341n22
Rasimus, Tuomas, 69nn34, 40
Ratcliffe, Rosie, 146n95
Ratzan, David, 229n68
Reale, Giovanni, 148n119
Reardon, Brian, 146n94
Rebenich, Stefan, xxin9, 179, 183n30, 184nn45, 49, 185n73, 187n110, 188n137, 189nn163, 166, 181
Reed, Annette Y., 68n28, 184n44
Reeser, Tood W., 274n51
Regev, Eyal, 151n157
Reinhartz, Adele, xxiin19
Renan, Ernest, 228n57
Renard, John, 360n15
Riedweg, Christoph, 312n1
Rigato, Maria-Luisa, 143n64, 144n74
Ringe, Sharon H., 44nn30
Robbins, Maria Mayo, 43n9, 45n37, 47n74
Roi, Biti, 341n31
Roig Lanzillotta, Lautaro, 118, 139n12
Roitman, Adolfo D., 94n21
Roll, Israel, 230n76
Roller, Matthew B., 112n31
Rose, M. Lynn, 17n14
Rosenblum, Jordan, 112n31
Rosen-Zvi, Ishay, 111n17, 225n34
Rosenzweig, Claudia, 227n49

Index

Rothstein, David, 93n10
Rousseau, Philip, xxin9
Rumsey, Patricia M., 45n40
Russell, James R., 318n70
Rutherford, Ian, 188n130
Ruttenberg, Danya, 16n10

Safranski, Benjamin, 146n91
Safronov, Yevgeniy, 221n1, 222n9
Sagnard, François, 68n27
Santoprete, Lucia Soares, 139n14
Sarkissian, A.O., 227n42
Satlow, Michael L., 92n5, 94nn30–31, 102, 111nn7, 13, 262, 272n22, 274nn38–41, 45
Sauter, Megan, 230n78
Sawyer, Deborah F., 313n11
Schäfer, Mary, 150n137, 227n48
Schäfer, Peter, 221n4, 227n48, 228nn56, 59, 229nn62–63, 341n29
Schalit, Abraham, 222n5
Schearing, Linda S., 313nn8, 11
Schechter, Solomon, 78–80, 93nn12–14
Schenk, Christine, 145n89
Schiffman, Lawrence H., 94n21, 221–22nn4–5, 224n29, 225n33
Schimmel, Annemarie, 359n7
Schlegell, B. R. Con, 360n20
Schmalzgruber, Hedwig, 273n29
Schmid, Nora K., xxin10
Schmidt, Konrad, xxin10, 312n1
Schmidt, Nora, xxin10
Schniedewind, William M., 94n34
Scholem, Gershom, 338n1, 339n14
Schoors, Antoon, 253n43
Schrader, Elizabeth, 143n64
Schroeder, C. Paul, 26, 44n18
Schroer, Silvia, 275–76nn68–71
Schuller, Eileen M., 44nn17, 30
Schumer, Nathan, 225n34
Schüngel-Straumann, Helen, 23, 43nn2, 5
Schüssler Fiorenza, Elisabeth, 56, 65n2, 66n9, 127, 144n75, 182n18
Schwartz, Daniel R., 221nn1, 4, 228n52

Schwartz, Joshua, 112n36
Schwartz, Marcus Mordecai, 251n21
Schwarz, Seth, xxin13, 112n34
Schwebel, Paula, 249n3
Scott, Joan Wallach, 100–101, 110n4, 111n8, 258, 271n11, 272n17
Scott, Joshua, ix–x, 221n1
Secunda, Shai, 274n50, 276n93
Segal, Michael, 273n31
Segal, Robert A., 341n22
Segovia, Fernando F., xxiin27
Seidman, Steven, 271n11
Seligman, Jon, 230n72
Sells, Michael Anthony, 359n2
Shapira, Ran, 231n81
Sharify-Funk, Meena, 359n1
Sheinfeld, Shayna, ix–xxi, 42n1, 47n67, 48n87, 141n44, 182n19, 221n1, 338n1
Shemesh, Aharon, 94nn26, 28
Sheppard, Eugene, 221n1
Shinan, Avigdor, 338n5
Shurchkov, Olga, x
Sidaway, Janet, 147n114
Sigismund Nielsen, Hanne, 112n30
Silvas, Anna, 150nn142, 150
Silvers, Laury, 359n4, 361n49
Simkovich, Malka Z., 224–25nn29–30
Simonetti, Manlio, 68n27
Simpson, Leanne Betasamosake, 181nn7, 9
Skolnik, Fred, 250n7
Sly, Dorothy, 32–33, 45n44, 46n46
Smith, Andrew P., 67n23
Smith, Dennis E., 112n31
Smith, Huston, 359n8
Smith, Kyle, 45n41
Smith, Leigh Eric, 348, 359n10
Smith, Margaret, 345, 359n3
Sordi, Marta, 148n120
Stahlberg, Lesleigh Cushing, 249n2
Standhartinger, Angela, x, 19nn63, 65, 44nn19, 23, 27, 141n44
Stanton, Graham N., 187n112
Starblanket, Gina, 185n75

Index

Starr Sered, Susan, 230n72
Stearns, Jenna, x
Stefaniw, Blossom, xxiinn24–25, 140n19
Stein, Batya, 250n4
Stein, David E. S., 92n3
Steinmann, Jean, 179, 181, 183n31, 189nn162, 185
Stemberger, Günther, 94n27
Stendahl, Krister, 253n47
Stern, David, 240, 250n6, 251nn15–16, 20
Stinchcomb, Jillian, x
Stökl Ben Ezra, Daniel, 229nn66, 67
Stone, Michael E., 44n20, 49, 252nn28–30, 253n32, 301, 312nn1–2
Strassfeld, Max K., 1, 14, 15, 15n1, 16n5, 19nn66, 68, 70
Stroumsa, Guy, xvi–xvii, xxin5, xxin15–16, xxiin21, 187n112
Suderland, Maja, 275n63
Sullivan, Nikki, 182n16
Sussman, Yaakov, 111n15
Szram, Mariusz, 140n28

Tabbernee, William, 145nn86–87
Tannen, Deborah, 74, 92n2
Taussig, Hal, 112nn30, 35
Taveime, Maarten, 189n156
Taylor, Joan, 143n64, 144n72, 146n95
Tchekhanovets, Yana, 231n80
Ter-Minasyan, Ervand G., 312n7
Ter-Petrosyan, Levon, 312n7
Tervahauta, Ulla, 66nn12–13, 139n14
Thomas, Christine, 44n23
Thomassen, Einar, 55, 65n6, 67n19, 68n29
Thompson, John B., 313n9
Thomson, Robert W., 209, 226n41, 227nn43–47, 312n7, 315nn32, 37, 318n63
Thornton, Dillon T., 144n72
Timotin, Andrei, 141n36
Toca, Madalina, 312n7
Tong, M Adryael, 221n1, 228n53
Topchyan, Aram, 226n41

Trevett, Christine, 145n87
Trible, Phyllis, 28, 45n3, 246–47, 253n44
Troiano, Mariano, 69n37, 139n14
Tromp, Jonathan, 43n14, 44nn6, 46n54
Trompf, Gary W., 67n25
Tuhiwai Smith, Linda, 181n7, 188n153
Tumanov, Vladimir, 47n69
Turner, Aimee, 226n40
Turner, John D., 65n7, 66n13, 68n29, 139n14
Turner, Stephen P., 101–2, 111n7
Tzamalikos, Panayiotis, 140n19, 149n130
Tzoref, Shani, 94n21, 95n37

Ulrich, Eugene, 93n18
Undheim, Sissel, 144n77
Upson-Saia, Kristi, 112n29

Vacca, Alison, x
Valentasis, Richard, 361n44
Valler, Shulamit, 338n5
Valve, Lotta, 141n45
Van Geest, Paul, 148n123
Van Lint, Theo M., 312n3
Van Nuffelen, Peter, xxiin23
Van Oyen, Geert, 313n8
Van Ruiten, Jacques T. A. G., 92n9
Varacini, Lorenzo, 179, 182n22
Veracini, Lorenzo, 189n164
Vessey, Mark, 172, 183n25, 184n59, 185n77, 186nn99, 101, 188n135, 189n180
Vital, Haim, 341n30, 342n33
Von Harnack, Adolf, 228n57
Vorpahl, Daniel, x, xx, 257–76
Vuilleumier, Sandrine, 140n27
Vuong, Lily, x, 37, 47nn71, 73, 76

Wacholder, Ben Zion, 78–80, 93n15
Wacker, Marie-Theres, 44n17
Wacquant, Loïc J. D., 272nn14, 16, 273n29
Wainwright, Elaine, 248, 254nn49–50

Index

Warren, Meredith J. C., x, xxiin27, 42n1, 43n15, 47n67
Warrior, Robert Allen, 188n141
Watts, Edward, 139n15
Weingarten, Susan, 223n18
Wendt, Heidi, 111n12
Wenger, Beth, 16n5
Wheeler-Reed, David, 144n77
Whitmarsh, Tim, 188nn149, 151
Wickham, Chris, xxin2
Widengren, Geo, 221n4
Wider, Kathleen, 140n18
Wilfand, Yael, 19n64
Williams, Craig A., 171, 185nn84–85, 186n90
Williams, Megan Hale, 186n99, 187n129, 189n182
Williams, Michael A., 58, 65n5, 66n12, 67n22
Williams, Rowan, 119
Wills, Lawrence M., 221n4
Wiseman, Timothy P., xxin2
Wood, Jamie, 184n60
Wortzman, Hannah, 34–35, 46nn53, 55–56

Wright, Benjamin G., 44nn28
Wright, Frederick A., 181n2

Xavier Pena, Joabson, 147n115
Xeravits, Géza, 276nn71, 83

Yaghoobi, Claudia, 360n38
Yamauchi, Edwin M., 66n14
Yarbro Collins, Adela, 144n72
Yardeni, Ada, 230n76, 231n78
Yli-Karjanmaa, Sami, 115, 138n2, 142n45
Young, Frances M., 184n59, 186n101
Yovel, Yossi, xxin14
Yuval, Israel Jacob, 228n59

Zahavy, Tzvee, 290
Zahn, Molly, 43n14
Zakarian, David, x, xviii, xx, 301–22
Zamagni, Claudio, 224n26
Zargar, Cyrus Ali, 360n38
Zekiyan, Boghos Levon, 317n62
Ziegler, Valarie H., 313nn8, 11
Zissis, Theodoros, 314n14
Zissu, Boaz, 230n71

About the Contributors

Matthew R. Anderson holds the Gatto Chair of Christian Studies at St. Francis Xavier, Nova Scotia, and has taught for over twenty years at Concordia University, Montreal. Anderson's Ph.D. in New Testament is from McGill University. His books include *Prophets of Love: The Unlikely Kinship of Leonard Cohen and the Apostle Paul* (2023), *Our Home and Treaty Land* (with Ray Aldred, 2022), *Pairings: The Bible and Booze* (2021), and *The Good Walk: Creating New Paths on Traditional Prairie Trails* (2024). Anderson teaches and researches ancient masculinity, Paul within Judaism, pilgrimage, and decolonizing biblical studies.

Bernadette J. Brooten, Ph.D., Dr. Theol., *h.c.* (Bern), Robert and Myra Kraft and Jacob Hiatt Professor *Emerita*, Brandeis University, directs the Feminist Sexual Ethics Project. She researches enslaved and slaveholding women in early Christianity, and female homoerotic desire and what may have been female-female marriage in the Roman world. Publications include *Women Leaders in the Ancient Synagogue: Inscriptional Evidence and Background Issues* (1982; 2020); *Love Between Women: Early Christian Responses to Female Homoeroticism* (1996; 2020); and, with Jacqueline L. Hazelton, editor: *Beyond Slavery: Overcoming Its Religious and Sexual Legacies* (2010). Fellowships include MacArthur, Fulbright, Harvard Law School, and Israel Institute for Advanced Studies.

Lavinia Cerioni is currently a Marie Curie Fellow at Aarhus University (Denmark) with the project "OriGen" on Origen of Alexandria's understanding of gender categories. She completed her Ph.D. in Theology and Religious Studies at the University of Nottingham in 2019. As a result, she has published her first monograph *Revealing Women: the Feminine in Gnostic*

Christian Texts (2021). Cerioni's interests lie in the field of Gnosticism, Origen of Alexandria, early Christian exegesis, and women's history.

Federico Dal Bo holds a Ph.D. in Translation Studies (Bologna, 2005) and a Ph.D. in Jewish Studies (Berlin, 2009). He is currently Senior Lecturer in Jewish Studies at the University of Modena and Reggio Emilia. His publications include *Massekhet Keritot: Text, Translation, and Commentary* (2013), *Deconstructing the Talmud: The Absolute Book* (2019), and *The Lexical Field of the Substantives of "Word" in Ancient Hebrew: From the Bible to the Mishnah* (2021).

Krista N. Dalton is Assistant Professor of Religious and Jewish Studies at Kenyon College. She is a cultural historian of religion, working primarily with the texts and traditions of Judaism within the ancient Mediterranean context. Her research analyzes the performance of rabbinic expertise and the cultivation of donor networks in late antiquity. Dalton is co-editor-in-chief of the digital journal *Ancient Jew Review*.

Kathy Ehrensperger is Research Fellow at the Faculty of Theology, University of Basel, Switzerland; she previously was Research Professor of New Testament in Jewish Perspective, at the Abraham Geiger Kolleg, University of Potsdam, Germany. Her publications and edited volumes include *Searching Paul: Conversations with the Jewish Apostle to the Nations* (2019), *Gender in Second-Temple Judaism* (with Shayna Sheinfeld, 2020), and she is the executive editor of the Encyclopedia of Jewish-Christian Relations.

Sari Fein is Visiting Assistant Professor in the Jewish Studies Program at Smith College. She completed her doctoral studies at Brandeis University with a dissertation entitled "Conceiving Motherhood: The Reception of Biblical Mothers in the Early Jewish Imagination." She additionally holds an MTS in Hebrew Bible/Old Testament from Harvard Divinity School and an MS in special education from CUNY Hunter College. Her teaching and research interests include women and gender in the Hebrew Bible and early Judaism, material culture of Jewish antiquity, and biblical reception history.

Sarit Kattan Gribetz is Associate Professor in the Theology Department at Fordham University and the Co-Director of Fordham's Center for Jewish Studies. Her book *Time and Difference in Rabbinic Judaism* (2020) received a National Jewish Book Award and a Jordan Schnitzer Book Award from the Association for Jewish Studies. She is now writing two books: *A Queen in Jerusalem: Helena of Adiabene through the Ages* and *Jerusalem: A Feminist*

History. Sarit received her A.B. and Ph.D. from the Department of Religion at Princeton University.

Andrew W. Higginbotham is a Ph.D. candidate at Hebrew Union College-Jewish Institute of Religion in Cincinnati, Ohio. He is presently Associate Professor of Science and Co-Chair of the Science Department at Ivy Tech Community College in Lawrenceburg, IN. Higginbotham's area of interest is Second Temple and early rabbinic Judaism, with special attention to the interpretive methodology of the tannaitic sources and the "Parting of the Ways" between rabbinic Judaism and early Christianity.

Juni Hoppe (Ph.D., University of Cambridge, 2016) is junior executive editor of the Encyclopedia of Jewish-Christian Relations (EJCR). She received her B.Sc. in Economics and M.St. in Jewish Studies at the University of Oxford. Her Ph.D. dissertation on Jewish, Muslim, and Christian trade networks in the Mediterranean deals with Cairo Genizah sources and Arabic papyri. Hoppe's research focuses on multireligious interactions in Antiquity, the Middle Ages, and the presence. She serves as the Director of the Intercultural Center Genezareth (IZG) in Berlin, Germany.

Matthew R. Hotham is an Assistant Professor of Religious Studies at Ball State University. His work focuses on the body and bodily comportment, examining how what a person eats, drinks, smells, sees, and touches is used to mark the boundaries of religious identity in both medieval Sufi literature and contemporary Euro-American contexts. Hotham's in-progress book manuscript, *Pig Fat, Goat Blood, and Dog Hair: Animals, Islam, and American Anxiety about Religious Difference*, investigates the relationship between Islamophobia, affect, and human-animal relations.

Ruth Kara-Ivanov Kaniel (Ph.D. Hebrew University of Jerusalem, 2010) is Senior Lecturer in the Department of Jewish History and Thought at the University of Haifa. She also serves as Research Fellow at the Tel Aviv Institute for Contemporary Psychoanalysis and at the Shalom Hartman Institute in Jerusalem. Her research deals with intersections between mysticism, gender, and psychoanalysis. She recently published *The Feminine Messiah: King David in the Image of the Shekhina in Kabbalistic Literature* (2021).

Sara Parks is Assistant Professor in Religious Studies at St. Francis Xavier University, Nova Scotia. She was formerly Assistant Professor in New Testament at Dublin City University, and a Leverhulme Fellow and Assistant Professor in New Testament at the University of Nottingham. Sara's Ph.D. in

Early Judaism is from McGill University (2016). Her recent books are *Gender in the Rhetoric of Jesus* (2019) and *Jewish and Christian Women in the Ancient Mediterranean* (with Shayna Sheinfeld and Meredith Warren, 2022), which won the Frank W. Beare award for an outstanding book in the area of Christian Origins, Post-Biblical Judaism, and/or Graeco-Roman Religions.

Ilaria L.E. Ramelli, FRHistS, holds two MAs, a Ph.D., a Postdoc, and various Habilitations to Ordinarius. She has been Professor of Roman History, Senior Visiting Professor (Harvard; Boston U.; Columbia; Erfurt), Full Professor of Theology and Endowed Chair (Angelicum), and Senior Fellow (Durham; Princeton; Sacred Heart U.; Corpus Christi and Christ Church, Oxford), Professor of Theology and of Philosophy (Durham, hon.; KUL; Stanford), and Senior Fellow/Member (MWK; Bonn U.; Cambridge). Recent books include *Patterns of Women's Leadership* (2021), *Eriugena's Christian Neoplatonism* (2021), *Lovers of the Soul* (2022).

Shayna Sheinfeld is Assistant Professor of Religion at Augsburg University (Minneapolis, USA). Her research emphasizes the vast diversity of Judaism in antiquity, including ancient constructions of gender. Sheinfeld is the author of multiple chapters and articles, including editing *Gender and Second-Temple Judaism* (with Kathy Ehrensperger, 2020). Most recently, Sheinfeld published *Jewish and Christian Women in the Ancient Mediterranean* (with Sara Parks and Meredith J.C. Warren, 2022), winner of the 2023 Frank W. Beare Award.

Daniel Vorpahl holds a Ph.D. in Jewish Studies and is working transdisciplinary in between this field and Religious Studies, Gender Studies, and Comparative Literature. Their academic education took place in Potsdam and Bamberg. Since 2020 Daniel Vorpahl works as a research assistant for the Chair for Hebrew Bible and Its Exegesis at the University of Potsdam. Their current interests of research involve the literary construction of gender and its religious relatedness in (post)biblical and rabbinic literature, discourse analytical reception studies on biblical themes and motifs, and the constructiveness of gender in religiously affine children's and young adult literature.

David Zakarian, D. Phil. (2015), University of Oxford, is an associate of the Faculty of Asian and Middle Eastern Studies there. He is the author of *Women, Too, Were Blessed: The Portrayal of Women in Early Christian Armenian Texts* (2021) and of several articles and chapters on the colophons of medieval Armenian manuscripts and the representation of women in late antique and medieval Armenian texts.